American Orchestras
in the Nineteenth Century

American Orchestras in the Nineteenth Century

EDITED BY John Spitzer

The University of Chicago Press

CHICAGO AND LONDON

JOHN SPITZER is professor of music history at the San Francisco
Conservatory of Music.

The University of Chicago Press, Chicago 60637
The University of Chicago Press, Ltd., London
© 2012 by The University of Chicago
All rights reserved. Published 2012.
Printed in the United States of America

Publication of this book was supported by a grant from the
H. Earle Johnson Fund of the Society for American Music.

21 20 19 18 17 16 15 14 13 12   1 2 3 4 5

ISBN-13: 978-0-226-76976-9 (cloth)
ISBN-10: 0-226-76976-3 (cloth)

Library of Congress Cataloging-in-Publication Data

American orchestras in the nineteenth century / edited by John
    Spitzer.
        p. cm.
    Includes bibliographical references and index.
    ISBN-13: 978-0-226-76976-9 (cloth : alkaline paper)
    ISBN-10: 0-226-76976-3 (cloth : alkaline paper) 1. Orchestra—
United States—History. 2. Music—United States—History.
I. Spitzer, John, 1945–
ML1211.4.A44 2012
784.20973—dc23

                                    2011030079

♾ This paper meets the requirements of ANSI/NISO Z39.48-1992
(Permanence of Paper).

This book is dedicated to the memory of Adrienne Fried Block, whose enthusiasm and insights into American music informed, inspired, and delighted her colleagues and many friends.

CONTENTS

ILLUSTRATIONS

TABLES

Introduction: Toward a History of American Orchestras in the Nineteenth Century

DEANE L. ROOT

In nineteenth-century America, the orchestra was as much a social institu-tion as it was a cultural one. Through its roles as a business and a social en-deavor, a motivation for and a mechanism of trans-Atlantic exchange, and an artistic medium, it touched broad sectors of the American population. Or-chestral activity reflected some of the most important developmental strains in the nation during that period. The history of the orchestra is a canvas for interwoven issues of class, gender, ethnicity, geography, identity, capitalism, labor, culture, leisure, inventiveness, influence, and power in the nation's first full century. The purpose of this introduction is to elucidate major historio-graphical perspectives of prior research on the nineteenth-century American orchestra in order to establish a framework for the issues addressed by the chapters in this volume.

The study of American orchestras is both a pursuit more than a century old and a new, wide-open field. As yet it lacks fundamental reference tools; there are relatively few case studies and fewer-still synoptic overviews. That is not to say that writers of earlier generations entirely ignored American orchestras or that their work was insignificant, but what they wrote about American orchestras was heavily conditioned by the events of their times, the writers' values and priorities, and the available resources.

Previous writers on nineteenth-century American orchestral history can be seen as belonging to three generations. Most authors of the earliest gen-eration, from the 1880s until World War I, had firsthand knowledge of or-chestral ensembles and performances during the latter part of the nineteenth century; some were music critics, who knew some of the musicians and cor-responded with individuals intimately involved in those ensembles. The sec-

I am deeply grateful for John Spitzer's many insights and abundant guidance in shaping the ideas and framework for this chapter.

ond generation, between the two wars, consisted of observers of American culture who elaborated the stories told by their predecessors into a "standard narrative," in which nineteenth-century orchestras were seen as a sort of prehistory to the success and prestige of American orchestras in the twentieth century. The third, postwar generation was writing at least in part for a new academic audience of music scholars and placed American music history alongside the developed narratives of European music history. Largely trained in and employed by university departments that granted doctoral degrees in musicology, they participated in scholarly associations whose publications and research interests were otherwise devoted almost exclusively to classical and earlier music. The narrative of orchestral development took shape in general histories of American music, supplemented by a few volumes devoted to specific orchestras. It shared an emphasis on "great men" and "great works," which characterized much of music study until the late twentieth century.[1]

Writing on American orchestral history can be said to have begun in 1883 with Frédéric Louis Ritter's *Music in America*.[2] Ritter (1834–91), an Alsatian immigrant who taught and conducted at Vassar College, drew on personal knowledge, contemporary periodicals, and interviews and correspondence with musicians to build his research files, which provided sometimes highly detailed information about organizations. He viewed America's musical history as a process of "cultivation" from "low" aesthetic taste and performance standards in the eighteenth and early nineteenth centuries toward greater audience expectations, higher vocal and instrumental performance standards, and familiarity with masterworks in his own day. Ritter's agenda was not to document all of American music but to assert America's upward trajectory toward cultural parity with Europe.

Ritter regards the development of orchestras as the primary force in elevating music in the United States. An account of the New York Philharmonic Society dominates his coverage (chapters 14, 19, and 24); in his day the New York Philharmonic was the only American orchestra that had proved itself capable of surviving as an institution. In addition, Ritter sees its cooperative business model, which made the performers responsible for setting and meeting their own artistic and financial goals, as a force for musical

1 · For analysis of this historiographical trait, see Lydia Goehr, *The Imaginary Museum of Musical Works: An Essay in the Philosophy of Music* (2007), and in particular her chapter "After 1800: The Beethoven Paradigm," 205–42.

2 · See Frédéric Louis Ritter, *Music in America* (1970). For an excellent discussion of Ritter and other authors who wrote comprehensive histories of American music, see Richard Crawford, *The American Musical Landscape: The Business of Musicianship from Billings to Gershwin* (1993), 3–37.

"progress." Beyond the Philharmonic, Ritter devotes a chapter to the orchestras that toured the United States in the 1840s and 1850s (chapter 17). A recurrent theme is the role of immigrant musicians—particularly those from Germany—in raising the level of performance, introducing better repertory, and inspiring the formation of new ensembles. Of the Germania Musical Society, which immigrated to the United States in 1848 and toured sporadically until 1854, he writes, "Their influence in awakening, even creating, a taste and understanding for the highest and noblest forms of instrumental music was invaluable."[3] Ritter gives only a couple of pages to the Theodore Thomas Orchestra, which he regards principally as a source of "lively" and "beneficial rivalry" with the Philharmonic. He sees Thomas as renewing and extending the efforts of the Germanians. While he acknowledges complaints about the domination of the New York Philharmonic by German musicians and German repertory, Ritter reads like an apostle for a religion of European masterworks when he writes that the Germania's concerts were "offerings on the shrine of true and beautiful art."[4] He thus suggests a parallel between the mission of orchestras and the goals of his contemporary social reformers and educators, all working to build and sustain progress in elevating culture on a national scale.

William S. B. Mathews (1837–1912), in *A Hundred Years of Music in America*, offered more of a midwestern perspective on America's music history, still framed by ideals of "progress" and "improvement" but now tinged with American social ideologies of inventiveness, competitiveness, and individual achievement. He argues that in the past century the United States had become self-sufficient, possessing great "stimulative power" in the persons of its "most distinguished workers."[5] That Mathews draws heavily on Ritter is apparent, though he does not normally identify his sources of information.[6] His chapter on "literary factors" reveals indebtedness to John Sullivan Dwight and other critics. Like Ritter, he believes that orchestras flourish in a capitalistic economy, but he is less reliant on religious metaphor and rather more systematic, descriptive, and biographic in his approach to orchestral history.

3 · Ritter, *Music in America*, 341. On the Germania Musical Society, see chapter III.4 in this volume.
4 · Ritter, *Music in America*, 343.
5 · W. S. B. Mathews, *A Hundred Years of Music in America* (1889), iv. On Mathews's career in Chicago, see chapter II.4 in this volume.
6 · Ritter's carefully documented account of the founding of the New York Philharmonic contains a curious error: he gives U. C. Hill's first name as "Uriah" rather than Ureli (Ritter, *Music in America*, 273). Later writers, such as Mathews, who repeat this error can be assumed to be basing their accounts on Ritter.

Mathews's history of orchestras is largely an account of the careers of their conductors, most prominently Theodore Thomas. His explanation for the success of Thomas's festivals and the Thomas Orchestra is that the conductor employed a "purely commercial" business model. Mathews's book was published in Chicago before Thomas moved there, and he gives great weight to Thomas's New York City performances, such as the orchestral series at Irving Hall and at Central Park Gardens. Mathews documents the contemporary reception of Thomas's activities, in contrast to later accounts that would cast Thomas's efforts as establishmentarian and educative.

The first history of an individual American orchestra was *The Philharmonic of New York: A Memorial* by *New York Times* music critic Henry Edward Krehbiel (1854–1923), published to celebrate the ensemble's jubilee year in 1892. Krehbiel goes beyond Ritter to mine the Philharmonic's annual reports and the memoirs of members and thus provides extensive and accurate details about the founding of the orchestra and its first fifty years. Filled with praise for the founders' vision, the subsequent members' faithfulness to the goal, and audiences' receptiveness to the music of the "classical masters," Krehbiel's book gives no ink to the strife over national or class agendas, rivalry with other ensembles, or orchestral developments in the rest of the country. Instead, Krehbiel compares the Philharmonic to the orchestras of Europe—to the Gewandhaus concerts in Leipzig and especially to the Vienna Philharmonic, founded, in "parallel" to the New York Philharmonic, in 1842.[7] Krehbiel's claim of "parallel" status (if not parity) validates and legitimizes the American orchestra by placing it in a European framework.[8]

An important influence on this first generation of writers was what music scholar Charles Seeger has called the "Make America Musical" movement.[9] Fed by the shared missions and energies of magazines such as *Musi-*

7 · Henry Edward Krehbiel, *The Philharmonic Society of New York: A Memorial* (1892), 17.
8 · Krehbiel's book spurred the writing of "official" histories of a few other orchestras, including M. A. DeWolfe Howe, *The Boston Symphony Orchestra: An Historical Sketch* (1914; rev. ed., 1931); Philo Adams Otis, *The Chicago Symphony Orchestra: Its Organization, Growth and Development, 1891–1924* (1924); and Frances Anne Wister, *Twenty-Five Years of the Philadelphia Orchestra, 1900–1925* (1925). The several histories of the New York Philharmonic would make a fascinating study in their own right. They include: James Gibbons Huneker, *The Philharmonic Society of New York and Its Seventy-Fifth Anniversary: A Retrospect* (1917) at the orchestra's 75th anniversary; John Erskine, *The Philharmonic-Symphony Society of New York: Its First Hundred Years* (1943) for the centennial; Bert Bial, *Focus on the Philharmonic* (1992) for the 150th; and particularly Howard Shanet's fine book, *Philharmonic: A History of New York's Orchestra* (1975), which attracted many scholars and archivists to the subject of orchestral history.
9 · Charles Seeger traced the movement's history in "Music and Class Structure in the United States" *American Quarterly* 9 (1957). I am grateful to Stephen R. Greene, "Visions of a 'Mu-

cal America and organizations including the National Federation of Music Clubs, the movement focused on establishing a taste for "Good Music," a concept articulated influentially in the 1890s by *New York Times* music critic W. J. Henderson.[10] The 1890s was also the decade in which several major northeastern cities established permanent orchestras, a product not only of the "Make America Musical" movement but also of the accumulation of capital in industrial centers and the United States' new confidence as a world power.

A later contribution by this first generation of scholars to the history of American orchestras in the nineteenth century appeared in 1904 from the pen of Louis C. Elson (1848–1920), a leading American editor of music magazines and teacher of music theory at the New England Conservatory. *The History of American Music* is organized by music genre rather than chronological period; orchestras are covered in the chapter on the history of American instrumental music from the eighteenth century to the twentieth. Elson's perspective is less on progress and development than on intercity rivalry and the durability or impermanence of organizations.

Elson admires the pioneering spirit of America's eighteenth- and early nineteenth-century orchestral musicians, and he notes the cultural benefits of the influx of musicians fleeing the European political upheavals in 1848. But all this is only a prehistory to the arrival of "Theodore Thomas, who has done more to raise the standard of music in American than any other man." "In all the [earlier] orchestral work in America," Elson asserts, "there was more of ambition than of true achievement." It was Thomas who raised the standard of his orchestra to "something akin to European technique and ensemble" and who first gave the American public "great musical works with something like their true reading."[11]

Elson's account seems imbued with a late-nineteenth-century ideology of manifest cultural destiny. He writes of cultural taste as if it were religious doctrine, describing Thomas's orchestral tours as "missionary work." His repeated references to "high" and "true" standards of art bespeak adherence to the "Good Music" movement, and his emphasis on institutional rivalry and "permanency" suggests the corporate values of the "Make America Musical" forces.[12]

A later account in a similar vein is the 1927 biography of Theodore Thomas

sical America' in the Radio Age" (Ph.D. diss., 2008), for bringing Seeger's article and the "Good Music" movement to my attention.

10 · W. J. Henderson, *What Is Good Music? Suggestions to Persons Desiring to Cultivate a Taste in Musical Art* (1898).

11 · Louis C. Elson, *The History of American Music* (1925), 58.

12 · Ibid., 59, 68.

by Charles Edward Russell (1860–1941) titled *The American Orchestra and Theodore Thomas*. Russell paints Thomas as a visionary conductor who initiated a "cultural revolution" in America. In order to imbue the story with even loftier significance, he begins by asserting that the American symphony orchestra was the very pinnacle of the nation's accomplishments, "our sign of honor among nations." Russell, an active political reformer with a prolific pen, is clearly of the "Make America Musical" camp. For him, Thomas is a Mosaic figure struggling toward his goal through a wilderness for more than forty years. Drawing on recollections and documents from the conductor's family and friends, Russell, in his more than three hundred pages of text, supplied a hagiographic account that indelibly colored subsequent histories, which saw Thomas as the necessary link between the primitive orchestras of the early nineteenth century and America's venerated orchestral institutions of the twentieth century.[13]

The first generation of histories of American orchestras was steeped in the social gospels of America's late nineteenth-century educated class. Among their themes were the importance of the orchestra as a sign of social and cultural progress, the missionary zeal to convert the American public to an appreciation of "good music," the assumption that European orchestras were an appropriate yardstick for American orchestras, and the paramount goal of financial "permanency." Many of these themes were taken up in retellings by subsequent generations.

The second generation of orchestral histories was initiated by W. Dermot Darby (1885–1947), the editor (along with composer Arthur Farwell) of *Music in America* (1915), to which Darby contributed a chapter titled "Instrumental Organizations in the United States." Darby had arrived in the United States from Ireland only six years earlier; he was thus the first of the authors considered here who had not personally witnessed American orchestras over a period of decades.[14] By Darby's time the national agenda had shifted sharply—politically, culturally, socially, and geographically. The United States was now a world political leader with a powerful corporate economic engine. Darby offers a businesslike record of results produced by America's "instrumental organizations." He summarizes received information on the "inadequate" interpretations and amateurism of the first part of the nineteenth century and the progress, beginning around the middle of the century, of orchestras in New York and Boston, but his chief contribution is new

---

13 · Charles Edward Russell, *The American Orchestra and Theodore Thomas* (1927), vii, v. This study was supplanted in the third generation of scholarship by Ezra Schabas, *Theodore Thomas: America's Conductor and Builder of Orchestras, 1835–1905* (1989).

14 · W. Dermot Darby obituary, *New York Times*, October 21, 1947. See also Richard Jackson, *United States Music: Sources of Biography and Collective Biography* (1973), 19.

information on the orchestras founded in the 1890s and thereafter in Chicago, Cincinnati, Pittsburgh, Minneapolis, San Francisco, and elsewhere. For Darby, writing in 1915, the story of the American orchestra is one of financial, civic, and artistic success: "Altogether, in orchestral matters America has sufficient reason to be proud of her attainments. Of course, one cannot argue from the existence of good orchestras the coincidence of a higher or widely diffused state of musical culture. They are to some extent the joint product of money and civic pride. But their educational influence is beyond question."[15]

A more nuanced and much more influential approach appeared in 1931 with *Our American Music* by John Tasker Howard (1890–1964). A prominent radio broadcaster and writer on music for popular magazines, Howard was adept at assembling bits of information and vignettes to tell stories succinctly; he later wrote exemplary documentary biographies of composers. He created the first history of the nation's music that plumbed the knowledge accumulated in research libraries and by bibliographers and historians and brought within its covers varied perspectives and multiple social and popular musical genres.[16] Much of Howard's detailed information about smaller and shorter-lived nineteenth-century orchestras and their musicians was new to readers. He gives extensive coverage to the American tour of Louis Antoine Jullien's orchestra in 1853–54, and he introduces the notion that American composers gained an idea of a "national consciousness" from Jullien's visit. Gone is the Germanophilia of Ritter and Krehbiel, influenced no doubt by the anti-German backlash resulting from World War I.

Nonetheless, Howard's treatment of Theodore Thomas echoes Elson and Russell. It begins with a two-page encomium casting Thomas as "an epic figure in American history" (note he does not say "music history"), "our first prophet of good music for the masses." And later, concerning the programming of American composers' works, he states: "It was because of Theodore Thomas that there are orchestras today to play the works of Americans, or of any composers."[17]

Howard's book culminated nearly half a century of writings on American orchestral history. The first and especially the second generation of authors had crafted a standard narrative of the topic, with mythic qualities. The following elements of this standard narrative are prominently articulated by Elson, Mathews, Russell, Darby, and Howard:

15 · Arthur Farwell and W[illiam] Dermot Darby, *Music in America* (1915), 201.
16 · By the time of his third edition (1946), Howard had become curator of the Americana Collection of the Music Division of the New York Public Library, with access to relatively vast numbers of original documents. He was the first of the panoptic historians of American music to get Ureli Corelli Hill's name right (p. 151).
17 · John Tasker Howard, *Our American Music* (1965), 280, 282, 289.

1. The United States through the 1870s was an orchestral wilderness strewn with artistically inadequate and impermanent ensembles.
2. The founding of the New York Philharmonic in 1842 and the brief career of the Germania orchestra at midcentury gave Americans their first taste for real (European) symphonic masterworks and good (German) musicianship. These became the hallmarks of high-quality orchestral culture.
3. Theodore Thomas, the hero of the narrative, educated American musicians and the public alike, fostering widespread appreciation of "good" music, establishing modern orchestral programming, and forcing artistic competition that raised standards throughout the country.
4. In consequence of this growth and development over the course of the nineteenth century, America embraced symphonic music, and many American cities established major permanent orchestras, which would be the cornerstone of America's musical culture in the twentieth century.

Some of the later accounts add a second great man to the narrative, Henry Higginson, who established the Boston Symphony in 1881 and financed it with his own fortune, thus pointing the way toward a system of philanthropic support for the American orchestra.

After Howard, a third generation of writers, coinciding with the formation of music departments in colleges and universities across the country after World War II, began to break away from this standard narrative. They sought to inject musicological research interests into their accounts and especially to emphasize what was original and distinctively American in nineteenth-century American music. For orchestral historiography, this meant reexamining the assumption by earlier writers that orchestras were an emblem of culture and that "good" music meant the European symphonic repertory. At the same time, these third-generation writers retained many of the themes, the high points, and some of the factual underpinnings of the standard narrative.

Gilbert Chase (1906–92), already an accomplished historian of Spanish and Latin American music, wrote a 1955 volume titled *America's Music: From the Pilgrims to the Present*, which became the textbook of choice for the newly initiated courses devoted to the nation's music history in institutions of higher education in the 1960s and 1970s. Whereas Howard for the first time had included coverage of folk and popular music along with classical compositions, Chase introduces the notion of a binary polarity between genteel and vernacular traditions in nineteenth-century American music. Chase sees the vernacular traditions as the most vigorous, interesting, and distinctively American music, and perhaps for that reason he neglects the history of orchestras almost entirely. He discusses the New York Philharmonic only in reference to early complaints that its programs excluded American compositions, and he mentions Theodore Thomas only concerning the 1876 U.S. centennial festival in Philadelphia.

Music in the United States: A Historical Introduction, by H. Wiley Hitchcock (1923–2007), is a slim but richly detailed textbook on American music, first published in 1969. Hitchcock adapts Chase's class-based dichotomy, replacing "genteel" with "cultivated," and views all of the nation's nineteenth-century musical history through this bipolar lens. But as a trained musicologist he recognizes the weight given to orchestras in European scholarly research, and he understands that ensembles of all kinds played a large role in musical life throughout the century. He discusses the "rise of public concerts and a mass audience"; he notes economic and business factors such as transportation infrastructure that influenced commerce, migration, and hence culture; and he acknowledges "Americans' attitudes as to the 'standard repertory'" stemming from the Germanians. He sees Theodore Thomas less as a cultural hero than as "an astute impresario and a canny program builder" with an "immense" influence on programming and standards of performance.[18]

Charles Hamm's (1925–) *Music in the New World* (1983) drew on U.S. bicentennial projects and introduced important variants to the standard narrative. His repertory-based approach broke with the traditional emphasis on ensembles and conductors, instead focusing attention on the music and in particular some of the American works that the major ensembles were *not* presenting. His gaze is fixed much more on what was being created new in America than on what was being imported from Europe, thereby rejecting the first premise of the standard narrative. Hamm's coverage of the visiting orchestras gives the Germanians and Jullien one page each but avoids notions that they elevated culture. The chapter on classical composition after the Civil War begins with the Boston May festivals and jubilees, creating the impression that these festivals (and those in Chicago, Philadelphia, and elsewhere) did as much as Theodore Thomas to raise audiences' demand for large ensembles and to infuse music into national civic agendas. Thomas, for Hamm, was more of an effect than a cause: "The period of Thomas's activity in the United States was thus a critical time in the evolution of the symphony orchestra into a permanent institution in a number of American cities and towns. Though the increased popularity of symphonic music would have undoubtedly come about even if Thomas had not come to the New World, there can be no denying him the role of being the single most influential in-

18 · H. Wiley Hitchcock, *Music in the United States: A Historical Introduction* (1988), 89, 90, 91–92.

dividual in this chapter of American music life."[19] The impetus came from a wider movement in American culture, within which Thomas created an orchestra and a career.

Richard Crawford (1935–), in *America's Musical Life: A History* (2001), a more recent general history of American music, devotes two chapters (chapters 14 and 15) to nineteenth-century orchestras and concert music. He embraces perspectives from the social sciences, introducing his section on mid-century concert life with a sketch of the socioeconomic and technological conditions that enabled change. He frames the visiting ensembles, including the Germania and Jullien, in the context of the economic motivations of impresarios who promoted orchestra concerts as part of a general development of "concert circuits." Crawford covers the New York Philharmonic in a section titled "New York and Theodore Thomas, Conductor of the Classics." His account is dispassionate: "Thomas viewed himself as an agent in the work of raising musical standards," who "labored to elevate public taste to the point where it would be worth gratifying" and who "accomplished one of the more complex balancing acts in the history of American music, by controlling [his own orchestra's] artistic and economic arms." Finally, Crawford is the only one among this series of historians to see the movement for "good" music as carrying some heavy cultural baggage: "During the 1870s ... the notion that such diverse elements as edifying music, entertaining music, and mammoth spectacle could be democratically intermixed lost ground to the view that edifying music deserved a forum all its own."[20] But, with all that, Crawford conforms in the main to the standard narrative of orchestral history, while drawing attention to its cultural- and social-history contexts.

The third generation of authors was influenced by a new genre of writing: book-length studies purporting to encompass all of American orchestral history.[21] John Henry Mueller (1895–1965) introduced a new perspective in 1951 with *The American Symphony Orchestra: A Social History of Musical Taste*. Compiled at a time when musicologists still focused principally on musical works, genres, and composers, it documents the programming history

19 · Charles Hamm, *Music in the New World* (1983), 317. A member of the planning group for the Rockefeller Foundation's New World Records project, Hamm organized his book around music available on sound recordings.

20 · Richard Crawford, *America's Musical Life: A History* (2001), 313, 307, 291.

21 · Perhaps the earliest of these studies was Henry Charles Lahee, *The Orchestra: A Brief Outline of Its Development in Europe and America, with a Description of the Instruments and Their Functions* (1925), but at only forty-eight pages and with limited distribution it did not have a national audience. Margaret Grant and Harman S. Hettinger, *America's Symphony Orchestras, and How They Are Supported* (1940), contains a chapter on symphony orchestras before 1900, largely derived from Ritter, but it primarily surveys the finances of twentieth-century organizations and argues for a National Bureau of Fine Arts.

of seventeen orchestras from 1842 through 1950. Mueller's premise, which he develops through a repertory database and analysis, breaks with the standard history by arguing that programming was determined not by the perceived greatness of a composer or piece of music but by sociological factors that drove audiences, musicians, and concert life in general. He traces long-term "trends" in the numbers of performances of certain composers in particular periods. His summary of late nineteenth-century orchestral history is derived from Ritter, Russell, Howard, and others.[22]

One section of Mueller's study discusses the role of orchestras as powerful not-for-profit institutions that promoted the public welfare through education, culture, and social services. Indeed, this concept had gained support during the 1930s, as federal income taxes began to increase and tax-free donations to nonprofit cultural institutions began to seem more attractive to wealthy Americans.[23] Philip Hart (1914–2000) examined the genesis and evolution of this model of the nonprofit orchestra in *Orpheus in the New World: The Symphony Orchestra as an American Cultural Institution* (1973), a study of the American orchestra as an institution through the 1960s. Hart's remains the most comprehensive book on the history of the American orchestra, drawing deeply on his professional knowledge as an orchestra administrator and a prominent figure in the American Symphony Orchestra League. His chapters on the nineteenth century, tellingly titled "Before Thomas," "Theodore Thomas—Conductor," and "Henry Lee Higginson—Patron," present the standard narrative derived from publications discussed above.[24] But Hart was the first to direct attention to the combination of charismatic orchestral conductors, patrons, and managers that emerged in the late nineteenth century as the characteristic organizational basis of American orchestras and to the roles of the musicians and their unions, especially following the Great Depression.

Most mid-twentieth-century writing on American orchestral history seems to have been motivated in large part by a desire to examine the best or standard practices by American cultural institutions at a time when the United States had become the world's most powerful nation militarily, eco-

22 · John Henry Mueller, *The American Symphony Orchestra: A Social History of Musical Taste* (1951). Twenty-two years later, Mueller's wife, Kate Hevner Mueller, added nineteen orchestras and extended the data through 1970 but abandoned the attempt to link programming with social history: *Twenty-Seven Major American Symphony Orchestras: A History and Analysis of Their Repertoires, Seasons 1842–43 through 1969–70* (1973).
23 · Judith Sealander, *Private Wealth and Public Life: Foundation Philanthropy and the Reshaping of American Social Policy from the Progressive Era to the New Deal* (1997), 5.
24 · Philip Hart, *Orpheus in the New World: The Symphony Orchestra as an American Cultural Institution* (1973).

nomically, and—through exported sound recordings, radio, television, and films—culturally. These books portray the American orchestra as a potent force for culture in a capitalist economy. As we have seen, much of the gaze of the third-generation writers was directed toward what were considered to be the "major" orchestras, thus ignoring the cultural context, the many smaller or shorter-lived orchestras, and orchestral ensembles beyond the grandest concert halls. Third-generation writers, with the important exception of Philip Hart, also demonstrated little interest in the musicians who played in American orchestras.

Joseph Horowitz (1948–), a prolific writer, cultural historian, and orchestral programmer, takes a different approach in *Wagner Nights: An American History*, using the cultural meanings of Wagner's music as a lens through which to see more deeply into the work of orchestras and musicians between the arrival of the Germania Musical Society in 1848 and World War I. While he largely expounds the standard narrative of rivalry and growth of the major ensembles, he recognizes the pervasiveness of orchestral music in New York in an array of venues, far beyond the Philharmonic and Thomas. His section on the Anton Seidl Society, for example, is among the first to reflect the role of women's organizations in orchestral culture and to point toward the potential of the vast number of topics and approaches open to new scholars.[25]

Building on the efforts of the first three generations of scholarship, a fourth generation of writers, steeped in cultural history and contextual musicology, has become interested in nineteenth-century American orchestral history. Beginning in the 1970s, publications on American music of all types mushroomed, encouraged at the local, state, and national levels by the nation's bicentennial programs, which emphasized America's cultural heritage.[26] Institutions such as the Institute for Studies in American Music at Brooklyn College, the Sonneck Society for American Music, and the Rockefeller Foundation's New World Records project promoted interest in American music and fostered a wide range of research and publication.[27] Access to previously

25 · Joseph Horowitz, *Wagner Nights: An American History* (1994). His *Classical Music in America: A History of Its Rise and Fall* (2005) extends his ideas to other composers and to other genres beyond the orchestra, addressing such topics as sacralization and "social control."

26 · For a historical perspective on the changes in American music studies during this period, see Dale Cockrell, "Can American Music Studies Develop a Method?" *American Music* 22 (2004).

27 · H. Wiley Hitchcock, founder of the Institute for Studies in American Music at Brooklyn College, began a newsletter in November 1971. The Sonneck Society was founded in 1975; it changed its name in 1999 to the Society for American Music (see http://american-music.org/sam/WhatIsSAM.php). New World Records was launched with a one-hundred-disc

unknown resources was aided by large-scale bibliographical projects funded by the National Endowment for the Humanities.[28]

The growth of American music studies coincided with a sea change in musicology as a discipline. A fundamentally new disciplinary approach arose, sometimes dubbed "contextual musicology," which encouraged the "thick description" of music and musical practices within a "web" of culture, in the influential metaphors of anthropologist Clifford Geertz.[29] A new road map for researchers of the nation's music history came from Richard Crawford in his 1984 valedictory address as president of the American Musicological Society, which he titled "Studying American Music."[30] Crawford asked some of the same questions that previous generations had asked:

- "What music have Americans made?"
- "Who has made music in America?"
- "What American music is the most important and why?"

The first three generations of authors about American orchestras in the nineteenth century had already addressed these questions by focusing on the repertory of "good" music, biographies of a pantheon of conductors and soloists, and masterworks. But Crawford added two more questions:

- "Where and in what circumstances has music been made here?"
- "How has the making of music here been financially supported?"

These questions point toward the study of nineteenth-century American orchestras in the context of social history and anthropology.

Members of the fourth generation, represented by the authors in this

bicentennial series of recordings that embraced the chronological and stylistic history of music in the United States. Thirty-five years later it was still issuing recordings.

28 · D. W. Krummel, Jean Geil, Doris Dyen, and Deane Root, *Resources of American Music History: A Directory of Source Materials from Colonial Times to World War II* (1981), identified a vast amount of source materials in libraries, archives, museums, local historical associations, and the holdings of private individuals and organizations, including orchestras themselves. "Music in Gotham," a project at the Graduate Center of the City University of New York, has assembled a rich archive of materials pertaining to music in New York City between 1862 and 1875.

29 · Clifford Geertz, "Thick Description: Toward an Interpretative Theory of Culture," in *The Interpretation of Cultures* (1973). See also Gary Tomlinson, "The Web of Culture: A Context for Musicology," *19th-Century Music* 7 (1984) 35–62.

30 · The talk was published as *Studying American Music: With a Bibliography of the Published Writings of Richard Crawford* (1985).

book, have taken *all* of Crawford's questions to heart as they seek to understand the full range of music and types of orchestras that Americans created and supported. They recognize that the answer to "who has made music?" must include not just composers, conductors, impresarios, and virtuosos but also the orchestral musicians who actually made the music night after night. In answer to "where has music been made," they recognize that a great variety of performance venues took orchestral music far beyond the concert hall. They revive the interest shown by nineteenth-century writers concerning orchestras' economic and business models, many of which were designed in response to shifting demographics and financial conditions in a rapidly urbanizing environment. As part of that interest they add a sixth question, "Who heard the music?"—and in answer to that question they have begun to pay close attention to the audience for orchestras, hardly mentioned by previous authors. When the current generation of writers asks what music was most important and why, they interrogate the nineteenth-century orchestral musicians, composers, and audiences—including women—about issues of class, gender, status, taste, authority, fashion, and other aspects of public behavior during those decades. In answer to Crawford's question about how music has been financially supported, these authors begin to show how political and economic history affected orchestras and musicians; they demonstrate, for example, that many orchestras and other cultural enterprises failed in America between 1837 and 1842 and again between 1857 and 1861 not because—as earlier writers had suggested—they lacked Germanic repertory and performance standards but because these were periods marked by bank panics and the constriction of capital.

In important ways this new understanding reinterprets even so basic a question as "which music was most important," seeking a culturally sensitive understanding of the meanings of individual compositions, analyzing the stylistic preferences of their audiences, and interrogating music critics' tastes and motivations. The first and second generations of writers sought to demonstrate that Americans could be educated to appreciate the canon of European orchestral masterpieces; the third generation sought to identify a parallel body of American compositions. But the fourth generation is not in the business of canon formation; these authors instead seek to know the breadth and depth of orchestral repertory. This does not mean that they have given up on the idea of "importance," just that their criteria for "importance" are what the people considered most important in the day, extending the approach pioneered by Charles Hamm.

This volume is the first to focus its attention on the period before the formation of permanent orchestras in the 1890s. Its understanding of the term "orchestra" embraces not only symphony orchestras but also theater orchestras, amateur orchestras, novelty orchestras, orchestras that furnished music in eating and drinking establishments, and other ensembles that participated in the varied forms of musical culture in the United States during the nineteenth century. Thanks to the bibliographic achievements of the 1970s and 1980s, the authors access a far greater variety of archival and library resources than have been used to support previous books on orchestral history. And contravening a tradition among American writers seeking to claim America's cultural independence, this book views the orchestras, their music, and their audiences as part of a trans-Atlantic culture, abandoning the standard narrative's Europe-versus-America dichotomy.

A cumulative effect of the chapters in this volume is to suggest that the earlier standard narrative about American orchestras in the nineteenth century—that they were sporadic, sparse, struggling to establish themselves, and entirely male—severely undervalued and misrepresented the richness and significance of orchestras in the web of culture. Earlier historians tended to treat the nineteenth century as the "prehistory" of the American symphony orchestra, a cultural institution that came into its own only in the twentieth century. Now we are in a position to understand that orchestral music and musicians were an important part of Americans' lives during most of the nineteenth century. The present authors try to understand the lives of men and women who played in those orchestras, look at the ensembles as part of the "businesses" of entertainment and culture, and examine orchestral history in the framework of ethnicity and national identification. Viewing the nineteenth-century American orchestra through these new lenses makes for a new, exciting, and entertaining story.

PART I

Ubiquity & Diversity

The Ubiquity and Diversity of Nineteenth-Century American Orchestras

JOHN SPITZER

Orchestras, in the second half of the nineteenth century, were an essential ingredient of American urban life. Before the advent of amplification or recorded sound, an orchestra (or a band) was needed to fill a large indoor space with sound, to provide continuity for a performance, to drown out other urban noises, and to add visual and aural glamour to a public event. A visitor to a medium-sized city in the 1880s—say Cincinnati, St. Louis, or Washington, D.C.—would have heard orchestras giving concerts in auditoriums and theaters; playing for operas; playing between the acts in the "legitimate" theater as well as for vaudeville and burlesque; and performing in parks, at resorts on the outskirts of town, and at a variety of special events, public and private. In New York, America's largest city, with a population of more than a million in Manhattan alone, hundreds of orchestras played on a daily basis in theaters, restaurants and beer gardens, concert halls, circuses, and amusement parks.

The ubiquity of the orchestra in nineteenth-century American cities forms a striking contrast to the rather narrow range of venues to which twenty-first-century orchestras are confined. American orchestras today give concerts in large halls to audiences of subscribers and regular patrons; they accompany singers and dancers at the opera and the ballet; and they make recordings and occasionally appear on television. Amateur and school orchestras play for friends and families. But it is rare today to hear a full orchestra of live musicians in the theater, in a restaurant, at an exhibition, in a public park, or at a dance; they have been replaced in these venues by smaller, amplified ensembles and by recorded music. "Orchestra" has come to mean "symphony orchestra," a large ensemble that plays a repertory of classics and aspiring classics in a concert setting for an audience of music lovers. The American orchestra today occupies a far narrower cultural niche than it did in the nineteenth century.

In the first half of the nineteenth century, only a few American cities—
New York, Philadelphia, and Boston—had enough resident musicians to put
together orchestras of any significant size. The musicians of St. Louis organized the "Polyhymnia," an ensemble of thirty-five members in 1845, but with
five clarinets, five flutes, and two each of violas, cellos, and basses, the orchestra was severely unbalanced.[1] Some of the players were professional musicians, others amateurs. The first concert of the Chicago Philharmonic in
1851 advertised a "Grand double orchestra OF TWENTY PERFORMERS" assembled from instrumentalists who played in the city's theaters and beer gardens.[2] By the 1870s and 1880s fifteen or twenty cities had grown large enough
to support a thriving entertainment industry and the orchestras that it required. Immigrant musicians, especially from Germany and, by the 1880s,
from Italy, arrived to staff the theaters, beer gardens, dance halls, summer
resorts, concert halls, and opera houses of Chicago, Cincinnati, Baltimore,
St. Louis, Pittsburgh, Detroit, San Francisco, and other cities. In addition,
orchestras made up of New York musicians crisscrossed the country with
opera companies, minstrel shows, and vaudeville troupes or set out on their
own to give orchestral concerts, usually with instrumental and vocal soloists.

Although symphony orchestras playing public concerts were an important component of urban musical life in the nineteenth century, this was only
one ingredient in an extensive and complex network of orchestral activities.
The personnel of orchestras in different venues overlapped extensively, so the
same violinist or clarinetist might play in the pit at the spoken theater one
night, in the opera orchestra the next, for a dance the next (hiring a substitute to take his place in the theater), back in the theater on Saturday evening,
and then "sacred concert" on Sunday. When a touring opera or a vaudeville
company arrived in town, both the violinist and clarinetist might be hired to
fill out the skeleton ensemble that traveled with the company. They might
also organize and lead their own orchestra to play for a party, an excursion,
or a dance. Repertory overlapped just as much as personnel. Opera overtures were played between the acts in the spoken theater; opera tunes were
arranged for dancing; dance music was played at orchestral concerts; and
movements of symphonies entertained patrons at the beer gardens.

Symphony concerts were usually organized by the musicians themselves,
who wanted to play symphonic repertory. The New York Philharmonic, a
succession of "Chicago Philharmonics," and a series of orchestras that called
themselves the Cincinnati Orchestra were all initiated by groups of musi-

1 · Ernst C. Krohn, *Missouri Music* (1971), 3.
2 · See chapter I.1 in this volume.

cians, often organized as profit-sharing cooperatives.[3] Sometimes amateurs took the lead, organizing concerts by professional musicians, as the Harvard Musical Association did, or forming an amateur orchestra reinforced with professionals, such as the Georgetown Amateur Orchestra in Washington, D.C. In other cases a conductor would organize a concert series as an entrepreneurial venture, hiring an orchestra that he paid with the proceeds from subscriptions and ticket sales. Hans Balatka's concerts in Chicago in the 1860s and Leopold Damrosch's 1877–78 series in New York provide examples of this kind of conductor-organized orchestral concert series.[4]

A symphony orchestra, however it was organized, needed to create an audience for the kind of music it wanted to play. By the mid-nineteenth century, American audiences had become familiar with theater music and operatic repertory, but for most listeners, "serious" orchestral music was still exotic. To recruit and keep audiences, orchestra musicians, conductors, and promoters offered a heterogeneous repertory: symphonies, tone poems, and concertos along with vocal numbers from operas, solo turns for members of the orchestra, and sometimes popular dance and novelty numbers as well. At the same time, the musicians tried to "educate" their audiences to appreciate and patronize symphonic music. In New York Theodore Thomas at his Terrace Garden concerts in 1867 advertised that on Tuesday and Friday evenings "the Second Part of the Programme will consist of compositions of a higher order, such as Movements of Symphonies, Classical Overtures, etc."[5] A few orchestras—for example, the New York Philharmonic and the Harvard Musical Association—programmed entire series of concerts consisting exclusively of "compositions of a higher order." The majority of American orchestral concerts, however, continued to offer audiences a more or less mixed repertory until the late nineteenth century.

Although concerts of symphonic music constituted only a fraction of the activities of nineteenth-century American orchestras, such concerts were the highest-profile activity that an orchestra could undertake, and they became increasingly popular and successful over the second half of the century. Tours by the Germania Musical Society from 1848 to 1854, by Louis Antoine Jullien's orchestra in 1853–54 and by the Theodore Thomas Orchestra from 1869 onward stimulated interest in orchestral repertory, raised standards of orchestral performance, and established orchestral concerts as a commer-

---

3 · See chapters V.3 (New York Philharmonic), I.1 (Chicago), and II.3 (Cincinnati) in this volume.

4 · See chapters II.3 (Harvard Musical Association), II.5 (Georgetown Amateur Orchestra), II.4 (Balatka), and III.3 (Damrosch) in this volume.

5 · See chapter II.2 in this volume.

cially viable form of entertainment.[6] Series of subscription concerts, which had been established in New York and Boston already in the 1840s, spread across the country after the Civil War. Cincinnati, Chicago, Philadelphia, Pittsburgh, Milwaukee, St. Louis, Baltimore, and Washington, D.C., initiated yearly concert series with orchestras whose personnel remained substantially stable from year to year. In a typical scenario, a philharmonic society or concert series would be formed with high hopes, musicians would be recruited, the enterprise would flourish for a few years, and then it would collapse in the face of economic hard times or internal disagreements. A few years later the orchestra would reconstitute itself with largely the same personnel, announce a new series, and try all over again. This scenario has been presented as a story of repeated failure to found "permanent" orchestras, but it also demonstrates the robustness of public demand for orchestral concerts in America's larger cities. And in some cities—New York, Cincinnati, and Chicago—the market was large enough by the 1880s and 1890s that two or more orchestras (often with overlapping personnel) offered competing concert series.[7]

Many of the orchestras that endured and became the ancestors of today's American symphony orchestras were founded between 1890 and the First World War, among them the Chicago Symphony (1891), the St. Louis Symphony (1893), the Cincinnati Symphony (1894), the Philadelphia Orchestra (1900), the Minnesota Orchestra (1903), the San Francisco Symphony (1911), and the Detroit Symphony (1914). In each of these cities (as in New York and Boston somewhat earlier) the "permanent" orchestra immediately became the most prestigious of the city's ubiquitous and diverse orchestras. It hired the best players (often importing them from New York or even from Europe); it programmed the greatest number of "compositions of a higher order"; and it was patronized by the city's social elites. Nevertheless, at the turn of the century, America's symphony orchestras were still connected by multiple bonds to other ensembles and orchestral activities. Because most symphonic seasons were short, many of the musicians continued to play in theater and opera orchestras and in touring ensembles. Because most of the orchestras did not yet have halls of their own, they tended to share venues (often theaters) with other kinds of entertainment. As well as their subscription seasons, most of the orchestras played popular concerts, where ticket prices were low, repertory was mixed, and food and drink were served along

6 · See chapters III.4 (Germania Musical Society), IV.1 (Jullien's orchestra), and V.2 (Theodore Thomas Orchestra) in this volume.

7 · See chapters III.3 (New York), II.4 (Chicago), and II.3 (Cincinnati) in this volume.

with the music. The categorical separation of American symphony orchestras from the mainstream of American entertainment did not begin in earnest until the advent of recorded sound, amplification, talking pictures, radio, and the other great transformations of American musical life in the twentieth century.

[1.1] Building the American Symphony Orchestra

The Nineteenth-Century Roots of a Twenty-First-Century Musical Institution

MARK CLAGUE

At Chicago Symphony Orchestra (CSO) concerts during the 2007–8 season, listeners enjoyed the artistry of approximately one hundred musicians, yet the number of players on stage represented less than 1 percent of the persons involved. Founded in 1890, almost a year prior to the ensemble's first performance, the Orchestral Association has administered the orchestra for more than a century.[1] In 2007 the association was managed by seven executive officers supported in turn by 141 trustees along with 441 governing members and 174 members of the Women's Association. It employed 140 full-time staffers who worked in thirty-eight separate departments ranging from Artistic Planning to Public Relations and Education to Archives. Donors included 153 corporate sponsors, 94 foundations and government agencies, and more than 15,000 individual contributors. In sum, 756 community leaders employed 140 staff members to support an orchestra of 101 players, revealing that for the 2007–8 season, each musician required the support of 1.5 administrators, 7.5 community leaders, and at least 150 individual donors.[2]

By contrast, when the Chicago Orchestra, as the CSO was originally known, played its first concert in 1891, its eighty-six musicians were led by conductor Theodore Thomas with the administrative support of Charles Norman Fay, de facto leader of the Orchestral Association's five-member executive board, plus a manager, a program book editor, and two librarians. Financial backing was provided by fifty-one businessmen known as trustees or "guarantors" who each pledged to pay for up to $1,000 of the orchestra's

---

1 · The Orchestral Association changed its name in 1996 to match the ensemble that it administers and since 2000 has been known as the Chicago Symphony Orchestra Association (see programs in the Chicago Symphony Orchestra's Rosenthal Archives).

2 · Statistics assembled from *Notebook: Chicago Symphony Orchestra, 2007–2008 Season,* 34, 40, 59, 61–64, 71–94, 96–103.

potential deficit.[3] So, in comparing the Orchestral Association of 1891 to its 2007 counterpart, we can immediately see that the institution has grown exponentially over the course of some 117 seasons, but disproportionately so in favor of leadership, staff, and, most dramatically, its donor base. In terms of human resources, the ensemble itself has increased by just 15 players, or only about 17 percent, while the staff has increased by 3,500 percent, from a handful to 140, and the donor base has expanded 30,000 percent.

The groundwork for this extraordinary growth and the subsequent success of the Chicago Orchestral Association's corporate model for the American orchestra can be traced to the nineteenth-century struggle to establish the orchestra as an American concert institution, a challenge that was particularly acute in Chicago. A history of this struggle offers a survey of organizational structures and tactics used by nineteenth-century arts leaders to establish musical institutions throughout the United States, as well as a richer appreciation of the social and personal dynamics that ignited these initiatives. The value of this history today lies in its ability to clarify the patterns and practices that characterize the contemporary American orchestral scene. Consequences of the choices made more than a century ago continue to influence the American orchestra's mission, leadership, and relationship to its community. By better understanding this history, its mythology and characteristics, arts advocates might better understand how these legacies both propel and burden the American orchestral scene today.

Six Models for the American Concert Orchestra

The corporate structure of Chicago's Orchestral Association, although a significant expansion on past models, was not a radical or new idea but represented a recombination and extension of nineteenth-century efforts. Six organizational models summarize early attempts to bring symphonic concert music to Chicago and move it toward a professional basis (see table I.1.1)—the club model, the cooperative model, the entrepreneurial model, the conservatory model, the concert society model, and, finally, the corporate model.[4]

The club model offered music making for nonprofessional musicians who paid membership fees, potentially including an initiation fee and regular

3 · Philo Adams Otis, *The Chicago Symphony Orchestra* (1924), 27–31. One thousand dollars in 1891 dollars is approximately $24,000 in 2010 dollars; http://www.westegg.com/inflation.
4 · Other organizational models could and are being proposed for orchestras today. Today's youth orchestras and retiree or "New Horizons" ensembles typically draw on the corporate, club, conservatory, and society models. Because these organizations are post-nineteenth-century entities, they remain outside the boundaries of this chapter.

TABLE I.1.1. Organizational models of nineteenth-century concert orchestras in Chicago

Type	Leadership	Musicians	Economic base	Ownership
Club	Volunteer	Amateur	Membership fees	Members
Co-op	Shared	Professional	Income	Members
Entrepreneurial	Leader	Professional	Income	Leader
Conservatory	Director / faculty	Faculty pros / students	Tuition + tickets (later, donations)	Director or corporation
Society	Volunteer member board	Professional	Tickets + membership dues	Corporation
Corporate	Civic board of nonmusicians	Professional	Tickets + donations	Corporation

Notes: Income includes both ticket sales for the orchestra's presentations plus payment for events sponsored by an outside organization, such as a business, a festival corporation, or a municipality. Ownership implies rights to the orchestra's assets as well as responsibilities for its debts.

dues, to participate. Members had other, usually nonmusical, employment, and any club earnings were reinvested in the organization. Administrative duties were undertaken by volunteers, although the full membership might be involved in decision making. A club's conductor might be paid, and especially prosperous clubs might hire professional musicians for principal chairs. Club ensembles played a limited set of concerts, but were primarily organized for the pleasure and artistic growth of participating members. Today's volunteer community orchestras follow the club model.[5]

In the cooperative model, professional musicians organized themselves into an orchestra with the dual purpose of making both music and money. The musicians themselves undertook organizational responsibilities for what was usually a limited series of concerts; they shared the financial risks; and they split the profits (if any) at the end of the season. Profits were typically divided equally (at least in Chicago), regardless of the role performed by any given individual. Thus concertmaster, second clarinetist, and conductor all received equal shares. Without a regular salary, most co-op players were required to find additional work, in music (such as in a theater orchestra) or in nonmusical fields.[6]

In the entrepreneurial model, an individual, often a charismatic impresa-

5 · Although not discussed extensively in this chapter because of its focus on professional ensembles, nineteenth-century Chicago did enjoy concerts by amateur clubs, such as the Haydn Society, which operated a sixty-member orchestra, including about ten professional musicians (see "The Haydn Society," *Chicago Tribune*, April 8, 1877, 9).

6 · The Germania Musical Society (1850–54) was a cooperative orchestra that sustained regular touring. See chapter III.4 in this volume. The New York Philharmonic was initially organized as a co-op, but it converted formally to the corporate model in 1912.

rio or conductor, assumed complete economic authority over an ensemble, receiving full benefit of the endeavor's success and accepting full liability for its failures. Such ventures might offer but a single performance or encompass a full concert season. Musicians in an entrepreneurial ensemble expected payment for all services—rehearsals as well as performances. Although paid professionals, many likely required additional employment. Only extremely successful entrepreneurial ensembles, what John Spitzer calls "enterprise orchestras," could offer a regular salary.[7] Owners often sought to mitigate their financial risks by partnering with local sponsors, such as a music store, theater, city government, or festival.

Connecting an orchestra to a school of music—the conservatory model—could strengthen each institution. The school gained a publicity vehicle that could feature and help to recruit exceptional faculty, while the orchestra gained rehearsal space, a steady revenue stream, the use of unpaid or minimally paid student musicians, increased ticket sales to students' family and friends, and an expanded mission that included education. The conservatory model used tuition rather than performance as an economic base. Instrumentalists might include students conducted by faculty or faculty accompanied and enhanced by local per-service professionals and exceptional students. In the nineteenth century, these nascent music educational endeavors operated less as public service institutions than individually operated, for-profit businesses owned by the schools' director(s). Into the twentieth century, the schools that thrived became nonprofit corporations. A school's orchestral concerts not only produced revenue but also served as a publicity vehicle for the institution and its most skilled performance faculty, helping to recruit students.

The concert society model—or simply "society" model as it was often called in nineteenth-century Chicago—used a music club structure to cover the costs of employing a professional orchestra. Members were music lovers or musical amateurs, and the society's leaders were organized as a board of member volunteers, sometimes including the group's paid conductor. Any revenue was reinvested in the society. Memberships, which comprised several types to include listeners and supporters and sometimes singers in an affiliated chorus, typically required an initiation fee and monthly dues. Members expected little or no income, although they did share ownership of the society's assets, such as its sheet music library or collection of auxiliary instruments. The society model developed to solve the problem of paying

7 · On "enterprise orchestras," see John Spitzer, "The Entrepreneur-Conductors and Their Orchestras" *Nineteenth-Century Music Review* (2008). Nineteenth-century enterprise ensembles in American music history include the professional bands of Patrick Gilmore and John Philip Sousa plus the touring orchestra of Theodore Thomas.

instrumentalists, initially for choral accompaniment. Because local theaters regularly employed instrumentalists, these jobs established a professional base salary for the skills of the city's limited number of qualified musicians. Chicago's better orchestral players required wages and did not typically play as community volunteers, thus making a top-notch orchestral club impossible. Although musicians were typically paid per service, nascent or especially precarious societies might offer extra performances as benefits to their conductor or players in lieu of service wages.[8]

The Chicago Symphony was one of the earliest examples of the corporate model, which has come to dominate the world of American professional orchestras. In the corporate model, a civic-oriented board of nonmusician directors supervised a professional staff and corps of musicians, including a typically charismatic conductor, for the benefit of its community. Musicians were professionals paid by service, with guaranteed minimum annual salaries in larger organizations. Seasons were longer than in other models, and there was more year-to-year continuity. Later organized as nonprofits, corporate orchestras combined the income-generating aspirations of a business with the social-service aspects of a charitable organization in what has come to be known as social enterprise.[9] The corporate structure was better able to withstand changes in leadership and weather economic uncertainty than the other models and became the primary institutional vehicle for orchestral performance in the twentieth century. The corporate model arose as the result of countless real-world experiments in institutional dynamics. Its story can be told in large part by rehearsing the attempts to bring a permanent professional concert orchestra to nineteenth-century Chicago.

Chicago's First Professional Orchestra

Chicago's first professional orchestra got its start with irregular gatherings of musicians at the home of violinist and banker Julius Dyhrenfurth (b. 1814), who on Thursday, October 24, 1850, gave the downbeat for the first season of the Chicago Philharmonic Society—a series of eight once-weekly perfor-

---

8 · The concert society had a long history in Europe going back to the eighteenth century. Examples include the early formations of the Royal Philharmonic in London, the Leipzig Gewandhaus, and concert societies in places such as Edinburgh, Manchester, and Amsterdam. See John Spitzer and Neal Zaslaw, *The Birth of the Orchestra: History of an Institution, 1650–1815* (2004), 203–4, 210–11, 242, 285–88, 414–16.

9 · See David Bornstein, *How to Change the World: Social Entrepreneurs and the Power of New Ideas* (2007); J. Gregory Dees, *Enterprising Nonprofits: A Toolkit for Social Entrepreneurs* (2001); and Alex Nicholls, *Social Entrepreneurship: New Models of Sustainable Social Change* (2008).

mances with an orchestra, largely made up of German immigrants to the city, all of whom were friends.[10] Programs included a potpourri of instrumental and vocal selections. The first concert, which dedicated Chicago's new Tremont Music Hall (located in the Tremont Hotel), included an orchestral medley of Donizetti's *The Daughter of the Regiment*, a song with vocal quartet accompaniment, a cello solo, a comic song and chorus, a vocal trio, a polka, a medley of "negro airs" composed by Dyhrenfurth, and a "French Grand Chorus" from Carl Maria von Weber's incidental music to *Preciosa* (1821).[11] The evening featured a "Chicago Waltz" composed for the occasion by cellist Carlino Lensen and performed by the composer to a guitar accompaniment.[12] Although there was no regular music criticism in the *Chicago Tribune* at this time, one attendee wrote to the newspaper in special praise of Lensen's "Chicago Waltz" as "the gem of the evening.... It was soft, tender, lulling, wafting the listener as gently as gossamer is borne upon the breeze, and anon carrying him round and round and up and up in a spiral motion delightful to feel."[13]

Despite a reported financial loss in its founding 1850 season, this first Chicago Philharmonic performed at least two eight-week concert seasons the following year (beginning in January and in October). In 1851 the orchestra adjusted its performance model to appeal to a broader entertainment-seeking audience. Each of the sixteen weekly concerts was offered in a promenade format: a concert of instrumental and vocal classics followed by a formal "promenade" and then a dance. Typically, the opening concert lasted from 7:30 to 9:00 p.m. Then came a fifteen-minute intermission in which the audience seats were cleared for dancing and a "saloon" was held, presumably to sell drinks to the dancers. The rest of the evening featured a "Grand Promenade Concert and Dance, Dyhrenfurth, conductor, Dean, caller."[14] The 1851 Philharmonic season culminated in a lucrative New Year's Eve ball patronized by eighty couples. In his memoirs *Tribune* critic George P. Upton recalled that at this final performance the orchestra comprised six violinists, two violists, a cellist, two bassists, pairs of flute, clarinet, and bassoon players, a trombonist, and two percussionists (playing cymbals and timpani).

10 · The 1850 *Tribune* account has apparently been lost, leaving only secondary sources for this event. See George P. Upton in *Musical Memories* (1908), 255, and Alfred Theodore Andreas, *History of Chicago* (1884), 1:498. Andreas (2:591–92) offers a detailed biography of Dyhrenfurth, who is described not as a professional musician but as a banker and school administrator who devised an influential system of accounting. His initial banking fortunes were destroyed by the 1857 crash.

11 · Andreas, *History of Chicago,* 1:498.

12 · Sources disagree on the spelling of the composer's name as either Lenssen or Lensen.

13 · Quoted in Upton, *Musical Memories,* 256.

14 · "Subscription Concerts," *Chicago Daily Tribune,* October 4, 1851, 1.

He praised the ensemble's musical growth, evidenced by the repertory of the evening's opening concert, which included Hérold's Overture to *Zampa,* a potpourri from Flotow's opera *Alessandro Stradella,* and the *Champagne Galop* (likely by Hans Christian Lumbye). These orchestral selections alternated with vocal selections from Verdi's *I Lombardi,* clarinet and piano solos, and a ballad titled "Child of Earth."[15]

Although called a "society," this initial Chicago Philharmonic was not organized on the concert society model but rather as the entrepreneurial effort of its conductor, Dyhrenfurth, who attempted to mitigate his financial risk by selling advance subscriptions to the entire season, thus assuring some revenue even before expenses (such as hall rental or music purchases) were incurred. His initial advertisement promised concerts only "if a sufficient number of subscribers can be found to insure the expenses."[16] For the first season, subscriptions cost $3 for all eight performances and entitled the bearer to admit "one lady and gentleman, with the privilege of one [additional] single ticket for 25c." By the fall of 1851, Dyhrenfurth had partnered with local businessman B. K. Mould and had increased the size of the ensemble to "a grand double orchestra of twenty performers."[17] Likewise, the subscription price increased to $5, with single tickets selling for $1 for gentlemen and half that for ladies. Figure I.1.1 shows a *Tribune* advertisement for the fall 1851 season that details the added vocal soloists along with a committee of gentlemen who were responsible for facilitating the formal promenade. Tickets were sold only at Mould's music store, thus serving to bring traffic to the shop.[18]

Despite the success of the final New Year's Eve performance, Upton reports that overall financial results were personally "disastrous" for Dyhrenfurth, who over the next two years "made several efforts to recoup himself, but at last abandoned the attempt to give regular seasons of concerts."[19] Upton's assessment may be distorted, however. Newspaper reports suggest that interest and attendance were strong at least at times: 175 of 200 subscriptions offered for sale at $5 in the fall of 1851 had been sold before October. Chicago historian A. T. Andreas suggests that the promenade concerts were discontinued not because of poor attendance but rather because "young people became more interested in dancing than in the music and came so late to

15 · Upton, *Musical Memories,* 257.
16 · Ibid., 255.
17 · Classified advertisements, *Chicago Daily Tribune,* October 4, 1851, 3. The date of October 6 is in error; the correct date—Tuesday, October 7—is confirmed by an announcement in the same paper on page 1.
18 · *Chicago Daily Tribune,* October 4, 1851, 1.
19 · Upton, *Musical Memories,* 258.

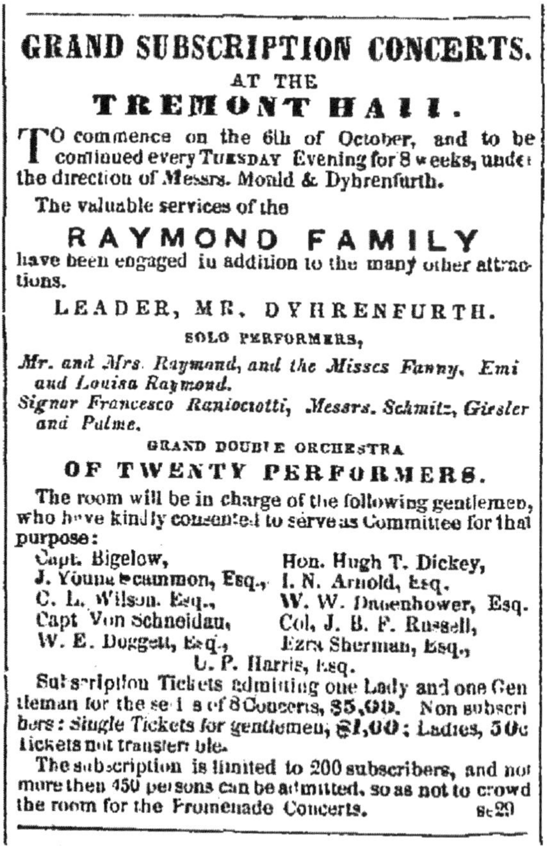

GRAND SUBSCRIPTION CONCERTS.
AT THE
T R E M O N T   H A L L .

TO commence on the 6th of October, and to be
continued every TUESDAY Evening for 8 weeks, under
the direction of Messrs. Mould & Dyhrenfurth.

The valuable services of the

R A Y M O N D   F A M I L Y
have been engaged in addition to the many other attrac-
tions.

LEADER, MR. DYHRENFURTH.

SOLO PERFORMERS,

*Mr. and Mrs. Raymond, and the Misses Fanny, Emi
and Louisa Raymond.*
*Signor Francesco Raniociotti, Messrs. Schmitz, Giesler
and Pulme.*

GRAND DOUBLE ORCHESTRA
OF TWENTY PERFORMERS.

The room will be in charge of the following gentlemen,
who have kindly consented to serve as Committee for that
purpose:

Capt. Bigelow,	Hon. Hugh T. Dickey,
J. Young Scammon, Esq.,	I. N. Arnold, Esq.
C. L. Wilson, Esq.,	W. W. Drucenhower, Esq.
Capt Von Schneidau,	Col. J. B. F. Russell,
W. E. Doggett, Esq.,	Ezra Sherman, Esq.,
	U. P. Harris, Esq.

Subscription Tickets admitting one Lady and one Gen
tleman for the set s of 8 Concerts, **$5,00.** Non subscri
bers: Single Tickets for gentlemen, **$1,00**; Ladies, **50c**
tickets not transferrable.
The subscription is limited to 200 subscribers, and no
more then 450 persons can be admitted, so as not to crowd
the room for the Promenade Concerts.   se29

FIGURE 1.1.1.
Advertisement for first
Chicago Philharmonic in
the *Chicago Tribune*,
October 4, 1851.

the concerts that Mr. Dyhrenfurth wisely discontinued them."[20] Andreas's
account is in accord with Upton's own characterization of Dyhrenfurth as
a musician of serious purpose and a man "stately in person and dignified in
speech.... Liberties were not taken with him."[21] Apparently not discouraged,
Dyhrenfurth initiated a fourth season, now of purely orchestral concerts, in
January 1852, again at Tremont Hall.[22]

20 · Andreas, *History of Chicago,* 1:498.
21 · Upton, *Musical Memories,* 278; one crack in Dyhrenfurth's austerity was his love for
mixing drinks at Germania Männerchor events, naming each after "dignitaries of the
Church—the bishop, archbishop, cardinal, and pope ... meant to indicate the increased
degree of excellence in each." Such sociality and camaraderie may have been key to the persistence of Dyhrenfurth's enterprises and the work of musicians from the German community generally.
22 · Andreas, *History of Chicago,* 1:498.

Chicago's Second Philharmonic

A new organization, Chicago's second Philharmonic Society, was not initially an orchestra at all. Founded in the fall of 1852, it did not present its first
concert until Thursday, January 6, 1853. The delay was due to the resigna-
tion of conductor G. P. Abell, who reportedly left because of the endeavor's
poor financial outlook.[23] Renewed under the directorship of Christopher
Plagge, this second society operated under a new business model and mission. Rather than a personal entrepreneurial venture, this Philharmonic was
organized as a "society" made up of the paying members of a large amateur
chorus whose members participated to improve their own musical abilities
as well as the taste of the community. As the *Tribune* announced: "We hail
with much satisfaction the debut of this Society composed as it is of the best
musical talent from our midst, and having for its object the most commendable one, of doing something towards the elevation of the standard of public
appreciation in matters of musical art, besides improving themselves in the
practice, and giving opportunity to the lovers of music to listen to the best
written."[24]

This second Philharmonic presented chiefly vocal music, including "glees,
solos, quartets and choruses." Its choruses in particular were praised in *Tribune* announcements and seem to have fit the newspaper's aspirations for
community taste. A "Grand Concert" on Monday, March 13, 1853, for example, included vocal compositions primarily by Mozart and Handel plus
instrumental selections featuring flute and piano solos. The second half
closed with Handel's "Grand Hallelu[j]ah Chorus."[25] Presumably in hopes
of reaching a larger audience, organizers moved the concerts to Warner Hall
and reduced ticket prices to fifty cents per couple. Whereas Dyhrenfurth
marketed to couples in offering functional dance music, this second Philharmonic seems to have targeted couples in order to attract a higher class of
listeners, using music for courting (but not dancing) and presenting sacred
vocal music, which in turn required more sober concert behavior (such as
timely attendance). A reviewer praised the ensemble's efforts and mission,
but also noted that "a good Orchestra was needed, and we trust that one may
soon be founded."[26]

By the fall of 1853, the anonymous reviewer's desire had been fulfilled,

---

23 · Upton, *Musical Memories*, 258.

24 · "Chicago Philharmonic Society," *Chicago Daily Tribune*, December 29, 1852, 3.

25 · "Amusements. Concert. Chicago Philharmonic Society," *Chicago Daily Tribune*,
March 11, 1853, 2.

26 · "Chicago Philharmonic Society," *Chicago Daily Tribune*, March 22, 1853, 3.

and Chicago Philharmonic Society concerts included an orchestra that alternated with and accompanied the "Society" (i.e., the chorus). Over the summer, an effort had been made to "place the Philharmonic Society on a substantial basis"; regular officers were elected and a board of directors appointed. The initiation fee for male members was set at five dollars, and the society petitioned the Illinois legislature for incorporation, which was eventually granted under the title of "an act to encourage the science of fiddling."[27] Although later mocked by *Tribune* music critic George P. Upton, this law is significant as the first incorporation of a musical organization in Illinois and an initial claim that such organizations were charged with the task of education. The petition itself embodied a desire on the part of the society's members to create an ongoing organization.

The first concert of this second year of the second Philharmonic was given on Monday, December 5, at Tremont Hall and included not only operatic overtures and choruses with orchestral accompaniment but also a full cantata — Andreas Romberg's *Lay of the Bell* (Lied von der Glocke, 1809), with Friedrich Schiller's poem as its text. Tickets were again sold on a subscription basis at Mould's music store, although a "limited number of tickets" were "sold at the door."[28] In February 1854 the society presented a benefit concert for its conductor, Plagge, seeking "an overflowing house . . . [to] testify a hearty appreciation to his merit." The need for a benefit suggests that whatever salary the society offered Plagge, it was not adequate payment for his time and effort.[29] Nevertheless, Andreas reports that the Philharmonic was "at this time in a flourishing condition," having "given a series of concerts which, aside from being popular and pleasing entertainments, had netted it handsome financial returns."[30]

In the fall of 1854, Carl Bergmann moved to Chicago and advertised for students. As principal cellist and sometimes director of the touring Germania Orchestra, Bergmann had visited Chicago in June 1853.[31] The directors of the society, already "acquainted with his reputation in the East," offered him the conductor's post. Bergmann's tenure lasted only two performances, the first on September 21, the second on November 21. Upton explains that the Phil-

27 · Upton, *Musical Memories*, 258.

28 · "Chicago Philharmonic Society," *Chicago Daily Tribune*, December 3, 1853, 2.

29 · "Christopher Plagge Musical Conductor of the Philharmonic Society," *Chicago Daily Tribune*, February 25, 1854, 2; advertisement, "Chicago Philharmonic Society," *Chicago Daily Tribune*, February 23, 1854, 2. See also Andreas, *History of Chicago*, 1:499.

30 · Andreas, *History of Chicago*, 1:499.

31 · "Philharmonic Society," *Chicago Daily Tribune*, September 21, 1854, 3.

harmonic musicians objected to Bergmann, but the cause of their dislike remains a matter of speculation.[32]

In January 1855, the society offered a benefit for its pianist Henry Lippert at Metropolitan Hall,[33] and, because the society lacked a permanent director, Dyhrenfurth reappeared to lead a short season of promenade concerts, closing with the city's first masquerade. Yet this renewed appeal to a broader audience did not revive the society; indeed, it may have exacerbated reported "internal dissensions."[34] A lengthy notice in the *Tribune* in February 1856 proposed an expansion of the society to include a new class of contributing members who would not sing with the group but would donate $10 per year to support the endeavor. Another proposal aimed to expand membership by reducing the initiation fee for men to $2 and fought perceptions of elitism by proclaiming that the society had "no notions of exclusiveness" and "earnestly desires . . . every person capable of taking part in its active work."[35] W. C. Webster of Buffalo was invited to direct the group's initial rehearsal, but this effort quickly ran its course, and by December 1857, a *Tribune* notice referred to the group as "the old philharmonic society."[36]

Chicago's Third Philharmonic Society

Yet a third Chicago Philharmonic Society was created in 1860 under the direction of Hans Balatka (1828–99); it was to become by far the most successful of the three.[37] It adopted the concert society model, again using dues-paying choristers and an audience of members to fill its coffers. Balatka had been introduced to Chicago in 1857 as director of the Northwestern Saengerfest.[38] He then served as director of the Milwaukee Musical Society, but in 1860 he joined the ranks of musicians that Chicagoans recruited away from

32 · Upton, *Musical Memories*, 259; here Upton suggests that the "German musicians" of the orchestra "did not like him and were forming cabals" against Bergmann; he attributes their opposition to "the fact that he was too great a musician for them to comprehend." Elsewhere Upton remarks that "Bergmann was not an industrious worker" and that he "gave himself up to an indolent, pleasure-loving manner of life, and this alienated many of his musical associates" (*Musical Memories*, 55).

33 · "Philharmonic Concert," *Chicago Daily Tribune*, January 26, 1855, 3.

34 · Upton, *Musical Memories*, 259.

35 · "Notice," *Chicago Daily Tribune*, February 2, 1856, 3.

36 · *Chicago Daily Tribune*, December 16, 1857, 1; Upton reports Webster's initials as C. W. (*Musical Memories*, 259).

37 · For Balatka and his orchestra, see chapter II.4 in this volume.

38 · "Annual Festival of the Northwestern Saengerbund," *Chicago Daily Tribune*, April 28, 1857, 2.

competing communities.[39] Balatka conducted a Mozart *Requiem* in Chicago on September 13, 1860, as a benefit for soprano Emmeline Garth and was persuaded to remain in the city to found this third Philharmonic.[40] By October 11 a slate of candidates for president, vice president, secretary, treasurer, librarian, and director (Balatka) had been nominated.[41] The official name of the new organization was the Chicago Philharmonic Society, and the group was structured similarly to concert societies in New York and Boston.[42] Members were divided into three categories: active (performers), contributory (audience), and honorary (presumably nonpaying members). A constitution set an initiation fee at $5 and required monthly dues of 50 cents. Members received three tickets to each concert for the season.[43] According to the *Tribune*, the mission of the society was to "promote and cultivate a taste for the higher branches of music."[44]

The third Philharmonic's first concert on Monday, November 19, 1860, featured Beethoven's Second Symphony, a chorus from Wagner's *Tannhäuser*, a quintet and chorus from Flotow's *Martha*, and a sextet from Donizetti's *Lucia di Lammermoor*. Only members were admitted to the audience.[45] By the second concert Bryan Hall was filled to its capacity (reportedly more than two thousand seats), and for the fourth concert "hundreds were compelled to stand during the whole performance."[46] The beginning of the American Civil War in April did not disturb the Philharmonic's plans; indeed, it ushered in a period of manufacturing prosperity and growth in Chicago that benefited the city's arts activity as a whole. Furthermore, Philharmonic concerts could be patriotic: "The Star-Spangled Banner" was performed to collective cheers in the seventh concert.[47] Altogether, the third Philharmonic's first season (1860–61) included eight regular monthly concerts plus a benefit for the instrumentalists. Repertory included overtures, opera arias, scenes, and choruses, and several complete symphonies (including Beethoven's Sec-

39 · "Death of Hans Balatka," *Chicago Daily Tribune*, April 18, 1899, 6.

40 · "Benefit," *Chicago Press and Tribune*, September 13, 1860, 1.

41 · Dyhrenfurth was among the officers of the third society (Andreas, *History of Chicago*, 2:591).

42 · For the organization of Boston concert societies, see chapters III.2 and V.1 in this volume. For New York, see chapter V.3.

43 · "The Chicago Philharmonic Society," *Chicago Press and Tribune*, October 11, 1860, 1.

44 · "First Philharmonic Concert," *Chicago Tribune*, November 19, 1860, 2.

45 · "Philharmonic Society," *Chicago Tribune*, October 27, 1860, 1.

46 · "Second Philharmonic Concert," *Chicago Tribune*, December 19, 1860, 1; "Fourth Concert of the Philharmonic Society, *Chicago Tribune*, February 11, 1861, 1; "The Dedication of Bryan Hall," *Chicago Press and Tribune*, September 18, 1860, 1.

47 · "The Seventh Philharmonic Concert," *Chicago Tribune*, May 15, 1861, 4, and Andreas, *History of Chicago*, 2:591.

ond, Fifth, and Sixth).[48] The Philharmonic's report of the year details that 284 members paid the initiation fee, while only 155 paid the full assessment of monthly dues. Extra ticket sales, including extra concerts with prima donna Inez Fabbri, brought total income to $3,525.50.[49] Reconciled against expenses ("including the cost of music and instruments, salary of the musical director, and of the musicians, advertising, printing, rent of hall, &c"), the season's revenue produced a surplus of $98.98.

Although the orchestra's sheen of novelty wore off in the next year, the ensemble continued to turn a profit, with 292 memberships and a $36.85 balance at the end of season two. Because of the time and expense of collection, monthly dues were eliminated for the second season, and ticket subscriptions that admitted three listeners (one man and two ladies) to each of five concerts were sold for five dollars.[50] As the ensemble grew, the society became increasingly professional and increasingly focused on instrumental music. Initially, many of the orchestra's musicians volunteered their services and received complimentary tickets in return. Soon, however, most musicians received a wage for both rehearsals and concerts. The chorus, which had initially provided the society's core members, was gradually distanced from concert participation. Instead, there was a special postseason performance of Mendelssohn's oratorio *Elijah*, featuring one hundred voices accompanied by the orchestra.[51] Over the summer of 1862, the choir was reorganized as the Chicago Musical Union, also conducted by Balatka but administered as a separate organization with its own board, members, and budget.[52] By the time season three began in the fall of 1863, the Philharmonic was a purely orchestral association. Season three saw 442 memberships providing for five regular "classical" concerts and two series of popular matinees leaving $81.47 in the treasury.[53] The Philharmonic's fortunes continued to rise as the 1863–64 season resulted in a $770 surplus, a balance peaking the following season when annual subscription rates were raised to ten dollars and the orchestra's account in May 1865 reached $1,485.[54]

When Confederate general Robert E. Lee surrendered at Appomattox Court House in April 1865, the Philharmonic was at its peak of success. In that same month, Crosby's Opera House opened in Chicago with a perfor-

48 · "The Philharmonic Society Concert," *Chicago Tribune*, June 25, 1861, 4.
49 · "Madame Fabbri's Concert," *Chicago Tribune*, January 19, 1861, 1.
50 · "The Philharmonic Society," *Chicago Tribune*, November 8, 1861, 4.
51 · "The Oratorio of Elijah," *Chicago Tribune*, May 13, 1862, 4.
52 · "Chicago Musical Union," *Chicago Tribune*, June 18, 1862, 4.
53 · "Philharmonic Society—Annual Meeting," *Chicago Tribune*, October 16, 1863, 4.
54 · "Philharmonic Society—Annual Meeting—Reports—Election of Officers," *Chicago Tribune*, May 10, 1865, 3.

mance of Verdi's *Il Trovatore* by Jacob Grau's star-studded traveling troupe from New York. Between April and June, Grau's company presented two separate seasons (nearly seven weeks) of opera, performing almost nightly. Union generals Grant and Sherman attended a performance of Donizetti's *The Daughter of the Regiment*, drawing cheers from the crowd as they were seated.[55] Building on the musical experience, choral repertory, and audience education of Chicago's Philharmonics, opera soon replaced orchestral music as the primary vehicle for musical art. The end of the war brought prosperity, security, and improved rail transportation to the north, thus facilitating the work of operatic touring companies. Crosby's Opera House triumphed, but the Philharmonic suffered.

The third Chicago Philharmonic Society announced a sixth season and began performing at the new opera house in the fall of 1865. This season exhausted the organization's financial surplus and put the orchestra in debt, despite a reduction in the number of concerts to four, the return of choral music, and the continuation of the more popular matinee season. Poor attendance at the opening concert of season seven on November 10, 1866, led the society's management to announce that unless enough subscriptions were sold to cover expenses, the 1866–67 season would be canceled.[56]

The orchestra gave one last concert in the opera house and then cut back its expenditures by using only local soloists and moving to the smaller Music Hall for the remainder of the season. Completing the year avoided any calls for refunds.[57] *Tribune* critic George Upton repeatedly proclaimed the death of the organization. His obituaries blamed a fickle public, ignorant of musical quality, for the ensemble's demise, but such a claim, even if basically true, oversimplifies the situation. Chicago seems to have possessed at least five separate musical publics: professional musicians, amateur singers who wished to participate in music making, casual listeners who desired familiar and functional light classics such as opera arrangements and dances, aspiring connoisseurs of classical or "scientific" music such as complete symphonies, and a "fashionable" public that sought events at which it could display its wealth and standing in Chicago's increasingly active society scene. When the Philharmonic engaged several of these publics, it thrived. Even when it focused on professional music making and instrumental classics, it remained viable, but only as long as the fashionable public joined forces with its connoisseur audience. Once fashion had shifted to opera, the enterprise failed.

While debates about repertory choices played out in the papers, what

55 · Upton, *Musical Memories*, 238–41.
56 · "The Philharmonic Society—Important Announcement," *Chicago Tribune*, November 23, 1866, 4. For the text of this announcement, see chapter II.4 in this volume.
57 · "Philharmonic," *Chicago Tribune*, January 4, 1867, 4.

eventually doomed the Chicago Philharmonic Society was, arguably, its very success. Having proved that classical music in Chicago could be profitable, the Philharmonic inspired competitors. As early as the 1850s, Chicago's musical dollars were targeted by a range of musical ventures — visiting opera troupes and instrumental virtuosi, local performers, persons offering musical instruction, and piano and organ sales. An efflorescence of musical opportunity in the second half of the nineteenth century competed in a limited but growing market. Chicago's Philharmonics were also victims of their own rising artistic standards. In the fall of 1868, Balatka reorganized the Third Philharmonic as the Orchestral Union, presenting concerts over the next two years. What doomed this new cooperative was not poor financial results, which Balatka valiantly overcame, but rather the direct comparison of his ensemble with the Theodore Thomas Orchestra. The orchestras performed back-to-back concerts, including overlapping repertory, at Chicago's Farwell Hall, with Balatka's ensemble performing first on Friday, November 26, 1869, and Thomas performing the next evening (see fig. I.1.2). Upton's discussion of the comparison was unequivocal and harsh.[58] He condemned the local product, stating that Thomas "is actually giving the grandest musical entertainments that Chicago has ever known."[59] By Thomas's farewell performance on November 30, Upton's review glorified the orchestra and its leader at the silent expense of Balatka's (and all other) previous efforts:

> [It was] such a performance as [Chicagoans] never heard before, as they may never hear again.... It was a revelation. Did we not all think we had heard an orchestra play before? And yet this was something new. You obtained musical possibilities for the first time — musical effects for the first time. You had a *crescendo* done for you. You first heard a musical *pianissimo*, and rarest of all rare things, you heard an orchestra play in time and tune. What a superb concert that was last evening! Everybody went out of that hall perfectly happy and loving everybody.[60]

Unfortunately for Balatka and the musicians of Chicago's series of philharmonics, the cooperative, entrepreneurial, and society models could not muster sufficient interest and local financial resources to match the artistic excellence of Thomas's touring enterprise orchestra.[61]

58 · For Upton's reviews of Balatka and Thomas, see chapter II.4 in this volume.

59 · "Amusements," *Chicago Tribune*, November 30, 1869, 4.

60 · "Amusements," *Chicago Tribune*, December 1, 1869, 4.

61 · As late as 1888, Balatka was still leading a Chicago-based concert society, namely, the Chicago Symphony Society (see "Music and Drama," *Chicago Tribune*, November 24, 1888, 5). Avoiding confusion with this group is one reason today's Chicago Symphony Orchestra

FARWELL HALL.

THEODORE THOMAS'

Grand Concert Organization

Of FORTY Celebrated Musicians, comprising all the
eminent Soloists of his great Orchestra, will give

THREE GRAND CONCERTS,

AT FARWELL HALL,

Saturday, Nov. 27,
Monday, Nov. 29,
Tuesday, Nov. 30.

Admission, $1.   Reserved Seats, $1 50.   The sale of
Reserved Seats will commence at Bauer's Music Store,
Crosby's Opera House, THURSDAY, Nov. 25.

FIRST PROGRAMME.

1. Overture—Tannhauser.................................Wagner
2. Allegretto—5th Symphony.........................Beethoven
3. Invitation a la Danse...................................Weber
        (Instrumentation by Hector Berlioz.)
4. Solo for Trombone—The Tear.......................Stigelli
        Mr. F. LEETSCH.
5. Traonmerie...Schumann
6. Grande Fantasie—Midsummer Night's
        Dream..Mendelssohn

PART SECOND.

1 Overture—William Tell...............................Rossini
2 Waltz—On the Beautiful Danube ....Strauss
3 Serenade for Flute and French Horn ....Titl
        Messrs. WRINRR and SCHMITZ.
4. {Polka Mazurka—Lob der Frauen,}
   {Polka Schnell—Jocus,   } ....Strauss
5. "Fackeltanz." No. 1, in B....................Meyerbeer

FARWELL HALL.

FIRST GRAND

SYMPHONY CONCERT

—OF—

H. BALATKA,

(Second Season,) FRIDAY EVENING, Nov. 26,

At Farwell Hall.

Subscribers' tickets, at $5, $9 and $12, at all the
Music Stores.
Single tickets, at the door, $1 50.

FIGURE I.1.2.
Chicago Tribune advertisements for Philharmonic and Thomas Orchestras at Farwell Hall, November 1869.

Co-op Orchestras in Chicago

The cooperative model emerged from Chicago's musicians unions rooted in its German musical community. As adaptations of the Turnverein and Männerchor traditions, the New World's nineteenth-century German community organizations put Enlightenment ideas of political and social engagement into practice through athletics and choral singing. Chicago's Männergesangverein of 1852 was among the city's earliest ethnic choral societies, and the Germania Männerchor (founded in 1865) and the Concordia (formed a year later) competed for a citywide audience; both ensembles used full orchestras to accompany their performances, which included symphonic and choral works as well as social dancing.[62] Some information about these more mainstreamed,

---

was originally called just the Chicago Orchestra. In 1881 Balatka began conducting a male chorus organized as the Mozart Society (see "The New Mozart Society Vigorously Entering the Field," *Chicago Tribune*, September 18, 1881, 18).

62 · Upton, *Musical Memories*, 270, 275–78. The Männerchor was formed after a German men's chorus performed to honor the funeral procession of President Lincoln. A Germania program reprinted in the *Tribune* indicates that an orchestra both accompanied the chorus

"Americanized" German musical organizations has been preserved by history, but contemporary records of German-influenced socialist culture in Chicago are comparatively rare. The tension between Chicago's integrated, so-called American, population and its more recent ethnic immigrants, especially Germans who came to the United States as refugees from the 1848 revolutions and brought their liberal, socialist, and anarchist ideas with them, has created gaps in the city's historical record. This suppression of radical German culture in contemporary accounts has relegated evidence of the cooperative or what might even be called the socialist model of orchestral culture to the margins.

As early as 1852, Henry Ahner, a cornet player formerly of the Germania Orchestra, began conducting orchestral performances in Chicago.[63] Andreas reports that "Henry Ahner's Saturday Afternoon Concerts" began in 1856 and credits Ahner with creating the city's "first full orchestra."[64] The *Tribune* first recognized these Saturday concerts on November 7, 1857, which saw the inauguration of a series of at least five weekly performances.[65] Tickets for the series were relatively inexpensive at one dollar for five concerts, with single seats priced at twenty-five cents. Far from marginal, these concerts were held at the newly renovated Metropolitan Hall, which in its day was known as Chicago's "largest and most pretentious public-room."[66] Notices in the *Tribune* through December 1857 suggest that Ahner's concerts ran at least until the end of that year.[67] Ahner's Saturday afternoon concerts came to an end early in 1858 with Ahner's unexpected death at the age of just thirty-three. An obituary published on February 4 laments the musician's death the previous morning due to a nine-day "attack of pneumonia ... aggravated by symptoms of typhoid fever."[68]

---

and played marches and other light works ("The Germania Maennerchor," *Chicago Tribune*, July 8, 1877, 10). The orchestra used by both organizations seems to have been the German music union's cooperative ensemble discussed below ("Concordia Maennerchor," *Chicago Tribune*, April 3, 1868, 4).

63 · Andreas describes a "series of concerts at Old Metropolitan Hall" given by Ahner in 1852 (*History of Chicago*, 1:498) as well as a series of Saturday afternoon concerts in the same location in November 1856 (1:500). Andreas later reports that a second season of orchestral concerts was given the next year led by a new conductor, Julius Unger (2:591).

64 · Otis (*Chicago Symphony*, 9) affirms the 1856 date for the creation of Ahner's ensemble and suggests that it linked the remaining musicians of the Chicago Philharmonic Societies with those of the Great Western and Light Guard Bands.

65 · Display advertisements, *Chicago Daily Tribune*, November 5, 1857, 1.

66 · Andreas, *History of Chicago*, 2:611.

67 · "Henry Ahner's Concert," *Chicago Tribune*, December 31, 1957, 1.

68 · "Death of Mr. Henry Ahner," *Chicago Daily Tribune*, February 4, 1858, 1. A retrospective article in Chicago's *Tribune* blamed Ahner's failure on German rivals. Calling Ahner an "excellent musician," the *Tribune* reports that "he came to Chicago and gave some orchestral concerts here with local players, but the opposition from the German musicians was too

The ensemble that played in Ahner's concert series seems to have largely escaped the notice of historians of classical music in Chicago, probably because of its name. Known as the Great Western Band (and only occasionally called the Great Western Orchestra), it appeared first in May 1856 under the baton of William Burkhardt and operated as a wind band or symphony orchestra as professional opportunities dictated.[69] Like other American ensembles founded by German émigrés, such as the Germania Musical Society and the New York Philharmonic, the Great Western Band was organized on a fully cooperative basis in which concert proceeds were divided evenly among all participants in a particular event. By October 1857 an orchestral version of this ensemble under the direction of Julius Unger performed light works and accompaniments for a vocal concert given by a visiting singer.[70] Ahner's own concerts began the next month with an ensemble now officially advertised as the Great Western Band. Something of a flexible pick-up ensemble, the Great Western Band appears associated with the German Music Verein or "Music Union," headed by Unger. This ensemble reconstituted itself as needed to serve the needs of specific musical employers and opportunities throughout the city, especially benefit concerts and picnics. The term "band" was used occasionally then (as now) as a colloquial synonym for "orchestra," but its use as an early economic model is more telling. In the cooperative sense used here, "band" refers to a "tribe" or banding together of musicians who work for mutual benefit. Indeed, later *Tribune* editorials that sought to inspire a permanent orchestra for Chicago used a capitalist argument to dismiss this "band" approach (i.e., the cooperative model), arguing that its equal distribution of profits among musicians, conductor, and venue staff failed to motivate excellence. Remarkably, the Great Western Band may in fact have been the most active performing organization in nineteenth-century Chicago.[71] Research remains to be carried out into the full range of activities of cooperative union ensembles, especially within the German community.[72]

much for him and he was obliged to abandon the attempt" ("A Chicago Orchestra," *Chicago Daily Tribune*, August 4, 1889, 28). Written in 1889, this article looks back on Chicago's music history through the distorted ethnic and class lens of the Haymarket killings of May 1886.

69 · "Serenading," *Chicago Daily Tribune*, May 22, 1856, 3.

70 · "Madame Johannsen's Concert on Saturday Evening," *Chicago Daily Tribune*, October 5, 1857, 1. This concert reportedly was the first in Chicago in which a solo singer was accompanied by a full orchestra.

71 · A search of the *Chicago Tribune* in the Proquest database returns more than two hundred hits on this ensemble's name prior to 1900.

72 · For more about the band and other co-op ensembles in Chicago, see Sandy R. Mazzola, "When Music Is Labor: Chicago Bands and Orchestras and the Origins of the Chicago Federation of Musicians, 1880–1902" (Ph.D. diss., 1984).

Orchestras at Chicago Music Schools

One of the first music schools in the United States, the Chicago Conservatory of Music, was established in June 1865 by Florenz Ziegfeld as an entrepreneurial effort to support his own teaching.[73] Born in Jever, Germany, Ziegfeld (father of the Broadway impresario of the same name) graduated from the Leipzig Conservatory in 1863. Having studied piano in one of Europe's most prominent schools which boasted such notable pedagogues as Ignaz Moscheles, Louis Plaidy, and Ernst Wenzel, Ziegfeld possessed an impeccable musical pedigree as well as firsthand experience with a leading school of music.[74] Settling in Chicago in November of 1863, he earned a living teaching piano privately,[75] and by 1865 he had established the first of at least two music stores.[76] In December of 1867, Ziegfeld presented a public "Soiree Musicale" concert by his pupils in partnership with Kimball's Music Store.[77] Ziegfeld's soirees became annual or even semiannual events attracting an increasingly fashionable audience.[78] Attached to a school, with a reliable audience of students and their families, and aspiring to establish highbrow credentials of excellence, Ziegfeld's soirees emphasized art music over a more popular, light classical repertory. Instrumental art music (works by Bach, Haydn, Mozart, Schumann, and Wagner), art song, and opera, especially bel canto (Schubert, Bellini, Donizetti, and Rossini), as well as virtuoso showpieces (works by Chopin, Liszt, and Gottschalk) appeared regularly on soiree programs.[79] Even before the school was large enough to staff

73 · "Musical," *Chicago Tribune*, May 24, 1865, 4; "Conservatorium of Music," *Chicago Tribune*, August 31, 1865, 1; Andreas (*History of Chicago*, 2:292) calls Ziegfeld's school the Chicago Academy of Music; "Musical," *Chicago Tribune*, April 25, 1967, 4. Chicago's Musical Union operated an earlier academy, beginning in 1859, but it focused on vocal instruction ("Musical Union Academy," *Chicago Tribune*, October 3, 1859, 1).
74 · Andreas, *History of Chicago*, 2:592.
75 · "Florence Ziegfeld," *Chicago Tribune*, February 17, 1864, 4. Three years later Ziegfeld had rented a studio in Chicago's premier venue, Crosby's Opera House. See "Musical," *Chicago Tribune*, April 25, 1867, 4.
76 · Advertisement, "Funeral March to the Memory of Abraham Lincoln," *Chicago Tribune*, May 6, 1865, 1; "Messrs. Ziegfeld, Gerard & Co's New Music Store," *Chicago Tribune*, April 18, 1866, 4.
77 · "Ziegfeld's Soiree Musicale," *Chicago Tribune*, December 22, 1867, 4. The paper praises both instructor and store owner for the fiscally inventive plan and plugs the "F. C. Lighte" piano.
78 · "Amusements," *Chicago Tribune*, June 7, 1870, 4.
79 · After Ziegfeld partnered with business manager W. A. Root (1870) and later George F. Root, popular songs published by Root and Cady appeared on Ziegfeld's soiree programs (see George P. Upton, "The World of Amusement," *Chicago Tribune*, May 29, 1870, 2).

a student orchestra, full symphonies by Haydn were performed in four-hand piano arrangements.[80]

In February 1869, Ziegfeld conducted Niels Gade's *Elverskud* cantata with soloists, orchestra, and a choir of eighty. Tickets were sold, and the *Chicago Tribune* promoted the event with two preview articles.[81] Few specifics about the orchestra are recorded by the *Tribune*, but its size as well as the paper's interest suggest it was professional because the school was not yet large enough to staff a "full orchestra" of students. By 1870 a "new" expanded Chicago Academy of Music was established in rooms at Crosby's Opera House. Its faculty included Hans Balatka (voice) as well as Dudley Buck and Louis Falk (piano, organ, and theory).[82] The Great Chicago Fire of October 1871 destroyed the academy's building, yet in just two weeks Ziegfeld reopened at a new location and was again advertising for students.[83] The school's student concerts resumed, helping to fill the void left by the fire.[84] In 1872, now partnering with songwriter and Lowell Mason–trained pedagogue George F. Root, Ziegfeld founded the Chicago Musical College, discarding the name Academy of Music, perhaps because it was used by several local theaters. By 1875, the college was presenting regular musical reunion recitals plus a season of eight public concerts and, following the precedent of Chicago's concert societies, had established an associate membership program to help fund a music library.[85] The State of Illinois recognized the college as a public educational institution the following year,[86] and soon its annual registrations numbered over one thousand pupils, who were taught by twenty-three instructors.[87]

In 1889 the college began sponsoring a professional orchestra by promoting a season of "faculty concerts" that featured the school's instructors as vocal or instrumental soloists accompanied by about forty of the city's pro-

80 · Ibid.; "Amusements," *Chicago Tribune*, December 10, 1873, 8; "Musical College Soiree," *Chicago Tribune*, October 14, 1877, 10.

81 · "Amusements: The Cantata Concert," *Chicago Tribune*, February 17, 1869, 4.

82 · Upton, "The World of Amusement," *Chicago Tribune*, July 10, 1870, 2; "Chicago Academy of Music," *Chicago Tribune*, October 26, 1870, 4.

83 · Advertisement, *Chicago Tribune*, October 25, 1871, 1.

84 · "The Chicago Musical College," *Chicago Tribune*, August 25, 1872, 8; "Musical: Church Benefit Concerts," *Chicago Tribune*, December 18, 1872, 7; "Modest Florence," *Chicago Tribune*, March 30, 1873, 3; "The Musical College Concert," *Chicago Tribune*, December 10, 1873, 8; "Amusements: Music: At Home," *Chicago Tribune*, February 21, 1875, 7.

85 · "Reorganization of the Chicago College of Music," *Chicago Tribune*, August 8, 1875, 3.

86 · "History of the Chicago College of Performing Arts," Roosevelt University website, http://www.roosevelt.edu/Home/CCPA/AboutCCPA.aspx.

87 · "Music," *Chicago Tribune*, June 5, 1881, 20; Andreas, *History of Chicago,* 2:592.

fessional musicians.[88] On April 22, 1890, for example, Ziegfeld himself conducted Bruch's Violin Concerto and piano concertos by Grieg and Tchaikovsky, plus Tosti's "Goodbye" and Verdi's "Celeste Aïda" with faculty soloists.[89] College and orchestra were mutually beneficial, attracting both audiences and future pupils while reinforcing the brand profile of each activity. The affiliation further elevated their shared mission, celebrating instrumental music and providing educational opportunities for students as well as the community at large. That Ziegfeld's initiative to link the orchestra, art music, and education was uncommonly successful is proved by the continued existence of his college, now renamed the Chicago College of the Performing Arts and since 1954 part of Roosevelt University.

Chicago's Orchestral Entrepreneurs

The entrepreneurial efforts of individual conductors and composers in Chicago to establish a series of orchestral concerts never sustained momentum. Dyhrenfurth's Chicago Philharmonic Society was the first of many such efforts. Better positioned were smaller, less expensive endeavors featuring solo artists and often presenting individual touring artists (such as pianists) sponsored by instrument manufacturers. The musical soirée, a variety evening featuring accompanied voice and small-scale instrumental chamber music, was also popular. However, as early as 1858, the aptly named J. M. Mozart directed an orchestra that competed successfully against the Great Western Band. Later, composer Silas G. Pratt organized a concert of his own works, and on Friday, April 17, 1874, he hired McCormick Hall and a forty-five-piece orchestra to present his complete first symphony (written when he was a student in Berlin) and four other of his compositions, including the tone poem *Magdalena's Lament* and a new march titled "Hail to New Chicago," plus vocal and instrumental selections by Wagner and Schubert.[90] Four years later—in December 1878 and early 1879—Pratt returned to McCormick Hall with a series of open rehearsals and concerts featuring works by Beethoven, Wagner, Mendelssohn, and other German masters, leavened with operatic excerpts and works by local composers, including Henry Grant Gleason and, of course, Pratt himself. Articles in the *Tribune* suggest sizeable attendance, but reviews describe the concerts as aesthetically disappointing

88 · "Music and Drama," *Chicago Tribune*, November 27, 1889, 4.
89 · "An Artistic Treat by Home Talent," *Chicago Tribune*, April 23, 1890, 6.
90 · "Review of Amusements," *Chicago Daily Tribune*, April 12, 1874, 7. Also performed were Pratt's serenade for male chorus, "Sailing the Sea," and his Polonaise for Piano (presumably with Pratt at the keyboard).

because of poor intonation and questionable tempo choices, owing to the limited skills of the artists and insufficient rehearsal. Adolph Rosenbecker presented orchestral concerts in 1878–79 under the management of Florenz Ziegfeld in McCormick Hall,[91] and in 1880–81, Adolph Liesegang offered a series of concerts with thirty-two players at Brands Hall, featuring classical and modern works by local composers;[92] in 1882, Liesegang led yet a fourth Chicago Philharmonic Society.[93] Yet by the 1870s, the touring Thomas Orchestra, which had begun almost annual visits to the city in 1869, had set a standard of excellence in orchestral performance that local efforts failed to match. Andreas blames the failure of Chicago to sustain a local orchestra on the precarious financial position of German immigrant musicians "obliged to eke out a living by playing in theaters, giving lessons, etc., engagements absorbing so much of their time that they have little leisure for practice, and can not be engaged in symphony or other transient concerts, except at such an advance upon their regular wages as to leave them a profit after paying a substitute."[94]

The most successful entrepreneurial concerts in Chicago using a local orchestra were the relatively frequent charity concerts performed by the Great Western Band and other musical societies for the benefit of the poor or for victims of natural disasters.[95] Tickets for these performances were typically 50 cents, twice the cost of the band's regular concerts, but expenses were minimal because the musicians were called on to donate their services. Also successful were the summer garden concerts organized by impresario George B. Carpenter featuring Theodore Thomas's orchestra in an informal setting at Chicago's enormous Exposition Building. Despite two weeks of cold rainy weather and a labor strike that paralyzed the city for a third week, Carpenter's first season of summer concerts in 1877 turned a profit, inspiring Thomas to return for fourteen more summer seasons.[96] Although these summer programs featured primarily light classics and dance music, Thomas did manage to program the complete Fifth, Sixth, and Seventh symphonies of Beethoven as well as complete symphonies by Gade, Haydn, Mozart, Raff, Schubert, and Schumann plus the American premiere of the Mozart Triple

91 · Andreas, *History of Chicago*, 3:640; "Music," *Chicago Tribune*, October 13, 1878, 10. Rosenbecker also conducted the Sunday afternoon concerts at Chicago's Turner Hall.
92 · Andreas, *History of Chicago*, 3:640.
93 · "The First Concert of the Philharmonic Society," *Chicago Tribune*, April 16, 1882, 8; "The Concert by the Philharmonic Society," *Chicago Tribune*, December 3, 1882, 20.
94 · Andreas, *History of Chicago*, 3:641.
95 · See, for example, "The Cantata Matinee," *Chicago Tribune*, July 24, 1869, 4, which describes a Great Western benefit for the Home for the Friendless.
96 · Otis, *Chicago Symphony*, 15.

Concerto.[97] It was the financial success of these summer concerts that laid the foundations for the creation of the Orchestral Association and, in turn, the Chicago Symphony Orchestra.[98] Thomas's success also inspired the cooperative orchestras (typically connected with musicians' unions) to mount similar popular series. In August 1877—following Thomas's first summer season—members of the Great Western Light Guard Band and Hand and Freiberg's Orchestra combined to form the sixty-piece Chicago Orchestra. The *Chicago Tribune* praised the development, hoping that a local orchestra drawing the best talent from across several cooperative ensembles could eventually match the artistic excellence of the Thomas Orchestra.[99] The original cooperatives appear to have continued to perform unabated, however, suggesting that the unified "Chicago Orchestra" was little more than a promotional vehicle intended to capture the audience cultivated by Thomas.

The Chicago Symphony—America's First Corporate Orchestra

In his 1924 history of the Chicago Symphony, longtime orchestra secretary Philo Adams Otis credits the founding of the ensemble to just two figures: conductor Theodore Thomas and businessman Charles Norman Fay. He writes, "To Theodore Thomas we must ascribe all honor as the founder of our Orchestra, but to Charles Norman Fay, a man endowed with a genius for organization and executive work, is due equal honor for the first thought of the Orchestra."[100] Otis thus recognizes that the venture's eventual success was determined by a combination of charismatic artistic leadership, a sound organizational structure, and effective mobilization of its features. Several studies of the American orchestras have fixated on the cult of the conductor, but in fact Fay's insight was to leverage Thomas's popularity to forge a corporate structure capable of outliving the orchestra's charismatic conductor.

Fay was a careful observer of Chicago's previous efforts to found orchestras and had, in fact, written to Thomas in 1879 for advice about forming yet another Chicago Philharmonic.[101] The failure of Thomas's own orchestra in 1888 and his declining reputation in New York when compared to ecstatic conductors such as Richard Wagner's protégé Anton Seidl made it possible

97 · "Amusements: The Close of the Summer-Garden Concerts," *Chicago Tribune*, August 5, 1877, 12. The Mozart "triple concerto" was probably the Sinfonia Concertante in A for violin, viola and cello, K. 320e, reconstructed from a Mozart autograph fragment and published in 1871. For more on the repertory of the Thomas Orchestra, see chapter V.2 in this volume.
98 · Otis, *Chicago Symphony*, 26.
99 · "Music," *Chicago Tribune*, August 12, 1877, 12.
100 · Otis, *Chicago Symphony*, 25.
101 · Rose Fay Thomas, *Memoirs of Theodore Thomas* (1911), 352–53.

to recruit the maestro for Chicago.[102] Vital to Fay's plan was a $50,000 annual guarantee fund that protected the nascent effort from debt in its first three years. The manner in which this fund was realized, however, had long-term implications for the success of the orchestra and the triumph of its corporate model. Essentially, Fay's Orchestral Association plan was an extended fundraising scheme, drawing on precedents from a range of charitable projects, music festivals, and building associations to create a sustainable venture that could navigate financial and leadership crises. The fact that Thomas had attracted substantial and profitable audiences in Chicago since 1869 helped Fay to recruit guarantors from among Thomas's fans and reinforced Fay's claim that the fund was not simply a donation but a guarantee against loss for an organization that would soon cover its expenses.

Fay's initial impulse was to raise the $50,000 guarantee by securing ten pledges of $5,000 each. With himself as the first signatory, Fay quickly secured the first $20,000 by approaching three other local business magnates, including department store owner Marshall Field, manufacturer Nathaniel K. Fairbank, and railroad car manufacturer George Pullman. In search of six others to complete the fund, Fay next approached Ferdinand Peck, a similarly impassioned music patron who had built Chicago's Auditorium Building, the orchestra's first home.[103] Peck urged Fay to broaden the orchestra's base of support by seeking fifty donors at $1,000 each.[104] During a social event sponsored by the Chicago Commercial Club, Fay secured nineteen signatories to this new plan and eventually found fifty-one supporters, slightly exceeding his goal. This move to expand the orchestra's base of support with a greater number of smaller contributions would become a recurring strategy that Chicago's Orchestral Association used to solidify and secure ongoing funding.

Dated December 16, 1890, the Orchestral Association's articles of incorporation proclaim its purpose as "the promotion of musical art in any and every lawful way and by any and every lawful means."[105] Such a broad charter reveals the experimental nature of the endeavor able to explore any means

102 · On Seidl, see Joseph Horowitz, *Classical Music in America* (2005), especially chapter 5.

103 · See Mark Clague, "Chicago Counterpoint: The Auditorium Theater Building and the Civic Imagination" (Ph.D. diss., 2002).

104 · Peck's advice drew on his experience with earlier cultural associations, including the Chicago Opera Festival Association founded on April 16, 1884 (see Andreas, *History of Chicago*, 3:651) and in 1886 the Auditorium Building Association (see Clague, "Chicago Counterpoint," 128). These had been influenced by the Chicago Musical Festival Association founded in February 1881 to promote Chicago's May Festivals in 1882 and 1884 (Andreas, *History of Chicago*, 3:649–50).

105 · The original copy of the articles of incorporation is held in the Chicago Symphony's Rosenthal Archives.

of promoting the orchestra (e.g., touring, building a new venue, founding a music school, creating a symphony chorus, sponsoring an opera festival, and so forth). The articles placed leadership responsibility in a five-member board of trustees, but Fay admitted in a 1916 letter to Otis that most association business was conducted over lunch at the Chicago Club, where he described his decisions to a single colleague who affirmed them.[106] In practical terms, then, Chicago's orchestra was at its origin very similar to the Boston Symphony Orchestra, as it was in many ways the project of a single man. In Boston, the orchestra was run by Henry Lee Higginson; in Chicago, by Charles Norman Fay.

Fay's plan worked, although the ensemble's guarantors were routinely called on to pay a bit more than their promised amount; they needed a total of $53,613 for the first season, $51,381 for the second, but just $49,000 for the third.[107] As the original three-year guarantee expired, the association hired Anna Millar as sales manager for associate memberships and started what it prosaically called the "Fund to Support the Orchestra." At meetings held during intermission at the November 30 and December 1, 1894, concerts, the trustees appointed a subcommittee to formulate a new financial plan.[108]

Rather than raise ticket prices and risk losing listeners, the association created an additional board of governing members—donors of $50 to $1,000 who would receive a proportionate vote in association business. Fully adopted by February 1895, the plan also increased the number of trustees from five to nine and created a three-person executive committee.[109] Although neither fund-raising nor subscription sales were as successful as hoped, player contracts were renewed, and the orchestra struggled onward. Annual deficits dropped to about $30,000 per year, of which donations from the governing members covered two-thirds, and the trustees managed the remainder through additional gifts and loans.

The move that secured the future of the Chicago Symphony was the construction of Orchestra Hall, which continues to serve as its home today. Thomas, according to his memoirs, had long been concerned that the cavernous Auditorium Building, with a seating capacity of 5,200 at that time, would challenge efforts to secure season subscriptions. Because there were always individual tickets available at the door, patrons were not compelled to purchase season subscriptions in order to secure seats to even the most popular concerts. Opening in December 1904, the new hall eased this problem by cutting seating capacity in half to 2,500. The smaller-capacity venue raised the

106 · Otis, *Chicago Symphony*, 28.
107 · Ibid., 37, 43.
108 · Ibid., 60–62.
109 · Ibid., 63–64.

value of subscriptions by limiting individual ticket sales to especially attractive events. Paradoxically, fewer tickets meant higher ticket income.

Possibly more important than subscription sales to the orchestra's economic dynamic, however, was the effect the building project had on the association's donor base. Eight thousand contributors, some giving as little as 10 cents, raised more than $569,000 to build the orchestra's new home.[110] Thomas had stoked the effort by threatening to leave Chicago if a new hall was not built, using the building project as a fund-raising gambit to yet again deepen and broaden Chicagoans' investment in the city's orchestra. The importance of this effort was proved when Thomas died not long after Orchestra Hall's dedication. Despite the tragic loss of its founder—the one and only musician Fay and his colleagues would support to create the ensemble—the orchestra's future was never threatened. Fay's organizational invention—the Orchestral Association—had transformed what had been the Theodore Thomas Orchestra into Chicago's orchestra, creating a permanent corporation from what could have been a mortal cult of personality.

The strengths of the corporate model derive from a synthesis of the entrepreneurial and concert society strategies. Such an approach provides two complementary economic tributaries for the organization—sales and donations. During the first three years of the Chicago Orchestra, ticket revenue from concerts, opera, and touring accounted for 59 percent of total expenditures, while the guarantee fund, essentially what became donations, made up the remaining 41 percent.[111] Remarkably, after the creation of the board of governors and its expansion of the orchestra's donor base, the proportion of the budget covered by ticket sales increased to nearly 72 percent.[112] Increasing community donorship increased community ownership and in turn strengthened commitment to and participation in the orchestra's activities.

This legacy, however, presents three complications for ensembles today. First, the ever-broader economic foundation of the corporate orchestra as a funding machine has expanded its mission to serve an ever-greater range of donors and goals, including economic development, artistic excellence, civic competition, education for the disadvantaged, and so forth. Such continual expansion threatens to dilute the focus of the ensemble on any particular goal and leads to inevitable conflicts. Second, the corporate model rejects the club model and dismisses amateurism. While the corporate orchestra thus emphasizes its professional credentials, it loses the rich connection to amateur members that the club and society models enjoy. Although Thomas and

110 · Ibid., 143 (see especially the table).
111 · Ibid., 37, 43, 57.
112 · Ibid., 70.

the Chicago press lamented the lack of informed and passionate core listeners in Chicago, such listeners were rejected as member-participants by the corporate model. Had the concert-society model, with its committed and active membership, been embraced, twentieth-century American orchestras might have forged much closer ties to educational efforts and schools of music, and the definition of a "service" (the unit of work performed by contracted instrumentalists that typically includes either a rehearsal or concert) might have been broadened to include coaching sessions for community orchestra musicians. Divisive debates in Memphis and Detroit over "service exchange" in which twenty-first-century professional musicians would be required to teach and perform other community service as part of their regular duties as symphony musicians might have been avoided entirely had amateurs and community service been more fully embraced by Chicago's influential model and musicians included in the orchestra's activities from the very beginning.[113]

Finally, by repudiating the cooperative model, the corporate model denies the possibility of musician-led leadership. The business magnates who populated the Chicago Orchestra's founding board were all bitter antagonists of organized labor.[114] Wage cuts imposed by the Pullman Palace Car Company during the economic depression of the early 1890s precipitated a nationwide strike, accompanied by armed conflict between the American Railway Union and U.S. government troops. Rampant fear of all forms of cooperative labor characterized the growing pains of Gilded Age business and immediately became an issue for the Chicago Orchestra. The Chicago musicians union objected to Thomas's plan to seed Chicago's new ensemble with New York musicians, primarily former members of his own Theodore Thomas Orchestra. Chicago's musicians, who had long hoped that a homegrown Philharmonic society would provide them with steady employment playing great music, realized and lost their hopes at one time. Thomas's memoirs confirm that "so many of the former [musicians of the Thomas Orchestra] were retained, that it might fairly be said that the Chicago Orchestra was, in reality, the original Thomas Orchestra."[115] In 1891 the Chicago Musical Society (i.e., the local union) threatened to have New York's union, of which Thomas was a mem-

---

113 · Mark Stryker, "Trust Issues at Root of DSO Strike Set to Begin Today," *Detroit Free Press*, October 4, 2010, E1; Joseph Horowitz, "Why Memphis Matters to Every American Orchestra," *The Unanswered Question* (ArtsJournal weblog), January 29, 2010, posted at http://www.artsjournal.com/uq/2010/01/why-memphis-matters-to-every-a.html.

114 · The Chicago Orchestra's board included George Pullman (railway cars) as well as other manufacturers such as Philip Armour (meatpacking) and Cyrus McCormick (farm implements).

115 · Thomas, *Memoirs*, 357.

ber, invalidate Thomas's contract with the Chicago trustees.[116] In the end a compromise was reached in which sixty musicians were brought from New York, and thirty local players were engaged. Nevertheless, the two groups of musicians remained separate, as only the former New York players toured with Thomas when the Chicago Orchestra left the city.[117] Thus Chicago's union immediately took on an antagonistic role in the ensemble's history, defending the interests of local musicians, confirming the fears of the orchestra's directors, and establishing a legacy of difference and division between administrators and players in the American orchestra that persists today.[118]

Chicago's Orchestral Association was a key development in the future proliferation of symphony orchestras in the United States. By the time of Thomas's death in 1905, orchestras in Philadelphia, St. Louis, Cincinnati, Minneapolis, and Pittsburgh had been founded on the Chicago model, and a few years later, the New York Philharmonic abandoned its cooperative model in favor of Chicago's corporate approach.[119] However, this corporate model, developed and implemented so successfully in Chicago, was built on previous efforts, based particularly on the concert society and entrepreneurial models. Despite their unique details, these different structures are consistent in their overall trajectory of increasing ambition, scope, and base of support. It is a story of artistry, entrepreneurship, sociality, cooperation, and community spirit. More than the work of any single composer, conductor, or soloist, the most significant contribution of nineteenth-century American culture to its orchestral tradition may well be the varied and adaptable institutional structures that have served to create and sustain symphonic music in the United States, now in its third century.

116 · Otis, *Chicago Symphony*, 30.
117 · Thomas, *Memoirs*, 370.
118 · See Stryker, "Trust Issues."
119 · Philip Hart, *Orpheus in the New World* (1973), 47, and Adam Galinsky and Erin V. Lehman, "Emergence, Divergence, Convergence: Three Models of Symphony Orchestras at the Crossroads," *European Journal of Cultural Policy* 2 (1995).

[1.2] Modeling Music
Early Organizational Structures of American Women's Orchestras

ANNA-LISE P. SANTELLA

Early orchestras, like much of nineteenth-century life in America, were segregated by gender. With the exception of a handful of harpists and organists—instruments traditionally taught to women and evocative of the Victorian idea of "the angel in the house"—women rarely performed in American orchestras until the last quarter of the nineteenth century.[1]

It is not so much that women were excluded from early orchestras but that in orchestras founded by men, the idea that women might be interested or qualified to perform was seldom considered. Women's participation in public-sphere activities, including musical performances, was severely limited, and the advisability of such participation was frequently questioned on both physiological and moral grounds. An 1895 article in *Scientific American*, for example, observed that even if women had proved to be creditable soloists, they did not have the stamina for orchestral performance and could handle "not more than a third, probably, of what men are able to do."[2] And even in respectable venues, the mere novelty of women appearing on the stage was often treated as a spectacle by audience and critics alike. This not only detracted from women's musical skills but also could force them into a sexualized role, a role that the press often underscored in reviews that focused on the women's orchestras' particular appeal to male listeners. This added weight to the suggestion that women's public performance was morally questionable.

Such treatment, however, only encouraged women to carve their own path. The women's orchestra movement was a direct response to the dearth

1 · On "angel in the house," see Sandra M. Gilbert and Susan Gubar, *The Madwoman in the Attic* (1979), 22. On organ and harp as women's instruments, see Christine Ammer, *Unsung: A History of Women in American Music* (2001), 12–33.

2 · "Orchestral Women," *Scientific American*, November 23, 1895, 327.

of public performance opportunities for women, particularly in ensembles, and it sought to walk the fine line between public performance and social respectability, between model femininity and model musicianship. Women's orchestras were not mere copies of their all-male predecessors. Rather, they emerged from women's own experiences and developed their own institutional structures and policies modeled on institutions in which women had already participated.

Two areas of women's public-sphere participation were particularly important in the development of women's orchestras. First, women gained crucial organizational skills and a limited access to the public sphere through women's clubs, which flourished in the years following the Civil War and peaked between 1880 and 1920, during which period approximately two million American women from all walks of life joined a club.[3] Music clubs were an important subset of the women's club movement. The first American women's club devoted to music, the Rossini Club, was founded in 1867 in Portland, Maine; the movement quickly ballooned and organized nationally.[4]

The second crucial area of women's public-sphere participation was as performers. Although women did not play in orchestras until the 1870s, they were involved in various types of performance throughout the nineteenth century, mainly in the theater as actors and singers, but also occasionally on concert stages as instrumental soloists, typically on piano or violin.

When the first American women's orchestras were founded in the 1870s, they followed one of two models, each arising from one of these areas of public-sphere expertise.

Institutional Models of Women's Orchestras

American women who wanted to play orchestral music were faced with a choice: either they could perform for pay as their soloist predecessors had done, or they could perform "serious" music with the artistic devotion of a women's music club study group. Male musicians generally didn't have to make such a choice, although they might have to play in more than one orchestra, making money in some and playing high-class music in others. But women's more circumscribed access to public life limited their options. Their choice led to two different organizational models for women's orchestras.

3 · Anne Ruggles Gere, *Intimate Practices: Literacy and Cultural Work in U.S. Women's Clubs, 1880–1920* (1997). See also Karen J. Blair, *The Clubwoman as Feminist: True Womanhood Redefined, 1868–1914* (1980), and Blair, *The Torchbearers: Women and Their Amateur Arts Associations in America, 1890–1930* (1994).

4 · George Thornton Edwards, *Music and Musicians of Maine* (1928), 140; Adrienne Fried Block and Carol Neuls-Bates, *Women in American Music* (1979), xix.

It is tempting to refer to these two models as "amateur" and "professional," as several scholars have done previously.[5] However, those terms are misleading. During most of the nineteenth century, the word "professional" was primarily associated with defined professions—doctor, lawyer, and clergy, for example—and was only occasionally used more broadly to refer to a paid position. Not until the early 1890s was the word used consistently to describe a musician who worked for money. The word "amateur" had not yet acquired its modern connotation denoting something of lesser quality or something to take less seriously. On the contrary, in the last third of the nineteenth century, "amateur" had associations with high ideals and devotion to a subject for love rather than for money.[6]

It is therefore more appropriate to designate the two models of women's orchestras as the "career" model and the "club" model. The career model was based on women's experiences as singers, actresses, dancers, and instrumental soloists on public stages before paying audiences. The priority of a career-model orchestra was to pay its members enough to make musical careers playing orchestral music. The club model was based on women's experiences in the private women's clubs. A club-model orchestra's priority was to play challenging classical repertory at a high level in respectable venues. Despite their different origins, both types sought to emulate male orchestras such as the Chicago and Boston symphonies, which did not need to make a choice between the two priorities.

These two models emerged in the last quarter of the nineteenth century. Both types sought a quality that would today be defined as professionalism—a blend of skill, success, and esteem. The two models evolved and eventually merged into a new, professional women's symphony model that was characteristic of women's orchestras founded in the twentieth century and, beginning in the 1940s, enabled women instrumentalists to gain entrance into orchestras once populated only by men. Table I.2.1 contrasts the most salient features of the career and the club models.

The Career Model

The career model was based on a combination of professional solo experience that some of the founders of early women's orchestras had and on their observation of male professional orchestras. Some of the key characteristics of the career model were the following:

---

5 · Judith Tick, "'Passed Away Is the Piano Girl': Changes in American Musical Life, 1870–1900," in *Women Making Music*, ed. Jane Bowers and Judith Tick (1986); Ammer, *Unsung*.
6 · See William Haley, "Amateurism" *American Scholar* 45 (1976): 253.

TABLE 1.2.1. Institutional models of American women's orchestras

	Career	Club
Founded	By entrepreneur	By small group with leader
Goal	Career	Self-improvement/social betterment
Class	Lower	Higher
Priorities/mission	Employment/popularity	Repertoire/charitable work
Touring	Often toured	No tours
Training	Private & conservatory	Mostly private
Venues	Vaudeville/theater/beer garden	Concert halls/private functions
Repertory	Mixed/popular	Mostly classical
Femininity	As marketing tool: novelty	As morally uplifting

- Orchestras subscribing to the career model were usually *founded and conducted by an entrepreneur*, who, if female, was usually a professional instrumental soloist (often a violinist) prior to her orchestra work. Many of the earliest orchestras, however, were founded or managed by men.
- Their *primary mission was employment*. Career-model orchestras tailored themselves and their repertory to the available work situations. These orchestras seldom had stated goals or mission statements.
- Most of the members were *lower middle class*—of a high enough class to have musical training, but low enough to be allowed to work outside the home.[7] Recent European immigrants were more likely to be in this type of orchestra. Most members were single and relatively young.
- Performers had a *mix of private and conservatory training*. Some came from families of musicians and had studied with relatives or played with a family ensemble.
- Career-model orchestras *performed in entertainment venues*. Typical settings included vaudeville houses, beer gardens, theaters, restaurants, hotels, and public parks.
- Career-model orchestras *toured as needed*. Not all groups toured, however. Some were attached to particular venues, such as theaters or beer gardens, as house orchestras.
- Most of their repertory consisted of "light" music: arrangements of symphonic works, especially opera overtures, instrumental solos, dance numbers, operatic arias, and popular songs.
- Career-model orchestras tended to *use their femininity as a marketing tool*, emphasizing the novelty of an orchestra made up entirely of women.

7 · "Class" is an ephemeral category in nineteenth-century America, where social mobility and shifting immigrant populations make it hard to pin down specific boundaries of classes.

The career model of women's orchestras appeared in the United States in the 1870s, before any club-model orchestras. Career-model orchestras seem to have been directly inspired by the Vienna Lady Orchestra and other European ladies' orchestras, primarily in German-speaking regions a decade or so earlier. Indeed, on its American tour of 1871, the Vienna Lady Orchestra itself exemplified the career-model orchestra.

CAREER MODEL CASE STUDY 1: THE VIENNA LADY
ORCHESTRA (FOUNDED 1867)

The 1871 American tour by the Vienna Lady Orchestra (VLO) sparked a veritable craze for women's orchestras.[8] Its American influence began even before the orchestra's arrival, when on June 29, 1871, a short article in the *New York Times* announced that the "famed" Vienna Lady Orchestra would make its American debut on September 11 at Steinway Hall in New York City. The brief history of the orchestra that accompanied the announcement emphasizes the orchestra's quality, both musical and social:

> [The Vienna Lady Orchestra] grew from a trio of performers, erst applauded in the Austrian capital in 1867. This trio consisted of Mlle. JOSEPHINE WEINLICH, pianist; Mlle. ELISE WEINLICH, violoncellist, and Mlle. ELISE GRUENER, violiniste [*sic*]. These ladies played classical music in a finished manner, and became favorites in the *salons*. The Empress took them under her patronage, and for some time they were in constant attendance at the Imperial Court.... Each member of this marvelous orchestra is fully capable of undertaking a solo part.[9]

This was a touring orchestra performing classical music, a type of ensemble already familiar and popular in the United States.[10] But unlike other touring orchestras, this orchestra was made up of women instead of men. Moreover, they were women associated with one of the great courts of Europe. This was elegant and highbrow entertainment, or at least that was

8 · In German, the Wiener Damen-Orchester or Erste Europäische Damenorchester.

9 · "Amusements: Notes of Music and the Drama," *New York Times*, June 29, 1871, 8. The article states that the information about the VLO is taken from the ensemble's press flyer. For more on the origins of the VLO, see "The Viennese Ladies' Orchestra," *New York Times*, July 27, 1874, 6; "Music and the Drama," *Appleton's Journal* 12 (August 22, 1874): 253.

10 · Among the best known of the touring orchestras were those of Louis Antoine Jullien, Theodore Thomas, and the Germania orchestra. See chapters IV.1, V.2, and III.4, respectively, in this volume.

the way the orchestra was sold to the American public by the impresario who brought the Vienna Lady Orchestra to the United States, Frederick Rullman. By the time they arrived in the United States in 1871, the Vienna Lady Orchestra had twenty-two members.[11]

According to a New York reporter, the ensemble made its debut before "a very large and fashionable audience."[12] Most critics noted the novelty of the VLO's performance. An unnamed reviewer for the *New York Times* observed:

> The spectacle was certainly a novel one. The platform was changed into a bower, and under the roses were sheltered, instead of the familiar *profanum vulgus* of music-makers, a score of blushing maidens attired in purest white, and armed, after the orthodox style, for their harmonious work. The sight of an instrumentalist of the gentler sex has little rarity about it, but the view of an organized force of female musicians was, until Monday, never offered in this country. On this fact was founded a very large share of the first success at the Vienna Lady Orchestra, and on it will rest their prospective triumphs.[13]

Rather than try to blend into a traditional male setting, the women of the Vienna Lady Orchestra feminized their performance space with flowers and white gowns in contrast to the unadorned black of nineteenth-century male orchestral attire. Moreover, the musicians changed costumes during the course of the concert, emphasizing the visual interest of their performance and reinforcing the point that the endeavor was a feminine one.[14] The orchestra sent a clear message with its visual presentation: This was not an orchestra of women aspiring to be men. This was a women's orchestra (see fig. I.2.1).

Although American reviews did not discuss Amann-Weinlich's conducting in any detail, European reviews presented a picture of a commanding figure who exuded confidence:

> Tall, thin, an expressive face, an ardent eye, the directress of the *Damen Orchester* is above all entirely mistress of her orchestra. Her musical capacities are varied. Composer, conductor, interpreter and directress all at once, accompanying on the piano when necessary, Mme. Amann-Weinlich repre-

---

11 · Arion, "Correspondence: New York," *Church's Musical Visitor*, October 1871, 2.

12 · "Amusements," *New York Times*, September 13, 1871, 5.

13 · Ibid.

14 · "You will soon have those twenty-two ladies in their handsome white dresses, which are changed during the concert, with you, and you can judge for yourself." Arion, "Correspondence: New York," 2.

FIGURE I.2.1. Josephine Amann-Weinlich conducting the Vienna Lady Orchestra at Steinway Hall, New York, 1871. *Frank Leslie's Illustrated Newspaper,* September 30, 1871.

sents the perfect type of grand priestess of the musical world. Her glance is sure, her arm vigorous, she knows the music by heart—as they say—and conducts from memory, for which we are grateful. Her intelligent face is not hidden behind the pages of a musical score, and one follows with interest the waves of harmony that unfold under her command to the applause of the public.[15]

Although the Vienna Lady Orchestra's American tour began in Steinway Hall, New York's foremost recital hall, and although they were marketed as an elite ensemble with royal connections, the orchestra did not give the elite performance critics were expecting. Nor was the ensemble as polished as critics had been led to believe, although several reviewers glossed over problems of artistry by emphasizing the novelty of the moment and the attractiveness of the performers. The instrumentation was also problematic, as noted by the critic for *Church's Musical Visitor*:

15 · "Concerts de la semaine: Le nouvel orchestre féminin," *L'art musicale* (France), December 4, 1873.

I have been disappointed seriously in relation to the merits of this orchestra, and regard the company, as a whole, rather below than above mediocrity. In the first place ... they had not the backbone of an orchestra. They had no brass, and no wind instruments whatever, save two flutes, a piccolo, and a chamber organ that was out of place. All the rest were stringed—a piano, out of place also, two violoncellos, and a double bass, all of reduced size, a harp, a viola, and first and second violins. Hence, the overtures were all wings, no body, and even these were wanting in color, smoothness, and artistic finish.[16]

The repertory also disappointed: instead of a symphonic program, the VLO presented a popular "mixed" program, which featured dance music, opera overtures, and song. This may be why, after mixed reviews in more formal music spaces, the VLO ended up performing in vaudeville houses and beer gardens, where they were immensely popular (see fig. I.2.2).[17]

The Vienna Lady Orchestra spawned a significant number of American copycat ensembles, many of which adopted the same or very similar names. By the 1880s, so many women's ensembles were performing as the "Vienna Lady Orchestra" or "Vienna Ladies Orchestra" that "Viennese" and "Vienna" became virtually synonymous with the genre.[18] The term "Vienna Ladies" must have been seen as marketable. Most of the groups called "Vienna Ladies" had no discernible association with Vienna, and some were not even women's ensembles, but rather mixed-gender groups.[19]

An examination of some of the groups performing under the name "Vienna Ladies Orchestra" or "Vienna Lady Orchestra" not only demonstrates the broad influence of the original Vienna Lady Orchestra but also offers a good picture of the variety of performance situations that career-model orchestras were likely to encounter. One "Vienna Ladies' Orchestra" performed at Abner's Summer Garden in Washington, D.C., in 1881.[20] Another "Vienna Ladies Orchestra" shared the bill with "Wainratta King of the Wire" and "The Lovely Galathea" at Koster and Bial's (New York) in a pure vaudeville spectacle in 1884. And in 1887, the year of Amann-Weinlich's death, one group billed as the "Vienna Ladies' Orchestra" appeared in an extended engagement at the summer garden at Kernan's Theater in Washington, D.C., while another provided music for an exhibition titled "Old London Street"

16 · Arion, "Correspondence: New York," 2.

17 · On concerts at New York's beer gardens, see chapter II.2 in this volume.

18 · This was also true in Europe, where there were several "Viennese" Lady Orchestras in the nineteenth century. See Margaret Myers, *Blowing Her Own Trumpet: European Ladies' Orchestras and Other Women Musicians, 1870–1950, in Sweden* (1993), 192.

19 · For an example, see "Amusements," *New York Times*, September 18, 1882, 7.

20 · "Amusements," *Washington Post*, September 11, 1881, 4.

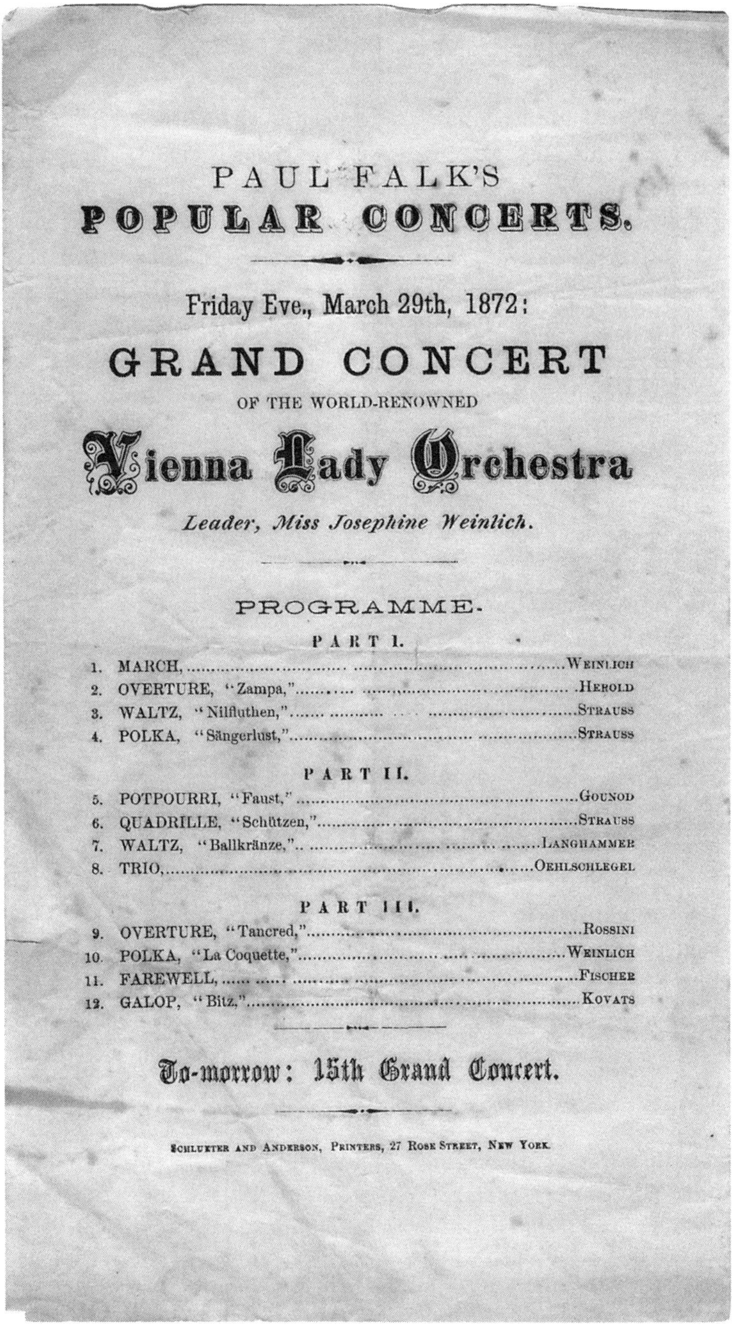

PAUL FALK'S
POPULAR CONCERTS.

Friday Eve., March 29th, 1872;

GRAND CONCERT

OF THE WORLD-RENOWNED

Vienna Lady Orchestra

Leader, Miss Josephine Weinlich.

PROGRAMME.

PART I.

1. MARCH, ... WEINLICH
2. OVERTURE, "Zampa," .... HEROLD
3. WALTZ, "Nilfluthen," .... STRAUSS
4. POLKA, "Sängerlust," .... STRAUSS

PART II.

5. POTPOURRI, "Faust," .... GOUNOD
6. QUADRILLE, "Schützen," .... STRAUSS
7. WALTZ, "Ballkränze," .... LANGHAMMER
8. TRIO, ... OEHLSCHLEGEL

PART III.

9. OVERTURE, "Tancred," .... ROSSINI
10. POLKA, "La Coquette," .... WEINLICH
11. FAREWELL, ... FISCHER
12. GALOP, "Bitz," .... KOVATS

To-morrow: 15th Grand Concert.

SCHLUETER AND ANDERSON, PRINTERS, 27 ROSE STREET, NEW YORK.

FIGURE I.2.2. Sample program from the Vienna Lady Orchestra's first American tour. Paul Falk's Popular Concerts, New York March 29, 1872. Harry Ransom Humanities Research Center, University of Texas at Austin.

on Broadway in New York.[21] Other similarly named ensembles performed in restaurants and orchestra pits and shared vaudeville stages with everything from acrobats to dancing mules.

Amann-Weinlich and her orchestra had captivated a nation. These and the American incarnations of the "lady orchestras," or "Damen Orchester" as they were often called, began in German American communities in the 1870s in the northeast, particularly New York, where they played in music halls, vaudeville theaters, and beer gardens.[22] All of these locations featured re-spectable entertainment geared toward families. And although it might have been inappropriate or even unseemly for a woman of a higher class to per-form in a beer garden, for talented women of a lower class it was a good, solid job, one whose popularity would ensure that the VLO's influence would con-tinue well into the twentieth century.

CAREER MODEL CASE STUDY 2: THE BERGER FAMILY
(1862–CA. 1880)

An even earlier American foray into the business of women's orchestras was made by the Berger Family, a mixed-gender ensemble that reinvented itself regularly in order to respond to public tastes of the moment. The Berger Family ensemble was made up of the children of Henry Berger, a German American church organist and organ builder based in York, Pennsylvania, and his wife Anna. Henry and Anna's six children—Henry, Anna Theresa, Louisa, Fred, Henrietta, and Bernhart—were all musical prodigies. They be-gan performing together as early as 1862, along with their music teacher's son, Ernest Thiele. Under the management of father Henry, they were contracted by the MacFarland Dramatic Company in early 1863, and by mid-1863, fol-lowing Henry senior's death, were touring with the Carter Zouave Company, a vaudeville troupe that most likely featured the Berger girls in their popular girl Zouave band.[23] After their contract ran out with the Carter Zouave Com-pany, the Bergers, now managed by mother Anna, began performing with the

21 · "Amusements," *Washington Post*, May 31, 1887, 2; "Amusements," *New York Times*, Au-gust 28, 1887, 5.
22 · Tick, "Passed Away Is the Piano Girl," 329–31.
23 · M. B. Leavitt, *Fifty Years in Theatrical Management* (1912), 3. Much of this information also appears in June Lloyd, "The Musical Young Bergers," *York Sunday News*, May 20, 2007, reprinted at York Blog as "York Berger Family Musicians Make it Big," www.yorkblog.com/ universal/2009/01/york-berger-family-musicians-m.html. The Carter Zouave band was a sort of parody in the flesh of a Civil War–era military band, with girls between ten and four-teen years of age appearing in military uniform, complete with muskets. An interview with the founder of the troupe, James Heneage Carter, titled "An Old Showman's Yarn," appeared in the *Washington Post*, September 23, 1883, 7.

Peak Family, a popular family of Swiss bell ringers, and eventually formed their own bell-ringing ensemble.

In early July 1871, the Bergers ran a classified ad in the *New York Times* in advance of a series of summer performances:

Engagement for the short summer season of
THE BERGER FAMILY
SWISS BELL-RINGERS
The only complete troupe of Swiss bell-ringers who
Have ever appeared in this country
A MAGNIFICENT CHIME OF 150 SWISS BELLS!
A STAFF OF PURE SILVER BELLS
PARLOR ORCHESTRA AND
SILVER CORNET BAND
the principal members of which are young ladies
THE BERGER FAMILY
will be assisted by the favorite Humorist
SOL SMITH RUSSELL[24]

The only hint that this might be a ladies' orchestra is the statement that "the principal members ... are young ladies." The group was, in fact, a family ensemble including both men and women, with several excellent female soloists, including cornettist Anna Theresa Berger.

As the publicity for the VLO intensified, the ads for the Berger Family's performances at Lina Edwin's theater, a vaudeville establishment, began to focus more on the female members of the ensemble. On Thursday, July 20, 1871, an advertisement appeared in the "Amusements" section of the classified ads in the *New York Times* that makes it clear that the ladies were now the ensemble's big selling point:

LINA EDWIN'S THEATRE
GREAT SUCCESS — EVERYBODY DELIGHTED
The most Elegant Entertainment in the City
EVERY EVENING THIS WEEK!
THE BERGER FAMILY SWISS BELL-RINGERS
LADY ORCHESTRA! LADY VIOLINISTS!
LADY CORNET PLAYERS! LADY HARPISTS!
YOUNG LADIES' SILVER CORNET BAND!
SOL SMITH RUSSELL.

24 · "Amusements," *New York Times*, July 10, 1871, 7.

And all the Favorites will appear
MATINEE SATURDAY AT 2 P.M.[25]

The Bergers performed in many ensemble configurations, generally all on the same program, as was typical of this style of vaudevillian ensemble. Although few descriptions remain of their performances, they most likely included light popular works interspersed with comedy. The ensemble billed in 1871 as a "Lady Orchestra" was most likely quite small—probably no more than eight players—and was probably more band than orchestra, as the novelty of talented female brass players accounted for a large share of the Bergers' popularity. Robert Grau, a music and drama critic, described the Bergers' 1871 tour as their first (and possibly only) "high class concert tour," a tour inspired by "the extraordinary musical talents of Anna Teresa Berger and her sisters."[26] It was, no doubt, helped by the newfound interest in women's instrumental ensembles fostered by the Vienna Lady Orchestra.

CAREER MODEL CASE STUDY 3: THE LADIES ELITE
ORCHESTRA (NEW YORK, 1880–CA. 1916)

The Ladies Elite Orchestra in New York offers a clearer example of the career-model women's orchestra. One of the most successful and popular American ensembles inspired by the Vienna Lady Orchestra's 1871 tour, the Ladies Elite was firmly associated with New York's German community and was rooted in the same European traditions as their model. The Ladies Elite was organized about 1880 by Marie Roller as the "Damen Elite Kapelle" at the Atlantic Garden, a popular beer garden in the Bowery that catered to German Americans.[27] Roller was a violinist who had been performing as a soloist with a variety of vaudevillian ensembles, including the Berger Family.[28] The Ladies Elite was soon taken over by Albert Eschert and later by his son Charles, at which point it was renamed "Charles Eschert's Elite Lady Orchestra." The Ladies Elite was a fixture at the Atlantic Garden from the 1880s until about 1916.

Little is known about the individual members of the ensemble or their backgrounds, but the group fits the description of the career model in most ways. Orchestra members were paid and performed regularly at the Atlantic

25 · "Amusements" (classified ad), *New York Times,* July 20, 1871, 7.

26 · Robert Grau, *Forty Years of Observation of Music and the Drama* (1909), 183.

27 · The Ladies Elite was also called the "Elite Lady Orchestra" and was occasionally billed as the "Wiener Damen Orchester," a name influenced, no doubt, by the popularity of the Vienna Lady Orchestra. On the Atlantic Garden, see chapter II.2 in this volume.

28 · "Berger Family and Russell," *Utica Morning Herald,* 1880 (exact date unknown). Facsimile obtained from Old Fulton NY Post Cards, http://fultonhistory.com/Fulton.html.

Garden, although they do not appear to have toured. Their repertory included a mix of light classical and popular tunes, not unlike the music performed by the Vienna Lady Orchestra.[29] And the Atlantic Garden marketed its lady orchestra as a novelty act. At the same time, the fact that the Ladies Elite Orchestra remained for more than three decades as what amounted to the house orchestra at the Atlantic Garden suggests that they performed their musical functions more than competently. Like their model, the Vienna Lady Orchestra, the Ladies Elite Orchestra seems to have been a successful combination of novelty and musicianship.

The Club Model

The second type of women's orchestra was modeled after women's clubs, which in the late nineteenth century were numerous, powerful, and nationally organized. Where the career-model orchestras subscribed to working conditions dictated by their male predecessors and struggled with men's conceptions of appropriate roles for women active in the public sphere, the club-model orchestras, like the women's clubs that inspired them, were organized and run for women and usually by them as well. They created structures that were based on women's needs, desires, skills, and self-conceptions of femininity. These orchestras, like women's clubs, were, as Karen Blair has stated, "a realm in which proper ladies flourished."[30] Many of the members of women's orchestras were involved with other women's clubs, both musical and otherwise. The club-model orchestra was based on their practical organizational experience.[31] The following are some of the key characteristics of the club model:

- Orchestras subscribing to the women's club model were usually *founded by a group of women*, sometimes under the musical or organizational leadership of a single person (male or female).
- The orchestra's stated goals tended to focus on *self-improvement, social betterment*, or both. The orchestra's mission usually included charitable work of some sort. The idea of social betterment assuaged concerns about the seemliness of women appearing on stage in public: they

29 · A program from 1877 lists music by Auber, Beethoven, Carl, Faust, Herrmann, Lumbye, Mendelssohn, Neibig, Resch, Strauss, Suppé, Verdi, and Wiegand. Figures II.2.5 and II.2.6 in this volume show Ladies Elite programs from 1877 and 1896.
30 · Blair, *The Clubwoman as Feminist*, 1.
31 · Founding an orchestra as a club, although characteristic of women's orchestras, was not, by any means, unique to them. In the nineteenth century, there were numerous amateur male and a few mixed ensembles organized on the club model. For an example of a mixed amateur orchestra in Washington, D.C., see chapter II.5 in this volume.

weren't performing, they were doing social work, which was a sanctioned feminine activity.

- Members came from the *upper and middle classes*. Sometimes they were from musical families, but often not. Many had families who encouraged them to pursue their talents beyond the level that would prepare them to be society women.
- Their *repertory emphasized highbrow music* rather than catering to popular tastes. This emphasis on highbrow music led the club-model orchestras to strive for full symphonic size and distribution. This sometimes meant an education component, where orchestra members taught girls to play needed instruments, particularly winds, brass, and percussion. Other times it meant male musicians were hired for performances, often relegated to the back row.
- Club-model orchestras were *community based*; they did not tour. As a result, this type of orchestra was more likely to include married women (although members were still mostly young and single).
- Performers were more likely to have been *privately trained* than educated in conservatories, which tended to prepare women to be music teachers. Because fewer members were conservatory graduates than in career orchestras, fewer had prior orchestral performance experience.
- Performance *venues were usually recital halls, private homes, and society events*.
- Club-model orchestras *used their femininity as uplift* by presenting themselves as wholesome, girlish or ladylike, chaste, well-bred, and pleasant. Such a presentation emphasized their femininity and reduced any sense of threat to traditional gender roles.

CLUB MODEL CASE STUDY: THE LOS ANGELES WOMEN'S
ORCHESTRA, 1893–1945

The early decades of the Los Angeles Women's Orchestra (LAWO) (fig. I.2.3), one of the longest-lived of the American women's orchestras, offer an example of the club model. The Los Angeles Women's Orchestra was organized in 1893 by Harley Hamilton, a male violinist who had come to Los Angeles on tour and stayed to work and teach. The orchestra began as a club of Hamilton's students to give them the "opportunity for the study of music written for symphony orchestras." Club members paid membership dues out of which Hamilton took his pay.[32]

32 · Catherine Parsons Smith, *Making Music in Los Angeles: Transforming the Popular* (2007), 59.

FIGURE I.2.3. The Los Angeles Women's Orchestra, Harley Hamilton, conductor. Huntington Library, San Marino, California.

The Los Angeles Women's Orchestra began with twenty-five members and gradually increased to nearly three times that many by the 1930s.[33] Like a women's club, the orchestra was run by a slate of elected officers.[34] The emphasis in the early years was on the learning of repertory, which meant that activities were focused on rehearsals rather than performances. This was typical of club-model orchestras, which tended to value self-improvement and personal excellence over public performance. The LAWO's relatively infrequent public appearances nearly all occurred in conjunction with charitable events. For example, a notice in the Los Angeles Times in 1906 announced that the orchestra would be performing for the first time in public in nearly three years in an earthquake relief benefit for the "San Francisco suffering ones."[35] Such long gaps between performances were explained by Cora Foy, the orchestra's president in 1907: "We don't give music in public until we are prepared, but we study it in its highest forms."[36]

Whereas club-model orchestras in other parts of the country could look to a local male symphony orchestra for inspiration and repertory, the LAWO was the first orchestra with any longevity in its city. Even after the founding of a male professional orchestra a few years later, also by Hamilton, women's clubs, as Catherine Parsons Smith observes, "formed the model around which much of the city's music activity was organized," and the LAWO remained an important part of the city's cultural life.[37]

The club format did not imply any lack of seriousness. Members of the LAWO took their music studies at least as seriously as paid musicians. Edna Foy (sister of Cora), a founding member of the group and its concertmaster for many years, dropped out of school at Hamilton's urging to focus more time on studying violin with him and later at the Royal Academy of Music in London. But Edna Foy struggled between her desire for a musical career on the one hand and her self-conception as a lady on the other. She played with the women's orchestra into the 1920s and, as Smith points out, could have had a musical career—she knew women who did—but she chose not to. The orchestra (run largely by the Foy sisters) seemed to take pride in its club status, believing that it held them to a higher standard than ensembles whose activi-

---

33 · Frédérique Petrides, "Los Angeles Group: A Tested Veteran," Women in Music 1 (1936); facsimile in Jan Bell Groh, Evening the Score: Women in Music and the Legacy of Frédérique Petrides (1991), 47.

34 · Smith, Making Music in Los Angeles, 70, 275n49.

35 · "Events in Local Society," Los Angeles Times, April 25, 1906.

36 · Estelle Lawton Lindsey, "Woman's Symphony Now One of Foremost Orchestras in the World," Los Angeles Record, 1907, quoted in Smith, Making Music in Los Angeles, 70.

37 · Smith, Making Music in Los Angeles, 70.

ties were governed by economics.[38] The Los Angeles Women's Orchestra was one of the most enduring of all women's orchestras. It was able to reinvent itself several times, including the adoption of a more careerist model in the 1930s, altering its priorities to fit changing times and community needs. It continued performing until at least 1945.[39]

Other less long-lived club-model orchestras never wavered from their original formation. The Women's Philharmonic Society of New York, founded in 1889 by Melusina Fay Peirce, stayed firmly within the women's club model. Even though its members—including Jeanne Franko of the "Five Famous Frankos" and Amy Fay, violinist and sister to Melusina—were professional performers or teachers, it functioned mainly as a philanthropic organization.[40] The New York Women's String Orchestra, founded in 1896 by Carl Lachmund, also adhered to the club model until it folded a decade later.

HYBRID MODEL CASE STUDY: THE FADETTES WOMANS
ORCHESTRA OF BOSTON (1888–1920; 1924)

One nineteenth-century American women's orchestra tried to have it all. Caroline B. Nichols, a violin soloist, founded the Fadettes Womans Orchestra of Boston with five of her friends in 1888 after performing for a short time in another "young ladies' orchestra" organized by Marion Osgood.[41] Although the Fadettes' beginnings reflect the club model, as they became more successful and gained public performance experience, they changed their priorities and shifted to the career model, a process that accelerated after they incorporated in 1895. Unlike groups that began in the professional sphere, the Fadettes were able to retain some of the attractive qualities of the club model; in particular, they remained self-managed throughout their long career, and they continued to use femininity as uplift.

---

38 · Ibid., 69–70.

39 · The latest mention of a LAWO concert I have been able to find appears in "Musically Speaking," *Los Angeles Times*, April 8, 1945, C-5; it documents a performance of Verdi's Requiem with the Santa Monica Choral Society at Santa Monica High School.

40 · Ammer, *Unsung*, 126.

41 · Osgood claimed her orchestra was founded in 1884, four years before the Fadettes started (Marion G. Osgood, "America's First 'Ladies Orchestra'" *Étude* 58 [1940]: 713). An 1893 article mentions both groups and states that Osgood was "the first woman in Boston, and probably in the whole country to organize a 'lady orchestra,' for business purposes" ("Women Musicians," *Musical Visitor* 227 [July 1893]: 184). This was not true, as demonstrated above. Like the Fadettes in their early years, the Marion Osgood Orchestra emphasized serious music and played primarily for social functions (Louis C. Elson, "Musical Matters: The Marion Osgood Testimonial Last Night," *Boston Daily Advertiser*, March 14, 1890, 2).

Evidence of the latter of these qualities is apparent in two pictures of the Fadettes that appeared in a publicity flyer issued around 1910 (fig. I.2.4). The first photo is a posed shot of the women in concert dress on a stage in front of a set that seems to evoke a Mediterranean villa. The second shows the women in traveling clothes, carrying their instruments and chatting in twos and threes. The music director at the front of the line serves as a mother figure; the male manager, a father figure, brings up the rear with the luggage. A small dog on a leash enhances the aura of domestic respectability. Pictures such as these addressed social anxieties about women in large ensembles on the public stage and concerns about them compromising their morality or femininity by playing in public for money. The text on the flyer affirms this message: it tells the history of the orchestra and doesn't fail to mention that although its director, Carolyn Nichols, was an excellent musician, she was also an excellent cook.

The Fadettes Womans Orchestra of Boston was successful by just about any measure: financial gain (they paid out more than $500,000 to more than six hundred performers), longevity (more than thirty years), number of concerts given (Nichols claimed more than six thousand between 1888 and 1920), fame (they appeared in major theaters nationwide), and breadth of repertory, which included what Nichols described as "many symphonies" and "all the classic overtures of 75 grand operas."[42] At the outset, the orchestra had only six members, but within two years had more than doubled their number to sixteen, at which point Nichols left her instrumental post and took up the conductor's baton.

Initially, the Fadettes conformed to the women's-club model. Their founding by a group of women was typical of women's clubs. And their decision to name themselves after the title character in George Sand's *La petite Fadette*— a fictional character whose musical interest emphasized her wholesome femininity—rather than after the ensemble's director or location was more clubbish than careerist.

The press seemed to agree. An 1890 review of a Fadette "reception and recital" spends approximately one-third of its ink on the delightfulness of the women in the Fadettes and two-thirds listing the social luminaries in the audience. Nowhere does it mention any of the repertory on the program. It does, however, list the names of ushers, "ladies receiving," and the women handing out the "dainty programs" to the guests. The orchestra "looked like a drift of lovely butterflies," opined the reviewer, "and the warmest compli-

42 · Blanche Naylor, *The Anthology of the Fadettes* (ca. 1937), 8–13. Naylor's book is held by the Special Collections of the Music Department of the Boston Public Library. It appears to have been printed in a limited edition to commemorate the Fadettes' fiftieth anniversary.

The Fadettes Womans Orchestra of Boston

CAROLINE B. NICHOLS, Conductor

HOW IT HAPPENED

IN the city of Boston some years ago, or to be more exact, in 1888, a young woman sat brooding over a shattered idyl. What it was is not important. It was one that comes to every woman at some time or other, and if the shattering of this particular dream has become commonplace, it loses none of its heartbreak. Different natures approach difficult problems in various ways. Some go round or crawl under while some stop short and others simply climb over, and once on the other side never halt. With Caroline B. Nichols the latter seemed the true method, and she still believes that it was the only way.

The problem of making a living was naturally the first to be considered. She was far from being ill-equipped for the battle. Her mother was behind her with years of experience, ready to advise and help with a kindly word in the right place, and she herself was blessed with a fund of wit and ability, coupled with strong constitution and good blood, that went a long way toward arming her for the struggle.

Her mother had been operator of famous hotels and summer resorts, and she had inherited much of her skill in the gentle art of cooking; so, she could cook. But while there is no art more worthy than cooking, she felt called to a different sphere. She had inherited musical temperament and talent from her father, who was a natural musician and a prominent leader in all musical enterprises and societies in Boston. She had been well educated in music, was a violinist of no mean attainment, and liked musical atmosphere. This was to be no pretty accomplishment, mind you, but a serious life business and possibly a career. A place on the concert platform as a successful soloist was only to be reached by years of endeavor, at much expense, and there was no one to offer to finance a budding genius and reap his or her reward in heaven. Music teachers were as plentiful as pupils; there was, of course, no place for a woman musician, however clever, in the regular orchestra of men.

The field of the young woman in music was too restricted for her. She decided to be a Leader and have an orchestra of her own; and what was more than that, it should be a GOOD orchestra and there should be none in it but women. This was a radical departure, and was frowned or laughed at and voted impossible by all who knew or were supposed to know about such things. The decision, however, had been made, and with this woman that of itself meant much.

She had musical girl friends, and it required little time for her to communicate her enthusiasm to them. The consequence was that an orchestra of six young ladies was soon organized, and after some practice went into the field as professionals. The business element of the undertaking was difficult, but it was not long before the clear-headed young leader mastered it and placed the enterprise upon a self-supporting basis.

They were young in those days, and when the question of a title came up it was settled in a rather poetic way that was thoroughly feminine. They chose the name "Fadette," the title character of one of George Sand's novels, who was a sprightly, cheerful, music-loving young girl who brought light and gladness into the hearts of all with whom she came in contact.

In 1890 their success made it an easy matter to induce others to join the ranks and the membership became fifteen. By this time the personal attractiveness, good character, and musical ability of the members had made for them many friends, and secured the support of the better class of music-lovers; they had all the engagements they could fill, and their lines lay in pleasant places as well. Their home city, known around the world for its exclusiveness, was proud of them, and they met, and met adequately, the demands of the music business in the grand old Commonwealth.

By this time The Fadettes had become very successful, and one of the original members who had acted as business manager, desiring to retire from business, sold the title, without consulting Mrs. Nichols, to a party who had ambitions to conduct a woman's orchestra. Finding that the orchestra as a whole had decided to make no change as far as leadership was concerned, the purchaser took her empty title to the courts to find out to whom it belonged. The courts decided that it remained with the originators; and so the controversy was settled for all time.

Immediately after this important decision still more members were added and the orchestra secured much of the valuable local business in the New England States. Most of the weddings, receptions, and other affairs in the most exclusive society were furnished with music by a quota of Fadettes, and they were engaged annually at the Expositions held in the huge Mechanic's Building, Boston. They also were substantially the only orchestra employed by the Women's Clubs of New England, and the orchestra in its entirety was to be heard at many of the great festivals where heretofore only men had been employed.

IN 1895 the idea of a business corporation suggested itself, and the State granted a charter, thus insuring to them exclusive right to their name, THE FADETTES. The business end of the orchestra being too much for the leader, she formed a partnership with one of the members who took over that department, leaving the Leader to attend only to the musical elements of the orchestra. To Miss Viola M. Dunn, therefore, may be credited much of the financial success that has been the portion of the organization, and she still acts as Treasurer and assistant manager and has charge of all the finances.

The old saying that two heads are better than one was never better illustrated than in this case, and the calm, level-headed Treasurer has saved the organization from many of the pitfalls that bestrew the pathway of all young financial propositions.

FIGURE 1.2.4. Caroline B. Nichols and the Fadettes Woman's Orchestra of Boston, publicity flyer. Special Collections, University of Iowa Libraries.

ments were paid the young players as their guests took their leave. Each received her meed of praise, from the first violins to the cornetist, whom one enthusiastic young man declared not only played divinely, but had the 'prettiest pucker' imaginable."[43] This so-called review, although it appeared in the *Boston Daily Globe* on a page with the other arts coverage, reads like one of the columns covering women's clubs in the society pages. Another review in 1893 calls them one of the "local music clubs."[44]

Like many club-model orchestras, the Fadettes occasionally performed for charitable endeavors. They served as the accompaniment for the production of a four-act play, *Esmeralda*, put on by the Young People's Fraternity of the Second Church in Boston in 1892 as a benefit for "the ward 16 day nursery" and in an 1894 musicale organized by the New England Women's Press Association to raise money for "Boston's suffering poor."[45]

It is difficult to make an accurate assessment of the Fadettes' repertory in the early years, as many of the reviews do not mention any music that the orchestra played. But those that do mention music indicate that the orchestra's focus was serious music—"concert work of a highly artistic order," wrote Marion Howard in the *Boston Daily Globe*.[46] A *Globe* reviewer listed the works in the program at the 1893 Chickering Hall concert as Raff, *Leonore* March; Nicolai, *Merry Wives of Windsor* Overture; Swepstone, Minuet; Hoffman, Serenade for Strings; Haydn, Finale to a symphony; Brahms-Moses, "Hungarian Rhapsody."[47] This program is typical of club-model orchestras. It includes a mix of short, lighter classical works that would fit well on a career-model program, but there is little evidence of more popular works or song. In early Fadettes programs, there is an emphasis on sections of symphonic multimovement works that looks more like an abridged version of the club model. Other Fadettes programs were similar and featured mostly excerpts from multimovement works. Unlike most club orchestras, however, the Fadettes almost never used soloists from outside the ensemble, a trait more typical of career orchestras.

In these early years, the group performed only in the greater Boston area, gradually expanding in the mid-1890s to perform at occasional events for women elsewhere in the northeast. An 1897 article about the ensemble in

43 · "Like a Drift of Butterflies," *Boston Daily Globe*, December 3, 1890, 4.

44 · "Concert by Ladies," *Boston Daily Globe*, March 29, 1893, 9.

45 · "Young People Present a Play," *Boston Daily Globe*, May 7, 1892, 9; "Personal," *Harper's Bazaar*, March 17, 1894, 207.

46 · Marion Howard, "The Fadettes," *Boston Daily Globe*, May 31, 1896, 28.

47 · "Concert by Ladies," *Boston Daily Globe*, March 29, 1893, 9. George Chickering was Caroline Nichols's brother-in-law.

Harper's Bazaar describes a busy concert schedule centered on women's clubs, outdoor festivals, and social events:

> During last winter, within two weeks they had played for four of the largest and most influential clubs in or about Boston, namely the Arlington Woman's Club reception, the Revere Woman's Club dance, the Boston Press Club theatre benefit, and the 999th Artillery's ladies' night, besides supplying the musical portion of the programme at the dramatic entertainment of the Woman's Charity Club, the reception of the Daughters of New Hampshire, and numerous weddings and evening parties. They often play for dancing at balls or "small and earlies," and are favorites for afternoon or evening musicals at the houses of the "smart set."[48]

At least some members of the Fadettes were, themselves, part of the "smart set." The same article reports on one of the players as being of "fine Maine stock, where her ancestors were among the early settlers," and the rest of the orchestra as being "all young women of character and strength of purpose."

Around the time of their incorporation in 1895, the Fadettes' profile began to change. Nichols handed over the business side of the group to Viola Dunn, the Fadettes' first clarinetist, who became Nichols's assistant and the orchestra's treasurer, leaving Nichols free to concentrate on musical activities and to study conducting. This marked the beginning of a shift to a more business-like approach to the orchestra's day-to-day operations. A legal dispute in the 1890s highlighted the transition that was taking place. One of the five "musical girl friends" who had joined Caroline Nichols to form the initial ensemble was a violinist named Ethel Atwood, who became the organization's first business manager, with the job of contracting and paying the musicians.[49] At some point in the 1890s Atwood left the group and sold the Fadettes' name to another woman, Mary E. Messer. Messer proceeded to organize her own ensemble and sued Nichols, who was still performing under the name "Fadettes." In March 1897, the case went before the Supreme Court of Massachusetts, which sided with Nichols, stating that in purchasing and using the name, Messer could only have intended to mislead the public.[50] By the 1890s, it seems, career considerations outweighed the "sisterhood" and the charitable intentions of the club model.

The ensemble increased in size slightly to between twenty and twenty-five on average and began touring in the summer of 1897; the tour included

48 · "The Fadettes," *Harper's Bazaar*, May 29, 1897, 30, 22, 447.
49 · "Women Musicians," *Musical Visitor* 22 (July 1893): 184.
50 · *Mary E. Messer v. The Fadettes* became a landmark in trademark law. The records of the trial appear in the *Lawyers Reports Annotated* (1897), 37:721–23.

a summer residency at Glen Echo Park, Washington, D.C., which was organized as a "national educational institute" by Mrs. Phoebe Apperson Hearst.
There appear to have been deficiencies in the organization and marketing
of the first Glen Echo concert, which Nichols claimed was attended by only
"about thirty people"; by the end of the Fadettes' three-month residency,
however, the press reported audiences of thousands. According to Fadettes
chronicler Blanche Naylor, "The street-car system proved to be inadequate
for the vast crowds that came to hear the Fadettes."[51] The Russian ambassa-
dor was so impressed by the Fadettes' performances that he presented Nichols with "a solid silver baton of exquisite workmanship."[52]

The following year, the Fadettes signed with the Redpath and Southern
Bureaus and spent the next several years touring the United States and Canada on the Chautauqua-Lyceum circuit.[53] In 1902, while the Fadettes were
preparing for one of their last Canadian concerts, they were scouted by B. F.
Keith, the legendary vaudeville impresario, who sent the manager of his Boston theater to a Fadettes' rehearsal. The manager engaged the ensemble for a
two-week tryout at Keith's theater, and then for a summer season, replacing
an ensemble of players from the Boston Symphony.[54]

Although the touring orchestra remained at around twenty players during
the vaudeville years, the ensemble's size doubled when playing concerts at
home in Boston. The Fadettes' willingness to adapt the ensemble to suit the
performance circumstances no doubt played a role in the group's longevity
and allowed them to maximize their repertory. Beginning around 1909, Boston and New York newspapers regularly advertised the Fadettes performing
in other vaudeville houses as well as Keith's and as the accompanying orchestra for theatrical productions.[55] The Fadettes continued touring in vaudeville
throughout the first two decades of the twentieth century.

The Fadettes also adapted their repertory to suit the new vaudeville setting. Although they still performed lighter classical pieces, they began to incorporate more popular tunes and even comedy. Vaudeville artist Joe Laurie
Jr. tells of "a bit where the all-girl group got mad and walked out and Caroline

51 · Naylor, *Anthology of the Fadettes*, 10–11.
52 · Emil Paur, "Music and Musicians," *Los Angeles Times*, October 10, 1897, 30.
53 · Naylor, *Anthology of the Fadettes*, 10.
54 · Ibid., 11.
55 · In 1909, for example, the Fadettes performed at Keith's in Boston in July and at Keith and
Proctor's Fifth Avenue Theater in New York in September. After their run at Keith and Proctor's, they appear to have remained in New York, performing at the Colonial Theatre in late
September and then, in October, at the Orpheum in Brooklyn and at the Alhambra. Similar
performance patterns continued through at least 1912, by which point they had played in
most of New York's major vaudeville houses.

replaced them, playing ten different instruments."[56] A 1909 performance at Keith's Theater in Boston included a march, *The Falcon,* by Chambers; *Morning, Noon and Night* (an overture) by Suppé; the Andante cantabile from Tchaikovsky's string quartet; excerpts from Bizet's *Carmen*; a "marche orientale" by Sellenick; *Innesfallen,* an Irish fantasy by Koppitz; and three more numbers. The printed program boasted that the Fadettes' music "represented that of all nations."[57] The Fadettes also took requests. A printed booklet was passed out at the door with a list of more than six hundred pieces. Audience members could find a piece on the list that they wanted to hear, write the name on a piece of paper, and send it up to Nichols, who "played the selection in the order in which it was received."[58]

In the later years of the Fadettes, Nichols became interested in film music accompaniment and, according to Naylor, "had very radical ideas of how music should be synchronized and fitted" to silent film.[59] The Fadettes spent six months working with a legendary impresario of the cinema, Samuel Rothafel (1882–1936), better known as "Roxy," at his first cinema in Minneapolis, Minnesota. Beginning around 1918, most of their advertised performances were accompanying films in Boston and New York theaters. They continued performing until at least 1924.[60]

The Fadettes' publicity materials suggest that their aims had changed somewhat by the end of their career, as had their model. A 1910 press flyer records this succinct mission statement:

Our Purpose: To please the Public
Our Aim: To make good popular music, and make good music popular
Our Ambition: To rank as the most complete and efficient Orchestra of
    Women Players in the World
Our Ideal: The Boston Symphony Orchestra
Our Watchword: Advancement

The last line of the statement, though, still acknowledges the group's origins as a women's music club: "Motto: 'Once a Fadette, Always a Fadette.'"

---

56 · Joe Laurie Jr., *Vaudeville: From the Honky-Tonks to the Palace* (1953), 67.
57 · "Playhouse News: Fadettes at Keith's," *Christian Science Monitor,* July 27, 1909, 6.
58 · Naylor, *Anthology of the Fadettes,* 12.
59 · Ibid., 11.
60 · A classified ad in the *Boston Daily Globe* advertises Caroline B. Nichols conducting the "Fadettes Orchestra" in the last five days of a production of *Secrets* starring Norma Talmadge at the Park Theatre (now known as the State Theatre) in Boston (*Boston Daily Globe,* July 27, 1924, 47).

The New Professional Model

The career and club models together defined early women's orchestras but could also limit them. Club-model orchestras were almost entirely self-sufficient and did not need to respond to public demand to stay in operation. Consequently, they had a tendency to be insular. Some of these orchestras were never held accountable for their quality because they played few public performances. On the other hand, the artistry of career orchestras was limited by a paycheck that depended on public whim and performance venues that were often less than dignified. A review of the Fadettes performing in one of B. F. Keith's theaters reports them sharing a program with a minstrel act, circus performers, and a troupe of trained dogs.[61]

As the Fadettes' career was coming to a close in the 1920s, a new type of model was forming, one that clearly defined itself as professional and modeled itself on what Mark Clague has described as the "corporate model" male orchestra.[62] This new breed of professional women's orchestras still dealt with some of the limitations of the earlier orchestras, most specifically with the difficulty in combining paying work with challenging symphonic repertory. But they adapted by defining their hard-won professionalism not simply by their paychecks but by multiple criteria, including membership in the musician's union, size of ensemble (the bigger the better), a repertory of complex symphonic works, performance venues at the center of the city (preferably the same hall where the local centerpiece orchestra played), and media attention.

The most prominent and successful example of the new professional model was the Woman's Symphony Orchestra of Chicago, which was founded in 1925 by a group of students at the Bush Conservatory of Music who, on "finding that careers were not open to them in the established symphony orchestras," to quote from one of their concert programs, "decided to organize one for women professionals."[63] Like the Fadettes in their later years, the Woman's Symphony Orchestra of Chicago exhibited qualities of both the club model (origin as small group, organizational structure, emphasis on challenging, highbrow repertory) and the career model (emphasis on payment, professionalism). There was no longer a need for women's orchestras to distance themselves from professionalism in order to create an orchestra of symphonic scope, nor was there a need to sacrifice pay in order to play challenging repertory.

61 · "Drama and Music," *Boston Globe,* July 15, 1902, 7.
62 · See chapter I.1 in this volume.
63 · Woman's Symphony Orchestra of Chicago, 1938–39 program book, Woman's Symphony Orchestra of Chicago Collection, Chicago Historical Society.

For this new generation of women's orchestras, the stage became a platform from which they could advocate for more opportunities for women and actually get them. The work of nineteenth-century women's orchestras had expanded women's performance opportunities and removed many of the barriers that had limited their work. In the twentieth century, women's orchestras began to see the project through to completion. In 1940, Helen Kotas, a horn player for the Woman's Symphony Orchestra of Chicago, made national news when she joined the Chicago Symphony Orchestra as principal horn, becoming the first female member of the CSO and the first woman to hold a principal position in a major orchestra anywhere in the country. By the end of 1944, at least twenty-five former members of the Woman's Symphony Orchestra of Chicago were performing in mixed-gender professional orchestras across the country.[64] And by the end of the twentieth century, there was a new model for women's orchestral performance, one that included both men and women.

64 · ["A former member ..."], *Chicago Daily News*, Tuesday, January 9, 1945, clipping in Woman's Symphony Orchestra of Chicago Scrapbook 7, Chicago Historical Society.

[1.3] American Orchestras and Their Unions in the Nineteenth Century

JOHN SPITZER

One European visitor to America in the centennial year of 1876 was Jacques Offenbach, who conducted his works in Philadelphia and in New York, where he appeared at Gilmore's Garden in Madison Square Park, leading an orchestra of American musicians. In a travel memoir he published the next year, he commented with amazement: "The musicians here have a vast and powerful organization, a society outside of which there is no salvation. Every individual who wants to play in an orchestra must first of all become a member. There are no exceptions, from the orchestra conductor to the drummer inclusive, everybody must belong."[1] Offenbach endeared himself to his orchestra at the first rehearsal by insisting that he too be allowed to join their "vast and powerful" organization: the Musical Mutual Protective Union of New York (MMPU).

To Offenbach, a musicians' union was a novelty. The "Association syndicale" of Paris musicians was not organized until December 1876, and this first attempt at a French musicians' union lasted only a few years.[2] In the United States, however, musicians' unions were already widespread, and they became increasingly powerful over the last quarter of the nineteenth century. It was a time of rapid growth in the entertainment industry. Orchestras and bands were formed to play in theaters, at concerts, for dances, for parades, in restaurants and saloons, and in countless other venues. It was also a time of growth for the American labor movement. Machinists, iron molders, carpen-

---

1 · Jacques Offenbach, *Offenbach en Amérique: Notes d'un musicien en voyage* (1877), 31. Gilmore's Garden was the original Madison Square Garden at Twenty-Sixth Street and Madison Avenue. The venue kept its name when it moved to its present location on Eighth Avenue in 1925.

2 · Joel-Marie Fauquet, "Les debuts du syndicalisme musical en France," in *La musique du théorique au politique* (1991), 224. See also Gabriel Lefeuvre, "L'Association des musiciens instrumentistes fondée en 1876," *Courrier de l'orchestre*, October 1, 1902, 6.

ters, plumbers, shoemakers, cigar makers, and more all formed unions during this period. Local unions of instrumental musicians were first organized in the 1860s. By the 1880s and 1890s there were musicians' unions in most large cities and in many smaller ones as well. At the end of the nineteenth century, most American orchestras were unionized.[3]

This chapter describes and explains the role that unions played in American orchestras in the nineteenth century—from the 1860s until about 1896, when the American Federation of Musicians (AFM) was organized and musicians' unions became part of the American Federation of Labor (AFL). The focus is on local unions rather than national organizations. Musicians' unions were organized city by city; the locals were self-contained and independent of one another. Until the end of the century, national organizations of musicians were weak confederations of strong local unions. The chapter ends with an attempt to assess what effect musicians' unions had on the history of American orchestras in the nineteenth century.

The Scope of the Musicians' Union Movement

Musicians' unions stated their purposes in the constitutions and bylaws they drew up when they organized themselves. The MMPU, which was founded in 1863, formulated its mission succinctly but carefully: "The object of this Union is to unite the instrumental portion of the musical profession for the better protection of its interests in General."[4] By "*instrumental* portion" the New York musicians meant that their union was intended for players of orchestral instruments, not for singers or pianists. By "musical *profession*" they meant that it was intended for professionals, not amateurs. By "*unite*" they

---

3 · The literature on nineteenth-century American musicians' unions is modest. It includes Abram Loft, "Musicians' Guild and Union: A Consideration of the Evolution of Protective Organization among Musicians" (Ph.D. diss., 1950); Sandy R. Mazzola, "When Music Is Labor: Chicago Bands and Orchestras and the Origins of the Chicago Federation of Musicians, 1880–1902" (Ph.D. diss., 1984); Anna Weldon Green, "Musicians' Union of San Francisco" (master's thesis, 1929); John R. Commons, "Types of American Labor Unions: The Musicians of St. Louis and New York," *Quarterly Journal of Economics* 10 (1906); James P. Kraft, *Stage to Studio: Musicians and the Sound Revolution, 1890–1950* (1996); James P. Kraft, "Artists as Workers: Musicians and Trade Unionism in America, 1880–1917," *Musical Quarterly* 79 (1995); Robert Schmaltz, "Organizing Orpheus: Protecting the American Orchestral Musician, 1890–1910," *Sonneck Society Bulletin* 25 (1999). Primary sources abound: printed materials issued by the unions (bylaws, price lists, and so forth); handwritten minutes and other records of unions; periodicals, especially the *American Musician*, which was for a time the official publication of the New York Musical Mutual Protective Union; and contemporary newspapers.

4 · Musical Mutual Protective Union, *Constitution and By-Laws* (1869).

meant that all musicians working in the city should belong to a single union. And, finally, *"protection"* meant that the union intended to see that New York musicians were treated fairly by their employers and were protected from outside competition. The constitutions of the Philadelphia Musical Association, the Washington Musical Protective Union, and several other musicians' unions around the country echoed this New York statement almost word for word.

There were traces of union activity in the 1850s in New York, Chicago, and San Francisco, and there were social and benevolent societies for musicians even earlier in New York, Philadelphia, and elsewhere. However, the first enduring union seems to have been the New York MMPU. In May 1863, the instrumentalists who played in New York's theater orchestras held a mass meeting "for the purpose of arranging a new tariff of prices for playing in the theatres and at balls."[5] The *New York Times* noted that the 150 or so musicians who attended the meeting included "musicians of every class" and that "by far the larger number of them [were] of German birth."[6] In July 1863, the musicians met again to approve the union's constitution and bylaws, to elect officers, and to issue the new price list.[7] It set prices at $12 per week in the Broadway theaters, $10 a week in the Bowery theaters, and $5 per service for balls. These rates represented a significant improvement on previous wages, which were variously reported as $7 to $10 per week in the theaters.[8] The union applied to the State of New York for a charter, which was granted in 1864.[9]

News of the MMPU and its success spread quickly to musicians in other American cities, who emulated the New York musicians by forming their own unions: the Philadelphia Musical Association in 1863, the Chicago Musicians' Protective Union in 1864, the Washington Musical Protective Union in 1865, and the Boston Musicians' Union before 1867. By 1872, when the first national Musicians' Protective Association was organized, there were musicians' unions in at least eight American cities. The new national organization attached membership figures for its member unions to its published constitution and bylaws:[10]

5 · *New York Times,* May 4, 1864, 5.

6 · Ibid., May 7, 1863, 8.

7 · *New York Musikzeitung,* July 10, 1863, 8; *New York Clipper,* July 4, 1863, 91.

8 · "Before this association was formed the best of musicians were glad to get engagements for from $7 to $10 a week; after its formation they fixed the price at $12" (*New York Tribune,* November 4, 1865). "The orchestral players at the theatres received nine dollars a week" (*New York Times,* November 2, 1865, 4).

9 · The MMPU's state charter and its amendments are discussed at length in Commons, "Types of American Labor Unions," 426–27.

10 · *Constitution and By-Laws of the Musicians' Protective Association of the United States* (1872), 27–51.

Local 1 – New York	813 members
Local 2 – Chicago	113
Local 3 – Baltimore	158
Local 4 – Boston	235
Local 5 – Philadelphia	549
Local 6 – Peoria, IL	17
Local 7 – Washington, DC	85
Local 8 – Louisville, KY	37

In 1892 almost fifty local music unions were represented at the seventh annual convention of the National League of Musicians (NLM).[11] Unions had sprung up in many midwestern and western cities—Cincinnati, Milwaukee, St. Louis, Kansas City, and San Francisco—and in small towns such as Beaver Falls, Pennsylvania; San Jose, California; and Belleville, Illinois. There were musicians' unions in manufacturing towns (Rochester, New York and Toledo, Ohio), in the mining camps (Butte, Montana and Leadville, Colorado), and in the South (Richmond, Virginia; Memphis, Tennessee; and Birmingham, Alabama). One city that did not appear on the 1892 list was Boston, where the union, one of the earliest in the United States, appears to have fallen apart in the early 1880s, perhaps in consequence of the founding of the Boston Symphony, which originally included members of Local 4 but soon became a nonunion orchestra.[12]

In 1896 there were two conventions—the eleventh convention of the National League of Musicians and the first convention of the rival American Federation of Musicians. Some locals sent representatives to both conventions, others to only one. In all there were musicians' union locals in eighty-nine different cities and towns (see table I.3.1).[13] Some cities, notably New York, Chicago, and Washington, D.C., had rival union locals, each of which sent a delegation to one convention. A new union in Boston was represented at the AFM convention. One city (St. Louis) had a separate local for "colored" musicians.[14] Neither the NLM nor the AFM convention reports gave membership figures for the locals in 1896. However, the AFM convention

---

11 · National League of Musicians, *Souvenir of the Seventh Annual Convention . . . 1892*, 35–36.

12 · See Mark DeWolfe Howe, *The Boston Symphony Orchestra* (1914), 65–71, 108–11, 157. See also *American Music Journal*, May 12, 1888, 123.

13 · *Souvenir* 4 (April 1896); American Federation of Musicians, *Proceedings of the [First Annual] Convention, Indianapolis, Indiana* (1896), 43–44.

14 · St. Louis AFM Local 44 (The Great Western Union) seems to have been the first all-black musicians' union—at least it was the first to affiliate with a national organization. Parallel segregated musicians' locals became common in the early twentieth century. See Leta Miller, "Racial Segregation and the San Francisco Musicians' Union, 1923–60," *Journal of the Society for American Music* 1 (2007); also Kraft, *Stage to Studio*, 30–31.

TABLE 1.3.1. Musicians' union locals in 1896

*Locals represented at 1896 National League of Musicians Convention
(in order by NLM local number)*

New York, NY	Musical Mutual Protective Union
Philadelphia, PA	Philadelphia Musical Association
Cincinnati, OH	Musicians' Protective Association
Chicago, IL	Musical Society
Milwaukee, WI	Musicians' Musical Protective Association
Detroit, MI	Musicians' Protective Benevolent Association
St. Louis, MO	Musicians Mutual Benevolent Association
Newark, NJ	Musical Mutual Protective Union
San Francisco, CA	Musical Mutual Protective Union
Paterson, NJ	Musical Protective Union
Pittsburgh, PA	Musical Mutual Protective Union
Washington, DC	Musicians' Protective Association
Baltimore, MD	Musicians' Protective Union
Syracuse, NY	Musical Protective Association
Los Angeles, CA	Musicians' Association
Kansas City, MO	Musicians' Protective Union
Grand Rapids, MI	Musicians' Mutual Protective Union
Omaha, NE	Musical Mutual Protective Union
Buffalo, NY	Musicians' Protective Association
Cleveland, OH	Musical Mutual Protective Association
Toledo, OH	Musical Protective Association
Denver, CO	Musical Protective Association
Rochester, NY	Musical Protective Association
Indianapolis, IN	Musicians' Protective Association
Louisville, KY	Musical Protective Union
Seattle, WA	Musicians' Mutual Protective Union
Memphis, TN	Musicians' Protective Union
Oakland, CA	Musicians' Union
St. Paul, MN	Musicians' Union
Beaver Falls, PA	Musicians' Protective Union
Belleville, IL	Musicians' Mutual Protective Union
Butte, MT	Musicians' Mutual Protective Union
Portland, OR	Musicians' Protective Union
Minneapolis, MN	Musicians' Association
Duluth, MN	Musicians' Protective Union
Fort Wayne, IN	Musicians' Protective Union
Saginaw, MI	Musicians' Protective Union
Pueblo, CO	Musicians' Protective Union
Sacramento, CA	Musicians' Protective Union
Dallas, TX	Musicians' Protective Union
Leadville, CO	Musicians' Protective Association
Birmingham, AL	Musicians' Protective Association
Evansville, IN	Musicians' Association
Quincy, IL	Musicians' Protective Union
Newport, RI	Musicians' Protective Union
East St. Louis, IL	Musicians' Protective Union
Orange, NJ	Musicians' Protective Union
San Antonio, TX	Musicians' Society
Fort Worth, TX	Musicians' Protective Union

TABLE I.3.1. (continued)

*Locals represented at 1896 National League of Musicians Convention
(in order by NLM local number)*

Erie, PA	Musicians' Association
Decatur, IL	Musicians' Protective Union
Salt Lake City, UT	Musicians' Mutual Protective Union
Utica, NY	Musicians Protective Union
Galveston, TX	Musicians' Protective Union
Auburn, NY	Musicians' Protective Union
Anaconda, MT	Musicians' Mutual Protective Union
East Liverpool, OH	Musicians' Mutual Protective Association
St. Joseph, MO	Musicians' Protective Association
Kansas City, KS	Musicians' Protective Union
Ottumwa, IA	Musicians' Protective Union
Oshkosh, WI	Musicians Union
Wheeling, WV	Musicians Mutual Protective Union
Raton, NM	Musicians' Union
Harrison, NJ	Musicians' Protective Association
Cripple Creek, CO	Musicians' Protective Association
Springfield, IL	Musicians' Association
Watertown, NY	Musicians' Protective Union
Sedalia, MO	Musicians' Protective Union
Houston, TX	Musicians' Protective Union
Peoria, IL	Musicians' Society
Hamilton, OH	Musicians' Protective Association
Reading, PA	Musical Association
Dubuque, IA	Musicians Protective Association
Bloomington, IL	Musicians' Protective Union

*Cities with locals at 1896 American Federation of Musicians Convention only
(in order by American Federation of Musicians' local number)*

Boston, MA	Musicians' Protective Union
Troy, NY	Musical Mutual Protective Union
Albany, NY	Musicians' Union
Akron, OH	The Local
Terre Haute, IN	Musicians' Protective Union
Anderson, IN	Musician's Protective Association
Port Huron, MI	Musicians' Union
Topeka, KS	Musical Association
Joliet, IL	Musicians' Protective Union
Elwood, IN	Apollo Union
Muncie, IN	Musicians' Protective Association
Racine, WI	Musicians' Union
St. Louis, MO	Great Western Union (Colored)
Marion, IN	Musician's Protective Union
Muscatine, IA	Musicians' Union

Sources: *Souvenir: Official Organ of the National League of Musicians of the United States* 4 (April 1896): 8; American Federation of Musicians, *Proceedings of the [First Annual] Convention,* Indianapolis, Indiana (1896), 43–44.

proceedings two years later tabulated the membership of seventy-seven locals and came up with a total of 9,152 member musicians. Given that many locals had still not joined the AFM, in particular the large New York and Philadelphia locals, it is probably safe to estimate the total number of unionized
musicians in the United States in 1896 at more than ten thousand.

Musicians' unions tended to resemble one another closely—they had
similar names, they used similar language in their constitutions and bylaws,
and they had the same structure of officers and committees.[15] In many cities
German musicians constituted the core of the early union. Musicians' guilds
were still active in Germany in the first half of the nineteenth century, and
immigrant musicians re-created aspects of the guilds—for example, pen-
sions and the price list—in their new homeland. The constitutions and proceedings of musicians' unions in Chicago, Cincinnati, and St. Louis were
initially published in German as well as English. The unions aimed to be inclusive, however, to "unite the instrumental portion of the musical profession," and they tried to avoid the possibility of multiple organizations based
on ethnicity. German was abandoned as an "official" language, and union affairs were conducted in English.[16]

Three Characteristics of Musicians' Unions

Nineteenth-century American musicians' unions shared three central features. These were as follows:

1. The closed shop. Every player in every orchestra—or in any other ensemble that played for money—had to be a union member. Members
   were prohibited from playing in an orchestra with nonmembers. The
   closed shop also excluded musicians who belonged to a union in a different city, although exceptions were frequent.
2. The price list. Each union published a schedule of rates for every sort of
   musical engagement in its jurisdiction—playing in an opera, at a dance,
   at a political rally, at a funeral, and so on. These were supposedly mini-
   mums; employers could pay higher rates if they chose.
3. The leader system. Orchestra leaders—that is, the men who organized
   and conducted bands or orchestras—were union members just like the
   players. In fact, they were often leaders of the union as well as of their orchestras.

---

15 · These similarities resulted from the movement of personnel from one city to another but
even more from conscious imitation, especially of the New York MMPU.

16 · *American Musician*, April 19, 1890, 7.

The *closed shop* was specified in the bylaws of most musicians' unions, probably all of them. The principle was stated thus by the Philadelphia Musical Association in 1865: "The members of this Association bind themselves, by signing the Constitution and By-Laws, to enter into no engagement and assist at no musical performance whatever with any professional musician or musicians who are not members of this Association. It shall, however, be understood that the members of this Association shall have the right to assist at the performance of traveling companies."[17] This language prohibits two things: a union musician cannot play in an orchestra (or a band) in which a nonmember plays. In addition, the union musician must refuse any engagement offered by a leader or conductor who is not a union man. The exception for traveling companies was needed because operas or minstrel shows often traveled with only a leader and a couple of first-chair players and then filled out the orchestra with local musicians in each city where they played.[18] The visiting musicians were union men, but they belonged to the union in a different city (usually New York). The Philadelphia Musical Association did not want to disrupt this system, which gave its members good work at good wages. By specifying that members were not allowed to play with nonunion "professional" musicians, the bylaws implicitly permitted members to play as reinforcements in amateur ensembles. This provision proved contentious, however, because Philadelphia's amateur ensembles often paid low wages. Unions in several other cities did not allow their members to play with amateurs at all.

The Philadelphia union enforced its closed shop provision with a sliding scale of fines: $4 for the first offense, $8 for the second, and "erasion" from membership in the union for the third offense.[19] These were substantial penalties. Four dollars was about what a musician would earn in two nights playing in the theater in Philadelphia; $8 was half a week's wages; "erasion" meant the man couldn't earn his living as a musician any more. This example from Philadelphia was typical. A closed-shop bylaw appeared in almost every union constitution and was enforced by similar fines and sanctions.

The purpose of the closed shop was to reserve jobs in orchestras and bands for members of the city's union and to maintain wage levels, since union members were also supposed to respect the price list. Thanks to the closed shop, the union functioned to a considerable extent as a musical hiring hall. Musicians' union offices were usually located in or near the saloons

17 · *Charter, Constitution and By-Laws of the Philadelphia Musical Association* (1865), article 13, section 1.
18 · See Commons, "Types of American Labor Unions," 430.
19 · *Charter, Constitution and By-Laws of the Philadelphia Musical Association,* article 13, section 1.

where musicians congregated. In New York these saloons lined East Fourth Street between the Bowery and Second Avenue, and the MMPU offices were upstairs from Victor Eckstein's Saloon at 64 E. Fourth Street. Leaders would come to East Fourth Street to hire men both for casual jobs and for standing orchestras.[20] The Washington, D.C., union in the 1890s rented a back room in a saloon at Tenth and E Streets Northwest as its clubhouse. Leaders would drop by around noon to fill out their orchestras for work that evening.[21]

To maintain the closed shop, the union had to make it relatively easy to join—otherwise many musicians would be left outside the union and would undermine the union's control of the labor market. To join the union, a musician had to be recommended by a member, play an audition, and pay an initiation fee. The audition was a sham in almost every case: the applicant played a scale or two for a committee, paid his fee, and was welcomed into the union. The initiation fee tended to be low and the dues reasonable. The exception was New York, where the initiation fee was raised to $100 in the 1890s; there was also a "six-month rule," which stated that a musician had to reside in the city for six months before he could be considered for membership in the Musical Mutual Protective Union.[22]

Although most American musicians' unions were founded by German immigrants, the closed shop principle was not used to exclude musicians of other ethnicities. Membership directories, orchestra rosters, and even lists of union officers from the 1870s and 1880s contain many non-German names. An article in the *New York Times* estimated in 1870 that 55 percent of MMPU members were of German origin, while 13 percent were French, 7 percent were Italians, 5 percent were Poles, 5 percent were Belgians, 4 percent were English and Irish, and only 2 percent were "Americans."[23] An 1890 article in the *American Musician* asserted that "many of our colored brethren" are

---

20 · "New York Musicians," *American Musician*, April 19, 1890, 7. Another place that functioned as a hiring hall for New York musicians was the Aschenbroedel Verein (Cinderella Society), a social and benevolent club for German musicians, which had a clubhouse at 74 E. Fourth Street, then at 144–46 E. Eighty-Sixth Street. See "Successful Career of the Aschenbroedel Verein of New York," *Souvenir* 4 (April 1896). Figure II.2.1 in this volume depicts musicians gathering on Fourth Street.

21 · Katherine Preston, *Music for Hire: A Study of Professional Musicians in Washington (1877–1900)* (1992), 47.

22 · Musical Mutual Protective Union, *Constitution and By-Laws* (1905), article 2, section 4; article 2, section 2.

23 · *New York Times*, December 18, 1870, 5. The *Times* also mentions "Swedes and Norwegians" at 5 percent, "Hollanders" at 4 percent, and "Spaniards, Portuguese and unknown nationalities about 2 per cent." The 55 percent figure for Germans is plausible; the others numbers may be little more than speculation.

represented in the New York MMPU.[24] Other musicians' unions that admitted black members included Boston, Detroit, and San Francisco.[25] On the other hand, the constitution of the Philadelphia Musical Association restricted membership to "white male person[s] … following the profession of music," and the Cincinnati Musicians' Protective Association specified "white male musicians recommended by the Examination Committee."[26] Thus in Philadelphia and Cincinnati, the closed shop principle was used to discriminate against women as well as black musicians. Other unions said nothing about sex or race in their bylaws, though they may have excluded women and blacks on an informal basis. A few unions are known to have had women members, for example, San Francisco, which admitted women beginning in 1887.[27] Women, in fact, played in many American bands and orchestras in the nineteenth century—most often in all-women ensembles such as the Boston Fadettes and the Ladies' Elite Orchestra in New York.[28] Many unions opposed these so-called lady orchestras, which were mostly nonunion, paid low wages, and took work away from union ensembles.[29] The National League of Musicians declared in 1888 that "the 'lady orchestras' have been the cause of much annoyance and pecuniary loss to many musicians" and proposed that musicians' unions should forbid their members from participating in performances with such orchestras either as soloists or as supernumeraries.[30]

The *price list* was the second central feature of nineteenth-century musicians' unions. Every union had a price list; in several cities there was probably a price list, formal or informal, before the union was even organized.[31] The Baltimore price list of 1872 (see fig. I.3.1) provides an example of a typical price list, although somewhat condensed because it was printed as a booklet

24 · *American Musician*, April 19, 1890, 7.

25 · Miller, "Racial Segregation," 164–65.

26 · *Charter, Constitution and By-Laws of the Philadelphia Musical Association*, article 2, section 1; *Constitution and By-Laws of the Cincinnati Musicians' Protective Association No. 1* (1898), article 4, section 1.

27 · Green, "Musicians' Union of San Francisco," 3.

28 · See Judith Tick, "Passed Away Is the Piano Girl: Changes in American Musical Life, 1870–1900," in *Women Making Music* (1986). On women's orchestras, see chapter I.2 in this volume.

29 · "The Question of the Employment of Women in Theater Orchestras," *American Art Journal*, September 12, 1891.

30 · *American Music Journal* 8 (March 3, 1888): 178.

31 · There must have been a price list in New York before 1863 because the report on the first meeting of the union says that it is being called for the purpose of arranging a *new* tariff of prices.

Musical Union

OF

BALTIMORE, MD.

1872.

ARTICLE XII.

PRICE LIST.

Sec. 1. BALLS.—held at the following Halls: Concordia, Masonic Temple, Monument, Raine's, Maryland Institute and Lehman's,—but longer than 4 A. M., $5 per man, leader $8. All other Halls, $4 per man, leader $8.

Sec. 2. BALLS with Concert.—$6 per man, leader $10; Rehearsals, $1 per man.

Sec. 3. BALCONY playing,—per hour, $1 per man.

Sec. 4. BANQUETS.—$5 per man, leader $9.

Sec. 5. BANQUETS with Hop.—$6 per man, leader $9.

Sec. 6. CONCERTS, Sacred, Symphony or Oratory,—$5 per man; Rehearsals. $2 per man.

Sec. 7. CONCERTS with Hop.—$5 per man, leader $10; Rehearsals, $1 per man.

Sec. 8. CITY PARK CONCERTS.—not longer than two hours, $3 per man, leader $5.—Fourth of July and other public days, $6 per man. leader $10.

Sec. 9. CIRCUS.—per day, $5 per man.

Sec. 10. COMMENCEMENTS.—$4 per man, leader $6.

Sec. 11. CHURCH MUSIC.—$2.50 per man, Rehearsal $2.50 per man. At churches where more than 6 masses occur during the year, $2 per man.

Sec. 12. CONCERT SALOONS.—per week, including one Matinee, $15 per man; extra Matinees, $2 per man.

Sec. 13. EXHIBITIONS.—not longer than three hours, $3 per man, leader $5.—By the week, (evening performances) $15 per man, leader $20. Matinees $2 per man extra.

Sec. 14. ESCORTS.—(extra occasions), not longer than two hours, $2 per man, leader $4; for every subsequent hour, $1 per man.

Sec. 15. EXCURSIONS.—(Water), half day, $4 per man, leader $7; whole day, $6 per man, leader $10.

Sec. 16. EXCURSIONS.—to White Rock Retreat, Holly Grove, Fair Haven and other places of the kind, per week, $18 per man leader $25.

Sec. 17. EXCURSIONS.—with Societies to distant cities,—one day, $8 per man, leader $9; two days, $10 per man, leader $13; three or more days, per day, $4 per man, leader $6. All expenses included in these cases.

Sec. 18. FAIRS.—held in halls,—see Section 13.

Sec. 19. FAIRS.—State or County.—per day, $4 per man, leader $6.

Sec. 20. FUNERALS.—$3 per man, leader $4.

Sec. 21. HOPS.—from 8 P. M. until 2 A. M. in the halls mentioned in Sec. 1, $4 per man, leader $8; in all other halls, $3 per man, leader $6. From 10 P. M. until 2 P. M., $3 per man, leader $6.

Sec. 22. THEATRICAL PERFORMANCES with Hop.—$4 per man, leader $6.

Sec. 23. KHAEXCHEN.—see Sections 21 and 22.

Sec. 24. LECTURES.—$2.50 per man, leader $4.

Sec. 25. OPERAS.—for single performance, $6 per man; Rehearsals, $1 per man extra; for short season, $5 per man for each performance.

Sec. 26. PRIVATE PARTIES.—$5 per man, leader $8.

Sec. 27. PROCESSIONS, Civil.—$5 per man, leader $10.

Sec. 28. ——— Torchlight [Fackelzug], not longer than four hours, $5 per man, leader $10.

Sec. 29. POLITICAL MEETINGS.—$4 per man, leader $6; if with Parade, $6 per man, leader $8.

Sec. 30. PARADES, Military.—not longer than six hours, $6 per man, leader $10 not longer than four hours, $4 per man, leader $7; each subsequent hour, $1 per man.

Sec. 31. PIC-NICS.—Day Pic-Nics until 6 P. M, $4 per man, leader $6; from 2 or 3 P. M. until 11 P. M., $6 per man, leader $7; from noon to 11 P. M., $8 per man, leader $9; with parade from hall direct to the Pic-Nic grounds, $1 per man extra; with general parade, $3 per man extra; with parade back to the city, $1 per man extra.

Sec. 32. RACES.—$3 per man, leader $5; with process' $5 per man, leader $7.

Sec. 33. SKATING PARKS.—not longer than two hours, $3 per man, leader $5.

Sec. 34. SOIREES.—see Sections 21 and 22.

Sec. 35. SERENADES.—one residence, playing no more than four selections, $1.50 per man, leader $2.50; for every subsequent residence, $1 per man. Should there be more than three, the leader can use his own discretion regarding the price.

Sec. 36. THEATRES.—single Performance, $3 per man, leader $5. Short season, by the week, $16 per man, leader $25. Regular season, per week (including one Matinee) $15 per man.

Sec. 37. TOURNAMENTS.—$6 per man, leader $8; with Ball, $10 per man, leader $15.

Sec. 38. UNTERHALTUNGS.-MUSIC, at private places.— from 4 P. M. to 10 P. M. $4 per man, leader $6. From 3 P. M. to 6 P. M., or from 8 P. M. to 11 P. M., $2.50 per man, leader $4.

Sec. 39. VARIETY THEATRE,—see Sec. 12.

Sec. 40. WEDDINGS.—$5 per man, leader $8.

Sec. 41. It shall be the duty of every leader or person making engagements, referring to Sections 1, 2, 4, 5, 7, 15, 19, 21, 23, 26, 31, 32, 34, 37, 38 and 40, to demand the usual privileges appertaining thereto.

Sec. 42. Each hour, once begun, shall be considered as full.

Sec. 43. Where the German is danced an extra charge shall be made at the discretion of the leader.

FIGURE I.3.1. Baltimore Price List, 1872, Peabody Archives, Johns Hopkins University, Baltimore, Maryland.

for members to carry in their pockets. It sets a rate for each type of work—balls, banquets, circuses, churches, fairs, and funerals, for example. The rate is by the job, not by the hour, though in some cases the job is rated at a set number of hours or until a certain time of the night, with additional hours being paid as overtime. For standing orchestras, such as theater orchestras, there are weekly rates, which tend to be a little lower than what the price would have been calculated as six or eight separate jobs. Rehearsals are extra—a dollar apiece—except for theaters, where a rehearsal rate is not given, probably because rehearsals in the theaters were unpaid.[32] The "German," a complex dance that could last up to an hour, calls for extra pay (see Sec. 43 in fig. I.3.1).[33] The list gives two prices for each job—one for rank-and-file players, the other for leaders. Leaders in Baltimore are paid from one and one-half times to double what the other players are paid, depending on the type of engagement. Price lists from most other cities specified leader prices with similar pay differentials. The union set leader prices to prevent leaders from skimming off exorbitant profits and to stop leaders from cutting their rates when they bid against one another for the same jobs. A few price lists differentiated between principal players and section players for opera, theaters, and concerts, but this was unusual.[34]

Price lists were supposed to be minimum prices. In theory, an individual player might demand more for a job, or an entire orchestra might be paid at higher rates. In New York in 1890, for example, the Metropolitan Opera paid above the price list; so did Tony Pastor's theater, as did the Gilmore band and the Theodore Thomas Orchestra.[35] But for most musicians the price on the list was the best wage they could hope for, and often they were paid less. The *American Musician* asserted in 1888 that "of the fifty theaters in New York and Brooklyn, there are but three, viz. Harrigan's, Daly's and the New Broadway, which pay the society prices."[36] A Baltimore musician explained to the newspaper how leaders and employers could get away with paying below scale:

32 · Theaters typically included one or more rehearsals as part of the weekly price. Price lists sometimes go into detail about when a rehearsal is part of the price and when it is extra.

33 · The New York MMPU (*Constitution and By-Laws* [1886], 23) and San Francisco (1888) similarly call for a premium of $2 per man "if the German is danced." The San Francisco price list also requires that theater musicians be paid an extra $5 per week "when, during a regular engagement, blacking up for Minstrel performances is required" (Green, "Musicians' Union of San Francisco," 153).

34 · The Philadelphia Musical Association price list of 1865 calls for first-chair players in the theaters to be paid $15 for a week of six evening performances, while second-chair players are paid $13 (see Minutes of the Executive Committee, March 14, 1865, Historical Society of Pennsylvania archives).

35 · "New York's Orchestra Players," *American Musician*, March 8, 1890.

36 · *American Musician*, May 5, 1888, 95.

"The leaders always had the advantage of the men. We had a price-list, which everybody was supposed to stick to. Some did, others did not; and if any of the leaders disobeyed any of the laws the men were afraid to bring charges against them from fear of losing future engagements."[37] Probably the Baltimore leaders were undercutting the very price list shown in figure I.3.1. Another way to evade the price list was for a leader to pay the listed price for the job but then to demand and receive a kickback from his musicians.[38]

Table I.3.2 compares a selection of nineteenth-century price lists. The earliest comes from New York in 1863, the year the MMPU was organized. The latest come from Pittsburgh, Pennsylvania, and Madison, Wisconsin, in 1907. The table includes only a few characteristic rates out of fifty or sixty different jobs on a typical price list. As with the Baltimore price list shown in figure I.3.1, the weekly rates are always lower than the single service rates. For example, in New York in 1877, for a week of six services in the opera orchestra, the musician makes $35 rather than $42, and for six services in the theater he makes $15 rather than $30. The steady income of a standing orchestra compensated for the lower per-service rate. This created an incentive for musicians who worked in theater orchestras to take casual jobs at the higher rates and hire substitutes at the lower rate to take their place in the theater. As a result, the personnel in the pit often changed from night to night.[39]

It is striking how similar the prices in table I.3.2 are from one city to another. From the 1870s into the 1900s, opera is worth $6 or $7 per service and $35 per week in most of the cities listed in the table. A theater orchestra pays $15 to $20 per week, as does an orchestra in a concert saloon. A ball is worth $5 or $6 per service; so is a parade, and so is a half day's work on an excursion boat. The only places where rates are significantly lower are Madison, Wisconsin, by far the smallest city on the list, and perhaps Cincinnati and Pittsburgh. In San Francisco, where musicians were in short supply, the rates seem a little higher. The similarity of prices may indicate that the unions shared their price lists with one another and believed that what was a fair price in one city ought to be fair in another as well. The similarity might also result from the fact that local musicians often played with traveling companies, which paid the rate of their home union—usually the New York MMPU. This may have drawn price lists all around the country toward the New York price list.

The only union in table I.3.2 for which the price lists extend over a period of time is the MMPU. On the basis of this New York series and a few reports from other cities, it seems as though prices were very stable from the

37 · Ibid., March 13, 1886.
38 · Commons, "Types of American Labor Unions," 429.
39 · On substitutes in New York theater orchestras, see chapter II.1 in this volume.

TABLE 1.3.2. Comparison of price lists

Place/date	Opera		Theater		Concert		Public park concert	Concert saloon	Ball	Parade	Boat excursion
	Service	Week[a]	Service	Week[a]	Service	Week[a]	Service[b]	Week	Service[c]	Service[b]	Service
Baltimore 1872	$6		$3	$16	$5		$3 (2 hrs)	$15	$5 (4 AM)	$6 (6 hrs)	$6
Chicago 1869	$6	$35		$18	$5				$5 (4 AM)	$5	$5
Chicago 1877	$6	$30	$3	$18 (8)	$5		$4		$5 (5 AM)	$4	$4
Cincinnati 1899	$5	$35	$3	$20 (8)	$5	$35 (7)	$4 (2.5 hrs)	$18 (8)	$4 (2 AM)	$7 (7 PM)	$6
Cleveland 1864	$3.50	$18			$4				$5	$3	
Los Angeles 1898	$6	$25	$3	$15 (8)	$5		$3 (3 hrs)	$16 (8)	$3 (12 AM)	$3 (2 hrs)	$4
Madison, WI 1907			$4	$18	$2.50				$2 (12 AM)		$2
New York 1863	$5	$15 (3)		$12	$2.50			$10 (6)	$5 (8 hrs)	$5	$5
New York 1877	$7	$35 (6)	$5	$15 (6)	$7	$35 (6)	$5		$6	$6	$6
New York 1881	$7	$35	$5	$15 (6)	$7	$36 (6)	$5		$6	$6	$6
New York 1886	$7	$35	$5		$7	$36 (6)	$5		$6	$6	$6
New York 1905	$7	$35	$5	$21 (9)	$7	$36 (6)	$5	$18 (7)	$6	$6	$6
Philadelphia 1865	$7	$20 (3)	$5	$15 (6)	$7			$15 (6)	$5 (4 AM)	$6 (6 hrs)	$6
Philadelphia 1904	$7	$35 (6)	$5	$20 (8)	$7		$4 (4 hrs)	$15 (6)	$5 (4 AM)	$6 (6 hrs)	$5
Pittsburgh 1907			$5	$25 (8)	$5		$4		$5 (2 AM)	$5 (4 hrs)	$5
St Louis 1903	$7	$35	$3	$19 (10)	$5	$36 (9)	$4 (3 hrs)	$18.50 (7)	$5 (4 AM)	$6 (4 hrs)	$6
San Francisco 1888	$7	$30	$5	$20 (8)	$8		$4	$20	$7 (4 AM)	$5 (2 hrs)	$5
Washington, D.C. 1865	$5			$15 (6)	$5			$16 (7)	$5 (4 AM)	$6 (9 hrs)	$6

a. Numbers in parentheses indicate services per week.

b. Number of hours in parentheses indicate maximum length of service.

c. Times in parentheses indicate time by which service must end.

1870s through the 1900s. There was an initial increase when the unions were first organized—the figures from the 1860s in New York, Philadelphia, and Washington are on the low side. But once established, the price lists scarcely changed. During most of the period, the unions seem to have been content to defend their price lists and did not aspire to increase the wages of orchestra musicians.

The *leader system*—the third important feature of nineteenth-century American musicians' unions —regulated the role of leaders and conductors in the unions. The leader was a man who hired musicians for a standing orchestra or for a temporary job, who provided and/or arranged the music, who led rehearsals, who conducted the orchestra in performance, and who paid the men their wages. Anyone could be a leader—that is, anyone in the union. All a would-be leader had to do was bid on a job, get the contract, and hire an orchestra. Often, musicians were leaders on one job, rank and file on the next. Successful leaders established themselves more permanently. They might lead their own band or orchestra, like the Theodore Thomas Orchestra in New York or Johnny Hand's band in Chicago. They might conduct at the same theater season after season. Some leaders had contracts at several theaters simultaneously—hiring assistants to conduct when they couldn't be present. In Baltimore one leader in the 1890s managed to secure the contracts for *all* the theaters in town.[40] To restrain this practice, unions sometimes added clauses to their bylaws that prohibited leaders from taking contracts for a season unless they led the orchestras themselves.

Leaders bid against one another for jobs—either a single job or a season—and if their bid was successful, they signed a contract with the theater manager, the producer, the city parks department, or whoever else the client was. The leader then signed a contract with each and every musician in the orchestra. These relationships are made explicit in a model contract distributed by the National League of Musicians in 1890 to member unions. In it the musician agrees "to perform the required duties of _____ player in the orchestra at the _____ Opera House or Theatre ... during the season of _____ weeks and days, commencing _____, as stipulated in the contract between the ... manager of the _____ Opera House, or Theatre and the said leader." The leader, for his part, would "draw from the ... manager of the said _____ Opera House, or Theatre, and pay the said musician ... $_____ per week for the season of _____ weeks."[41] Thus, an orchestra

40 · See Commons, "Types of American Labor Unions," 430; also American Federation of Musicians, *Proceedings of the Third Convention, Louisville, Kentucky* (1898), 50.

41 · National League of Musicians, *Proceedings of the Convention of the National League of Musicians ... 1890*, 63. The contract also states that the leader will conform to the price list of the local union.

musician's contract is with the leader, not with management. A space is left at the bottom of the page for the theater manager to "endorse" the contract. This model contract probably was not often used word for word, but it gives an idea of the tens of thousands of individual contracts that regulated American orchestras in the nineteenth century.

Leaders were the linchpins of the system. They were working musicians who in most cases appeared with their orchestras in performance, often functioning as instrumental soloists as well as conductors. But leaders were also executives in the sense that they hired and fired and gave orders in rehearsal and performance. And they were entrepreneurs who bid on jobs, signed contracts, and sometimes put their own capital at risk.[42] Leaders were responsible to management for providing music as contracted; they were responsible to the musicians for leading them in performance and paying their wages; and they were responsible to the union for enforcing the closed shop and maintaining the price list. Through the leaders, the union could control both the workplace and the musical labor market.

The problem was that in many cases the leaders controlled the union. In most cities the majority of the union officers and the members of the executive committees were or had once been leaders. The leaders "had the advantage of the men," as the Baltimore musician above put it, and they ran the union to their own purposes. Because the leaders bid against one another for jobs, however, and because men alternated between being leaders and rank and file, a leader couldn't press his advantage too far. The minutes of union executive committee meetings, are full of complaints by leaders accusing one another of cutting prices, underbidding, hiring nonunion musicians, and otherwise trying to gain unfair advantage over one another. Rivalries between leaders served as a check on their power and enhanced the influence of the rank and file in the union.

Most of the well-known American conductors of the late nineteenth century were leaders and belonged to the union. Patrick Gilmore, Theodore Thomas, Walter Damrosch, and Victor Herbert all belonged to the New York MMPU. Several of these men were charged with violations of union regulations and brought before the Executive Committee. In 1885 Theodore Thomas was charged with violating the union's six-month residency rule when he hired Felix Bour, an oboist, directly from Belgium to play in the

---

42 · It was unusual in the nineteenth century, as it is today, for executives or entrepreneurs to belong to the same union as the men whose labor they bought and sold. The only comparable situation was the building trades, where foremen usually belonged to the union. However, contractors in the building trades did not belong to the union. See Solomon Blum, "Trade Union Rules in the Building Trades," in *Studies in American Trade Unionism*, ed. J. H. Hollander and G. E. Barnett (1905).

Thomas Orchestra. The union levied fines both on Thomas and on his musicians for playing with a nonmember. Thomas took the matter to court and got the fines rescinded.[43] Walter Damrosch in 1893 was not so lucky when he imported a Danish cellist to play in the New York Symphony. The MMPU forbade the members of the orchestra—all union members, as was Damrosch himself—to play with the new cellist, who had not lived in New York for the requisite six months and therefore could not join the union. At the orchestra's next concert, according to the *New York Times*, "Mr. Damrosch lifted his baton and waved it for the musicians to begin, but not a note came in response. A few violinists instinctively lifted their violins to the shoulder, but that was all. The fifty-three musicians would not play."[44] Damrosch resigned from the union in protest but then backed down and paid his fine, saying that "his sympathies were with the union" and that he deeply regretted the whole affair.[45] The union, for its part, allowed the cellist to perform with the orchestra as a soloist while he waited out his six months.[46]

This pattern of American conductors belonging to the union and functioning as leaders began to change at the beginning of the twentieth century. Leopold Stokowski, when he took over the Cincinnati Symphony in 1909, became a member of the Cincinnati Musicians' Protective Association.[47] Gustav Mahler, on the other hand, who conducted at the Metropolitan Opera in 1908 and the New York Philharmonic in 1909, did not join the MMPU as Offenbach had done thirty years earlier, even though the players in both orchestras were union members. Perhaps Mahler was covered by the clause in the MMPU bylaws that stated: "Eminent composers, conductors or instrumentalists … shall be eligible to honorary membership in the Musical Mutual Protective Union if recommended by the Board of Directors."[48]

Strengths and Weaknesses of Nineteenth-Century Musicians' Unions

Musicians' unions in nineteenth-century American orchestras—based on the closed shop, the price list, and the leader system—were successful, stable, and durable. By far the majority of orchestras were unionized: opera

---

43 · See Loft, "Musicians' Guild and Union," 305–11.
44 · *New York Times*, December 18, 1893, 4.
45 · Ibid., January 20, 1894, 2.
46 · Ibid., December 23, 1893, 12.
47 · Oliver Daniel, *Stokowski: A Counterpoint of View* (1982), 10.
48 · *Constitution and By-Laws of the Musical Mutual Protective Union* (1886), article 2, section 9. If Mahler became an "honorary member" of the MMPU, the event went unnoticed in the press. This mechanism may have been used for other European conductors who worked in New York.

orchestras, concert orchestras, theater orchestras, touring orchestras, and all sorts of temporary and casual orchestras. Jobs were filled, musicians were paid, and the ever-expanding market for music was satisfied. Strikes were exceedingly rare. In some cities there was a strike when the union was first organized; there was a later, unsuccessful strike against the New York theaters in 1865 and a brief strike in Chicago in 1868.[49] But thereafter problems were typically addressed and solved contract by contract—between managers and leaders or between leaders and players—rather than by strikes. The absence of strikes was a sign of the unions' strength, but it was also a sign of their weakness.

The weaknesses of nineteenth-century American musicians' unions were structural. Because leaders belonged to the union and were very influential, it was hard to raise wages or even to enforce the price list. On the whole it was in the leaders' interest to keep wages low. Because musicians' contracts were with leaders rather than with management, there was no room for collective bargaining. The fact that musicians' unions were exclusively local became a weakness too, as theater circuits developed and more and more shows toured around the country. Travel created new challenges: for example, union members migrated from one city to another looking for work, and orchestras on tour took work away from local musicians all around the country. It was mainly to address problems of travel, as well as to lobby the federal government on issues of concern to musicians, that local musicians' unions formed a series of national organizations in the last quarter of the nineteenth century.[50]

From 1871 to 1875 there was a Musicians' Protective Association of the United States, little more than an annual meeting of six or eight local unions. The National League of Musicians, a more active confederation of local unions, was organized in 1886 and lasted until 1903. The NLM was dominated by its largest member union, the MMPU of New York, and ironically the MMPU was the source of many of the travel problems. It refused to recognize the "travel cards" of union musicians from other cities who came to New York looking for work. It "colonized" the territory of neighboring jurisdictions, taking work away from members of other unions. And almost all touring companies—operas, minstrel shows, vaudeville, and burlesque, as well as the Theodore Thomas Orchestra—operated out of New York with

---

49 · On the 1865 New York strike, see chapter II.1 of this volume. There were additional strikes in Chicago in 1888, 1892, and 1896.

50 · Musicians' unions lobbied the government on two big issues: (1) to prevent military bands on the federal payroll from hiring themselves out in competition with the local union; and (2) to prevent managers and entrepreneurs from importing European ensembles, again in competition with American musicians.

orchestras composed of MMPU members. Local unions all over the country complained that these traveling orchestras of New York musicians took the best jobs away from their members. In 1888, for example, the St. Louis Musicians' Association took issue with the fact that the organizers of the Saengerfest in St. Louis had imported the Theodore Thomas Orchestra to play at its summer festival instead of using a St. Louis ensemble. Worse yet, Thomas proposed to expand his orchestra with a large contingent of extra musicians from New York instead of hiring local musicians, as was customary.[51] The president of the St. Louis union took the grievance to the NLM, which characteristically declined to act. Unrestricted travel served the interests of the New York union and its members, and therefore the NLM paid lip service to regulating travel but left the system the way it was.[52]

In 1896 several musicians' unions broke away from the National League of Musicians, affiliated themselves with the American Federation of Labor, and created the American Federation of Musicians. Between 1896 and 1903, the AFM and the NLM competed, with more and more unions leaving the NLM and joining the AFM. In 1903 the last holdout — the New York MMPU — became an AFM local, and the National League of Musicians disbanded. The American Federation of Musicians survives to this day.

The conflict between the AFM and the NLM has been portrayed as a struggle between a trade union and a professional society. Some commentators argue that the AFM regarded orchestra musicians as "workers," whereas the NLM considered them to be "artists," and that this is the reason the NLM was unwilling to affiliate with the AFL.[53] This argument is somewhat misleading. In the heat of the struggle between the two organizations in the 1890s, the NLM officers did call their opponents "mechanics" and "labor musicians,"[54] while the AFM insisted that however much an orchestra musician might consider himself to be an "artist," he still worked for wages and would benefit by allying himself with other wage-workers.[55] Much of the time, though, the "artists" in the National League of Musicians and the New York MMPU talked and acted exactly like trade unionists. For example, when the Strauss orchestra came to the United States in 1890 under the direction of Johann's younger brother Eduard, the NLM claimed that the mu-

51 · *American Musician*, March 10, 1888, 198.
52 · Loft, "Musicians' Guild and Union," 360–64.
53 · Ibid., 373 ff.; Kraft, "Artists as Workers," 526; Robert David Leiter, *The Musicians and Petrillo* (1953), 14–15.
54 · *New York Times*, March 9, 1896, 2; *National League of Musicians Proceedings*, 1897–98, quoted in Loft, "Musicians' Guild and Union," 381.
55 · *Union Record* (St. Louis), September 28, 1889, quoted in Green, "Musicians' Union of San Francisco," 17.

sicians in Strauss's orchestra were *not* "artists" but "workers" and therefore subject to the provisions of the Foran Act, which forbade the importation of foreign contract labor.[56] Similarly, the AFM unions insisted that musicians were both artists *and* workers. Owen Miller, president of the St. Louis Musicians' Association, availed himself of the vocabulary of phrenology to declare that orchestra musicians worked for low wages because their "artistic musical bump" was more highly developed than their "bump of accumulation."[57] Musicians, Miller argued, should consider themselves professionals, like doctors and lawyers, who regulated their affairs by means of national organizations very much like the AFM. The "artists" versus "workers" issue seems to have been created more by the press than by either the AFM or the NLM. The real disagreements between the two organizations were whether musicians' unions should affiliate with the American Federation of Labor and whether the New York MMPU would continue to run the national organization for its own interests.

Orchestras and Unions

What effect did musicians' unions have on the development of American orchestras in the nineteenth century? Did the three central features of the unions—the closed shop, the price list, and the leader system—promote or inhibit the formation of orchestras and their success? Did they make American orchestras different from French or English or Italian orchestras, which were not unionized?[58]

The effects of the unions differed according to the type of orchestra. Union musicians in most American cities played in a broad spectrum of orchestras and bands, from symphony orchestras to theater orchestras, to orchestras in parks and resorts, to dance bands, to orchestras for excursions, weddings, and hops (see fig. I.3.1). Typically, the same musician played up and down along this continuum according to his skill level, his connections,

56 · *New York Times,* February 14, 1890, 1. The U.S. Treasury Department decided that the musicians of the Strauss orchestra were indeed artists, and the orchestra played in New York and elsewhere in the United States.

57 · *American Musician,* July 14, 1888, 39.

58 · Unions were not formed in English orchestras until the Amalgamated Musicians' Union in 1893. There were short-lived musicians' unions in France from 1876 on, but an enduring organization, the Chambre syndical des artistes-musiciens, did not emerge until 1902 (Fauquet, "Debuts du syndicalisme musical"). German orchestras were unionized in the second half of the nineteenth century, at about the same time as American orchestras. See Martin Jacob Newhouse, "Artists, Artisans, or Workers? Orchestral Musicians in the German Empire" (Ph.D. diss., 1979).

and the available work. For this discussion it is convenient to distinguish between three types of orchestra:

1. Casual orchestra—an orchestra or band formed for a single job, for example, a dance, a parade, or the performance of an oratorio;
2. Seasonal orchestra—for example, a theater orchestra, an orchestra hired for a series of concerts in a public park, or an orchestra organized for a touring opera;
3. Concert orchestra—a standing ensemble established to give public concerts under its own name, for example, the Theodore Thomas Orchestra, the Gilmore Band, or the New York Philharmonic.[59]

Musicians' unions were originally established in the context of casual orchestras, and this is where the system probably worked best. The closed shop centralized and regulated the supply of musical labor. By reserving work for union members while making entry into the union relatively easy, the unions fostered the formation in many American cities of a pool of players large enough to meet the demand for casual work. The price list, even though it was poorly enforced, seems to have helped keep wages at steady levels and prevented reductions during times of economic distress. European reports on American music often noted that orchestra musicians were better paid in the United States than in Europe. A German musician residing in New York wrote home to the *Deutsche Musikerzeitung* in 1873: "I was lucky enough to get a job playing viola in a theater for 20 dollars a week and I make even more giving lessons, which adds up to $160 or 200 Prussian Thalers per month. My living expenses are $50 per month. When I was in Paris, I earned 150 francs, i.e. 40 Thalers per month, more or less what I would earn in Berlin or Hamburg, and spent every penny on living expenses. Here I save three-quarters of my income."[60] Moreover, the leader system also seems to have functioned efficiently for casual orchestras because it combined the roles of contractor and conductor, because the union regulated competition between leaders, and because it offered entrepreneurial opportunities to ambitious musicians. In cities across the country, musicians' unions helped create and maintain a lively world of casual bands and orchestras in which instrumentalists could put together a decent living and aspire to improve their lot.

For seasonal orchestras the unions also worked reasonably well, although there were some characteristic problems. The closed shop helped theaters

---

59 · This is only one possible typology of nineteenth-century American orchestras. For another typology, see chapter I.1 in this volume.

60 · *Deutsche Musikerzeitung*, March 20, 1873, 99.

keep more or less the same personnel year after year. The price list kept wages at a decent level compared to other trades, but it also had the effect of making American theater orchestras relatively small compared to Europe, where wages were lower.[61] The lax enforcement of the price list and the differential between seasonal and casual rates led to chronic substitution, which almost certainly lowered the level of performance in the theaters and other seasonal orchestras.[62] The leader system protected players in seasonal orchestras from direct exploitation by theater and concert managers. Leaders were not necessarily more generous than managers, but they were union members, and they competed with one another for players and for jobs in the context of the union. The fact that leaders were union members also seems to have made relations between conductors and players in American orchestras somewhat more egalitarian than in European orchestras. An immigrant German theater musician to New York commented in 1874 about how surprised he was to find himself sitting next to his conductor in a saloon "chatting easily and comfortably, just as one would with any other human being."[63]

Musicians' unions functioned perhaps least well for concert orchestras, and particularly poorly for philharmonic societies and symphony orchestras. The closed shop tended to protect the jobs of inferior players, especially when they held union office; it discouraged the movement of musicians from one city to another; and it made it harder to import players from Europe. It was difficult outside of New York City to put together an adequate symphony orchestra with local players. The exception was the Boston Symphony, which remained steadfastly nonunion and hired European players freely. The price list was not much of an issue for big New York–based ensembles such as the Thomas Orchestra, the Sousa Band, or Damrosch's New York Symphony because they paid over scale in any case. But the price list raised the start-up costs for a concert orchestra in regional centers such as Chicago, Cincinnati, and Pittsburgh, all of which initially had to staff their orchestras with players imported from New York. Concert orchestras, unlike theater orchestras, had to pay the musicians for rehearsals, so concerts were chronically underrehearsed. Thus, outside of New York (and Boston), the price list exerted a dampening effect on symphonic initiatives and activities. As for the leader system, it was almost entirely unsuited for concert orchestras. A man who

---

61 · See ibid., October 13, 1872, 324.

62 · This problem cannot be blamed entirely on musicians' unions, because substitution (called "deputization") was also typical of French and English orchestras, which were not unionized.

63 · *Deutsche Musikerzeitung*, March 22, 1874, 90. In Germany, where the musicians' union was already strong by the 1870s, leaders and conductors were not members of the union. The leader system seems to have been unique to the United States.

could put together an orchestra, book dates, negotiate contracts with management and players, and hold union office might not be a very good conductor. Concert orchestras required a conductor who knew the repertory, classical and modern, who could prepare a score and get the orchestra to play it, and who could socialize effectively with patrons and potential donors. Such men often preferred to leave entrepreneurial, managerial, and union affairs to others.

Of the three types of American orchestra—casual, seasonal, and concert—musicians' unions fostered the success and well-being of the first two types and of the musicians who played in them. American symphony orchestras were formed and grew during the nineteenth century in spite of the unions.

PART II

The Orchestra & the American City

Orchestras: Local versus National

JOHN SPITZER

Before the Civil War, most American orchestras were local in scope: they operated within the boundaries of a single city and its immediate vicinity. Orchestras developed city by city as urban populations grew; as theaters, beer gardens, and other entertainment venues came into being; and as a critical mass of musicians—many of them German immigrants—settled in America's cities. Everywhere, orchestras took the same forms: standing orchestras in the theaters, ad hoc orchestras for special occasions, and concert orchestras that gave a short season of "classical" music, usually by subscription. In each city all these orchestral activities were staffed by the same musicians, who held steady jobs in the theaters and then took as much additional work as they could get. By 1865 an orchestral "scene" along these lines had come into being in most American cities, including New York, Boston, Philadelphia, Washington, D.C., Baltimore, Richmond, Cincinnati, Chicago, Milwaukee, St. Louis, San Francisco, and many more in between. In Boston there were at least four theaters, the Harvard Musical Association orchestra, and a Handel and Haydn Society, which hired orchestra musicians for choral performances. Cincinnati had two major theaters, a sporadic philharmonic orchestra, and periodic choral festivals with amateur singers accompanied by an orchestra of musicians from the theaters. In Chicago there were two theaters with standing orchestras, and a third (Crosby's Opera House) opened in 1865. There was also a Philharmonic Society, as well as many concerts organized by musicians on a cooperative basis.[1] New York, meanwhile, had by far the greatest number of theaters in the country—eight or ten theaters with standing orchestras (including the Astor Place Opera House)—and correspondingly the most orchestral musicians; estimates in 1865 ranged from

---

1 · See chapters V.1 (Boston), II.3 (Cincinnati), and I.1 (Chicago) in this volume.

eight hundred to twelve hundred.[2] There had been three New York Philharmonic Societies, of which the third, founded in 1842 as a musicians' co-op,
endured to become America's first "permanent" concert orchestra.[3] In cities
across America during the first half of the nineteenth century, orchestras developed in parallel, linked by the movement of musicians and listeners, but
separated by distance, poor transportation, and regional isolation.

Already during the 1840s, however, national developments had begun to
intrude into local orchestral scenes. Singers and instrumental virtuosos, managed by impresarios such as Bernard Ullman and P. T. Barnum, undertook
multicity tours. For accompaniment they traveled with a pianist, but they
were often joined by a local orchestra when available. Operas also toured in
the 1840s, usually just a few traveling stars, but occasionally as entire companies with full casts of singers. In most cases these touring operas were accompanied by the orchestras of the theaters where they appeared, but a few
companies brought entire orchestras with them. Opera companies based in
Havana toured in 1843 and again in 1847 to several American cities, accompanied both times by orchestras of twenty-five to thirty members who came
with the troupe from Cuba.[4] In 1850–51, Max Maretzek's Astor Place Opera
company, after a four-month season in New York, traveled with a "Grand Orchestra" of New York musicians to Boston; Charleston, South Carolina; and
Augusta, Georgia.[5] Because these traveling orchestras performed the same
operas night after night, they gave better performances than local theater orchestras, whose rehearsal time with the visiting singers was extremely limited.

Orchestras also began to tour on their own in the 1840s. Two German
orchestras, the Steyermark Musical Company in 1847 and Joseph Gungl's
Orchestra in 1848, played in New York and a few East Coast cities before returning to Europe. The Germania Musical Society, on the other hand, immigrated en masse to the United States in 1848 and traveled widely in America
before it disbanded in 1854. These touring orchestras occasionally competed
with local musicians for work. For example, when Jenny Lind sang in Baltimore and Washington, D.C., in 1850, she hired the Germania Orchestra to
accompany her in preference to the local theater musicians. The most ambitious European orchestral visit occurred in 1853–54, when Louis Antoine
Jullien led his orchestra in a tour that began in New York and reached twenty
American cities in ten months.[6] Jullien, however, brought only first-chair

2 · *New York Times*, September 21, 1864, 5; *New York Tribune*, November 1, 1865, 5; *New York Herald*, November 2, 1865, 4.

3 · On the prehistory of the New York Philharmonic, see chapter IV.2 in this volume.

4 · Katherine K. Preston, *Opera on the Road* (1993), 118–22, 131–34.

5 · Ibid., 161–213.

6 · See chapter IV.1 in this volume.

players and soloists with him from Europe; the other musicians were recruited in New York from the pool of available instrumentalists—some of the same players who had gone on the road with Maretzek's opera company two years earlier.

This system, in which orchestras were assembled in New York to accompany singers, dancers, and other entertainers on national tours, became common after the Civil War and persisted through the end of the nineteenth century. Some of these were "skeleton" orchestras, consisting of a leader and a few first-chair players, to be filled out with local musicians in the cities and towns where they played.[7] English-language opera companies—such as Caroline Richings's company (1860s–70s), the Kellogg English Opera Company (1873–77), and the Emma Abbott Company (1878–91)—usually operated in this way.[8] Orchestras for foreign-language opera on tour were more likely to be complete and did not need to rely on local musicians. The Mapleson company (1878–86) and the Metropolitan Opera (1884–) toured with their own orchestras, composed mostly of New York musicians, as did Jeannette Thurber's English-language American Opera Company (1885–87). Operettas and musical spectacles often took orchestras with them when they toured, and so did the elaborate traveling minstrel shows, such as Haverly's or Primrose and West's.[9] Vaudeville, on the other hand, and spoken drama toured with stage performers only and relied on the house orchestras in the theaters where they played to provide musical accompaniments. Although local instrumentalists occasionally complained about losing work to visiting orchestras of New York musicians, they seldom resisted in any organized way, first because shows that toured with skeleton orchestras provided local musicians with lucrative employment and second because the National League of Musicians was controlled by the New York local and refused to place any restrictions on traveling orchestras.[10]

The most important orchestra working out of New York in the second half of the nineteenth century was undoubtedly the Theodore Thomas Orchestra, which began its yearly tours in 1869 and continued until 1889. Thomas's first tour brought the orchestra to twenty cities around the Northeast and as far west as Chicago. Later tours took the orchestra to the South, the Midwest, and even to San Francisco, traveling by rail along what came to be called the

7 · See John R. Commons, "Types of American Labor Unions," *Quarterly Journal of Economics* 20 (1906): 420.

8 · See Katherine K. Preston, "Travelling Troupes—5: The USA," in *The New Grove Dictionary of Opera* (1992); *Oxford Music Online*, www.oxfordmusiconline.com.

9 · On operetta and spectacles, see Deane L. Root, *American Popular Stage Music, 1860–1880* (1981), chaps. 3–4. On postwar minstrelsy, see Robert Toll, *Blacking Up* (1974), chap. 5.

10 · See chapter I.3 in this volume.

"Thomas Highway." In the larger cities along the route, the Thomas Orchestra sometimes collaborated with local singers in grand festivals of choral repertory. But the orchestra—well-trained, self-sufficient, and comprising some of the best musicians in New York—rarely engaged local instrumentalists as substitutes or reinforcements. Relations between the Thomas Orchestra and local ensembles and concert societies in cities along the Thomas Highway were fraught with tension. Critics everywhere recognized that the performances of the Thomas Orchestra were far superior to anything their local orchestras could achieve. At the same time, advocates of local groups recognized that a visit from the Thomas Orchestra could create new audiences and higher expectations for their own ensembles. "Wherever Theodore Thomas and his orchestra go," declared a Pittsburgh newspaper, "they will sow seeds that will bring forth good fruit,... inspire a love for a high order of music [and] promote local organization."[11] Local musicians often complained that the Thomas Orchestra took away paying jobs that would otherwise have been theirs. The St. Louis musicians' union, for example, boycotted the local Saengerfest (choral festival) in 1888 because the organizers had brought in the Thomas Orchestra to accompany the chorus rather than hiring local musicians.[12] Even worse, Thomas gained the allegiance of elite patrons in cities throughout the country, for whom it was often easier to import an ensemble from New York than to build a local orchestra. Competition with Thomas for patronage was a serious problem in Cincinnati, Chicago, St. Louis, and elsewhere for almost two decades.

The Thomas Orchestra and the orchestras of New York musicians that toured with opera companies and other shows were part of a national centralization of the entertainment industry that took place in the second half of the nineteenth century. By the 1880s it might have seemed as though American orchestras might soon operate out of New York, just as the spoken theater was run by a New York "syndicate" and just as vaudeville was consolidated into four or five national "circuits." In the case of orchestras, however, the countervailing local forces were strong. Orchestras were a necessity for hundreds of theaters, and the expenses of travel (railroad fare, lodging, meals, and so forth) were relatively high compared to musicians' wages. As the number of theaters in a city or town grew, the number of musicians increased as well. The demand for concert music grew similarly—both subscription concerts and more casual garden and promenade concerts—and this demand too was satisfied primarily by local musicians and local orchestras. When the

11 · *Pittsburgh Evening Chronicle*, as quoted in Rose Fay Thomas, *Memoirs of Theodore Thomas* (1911), 58–59.

12 · *American Music Journal*, February 18, 1888, 128; see also ibid., March 10, 1888, 198.

Thomas Orchestra or another New York–based ensemble finished its run in a city, local ensembles rushed in to fill the vacuum. For American orchestras, unlike vaudeville or spoken theater, national consolidation remained a distant goal.

Something like a tipping point in the orchestral balance between New York and the rest of the nation came in the 1880s and 1890s, when several American cities managed to launch local orchestras that have endured until the present. The Boston Symphony Orchestra was the first in 1881; then followed the Chicago Symphony, led by Theodore Thomas, in 1891, the St. Louis Symphony in 1893, Cincinnati in 1895, Pittsburgh in 1895, and Philadelphia in 1900.[13] The St. Louis and Cincinnati orchestras were formed from local instrumentalists who played in the theater orchestras and in previous, shorter-lived concert societies. The Chicago Symphony, on the other hand, consisted mainly of former members of the Theodore Thomas Orchestra— New York musicians who moved to Chicago with their leader and took jobs in the orchestra over the protests of local instrumentalists. The Philadelphia Orchestra and the Boston Symphony were initially composed entirely of local musicians, but after a few seasons both began to lay off weaker players and import younger and stronger musicians, not just from New York but also from Europe.[14] In Pittsburgh there were not enough good musicians available locally to form an orchestra, and first-chair players were brought in each year for the duration of the season, mainly from New York.[15] All these orchestras enjoyed generous financial support from local patrons, who guaranteed yearly contributions to cover deficits.

The dissolution of the Thomas Orchestra in 1889 and the creation of permanent orchestras in several major American cities in the closing years of the nineteenth century did not end the dynamic between New York and the rest of the nation. Operas, musicals, and other shows still went on the road with orchestras recruited in New York, although the number of road shows declined markedly after 1900 as the motion picture industry came into being.[16] Concert orchestras based in New York (e.g., Damrosch's New York Symphony and, after 1910, the New York Philharmonic) continued to

13 · The St. Louis Symphony was organized in 1893 as the St. Louis Choral-Symphony Society. The orchestra separated itself from the chorus in 1907 (Ernst C. Krohn, *Missouri Music* [1971], 170–71). The Pittsburgh Symphony was defunct between 1910 and 1926.
14 · M. A. De Wolfe Howe, *The Boston Symphony Orchestra, 1881–1931* (1931), 64, 71; "Think They Need Outside Musicians," *Philadelphia Inquirer*, September 26, 1901, 8; "Personnel of the Philadelphia Orchestra," *Philadelphia Inquirer*, November 15, 1901, 8.
15 · Richard James Wolf, "A Short History of the Pittsburgh Orchestra, 1896 to 1910" (master's thesis, 1954), 107–9.
16 · Alfred L. Bernheim, *The Business of the Theatre* (1932), 75–84.

tour across America, as did New York–based bands, such as those of Sousa, Creatore, and Goldman. But local symphony orchestras organized along a "corporate" model, with a board of guarantors and a large base of subscribers, proved successful and durable.[17] The pioneering concert orchestras of the late nineteenth century were followed in the twentieth by additional local orchestras organized along similar lines—Minneapolis (1903), San Francisco (1911), Detroit (1914), Cleveland (1918), Los Angeles (1919), and many others. These local orchestras toured both regionally and nationally. The Boston Symphony traveled around New England beginning in its second season and then nationally from 1887 on.[18] The Chicago Symphony toured in the Midwest from its very first season (1891–92) and played in Boston and New York in 1896 and thereafter.[19] By the early decades of the twentieth century, then, the world of American orchestras had become pluralistic, with flourishing communities of orchestral musicians in hundreds of cities and towns and permanent orchestras in many of the larger cities. Several of these ensembles could reasonably claim to be as good as or better than any orchestra in New York. The dynamic of New York versus the nation had been replaced by an orchestral pluralism that remained the pattern for American orchestras in the twentieth century.

17 · On the "corporate" model of organization, see chapter I.1 in this volume.
18 · Howe, *Boston Symphony Orchestra*, 65, 74–75.
19 · Ezra Schabas, *Theodore Thomas: America's Conductor and Builder of Orchestras, 1835–1905* (1989), 192–93, 220–21.

[II.1] Invisible Instruments
Theater Orchestras in New York, 1850–1900

JOHN GRAZIANO

The orchestra, for many concertgoers, is defined as a large ensemble that per-forms symphonic music.[1] It is the featured "performer" at a concert, some-times playing by itself, sometimes accompanying one or more soloists. The orchestra can also be limited by size, instrumental grouping, or both—for ex-ample, a chamber or string orchestra,. In opera, operetta, ballet, and musicals, the orchestra players usually are not seen; the group serves primarily as ac-companist to the singers, though it is allowed, in many instances, to have a mo-ment of glory playing an overture, an intermezzo or an *entr'acte*. Symphonic music, opera, and ballet, where music is an intrinsic part of the production, provide the basis of employment for most "classical music" instrumentalists today. In the nineteenth century, orchestral musicians had another means to support themselves: as members of orchestras that provided live music for performances of spoken plays. Nonmusical theater today seldom employs live musicians, although audiences may still hear recorded music at the start of a play, after the intermission, and sometimes during or between scenes.

For many professional musicians today, playing in an orchestra is a full-time, year-round job. The major orchestras and opera companies offer fifty-two-week employment, although smaller orchestras usually have shorter sea-sons and pay their musicians only for the weeks they actually perform. In the nineteenth century, American professional concert orchestras offered only sporadic, part-time employment, whereas theater orchestras provided more and steadier work. Professional instrumentalists who did not work in thea-ters might earn their livings instead by giving lessons privately or by working at music conservatories that were established in their cities.

In New York, which by the 1860s was the largest city in the United States,

---

1 · See chapter 1 of John Spitzer and Neal Zaslaw, *The Birth of the Orchestra: History of an In-stitution, 1650–1815* (2004) for various definitions of "orchestra."

the scene was somewhat different due to the multiplicity of simultaneous events for which instrumentalists were needed. The New York Philharmonic, until late in the century, gave only five or six programs a year. Many of its members, however, also played in the Brooklyn Philharmonic, in Carl Bergmann's orchestra (which often scheduled the same works), in the many "sacred" concerts scheduled on Sundays in concert halls and beer gardens, and in occasional concerts given by various local artists. The New York Philharmonic functioned as a cooperative until 1909, splitting the profits at the end of the season, which meant that the members' income was uncertain.[2] The other orchestras paid per performance. The only New York orchestra whose musicians had jobs that provided adequate year-round compensation was the Theodore Thomas Orchestra.[3] For instrumentalists not fortunate enough to be in the Thomas Orchestra, the most secure employment was playing in the pits of the many theaters in New York City, where orchestras provided musical accompaniment for plays, pantomime, variety shows, musicals, and the circus. The jobs provided the musicians with a steady, though relatively low, income throughout the winter season and, in some cases, into the summer. Although these musicians' participation in musical enterprises such as vaudeville and pantomime is well known, their regular and evidently expected presence in nonmusical theater settings is somewhat surprising. In this chapter, I explore the contributions and working conditions of this latter group of musicians, those who labored in New York theater orchestra pits. I also examine the types of music that audiences heard in those houses where spoken dramas and comedies predominated. My examples are drawn mostly from the years 1860 to 1875, with a few later citations that demonstrate how the same practices continued through the end of the century.

Theater Orchestras as a Source of Income

New York, in the mid-nineteenth century, boasted no fewer than seven theaters in which dramas and comedies were performed, and almost all of them

2 · See Howard J. Shanet, *Philharmonic: A History of New York's Orchestra* (1975), 92.

3 · See Charles Edward Russell, *The American Orchestra and Theodore Thomas* (1927), 57–59; and John H. Mueller, *The American Symphony Orchestra: A Social History of Musical Taste* (1951), 44. Ezra Schabas notes that Thomas "failed in his attempts for exclusivity—that his orchestra members play for him and no one else.... His plan was based on a doubtful assumption ... since he could not [in the 1860s] as yet provide work on a year-round basis. He never gave up trying, however, and finally imposed an exclusivity of sorts on his players in his Chicago years" (*Theodore Thomas: America's Conductor and Builder of Orchestras, 1835–1905* [1989], 31). At its founding in 1881, the Boston Symphony was organized on the Thomas model, offering its musicians full-time employment. See M. A. De Wolfe Howe, *The Boston Symphony Orchestra 1881-1931* (1931), 16.

employed an orchestra. The size of the orchestra undoubtedly varied with the importance of the theaters and their presentations. Because the orchestra played for seven or eight performances a week, a season's employment in one of these orchestras—thirty-six to forty weeks—could provide much of a musician's yearly income. As might be expected, these jobs were populated by some of the best musicians in town, including members of the New York Philharmonic. According to an article published in the *New-Yorker Staats-Zeitung* in July 1863, theater musicians were paid $12 per week at the Broadway theaters and $10 per week at the theaters in the Bowery.[4] Although they were hired for the season, musicians were allowed, without the leaders' permission, to hire substitutes for their pit positions when jobs in other, higher-paying orchestras became available. During much of the regular season, from October through the beginning of May, the best musicians could play with various opera companies—including Maretzek's, Grau's, and Anschütz's—with performances on Mondays, Wednesdays, Thursdays or Fridays, and Saturday matinees and evenings. Opera companies had a higher pay scale. The first and second clarinets, for example, were paid $15 and $12 per week, respectively, for three opera performances. Extra performances were billed at $3 each. A first clarinet, then, could earn $21 for a week with five operas and add another $3 to $4.50 for the theater performances that did not conflict, for example a Tuesday evening or a Wednesday matinee. He could also play in one of the Sunday sacred concerts, of which there were many, where he would earn $5 for one performance.[5] In a busy week, the clarinet player might earn $34. In 1863, $34 had approximately the same purchasing power as $600 does in 2010, resulting in a yearly income of something like $25,000.[6] Today this sum would be considered to be on the low end of salaries, but in the context of the 1860s, when working-class families earning no more than $10 a week were able to survive, the income of the hypothetical clarinetist would have been considered middle class. The ordinary pit musician's weekly salary of $12 was barely beyond that of a skilled laborer. In the early 1850s, though, only something like $300 to $600 annually was needed to sustain a family

4 · *New-Yorker Staats-Zeitung,* July 10, 1863, 8. According to Rosemarie K. Bank, the theater carpenter at Wallack's Theatre on Broadway made $15 per week in 1857, while the orchestra conductor was paid $30 a week plus one benefit per season; see *Theatre Culture in America, 1825–1860* (1997), 95. In the 1850s "first-class" pit musicians' salaries were usually less than $10 a week. See chapter I.3 in this volume.

5 · On New York's Sunday sacred concerts, see chapter II.2 in this volume. On musicians' wages, see chapter I.3 in this volume.

6 · According to MeasuringWorth.Com, $34 in 1863 had the same purchasing power as approximately $609 in 2010, http://www.measuringworth.com/ppowerus/. The yearly income figure supposes that our hypothetical clarinetist was able to fill his schedule for about 40 weeks of the year.

of five.[7] Small luxuries, such as theater tickets, were within a skilled laborer's means. However, during the Civil War, "living costs outstripped money wages; the result was that in 1864 real wages were less than three-fourths their 1860 level."[8]

In the 1860s, theater orchestras in the more prestigious houses ranged in size from thirteen to nineteen players.[9] The principal violinist, called the "leader," usually served as composer, conductor, and arranger.[10] The four most important pit orchestras in New York were described in an 1863 article in the *New York Tribune*—unsigned but very likely written by William Henry Fry (1815–64), composer and long-time music critic for Horace Greeley's *Tribune*.[11] At Wallack's, the orchestra was led by Robert Stoepel (1821–83), a German immigrant who came to the States in the 1850s.[12] British composer Thomas Baker (1822?–88) was in residence at Laura Keene's theater. From the 1860s through the 1880s, he was regarded by some as the best of the composer-conductors, with a large number of published compositions in the lighter vein. An article in the *New York Clipper* claimed that Baker was the first theater orchestra conductor in the United States to use a baton.[13] Edward Mollenhauer (1827–1914) at the Winter Garden was known as a virtuoso violinist and composer. He and his brother Frederick, also a virtuoso violinist, had joined Louis Antoine Jullien's orchestra in London; after touring the United States with Jullien in 1853–54, both brothers decided to emigrate. Harvey Dodworth (1822–91) at Niblo's was one of four brothers who were central to the musical scene in nineteenth-century New York. Their father, Thomas, had emigrated from England, arriving in 1828. Several members of the family were founding members of the New York Philharmonic, and Harvey was the leader, through most of the century, of the Dodworth Band, which gave many concerts around the city and was connected to various military regiments.[14]

As seen in table II.1.1, Stoepel's orchestra at Wallack's was the largest

7 · Bank, *Theatre Culture*, 92.

8 · Clarence Dickinson Long, *Wages and Earnings in the United States, 1860–1890* (1975), 61.

9 · This number of players correlates with the size of theater orchestras going back to the eighteenth century. See Spitzer and Zaslaw on the size of orchestras at the Comédie-Française and Comédie-Italienne (*Birth of the Orchestra*, 192–93).

10 · During this period, some orchestras were led by conductors with a baton, and others were led by the "concertmaster" (leader). In this chapter, I use the terms interchangeably.

11 · *New York Tribune*, January 22, 1863, 3.

12 · Michael V. Pisani, "Composing in the Theater: The Work of a Late Nineteenth-Century New York Music Director" (conference paper, CUNY Graduate Center, 2004).

13 · *New York Clipper*, December 12, 1863, 216. Most American theater orchestras during this period were led from the first violin stand.

14 · See Frank J. Cipolla, "Dodworth," in *New Grove Dictionary of American Music* (1984).

TABLE II.1.1. Instrumentation of four theater orchestras in 1863

Stoepel at Wallack's Theatre	Baker at Laura Keene's Theatre	Dodworth at Niblo's Garden	Mollenhauer at the Winter Garden
19 players	16 players	16 players	13 players
3 first violins	3 first violins	2 first violins	2 first violins
2 second violins	2 second violins	2 second violins	1 second violin
1 viola	1 viola	1 viola	1 viola
1 cello	1 cello	1 cello	1 cello
1 bass	1 bass	1 bass	1 bass
1 flute/piccolo	1 flute/piccolo	1 flute/piccolo	1 flute/piccolo
1 oboe	1 oboe	1 oboe	2 clarinets
2 clarinets	2 clarinets	1 clarinet	2 trumpets/cornets
1 bassoon	2 cornets	2 trumpets/cornets	1 trombone
2 trumpets/cornets	1 trombone	2 horns	1 drums
2 horns	1 drums	1 trombone	
1 trombone		1 drums	
1 drums			

Note: This chart is derived from an article on theater orchestras in the New York Tribune, January 22, 1863.

among New York theaters, with a woodwind choir that included two clarinets, as well as flute, oboe, and bassoon and a brass section with double trumpets and horns. With an instrumentation that was similar to that of a standard orchestra, Stoepel was able, in his arrangements, to approximate the original sound of many works from the concert and operatic repertories. Fry notes that "the three first violins are unusually powerful. . . . Of the details of the orchestra we should say that its string instruments are all well supplied . . . and the violoncello is one of the finest that we have anywhere heard. The wood wind instruments are also especially good. The brass are not so good, in any particular. The character of the music here is unquestionably the best in the city. The conductor, Mr. Stoepel, has made himself a reputation (outside of his position as a composer) by his arrangements of selections from operas, which form the leading features of his entre-acts."[15]

Baker's sixteen-piece orchestra at Keene's lacked a bassoon and the two horns, which, as discussed below, would have required him to rewrite many passages in pieces his orchestra played. Fry comments that "the essential defect here is the absence of horns, the consequence of which is to leave the harmonies thin and unsubstantial. Without them the orchestra becomes more of a skeleton. . . . Mr. Baker's purpose, however, is to offer music which shall depend for its effect upon the brilliancy with which its melodies are expressed—dance-music and the lighter operatic trifles. For this intention his

15 · *New York Tribune*, January 22, 1863, 3.

orchestra answers very well, especially as his musicians are clever performers. But it would be impossible for him to realize any more serious musical idea.... Baker frequently adds to the keenness of his solo effects by introducing the flageolet, a high wind instrument of wood, less piercing than the piccolo, or small flute (which in theater orchestras is played by the regular flutist when resonance or emphasis is required and somewhat more flexible."[16]

Dodworth's ensemble at Niblo's also comprised sixteen instruments, but with one fewer first violin and clarinet, he was able to include the two horns. In comparing him with Baker, Fry suggests that "he too, like Mr. Baker, gives most attention to light and sparkling dance music, or its equivalent, and his performances are always popular. The defect of his orchestra is its extreme numerical weakness in wood instruments, as that of Mr. Baker's is in those of brass. There are often musical occasions which demand that the sound shall temporarily proceed from the strings, from the wood, or from the brass alone, to secure particular, and sometimes important effects.... Certain effects, then, are here forbidden, and the reliance is upon vigorous ensembles, with plenty of dash and spirit in the themes. In certain selections from Richard Wagner's opera, which have recently been presented by Mr. Dodworth, and, on the whole, very capitally outlined, the deficiency of which we speak is peculiarly apparent."[17]

Mollenhauer, with only twelve other players, had the smallest of these orchestras; he lacked an oboe and a bassoon and had only one second violin. Fry does not reckon with the possibility of doublers in these orchestras, though he may be hinting at it when he mentions the cleverness of Baker's players. Many musicians during this period were proficient on more than one instrument. Harvey Dodworth, for example, played violin in the New York Philharmonic but was principal cornet and leader of the Dodworth Band. His brother Allen (1817–96) also played violin in the Philharmonic and was known as a gifted piccolo player as well.[18] Fry notes that "the chief value of Mr. Mollenhauer's orchestra at the Winter Garden is to supply accompaniments for his exquisite solo violin playing. He is a 'star' rather than a general conductor, and is sustained much after the manner of ordinary theatrical stars. When he does not himself play, the orchestra is given over to the most demonstrative dance music, in which it is vigorous and not over delicate."[19]

Orchestra leaders normally contracted to stay at one theater for a season, or for multiple seasons, although they frequently moved to a different house (or sometimes to another city) at the end of a season. Their employment

16 · Ibid.
17 · Ibid.
18 · See Cipolla, "Dodworth."
19 · *New York Tribune*, January 22, 1863, 3.

agreements were usually negotiated with the manager or lessee of a theater. When a lessee's contract ended, the conductor had to advertise for a new position. Thus, when Laura Keene decided to end her tenure at the theater named for her, Baker published the following advertisement in the *New York Herald*: "Mr. Thomas Baker, Musical Director of Laura Keene's theatre, begs to announce that his engagement with the above theatre will terminate in a few days. He will then be happy to negotiate engagements for the summer season, with or without orchestra."[20] On June 6 the *Clipper* announced that Baker "has been secured by Mrs. John Wood," who took over the theater from Laura Keene.[21]

When pit musicians played with the Philharmonic or another orchestra, their efforts were accepted as high art, even when they played popular dances by Lanner, Gungl, and Strauss. But when they were not the main attraction, audiences were usually unaware of their efforts except when people heard a wrong note or some other mistake. Fry gives credit to the efforts of these "invisible" musicians playing in "invisible" orchestras:

If there be one department of a first-class theater from which more is expected and to which less is awarded than any other; the labors of which are always depreciated or misunderstood by the public; whose errors are promptly noted while its merits pass unrecognized; the really good or bad qualities of which are overlooked in favor of accidental ear-catching effects; the importance of which is held secondary, not only by the general visitor but by those who should better understand its value, and by whom it ought to be regarded as primary, it is the orchestra.... Upon its particular virtues or defects, a vast and comprehensive indifference is bestowed. Of its general worth there is an undefined idea, which no person takes pains to make distinct, either to himself or anybody else. It fills the gap between the acts; makes "waits" endurable; shrouds fragmentary conversations, which may or may not be of importance to third parties, from the obtrusive ear of the community at large; serves often to adorn a tale, if not to point to a moral; gives opportunity for the practice of musical rudiments in galleries and elsewhere, which are improved by marking time in familiar tunes with feet and sticks, or vivifying the melody with obligato of whistle au natural; and in other similar ways exercises its humble and not over-dignified functions.... We consider the average performances of the orchestras at our best theaters much too interesting to pass unheeded.[22]

20 · *New York Herald*, May 8, 1863, 7.
21 · *New York Clipper*, June 6, 1863, 211.
22 · *New York Tribune*, January 22, 1863, 3.

In describing the orchestra's role during the performance, Fry, with his sardonic comments on time-beating in the galleries, gives us an added insight into raucous audience behavior during the intervals between scenes when the curtain was lowered.

As noted above, when a better-paying job was offered, players were allowed to opt out of their contracted performances in the theaters. This led to one serious problem noted by the critics—the abuses generated by hiring substitute players. In 1865 a commentator for the *New York Clipper* noted that there were "several places of amusement where there are three to four substitutes every night, and in the height of the ball season, in January and early February, nearly double that number. At their present fixed rates ($14 a week and with what they make by putting on substitutes), some of them get over $30 a week, a pretty good salary when it is taken into consideration that nearly every one of them has a day business beside."[23] An unsigned article several years later in the *New York Herald* opines that "we have the pernicious custom of allowing the regular members of the orchestra to go off to a ball or a concert for a few dollars on any night they please, leaving miserable substitutes in their place. There are many theatres in this city where one-third of the orchestra every night consists of substitutes.... We have a thorough, painstaking musician as leader, who vainly scowls at reckless 'subs,' over whom control is out of the question, and who is constantly hampered into inefficiency by the parsimony and interference of the manager. The result is that the fiddles, clarionets, horns, and even kettle drums are always on bad terms or seem anxious to outstrip each other in the race for the 'double barred' goal."[24]

Because there were no established fees for performing in the theaters, concerts, and other entertainment venues, managers often asked instrumentalists to accept engagements that paid less than the rates set forth above. In 1863 the musicians formed a union, the Musical Mutual Protective Union, "for the purpose of arranging a new tariff of prices for playing in theatre and at balls." "They claim," the *Times* stated, "that they are ridiculously underpaid at the former, and overtaxed by rapacious conductors at the latter. A musician (first class) seldom gets more than $8 or $9 at a theatre. For playing all night at a ball he is supposed to receive $5, but when the customary deductions have been made there is rarely more than $3.50 left for the performer."[25] This last, rather curious comment deserves some attention. What were "customary" deductions? We know that services at a ball went on for many hours,

23 · *New York Clipper*, November 4, 1865, 228.
24 · *New York Herald*, December 29, 1867, 4.
25 · *New York Times*, May 4, 1863, 5.

sometimes into the wee hours of the next day. The musicians undoubtedly needed to eat and drink during this time. It is possible that they were required to *buy* any food and drink they consumed, for in the contract demands of 1865 (see below), there was a specific provision that "always a supper" was part of the payment at a private party.

Many of the union members were German, and the union undoubtedly followed the guild model that was common in German and Scandinavian cities. An 1865 article in the *Clipper* noted that "before this association was formed the best of musicians were glad to get engagements for from $7 to $10 a week; after its formation they fixed the price at $12, and in a short time [about a year later] at $14."[26] These raises would have barely kept up with inflation during the war. By the end of the war, the pit players believed they were entitled to receive yet another raise.

In October 1865, the union asked that the rates be increased as follows: "All theatres in New York and Brooklyn to pay each musician $20 per week. Barnum's Museum for six afternoon and six evening performances $30. Single theatrical performances $5. Leaders not to receive less than $40. Repetiteurs not less than $25." The *Tribune* reported that "about 1,000 musicians were present, and the [Germania Assembly Rooms], which is about the size of Irving Hall, appeared to be filled with orderly and well-dressed people. . . . It was agreed with almost perfect unanimity to adhere to the demand made for $20 a week for playing in the theatres."[27] On November 1, 1865, those instrumentalists who were members of the association went on strike. The leaders of the major theater orchestras—Stoepel, Dodworth, Baker, and Mollenhauer—all took the side of management and resigned from the union.[28] Some negotiations with the theater managers evidently took place, because the *New York Post* reported that "the scale of prices resolved on is in some points lower than previously announced. Players in theatrical orchestras, however, still claim $20 a week, at circuses and concert saloons $18, private parties $8 for one man, $15 for two, $21 for three men, and always a supper. For playing a funeral $4 will be charged; at a target excursion, $5; at a concert, $7; and a public rehearsal, $3." "If the managers have held out against the musicians," the *Post* commented, "the musicians are quite as pertinacious as the managers."[29]

On November 7 the *Times* reported that "after a stormy session and some debate, the society resolved to levy a tax of one dollar on each member to support the strikers" with their regular $14 salaries. The article commented

26 · *New York Clipper*, November 4, 1865, 228.

27 · *New York Tribune*, November 7, 1865, 4.

28 · *New York Post*, November 7, 1865, 5.

29 · Ibid.

that "it only remains for time and the longest purse to determine the winning side in the contest."[30] The union also said that it would "stand" all lawsuits.[31] This tough stance led the *Clipper* reporter to muse that "several of the managers have determined to let their entire orchestra go sooner than be imposed upon by them, and to put pianos in their place." With more than a touch of xenophobia, the article continued, "A piano, one violin and a cornet will afford considerable music and is the only way to bring these *foreign* fiddlers to their right senses" (emphasis added).[32] Two days later, the *Post* reported that "Mr. Mollenhauer has reorganized his orchestra."[33] At least one newspaper, the *Post*, was more sympathetic to the musicians' cause, saying that they should be making at least as much as craftsmen, because their profession required many years of training. But the article also noted that if the costs associated with musicians rose, the theater managers might consider doing without them.[34]

At a meeting of the Managers' Association, reported by the press on November 9, the dispute escalated: with a bit of saber-rattling bravado, the theater managers voted that instead of following the union's price list as before, the leaders of orchestras "shall be invested with the authority to engage musicians at such salaries as their status as musicians justifies, the salaries ranging from $10 to $30 or $40 per week, according to their ability. Thus the first class orchestral players will receive a proper remuneration, and the fourth rate player will not be overpaid."[35] Two weeks into the strike, the *New-Yorker Staats-Zeitung* noted that "the public is not interested in the strike."[36] Although the strike appears to have continued into the beginning of December, it became clear that the managers had the upper hand, as their orchestras were populated with nonunion musicians. Rather than coming to a negotiated conclusion, the strike "ended in a compromise" sometime in December, leaving most of the instrumentalists without a raise but back in their old jobs. A decade later the theater musicians' wages remained at what they had been before the strike in 1865.[37] On the other hand, the theaters remained closed to nonunion musicians, and the leaders—Stoepel, Dodworth, Baker, and Mollenhauer among them—rejoined the union.

30 · *New York Times*, November 7, 1865, 8.

31 · *New York Clipper*, November 4, 1865, 228.

32 · Ibid. Although German immigrants were the largest ethnic element in the mix of pit musicians, it is clear that non-Germans were also employed in these orchestras.

33 · *New York Post*, November 7, 1865.

34 · Ibid., October 31, 1865, 2.

35 · *New York Tribune*, November 9, 1865, 5.

36 · *New-Yorker Staats-Zeitung*, November 14, 1865, 8.

37 · See chapter I.3, table I.3.2, in this volume.

The strike led to several lawsuits, one of which, *Otis v. Stuart*, sheds considerable light on the relationship between musicians, conductor, and management in the New York theaters.[38] At the end of the job action, a drummer named Otis sued the manager of the Winter Garden for the pay he lost when he went on strike. The manager, Mr. Stuart, responded that he was not involved with the hiring or payment of the musicians, that his contract was with the orchestra leader, Robert Stoepel, rather than with the individual musicians.[39] The court held the following: (1) The management of the house had no part in hiring or paying the members of the orchestra; those actions were the responsibility of the leader; (2) The musicians were hired by the leader for the season, rather than by the week, though a player could be dismissed for cause at any time; and (3) When there was a contract dispute, management could hold the leader responsible for a breach of contract.

Stoepel testified that he received $271 per week from the theater manager. This amount does not appear to reflect the 1863 pay scale.[40] If Stoepel's orchestra in 1865 still consisted of nineteen musicians (eighteen instrumentalists plus himself as leader), at $14 per week per man (excluding the leader), the payroll would have been $252, leaving $19 unaccounted for.[41] It is possible that the remaining money might represent Stoepel's salary plus his fee for contracting with the musicians, but the leader usually received double the rate of his players.[42] It is also possible that the extra money was used to pay the best players more than the basic contracted wage.[43]

Theater Orchestra Repertory

Theater orchestras were an important constituent in the production of plays. They provided the glue that held together scene changes and ends of acts, and they underscored dialogue as needed. Our knowledge of the specific music performed by theater orchestras during the play is mostly limited to the pieces programmed around the play; very little of the incidental music to the shows, with the exception of a few songs, has been examined. Information about some of the programmed repertory, however, can be gleaned

38 · For the full text as reported in the *New York Times*, see the appendix in this chapter.

39 · Robert Stoepel is listed in table II.1.1 as conducting at Wallack's, but in 1864 he moved to the Winter Garden, where he remained through the 1866–67 season.

40 · See Chapter I.3, table I.3.2, in this volume.

41 · It is not clear from the news reports whether the leader's salary was included in the sum paid by the manager or whether he received his salary separately.

42 · See chapter I.3 in this volume. This ratio remains in the musicians' demands in 1865, where they indicate that the leader should make no less than $40 a week, that is, twice the salary of $20 that they went on strike for.

43 · See "Knight of Bow and Baton," *New York Times*, October 6, 1878, 5.

from advertisements, programs, and reviews. In his groundbreaking study of American popular stage music between 1860 and 1880, Deane Root examined some surviving programs to document the types of music played in the theaters and how music was used in various productions.[44] Other programs and reviews, which are discussed below, add to our knowledge of the variety and extent of the works performed at the theaters.

As Fry notes (see above), the music played by pit orchestras had two important functions. The first was to perform incidental music, usually composed or chosen and arranged by the leader, to the spoken play being performed. Benjamin Deane, who had served as leader in a number of New York theaters during the 1860s and 1870s, was asked by a *New York Times* reporter whether orchestra leaders were "expected to be composers to any considerable degree." He responded that "their work is rather arranging than composing, although there are few if any who do not write some original music, and some of them a great deal."[45] One conductor known for his original incidental music was Stoepel. When the play *Pauline* was performed at Wallack's in 1863, his contribution was noted by the reviewer for the *Times*: "We must not neglect to add that the incidental music, by Robert Stoepel, gives great intensity to the tragic scenes of the work." Simultaneously, Stoepel's incidental music for *Leah the Forsaken* was being heard at Niblo's Theatre, where Dodworth was conducting. "Some effective and appropriate musical *morceaux* have been written by Robert Stoepel, and contribute in a large measure to the completeness of the production," said the *Times* review.[46] While Stoepel appears to have written original music for many of his shows, it seems, from the evidence available, that Baker, for the most part, was known for his adaptations of other composers' works. In his 1878 interview, Deane gives the following anecdote about Baker's incidental music to *The Black Crook* (1866):

It is related of Tom Baker that Barras [the author of the play] got him to arrange the music for "The Black Crook," and he went down to Niblo's to rehearse it, although Dodworth was then leader there. As the rehearsal progressed, the members of the orchestra maintained a muttered rumble of recognitions as each new passage was attacked. "Rossini!" "Meyerbeer!" "Mendelssohn!" "Verdi!" broke forth here and there among them, until the incantation scene was reached when there was a choral burst of "Weber!" but the boldness of that portion of the musical Boucicaultization stunned them into comparative silence through the rest of the rehearsal. Baker only

44 · Deane L. Root, *American Popular Stage Music 1860–1880* (1981), 41–46.

45 · "Knight of Bow and Baton," *New-York Times*, October 6, 1878, 5.

46 · *New York Times*, January 6, 1863, January 5, 1863, 7.

laughed good-naturedly, admitted that he had appropriated his incantation music from "Der Freischuetz" and other portions from other works, and added, "but none of the others were smart enough to do it, and you have to admit that it is good music."[47]

The orchestra's other important function was to provide "external" music that would entertain the audience when nothing was happening on the stage. This practice undoubtedly reflects the custom of earlier times, particularly in British theaters. While the audience was streaming in, the orchestra usually played an overture from a familiar opera. During the intermissions, the audience might hear a symphonic suite of well-known excerpts from a different opera and a medley of popular tunes. As the audience exited at the end of the show, a set of cotillion dances, such as a quadrille, or another popular dance, such as a waltz, might be played. The music performed was considered an audience "draw": the titles of the various pieces were usually listed in theater programs and in some newspaper advertisements and on handbills. For example, at Niblo's Theatre in the mid-1860s, the orchestra, under Dodworth's baton, performed Auber's overture to *Fra Diavolo* before a "new and powerful Drama" by Charles Gayler. During the intermissions between the acts, they played selections from Meyerbeer's *Dinorah* and, at the conclusion, a medley of "popular airs" arranged by the conductor, plus a set of dances, the *Irving Lancers*, which Dodworth also wrote.[48] There is no mention of music during the drama itself, though one can speculate, on the basis of other shows, that the orchestra provided underscoring at times and possibly accompanied one or more of the actors in an interpolated song or two. Another program lists the overture to Flotow's opera *Sophia Catherine* (1850), a selection of "gems" from Verdi's *Aroldo* (1857), a medley of popular songs arranged by Dodworth, and the *Bridal Eve Polka* by the American pianist-composer Harry Sanderson (1837?–71).[49] In November 1863, a playbill for Shakespeare's *Coriolanus* at Niblo's Theatre, starring the noted American actor Edwin Forrest (1806–72), notes that "prior to the Tragedy, the Overture to Coriolanus by Beethoven Will be given." The conductor once again was Dodworth. At Wallack's Theatre, the music heard for the comedy *Single Life* by John Baldwin Buckstone (1802–79) included the overture to Flotow's *Alessandro Stradella* (1844); selections from Petrella's once popular but now forgotten opera *Jone* (1858), based on Bulwer-Lytton's *Last Days of Pompeii*; a waltz, *Dreams on the Ocean*

47 · "Knight of Bow and Baton." "Boucicaultization" refers to the Irish playwright Dion Boucicault (1820–90), who was accused of piecing together his plays from bits and pieces of other playwrights' works.
48 · Undated handbill, author's collection.
49 · Program, author's collection.

(1855), by Josef Gungl; a quadrille based on Weber's overture *Jubel*; and a polka, the *Militaire*, composed by Edward Mollenhauer.

Much of the music that theater orchestras played was familiar to their audiences. Flotow's opera *Stradella* had premiered in New York in 1853 and was being performed by Carl Anschütz's German opera company during the fall of 1862. Later in the season, on April 6, 1863, Petrella's *Jone* was premiered by the Maretzek company.[50] Gungl had visited the States during the 1848–49 season, and a few of his dances, including *Dreams on the Ocean*, remained extremely popular through the 1870s. Finally, Mollenhauer's polka might have been heard at the many balls and galas that filled the halls every year before Lent or at a band concert, where dances were often programmed as the final number.

Given the general lack of rehearsal time and the many substitute players who populated the pit orchestras, leaders may not have always picked appropriate music for the dramas being presented. A critic writing in the *New York Herald* in 1867 complained:

> If the play be "Hamlet," "Midsummer Night's Dream," "Lear" or "Othello," we are sure to have a tripling [trifling?] polka, with mocking bird accompaniment, a negro melody or a set of quadrilles, none of which is certainly in keeping with the subject of the drama.... Leaders of orchestras are also too much in the habit of inflicting upon the audience their own compositions, which are, as a general rule, the veriest trash that ever fiddler bowed or hornblower tooted. The managers also must needs step within the charmed circle of composers and place themselves beside Auber, Rossini, Gounod and Flotow, with the "esq." attached to their names. Imagine the titles "Overture to Massianello, Auber," and "The Swallow Tail Schottishe,—, Esq., manager," placed side by side on a programme! Conceit and assurance can go no further.[51]

Some of the problems alluded to by the critic may have been the result of the repertory system, where two (or more) different plays might be presented by the company every week.[52] The external music for the first presentation might not suit the second. Or, in the case of a theater at which a new play did not attract an audience and was quickly dropped after one or two per-

---

50 · The New York production of *Jone* was only the third to be heard outside of Italy. It was preceded by performances in Malta (1861) and Havana (1862).

51 · *New York Herald*, December 29, 1867, 4.

52 · For example, at Fox's Old Bowery Theater, plays alternated during the week. Sometimes the most popular play would be presented all week, and the shorter works changed. At a few theaters, the program was changed midweek.

formances in favor of one that previously had proved popular, the music also might be viewed as inappropriate.[53]

When a piece composed or arranged by an orchestra leader achieved some popularity, it might be published, giving the composer-arranger the possibility of additional income. Such is the case with two 1868 publications by Thomas Baker: his *Lanciers Quadrilles* and his arrangement of pieces from *The Black Crook*. Although he had not been the conductor at Laura Keene's since 1863, the cover of the *Lanciers* reminds the public of the composer's connection to the famous actress's company. In the intervening years, while he served as conductor for Mrs. John Wood at the same theater, now named the Olympic, he probably programmed these dances a number of times at the end of the play so that audiences heard them as they left the theater. Theatergoers who heard the piece might have expressed an interest in purchasing the music, particularly if the intricate dance steps were included. Baker's royalties from the *Lanciers Quadrille* certainly would have contributed to his annual income, so it was in his best financial interests to promote sales of the sheet music. Somewhat surprisingly, his version of the dances is virtually identical to another publication of the quadrille that is attributed to Harvey Dodworth. Dodworth's version must have been very popular, providing him with continuing income, because his self-published music was reprinted no less than twenty-two times. Baker's arrangement of "gems" from *The Black Crook* "as played at Niblo's Garden" was undoubtedly an attempt to profit from the immense popularity of the show in the 1860s.

The performance of operatic selections and overtures by an orchestra of less than twenty instruments might seem a bit odd to us today. But it is useful to remember that military bands, which usually numbered in the twenties, regularly played these same selections in park and armory concerts and at a variety of social functions and that fully staffed orchestras of sixty or more players, while desirable, were not always economically feasible. Opera orchestras were similarly modest in mid-nineteenth-century New York. Anschütz's opera orchestra generally numbered thirty players, and Maretzek's was usually forty strong. When Thomas started his orchestra in the early 1860s, it too comprised only thirty players.

To perform Beethoven's *Coriolanus* Overture or selections from Meyerbeer or Verdi operas with the orchestras shown in table II.1.1 would have

---

53 · For the last week of the 1862–63 season, Laura Keene mounted a very expensive production of an original pastiche, *Tibb; or, the Cat in the Crinoline*. Although the "buzz" was quite favorable in advance, when the show opened (on May 4) it was deemed "one of the most decided fizzles, or catastrophes, of the season" (*New York Clipper*, May 16, 1863, 38). It was withdrawn after one performance, and *Our American Cousin*, a guaranteed hit, replaced it for the rest of the week.

required some adjustments in the score. Arrangements of symphonic and opera music from the first half of the nineteenth century would not have been too difficult to accomplish. In his performance of Beethoven's overture to *Coriolanus* at Niblo's in 1863, for example, Dodworth would have had to adjust the orchestration to account for the lack of double winds by making changes in the string parts to accommodate the lines for which he had no instruments. The addition of two valve horns, two trumpets/cornets, and a trombone would have allowed him some additional flexibility. The essential sound of the piece would not have been violated, and for audiences who might have heard the original orchestration once or twice at best, Dodworth's version would have provided an acceptable substitute.

Theater Orchestras in the 1890s

It is beyond the scope of this chapter to examine in detail the role of the theater orchestra during the remainder of the nineteenth century. However, one can make a number of general observations based on a limited examination of newspaper reviews from 1892 and 1897 of spoken theater presentations. Theater orchestras of the 1890s were still providing the "external" music they had furnished in the 1860s, as well as the incidental music and accompaniments for spoken drama. Familiar repertory now included overtures from Offenbach and other composers' operettas, and the dance music no longer included quadrilles. Waltzes and polkas could still be heard after the play, but many orchestras now performed marches or arrangements of popular tunes as their final numbers. Although mention of the orchestras is infrequent, sometimes a review offers a bit of insight. For example, in April 1892, in a review of the melodrama *The Golden Ladder* by Wilson Barrett (1846–1904) and George R. Sims (1847–1922), the reviewer gives his readers a description of the action and the involvement of the orchestra: "The calculating villain fixes Thornhill's revolver so that it shall appear that the forthcoming murder is a suicide, when—eh! A whistle from the outpost! A second's delay, and Thornhill, who has just come to, turns the weapon on the enemy. In the calcium, and with Hungarian music from the orchestra, this is effective."[54] For the comedy-drama *Count Caper* by the playwright-director Herbert Hall Winslow (1865–1930), which starred Charles T. Ellis, the reviewer refers to the interpolated songs that the orchestra accompanied: "Of the play, it is not necessary to speak at any length. It suffices to introduce the

---

54 · *Dramatic Mirror*, April 9, 1892, 2. "Calcium" refers to the calcium lamps that were used as spotlights beginning in the 1860s.

songs, dances, and yodels of Mr. Ellis"[55] A week later, it was announced that Ellis had introduced two new songs, "I Love You All" and "Putty Soon."[56] Another instance of an interpolated song was seen at Augustin Daly's theater in May 1892 on one part of a triple bill; the farcical sketch *The Lawyer's Fee* included a song "voiced by Miss Vokes in her inimitable fashion and danced as she alone can with perfect safety."[57] In October 1892, a reviewer for the *Dramatic Mirror* commented on the incidental music that a "Mr. Tomaszewicz" had written [arranged?] for Shakespeare's *Henry VIII*, starring the famous actress Helena Modjeska (1840–1909). He also mentioned some of the external music, which he found inappropriate: "If the object of *entr'acte* music is to divert attention, some of that furnished by the orchestra accomplishes that aim. 'Sally in Our Alley' was one of the melodies, Monday night."[58]

Music played during the intermissions was still an important draw for audiences. At a performance of *Deborah* (the German play, here translated, that provided the basis for Daly's *Leah the Forsaken*), the reviewer notes that "a feature of the evening was the cornet solo played by John C. Martin between the first and second acts. It was heartily encored."[59] Perhaps the most unusual (and possibly unscheduled) intermission event occurred during a performance of *Jane* in September 1892:

> For ten minutes last evening Lottie Collins had the Standard stage all to herself between the second and third acts of Jane. Curiosity drew a large house, many of the auditors dropping in for the song and dance, and filing out after it.... Miss Collins is tall and active. She wears a preposterous hat and an impossible blonde wig. Black hose and black gloved arms are much in evidence. She has an odd personality, plenty of assurance, and no end of *verve*. While she sings she makes jerky gestures from the elbows, and when she dances she moves her understandings with great rapidity and some audacity. Her mouth is like Mercutio's wound, not so deep as a well nor so wide as a church door—but it serves the purpose of "Ta-ra-ra."[60]

The writer implies that some of the public was aware that Collins was going to appear that night because many people were present in the theater only for her performance. Presumably the orchestra had not rehearsed with the unan-

55 · Ibid., April 23, 1892, 2.

56 · Ibid., April 30, 1892, 2. No review appeared in the *New York Times*.

57 · *Dramatic Mirror*, May 14, 1892, 2.

58 · Ibid., October 15,1897, 2.

59 · Ibid.

60 · Ibid., September 24, 1892, 2. Collins became known as the originator of the song "Ta-ra-ra-boom-ti-ay."

nounced star; most likely they were reading their parts for the first time during the performance. It is entirely possible that other performers made similarly "unannounced" intermission appearances at various New York theaters in the 1890s, but verification of that speculation awaits further research.

In addition to their regular duties, the pit musicians were also expected to respond to emergencies in the theater. During a performance of the comedy *Dr. Bill* in October 1892, "sparks from electric lights dropped upon the wings. The curtain was instantly lowered. Several persons made a rush for the doors, while cooler heads called upon the audience to be seated. Excitement subsided when Manager Sammis stepped upon the stage and requested the orchestra to play."[61]

The labor issues that had plagued New York orchestras during the first half of the 1860s still remained unresolved in the 1890s; pit musicians were still underpaid. A brief article in the *Dramatic Mirror* notes that a performance of the play *Rose Michel* was almost cancelled: "Some trouble with the Central Labor Union over the stage hands and orchestra came near preventing the performance last night but things were patched up and the play was given on schedule time."[62]

Conclusions

Theater orchestras, as we have seen, *were* the glue that held shows together. They were hired to play external music—the overtures, *entr'actes*, and exit music—and to play the incidental music necessary for the spoken shows that were scheduled at their theaters. Though small compared to concert orchestras, they performed symphonic overtures and operatic excerpts in adequate arrangements, written by their conductors, that attempted to preserve the spirit of the original piece. Although the hours were long, working in a theater orchestra provided New York instrumentalists with a steady, if modest income for eight to nine months of the year, which could be supplemented during the regular season by jobs in the various symphonic and opera orchestras of the city and in the summer months by playing concerts in parks and in the many pleasure gardens that dotted the city.

Theater musicians were looked on with disdain by many in the entertainment profession, including theater managers, and were often characterized as below-average players, even though many of them played in concert orchestras. The *New York Times* reporter who interviewed Benjamin Deane in 1878 asked the old orchestra leader whether it was true that "the vast ma-

---

61 · Ibid., October 8, 1892, 2.
62 · Ibid., December 18, 1897, 16. No article on the job action appeared in the *Times*.

jority of theatrical orchestra performers are of a dull, mechanical kind, who seem to view musical labor as merely a handicraft." Deane answered, "Well, I cannot deny that some are a good deal that way, but there are many who have a real love for music, and hardly any who do not take a lively interest in a good passage put before them. . . . Almost any one, even a musical enthusiast," Deane continued, "might be pardoned for yawning and discontent when kept late—on a bad night, when he knows he has a long way to go to get home—merely to snap off a 'pizzicato' or rattle a 'hurry' toward the end of a long piece that has become an old story to him." Deane finished with an anecdote that can still be heard in orchestra pits today: "Your question reminds me of a story I have heard of an amateur musician—a very impulsive, enthusiastic sort of chap—who heard at the theatre, between the acts, a piece of music which pleased him so much that at its close he glided down to the German trombone-player, and eagerly whispered to him: '. . . Tell me, my friend, what was the name of that truly inspired piece?' And the solemn Teuton, referring stolidly to the page before him still, made answer: 'Dot was nummer dhirteen, green books.'"[63]

As more details are amassed and researchers learn more about the specific productions of spoken plays in the second half of the nineteenth century, they will be able to draw out and refine the theatrical contexts in which music was heard and document the significance and influence of these invisible instrumentalists on stage (and screen) presentations in the early twentieth century.

63 · "Knight of Bow and Baton."

APPENDIX II.1.1 *The Musicians' Strike-Action against the Proprietor of the Winter Garden Theatre—The Value of Services*[64]

Second Judicial District Court—Jan. 6, 1866
Before Judge Kevelin

Otis vs. Stuart—This case, which arises out of the recent strike of the musicians, was heard yesterday at the Second Judicial Court, before Judge Kevelin. The plaintiff Otis claimed $14, being one week's salary, from the defendant, the manager of the Winter Garden Theatre, being the salary for the week in which the musician's strike took place. On his examination by Mr. Cozens, the plaintiff stated that he was engaged as a drummer in the orchestra by Mr. Robert Stoepel at a salary of $14 a week, being the price fixed by the Musicians' Union; that he had played down to Oct. 20, and had received his salary down to the last week; he had since demanded that, but had been informed by Mr. Stoepel that it would not be paid.

[Otis] *Cross-examined by Mr. Dunphy*—The reason Mr. Stoepel had stated for non-payment was that he had broken his engagement; he did not consider himself engaged otherwise than by the week; nothing was paid to him of the season; did not know Mr. Stuart, and never made any engagement with him; had always received his pay from Mr. Stoepel; had never been paid by Mr. Stuart or his Treasurer.

Mr. Myers examined—He stated he was a violin player in the orchestra; had known Mr. Stoepel to discharge persons from the orchestra during the season; had the honor of once being introduced to Mr. Stuart, but it was on a literary matter unconnected with business; had always been paid by Mr. Stoepel; never received payment from Mr. Stuart or his Treasurer.

Mr. Stuart examined—He had known Mr. Stoepel for many years; he was the leader of the orchestra; had made an engagement with him to furnish an orchestra and to direct it for $271 a week; he had every confidence in Mr. Stoepel; he made the engagement with him only; knew nothing of the plaintiff in this case; he had never seen him to his knowledge; had never exercised the right of engaging or discharging members of the orchestra; that belonged solely to Mr. Stoepel; had not received any notice from the orchestra of their intention to leave, but he had from the Secretary of the Musical Union; the night before the orchestra left, he spoke to Mr. Stoepel, and he told him they would not leave that

64 · *New York Times*, January 7, 1866, 8.

night, but they would go soon, if they did not receive the increased salary; told Mr. Stoepel, when they left, that he looked to him alone, and though he had a great personal regard for him, he would hold him responsible for the breach of contract in being left without an orchestra; the engagement was for the season; the season, as defined by Mr. Wallack, was from thirty-six to forty weeks.

Mr. Stoepel examined—He had engaged the plaintiff to play the drums for fourteen dollars a week in the orchestra; had engaged him for the season; he had distinctly told him so; the engagements were made by him, and he discharged also, but only where just cause existed; he had once discharged the plaintiff for continued impertinence; he had agreed to provide Mr. Stuart with an orchestra for $271 a week; he considered that he engaged the musicians for Mr. Stuart; had receipted always for the full amount himself; Mr. Stuart was responsible to him.

Mr. Baum, the clarionet-player in the former orchestra, testified that he considered himself engaged by the week, and not for the season; he had not heard anything of season.

Mr. Stoepel, recalled, testified that before the close of last season he had distinctly engaged the last witness for the season, and that his statement was untrue in that respect.

Mr. Stuart then read a resolution of the Musical Union of July, in which they fully admit that their contracts are for the season, and allege their fidelity in keeping them as such as a guarantee for the future.

After the testimony was all in, Mr. Dunphy, counsel for the defendant, made a motion to the court for a dismissal of the complaint on the ground:

First—That it appeared by the evidence that the manager made an agreement with Mr. Robert Stoepel to furnish his theatre with an orchestra for $271 per week; that it was he who hired the men, and that under such circumstances there was no legal liability on the part of the defendant to pay.

Second—That if Mr. Stoepel could be considered to be the agent of the defendant, the hiring was for a season, and if the plaintiff broke such engagement by refusing to play for less than $20 per week, he could not recover.

Mr. Cozzens and Mr. Merritt argued in opposition. The Judge took the papers and reserved his decision.

[11.2] Beethoven and Beer

Orchestral Music in German Beer Gardens in Nineteenth-Century New York City

JOHN KOEGEL AND JONAS WESTOVER

> The Germans of New York are a very steady, hard-working people, and withal very sociable. During the day they confine themselves closely to business, and at night they insist upon enjoying themselves. The huge Stadt Theatre draws several thousand within its walls whenever its doors are opened, and concerts and festivals of various kinds attract others. But the most popular of all places with this class of citizens is the beer garden. Here one can sit and smoke, and drink beer by the gallon, listen to music, move about, meet his friends, and enjoy himself in his own way—all at a moderate cost.[1]

James McCabe painted this evocative portrait of New York's German beer gardens in 1872. In *Lights and Shadows of New York*, McCabe discusses a great many things, both commonplace and notable, about the city and its diverse populations, including the very large German community. In McCabe's time, much of German New York's population and commercial life were centered on the Lower East Side, especially on or near the Bowery, an area so heavily German that New Yorkers often referred to it as "Klein Deutschland" (Little Germany). The neighborhood was home to numerous German- and English-language theaters, as well as hundreds of German and American beer gardens, music and dance halls, saloons, club and society halls, and concert saloons.[2] In contrast to the concert saloons, which attracted a primarily male clientele from a wide range of ethnic backgrounds, and which in many instances facilitated prostitution, the beer gardens generally emphasized a family at-

---

1 · James D. McCabe, "The Beer-Gardens," *Lights and Shadows of New York* (1872), 550.

2 · On the Bowery theaters, see John Koegel, *Music in German Immigrant Theater: New York City, 1840–1940* (2009). Alvin F. Harlow (*Old Bowery Days: The Chronicles of a Famous Street* [1931]) paints an evocative picture of the Bowery, but the information he presents is incorrect in places.

mosphere.[3] Thousands of theatrical and musical entertainments were given in the beer gardens, especially during the popular Sunday sacred concerts.

Although specific details about the beer garden orchestras are relatively scant (e.g., instrumentation and names of musicians), the repertory they performed was often advertised or reviewed in local German American newspapers, especially the *New-Yorker Staats-Zeitung*, and printed programs were distributed to audiences. Because the orchestras that played in theaters, beer gardens, concert saloons, and society halls vastly outnumbered those playing symphonic repertory in concert venues such as Steinway Hall or Irving Hall, it is essential to understand the role of these ensembles in the city's musical life. Public support for orchestral music in popular venues was an important factor in the development of symphony orchestras in the United States and the acceptance of the symphonic repertory. Thus, some of the roots of the contemporary American orchestra are found in the nineteenth-century German American beer halls on the Bowery.

"Cheap Amusements": Venues, Ensembles, and Musical Repertory

On October 24, 1867, the *New York Times* published an article titled "Cheap Amusements." In picturesque prose the author described an audience that usually did not attend the opera or symphony but heard operatic and symphonic music in the popularly oriented performance venues: "If you want to find this great auditory ... you must go to 'Tony Pastor's,' in the Bowery, or to the 'Theatre Comique,' or to 'Butler's,' or the 'Eighth-Avenue Opera House,' or to the German Turner theatres scattered over the City, the beer gardens, and the minstrel halls." "Besides the cheap theatres and the minstrels," the article continued,

> there are cheap amusements for which no entrance fee is demanded. Elaborate halls and gardens are in existence in the Bowery, on Eighth Avenue, and along Broadway, with stages, scenery, and performances, which one may behold without being obliged to buy a ticket. The proprietor only requires that the visitor shall "order something." The auditorium is a confused mass of small tables, surrounded by chairs, and the audience a straggling, talking, smoking and drinking, but orderly, mob. In the middle of the din created by shuffling waiters, clicking glasses, orders bawled out, scraping feet, and mugs rapping on tables, a persevering orchestra performs "selections from favorite operas," and daring performers come forth to sing, dance, or talk.[4]

3 · Brooks McNamara, *The New York Concert Saloon: The Devil's Own Nights* (2002).
4 · "Cheap Amusements," *New York Times*, October 24, 1867, 8.

At the beer gardens this "great auditory" heard instrumental and vocal ensembles of varying sizes and different types. Although newspaper advertisements are inconsistent in the information given about performers and ensembles, details published in the *New-Yorker Staats-Zeitung* provide important information. For example, the paper announced in 1863 that on December 6 at the Cosmopolitan Music Hall an orchestra of thirty musicians would perform.[5] This was probably a special performance, with an orchestra somewhat larger than the one that played at this venue throughout the year. Similarly, on December 25, 1864, the proprietor of the Germania Assembly Rooms advertised a performance by a thirty-member orchestra. This was a special Christmas concert, and it added six people to the twenty-four-musician orchestra that normally played at the Germania Rooms for Sunday concerts.[6] Events requiring large instrumental and vocal forces of upward to 150 musicians were usually booked in larger venues, such as the Academy of Music or the Metropolitan Rooms (156–160 Hester Street). Newspaper advertisements also mention small ensembles, such as string quartets and quintets and male vocal quartets. The usual number in beer garden orchestras ranged from about ten to twenty musicians, divided more or less equally between strings and winds. And a piano was often available.

By the second half of the nineteenth century, the majority of New York City's instrumentalists were German immigrants, and the musicians who played in the beer garden orchestras were overwhelmingly German. They reflected a cross section of backgrounds and abilities, from well-known soloists and members of the New York Philharmonic to part-time musicians who waited at the Musical Exchange—down the block from the musician's union hall on East Fourth Street—to pick up casual work. William Allen Rogers (1854–1931) depicts the scene in one of his evocative pen-and-ink drawings (fig. II.2.1). Work in the beer gardens was relatively well paid. In 1863 the *New-Yorker Staats-Zeitung* printed the recently established pay scale for New York instrumentalists, including the rates for "concert salons," which included beer gardens as well as other concert venues that served food and drink. A week of afternoon concerts including Sundays paid $15, more than the weekly rate for the Broadway theaters ($12) or the theaters on the Bowery ($10).[7] From the 1860s on, most orchestra musicians at the beer gardens

---

5 · Advertisement, *New-Yorker Staats-Zeitung*, December 6, 1863, 8.

6 · Ibid., December 25, 1864, 6.

7 · *New-Yorker Staats-Zeitung*, July 10, 1863, 8. The fee schedule, union regulations, and a list of union members are given in *Constitution der Musical Mutual Protective Union: Gegründet den 23. April 1863* (1863). The pay scale for the beer gardens was higher because afternoon performances there prevented the musicians from giving lessons or taking other work. When

FIGURE II.2.1.
William Allen Rogers, "The Musical Exchange, 4th Street near 3rd Avenue," pen-and-ink drawing, also published as a lithograph in *Harper's Weekly*, August 4, 1888.

were members of the Musical Mutual Protective Union, the New York musicians' union.[8]

Performances at the beer gardens and other concert venues in Klein Deutschland attracted mainly a German clientele, but members of other ethnic groups also patronized them. Most German beer gardens were indoor establishments decorated with plantings, but the buildings sometimes had outdoor covered areas, gardenlike, attached to the principal performance area. Many offered dramatic entertainments in addition to regular orchestral, band, and vocal concerts. There were also some entirely outdoor venues offering beer, food, and music, notably Sulzer's Harlem River Park and the beer gardens in Jones's Wood, located on the Upper East Side of Manhattan considerably north of Klein Deutschland. Each of these spaces had its target audience, clientele, or membership. For example, the German Volksgarten at 45 Bowery, next to the Stadttheater, was a middle-class promenade and dance space as well as a theater. Gaming took place in connected rooms, and there were also bowling alleys, billiard tables, panoramic views of scenes from history and nature, and other entertainments. The orchestra played from a balcony or from the pit in front of the stage. In April 1859 the *New York Herald*

---

musicians were engaged only in the evening, the pay scale was $10 per week, the same as the Bowery theaters. Compare table I.3.2.

8 · On the Musical Mutual Protective Union, see chapters I.3 and II.1 in this volume.

called the Volksgarten the "most popular resort of the children of the Fader-
land" and noted that "as soon as the [orchestral] music began the din of many
loud voices was stilled."[9]

Three venues will serve here as models for the wide range of entertainment spaces available to New York's German audiences: the Café Chantant
Caffe und Wein-Salon on Chrystie Street; Widow Anna Schürmann's Wein,
Lagerbier, und Conzert-Salon at 145 William Street; and Paul Falk's Broadway Garten at 545 Broadway.[10] The bottom tier of establishments is represented by the Café Chantant, located in the heart of Klein Deutschland at
27½ Chrystie Street (near Hester Street). Its French name advertised that it
tried to model itself on the fashionable Parisian venues of the same name. A
"comic song concert" at New York's Café Chantant in 1865 featured the singers Hermann Wachtel and Fräulein Amonia (*sic*) with an orchestra directed
by Herr Heim, plus the magician Herr Müller.[11] Wachtel and Herr Koenig
were the proprietors of the establishment. Although admission was free, the
audience was expected to buy refreshments. The advertisement in the *New-
Yorker Staats-Zeitung* listed four musical numbers: Weber's overture to *Der
Freischütz*, the songs "Jetzt komm ich" (sung by Wachtel) and "Vöglein" (by
Amonia), and an aria from *Das komische Mädchen*. Very likely additional orchestral numbers were performed as *entr'actes* and accompaniment to Herr
Müller's magic show. With its mixture of music and magic, this kind of program seems closer to a variety show than a concert. Other bottom-tier venues were so small that they did not even have a name. Advertisements often
indicated that these were located in the "basement" or "below" a shop. Even
here, though, the notices in the *New-Yorker Staats-Zeitung* usually advertised
some sort of musical entertainment.

Anna Schürmann's Wein, Lagerbier, und Conzert-Salon was one of the
middle-tier venues, and one of the few to advertise consistently throughout the 1860s in the *New-Yorker Staats-Zeitung*. Schürmann, who offered free
daily shows at three o'clock in the afternoon, took a novel approach to promotion. Each week she published a new poem in the *Staats-Zeitung* extol-
ling the virtues of her establishment. The poem encouraged the newspaper's
readers to relax at her beer garden, listen to good music, and quaff a stein
of beer. Schürmann employed two conductors, Herr Schwensech (1862–65)
and the curiously named Herr Adagio Meyer (late 1865 until at least 1869).
Both men included their own compositions in the repertory they conducted,
and Schwensech later worked at other locations, probably conducting the

9 · "Teutonic Sunday Amusements," *New York Herald*, April 25, 1859, 1.

10 · The term "salon" in this context is synonymous with beer garden and should not be con-
fused with the "concert saloon."

11 · Advertisement, *New-Yorker Staats-Zeitung*, December 21, 1865, 6.

same kind of group for different proprietors. Information about the size and composition of their orchestras is unavailable. Judging by the free admission (but required purchase of refreshments), the regular advertisements in local newspapers, and the emphasis on light orchestral and vocal music, we can assume that Frau Schürmann's salon was probably somewhere in the middle rank of quality and importance in relation to other beer gardens.

The Broadway Garten represented the highest tier of beer garden. A large orchestra gave full-scale concerts there, most often on Sunday, when they were billed as "sacred concerts." The orchestra was led for many years by New York Philharmonic conductor Carl Bergmann and included several members of the Philharmonic. Although the performance level of the orchestra was probably higher than that of other ensembles in Klein Deutschland, the repertory was mostly the same. Bergmann's concerts of the early 1860s stressed a combination of movements from symphonies or concertos, operatic arrangements, dance music, and popular ("light classical") orchestral pieces. The programs were long, and there were two intermissions, which gave the orchestra a chance to rest and encouraged the audience to purchase liquid and solid refreshment. Unlike some venues, where admission was free, the price of a ticket to the Broadway Garten was fifteen cents, which admitted a gentleman and a female companion. Buying a ticket also allowed patrons the privilege of reserving seats in advance. Below is the program of a typical Bergmann "sacred" concert at the Broadway Garten given in early November 1863:[12]

Program 1. Sacred Concert, Broadway Garten, November 1863, cond. Carl Bergmann

PART I
Giacomo Meyerbeer: *Krönungsmarsch* [from *Le Prophète*]
Gaetano Donizetti: Overture to *La fille du régiment*
Johann Strauss [Sr.]: Waltz, *Myrthen*
Charles Gounod: Selections from *Faust* (arranged by Carl Bergmann)

PART II
Meyerbeer: Introduction from *Robert le Diable*
Hans Christian Lumbye: *Reunions Galop*
Felix Mendelssohn: *Lieder ohne Worte* (arranged for orchestra and two solo cornets)
Johann Strauss [Sr.]: *Carnival Quadrille* [*Souvenir de Carneval?*]

12 · Ibid., November 8, 1863, 6.

PART III

Adolphe Adam: Overture to *Le roi d'Yvetot*
Fromental Halévy: Romance from *Der Blitz* [*L'éclair*]
Carl Bergmann: *Louisen Polka*
Johann Valentin Hamm: *Frankfurt Schlitzenfest March*

This concert was notable for Bergmann and for New Yorkers because it was the first time that music from Gounod's *Faust* was heard in the city in an orchestral arrangement.[13] It preceded the New York stage premiere of *Faust* at the Academy of Music on November 26 and Theodore Thomas's performance of an arrangement from the opera in late November.[14] Bergmann's concerts also featured novelties such as *Paganini in China*, performed during the 1864–65 season. Bergmann's division of the program into three parts, his mixed programming, and the orderly, respectable atmosphere were all designed to attract middle-class and elite patronage, a model soon to be borrowed and expanded on by Theodore Thomas in his concerts at Terrace Garden and Central Park Garden (see below).

Policing the Sabbath: Sacred Concerts and the Law

Bergmann's "sacred concert" did not include a single piece of religious music. It was billed as "sacred" because city and state statutes, the so-called blue laws, prohibited theatrical performances and other public entertainments on Sundays.[15] The blue laws were promulgated in the mid-nineteenth century and remained on the books for many decades. The Penal Code of New York State, Title X, Section 277, still in force in 1902, included a long list of what was not to be performed on the Sabbath: "The performance of any tragedy, comedy, opera, ballet, farce, negro minstrelsy, negro or other dancing, wrestling, boxing with or without gloves, sparring contests, trial of strength, or any part or parts therein, or any circus, equestrian or dramatic performance or exercise, or any performance or exercise of jugglers, acrobats, club performances or rope dancers on the first day of the week is forbidden."[16] "Con-

---

13 · Earlier in 1863, Louis Moreau Gottschalk had played the waltz from *Faust* in a piano arrangement. Gottschalk's piano arrangement *Valse de Faust* (New York: Beer and Schirmer, 1863) was published under the pseudonym Oscar Litti.

14 · On Thomas's performance of the *Faust* arrangement, see "Amusements," *New York Times*, November 30, 1863, 4.

15 · On the temperance and Sabbatarian movements, see John W. Frick, *Theatre, Culture, and Temperance Reform in Nineteenth-Century America* (2003); Alexis McCrossen, *Holy Day, Holiday: The American Sunday* (2000).

16 · *The Penal Code of the State of New York in Force December 1, 1882* (1902), 73.

certs" are not on the list and thus potentially could be presented on Sundays so long as they had nothing to do with tragedy, comedy, opera, ballet, and so forth. Entrepreneurs and performers got around the blue laws by advertising Sunday entertainment as "sacred concerts," though they were not always concerts. Unlike the Parisian Concert spirituel in the eighteenth century, New York sacred concerts rarely contained any sacred music.

A tongue-in-cheek report published in the *New York Times* in 1889 mentions that instead of performing Cherubini's Mass in A Minor and Mozart's Requiem as listed on the program at an unidentified theater, the orchestra actually played "Johnny Get Your Gun" and the Irish song "Fifteen Dollars in My Inside Pocket," by Harry Kennedy.[17] This same report noted that at Koster and Bial's Music Hall, the orchestra's rendition of Bach's "Easter March" sounded suspiciously like the "Razzle Dazzle Symphony" from Charles Hoyt's popular 1888 farce comedy *The Brass Monkey*. Contemporary reports suggest that Sunday theatrical sacred concerts were given without costumes, without lowering the stage curtain, and without visibly shifting scenery. Some managers even posted signs directing audiences not to applaud, though how often this rule was followed is not known.

These sacred concerts were very important to the social and musical life of Klein Deutschland. Sunday concerts were well established all over Germany, and German immigrants in New York expected to be able to attend similar musical entertainments in Gotham. Events billed as "sacred concerts" actually included performances of operas and plays, popular and light classical orchestral music, excerpts from the standard symphonic repertory, band music, vocal and instrumental music for small ensembles, and dance music, whether for dancing or just for listening—not to mention zither players, Tyrolean and yodeling acts, musical puppet theater, singing dwarf acts, and solos on novelty instruments such as "magical harmonica."[18] The predominantly European theatrical and musical repertory of the German sacred concerts contrasted sharply with popular American theatrical entertainments such as minstrelsy and variety/vaudeville acts. The institution of the sacred concert highlighted the sharp contrasts in ethnic values and expectations that New Yorkers experienced on a daily basis, as well as the intersections and accommodations between low-, middle-, and high-brow culture. Figure II.2.2 shows a typical though modest New York German beer garden of the 1860s. Onstage a man plays piano, a woman the guitar. Some of the guests may be listening, but most are smoking, eating, drinking, or socializing. On the right

17 · "Beer Flowed Yesterday. The Saloons Were Not Closed Very Tight," *New York Times*, August 12, 1889, 1.
18 · The "magical harmonica" was played by a Herr Zirom; advertisement, *New-Yorker Staats-Zeitung*, January 17, 1864, 8.

FIGURE II.2.2. A German Wirthschaft, *Illustrated London News*, December 3, 1864.

a banner advertises a "shooting gallery," a common feature in such locales, and a waiter carries a fistful of beer steins for thirsty customers.

To the denizens of Klein Deutschland the scene in figure II.2.2 seemed natural and *gemütlich* (cozy)—perhaps it reminded them of home. To many Protestant Anglo-Americans it was scandalous. "In the first half of the nineteenth century," said John W. Frick, "no single issue—not even the abolition of slavery—had a greater capacity for arousing the American passion than did the cause of temperance."[19] In the minds of the righteous, the German (and American) theater, entertainment, and saloon district centered on the Bowery was a den of iniquity.[20] Organizations such as the New York Sabbath Committee and their allies in the temperance movement aspired to control the entertainments of the working-class (especially immigrant) population and to police the behavior of women in public spaces, especially women musicians and the "waiter girls" in the concert saloons. Attempts to prohibit Sunday performances were opposed by the German American community, which generally supported public entertainments on the workingman's day of rest. The strong desire for recreation and entertainment on Sunday, especially among the working classes, conflicted with Sabbatarians' insistence on a cessation of these activities on that day.[21] As a result, German managers such as Gustav Lindenmüller, Charles Eustachi, and Otto Hoym became periodic targets of the temperance reformers and police.[22] Hoym, director of the New York Stadttheater (and one of its principal actors), as well as Lindenmüller, proprietor of the Odeon Winter-Garten und Conzert-Salon, were charged in 1860 with violating the Sunday blue laws and were forced to defend themselves in court. A series of reports of their legal troubles appeared in the *New York Times* and other newspapers and journals during the second half of 1860 and into 1861.[23]

19 · Frick, *Theatre, Culture, and Temperance Reform*, 1.

20 · In 1859 *Harper's Weekly* published the five-part series titled "Sketches of the People Who Oppose Our Sunday Laws." The first article portrayed "A Sunday Evening Sacred Concert" (October 8, 1859, 641–42). The second was "Sunday Evening in a Beer Garden" (October 15, 1859, 657–58). The third article described a Sunday sacred concert at the Stadttheater (October 22, 1859, 673–74) and the fourth a Sunday at Jones's Wood, the well-known pleasure grounds (November 5, 1859, 707–8). The last installment in the series was "Sunday in Chatham Street" (November 19, 1859, 739–40).

21 · McCrossen, *Holy Day, Holiday*.

22 · Gustav Lindenmüller was a "48er" from Berlin who had been involved in the revolutions of that year before his emigration. See "Lindenmüller's Erdenwaller in New York" in *Amerika, wie es ist. Ein Buch für Kunde der neuen Welt* (1854), 40–42, available at http://pds .lib.harvard.edu/pds/view/4676810. Charles Eustachi was the proprietor of the very active Volkstheater at 515–19 Fourth Street.

23 · "Disregarding the Sunday Law," *New York Times*, May 1, 1860, 8; "Enforcement of the Sunday Law: The German Theatres," *New York Times*, June 16, 1860, 6; "Constitutionality of the Sunday Law," *New York Times*, June 22, 1860, 3; "Oyer and Terminer," *New York Times*,

The Society for the Reformation of Juvenile Delinquents, the recipient of the fees generated from obligatory theatrical licensing, led the campaign against these German (and other) venues, accusing managers such as Hoym and Lindenmüller of being atheists because they offered Sunday performances and because they sold beer on the Sabbath. The New York Sabbath Committee issued numerous tracts advocating the cessation of almost all commercial and entertainment activities on Sundays.[24] Several of these Sabbatarian tracts were published in German and distributed through German American churches and social organizations. Temperance publications such as the Methodist *Christian Advocate and Journal* and Presbyterian *New York Evangelist* attacked Lindenmüller, who responded by issuing a "Constitution of the Religious Sect Called the 'German Shaker Association.'" Lindenmüller claimed that his musical and theatrical entertainments were religious worship, that his customers were a congregation, and that his theater was thus beyond the jurisdiction of the police.[25] On Sunday, November 4, 1860, Lindenmüller offered his flock a magnificent "double" sacred concert in which two full ensembles—a wind band and an orchestra—performed arrangements of operas by Rossini, Cherubini, Weber, Lortzing, Auber, Bellini, and Verdi and dance music by Lanner, Strauss, Gungl, and others. Band and orchestra played concurrently in two adjacent halls at the Odeon beer garden/concert–dance hall complex—the band in the Ball-Saal and the orchestra in the Winter-Garten und Conzert-Salon.[26] At the bottom of the program Lindenmüller addressed his "beloved public" in a mixture of German and English:

> My beloved public: As you can see for yourselves, I have not become at all disheartened despite the blow I recently suffered. We can't hold church any more — so, in the meantime, we'll play music.... You alone, my beloved public, have it in your power to determine whether my new enterprise is to blossom or to wilt. In the pleasant hope that the former will be the case, our new ballroom will be opened tomorrow, Monday evening at 8:00, with a friendly BALL to which I extend to you, my friends and patrons and your families a most earnest and courteous invitation. For my part, I will make

July 4, 1860, 2; "Law Reports," *New York Times*, October 1, 1860, 2. The controversy continued on into 1861, 1862, and 1863 and was reported on in the *New York Times* and other local newspapers.

24 · See the collection of twenty tracts, also published separately between 1857 and 1863: New York Sabbath Committee, *First Five Years of the Sabbath Reform, 1857–62* (1862). These Sabbatarian tracts provide important details about German performance venues.

25 · "Court of Oyer and Terminer: German Shaker Constitution," *New York Times*, November 18, 1860, 2; "Sunday Theatres Doomed," *New York Observer and Chronicle* 38 (November 29, 1860): 378; "The Lager Bier Dodge," *New York Evangelist* 31 (November 29, 1860): 4.

26 · Program in the Harvard Theatre Collection, Harvard University.

every effort to arrange all aspects in such a way that you will think back on your experience with great pleasure for a long time. By the same token, I will take the liberty of charging no admission fee for tomorrow's inaugural ball counting instead on a strong attendance, and I remain in this hope your most devoted Gustav Lindenmüller.[27]

The controversy that raged in 1860 and 1861 was a prelude to the Anti-Concert Saloon Bill passed in 1862 by the New York state legislature, which, as Gillian Rodger has shown, resulted in many changes, including the ban of the sale of alcohol in public theaters.[28] Police surveillance of performance venues intensified after the passage of the Anti-Concert Saloon Bill, and police raids and fines were motivated as much by a desire to stamp out Sunday celebrations and prostitution as by actual violations of ordinances. Some police records survive that give details about musical performance.[29] A police report from 1887 describes the seven-member orchestra that performed popular selections at the Bijou Cafe concert saloon (61 West Fourteenth Street). Six women and one man played first and second violin, bass, cornet, flute, clarinet, and piano for an audience of about 150 persons. Nearly half the audience were women "who were apparently prostitutes, from their actions and language."[30] Despite the official pressure, German American resistance to the Sunday blue laws continued for many years, and later impresarios such as Adolf Neuendorff (director of the Germania Theater) and William Kramer of the Atlantic Garden fought vigorously for the right to give performances on Sundays (see below).

The *New York Herald* pointed out in 1860 the hypocrisy inherent in the Sunday blue laws, arguing that "a man is tried and condemned in one of our courts for doing ... on a Sunday what ... he might have done with impunity on the other six days of the week."[31] Some community leaders advocated

27 · English translation of excerpt of German original, from the program in the Harvard Theatre Collection. The interpolated English words do not appear in this excerpt.
28 · Gillian Rodger, "Legislating Amusements: Class Politics and Theater Law in New York City," *American Music* 20 (2002); Rodger, *Champagne Charlie and Pretty Jemima: Variety Theater in the Nineteenth Century* (2010). Theater licensing is also discussed in Daniel Czitrom, "The Politics of Performance: From Theater Licensing to Movie Censorship in Turn-of-the-Century New York," *American Quarterly* 44 (1992).
29 · Police reports relating to theater licensing are available on microfilm at the New York City Municipal Archives, filed under "Mayors Papers," organized chronologically according to the term of the individual mayor, and then under the category "Police Department, Licensing of Theatres." See http://www.nyc.gov/html/records/home.html.
30 · Report filed January 11, 1887, Mayor Abram S. Hewitt Papers, Police, Dept. of, Licensing of Theatres, 1881–1882, box 1366, folder 245, New York City Municipal Archives.
31 · "The Late Conviction under the Sunday Law," *New York Herald*, November 23, 1860, 4.

other entertainments for the working classes in place of saloon culture and argued that the higher-class German beer gardens did not exercise the pernicious influence that the concert saloons and regular saloons did. Figure II.2.3, an illustration by William Glackens for *Harper's Weekly* in 1900, depicts the "typical" New York beer garden as a family-oriented affair, with an intergenerational atmosphere, joyous conviviality, a well-dressed audience, bright lights, copious consumption of food and drink, and, equally important, a large orchestra on the stage playing what is very likely a Sunday sacred concert. James McCabe portrayed the Atlantic Garden in a similarly positive light and offered a forceful argument for both beer and Beethoven:

> The consumption of the article here nightly is tremendous, but there is no drunkenness. The audience is well behaved, and the noise is simply the hearty merriment of a large crowd. There is no disorder, no indecency.... They come here with their families, spend a social, pleasant evening, meet their friends, hear the news, enjoy the music and the beer, and go home refreshed and happy.... It is a decided advantage to the people who frequent this place, whatever the Temperance advocates may say, that men have here a resort where they can enjoy themselves with their families, instead of seeking their pleasure away from the society of their wives and children. The buzz and the hum of the conversation, and the laughter, are overpowering.... Suddenly the leader of the orchestra raps sharply on his desk, and there is a profound silence all over the hall. In an instant the orchestra breaks forth into some wonderful German melody, or some deep-voiced, strong-lunged singer sends his rich notes rolling through the hall. The auditors have suddenly lost their merriment, and are now listening pensively to the music, which is good.[32]

The Atlantic Garden

The Atlantic Garden, which McCabe depicted in such glowing terms, opened in 1858 at 50–54 Bowery, next to the English-language Bowery Theater.[33] It immediately became one of Manhattan's leading German performance spaces, where music, theatricality, and beer combined in an atmosphere of *Gemütlichkeit* (snugness, sociability). It could accommodate considerably more than a thousand people and was noted for the wide range of events held

32 · McCabe, *Lights and Shadows*, 551–53.
33 · For more on the Atlantic Garden, see Koegel, *Music in German Immigrant Theater*, chap. 3; also see David Freeland, *Automats, Taxi Dances, and Vaudeville: Excavating Manhattan's Lost Places of Leisure* (2009).

A TYPICAL NEW YORK BEER-GARDEN.

FIGURE 11.2.3. William Glackens, "A Typical New York Beer-Garden," *Harper's Weekly*, July 21, 1900.

there.[34] The Atlantic Garden was said to be located on the site of the famous eighteenth-century Bull's Head Tavern, where George Washington briefly had his headquarters in 1783 at the conclusion of the American Revolution. In the early nineteenth century, the New York Theater Hotel was erected on the site.[35] William Kramer (Wilhelm Kraemer) remodeled and expanded the building as the Atlantic Garden. Throughout most of its history, it served as a high-class beer garden, music hall, and variety and vaudeville performance space. In addition, performances of German plays were given there periodically during the 1860s and in later decades.[36] It was also the fashionable place for parties after performances at the Bowery Theater next door.

Kramer purchased the Bowery Theater in 1878 and reopened it in 1879 as the Thalia Theater, dedicated to German-language performances.[37] A door was opened on the second floor to connect the galleries of the theater and beer garden, making it easy for theater patrons to have a drink during the intermissions between the acts of German-language plays and operettas. Throughout the Atlantic Garden's long history, lager beer flowed freely, and the strong German American thirst for beer assured Kramer's financial success. On Sundays, when the excise laws prohibited the sale of lager beer and stronger beverages, Kramer sold Weissbier, which had a lower alcoholic content.[38] The Atlantic Garden's extensive menu offered a varied German and American cuisine—Wiener Schnitzel (thirty-five cents); pigs knuckles (twenty-five cents); sirloin steak (forty-five cents), and so forth. The consumption of lager beer was essential to the atmosphere at the Atlantic Garden and other German American spaces, where sociability and performance were paramount and intertwined and where the profits from the sale of drink and food (in that order) enabled proprietors such as Kramer to offer free admission.

Musical entertainment at the Atlantic Garden was provided for many decades by the Damen Elite Kapelle, or Vienna Elite Lady Orchestra, a renowned orchestra of about a dozen women musicians who performed or-

34 · Julian Ralph, "The Bowery," *Century Illustrated Monthly Magazine* 43 (1891): 236; Junius Henri Browne, *The Great Metropolis: A Mirror of New York* (1869), 158–74.
35 · "Theatrical History Made on the Old Bowery's Stage," *New York Sun*, July 2, 1916, 5–6.
36 · Carl Eugene Marquardt, "The German Drama on the New York Stage" (Ph.D. diss., 1915); unpaginated performance chronology for the Atlantic Garden.
37 · On the Thalia Theater, see Koegel, *Music in German Immigrant Theater*, chap. 4.
38 · Lager beer has an alcoholic content of about 4 to 5 percent, Weiss beer 1 to 2 percent. To accommodate his patrons, Kramer sometimes illegally sold Pilsner beer on Sundays as Weiss beer. "What Weiss Beer Is: It Is Not Beer, and Its Sale Is Not Prohibited," *New York Times*, May 14, 1876, 12; "Well Watered Weiss Beer," *New York Times*, January 16, 1883, 8; "It Was Weiss Beer: The Atlantic Garden Permitted to Keep Its License," *New York Times*, February 18, 1885, 3.

FIGURE II.2.4. Atlantic Garden Lady Orchestra. John Jennings, *Theatrical and Circus Life*, 1882.

chestral works and accompanied popular singers and instrumental soloists (see fig. II.2.4).[39] Marie Roller was the first director of the ensemble, which was formed in the aftermath of the visit to New York in 1871 of the Vienna Lady Orchestra and their concert series at Steinway Hall.[40] The original Vienna Lady Orchestra toured the United States and provided the model for the formation of other women's orchestras throughout the country, including those at several competing German beer halls on the Bowery. Albert Eschert took over the orchestra from Roller some years later; his son Charles replaced him as director, probably in 1884. Charles Eschert continued to direct the Lady Orchestra until the turn of the century. Besides the Lady Orchestra, other musicians also performed at the Atlantic Garden, including Tyrolean singing groups and instrumental ensembles such as F. Leiboldt's famous military band and cornet soloist and conductor Alessandro Liberati (1847–1927).

Figure II.2.5 reproduces a program for an 1877 orchestral performance at the Atlantic Garden by Marie Roller and the Damen Elite Kapelle. Like

39 · Before the establishment of the Lady Orchestra at the Atlantic Garden in the early 1870s, the orchestra there was apparently all-male, and a Herr Heydenreich was the conductor for the 1863–64 season. In November 1863, he brought in a specialty ensemble performing "Janissary" music to entice crowds to the venue.

40 · On the Vienna Lady Orchestra and its American imitators, see chapter I.2 in this volume.

ATLANTIC GARTEN.

50 BOWERY, 50

Sonntag, den 8ten September, 1877.

Großes Sacred Concert,

des beliebten Wiener

Damen Orchesters,

unter Direction der Frln. Maria Roller.

Anfang ½8 Uhr.   **Anfang ½8 Uhr.**

——:—o—:——

PROGRAMM

I THEIL

1. En avant Marsch..Lumbye
2. Ouverture „Prometheus"...............................Beethoven
3. Benefice Quadrille..Resch
4. Traumbilder Fantasie.....................................Lumbye
5. Val ska Polka Mazurka......................................Neibig
6. Quartett aus Feensee..Auber

II THEIL.

7. Amicitia Marsch ....Wiegand
8. Flotte Burschen Ouverture.................................Suppé
9. Romanze für Glassharmonium.
   Vorgetragen von Frln. Kattie Liebhold.
10. Geschichten aus dem Wiener Wald, Walzer.........Strauss
11. Hochzeitsmarsch aus Sommernachts-traum.....Mendelsohn
12. Polka Capriciosa, Solo für Xilophon.
    Vorgetragen von Frln. Bertha Eschert.
13. Variatio delectat, Potpourri..............................Faust

III THEIL

14. Kayser Jäger Marsch.......................................Strauss
15. Arie aus Ernani ....Verdi
16. Les Inséparables, Polka................................Herrmann
17. Reiter Galopp..Carl

Achtungsvollst

W. Kramer.

N. B.—Dem verehrlichen Publikum die ergebenste Anzeige, daß während der Sommer Saison jeden Montag Matinee Concerte des Wiener Damen Orchesters bei freiem Eintritt stattfinden werden.

FIGURE II.2.5. Atlantic Garden Sacred Concert program, 1877. Harvard Theatre Collection.

Carl Bergmann's Broadway Garten concert mentioned above, it is billed as a sacred concert, and the program is similarly divided into three sections, with lengthy intermissions designed to encourage the purchase of food and drink. Compared to the Bergmann concert (or to Theodore Thomas's Central Park Garden concerts discussed below), the Damen Elite Kapelle program seems to put more emphasis on popular repertory. However, the Lady Orchestra did play more musically substantial works, as represented in the 1877 program by Beethoven's *Creatures of Prometheus* Overture. The German language and Gothic script in this 1877 program make it clear that much of the audience at the Atlantic Garden must have been German speakers. This contrasts with the Atlantic Garden program from 1896 reproduced in figure II.2.6. In this later program the language is English throughout, the typeface is modern, and the program is more mixed, with a dancer and various novelty acts. The instrumental soloists are still women (except for director Charles Eschert on xylophone), and although most of them have German surnames, several have American first names, such as trombonist Lizzie Spargur. By 1896 the Atlantic Garden audience seems to have been more comfortable in English than in German, either because more non-Germans were attending the Sunday concerts or because second- and third-generation German Americans in New York preferred to speak English. These changes seem to reflect the gradual assimilation of the German American community into an American mainstream.

During the day, and other times when the Elite Lady Orchestra was not playing at the Atlantic Garden, the "Mammoth Pneumatic Orchestrion" provided music for patrons. The orchestrion, manufactured by M. Welte and Company in Freiburg, Germany, was a mechanical instrument that imitated the orchestra, with organ pipes controlled by pinned cylinders (see fig. II.2.7).[41] In 1869 the Atlantic Garden orchestrion, according to the *New York Times*, was the largest in the world.[42] William Kramer probably ordered his instrument from Welte's New York City showroom, which opened in 1865. Kramer purchased a second orchestrion sometime later. These mechanical instruments were used for many decades and were invariably mentioned in accounts of the Atlantic Garden. The orchestrion played much the same repertory as the Damen Elite Kapelle: operatic overtures and potpourris, marches, polkas, and other popular pieces. Kramer encouraged the audience to sing and dance to the music provided by the orchestrion, just as if it

41 · See Tim Trager, "Welte Orchestrions at Atlantic Garden," http://mmd.foxtail.com/Pictures/welte1.html; Arthur A. Reblitz, *The Golden Age of Automatic Musical Instruments* (2001); "M. Welte and Söhne Orchestrions," http://www.mechanicalmusicpress.com/history/welte/wt_index.htm.

42 · "Among the Germans," *New York Times*, January 1, 1869, 8.

ATLANTIC GARDEN,

WILLIAM KRAMER, Proprietor..................................Established 1858.

GRAND

Vocal & Instrumental Concert

Every Evening at 7.30.

Every SUNDAY. **MATINEE FROM 2.30 TO 6 P. M.** **Every SUNDAY.**

GIVEN BY

CHARLES ESCHERT'S

ELITE LADY ORCHESTRA,

Miss Eleanore Bloomfield. ....Violin Soloist.
Miss Lilian Bailey ....Bell Soloist.
Miss Margaret Hittner ....Flute Soloist.
Miss Emma Glasberger...................Clarionet Soloist
Miss Lizzie Spargur ....Trombone Soloist.
Mr. Charles Eschert.............. ....Xylophone Soloist.

First Appearance of the Great Novelty Musical Sketch and
Change Duettists,

THE TWO CARLES.

Great success of the Great Transatlantique Transformation Dancer
Miss EDITH CRASKE,

First Appearance of the Grand Opera and Concert Singer,
Miss Imogene Comer.

First Appearance of the German Chansonette,
Miss JOHANNA WEGNER.

PROGRAMME ON SECOND AND THIRD PAGE.

FIGURE 11.2.6. Atlantic Garden Sacred Concert program, 1896. Harvard Theatre Collection.

THE WORLD'S FAIR FIRST PRIZE

Mammoth Pneumatic Orchestrion

The Orchestrion is the greatest instrument of its kind in the world and built expressly for the Columbian Exposition and was awarded with the First Prize. Height, 26 feet; depth, 8 feet; length 18 feet.

The Orchestrion plays every day from 10 A. M. to 7 P. M.

ADIMISSION FREE.

FIGURE II.2.7. Atlantic Garden Orchestrion. Harvard Theatre Collection.

were a live orchestra. Occasionally orchestrion and orchestra combined in formal concerts, alternating with one another and with vocal soloists, quartets, and other acts. A solo orchestrion concert in 1865 included arrangements of operatic music by Hérold (*Zampa*), Weber (*Oberon*), and Meyerbeer (*Le Prophète, L'Africaine*), as well as dance music.[43] On January 14, 1866, the Atlantic Garden presented a vocal concert conducted by Herr Wiedemann, with the assistance of a "double quartet of the best singers in New York" singing German partsongs, with interludes played by the orchestrion.[44] Just as the police shut down live performances at the Atlantic Garden for blue law violations, they occasionally prohibited Sunday orchestrion concerts. "On Sunday, the 14th of this month," the *New-Yorker Staats-Zeitung* reported in January 1866, "the orchestrion performance at the Atlantic Garten was stopped by the police."[45]

By the turn of the century, the Atlantic Garden had become a venue where vaudeville performers such as Harry von Tilzer, Emma Carus, Harrigan and Hart, and Cole and Johnson played to large mixed German and American audiences. Edward B. Marks, the song plugger turned music publisher, was a frequent habitué of the Atlantic Garden in the 1890s.[46] Marks's job took him to numerous entertainment establishments, where he would encourage performers to play and sing the songs published by his firm (Joseph W. Stern) in order to establish them as hits and to encourage sheet music sales. At the Atlantic Garden, Marks passed out printed slips to the audience with the song's lyrics so that the crowd could sing the refrain along with the vocal soloist and the Lady Orchestra. To assure the orchestra members' cooperation, Marks plied the ladies with free drinks.

During its heyday, the Atlantic Garden was ranked by newspaper reports and city guides as the best German beer garden and music hall in New York, and these accounts often mentioned the festive and orderly air that prevailed there as well as its family atmosphere. By the turn of the century, however, the neighborhood had changed dramatically. Much of the German American community had moved away from the Lower East Side to uptown Manhattan and the outer boroughs and nearby New Jersey cities, and, as a result, the Atlantic Garden had fallen on hard times.[47] It played Yiddish vaudeville for a while and then presented boxing matches and motion pictures. New immi-

43 · Advertisement, *New-Yorker Staats-Zeitung*, December 21, 1865, 8.

44 · Ibid., January 14, 1866.

45 · Ibid., January 20, 1866.

46 · Edward B. Marks, *They All Sang: From Tony Pastor to Rudy Vallée* (1935), 4–9, 30, 111.

47 · "Thalia and Historic Atlantic Garden Give Way to Progress of Trade," *New York Tribune*, June 16, 1916; "Atlantic Garden Changes Its Ways," *New York Times*, October 4, 1910, 5.

grants, many of them Eastern European Jews, looked to the nearby Yiddish and American theaters for their entertainment instead of the beloved old German beer garden with its famous Lady Orchestra.

Summer Orchestral Concerts at Terrace Garden and Central Park Garden

When the Terrace Garden first opened in 1866, it was considered to be on the periphery of the main part of the city. That was probably part of its attraction to audiences seeking a respite from the high density of the areas to the south in Manhattan. Also called the Lexington Avenue Opera House, the Terrace Garden Theater was a complex of buildings located between Third and Lexington Avenues and extending from East Fifty-Eighth Street to East Fifty-Ninth. During its almost sixty years of existence, it was one of the premier performance venues and social gathering places for New York's German American community, and it was also used by other ethnic groups. Besides the theater, which could be used as an indoor concert space, Terrace Garden had a gardenlike, open-air performance space with a stage large enough for a sizeable orchestra. It was in this open-air theater at the Terrace Garden that Theodore Thomas, in the summers of 1866 and 1867, originated his groundbreaking series of popular summer orchestral concerts.

A program from a concert given at the Terrace Garden on August 2, 1867, is shown below.[48] Though this was a Friday evening concert, it was similar to those that Thomas offered on Sundays, with the same three-part division as in the earlier beer garden concerts. The first part contained brilliant and vigorous pieces that could cover up the noise of late arrivals. During the middle segment, Thomas presented substantial symphonic works, including movements from Beethoven's Third and Fifth Symphonies, and here he expected the audience to be especially attentive.[49] If they wished to talk, drink, or smoke, they could move to the separate outdoor garden area, away from the concert stage. The third section consisted of lighter dance pieces intended to lighten the mood and send the audience out into the night in a jovial and relaxed state.[50]

48 · From the program in the Harvard Theatre Collection.

49 · The program in the Harvard Theatre Collection includes the following notice: "Every Tuesday and Friday Evenings. The second part of the program will consist of compositions of a higher order, such as movements of symphonies, classical overtures, etc."

50 · Thomas's three-part "crescent-shaped" programs, with the more substantial pieces performed in Part II, are discussed in H. Wiley Hitchcock, *Music in the United States: A Historical Introduction* (2000), 95–97.

Program 2. Theodore Thomas's Popular Garden Concert—August 2, 1867

PART I

1. Overture, *Semiramis* [*Semiramide*]   Rossini
2. Waltz, *Josephinen*   Matzka
3. Polka Mazurka, *Libelle* (new)   Strauss
   Polka, *Wildfire* (new)   Strauss
4. Fantasie, *Don Giovanni*   Mozart

PART II

5. Overture, *Jessonda*   Spohr
6. Andante from the Fifth Symphony (by request)   Beethoven
7. Scherzo, *Midsummer Night's Dream*   Mendelssohn
8. Last movement from the *Eroica* Symphony   Beethoven

PART III

9. Overture, *Rienzi*   Wagner
10. Styrian Laendler, "S Hoamweh"   Lanner
    With Violin Obbligato by Theodore Thomas
11. Polka, *Bauern*   Strauss
12. Galop, *Lafayette*   Muller

Although Thomas left the Terrace Garden after the 1867 season, the venue continued to offer outdoor summer performances. Audiences flocked to the orchestral concerts and German-language operetta performances from the 1870s through the 1890s. A substantial contingent of English speakers joined the Germans at the Terrace Garden, a sign of the assimilation of German and Anglo-American music cultures in New York. As the *New York Times* noted, it was "a popular resort for Germans who love operetta of a summery kind and for Americans who are fond of light music with accompaniment of fluent and luminous beer."[51] The Terrace Garden offered musical and dramatic performances as well as dancing year round. It boasted a large indoor theater that doubled as a ballroom, in addition to an elegant restaurant, bar rooms including an "Old German Bierstube," lounges, bowling alley, and outdoor garden on the ground level to which the doors of the theater opened. Thanks to this arrangement, theater patrons could visit the garden during the intermissions of an operetta or between vaudeville acts. They could order refreshments and listen to well-performed popular orchestral music and then return to the main theater at the end of intermission.

51 · "Music," *New York Times*, May 23, 1897, 12.

In addition to orchestral concerts, operettas, and vaudeville, the Terrace Garden was the site of literally thousands of German social activities and dances given by countless *Vereine* (social clubs) during its long existence.[52] In its form and function, the Terrace Garden resembled the multipurpose nineteenth-century performance spaces in Berlin that specialized in operetta and light orchestral music, such as the popular Kroll, Wallner, Flora, and Victoria Theaters. Even more than the Atlantic Garden, it was representative of the German and American interest in creating multifunctional theatrical and entertainment spaces that would maximize artistic, social, and economic possibilities.

Theodore Thomas and his orchestra left the Terrace Garden in 1867 and moved for the 1868 summer season to another, yet more elegant beer garden, the Central Park Garden, where he remained until 1875. The building was located on Seventh Avenue between West Fifty-Eighth and Fifty-Ninth Streets a block south of Central Park. The ubiquitous James McCabe described Central Park Garden as "more of an American institution" than the beer gardens of Klein Deutschland:

It consists of a handsome hall surrounded on three sides by a gallery, and opening at the back upon grounds of a moderate size, tastefully laid out, and adorned with rustic stalls and arbors for the use of guests. At the Atlantic Garden the admission is free. Here one pays fifty cents for the privilege of entering the grounds and building. During the summer months nightly concerts, with Saturday matinées, are given here by Theodore Thomas and his famous orchestra—the finest organization of its kind in America. The music is of a high order, and is rendered in a masterly manner. Many lovers of music come to New York in the summer simply to hear these concerts. The place is the fashionable resort of the city in the summer. The audience is equal to anything to be seen in the city. One can meet here all the celebrities who happen to be in town, and as every one is free to do as he pleases, there is no restraint to hamper one's enjoyment. You may sit and smoke and drink, or stroll through the place the whole evening, merely greeting your acquaintances with a nod, or you may join them, and chat to your heart's content. Refreshments and liquors of all kinds are sold to guests; but the prices are high. The Central Park Garden, or, as it is called by strangers, "Thomas's Garden," is the most thoroughly enjoyable place in the city in the summer.[53]

52 · *Appleton's Dictionary of New York and Vicinity* (1880), 120.
53 · McCabe, *Lights and Shadows*, 554.

Missing from McCabe's account is any mention of German immigrants, German performers, or German beer. Although he acknowledges Central Park Garden's origins, he does not call it a "beer garden." Instead, he emphasizes its elegance, its Americanness, and the superior quality of the music. In essence, however, it was a high-class beer garden.

Thomas's summer concerts at Central Park Garden in the 1870s represented a focal point of orchestral activity in New York, indeed in the United States. Thomas and his orchestra performed most of the standard orchestral repertory from the late eighteenth century to his day and played many American premieres of the latest works. He offered nights devoted to the works of Wagner, Schumann, Mozart, Schubert, Mendelssohn, Beethoven, and other major composers. Between 1868 and 1875, Thomas gave 1,125 orchestral concerts at Central Park Garden.[54] In eight seasons, Thomas's Central Park Garden concerts gave New Yorkers many more performances of a much broader orchestral repertory than the New York Philharmonic did in the entire nineteenth century.

Most of the writing on Thomas emphasizes his role as an innovator in the repertory he championed and the manner of his programming.[55] There is a good deal of truth to this view, but it needs to be adjusted in light of recent research. Thomas's 1866–67 Terrace Garden summer concerts and the Central Park Garden concerts of 1868–75 came out of a well-established tradition of music in German beer gardens, from Widow Schürmann's Wein, Lagerbier, und Conzert-Salon to the Broadway Garten, the Atlantic Garden, and countless other venues. The repertory that the Thomas Orchestra played and the structure of his programs resembled those of the sacred concerts at German beer gardens in earlier years, especially in the concerts conducted at the Broadway Garten by Carl Bergmann.[56] Because Thomas gave his summer concerts at the Terrace Garden and Central Park Garden, neither of which was located in the main centers of German life on the Lower East Side and in Yorkville, he was able to attract a greater mix of ethnicities to his concerts than impresarios in Klein Deutschland had been able to do earlier. However,

54 · Edwin T. Rice, "Thomas and Central Park Garden," *Musical Quarterly* 26 (1940).
55 · Hitchcock, *Music in the United States*, 95–97. Other coverage of Thomas's concerts is included in Ezra Schabas, *Theodore Thomas: America's Conductor and Builder of Orchestras, 1835–1905* (1989); Joseph Horowitz, *Classical Music in America: A History of Its Rise and Fall* (2005); and Richard Crawford, *America's Musical Life: A History* (2001). See also chapter V.2 in this volume.
56 · Matthew Reichert's dissertation on Carl Bergmann ("Carl Bergmann in New York: Conducting Activity, 1852–1876" [D.M.A. diss., 2011]) establishes that conductor's essential role in the development of orchestral music in New York City.

German Americans continued to support these summer orchestral concerts even after they moved uptown.

One reason for this multiethnic support was Thomas's growing stature throughout New York's musical establishment. Another was the location of both the Terrace Garden and Central Park Garden. The New York and Harlem Railroad had reached the Upper East Side of Manhattan by 1834, with a northern terminus at East Eighty-Sixth Street, so those living on the Lower East Side could reach the Terrace Garden in the 1860s and later. By the 1870s, a main area for New York's German American population was Yorkville, centered on East Eighty-Sixth Street. Yorkville's German Americans found it easy to venture beyond the southern borders of their enclave to attend performances and celebrations at the Terrace Garden on East Fifty-Eighth Street. When the Third Avenue elevated line opened in 1878, the Terrace Garden became readily accessible to theatergoers throughout Manhattan, both German and non-German. They could also easily travel to Central Park Garden on the west side of Manhattan on public transportation.

The multifaceted history of the German American and American performance spaces—both the major venues, such as Lindenmüller's, Atlantic Garden, Central Park Garden, and Terrace Garden, and the places of lesser fame, such as the Café Chantant Caffe und Wein-Salon and Widow Anna Schürmann's Wein, Lagerbier, und Conzert-Salon—demonstrates the fluid and complicated interethnic and interclass nature of theatrical and musical repertories and audience patronage. Symphonic music by Beethoven and other classical composers as well as popular dance-inspired music by composers of light orchestral music were always accompanied in the German beer gardens by "fluent and luminous lager bier." This cultivation of sociability through music and drink was a highlight of the culture of entertainment in nineteenth-century German New York, and it continued into the twentieth century. Many of the features of the beer garden orchestras—frequent performances staffed by professional musicians, mixed repertory, three-part programs—became models for the concert orchestras that formed in the United States in the last decades of the nineteenth century.

[II.3] Performances to "Permanence"

Orchestra Building in Late Nineteenth-Century Cincinnati

KAREN AHLQUIST

Anyone who attends symphony orchestra concerts today can well appreciate the complex conditions that bring the players and the audience together: a large number of trained musicians organized into a fixed and stable membership; a respected artistic leader; a competent and committed management; a clear and workable relationship between management and the players; an accurate assessment of the market for performances; a series into which individual concerts can be placed; a balance between innovation and tradition in repertory; and financial backing sufficient to offer the players steady employment and—most important for the cause of art—to permit adequate rehearsal time to achieve a high musical standard. Finally, clear beliefs about the importance of a symphony orchestra and the music it plays are essential to publicity, fund-raising, and community respect. These conditions are the building blocks of a "permanent" orchestra—an orchestral organization that offers the community high-quality performances of symphonic music in perpetuity.

The history of American symphony orchestras in the nineteenth century suggests that it took decades to create and support the conditions listed above and thus establish a permanent orchestra. The first orchestra with all or most of the characteristics above was the Boston Symphony Orchestra, founded in 1881, followed by the Chicago Symphony in 1891. The New York Philharmonic, despite its continuous operation since 1842, did not qualify as a permanent orchestra in the above terms until the first decade of the twentieth century. This chapter explores the developing idea of orchestral permanence in the years before the creation of the Cincinnati Symphony Orchestra (CSO) in 1894. Arguably the most culturally ambitious city beyond the Appalachians, the "Queen City of the West" on the Ohio River established a series of orchestral organizations before the CSO, each one's successes and failures marking a new understanding of "permanence."

Post–Civil War Cincinnati could well be called a city of strong musicians. As a third of the so-called German triangle (with St. Louis and Milwaukee), beginning in the 1830s it attracted large numbers of musical immigrants, especially after the European revolutions of 1848. Already before this time, Cincinnati had an active public musical life. But the Germans were expert at creating demand for musical performance and an interest in music study among both the immigrant and the native-born populations. Putting together performances of difficult "classic" works and the latest music from Europe piqued the curiosity of potential listeners and inspired pride among economic and civic leaders sensitive to culture as a source of prestige. Scholars of Cincinnati's history have recognized the significant role of musical institutions—the Conservatory of Music (1867), May Festival (1873), College of Music (1878), Music Hall (1878), and Cincinnati Symphony Orchestra (1894)—in forging the city's identity and serving as sources of its reputation and pride.[1]

Under German leadership, the city also hosted a Saengerfest with orchestral accompaniment as early as 1849 and assembled small concert orchestras beginning in 1856.[2] These orchestras' performances of new music, as well as a growing canon of works from the past, were judged as generally, if not uniformly, satisfactory in the Cincinnati press. Many of the instrumentalists involved taught privately or at the conservatory or the college.[3] The college in particular sought to bring orchestra concerts to the public under the musical leadership of the most prominent American conductor of his time, German-born Theodore Thomas (1835–1905), its founding music director. Thomas had begun to take his New York–based orchestra on tour in 1869, tours that eventually reached the West Coast and ran so frequently that their routes became known as the "Thomas Highway." Touring was central to Thomas's goals of stabilizing the orchestra's membership, supporting adequate rehearsal time for high-quality performances, and raising the status of instrumental vis-à-vis vocal music across the country. The Thomas Orchestra began to persuade Americans of the power of a classical repertory and its

---

1 · Louis R. Thomas, "A History of the Cincinnati Symphony Orchestra to 1931" (Ph.D. diss., 1972); Robert C. Vitz, *The Queen and the Arts: Cultural Life in Nineteenth-Century Cincinnati* (1989); and Michael Charles Cahall, "Jewels in the Queen's Crown: The Fine and Performing Arts in Cincinnati, Ohio, 1865–1919" (Ph.D. diss., 1991). I am particularly grateful for the extensive research notes of Professor Joseph Holliday, a history professor at the University of Cincinnati; his notes are held at the Cincinnati Historical Society Library.

2 · Frédéric Louis Ritter, *Music in America* (1883), 377–79; Joseph E. Holliday, "The Cincinnati Philharmonic and Hopkins Hall Orchestras, 1856–1868," *Bulletin of the Cincinnati Historical Society* 26 (1968). Ritter conducted the 1856 orchestra in Cincinnati.

3 · The conservatory and the College of Music merged in 1955 to form the Cincinnati College-Conservatory of Music, integrated into the University of Cincinnati in 1962.

necessity to an adequately cultured population.[4] Thomas and his group performed in Cincinnati on their first tour, and, as elsewhere, they inspired an
interest in orchestral concerts in the city, especially among musicians.

Cincinnati's greatest musical claim to fame and influence in the period
was not concerts, however, but a festival tradition that grew quickly over
the course of the 1870s, bringing together amateurs and professional musicians, both Anglo-Americans and German Americans. At its center stood
the five-day May Festival, established in 1873 by a committee of wealthy and
committed civic leaders and presented annually today.[5] Appointed music director of the May Festival, Theodore Thomas brought his orchestra to Cincinnati for the event, supplementing it with musicians from Cincinnati and
other cities, to create huge choral and orchestral performances that could
not be mounted with local resources alone—Beethoven's Ninth Symphony
and excerpts from the operas of Wagner, for example.[6] To house the festival
participants and audiences of thousands, Cincinnatians built Music Hall, an
auditorium that could accommodate up to six thousand people, including
standing room, and is still in use today. The festival received national attention and even approbation from New York: an author for *Scribner's Magazine*
wrote, "With one enormous stride[,] pork-packing Ohio overtook aesthetic
Massachusetts, and in the next festival … it will rival … the most ambitious
efforts of New York or Boston, and even the achievements of the great choral festivities of England."[7] All accounts report the Cincinnatians as gratified.

A simultaneous local effort was the Cincinnati Grand Orchestra, sometimes known more simply as the Cincinnati Orchestra, founded in 1872 even
as the May Festival was being planned for the following spring. The success of
the festival and Thomas's repeated visits with his orchestra notwithstanding,

4 · On Thomas, see Philip Hart, *Orpheus in the New World* (1973), chap. 2; Theodore Thomas,
Theodore Thomas: A Musical Autobiography (1905); Rose Fay Thomas, *Memoirs of Theodore Thomas* (1911); Charles Edward Russell, *The American Orchestra and Theodore Thomas*
(1927); Ezra Schabas, *Theodore Thomas: America's Conductor and Builder of Orchestras, 1835–
1905* (1989); Joseph Horowitz, *Classical Music in America* (2005), 32–37, 163–71. Also see
chapter V.2 in this volume.
5 · Thomas conducted every May Festival through 1904. For an overview, see Karen Ahlquist,
"Musical Assimilation and 'the German Element' at the Cincinnati Sängerfest, 1879" (*Musical Quarterly* 94 [2011]: 389–90).
6 · See Karen Ahlquist, "Playing for the Big Time: Musicians, Concerts, and Reputation-
Building in Cincinnati, 1872–82," *Journal of the Gilded Age and the Progressive Era* 9 (2010).
7 · "Theodore Thomas," *Scribner's Monthly* 9, no. 4 (February 1875). New York had held a
large festival in 1873 under immigrant conductor Leopold Damrosch. The chorus was the
Boston Handel and Haydn Society. The English choral festival tradition dates from the Three
Choirs Festival, founded about 1715.

the Cincinnati Orchestra presented a subscription series from 1872 to 1878 of five or six concerts per season under the management of Louis Ballenberg, a local flutist with strong entrepreneurial interests. Born in Hamburg in 1840 and a Cincinnati resident from 1854 on, Ballenberg began his career as a cigar salesman while playing in the orchestra at Pike's Opera House. By 1880 he had given up cigars, listed himself in the city directory as a musician, and in 1881 became manager of Pike's itself.[8]

The conductor of the Cincinnati Grand Orchestra for most of the 1870s and 1880s was Michael Brand (1849–1904). Born in New York into a German-speaking musician family and raised in Cincinnati, Brand played stringed instruments and trumpet, but was primarily a cellist. As a young man, he lived in New York, studied with conductor Carl Anschütz, and played in the Thomas Orchestra.[9] Decades later, a Cincinnati journalist could still quip, "When Thomas wants a good, first-class 'cellist he telegraphs for Mr. Brand."[10] The players were local musicians, European- and American-born, who played in the theaters, hotels, beer gardens, and other venues and taught music. Organizing concerts on their own initiative, Ballenberg and Brand created a management alternative to the city's elites, who set up and supported the May Festival, and to Thomas and his New York–based orchestra. They and their players publicly worked through problems of venue (especially size), range of repertory, standards of performance quality, audience, and especially financial backing that could increase the possibility of a concert-giving orchestra's success. In so doing, they kept the name "Cincinnati Orchestra" in front of the public for a generation. Indeed, the long-term existence of a group of musicians under this name behooves us to see them not as one of a list of predecessors of the CSO of 1894 but as a well-known and integral part of the same ongoing urban musical life.

The May Festival's successes in 1875 and 1878, however, undermined the local orchestra's efforts. Simply put, Cincinnati in the 1870s lacked enough strong players to offer the enormous, spectacular, and expensive performances of a large repertory, including premieres, that the festivals offered. The national publicity that the May Festival received encouraged replication of the same model: weeklong, locally organized festivals performed by local choral singers, local and imported vocal soloists, and an orchestra made

8 · Cincinnati city directories, 1879–81, available at http://virtuallibrary.cincinnatilibrary .org/VirtualLibrary/vl_CityDir.aspx; obituary, *Cincinnati Enquirer*, May 30, 1908, 8; Joseph E. Holliday, "Notes on Samuel N. Pike and His Opera House," *Bulletin of the Cincinnati Historical Society* 25 (1967): 176.
9 · United States Census, 1870; obituary, *Cincinnati Enquirer*, August 5, 1904.
10 · *Cincinnati Times-Star*, May 8, 1890, 3.

up largely of instrumentalists brought in from elsewhere. Indeed, by 1882, Thomas's orchestra, traveling soloists, and local choruses offered May Festivals with overlapping repertory over the course of the month in New York, Chicago, and Cincinnati. Cincinnati's purported uniqueness as a musical city was undermined by the capacity of other cities to do the same thing and do it at least as well.[11]

The idea of concert series performed by a local orchestra had taken hold, however, and the absence of local players from the orchestra of the 1878 May Festival annoyed many Cincinnatians.[12] Among the annoyed was the ambitious George Ward Nichols, president of the College of Music, which was then in the planning stages. Nichols enticed Thomas to drop most of his New York engagements and move to Cincinnati with his family by offering to "widen the school so as to make it a school for orchestra."[13] In October 1878 the college's board of directors issued a circular announcing an ambitious series of twelve programs of a "new Thomas Orchestra, ... composed of the best musicians in Cincinnati, including the professors at the head of the various string departments in the college."[14] According to a review in the *Cincinnati Gazette*, the audience at the first concert recognized many of the musicians "as the same who for the past five years, under difficulties and discouragements at times, had held together, and had given many pleasing entertainments" as the Cincinnati Grand Orchestra.[15] Neither of the orchestra's two seasons was successful, however, and the second was criticized in the press for inferior performance quality. Before this season had been completed, Thomas left his College of Music post in a widely reported dispute with Nichols and returned to New York.[16] The college dropped orchestra concerts from its agenda, and instead, from 1881 to 1884, it mounted an opera festival. The performances featured international stars on tour, accompanied (like the May Festivals) by a traveling orchestra supplemented by

11 · Ahlquist, "Playing for the Big Time," 161–63.

12 · Ibid., 156–57.

13 · George Ward Nichols to Theodore Thomas, quoted without date in Schabas, *Theodore Thomas*, 88.

14 · Quoted in the *Cincinnati Gazette*, October 19, 1878, 10. See also A. Howard Hinkle, "History of Orchestras in Cincinnati," *[Church's] Musical Visitor*, February 1895, 40.

15 · *Cincinnati Gazette*, November 8, 1878. The author was probably Henry E. Krehbiel, later a distinguished critic in New York.

16 · The quarrel received front-page press attention and commentary nationwide. For summaries, see the pamphlet issued by the College of Music, "Correspondence Connected with the Withdrawal of Mr. Theodore Thomas from the College of Music of Cincinnati" (1880); Schabas, *Theodore Thomas*, 97–101; Michael C. Cahall, "Battle on Mount Olympus: The Nichols-Thomas Controversy at the College of Music of Cincinnati," *Queen City History* 53 (1995); Vitz, *Queen and the Arts*, 112–17.

forty-two local instrumentalists.[17] As in the May Festivals, Cincinnati's top musicians had the opportunity to play in high-quality performances of significant repertory, but unlike the Cincinnati Orchestra, under nonmusician management.

Meanwhile, as the 1880s progressed, a sharp economic downturn, growing class divisions, political upheavals that established machine government in Cincinnati, and labor unrest preoccupied local political leadership.[18] From 1878 to 1884, the city's major employers replaced much of their support of cultural institutions, such as the Musical Festival Association, Music Hall, the College of Music, and the Art Museum, with participation in reform groups such as the Good Government Club, the Civil Service Reform Association, and the Committee of 100.[19] Cincinnati's largest musical contributor, Reuben Springer, who had built Music Hall and underwritten much of the May Festival and the College of Music, died in 1884. The college opera festival died with its founder, College of Music president George Ward Nichols, in 1885. The goal of attaining national prestige through cultural achievement grew more marginal in the city.

Under such conditions it was not clear how (or even whether) Cincinnati would support regular orchestra concerts performed by local musicians. At the opening of the college orchestral concerts under Thomas in 1878, the local music periodical, *Church's Musical Visitor*, reported, "The Cincinnati Orchestra will not disband. It will continue to exist as a separate organization entirely distinct from the College of Music band under Mr. Thomas."[20] And, indeed, the orchestra did not disband: even as the college opera festivals headlined the city's musical efforts, local musicians under Ballenberg solicited subscriptions for a series of classical orchestral concerts at Pike's Opera House. An attempt in 1880 supported by the Cincinnati Musical Club failed for lack of the required seven hundred subscriptions at $5 each. Ballenberg's independently proposed seasons in 1882 and 1883 also failed for lack of subscribers.[21]

17 · The players are listed in the *Cincinnati Enquirer*, February 12, 1881. For details on the opera festivals, see Ahlquist, "Playing for the Big Time," 159–61, and Joseph E. Holliday, "Cincinnati Opera Festivals during the Gilded Age," *Bulletin of the Cincinnati Historical Society* 24 (1966).

18 · Steven J. Ross, *Workers On the Edge: Work, Leisure, and Politics in Industrializing Cincinnati, 1788–1890* (1985), 240–42, 252 (on unions); Zane L. Miller, *Boss Cox's Cincinnati: Urban Politics in the Progressive Era* (1968).

19 · Jeffrey Haydu, "Business Citizenship at Work: Cultural Transposition and Class Formation in Cincinnati, 1870-1910," *American Journal of Sociology* 107 (2002). Note especially the table of organizations on page 1447.

20 · *Church's Musical Visitor*, November 1878.

21 · Letter from Louis Ballenberg and Michael Brand to Lucien Wulsin, October 8, 1880, in Wulsin Family Papers, series 1, box 23, folder 8, Cincinnati Historical Society Library (here-

The year 1884 appeared more promising. Peter Neff, a College of Music board member (and later president of the college, following the death of Nichols), and Lucien Wulsin of Baldwin Piano proposed a Cincinnati Philharmonic with a new organizational structure—a cooperative modeled on the New York Philharmonic.[22] Neff even contributed $50,000 of his personal fortune to the organization. A newspaper account lists forty-five players who signed an agreement to form the orchestra: fifteen were veterans of the 1872 Cincinnati Orchestra (Brand and Ballenberg among them), and others were new college faculty members or young musicians who had grown up in the city.[23] Table II.3.1 shows the Philharmonic of 1884 in the context of a succession of Cincinnati concert orchestras.

The Philharmonic's first performance opened the college's new hall, the Odeon, which seated about fifteen hundred people, a sharp contrast to the cavernous Music Hall.[24] The conductor was Henry Schradieck, a longtime violinist in the Leipzig Gewandhaus and a new resident of Cincinnati. Schradieck led a program of familiar works: Weber's *Euryanthe* overture, Mendelssohn's G Minor Piano Concerto, and a "master-piece of the immortal Beethoven," Symphony no. 7.[25] The remainder of the Philharmonic's subscription concerts were led by Michael Brand, elected by the musicians. Reviews called the performances "unequal [i.e., uneven], . . . at times admirably clear and poetic, then suddenly lapsing into crudity."[26] In 1885 the players elected Schradieck and violist John Broekhoven as codirectors over Brand, whose partisans threatened to leave the orchestra.[27]

A year later, the members returned Brand to the conductorship of the Philharmonic in a split vote against Schradieck, which probably led to the college's establishment in 1886 of its own orchestra, made up of "the forces

after CHS); *Cincinnati Commercial*, April 30, 1882; Thomas, "History of the Cincinnati Symphony Orchestra," 71–72.

22 · *Cincinnati Enquirer*, October 25, 1885, 12; undated letter from Henry E. Krehbiel to Lucien Wulsin, Wulsin Family Papers, series 1, box 22, folder 1, CHS, quoted in Thomas, "History of the Cincinnati Symphony Orchestra," 79.

23 · *Cincinnati Enquirer*, July 1, 1884.

24 · *Cincinnati Commercial Gazette*, October 26, 1884, 13. On the Odeon, see Anne W. Baxter, "Showplace of Central Parkway: The College of Music Administration Building," *Queen City Heritage* 57 (1999). The Philharmonic paid rent to the college for use of the Odeon (receipts, 1884, Wulsin Family Papers, series 1, box 23, CHS).

25 · *Cincinnati Commercial Gazette*, October 26, 1885, 3; October 28, 1885, 5.

26 · *Courier* [College of Music of Cincinnati] 3, whole no. 31 (September 1884), 472–73. See also no. 33 (November 1884), 505; no. 34 (December 1884), 519; no. 37 (March 1885), 566; 4 whole no. 41 (July 1885), 633.

27 · *Courier* 4, whole no. 42 (August 1885), 643, excerpted in the *Cincinnati Commercial Gazette*, August 16, 1885, 13.

TABLE II.3.1. Cincinnati concert orchestras to 1894

Seasons	Name(s)	Conductor(s)	Number of players	Management or sponsorship	Remarks
1856	Philharmonic I	Frederic Ritter, Carl Barus	26	Self-managed	
1872–ca. 93	Cincinnati [Grand] Orchestra	George Brand[a], Michael Brand	25–70	Louis Ballenberg as enterprise orchestra	Subscription series 1872–78
1873–to date	Cincinnati May Festival	Theodore Thomas through 1904	90–190	Cincinnati Musical Festival Association	Subsequently held in 1875, 1878, then biennially, then annually from 1967
1878–80	College of Music Orchestra I a.k.a. Thomas Orchestra	Theodore Thomas	Unknown	College of Music	Thomas withdrew
1882, 83	Attempted subscription series	Michael Brand	Unknown	Ballenberg	Canceled for lack of subscriptions
1884–86	Philharmonic II	Henry Schradieck, John Broekhoven, Michael Brand	48–58	Independent cooperative	Usurped by College Orchestra II
1886–88	College of Music Orchestra II	Schradieck	Unknown	College of Music	College withdrew
1888–fall 1890	Cincinnati Orchestra "pops" and symphonic concerts	Brand	ca. 60	Ballenberg	Ballenberg withdrew in December 1890
1890–95	Cincinnati Orchestra Company[b]	Brand	ca. 60	Brand	Mostly pops in Music Hall
1894–to date	Cincinnati Symphony Orchestra	Frank Van der Stucken	56 in first season	CSO board drawn from membership of Ladies Musical Club	Concerts from January 1895

a. George Brand conducted the first season only.

b. Ballenberg retained the rights to the name "Cincinnati Orchestra."

of the College" and "the best orchestral players in the city."[28] The new orchestra led to the prompt demise of the Philharmonic, which received no college funding. Whereas the Philharmonic management had included musicians, the College of Music's General Committee of Arrangements comprised mainly nonperformers, including Peter Neff, music publisher John Church, newspaper publisher Charles P. Taft, Lucien Wulsin (as treasurer),

28 · *Cincinnati Commercial Gazette,* June 19, 1886, 4; *Courier* 6, whole no. 54 (August 1886), 93.

and others. The fifty-eight-member ensemble included advanced string students as a means of training future professional orchestral players, which, the college asserted, made the concerts essential to its educational mission.[29] Seeing college sponsorship as offering the orchestra "a solid pedestal upon which to ... do whatsoever it will in the service of high art," the ever-optimistic College of Music *Courier* claimed that "Cincinnati has a good percentage of art-enthusiasts who feel and value the fascinations of grand abstract music"—that is, symphonies and other large works for orchestra only.[30] Nevertheless, after only two seasons (1886–87 and 1887–88) with indifferent attendance, the college bowed out, again leaving the city without an orchestral concert series. In abandoning its attempt to underwrite an orchestra, the college alluded to the discipline problems that can come from working with part-time players: "[The college] had no controlling influence over the musicians, who came and went as they saw fit, appearing, however, with commendable promptitude on salary day." In short, "it has no contingent Higginson"—the Boston Symphony Orchestra's founder serving as a euphemism for an endowment. [31]

The lack of an endowment did not deter the players, however. Even as the Philharmonic and the College of Music orchestras were failing, the Cincinnati (sometimes "Grand") Orchestra maintained its musical presence—and its name—well into the 1890s. When an ensemble was needed for a variety of musical tasks, Brand and his "band" were close by and ready to take the job. From 1885 on, manager Ballenberg—by now thought of as "our veteran impresario"—kept an office at John Church's publishing house and music store while still managing Pike's Opera House.[32] Engagements such as summer performances at the city's hilltop "resorts" that surrounded the riverfront downtown, concerts at the zoo, and ceremonial and entertainment performances at most of the Cincinnati Industrial Expositions were awarded by contract.[33] Long engagements, such as summer concerts series, offered the players reliable, if temporary, income, keeping the orchestra together at home, much as Thomas's engagements did on the road.

A typical summer program offered a full evening of music with two intermissions, allowing patrons to obtain refreshments, socialize, and enjoy the

29 · *Courier* 6, whole no. 55 (September 1886), 105–6.
30 · *Courier* 7, whole no. 57 (October 1886), 140; season announcement flyer, Wulsin Family Papers, series 1, box 23, CHS.
31 · *Courier*, n.s. 3, no. 1 (November 1888), 10.
32 · *Cincinnati Commercial Gazette*, March 15, 1885; Cincinnati city directory, 1885.
33 · *Cincinnati Commercial Gazette*, April 24, 1887, 14; *Cincinnati Times-Star*, September 2, 1889, 8.

view. As with Theodore Thomas's three-part summer programs in Cincinnati and elsewhere, the second section offered the most challenging music, including a full symphony and often a piece for strings alone. The program opened with an often-played overture by Beethoven, Weber, or Mendelssohn, sometimes included music by an orchestra member, and ended with a galop or a waltz by Johann Strauss Jr.

Although Brand's ensemble was sometimes billed as the Cincinnati Orchestra Reed Band, many, if not all, of the players were undoubtedly the same regardless of the instrumentation: instrumentalists at the time were expected to be "double-handed," that is, proficient on both strings and winds.[34] For example, an 1899 union directory lists five members of the Brand family playing both violin and a wind or percussion instrument and two well-regarded oboists also playing violin.[35] The orchestra's summer activities were understood as lighter fare than symphonic concerts but were respected nonetheless; as a newspaper editorialized in 1887, "From a musical and critical standpoint the utmost satisfaction will be generally entertained if the [summer] contract is awarded by the city Board of Public Affairs to that orchestra bearing the title of our own city [i.e., the Cincinnati Orchestra], the musical reputation of which it has enhanced for so many years."[36]

Perhaps the most surprising Cincinnati Orchestra activity was a large amount of travel, evidence of its strong regional reputation and its place in a broad musical network. As early as 1880, the orchestra performed in Chicago's McCormick Hall.[37] In 1883 it spent the summer at New York's Brighton Beach rather than on Cincinnati's hilltops. In November 1885, it served as the orchestra at the inaugural music festival for the new concert hall in Cleveland.[38] At this event, its role was exactly the same as that of the Thomas Orchestra at the Cincinnati May Festival—providing a reliable orchestra for choral accompaniment and independent instrumental performance. The following spring it returned to Cleveland for that city's May Festival, performing Berlioz's *Damnation of Faust* and other works, with Brand conducting all of the nonvocal music.[39] During the 1885–87 seasons, the Cincinnati Orchestra performed at festivals in Nashville, Tennessee; Dayton, Ohio; Springfield,

34 · See Raoul Camus, "Bands" in *New Grove Dictionary of American Music* (1986).

35 · *Directory of the Cincinnati Musicians' Protective Association No. 1 A.F. of M. No. 1* (1899), 26–34. Michael Brand led the Grand Opera House orchestra from the first violin seat.

36 · *Cincinnati Commercial Gazette*, April 24, 1887, 14. The article states that the concerts were supported by an endowment.

37 · *Cincinnati Gazette*, August 21, 1880.

38 · *Cleveland Press*, November 10 and 11, 1885, 1; *New York Times*, November 10, 1885, 1.

39 · *Cleveland Plain Dealer*, May 9, 1886, 3; May 13, 1886, 8; May 14, 1886, 8.

Ohio; and Columbus, Ohio (the last a German Saengerfest, probably one of
several the orchestra played).[40] Remarkably, the 1886–87 season's travel took
place without Brand, who spent two years in the New York Philharmonic
under Thomas, appearing in Cincinnati as principal cellist of the May Festival orchestra in 1888.[41] As late as 1893, under Brand and the name "Cincinnati Orchestra Company," it was the only non-Chicago ensemble engaged
for the Chicago World's Columbian Exposition's entire six-month run, giving
two free concerts daily except Sunday.[42] Press reports made these activities
known to Cincinnati's residents.

The local orchestra was also understood as essential for important ceremonies and notable events. In 1888 the Cincinnati Orchestra—not the
New York–based Thomas musicians—joined the May Festival Chorus at
the opening ceremony of the Centennial Exposition to celebrate the city's
founding in 1788. A ten-year-old girl "stepped to the side of the stage, and
pressing an electric button, gave 12 signals on the gong and put in motion the
ponderous machinery of the Exposition"; cheers and the "Hallelujah Chorus" followed.[43] Throughout the exposition, the Cincinnati Orchestra, often
as a reed band (still led by Brand), performed regularly at Music Hall, itself
part of the exposition grounds.[44] In 1889 the orchestra performed at an elaborate celebration honoring Cincinnati's distinguished rabbi Isaac Mayer Wise
at the Plum Street Temple. The press described two pieces for chorus and orchestra composed for the occasion along with music by Meyerbeer, Rossini,
Handel, and Weber liberally placed among the speeches and presentations.[45]

Despite the Cincinnati Orchestra's performance opportunities and its
regional notoriety, however, locally produced formal concerts were lacking after the College of Music orchestra failed in 1888 (table II.3.1). That fall,

40 · *Cincinnati Commercial*, April 4, 1883; *Cincinnati Commercial Gazette*, November 8, December 20, 1885; January 24, March 28, May 13, May 14, May 30, 1886; July 28, 1887; [*Church's*]
Musical Visitor, January, February, April, June 1886; March 1887. Brand was in Cincinnati in
the summer of 1887 and may have performed at the Saengerfest in July.

41 · [*Church's*] *Musical Visitor*, May 1886; *Cincinnati Commercial Gazette*, August 21, 1887;
May 16, 1988; New York Philharmonic and May Festival programs, 1888, New York Philharmonic Archives and Cincinnati Historical Society.

42 · Sandy R. Mazzola, "Bands and Orchestras at the World's Columbian Exposition,"
American Music 4 (1986): 415.

43 · *New York Times*, July 5, 1888, 5.

44 · Ballenberg was the impresario for the orchestra's engagement and presented the music
and entertainment committee with afternoon and evening concert programs. Newspapers
published concert programs in advance; see, for example, *Cincinnati Commercial Gazette*,
July 6, 1888, 5.

45 · *Cincinnati Enquirer*, April 7, 1889, 12; *Cincinnati Commercial Gazette*, April 7, 1889, 15;
New York Times, April 7, 1889, 2.

Ballenberg stepped in again as entrepreneur, offering "people's popular concerts" by the Cincinnati Orchestra in Music Hall and adding well-attended
symphonic programs at the Odeon in 1889.[46] Having promised to include
music by American composers, Ballenberg opened the five-concert symphonic series with George Whitefield Chadwick's Symphony No. 2.[47] For the
popular concerts, employers (notably brewers) bought hundreds of transfer-
able season ticket books for employees, while traditional supporters of symphonic music bought books in smaller numbers.[48] The "pops" were said to
be modeled on popularly priced concerts at London's Covent Garden Opera
House. That is, they were not expected to consist of an entirely different repertory of "popular" music but rather a mixture of "classical" and "popular"
selections, presented in casual surroundings as "music for the people." "Think
a popular audience can't enjoy a concerto?" gushed the *Cincinnati Times-Star*
after a performance of Liszt's Piano Concerto in E-flat.[49]

Indeed, the concerts were successful. However, in the fall of 1890 Ballenberg moved them to the smaller Pike's Opera House, raised prices, and
enjoined the orchestra to perform a "higher class" of music. The change
quickly proved a financial failure. In December Ballenberg withdrew from
the orchestra's management, breaking his long professional relationship with
Brand. The orchestra quickly reorganized under its own management and
was performing again under Brand by January.[50] The popular Sunday concerts featured the usual blend of Strauss waltzes, overtures by Beethoven
or Weber, and newer music, sometimes by local artists. They also featured
prominent soloists; for example, in January 1891, violinist Maud Powell and
contralto Olive Fremstadt performed on consecutive Sundays.[51] The Sunday concerts were underwritten by Frank Tuchfarber, who ran a successful
chromolithography company, allowing Brand to make good on a promise to
pay the musicians promptly, which Ballenberg had not always been able to
do.[52] As a reporter noted, however, "[The ensemble] is the same old Cincinnati Orchestra."[53] The word "old" here appropriate; there had been a Cin-

46 · *Cincinnati Commercial Gazette*, December 2, 1888; *Cincinnati Times-Star*, October 14,
1889, 8; October 19, 1889, 5; November 14, 1889; November 15, 1889; Thomas, "History of the
Cincinnati Orchestra," 86–90.
47 · *Cincinnati Times-Star*, November 14, 1889.
48 · *Courier* 5, no. 1 (October 2, 1890); *Cincinnati Commercial Gazette*, October 10, 1891, 14.
49 · *Cincinnati Times-Star*, October 2, 1889, 3.
50 · *Cincinnati Enquirer*, December 30, 1890, 8; January 3, 1891, 8. The January article asserts
that a group of classical music admirers persuaded Ballenberg to make the change.
51 · *Cincinnati Times-Star*, January 16, 17, 18, and 25, 1891.
52 · Ibid., December 6, 1890, 2; January 3, 1891, 8; January 8, 1891, 8. Tuchfarber was still supporting the concerts in 1894; see the *Cincinnati Times-Star*, April 13 and 24, 1894.
53 · *Cincinnati Times-Star*, January 17, 1891.

cinnati Orchestra under Ballenberg, Brand, or most often both for nearly twenty years.

From the mid-1880s, then, Cincinnati audiences heard three local orchestral organizations with three names: the Cincinnati Philharmonic, the College of Music Orchestra, and the Cincinnati Orchestra. Among them, these ensembles performed every function expected of an orchestra except theatrical and operatic accompaniment. The Philharmonic and the College of Music Orchestra had at least twenty-eight players in common.[54] Overlapping membership with the Cincinnati Orchestra cannot be ascertained because there seem to be no Cincinnati Orchestra rosters after 1878. So, for example, when Brand was ousted as Philharmonic conductor in 1885 and apparently left the orchestra, we do not know whether "his" players left with him as they threatened to do or remained in both the Cincinnati Orchestra and the Philharmonic. We do know, however, that the Cincinnati Orchestra was advertised in Cleveland as comprising seventy members, along with four nonmembers (all College of Music faculty) identified by name.[55] Furthermore, the College of Music Orchestra's flutist was Louis Ballenberg, the Cincinnati Orchestra's manager, a fact that suggests that personnel may have overlapped extensively among the three ensembles. Hidden under the perception of false starts, conflict, and failure was an ongoing concert orchestra in Cincinnati, made up of many of the same musicians and appealing to many of the same audiences.

The Cincinnati Orchestra's activity notwithstanding, its tenuous financial condition kept the idea of a "permanent" orchestra in front of the public. In 1885 the *Cincinnati Enquirer* insisted that "a permanent orchestra long [had] been and [was] a crying necessity, ... [despite] the indomitable pluck and almost more than mortal patience of Mr. Ballenberg, whom the credit of keeping it together is undoubtedly due."[56] The frustration of this writer was undoubtedly fed by the increased numbers of visits from out-of-town orchestras. Thomas's ensemble, which had performed in Cincinnati intermittently since 1869, came in even-numbered years for the May Festival, and in 1883 and 1885 for smaller, three-concert festivals run by his steadfast local supporters, the Festival Association. In 1888 it played a "summer nights" season with a fifty-six-member ensemble "identical with Mr. Thomas' orchestra during the past season in New York City."[57] Thomas also came for *Messiah* performances in 1889, and in 1891 he appeared twice with his new "Theodore

54 · Thomas, "History of the Cincinnati Symphony Orchestra," appendix 2, 737–44. Thomas does not provide complete rosters.

55 · *Cleveland Plain Dealer*, May 9, 1886, 3.

56 · *Cincinnati Enquirer*, October 25, 1885.

57 · Letter from Milward Adams, summer night concert manager, to Louis Ballenberg, April 18, 1888, Centennial Exposition of the Ohio Valley, Mss 684, box 8, CHS.

Thomas Chicago Orchestra" [i.e., the Chicago Symphony].[58] These visits elicited calls for a reliable Cincinnati equivalent. Thomas's star in Cincinnati had fallen precipitously in the 1880s, fed by assertions of his lack of interest in the May Festival, his alleged ill-treatment of the festival chorus, and his refusal to use more than a token number of local players to supplement his traveling orchestra. Perhaps most important, the press complained about the money that went to Thomas and his New York players instead of helping Cincinnatians make progress on their own. "The common sense position [is] that the growth of home music must come through the stimulation of innate force and vitality," wrote one commentator in 1886, "not from the borrowed strength of exotics."[59] Indeed, by this time it was becoming clear that the city's "serious" musical life need no longer depend on Theodore Thomas. A reporter's assertion in 1889 that "the orchestra that Theodore Thomas had here last was in no essential sense the superior of our own Cincinnati orchestra" may have not been literally accurate, but increasing amounts of listening experience were helping music lovers consider such statements on the basis of their own knowledge.[60]

Thomas was old hat; the Boston Symphony was not. Cincinnatians heard the sixty-member orchestra at the College of Music's Odeon in 1886, 1887, and thereafter every year from 1889 to 1894.[61] The orchestra's opening program offered a largely familiar and comparatively unthreatening repertory of music by Weber, Beethoven (Fifth Symphony), Robert Schumann (piano concerto), Max Bruch (violin concerto), and Edvard Grieg, among others.[62] It also presented yet another orchestra model—identified with a city rather than an individual leader such as Thomas and steeped in a rapidly canonizing repertory from the past at the expense of new and "radical" works by composers such as Wagner and Liszt, whose music Thomas favored. This model appeared attainable to Cincinnatians, because pieces by Beethoven, Schumann, and others, which did not require large numbers of wind and brass instruments, had been played successfully for at least two decades by the city's own musicians.

58 · *Cincinnati Times-Star*, August 24, October 8, and October 30, 1889; March 1 and December 30, 1892; January 6, 1893. Cincinnati native Julia Rivé-King was piano soloist in these Chicago Symphony concerts.

59 · *Cincinnati Commercial Gazette*, June 27, 1886. See also ibid., May 26, 1886.

60 · *Cincinnati Times-Star*, December 14, 1889.

61 · Ibid., May 14 and 15, 1889; January 24, May 11, December 15, 1891; January 11, May 6, 1892; April 13, May 1, 8, 11, and 12, 1893; *Cincinnati Commercial Gazette*, May 15, 1889, May 7, 1890, May 12, 1891; *Cincinnati Enquirer*, May 8, 1890. Ballenberg managed the Boston Symphony Orchestra's 1891 engagement.

62 · *Cincinnati Commercial Gazette*, April 17, 1886, 8; *Courier* 5, whole no. 51 (May 1886): 51; *Cincinnati Enquirer*, May 8, 1891, 4.

Cincinnatians quickly took note of the Boston Symphony Orchestra as a model for a "permanent" orchestra in an American city. Reviewers offered detailed praise of performances of familiar repertory, equated high-quality performance with adequate rehearsal time, saw a need to free players from nonsymphonic employment, and sometimes called for a Cincinnati equivalent of Boston's Henry Lee Higginson to "provide an endowment fund for a permanent orchestra, who shall have no other aim than that of perfecting themselves in ensemble playing."[63] In 1890 Higginson even made headlines: "CINCINNATI'S HIGGINSON, IT SEEMS HE IS YET TO BE DISCOVERED. Badly Wanted to Build Up a Great Orchestra."[64] Compared to the Thomas model of an orchestra that was ongoing but obliged to tour nationally in order to offer its musicians full employment, the Boston Symphony Orchestra model seemed to offer Cincinnati the possibility of an orchestra that was both permanent and local—if only a local Higginson could be discovered.

The number and variety of outside orchestras that played in Cincinnati continued to grow in the 1890s, and the World's Columbian Exposition in 1893 brought orchestras on their way to or from Chicago. In addition to the Boston Symphony, Walter Damrosch's New York Symphony appeared in 1892 and 1893, and the Metropolitan Opera Orchestra performed an all-Wagner program in 1893. What Cincinnati had been able to provide locally, however, was something less. The results of the end of the Ballenberg-Brand partnership were evident by the fall of 1892, when the Cincinnati Orchestra Company string ensemble (Brand's group) performed on Sunday afternoons, while a Bellstedt-Ballenberg "military" band offered biweekly concerts on Sunday evenings, both at Music Hall.[65] The existence of the two ensembles testified to the breadth of the orchestral talent base in Cincinnati. Nevertheless, it remained clear that this city, which had long prided itself on its cultural achievements, needed an energetic, broad-based, and sustained effort to harness that talent. Cincinnati's Higginson, it was by now apparent, did not exist.

That energy came from a new quarter. A group of upper-class women headed by Helen Herron Taft (Mrs. William Howard Taft) organized themselves as the board of the Cincinnati Symphony Orchestra in 1894. All were members of the Ladies Musical Club, founded in 1891 for the education of its members and the improvement of Cincinnati's musical life. That a group of woman suddenly assumed leadership of Cincinnati's orchestral activities may seem astonishing; however, female members of Cincinnati's elite had

63 · *Cincinnati Commercial Gazette*, April 26, 1887.
64 · *Cincinnati Times-Star*, November 29, 1890.
65 · *Courier*, November 1892, 10. See also the *Cincinnati Times-Star*, September 24, October 23, 1892.

been successfully managing artistic enterprises at least since their locally publicized contributions to the Women's Building at the Philadelphia Centennial Exhibition of 1876 and the founding of Rookwood Pottery by Maria Longworth Nichols (wife of George Ward Nichols) in 1880. Female artistic activity was not unique to Cincinnati, although it was more prominent there than in some other cities. Historian Karen Blair explains how the extensive network of female arts clubs after 1890 created "an invisible amateur arts subculture whose members were serious and knowledgeable but invisible and incapable of challenging the powerful mainstream."[66] By redefining their traditional roles as keepers of home and family to include whole communities, Blair argues, women's clubs could realize ambitious projects, such as the CSO, that challenged their skills and created leadership roles in support of the mainstream as they defined it.

The Cincinnati women fit Blair's model, except that they were far from invisible. Within two years of its founding, their club had managed tour performances by eminent classical music artists and groups as large as the Boston Symphony Orchestra. It was evident to all the involved parties, male and female, that these women had the management experience and will to succeed sufficient to take on yet another attempt at a permanent orchestra in Cincinnati.[67] As Cincinnati cultural historian Robert Vitz summarizes, "The [Ladies Musical] club provided a new network of relationships that in large part bypassed the male-dominated connections which had entangled previous efforts, and through this network the club tapped the city's deep, latent musical energies in a new way."[68]

In January 1895, the CSO performed its debut concert in Pike's Opera House (still under Ballenberg's management). The season consisted of nine concerts under three guest conductors: Henry Schradieck, who after leaving Cincinnati in 1888 had spent several years in Europe; the well-known Wagner advocate Anton Seidl; and Texas-born, European-educated Frank Van der Stucken. With Seidl not interested in the position of director, Van der Stucken quickly became the board's favorite. Appointed music director in 1895, he served until 1907.[69] The orchestra's first *assistant* conductor and principal cellist was Michael Brand, who had withdrawn from consideration

66 · Karen J. Blair, *The Torchbearers: Women and Their Amateur Arts Associations in America, 1890–1930* (1994), 4. For specifically musical activities among clubwomen, see Linda Whitesitt, "Women as 'Keepers of Culture': Music Clubs, Community Concert Series, and Symphony Orchestras," in *Cultivating Music in America: Women Patrons and Activists since 1860*, ed. R. Locke and C. Barr (1997).

67 · Thomas, "History of the Cincinnati Symphony Orchestra," 99.

68 · Vitz, *Queen and the Arts*, 126.

69 · Ibid., 129–30.

as music director.[70] The original roster included forty-nine local players, including twenty-eight from the Philharmonic of 1884 but only four from the original Cincinnati Orchestra of 1872.[71] Many of these players had performed under Thomas at festivals in Cincinnati, Chicago, and New York and in subscription concerts under Thomas's direction in the early 1880s.[72] In addition, seven players were brought from New York. Louis Ballenberg was not a member.

The opening program on January 17, 1895, consisted entirely of well-known music by canonic composers: Mozart's Symphony no. 40; Schumann's Symphony no. 4; overtures by Beethoven and Weber; and vocal pieces by Haydn, Schubert, and Mendelssohn sung by American soprano Lillian Blauvelt.[73] The next day, however, the orchestra performed an all-American program featuring Edward MacDowell performing his Second Piano Concerto.[74] Estimates suggest that concert attendance in 1895 was roughly the same as at past formal concerts of the Cincinnati Orchestra, the College of Music Orchestra, and the Cincinnati Philharmonic, ranging from about five hundred to one thousand.[75]

Like its local predecessors, the Cincinnati Symphony Orchestra was far smaller than the May Festival orchestras, and it performed in Pike's Opera House rather than in the larger Music Hall. It seems that the city had finally managed to match a supply of symphonic series concerts with a realistic assessment of potential demand, rather than try to "civilize" a broad population. The idea of "music for everyone" made a quick return, however. By 1899, Van der Stucken was conducting the CSO in popular concerts—smoking permitted and evening dress not required—in a hotel pavilion outfitted with table seating. Rather than advertising itself as the CSO, for these popular concerts the orchestra was billed as "The Cincinnati Orchestra."[76] In 1905 the CSO was performing symphonic concerts (two performances per program) with soloists such as Fanny Bloomfield Zeisler and Eugene Ysaÿe *and* lighter programs on Sunday afternoons at Music Hall exactly as had been done under Brand and Ballenberg. The popular series offered music by Herbert, Leoncavallo, MacDowell, Beach, Van der Stucken himself, Wag-

70 · *Cincinnati Times-Star*, May 9, 1894.

71 · Thomas, "History of the Cincinnati Symphony Orchestra," 137; roster, 139–41. The Cincinnati Orchestra 1872 roster is given in the *Cincinnati Enquirer*, December 18, 1872.

72 · Ahlquist, "Playing for the Big Time," 161–62.

73 · A facsimile of the program is found in *Cincinnati Symphony Orchestra: Centennial Portraits* (1994), 25.

74 · *Cincinnati Commercial Gazette*, January 19, 1895; *Cincinnati Enquirer*, January 19, 1895.

75 · Thomas, "History of the Cincinnati Symphony Orchestra," 166, 173, from CSO board minutes, May 13, 1895, and the *Cincinnati Commercial Gazette*, November 30, 1895.

76 · Flyer, Ladies Musical Club/Orchestra Association scrapbook, CHS.

ner, Verdi, Brahms, and other well-known modern composers.[77] One can see the connoisseurs being offered larger musical structures and canonized repertory, while those with less sophisticated tastes learned about living composers, including Americans. The Cincinnati Orchestra's approach to its performance—subscription concerts, flexibility in repertory, smaller and varied venues (including informal settings), audience outreach, and eventually touring—set the precedent for the CSO.

With so many similarities between the Cincinnati Orchestra and the CSO, then, why did the CSO succeed in achieving "permanence" where earlier efforts had not? The answer is simple: adequate financial support. Underwriting musical performance with guarantee funds dated from the May Festival; the College of Music orchestra of 1886 had a guarantee fund, as did Brand's popular concerts of the early 1890s.[78] Unlike these organizations, however, the CSO board solicited donations from a broad range of the local population in amounts as small as $5, thereby creating not only financial backing but also a larger number of individuals—potential concertgoers—identified as having a stake in the enterprise.[79] The time and money that the women and their supporters invested in the Cincinnati Symphony Orchestra provided a financial cushion and a level of administrative support that a musician-entrepreneur such as Ballenberg did not have. The CSO board also relieved the College of Music from further involvement in professional orchestra management. And finally, under its independent board, the CSO began to provide an effective artistic and financial counterweight to Theodore Thomas in spite of his support from the May Festival Association and his presence at the festivals through 1904. In so doing, Cincinnati not only established an orchestra but also tacitly displaced the music festival from the center of its musical effort.

Meanwhile, what of the players? One may argue that they kept the idea of a symphony orchestra alive at a time when Cincinnati's civic leaders, preoccupied with social and economic problems from the mid-1880s, lacked the will to sustain new efforts in the area of culture. As professionals, the players wanted to play and, if possible, earn a living, while making satisfying music. The most visible example of the instrumentalist's predicament was undoubtedly Michael Brand. In retrospect he seems to have been a first-rate cellist and an average conductor, but the Cincinnati press presented him repeatedly as an excellent musician stymied by lack of opportunity. "Why is Brand stuck sawing away in a theater orchestra?" a reporter asked rhetorically in 1890. He

77 · *Courier*, n.s. 5/6, March 15, 1905, 6–7.

78 · *Cincinnati Commercial Gazette*, July 13, 1885. The May Festival guarantors were called on to contribute to debt reduction for the first time following the festival of 1884.

79 · The strategy of broadening the orchestra's base of support had been carried out successfully by the Chicago Symphony in 1891–92. See chapter I.1 in this volume.

would be a wonderful conductor and make splendid music if only money could pay for sufficient rehearsal time to achieve high artistic goals. This "if only" underlay the wish for a Higginson to buy that time, a wish that came true not through an individual wealthy benefactor but through dozens of zealous clubwomen with money, energy, commitment, and social capital to spare.

In 1881 the members of the Cincinnati Orchestra, Brand and Ballenberg's ensemble, organized themselves and other local musicians, as the Cincinnati Musical Protective Union. Union activists at the national level as well, they were charter members of the National League of Musicians in 1886, and in 1896 they threw in their lot with organized labor by joining Samuel Gompers's American Federation of Labor as the American Federation of Musicians Local 1.[80] With that action, the players tacitly accepted a division between musical and institutional responsibilities. Now organized to protect their own interests, they left organizing and funding the CSO to civic leaders and nonmusicians. The generation of the 1890s contained no musician-impresario such as Louis Ballenberg. For its part, the orchestra's management came to understand the limits of formal culture as a civic-reputation enhancer in the United States, thereby increasing the possibility of establishing a professional concert orchestra sustainable in proportion to community interest.

Over time, the CSO became a "permanent orchestra"—an ensemble with a regular membership of local professional musicians performing in a locally produced concert series. Yet in important ways, "permanence" could be said to date from 1872. The Cincinnati Orchestra's years of struggle for a place in front of the public gave the players, would-be organizers, and potential audience members a chance to understand what an orchestra had to offer as a musical instrument; a vehicle of artistic presentation and interpretation; a community of performers; and a social, economic, and institutional structure. In particular, the strongest advocates of the orchestra as an exclusively high-art vehicle learned that lightening the repertory on occasion could broaden the audience base and boost the musicians' income by offering them more work, thereby supporting the institution itself. Today's CSO offers outdoor pops concerts and holiday entertainment, as do the Boston Symphony, the National Symphony, and many other major American orchestras. Yet the idea that a single organization could please a broad public while fostering the acceptance of a high-art repertory was not an inevitable development. Rather, it grew from a mutual recognition of the possibilities and practicalities of a broadly significant art.

80 · See chapter I.3 in this volume. Still A.F.M. Local 1, the Cincinnati union is known today as the Cincinnati Musicians Association.

[II.4] Critic and Conductor in 1860s Chicago

George P. Upton, Hans Balatka, and Cultural Capitalism

JAMES DEAVILLE

Music criticism in mid-nineteenth-century America was far from professional, as Mark Grant has shown in his study of music critics in the United States.[1] Orchestra concerts were often reviewed by nonmusician newspaper editors or local musicians, and criticism itself served purposes other than providing expert opinions.[2]

A symbiotic relationship existed between the press and musical institutions in every American city. As an urban center developed, so did the "official" institutions of its musical life: churches, orchestras, music schools, choruses, opera companies, and so on.[3] Accompanying the establishment of these music-cultural entities was the press, which initially functioned as a vehicle for the promotion of the local musical scene by disseminating information about events, the organizations that sponsored them, and the audiences that heard them. Articles about music in the early stages of a city's press often read more like advertisements or society columns than informed musical judgments.[4] Eventually, newspapers began to engage professional music

For their valuable assistance with this chapter, I am indebted to Hilary Shrubb, Mark Clague, E. Douglas Bomberger, Eric Hung, and John Spitzer. I am grateful to the Newberry Library, the Chicago Public Library, and the Chicago Historical Society (now the Chicago History Museum) for access to their valuable holdings.

1 · Mark N. Grant, *Maestros of the Pen: A History of Classical Music Criticism in America* (1998).

2 · For a discussion of the situation in early nineteenth-century Chicago, see James Deaville, "The Origins of Music Journalism in Chicago: Criticism as a Reflection of Music Life," in *American Musical Life in Context and Practice to 1865*, ed. J. Heintze (1993).

3 · Other, less official vehicles for musical expression and entertainment existed, such as taverns and dance halls, which presented an assortment of vernacular musics. Such performances were rarely documented in the press.

4 · This dynamic relationship exists even today, observable in smaller markets where professional levels of musical institutions and music criticism have never emerged, where small

critics—for example, Henry C. Watson (1815–75) in New York and William Foster Apthorp (1848–1913) in Boston—and specialized journals, such as the *Message Bird* (New York), *Dwight's Journal of Music* (Boston), and the *Chicago Musical Review*, highlighted the city's musical activities for a geographically broader audience.

In this symbiotic relationship, the critic and newspaper benefited in turn from what Pierre Bourdieu calls the "symbolic capital" of the "cultural businessman."[5] Bourdieu persuasively argues that "cultural businessmen" add considerable value to works of art:

> Who is the true producer of the value of the work—the painter or the dealer, the writer or the publisher, the playwright or the theatre manager? The ideology of creation ... conceals the fact that the cultural businessman (art dealer, publisher, etc.) is at one and the same time the person who exploits the labour of the "creator" by trading in the "sacred" and the person who, by putting it on the market, by exhibiting, publishing or staging it, consecrates a [cultural] product.... He is the person who can proclaim the value of the author he defends ... and above all "invests his prestige" in the author's cause, acting as a "symbolic banker" who offers as security all the symbolic capital he has accumulated.[6]

If we substitute the words "newspaper" and "critic" for Bourdieu's "theatre" and "manager," we find a compelling argument for the symbiotic relationship between the press and musical institutions. The newspaper and critic accumulate "symbolic capital" (authority and prestige) in the eyes of the public; with this capital they establish and "consecrate" the value of cultural products—works by a composer, concerts by an orchestra, the activities of the conservatory, and the like. In the early years of music criticism in America, this creation and accumulation of cultural capital was a matter not only of personal profit for the newspaper and the critic but also of participation in

community ensembles perform to "lower standards," and press coverage is limited to "puffs" in the weekly neighborhood paper.

5 · Pierre Bourdieu, "The Production of Belief: Contribution to an Economy of Symbolic Goods," in *The Field of Cultural Production*, ed. Randal Johnson (1993), 76. In his essay "Cultural Entrepreneurship in 19th Century Boston: The Creation of an Organizational Base for High Culture in America" (*Media, Culture, and Society* 4 [1982]), Paul DiMaggio invokes Bourdieu's notion of "cultural capital" in discussing the role of "capital" in musical development in one urban cultural context. However, he applies the concept narrowly in the sense of "economic capital" (actual money) rather than Bourdieu's more nuanced identification of "cultural capital" and the symbolic economic relationships embodied therein.

6 · Bourdieu, "Production of Belief," 76–78.

the task of building the city. The pioneering generations of music critics regarded themselves as significant contributors to the progress and prosperity of their communities and the nation.

This chapter is an attempt to apply these principles to the relationship between critics and musical institutions in the emerging cultural landscape of Chicago, a city with a rich set of traditions in its press and musical life.[7] It examines the symbiosis in Chicago during the 1860s between a groundbreaking music critic on the one hand, George P. Upton, and a pioneering conductor, Hans Balatka and his Philharmonic Society, on the other.

In histories of American music, George P. Upton is inextricably linked to the conductor Theodore Thomas.[8] Upton became a fervent Thomas supporter after hearing the conductor's first Chicago concert in 1869; he wrote enthusiastic reviews in the *Chicago Tribune* of the concerts that the visiting Thomas Orchestra played in the 1870s and 1880s; he helped persuade Thomas to relocate to Chicago in 1891; and he edited Thomas's memoirs after the conductor's death.[9] Before 1869, however, Upton was involved in a similarly symbiotic relationship with another conductor, Hans Balatka.

Beginning in 1861, Upton assumed the role of cultural agent for Balatka and his Chicago Philharmonic Society, publishing announcements, commentary, and favorable reviews. In Bourdieu's terms, he "consecrated" and "proclaimed the value" of Balatka, the orchestra, and its concerts. In turn, Balatka and the orchestra increased Upton's cultural capital to the extent that the critic was recognized as having "made" the Philharmonic Society and shaped Chicago taste. The orchestra struggled financially after 1865, and while Upton continued to support the enterprise, he began to adopt a more critical tone. After the collapse of the Philharmonic in 1867, Upton's support for Balatka and his concerts became more guarded. When, in November 1869, Theodore Thomas visited Chicago with his orchestra and played three concerts, Upton proclaimed it "the finest musical event Chicago has ever known," withdrew his support from Balatka, and backed the visiting conductor and ensemble as a model for a successful professional orchestra. In Bourdieu's terms, Upton built up symbolic capital from 1862 to 1867 and invested it in Balatka's prestige. He withdrew that capital from Balatka over the next two years, until the fall of 1869, when he reinvested it in Theodore Thomas.

7 · See Mark Clague, "Chicago Counterpoint: The Auditorium Theater Building and the Civic Imagination" (Ph.D. diss., 2002). See also chapter I.1 in this volume.
8 · See, for example, Joseph A. Mussulman, *Music in the Cultured Generation: A Social History of Music in America, 1870–1900* (1971), 77–79.
9 · Theodore Thomas, *Theodore Thomas: A Musical Autobiography* (1905).

Critic and Conductor

Born near Boston in 1834, George Putnam Upton had no musical education
except what he taught himself, and he is not known to have played any musical instrument.[10] His musical knowledge came mainly from reading and from
concert attendance. Upton did, however, have a good deal of literary ambition and experience. Graduating from Brown University in 1855, he moved
the next year to Chicago, where he was immediately engaged as a local reporter by the *Daily Native Citizen*. He soon moved to the *Chicago Evening
Journal*, where he developed a column that covered the Chicago scene, including entertainment. In November of 1861, Upton took a position at the
Chicago Tribune, the newspaper with which he would be associated for the
rest of his career. He was initially hired as city editor and subsequently became news editor in 1863. As such he was required to cover political events
as well as "amusements" and other cultural "happenings" in Chicago. Despite his many other responsibilities at the *Tribune* (including reports from
the front during the Civil War and a full-length book on the Great Chicago
Fire[11]), Upton consistently wrote the paper's music criticisms throughout his
long career. Beginning in 1867, his reviews appeared in a weekly column, "Letters of Peregrine Pickle," which commented on the city's social and cultural
scene in a light, satirical style that masked Upton's power of consecration.[12]

Upton retired as the *Tribune*'s chief music critic in 1881, but "cultural businessman" that he was, he remained involved in the music-critical scene both
locally and nationally. Locally he was deeply involved in the creation of the
Chicago Symphony and the construction of the Auditorium Theatre (1889)
and Orchestra Hall (1904). He lived long enough (until 1919) to see the fruits
of his investments in Chicago's musical culture grow to maturity. In books
such as *The Standard Symphonies* (1889), *Musical Memories: My Recollections
of Celebrities of the Half Century, 1850–1900* (1908), and *Standard Musical Biographies* (1910), Upton deployed the symbolic capital he had accumulated
over the years in Chicago to speak to a national audience of music lovers.

Hans Balatka was born in Moravia (Hoffnungsthal, near Olmütz, now
Olomouc) and trained as a musician there and in Vienna.[13] Involved in

10 · Upton's life and music criticism are meticulously documented in a dissertation by Mary
Ann Feldman: "George P. Upton: Journalist, Music Critic and Mentor to Early Chicago"
(Ph.D. diss., 1983). On Upton's early life, see pp. 94–100.
11 · James W. Sheahan and George P. Upton, *The Great Conflagration* (1872).
12 · Upton took the character of Peregrine Pickle from Tobias Smollett's novel *The Adven-
tures of Peregrine Pickle* (1751).
13 · Some confusion exists over Balatka's birth date: February 26, 1825, or March 5, 1826, 1827,
or 1828. Sources for the four dates are (in the order as listed above): Thomas H. Schleis, "Ba-

the revolution of 1848, he fled to Hanover and then to the United States in April 1849. Settling in Milwaukee by 1851, Balatka directed the *Musikverein* there for nine years. His performance in 1860 of Mozart's Requiem at the Northwest Saengerfest in Chicago was so successful that several prominent Chicagoans persuaded him to relocate.[14] Balatka became director of the newly formed Philharmonic Society in the fall of 1860, and his first concert with them took place on November 19.[15] He continued as the group's director until its dissolution in 1867 and then led various instrumental and choral ensembles in Chicago (including an orchestra similar to the Philharmonic Society), until the great fire of October 1871, after which he returned to Milwaukee. After sojourns in Milwaukee and St. Louis during the 1870s, the conductor settled again in Chicago and in 1879 established the Balatka Academy of Musical Art (later Balatka Musical College), to which he dedicated the last twenty years of his life.[16] Balatka was in demand as director of many Chicago vocal and instrumental ensembles during the 1860s and again in the 1880s and the 1890s. Karl Merz wrote in *Brainard's Musical World* that "as a director he is a man of force who knows what he is about to do and who goes and does it. We saw Mr. Balatka several times at the head of orchestras, and we at once noticed that ease and surety that distinguishes his wielding the baton. He is a fine disciplinarian of the forces under him."[17] Other commentators felt compelled to qualify their praise of Balatka—they seemed to share a sense that he could have been better. Critic W. S. B. Mathews, who had followed Balatka's career from the 1860s on, commented in an obituary: "[Balatka] was generally at cross purposes with life and his art. Only now and then did he find an adequate place for the exercise of his best talent. He was a musical conductor only a little short of greatness."[18] Balatka died in Chicago on April 17, 1899, four years after having celebrated his fiftieth anniversary as conductor with a "music festival" in the Auditorium Theatre.[19]

latka," *New Grove Dictionary of American Music* (1986); J. J. Schlicher, "Hans Balatka and the Milwaukee Musical Society," *Wisconsin Magazine of History* 27 (1943): 40; Louis C. Elson, *The History of American Music* (1915), 328; and W. S. B. Mathews, ed., *A Hundred Years of Music in America* (1889), 496.

14 · [Karl Merz], "Hans Balatka," in *Brainard's Biographies of American Musicians* (1999), 20.

15 · This was the third and last Chicago Philharmonic Society. See chapter I.1 in this volume.

16 · Francis Cheney Bennett, *History of Music and Art in Illinois* (1904), 50. Under his son Christian's leadership, Balatka's college survived well into the twentieth century.

17 · *Brainard's Biographies*, 21.

18 · W. S. B. Mathews, "Editorial Bric-a-Brac," *Music* 16 (June 1899): 196.

19 · "The Hans Balatka Jubilee," *Chicago Daily Tribune*, March 10, 1895, 12.

Investing in Culture

Chicago, during the 1860s, was in the midst of a tremendous growth spurt, which altered not only the city's urban topography but also its cultural institutions. John S. Wright, writing in 1870, portrayed the work of those engaged in civic development as a moral imperative: "It should be and is our hope and aim, that this young City, made up in large measure of the most active, energetic, enterprising of the older States, should set other cities an example of what may and should be done by these centres of civilization, to improve and elevate humanity."[20] Another civic historian, I. D. Guyer, explained that artistic enterprises were just as important as "bricks and mortar" in this work of improvement and elevation: "One of the most powerful civilizers is Music. . . . Let a community be well supplied with Pianos or Melodeons, and a visitor requires no higher evidence of its high intelligence and excellence. That refined communities prosper, in a material point of view, more than those where the refining influence of music and education are less regarded, is a well-conceded fact."[21] The establishment of Balatka's Philharmonic Society in 1860, the opening of Lyon and Healy's music store in 1864, and the erection of Crosby's Opera House in 1865 were each important steps in making Chicago a prosperous community and center of civilization.

When George P. Upton began working at the *Chicago Tribune* in 1861, Hans Balatka and the Chicago Philharmonic Society were about to begin their second season. In what appears to be his first extended commentary on the orchestra, a preview of the orchestra's upcoming season, Upton emphasizes the orchestra's importance in civic progress: "We claim to be the metropolis of the Northwest — not only in a commercial point of view but as a centre of art and taste and refinement. The establishment of one institution after another has already effected much toward this end, but we look to the success of the Philharmonic Society as adding one of the most substantial and commendable claims to popular favor as well as a most solid and enduring monument to our taste and cultivation."[22] Musical monuments could only endure if they were continually re-created by organizations such as the Philharmonic and validated by opinion, especially as represented by the press. Upton and the *Tribune* gave value to the conductor's and ensemble's work for the citizens of Chicago. At the same time, by convincing the public

---

20 · John S. Wright, *Chicago: Past, Present, Future* (1870), 261.

21 · Isaac D. Guyer, *History of Chicago* (1862), 109.

22 · "The Philharmonic Society," *Chicago Tribune,* November 8, 1861, 4. The article is not signed by Upton. Feldman suggests that Upton wrote a good deal of unsigned criticism in his early years at the *Tribune* ("George P. Upton," 141–42).

of the value of the "cultural goods" offered, Upton laid the foundation for his own accumulation of symbolic capital (i.e., authority as music critic).

Upton covered the third concert of the 1861–62 season with a series of four articles: an announcement of the time, place, program, and personnel (January 16); a detailed analysis of the featured work on the program, Beethoven's Symphony no. 7 (January 17); a description of the other pieces on the program (January 20); and finally a review of the concert itself (January 21). In his preview of "the beautiful and wonderful A-major symphony of Beethoven," Upton promises the audience "the wildest hilarity and most exciting jubilees."[23] Then he establishes his authority by drawing on a recognized and respected source for the Beethoven explanation: *Dwight's Journal of Music*, from which he quotes Richard Wagner's well-known characterization of the last movement as the "very apotheosis of the dance."[24] Thus, Upton draws on New German ideology as conveyed in the national musical press to educate (and impress) the public of the frontier city.[25] In doing so, he anticipated Balatka's (and eventually Thomas's) promotion of Wagner and Liszt in Chicago, where their music would find eager auditors in the following decades.

Upton's next column acquaints the audience with the remainder of the program. In Weber's "Invitation to the Waltz" (orchestrated by Berlioz), listeners can look forward to "a kind of dialogue ... between the violoncellos which may be fancied to represent the gentlemen, and the clarionets the ladies."[26] The critic also assures his readers that the vocal soloist "will make a favourable impression" and that the orchestra "will be larger and more effective than ever before." When he comes at last to review the concert, Upton proclaims that "a large and brilliant audience was in attendance" and proceeds to his juridical duties. He acknowledges that "little defects were of course apparent" in the orchestra, particularly "rather impulsive execution upon the part of the stringed and a lack of accuracy in the wind instruments."

23 · "Third Philharmonic Concert," *Chicago Tribune*, January 17, 1862, 4.

24 · Unfortunately, Dwight had not gotten the translation quite right. Wagner's phrase "the ideal of bodily movement [*Leibesbewegung*] embodied in tones" comes out in Dwight and thus in Upton as a "movement of love [*Liebesbewegung*] ideally embodied in tones." "Beethoven's Symphonies, by a 'Friend of Art,'" *Dwight's Journal of Music* 7 (June 30, 1855): 97. Wagner's original passage reads as follows: "Diese Symphonie ist die Apotheose des Tanzes selbst: sie ist der Tanz nach seinem höchsten Wesen, die seligste That der in Tönen gleichsam idealisch verkörperten Leibesbewegung" (*Das Kunstwerk der Zukunft* [1850], 90).

25 · On the reception of Wagner and Liszt in the United States in the 1860s, see James Deaville, "'Westwärts zieht die Kunstgeschichte': Liszt's Symphonic Poems in the New World," in *Identität—Kultur—Raum*, ed. S. Ingram, M. Reisenleitner, and C. Szabó-Knotik (2001).

26 · "The Third Philharmonic Concert," *Chicago Tribune*, January 20, 1862, 4.

But the "general effect" was "most excellent." At the end Upton comes to Hans Balatka, whom he praises for the "careful labor" he has bestowed on the orchestra and for being a "thorough musician."[27] Four newspaper articles for one concert is a significant investment of cultural capital. Upton's aim is to proclaim the value not just of this one concert but of the entire enterprise— the Philharmonic Society, the concert music scene in Chicago, and classical music generally.

Upton availed himself of the final concert of the 1861–62 season on March 25 to assess the season as a whole. He praises the breadth of the repertory, the accomplishment of the soloists (all of them local), the improved performance standard of the orchestra, and finally the "genius" of Mr. Balatka, to whom "a large portion of our enjoyment is justly due."[28] Above all, Upton praises the city of Chicago for supporting such a worthy undertaking:

> We believe that such an organization [the Philharmonic Society] exists in but five cities of the Union—New York, Chicago, Boston, Philadelphia and St. Louis—and that Chicago stands second in the list, New York alone taking precedence. It is an important step for our Society to have achieved this result with its second season, the New York Philharmonic Society having been in operation for some fifteen years; but *it is established* with us now.... We have had nothing before which has so continuously brought together the very *elite* of our society, and it has only been necessary to glance around the Concert hall to become convinced that the intelligence, beauty, and refinement of the city have rallied *en masse* to the support of so worthy an association.[29]

The comparison with New York was a familiar trope for Chicago readers, as was the corollary that Chicago was more enlightened, more progressive, and more public spirited than its East Coast rival.

The same optimism echoes in Upton's season-opening and closing reviews for several ensuing years of Philharmonic concerts—he consistently refers to the orchestra's progress and Balatka's hard work as synecdoches for Chicago enterprise:

> [Balatka] has consolidated and brought into complete working union the best musical talent in our midst, and has given us a series of entertain-

27 · "Third Philharmonic Concert," *Chicago Tribune*, January 21, 1862, 4.
28 · "The Closing Philharmonic Concert," *Chicago Tribune*, March 26, 1862, 4.
29 · Ibid., italics in original. Upton's arithmetic is faulty. By 1862 the New York Philharmonic had been in existence for twenty years, not fifteen.

ments ... decidedly the most chaste and thoroughly elevated in tone of which we have ever enjoyed. . . . We hope to see the Philharmonic established as an institution in our city.[30]

The Orchestra exhibited a decided improvement over previous seasons, both as regards numerical force and artistic skill. Under the admirable training of Balatka they have steadily advanced until now, at the beginning of the third season, there appears but little to be accomplished.[31]

Taken as a whole, the concerts of the Society this season have been fully equal, if not superior to those of any previous season. We hope and think that the musical taste of the city has been elevated, and that the Treasury of the Society has been increased in financial interest.[32]

Did Upton's readers really believe that the Philharmonic programs and Philharmonic concerts and Philharmonic audiences were getting steadily better, concert by concert, season by season? Given the optimism of the era, especially in Chicago, perhaps they did. Upton was fulfilling his role as cultural businessman by convincing the consumers (audience) of the value of the cultural commodity (Philharmonic Society) in which he had invested his symbolic capital. In turn, Upton gained recognition as an authority who could consecrate cultural goods and institutions, a position he maintained above any possible complaints of "puffery" through his visible maintenance of standards: these included occasional critiques of guest soloists (the orchestra received only light reprimands) and humorous jibes (usually mild) aimed at audience behavior.[33] Indeed, the element of wit increasingly entered his reviews as he established himself and became more comfortable writing about the arts in the wide-ranging Peregrine Pickle columns. Thus Upton could support the orchestra and encourage its public while displaying his ability as juridical critic and droll arbiter of taste.

30 · *Chicago Tribune*, April 28, 1862.
31 · Ibid., November 26, 1862.
32 · Ibid., April 8, 1864.
33 · Chastising the unruly audience at one concert, Upton writes, "At the close of the piece next to the last, the snobs and snobesses commenced retiring from the hall, as usual, to the deep annoyance of the orchestra and those who preferred to remain. To tell these unmannered people of the utter disgust which their conduct excited among the respectable portion of the audience, we fear would be but to increase their aptitude for such performances" ("Amusements: Philharmonic Concert," *Chicago Tribune*, January 19, 1864, 4).

Deconsecrating the Philharmonic

For their 1865–66 season Balatka and the Philharmonic moved from Bryan Hall to Crosby's recently completed opera house. The larger hall, plus the competition with visiting opera troupes, put a severe financial strain on the society. By the end of the season the losses totaled almost $1,500 (receipts: $6,292.50, expenses: $7,734).[34] Undaunted, Upton published his customary preview of the coming year (1866–67), promising "a very excellent programme for the season," with a "fresh repertoire, full of novelties."[35] He notes that fewer opera companies plan to visit Chicago, and thus the Philharmonic will largely "have the field to themselves." He also remarks, somewhat cryptically, that "the 'dead lethargy,' which seemed to have taken possession of the management, has been dissipated." At the end of his preview, Upton reminds his readers that "this is our home society, and ... its encouragement should always take the preference over foreign entertainments.... We are confident that its concerts will reach even to the standard of the Eastern Philharmonic societies, if not surpass them, and we, therefore, appeal to all our lovers of music to promptly fill up the subscription list."

Early in November (1866), Upton reported that sales of season subscriptions were not progressing as hoped. To encourage people to come to the Philharmonic's opening concert, he draws on his now-familiar rhetoric of superlatives: "one of the best ever given in the city"; "orchestra has been thoroughly reorganized"; "has done so much to cultivate musical taste in our midst."[36] The concert on November 10 featured twenty-four-year-old violinist Camilla Urso, and Upton proclaims the next day that it has been "a pronounced musical success."[37] The soloist was obliged to play three encores; the orchestra was "excellently balanced"; "Mr. Baier's usually refractory horn" had acquired a new "smoothness of tone." Upton saves the bad news for the review's final paragraph. The engagement of Camilla Urso has been a "heavy expense" for the society; if the concerts are to continue, the public must "second them in their efforts" by subscribing to the remainder of the season.

Twelve days later, on November 23, 1866, Upton printed an "Important Announcement" in the *Tribune*: "Only a portion of the tickets necessary to guarantee the expenses of the season have been sold." Unless enough subscriptions are in hand by December 1, "no further attempts will be made to

34 · "Philharmonic," *Chicago Tribune*, May 15, 1866, 4.
35 · "The Philharmonic Season," *Chicago Tribune*, October 21, 1866, 2.
36 · "The Philharmonic Concerts," *Chicago Tribune*, November 2, 1866, 2.
37 · "Amusements," *Chicago Tribune*, November 11, 1866, 4.

give concerts this season."[38] He observes that the managers of the society, "who are men of business," cannot afford to risk more money in the enterprise, and he hopes that the public would "see it in this light, and avert the disgrace of such a musical failure." "If we cannot support our Philharmonic concerts," Upton concludes, "we had better revert to negro minstrelsy, and have done with any pretension of being a musical people."

The "Important Announcement" marked a turning point in Upton's attitude toward the Chicago Philharmonic Society. Over the next two months (December 1866–January 1867), Upton systematically withdrew his "cultural capital" from Balatka and the Philharmonic. He began with a "Feuilleton" published November 25.[39] In it Upton explains that the Philharmonic's failure was not due to the indifference of the Chicago public but rather to at least three mistakes that Balatka and the Philharmonic management have made: (1) selling only season tickets rather than tickets for individual concerts; (2) not making the orchestra's rehearsals public and selling tickets to them as "public rehearsals"; and (3) programming a repertory that "only a small class of the public can appreciate, or even enjoy." "Had the suggestions advanced in these columns at different times been acted upon," Upton continues, "the Philharmonic Association would scarcely have encountered its present difficulties." In this final ungracious remark, the critic does more than say "I told you so." He preserves the cultural capital he has built up over six years of reviewing the Philharmonic, but withdraws that capital from the orchestra. Because they have rejected his advice, the failure is theirs, not his.[40]

As the weeks went by, Upton's criticism grew abusive. The orchestra is "getting music out of the bottom of the barrel."[41] The Philharmonic's plan to substitute chamber works for more expensive orchestral numbers is "a kind of hermaphrodite blending of the chamber concert and the full concert."[42] When management proposed, at the beginning of the new year, to cut costs by reducing the size of the orchestra, Upton declared that the Philharmonic Society had reached the end of its useful life: "When the professor of physiology puts a current of electricity into the leg of a dead frog, the artificial sprightliness of the defunct rana is very amusing. Hot lard has the same effect on dead eels. But I do not think even electricity and hot lard will save the Philharmonic Society. And now somebody is trying to galvanize them into

38 · "The Philharmonic Society: Important Announcement," *Chicago Tribune*, November 23, 1866, 4.
39 · "Feuilleton," *Chicago Tribune*, November 25, 1866, 2.
40 · In fact Upton had not made any of his three suggestions in previous columns about the orchestra. This is the first time they appear.
41 · "The World of Amusement," *Chicago Tribune*, December 23, 1866, 2.
42 · "Philharmonic," *Chicago Tribune*, January 4, 1867, 4.

life again by giving [concerts] in a smaller hall with a half orchestra. It won't do. The body should be removed to the tomb of the Capulets."[43] From this point forward, Upton referred to the orchestra as the "late Philharmonic" and its performances as "posthumous concerts."

When the "late" Philharmonic dared to give a "posthumous" concert in February 1867, Upton's review was extremely harsh. There were many empty seats; the performance was "mournful, uneven, cold, and wanting in … life"; Balatka's "unimpassioned marking of time" was followed "sometimes precisely, sometimes not, by the orchestra."[44] Beethoven's Second Symphony was played "mechanically," except for the "brutal" horns that made "wretched work" of the larghetto. Upton saved his harshest words for Mrs. Carrington, the vocal soloist: "It is worse than folly for a singer of her calibre to attack such ambitious music as the *Ah! quel giorno*. She is not able to sing it now, and she never may be."[45] A concert a year later (April 1868) was "haunted" and "mournful." The audience consisted mainly of the Germania Männerchor, which shared the bill, and their families and friends. "Balatka was mounted on a cracker-box with a baton in his hand, amusing the ghost."[46]

Upton later took pains to deny "that stupid old charge that I killed the late Philharmonic."[47] He had "warned it many a time," he acknowledged, "that if it did not correct certain radical faults it would die." But the managers would not listen. "When the physician tells his patient that if he persists in a certain course he will die … is the physician responsible for his death?" Here Upton simultaneously takes credit for the death of the Philharmonic and denies any responsibility. The cultural businessman-critic-physician was not only protecting the citizens of Chicago from the orchestra's mechanical playing and brutal horns; he was also preserving the symbolic capital that he had acquired as the city's leading arbiter of taste. Upton was careful not to blame conductor Balatka for the orchestra's demise. He asserted his "sympathy" for the conductor; he acknowledged Balatka's indefatigable energy and diligence.[48] At the same time he avoided any outright endorsement, and his tone became manifestly condescending: "Mr. Balatka's heart is in the right place.… He is striving in the right direction.… I admire his pluck."[49] Upton declared his faith in Balatka, but he was not about to invest any more of his hard-earned cultural capital in a failed enterprise.

---

43 · "The World of Amusement," *Chicago Tribune*, January 6, 1867, 2.
44 · "Amusements," *Chicago Tribune*, February 19, 1867, 4.
45 · "Ah! quel giorno" comes from act 1 of Rossini's *Semiramide*.
46 · "The World of Amusement," *Chicago Tribune*, April 5, 1868, 2.
47 · Ibid., December 5, 1869, 2.
48 · "Music in Chicago," *Chicago Tribune*, November 20, 1868, 2.
49 · "The World of Amusement," *Chicago Tribune*, December 5, 1869, 2.

New Critic in Town

In October 1868, Balatka gave up on the Philharmonic and announced a season of concerts by an ensemble that he called an "Orchestral Union," which was composed of many of the same players but organized on a season-by-season basis. In his column, Upton printed an open letter by Balatka and A. J. Vaas, leader of Chicago's Great Western Light Guard Band and first violinist in the Orchestral Union, in which the two announce a season of five subscription concerts by a forty-piece orchestra. Their repertory will encompass "almost exclusively new compositions of the highest order, both of the classic and modern school." Upton's only comment was to refer once again to the "death and burial of the late Philharmonic" and to add that the new form of organization "must compel success."[50]

The critical vacuum left by Upton's reluctance to invest any more cultural capital in Balatka and the orchestra was filled to a certain extent by the arrival in Chicago of a new critic. William Smythe Babcock (W. S. B.) Mathews (1837–1912) settled in Chicago in 1867, with primary employment as piano teacher and organist, a vocation he had pursued previously in New York State, Georgia, South Carolina, and Alabama. In addition, from 1859 on he had been a frequent contributor to *Dwight's Journal of Music* under the pseudonym of "Der Freyschutz."[51] In November 1868 the Chicago music dealer Lyon and Healy established the *Musical Independent* and engaged the newly arrived Mathews as its chief editor.[52] Because Mathews was new in town, Balatka's concerts with the Orchestral Union presented an opportunity to begin the process of capital accumulation. His review of the Balatka orchestra's opening concert—positive, enthusiastic, and charitable—sounds like the reviews Upton had been writing of the Philharmonic five years before:

> CHICAGO—Mr. Balatka's First Symphony Concert was given Nov. 20. The principal features were Mendelssohn's A minor Symphony and Wallace['s] Loreley Overture. The orchestra of forty pieces played better than at any similar concert here, and the concert as a whole was an eminently enjoyable one. The vocal pieces performed were by Miss Kunstz [?] of Indianapolis, who had an uphill time of it trying to sing against the enthusiastic blowing and scraping of the orchestra. *Piano* next time, gentlemen! We regret to say

50 · Ibid., October 4, 1868, 2. On the Great Western Band, see chapter I.1 in this volume.

51 · See the article on Mathews in his *A Hundred Years of Music in America*, 403.

52 · After the fire, the *Musical Independent* ceased to exist, but Mathews continued to write music reviews for the *Chicago Herald*, the *Chicago Record*, and the *Chicago Tribune*. He became editor of *Etude* in 1885, and in 1891 he founded the influential Chicago-based journal *Music*, where he was editor in chief as well as a prolific contributor.

that this concert was not so well attended as it ought to have been. Mr. Balatka was a loser by the operation. Let us rally to the next ones, and save him from loss by so praiseworthy an undertaking as the production of first-class concerts here.[53]

Mathews identifies the repertory, praises the performance in general, criticizes a detail, expresses regret over poor attendance, and exhorts readers to do better next time. The review plays on civic pride, couched in a casual, enthusiastic tone.

Upton, in his review of the same concert, was more circumspect. The audience was "fair"; the execution of the orchestra was "creditable."[54] Upton gives a two-paragraph account of Mendelssohn's *Italian* Symphony, which has not been heard before in Chicago, praises the soprano, Miss Kunst [?], for her "very strong, good voice." The audience, Upton agrees, was "not as large as it should have been."[55] "Can it be possible," Upton asked a few days later, "that in this great city of 300,000 people 700 cannot be found with taste enough to support good music?"[56]

For the balance of the 1868–69 season Mathews and Upton traded reviews of the Balatka concerts. As a newcomer to the city and its music-critical scene, Mathews needed to introduce himself to Chicago readers and establish his cultural capital. Thus, his reviews tend to criticize performances only cautiously, and then couched in good-natured admonitions. Upton, on the other hand, had already accumulated a good deal of capital in Chicago; his task was to avoid dissipating that capital on another "losing" venture like the Philharmonic. Stimulated perhaps by the competition, Upton, in his reviews from the 1868–69 season, exceeded his prior music-critical work in quantity of information and authoritative judgments. Upton did not publicly reference or even allude to Mathews's reviews, and Mathews likewise ignored Upton. It is unlikely that readers would have compared them: Upton's assessments were on newsstands the day after the concert, whereas Mathews's reviews in the *Musical Independent*—a monthly publication—appeared at least one month after the concert, which meant that his critique of the late November concert came out in the January issue, that for the late December concert in February, and so on. This gap between event and publication probably led Mathews to make his reviews more concise.

Both critics approved Balatka's choice of repertory, which valorized Austro-German composers, with Beethoven occupying the central position. The con-

53 · "Monthly Summary of Musical Doings," *Musical Independent* 1 (January 1869): 89.
54 · "Amusements," *Chicago Tribune*, November 21, 1868, 4.
55 · Ibid.
56 · "World of Amusement," *Chicago Tribune*, December 6, 1868, 2.

ductor introduced established works to Chicago listeners, such as the Symphony no. 9 in C Major by Schubert and Mendelssohn's *Italian* Symphony, but he also promoted the newest musical products of Germany, in particular Liszt and Wagner.[57] Upton and Mathews both gave positive reviews to Liszt's symphonic poem *Tasso* on the December program.[58] Upton praises Liszt's "superb" storytelling in music.[59] Mathews feels that *Tasso* lacks "real melodic wealth" in comparison to Mendelssohn or Schubert. But he perceptively articulates the formal principles of Liszt's style: "unity of origin" (thematic transformation) and "unity of membership" (sonata form).[60] Neither critic seems to be affected by the hostile *Lisztrezeption* typical of East Coast critics.[61]

The most substantial divergence between the two sets of reviews of Balatka's 1868–69 season resided in the critics' attitudes toward the Chicago public, readers, and concertgoers. Upton, whose concern was to preserve his cultural capital, casts himself in the role of juridical critic and guardian of taste, urging both orchestra and audience to rise up to his level. In a retrospective comment on the orchestra's December concert, he praises the conductor but excoriates the audience: "Mr. Balatka … has been giving some of the best music ever heard here, under the mistaken idea that there were people enough of taste in this great city of 300,000 people to pay him for his trouble and labor. At the first concert he lost about $250, and as for the second concert, he sold just one more ticket than at the first; his losses at the second can be quite easily computed. … He must make his concerts 'the thing to do' … or else he must bring his programmes down to the standard of musical taste in the community and in place of symphonies, which people here don't know from sardines … treat his audience to the harmless measures of a twiddling polka."[62] Mathews, who could not afford to speak to his newly acquired readers in such a tone, took a line of "education" and "uplift." In an extended promotional piece appended to the review of Balatka's December concert, he expounds on the educational value of orchestral concerts:

> Any sort of a piano lesson here costs from a dollar and a half to three dollars. You get a few hints on scales, and a more or less careful drill on a few lines of

---

57 · Deaville, "'Westwärts zieht die Kunstgeschichte.'"

58 · *Tasso* had received its first American performance on March 24, 1860, under Carl Bergmann in New York; Balatka's in Chicago appears to have been the work's second orchestral rendition in the New World.

59 · "Amusements," *Chicago Tribune*, December 23, 1868, 1.

60 · "Monthly Summary of Musical Doings," *Musical Independent* 1 (February 1869): 121.

61 · Dwight, for example, rejected Liszt's orchestral works as "tedious, overstrained, unedifying" ("Liszt Criticized by an Admirer," *Dwight's Journal of Music* 15 [1859]: 102).

62 · "The World of Amusements," *Chicago Tribune*, December 27, 1868, 2.

some piece. If the teacher be not in a hurry, he may play one piece for you. You have learned something, to be sure. You have put a brick or so into the fabric of your musical education. Suppose you pay a dollar to go to a symphony concert. What do you hear? Why at the second, we had the beautiful music to "Midsummer Night's Dream," by Mendelssohn, Liszt's "Tasso," various songs, and the spirited ... Overture to "Zampa." In listening to this you do not acquire the ability to strike any more keys in a given time, than you possessed on leaving home. But you do get ideas in relation to style of performance, the true perspective of the works played, which you can never learn from pianoforte arrangements. In short, if you have added no bricks to ... your musical education, you have at least learned how to embellish the completed portion of the building, and so render it more comely.[63]

Here the critic steps down from his juridical podium and addresses the concertgoing public as a group of peers, fellow workers in the city's cultural atelier. Mathews invokes the "bricks and mortar" image of Chicago's civic progress in order to entice the public to attend Balatka's concerts.

Faced with competition from Mathews and the *Musical Independent* during Balatka's 1868–69 season, Upton was determined to preserve the cultural capital he had accumulated over the previous eight years. He positioned himself as a strong advocate of the orchestra's repertory, classical and modern, and as a stern critic of public taste. When it came to the orchestra and the conductor, Upton kept his distance. He was more charitable than he had been during the last two seasons of Philharmonic concerts, yet nowhere near as enthusiastic as in the early 1860s about the quality of Chicago musicians and the prospects for a successful Chicago-based concert orchestra.

The Messiah Appears

Balatka entered into the 1869–70 season with optimism for his "Orchestral Union" concert series: in a press release of September 12, 1869, the conductor announced a second season of concerts, with the promise that "all orchestral works to be performed during the coming season will be *entirely* new to Chicago, without exception."[64] Among the anticipated repertory was *Les Préludes* of Liszt, a symphony by Rubinstein, Wagner's overture to *The Flying Dutchman* and prelude to *Lohengrin*, and "marches by Liszt, Gade, Raff, Lassen, etc.," as well as symphonies and overtures by Haydn, Mozart, Beethoven,

63 · *Musical Independent* 1 (February 1869): 102–3.
64 · "The World of Amusement," *Chicago Tribune*, September 12, 1869, 2.

and Mendelssohn. Upton published Balatka's "pronunciamento" verbatim and without comment.

On November 7, Upton informed his readers that a "letter from New York" had notified him that "Theodore Thomas will bring the whole of his New York orchestra here this month."[65] The year 1869 was the first in which Thomas took his New York–based orchestra on tour—to Boston, Providence, Pittsburgh, Cincinnati, St. Louis, Chicago, and several more cities in between. In Chicago the orchestra was scheduled for three concerts at Farwell Hall, beginning on Saturday, November 27. Meanwhile, Balatka's first concert of the 1869–70 season took place on Friday, November 26, and Upton's review appeared in the next day's paper. He describes and praises Mendelssohn's *Reformation* Symphony; he compliments the piano soloist for "precision and clearness"; he pans Lindpaintner's *Jubilee Overture*, "which was evidently written when Mr. Lindpaintner was either very drunk or very crazy."[66] Balatka's orchestra receives no quarter from the critic. It is smaller than in the previous season; the brass overpower the strings; the players seem unfamiliar with their parts; the ensemble is ragged. Although he does not mention Theodore Thomas, Upton seems to be comparing Balatka and his orchestra in advance to the renowned orchestra he will hear that evening.

The first Thomas concert took place on Saturday, and Upton was not able to publish his review in the Sunday paper. Instead, he returned to Balatka's Friday evening concert, comparing it to "those dying days of the late Philharmonic."[67] Now the comparison to the Thomas Orchestra becomes explicit: "Theodore Thomas ... before this [column] meets your eye ... will have introduced his splendidly-trained orchestra to the Chicago public. ... If we can't support a home orchestra," Upton declares, "the next best thing is to support a foreign orchestra."[68]

Upton's review of the Thomas Orchestra's Saturday concert appeared in the Monday paper. In it the critic consecrates Thomas and the orchestra in the very first sentence: "The first concert by Theodore Thomas' unrivalled orchestra on Saturday evening was, without exception, the finest musical event Chicago has ever known, and we can only regret that there were not more to hear such an absolutely perfect performance of music. It is an episode which may never happen again in a life-time."[69] Upton proceeds to give his readers

65 · Ibid., November 7, 1869, 2.
66 · "The Symphony Concert," *Chicago Tribune*, November 27, 1869, 4.
67 · "The World of Amusement," *Chicago Tribune*, November 28, 1869, 2.
68 · Ibid.
69 · "Amusements: Theodore Thomas' Concert," *Chicago Tribune*, November 29, 1869, 4. Little did Upton suspect at this time that Thomas would become a regular visitor to Chicago and would eventually conduct the city's standing orchestra.

a brief biography of Thomas, a capsule history of the orchestra, and a glowing encomium of its performance: "perfect whole," "bows move in perfect
unison," "delicious expression," "perfect truth of detail," and so on. Not until
the fourth paragraph does Upton discuss the program, which included the
overture to *Tannhäuser*, the allegretto of Beethoven's Eighth Symphony, the
William Tell Overture, an arrangement of Schuman's "Träumerei," a couple of
virtuoso turns by soloists from the orchestra, and several Strauss waltzes.[70]
Although he did not mention Balatka or the Balatka orchestra in this or the
following reviews of Thomas's next two concerts, Upton made it abundantly
clear that the cultural capital he had withdrawn two seasons earlier from Balatka and the Philharmonic would now be invested in Theodore Thomas: "If
Theodore Thomas should remain here a week, the musical people of Chicago
might ... learn that he is actually giving the grandest musical entertainments
Chicago has ever known, or ever will know again, for all that."[71]

Dazzled by this revelation, as the story was later told, George Upton
abandoned his advocacy of local music and became apostle of Theodore
Thomas.[72] The facts, as narrated above, tell a somewhat different tale.
Upton had given up on local orchestras (and on local audiences) some three
years earlier, at the end of 1866. At that moment he condemned the Philharmonic Society to "death," adopted a cautious attitude toward Balatka, and
refused to invest any more of his "cultural capital" in a local concert series. In
his reviews of Balatka's 1868–69 season, Upton, unlike Mathews, maintained
a tone of critical detachment and watchfulness, waiting for an opportunity
to make a new and better investment. In November 1869, before Upton had
heard the Thomas Orchestra play a note, he was already singing the maestro's
praises and calling for the Chicago public to shift its allegiance to "a foreign
orchestra."[73]

Thirty years later, when he was writing his biography of Theodore Thomas,
Upton would remember Balatka and the Philharmonic in a somewhat different light: "[Through the Philharmonic concerts] Balatka soon found himself famous, and the musical lion of the city.... [The Philharmonic] accomplished an important work in the education of the people and in preparing

70 · An arrangement of "Träumerei" (a different one) had been heard at Balatka's concert
the night before. At its second concert the Thomas Orchestra played a movement from Mendelssohn's "Reformation Symphony," likewise performed at Balatka's concert. These might
be coincidences, but they might also have been part of a strategy by Thomas to show up the
local orchestra.
71 · "Amusements: Theodore Thomas' Second Concert," *Chicago Tribune*, November 30,
1869, 4.
72 · Feldman, "George P. Upton," 183–91. Also George P. Upton, *Musical Memories* (1908),
266–68.
73 · "The World of Amusement," *Chicago Tribune,* November 28, 1869, 2.

them for the new leader soon to come, who was to make Chicago a musical center. Mr. Balatka gave a few concerts in 1869, and then abandoned the field, the Thomas Orchestra having arrived in the same year. To ... Balatka [along with two earlier conductors] is due the credit of preparing the way for the greater skill and higher interpretative ability of Mr. Thomas and the greater perfection of his instrumental force."[74] Here Upton positions the older conductor (Balatka) as a prophet for the messiah to come (Thomas). Balatka, whom Upton had deconsecrated in the late 1860s, is reconsecrated in retrospect in a way that confirms the greater value of Thomas. Looking back at Chicago in the 1860s, Upton forgives himself his youthful enthusiasm: for Balatka, for the Chicago Philharmonic, for the illusion that Chicago could compete successfully with New York. His investment of cultural capital in Balatka, Upton implies, was not a mistake or a lapse. It was a down payment on a cultural investment that would eventually prove much more profitable for Upton, for the *Tribune*, and for Chicago.

74 · Thomas, *Theodore Thomas*, 317–18. The earlier conductors whom Upton mentions along with Balatka as preparing the way for Theodore Thomas are Henry Ahner and Julius Unger, both of whom led Chicago orchestras in the 1850s. See chapter I.1 in this volume.

[II.5] Amateur and Professional, Permanent and Transient

Orchestras in the District of Columbia, 1877–1905

PATRICK WARFIELD

In January of 1905, Oscar G. Sonneck, then head of the Music Division at the Library of Congress, wrote to the editors of the *Washington Post*: "It seems incredible that the Capital of the United States should not be willing to support a symphony orchestra.... All who love good music and know its uplifting power on a community should contribute their share, be it ever so small, and should induce even their unmusical friends do the same toward the establishment of a permanent orchestra."[1] Sonneck was responding to an appeal from a local ensemble, which warned that without greater financial support, it would "in all probability go permanently out of existence with the stamp of failure upon it."[2]

Such exchanges were commonplace in District of Columbia newspapers throughout the late nineteenth and early twentieth centuries. Local musicians would announce a new permanent orchestra, and an inaugural concert would be given to great fanfare before a sympathetic press. After a season or two, a circular would be issued seeking additional funds, and in short order the ensemble would disintegrate, sometimes with a farewell concert but just as often without comment. Blame was then assigned to Washington's cultural naiveté, the lack of an acceptable concert venue, or the difficult financial times. Finally, the press would lament: "The shores of Washington are strewn with the wrecks of musical endeavor."[3]

Such stories of a national capital unable to sustain a permanent professional orchestra are gloomy only when one is concerned with institutional permanence and fixated on professionals. Once other models of orchestral success are admitted, however, late nineteenth-century Washington proves

1 · O. G. Sonneck, "Views of People on Various Subjects," *Washington Post*, January 30, 1905, 9.

2 · "Plea for Orchestra," *Washington Post*, January 25, 1905, 10.

3 · "Is Washington a Musical City?" *Washington Post*, April 17, 1905, 6.

to have been home to a host of ensembles, a fact noticed by the *Musical Courier*: "Although Washington is a little place, she is well supplied with local orchestras. There are the Philharmonic Orchestra, under William H. Santelmann; the Marine Band Orchestra, also under his direction; the Georgetown Orchestra, directed by Josef Kaspar, and the Haley Orchestra, not counting bands and several small orchestras."[4] Two such local ensembles are of particular interest: the Georgetown Amateur Orchestra, which welcomed nonprofessional players, and the Washington Symphony Orchestra, which went through several brief incarnations. Taken together these ensembles demonstrate that the tendency to privilege permanence and praise professionalism can cause us to undervalue the orchestral life of an American city.

An Amateur Ensemble: The Georgetown Orchestra

After serving as the unified District of Columbia's first governor, Henry David Cooke (1825–81) settled in the west part of the district and made a name for himself as a local benefactor. In what must have been a particularly pleasing donation, he opened his parlor to rehearsals by a trio of chamber musicians beginning in 1877. None of the men who gathered in the Cooke home were professional players; rather, their meetings were a way of pursuing music "as a recreation and pleasure in the evening, after their regular avocations of the day were over."[5] This trio consisted of the host's own son, financier Henry David Cooke Jr. (violin), painter Charles S. Hein (piano), and dentist Francis Sinclair Barbarin (cello).[6]

It did not take long for other friends to join this group of chamber musicians, and by the early 1880s they had formed a small orchestra: "The enjoyment experienced by these gentlemen, and the improvement they derived from their practice attracted the attention of other performers, and so gradually their number increased until they found they had a very fair orchestra."[7] This new ensemble presented its first concert on January 19, 1882, at Curtis

---

4 · *Musical Courier* 42 (May 29, 1901): 29.

5 · "The Georgetown Amateur Orchestra," *Washington Star*, April 25, 1885.

6 · Barbarin was not unknown in Washington's artistic community, as he had served as assistant curator at the Corcoran Gallery since 1874; he would become the gallery's curator in 1889. Several histories of the Georgetown Amateur Orchestra appeared in the press. See especially Ray C. B. Brown, "Fostering of City's Musical Growth throughout Years No Easy Task," *Washington Post*, December 6, 1937, AN17.

7 · "The Georgetown Amateur Orchestra," *Washington Star*, April 25, 1885, 2. The Historical Society of Washington, D.C., owns a photograph, probably from the late 1870s, labeled "Original Georgetown Amateur Orchestra." It shows eight well-dressed men with instruments. Three have violins or violas, and there are also two flutes, one cello, a guitar, and an alto horn.

Hall in Georgetown, with the leader of the Albaugh Opera House orchestra, Robert Camp Bernays, serving as conductor.

With regular performances and steady paychecks, theater orchestras served as one of the best musical employers in the District of Columbia. Even so, it was often necessary for theater musicians to supplement this income, and Bernays chose to aid a number of Washington's amateur clubs by providing music lessons to their members. It is thus likely that two of the musicians at that first Georgetown Amateur Orchestra concert came from the Bernays studio: a young Hermann Rakemann, who "performed a violin solo so well as to elicit an encore," and "a little miss of not more than ten summers, Miss Lillie Parsloe by name," who played "upon a viola with perfect unconcern and apparent correctness."[8]

In 1885 the ensemble accompanied a production of Gilbert and Sullivan's *Patience*, which was "rendered entirely by ladies and gentlemen prominent in society."[9] This benefit performance for the orchestra raised its profile considerably. According to the *Washington Star*, the ensemble had given the city complete symphonies by Haydn and Beethoven at a time when "no local assemblage of musicians had ventured upon symphonic work."[10] The *Washington Post* proudly announced that the Georgetown Amateur Orchestra had "demonstrated that it is the best organization of its kind."[11] With their new success the group established a subscription series, and annual dues of five dollars entitled passive members to four tickets to each of the season's four concerts. The press urged Washingtonians to sustain their orchestra and gain the "knowledge that they are aiding to support a most excellent and successful educational organization."[12]

In November 1886 the ensemble turned to a new conductor and engaged one of the most active professional musicians in late nineteenth-century Washington, Josef Kaspar (1858–1936). Kaspar took up the baton on condition "that he be allowed to have absolute control of the orchestra."[13] The new conductor immediately set to work transforming the ensemble from a social club into a well-rehearsed local symphony. His musical standards were higher than some of the players had expected: "The very first rehearsal proved too rigorous for several members and they resigned. A few who were incapable

8 · "Amusements," *Washington Post*, January 20, 1882, 2.
9 · "A Society Event," *Washington Post*, March 29, 1885, 2.
10 · "The Georgetown Amateur Orchestra," *Washington Star*, April 25, 1885, 2.
11 · "Amusements," *Washington Post*, February 14, 1885, 2.
12 · "The Georgetown Amateur Orchestra," *Washington Post*, May 23, 1886, 8.
13 · "Kaspar Takes the Baton," *Washington Post*, November 21, 1886, 2. That same year, Kaspar's wife, Annie Roemer, created the leading role in *The Queen of Hearts,* an operetta by Marine Band leader John Philip Sousa.

of performing upon their instruments were allowed to step aside, and others who were second-rate musicians were spurred on to better work."[14] Kaspar replaced these players and expanded the ensemble to fifty instrumentalists. Although most of the musicians were still amateurs, Kaspar announced that "professional players will be engaged to supply deficiencies."[15]

Programs from the mid-1880s reveal a steady increase in the number of professional musicians aiding the Georgetown amateurs. They also reveal that Kaspar, who served "without remuneration," created demanding programs that mixed complete symphonies with popular selections.[16] At a concert in December of 1887, the ensemble opened with Mendelssohn's *Scottish Symphony*. It then accompanied a local vocalist in a selection from Gluck's *Orphée et Eurydice*. This was followed by a movement from Anton Rubinstein's Violin Concerto, a *Norwegian Rhapsody* from Johan Svendsen, a song by Dudley Buck, Camille Saint-Saëns's *Jota aragonese*, and a "patrol" based on Louis Desormes's *En revenant de la revue*. Such programs were fairly typical of late nineteenth-century Washington, and Kaspar often included both complete symphonies and individual movements from Beethoven, Schubert, and Mendelssohn.[17]

In 1889 the press praised the orchestra's decade-long contributions to Washington's cultural education: "For nearly ten years the public rehearsals have been attended by large audiences, the number at each concert for the last three years averaging 1,500 people. They have listened to programmes which have been, in the main, well and judiciously chosen, and by studious attention have advanced in the knowledge of musical compositions. To be sure, the ensemble playing is not faultless, and there is often a painful amateurishness about the work of the soloists, and yet, despite this fact, I believe it is not extravagant to say that the Orchestra has been influential in educating a great mass of people to the enjoyment and intelligent appreciation of such organizations as the band which Mr. Gericke lately directed."[18]

Kaspar led the Georgetown Amateur Orchestra for nearly a decade, and when he resigned in 1894, the ensemble turned to the young musician who

14 · "Music and Musicians," *Washington Post*, November 13, 1887, 5.

15 · "Kaspar Takes the Baton," *Washington Post*, November 21, 1886, 2.

16 · "Professor Kaspar's Tenth Anniversary," *Washington Post*, May 4, 1890, 12.

17 · Several printed programs can be found in the scrapbooks compiled by orchestra member Mattie Saxton, now in the Washingtoniana Division of the Martin Luther King Jr. Memorial Library in Washington, D.C. The orchestra performed many of the European classics that were favorites of late nineteenth-century Americans, including works by Bizet, Chopin, Dvořák, Gade, Gounod, Grieg, Raff, Eduard Strauss, Ambroise Thomas, and Weber.

18 · "In Its Tenth Season," *Washington Post*, December 1, 1889, 12. The "band" referred to here is the Boston Symphony, which Karl Gericke led in a concert of works by Haydn, Wagner, and Moskowski at Washington's Congregational Church on January 18, 1889.

had soloed at their first concert in 1882. Hermann Rakemann was now a well-known Washington violinist, and he continued Kaspar's reforms by increasing the frequency of rehearsals and enlarging the ensemble to some seventy-five players.[19]

Washington had seen orchestras come and go, often surviving only a season or two, but the Georgetown amateurs held together for nearly two decades. By the 1890s the ensemble was recognized as one of the city's greatest artistic accomplishments: "Washington may well be proud of the Georgetown Orchestra. Few cities in the land can boast of an amateur organization so closely approaching a professional standard."[20] One critic was especially proud of this local ensemble. In 1894 he compared the Georgetown amateurs to the Boston Symphony and thanked them for occasionally providing audiences with a "number of less length and greater melodic brilliance." The Georgetown amateurs could even boast "twenty-four violins, a larger number than the symphony orchestra brings here."[21]

In 1895 the Georgetown Amateur Orchestra, at least temporarily, came to an end. The *Washington Post* announced, "From present indications the Georgetown Orchestra has played its last season, it being the general impression of the members that it will not be continued next year." No explanation was given other than that the ensemble had completed its "missionary work in bringing local musical people up to a love of orchestral performances."[22] The amateurs met in October and held rehearsals, but they gave no further concerts.[23] For the time being, the Georgetown Amateur Orchestra was gone.

Membership

Although theater orchestras were an important source of income for local musicians, Washington's most lucrative musical employment was to be found in the United States Marine Band. In addition to providing players with a stable paycheck, this ensemble acted as a clearinghouse for musical employment within the District of Columbia. Concert programs from the nineteenth century reveal that Marine Band musicians were involved in al-

19 · "Under a New Leader," *Washington Post*, December 24, 1893, 9; and "Concerts and Entertainments," *Washington Post*, February 1, 1894, 5.
20 · "A Creditable Performance," *Washington Post*, January 5, 1895, 4.
21 · "Concert of the Georgetown Orchestra," *Washington Post*, April 1, 1894, 20.
22 · "Musical Topics," *Washington Post*, July 28, 1895, 7. It was clear that Rakemann planned to leave the orchestra and form his own professional ensemble.
23 · "Musical Topics," *Washington Post*, October 27, 1895, 18; ibid., November 15, 1896, 18.

most every aspect of the city's musical life.[24] It is hardly surprising that when Josef Kaspar sought to expand his amateur orchestra with more solid players he turned to the "President's Own." The list below shows the orchestra's roster as printed in a program from 1886. Of the forty-seven players listed on it, six were members of the Marine Band (Francis Lusby, Franklin Pearce, Charles Thierbach, Louis Tillieux, and Salvatore and Vincent Petrola). Later rosters included so many Marine Band musicians that in 1891 the orchestra had to arrange its concert schedule to finish the season "before the 1st of April, when the Marine Band, from which the brass and wood wind of the orchestra are obtained, will leave on a six week's tour."[25]

Membership of the Georgetown Amateur Orchestra, December 28, 1886

1st Violin	*Violoncello*
H. D. Cooke	I. Thos. Davis Jr.
E. Szemelenyi	J. H. Alexander
F. Weiler	Chas. Thierbach
J. R. Hill	Carl Fischer
T. Nordlinger	Ernest Lent
Dr. George Arthur	A. E. Knorr
Emil Kubel	*Contra Bass*
Miss Birdie Lucas	A. W. Tyler
Miss Nona Stosch	H. Schuldt
2nd Violin	L. Brandt
T. E. Rogers	*Flute*
F. C. Schaefer	E. W. Stone
Carl Keferstein	H. Schutter
C. H. Seaton	*Oboe*
Miss Mattie Saxton	C. S. Hein
Miss Emma Prall	O. L. Wolfsteiner
Viola	*Clarinet*
W. H. Burr	T. M. Fields
Geo. K. Finckel	Wm. Jardine
R. C. Stearns	*Cornet*
A. Fischer	Wm. Long
	J. R. Gibson

---

24 · For more on the Marine Band's place in Washington's musical culture, see Patrick Warfield, "John Esputa, John Philip Sousa, and the Boundaries of a Musical Career," *Nineteenth-Century Music Review* 6 (2009).

25 · "Music and Patriotism," *Washington Post*, November 22, 1891, 14.

Horns
N. D. Adams
L.Tillieux
S. Petrola
V. Petrola
Trombone
F. H. Barbarin
W. C. Babcock
F. Pearce

Tympani and Drums
F. Lusby
S. Tanhauser
Bassoon
J. Ulke
J. Henings

Not all professional players in Washington were military or theater musicians, however. Given the city's large number of musical amateurs, there was great demand for professional instructors, and several musicians managed to cobble together an existence by running music studios and working with amateur groups. More often than not, these men (and women) were European born and trained, and they frequently used that background to their professional advantage. Kaspar, who had studied in Prague and maintained a violin studio in Washington, clearly belonged to this class of teacher-professionals.[26]

A particularly interesting example is Ernest Lent (1856–1922), who briefly led the orchestra. Lent was a German immigrant who came to New York to join the Metropolitan Opera Orchestra as principal cellist in 1883. He moved to Washington the next year to open a music studio, and his 1884 card boasts of training at the Royal Conservatory in Leipzig and advertises lessons in piano, violin, cello, and composition. Lent was also a member of New York's Manuscript Society and its corresponding secretary in Washington, where he evidently had some success as a composer.[27] To support himself Lent was active in a number of Washington's musical associations, both professional and amateur. In addition to the Georgetown Amateur Orchestra, he led the Washington String Orchestra, the Ladies String Quartet, and the

26 · Information about Kaspar can be found in "Professor Kaspar's Tenth Anniversary," *Washington Post*, May 4, 1890, 12; and "Josef Kaspar, Noted Teacher and Orchestra Director, Dies," *Washington Post*, March 20, 1936, 14. Kaspar was successful enough to be able to purchase a summer home in the Blue Ridge Mountains, where he laid out the grounds of Mont Salvat in three movements: a formal park (*maestoso*), a homestead (*symphonia domestica*), and a "rugged stretch of ground" (*finale allegro*). A "winding path led to Valhalla and a Bruennhilde Rock," overlooking the Shenandoah Valley.
27 · See E. Douglas Bomberger, *"A Tidal Wave of Encouragement": American Composers' Concerts in the Gilded Age* (2002), 208. Elise K. Kirk suggests that Lent's 1898 performance of his own Piano Trio was one of the first times serious chamber music had been brought to the president's home; see her *Music at the White House: A History of the American Spirit* (1986), 158–59.

Lyric (Vocal) Quartet. He played with a professional chamber music society known as the Philharmonic Club, took part in a series of Working People's Concerts, and provided music for Oscar Sonneck's lectures at the Library of Congress.[28]

Both Kaspar and Lent seem to have lacked regular orchestral employment, but they were prominent teachers in Washington, and their names are frequently found as conductors, performers, and composers, often in amateur circles. They were presumably paid for their services or used the city's amateur clubs to enlarge their private studios. Several other musicians from the above roster also fit into this group of professionals among the amateurs. These include Robert Stearns, who conducted the orchestra on one occasion, the instrument maker Emil Kubel, and William Burr, William Long, and Henry Schuldt, each of whom listed his occupation as "musician" in the city directory. These professional players account for twelve of the forty-seven musicians listed in the roster.

This was an amateur orchestra, however, and many of its members really were amateurs. Like the professional musicians, these amateurs fell into two groups. First, there were those for whom music was very nearly a vocation, but whose principal jobs were not musical in nature. Ernest Szemelényi Jr. (1852–1919) was a model of this type of player. Szemelényi's father was a Hungarian immigrant and a prolific composer of parlor music. We can assume that the son studied with the father before enrolling at Harvard, where he appears to have been a student of John Knowles Paine and a frequent vocalist prior to his graduation in 1875.[29] He taught briefly in New York (having the young Civil Service commissioner Theodore Roosevelt as a pupil). Then in 1881 Szemelényi won a post as translator in the D.C. Patent Office, a position he would occupy for most of the rest of his life.

Szemelényi was hardly a simple public servant. A profile published in 1891 was correct in reporting that since his "advent in Washington there have been few musical undertakings in which he has not taken an active part."[30] In addition to serving as conductor of the Georgetown Amateur Orchestra, Szemelényi was a periodic concertmaster, violinist, violist, or pianist with a variety of other amateur groups, including the Choral Society, the Richard

28 · The 1905 Working People's Concerts were organized by Maria von Unschuld and sponsored by the American Federation of Labor for the purpose of "giving the best class of music by good artists at modest prices." See "Miss Unschuld's Concert," *Washington Post*, March 13, 1905, 2.

29 · Szemelényi's connection to Paine is uncertain, but a collection of pieces by Paine's students, now at the Houghton Library at Harvard University, includes a short song in manuscript by E. Szemelényi Jr. titled "Put Forth Thy Leaf."

30 · "Leads as an Amateur," *Washington Post*, November 15, 1891, 14.

Wagner Society, the Travel Club, the German Club, and the French Club. In short, Szemelényi, although not a professional musician, was hardly an amateur. He was the product of a musical family, was well trained as a musician, and took part in a wide range of musical events. He had a regular nonmusical source of income, but was constantly active in musical circles.

Another vocational amateur was Albert W. Tyler, a veteran of the Civil War who worked his way up from watchman to clerk in the Treasury Department. He was a remarkably active musician who "was connected at different times with numerous musical organizations."[31] In addition to playing double bass in the Georgetown Amateur Orchestra, Tyler directed Heald's American Band and served as president of the Washington Musical Assembly, No. 4. Much the same could be said of Edward W. Stone, the orchestra's librarian and flutist. He does not appear to have been a professional musician, but he was devoted to the ensemble. The *Washington Post* observed, "It is only justice to say that the orchestra was kept alive during one or two periods of disaster solely by his energy and persistence."[32]

Perhaps the most interesting type of musician was the true amateur, the player for whom the orchestra was a periodic social event and artistic outlet. More often than not, such players were highly educated musically (often by artists such as Robert Bernays, Josef Kaspar, and Ernest Lent); they were usually from wealthy families and frequently well connected in Washington's political and business life. All of the orchestra's founding members fit into this group, as do most of the remaining players listed in the above roster. Because many of the ensemble's early members were residents of Georgetown, it is not surprising to discover that they often had jobs in government, an aspect of the ensemble not lost on the press: "The interesting fact remains that on its bead-roll of honor are men prominent in our official, social, and business life."[33]

A brief tally of the remaining musicians from the roster reveals just how prominent these true amateurs were in Washington. John Hill was the chief of the Engraving Division at the Bureau of Engraving and Printing, and Ferdinand Weiler was the chief of the Loan Division in the United States Treasury. The treasury was also represented by Thomas Rogers, the superintendent of the National Bank Redemption Agency. There were a significant number of clerks in the orchestra, including Frank Schaefer, Charles Seaton, and Wallace Babcock. James Alexander was a clerk in the Post Office Department and the brother of Congressman De Alva Alexander from New York.

31 · "A Good Citizen Gone," *Washington Post*, March 7, 1892, 2.
32 · "His Work for Harmony," *Washington Post*, October 11, 1891, 14.
33 · "Good Amateur Music," *Washington Post*, January 31, 1891, 5.

The military was also well represented. George Finckel was chief clerk in the Quartermaster-General's office, James Gibson was a clerk in the War Department, and Dr. George Arthur was a U.S. Navy surgeon. Other federally employed members included I. Thomas Davis Jr. and Augustus Knorr, chemists in the Department of Agriculture, and Nelson Adams, a clerk in the Government Printing Office and presidentially appointed notary public.

Several orchestra members were in real estate or construction. Carl Keferstein was a well-known architect, Tyler Nordlinger a real estate developer, Otto Wolfsteiner a builder, and Julius Ulke a draftsman; William Jardin worked for the Washington Granite Company. Others were connected with the visual arts, such as F. S. Barbarin, who became curator of the Corcoran Gallery, painter Charles S. Hein, and H. Schutter, who had the intriguing job of superintendent of painting at the Post Office. Of the rest, Anthony Fischer was a mining engineer, Louis Brandt a tailor, and Francis Hyde Barbarin (Dr. Barbarin's son) a bookkeeper.

The bulk of the orchestra's players were men, but there were also several young women in the ensemble, most of whom came from Josef Kaspar's violin studio. Over its history the ensemble included a number of women belonging to prominent families. Miss Mabel Clare Money was the youngest daughter of Senator Hernando DeSoto Money of Mississippi. Some went on to pursue professional careers in music. Mattie Saxton, for example, moved to New York to study violin with Edward Arnold before her untimely death from tuberculosis. Birdie Lucas had a successful career as a local soloist. Nona Stosch (1872–1956) achieved much more fame. After training with Bernays and Kaspar, she traveled to Europe to pursue a musical education and began a concert career as Leonora von Stosch. She gave up the violin after her marriage to Sir Edgar Speyer, but in 1927 won the Pulitzer Prize for Poetry as Lady Leonora Speyer.[34] Finally, Ernest Lent's daughter was the well-known concert violinist Sylvia Lent (ca. 1907–72).[35]

The press could not resist commenting on the visual benefits that the women brought to the orchestra's concerts: "It is wholly without the bounds of competent criticism to speak rationally of a performance which deliberately intrenches [sic] itself behind a double-banked row of blushing young womanhood, mostly still in the 'teens, a charm of 'waving arms and woven faces,' wielding the bow like so many virgin Dianas."[36] But the presence of women was also a source of local pride. In writing that German orchestras were considering the addition of women, the *Washington Post* noted that this

34 · On Speyer's Washington career, see "They Play the Violin," *Washington Star*, March 12, 1892, 7.

35 · Sylvia Lent would marry the critic Alfred Frankenstein.

36 · "Good Amateur Music," *Washington Post*, January 31, 1891, 5.

District of Columbia ensemble was well ahead of the curve: "America will probably lead in this as in other reforms, and at present the Georgetown Orchestra is probably the largest and most important organization of its kind in which women are admitted on an equal footing with men."[37]

Amateur Reception

What did audiences think of this assortment of men and women, amateurs and professionals? Hundreds of reviews of the orchestra have been preserved, but just one major event reveals the public's impression. The 1888 election of the New Yorker Levi P. Morton to the vice presidency of the United States led the New York–based cultural philanthropist Jeannette Thurber to take a new interest in the musical life of Washington, D.C. She and Mrs. Morton conspired to equip the capital with a concert hall that would "elevate the standard of culture in this country." The press agreed that the election of Benjamin Harrison might finally allow Washington to construct the much-needed venue: "The change of Administration, with its infusion of new blood in the city, may, however, bring about the erection of the much-desired building."[38] The Thurber-Morton enterprise was soon realized with the opening of Lincoln Hall on December 20, 1889.

But Thurber was not finished with the capital. She recognized that if the city was to have a permanent and professional orchestra, it would be best to engage Washington's large population of amateur musicians. In January of 1890 she and Major John W. Powell (another musically inclined amateur and director of the U.S. Geological Survey) floated a proposal. They promised that if all of the city's amateur orchestral and choral organizations would band together, they would have access to Lincoln Hall as well as conductors and section leaders from New York and Boston.[39]

This scheme never materialized, but it did lead to a number of telling reactions in the papers. The most vicious letter was signed by Naphtali Nordlingler (probably a relative of Tyler Nordlinger, an amateur violinist, real estate developer, and Georgetown Orchestra member). Nordlinger's argument focused on local pride. He began by charging that "either through ignorance of the exact condition of local musical affairs, or the misrepresentation of some

---

37 · "Musical Notes," *Washington Post*, November 25, 1900, 20. Women were not unknown in nineteenth-century American orchestras, but as Anna-Lise P. Santella shows in this volume (chapter I.2), they most often appeared in all-woman ensembles.
38 · "A Music Hall Possible," *Washington Post*, March 24, 1889, 10.
39 · "Music and Music Lovers," *Washington Post*, January 19, 1890, 12; "Mrs. Thurber's Ideas," *Washington Post*, January 20, 1890, 6.

cackling 'deletante' [*sic*], her ideas were unpractical and tended in the wrong direction."[40] Thurber's offer of a professional conductor was unneeded, inspired by an "ignorance of the make-up, condition and temperament of an amateur orchestra." Celebrated conductors could never hope to "cope with the thousand and one difficulties which surround the efforts of an amateur band," and quite simply there was no need to bring in New Yorkers to prop up the ensemble. Not only did the orchestra take pride in its amateur status, but Washington was fully capable of supplying expert players: "If the orchestra desired a professional first violinist there are in Washington several competent men to select from without calling on New York." If Thurber believed that Washington's musical culture was incomplete without a professional ensemble, Nordlingler suggested the opposite: "Let not, however, the public believe that the standard of musical culture here is not high. We have a discriminating and intelligent public—musical societies as well as individuals of recognized ability." Indeed, Washington did not even need a New Yorker's money; the capital had its own philanthropists: "It will not be so far in the future when some or one of our own music-loving citizens will, 'Higginson-like,' give the financial impetus to the establishment of a professional orchestra."[41]

It is striking just how much Washingtonians rallied around this amateur ensemble. They were understandably proud of the accomplishments of their friends and neighbors, but they also defended the musical benefits of an amateur orchestra. One writer suggested that a group of amateurs could coexist more harmoniously than an ensemble of professionals: "In the first place, the active members are under no expense; in the second place, all quarrels or jealousies are instantly suppressed, and, thirdly, its composition is thoroughly democratic. Rich and poor play side by side, and social inequalities are lost sight of on the common plane of music."[42] Another critic suggested that the performances themselves benefited when the players were volunteers instead of employees: "It is a pleasure to hear orchestral music where it is evident that performers are appreciative, intelligent men and not automations, where they and their conductor interpret *con amore* and not at so much per hour."[43] As a result of its amateur members, the orchestra "has risen, step by step, to a position now on a plane unattained, perhaps, by any similar amateur musical organization in this country."[44]

40 · All quotations in this paragraph are from Naphtali Nordlingler, "From the Amateur's Standpoint," *Washington Post*, January 26, 1890, 10.

41 · The reference is to Henry Lee Higginson, the businessman who founded the Boston Symphony Orchestra in 1881.

42 · "Kaspar Takes the Baton," *Washington Post*, November 21, 1886, 2.

43 · "Some Musical Matters," *Washington Post*, February 15, 1885, 2.

44 · "Amusements," *Washington Post*, February 14, 1885, 2.

The story of the Georgetown Amateur Orchestra and its local reception in the 1880s and 1890s reveals that Washington had a symphony of which to be proud, and its inhabitants were able to enjoy orchestral music performed by their friends and neighbors. The Georgetown Amateur Orchestra's twenty-year history and remarkable continuity in membership effectively qualified it as Washington's permanent orchestra, at least in comparison to its professional rivals.

A Transient Ensemble: The Washington Symphony Orchestra(s)

The Georgetown Orchestra was hardly the only amateur ensemble in the District of Columbia. On November 14, 1886, the *Washington Post* announced: "The Washington Symphony Orchestra's first concert will take place on the 30th and will be for the benefit of the Nurses' Training School."[45] This first incarnation of the Washington Symphony Orchestra was led by none other than Robert Bernays, who had just been replaced as conductor of the Georgetown amateurs. In forming the Washington Symphony, Bernays was looking to create a musical outlet for his private students, and like Josef Kaspar, he turned to the "judicious employment of several professionals" who "did much to steady" his new ensemble.[46]

This early version of the Washington Symphony did not establish a regular concert routine, but rather appeared sporadically throughout the late 1880s. Perhaps its most impressive performances came in 1888 when Bernays took a seat as concertmaster and handed the baton to the leader of the Marine Band, John Philip Sousa.[47] Surviving programs indicate that Sousa led Sunday concerts of light classical works at the New National Theatre and directed the orchestra in conjunction with Washington's Choral Society in a performance of John Francis Barnett's cantata *The Ancient Mariner*.[48] Sousa would lead a number of semiprofessional organizations in Washington, including the Philharmonic Society, a choral organization often accompanied by players from the Marine Band.[49]

Even Sousa could not hold the Washington Symphony together for long. Attracting audiences meant playing "music of the lightest, frothiest charac-

45 · "An Oratorio Society," *Washington Post*, November 14, 1886, 2.

46 · "Amusements," *Washington Post*, December 1, 1888, 2. A roster of Bernays's orchestra was printed in "A Round of Concerts," *Washington Post*, November 28, 1886, 2.

47 · "Amusements," *Washington Post*, February 12, 1888, 4. Bernays married his conductor's sister, Elizabeth Sousa, in January 1890.

48 · Programs, Fowles Scrapbook, United States Marine Band Library, 8, 11.

49 · See unlabeled clippings in the Sousa Scrapbook, Blakely Papers, Manuscripts and Archives Division, New York Public Library.

ter," and Sousa could not get his professional players to donate their services unless the repertory was worthy of their attention: "The men who really desire to add to their musical education by reading meritorious works, even at some sacrifice, are not willing to lose time and money without adding to their intelligence."[50] The Bernays-Sousa Washington Symphony vanished by the late 1880s.

The next incarnation of the Washington Symphony Orchestra came in February of 1902 when the famous composer of comic opera, Reginald de Koven, attempted to form a new orchestra for the District of Columbia. Recently married to the daughter of Illinois senator Charles B. Farwell, de Koven had joined the city's social circles and was determined to harness local talent and "put a permanent orchestra on a sound and practical basis."[51] His plans were grand; de Koven hoped to raise $300,000 to establish a sixty-five-piece ensemble and a self-sustaining concert hall. After fifteen rehearsals and considerable press, the orchestra gave its first concert on April 28, 1902, with pianist Ignacy Paderewski as soloist. The *Washington Star* noted that the city had heard "symphonies played by Washington musicians" before, as "the Georgetown Orchestra has done that for many years." The new ensemble was different in that it "starts out with the symphony as its basis of operations, and one may expect one composition of that character at each concert."[52]

De Koven's enterprise generated considerable buzz; announcing a "New Epoch in Music," the *Washington Post* published the orchestra's roster on April 27, 1902. A glance through the names reveals that de Koven drew his men from the same sources his predecessors had used: strings from the city's theater pits and winds from the United States Marine Band. Violinists Chris Arth Jr. and Raymond Schroeder, as well as violist Charles Donch, came from the National Theater. Violinist Sol Minster was music director at the Columbia and Belasco Theaters, and his section mate Victor Johnson led the orchestra at the Lafayette Square Opera House.[53] The Marine Band gave the orchestra nearly half its musicians, and William H. Santelmann, the band's leader, became the orchestra's associate conductor. These men, as well as several others who listed their occupation as musician or music teacher in the city directory, reveal an orchestra consisting of local, professional musi-

50 · "A Memorable Musical Season," *Washington Post*, March 11, 1888, 7.

51 · Reginald de Koven, quoted in "For a Symphony Orchestra," *Washington Post*, February 12, 1902, 10. A more detailed look de Koven's Washington Symphony appears in Orly Leah Krasner, "A Capital Idea: Reginald de Koven and the Washington Symphony Orchestra," in *Music, American Made: Essays in Honor of John Graziano*, ed. J. Koegel (2011).

52 · "Symphony Orchestra," *Washington Star*, April 29, 1902, 5.

53 · Robert Bernays had used some of the same theater musicians (including Victor Johnson and Sol Minster) in his version of the Washington Symphony.

cians. In this way, the new Washington Symphony Orchestra was quite different from the Georgetown amateur ensemble.

But such an ensemble of professionals faced a serious problem. Marine Band players, with their guaranteed government salaries, could presumably underbid any civilian for musical work within the District of Columbia. The musician's union—Local 161 of the American Federation of Musicians—viewed this as a threat, and their rules therefore prohibited members from playing alongside military musicians. This regulation was often quietly ignored, but a composer as well known as de Koven presented all-too-visible a target.[54] In June of 1902, a few months after the Washington Symphony's inaugural performance, the American Federation of Musicians recommended that its locals boycott de Koven's compositions so long as he employed enlisted men in his orchestra.[55] The *Washington Post* immediately recognized the danger: "If the Marine Band is to be debarred from participating in the concerts because the men are ineligible to membership in the federation, or per contra the union men are to be excluded, the concerts are impossible." Furthermore, it was hardly fair that de Koven's fame forced him to "bear the brunt of this ungallant attack."[56]

The orchestra met in October and put the situation to a vote. With the Marine musicians abstaining—an action "deserving of much commendation"—the Washington Symphony disbanded itself and reorganized without its military members. The Marine Band's assistant leader, Walter F. Smith, noted that the orchestra had little choice and that the result was "a case of accepting the lesser of two evils. The absence of the band from de Koven's orchestra will be a detriment, but not so great a one as a boycott against his music."[57] In less than a year, this permanent ensemble had given a single concert, dissolved, and reformed as the De Koven Orchestra. The AFM subsequently dropped its boycott.[58]

Despite the name change, the orchestra was still commonly referred to as the Washington Symphony, and during the season of 1902–3, it gave five monthly concerts on Tuesday afternoons and made one "popular" Sunday

54 · Given Washington's large supply of military musicians, there was frequent conflict with the union, which led to several efforts to legally separate military and civilian musicians. See, for example, "The Marine Band versus Civilian Bands," *Musical Courier* 44 (February 12, 1902): 27.

55 · "Proposed Boycott on De Koven's Music," *Washington Post*, June 5, 1902, 10.

56 · "The World of Amusement," *Washington Post*, June 8, 1902, 30.

57 · "Marine Band Dropped," *Washington Post*, October 16, 1902, 2.

58 · "De Koven Boycott Lifted," *Washington Post*, October 18, 1902, 12. De Koven commented on this situation in "Reginald de Koven," Musical Courier 47 (September 2, 1903): 12.

evening appearance.[59] But the dismissal of the Marine Band caused a significant problem. While string players could still be found locally, many of the winds now had to be supplied by bringing in union musicians from other cities.[60] Despite local players willing to work for "a minimum of remuneration" and a conductor "receiving no compensation," the orchestra's first season ended with losses totaling $10,000. Some twenty benefactors covered this deficit, but such a "condition of affairs is certainly unjust and unsatisfactory, and the public should not require this handful of enthusiasts to bear such loss another season."[61]

Still, de Koven struggled on. The season of 1903–4 consisted of five monthly concerts on Friday afternoons. The Sunday evening popular concerts had proved so successful that the orchestra gave eleven of them.[62] In a clever gimmick, de Koven allowed one concert to be programmed by audience vote. The selected works in order of popularity were Grieg's *Peer Gynt Suite*, the largo from Handel's *Xerxes*, and the intermezzo from Mascagni's *Cavalleria Rusticana*. De Koven congratulated Washington because he "received only one request for rag-time, and the person who asked for it apologized for doing so."[63] Despite this grand season, the absence of Marine Band musicians remained a fundamental problem. Forced to import players from other cities, the orchestra had to guarantee them a salary. This increased the operating budget so dramatically that the treasurer was forced to concede that "even were every seat in the house sold for each performance, there would still remain a considerable deficit."[64]

59 · The Tuesday concerts were held on December 9, January 6, February 10, March 10, and April 21. The Sunday concert was on April 12.

60 · "The World of Amusement," *Washington Post*, November 1, 1903, FP6. Some of the imported players were named in "Symphony Orchestra," *Washington Post*, November 15, 1903, L5.

61 · Edward H. Droop, "Symphony Orchestra," *Washington Post*, April 5, 1903, B6. Droop was the orchestra's treasurer and general manager.

62 · The Friday concerts were held on December 11, January 15, February 12, March 18, and April 15. The popular concerts were held almost weekly on January 3, 17, and 31; February 14, 21, and 28; March 6, 13, and 27; and April 3 and 24. The orchestra also gave three joint concerts with local choirs (December 13 and 27 and April 10). In February de Koven was named conductor of the Carroll Institute Choir, further facilitating such collaborations. "De Koven's Musical Coup," *Washington Post*, February 13, 1904, 7.

63 · "Plays Request Numbers," *Washington Post*, February 29, 1904, 7. The orchestra's role in saving Washington from the new popular music had been noted in the *Musical Courier*: "Permanent orchestras are the very features that are necessary in the large cities of America for the permanent education of the people in good music. They are the best cure for the rag-time proposition" ("The Washington Orchestra Question," *Musical Courier* 46 [January 21, 1903]: 10).

64 · E. H. Droop, "Appeal for Symphony Orchestra," *Washington Post*, April 17, 1904, A8.

For the third season, de Koven put all of his chips on the table. Five monthly concerts were planned, with each to be repeated in Baltimore. The weekly popular concerts would be expanded to include a series of Wednesday promenade matinees and six young people's performances. Because this plan required more rehearsal time, de Koven decided to bring in orchestral musicians from Boston, New York, Chicago, and Cincinnati and to keep them in Washington not just for the concerts but on salary for eighteen weeks. To cover the projected $40,000 cost, de Koven established the Washington Symphony Orchestra, Incorporated stock company. The capital would now have an official orchestra, and the press was pleased to report that "Washington is one of six cities of America that have permanent orchestras."[65]

De Koven's efforts were heroic, and he was clearly willing to weather financial risks, but in January 1905 he received an unexpected blow from Washington's elite. The highest-profile engagement of the season would be Theodore Roosevelt's inauguration, and a music committee solicited bids for the inaugural ball. De Koven offered his symphony for $1,800 but was outbid by William Haley, who promised to provide his band for $200 less. De Koven was also underbid for a series of inaugural concerts, which went instead to the Marine Band.[66]

De Koven was furious. In a letter to the *Washington Post*, he argued that the decision was "so prejudiced and pitiably provincial that any thinking man ... will call absolutely every action in question."[67] The conductor took the affair personally: "I have neglected my profession, which has earned me a livelihood for many years, cut my professional income in half, given my entire time, thought, and energy for three years without compensation" to the Washington Symphony. "I cannot but feel that the result of my sincere effort has been that the Washington public ... prefers Haley's Band ... to the Washington Symphony Orchestra, and thereby declines to recognize an organization which, through its supporters, has spent $30,000 during the last three years to further the cause of good music in Washington.... I can only accept the verdict thus rendered of the total failure of my efforts."[68]

65 · "Gave Concert in Baltimore," *Washington Post*, November 20, 1904, 2; "Campaign for Music," *Washington Post*, November 27, 1904, 11. The quotation is from "Permanent Orchestra," *Washington Post*, November 18, 1904, 4.

66 · "Inaugural Day Music," *Washington Post*, January 26, 1905, 2.

67 · Reginald de Koven, "Mr. De Koven Protests," *Washington Post*, January 26, 1905, 2.

68 · Reginald de Koven, "Gives Way to Haley," *Washington Post*, January 31, 1905, 12. The situation elicited considerable debate in the press, including another fight with the union. This time the union took de Koven's side and questioned the right of the Marine Band to bid on the inaugural performances. See "Parade Plans Ripen," *Washington Post*, January 13, 1905, 2; Percy S. Foster, "Chairman Foster Denies," *Washington Post*, January 27, 1905, 2; "Inaugural Music Discord," *Washington Post*, January 29, 1905, 2; "Says Protest Was Made," *Washing-*

The ensemble's February concert was advanced to January "owing to the financial troubles" of the orchestra, which issued a circular wherein it lamented declining audiences and complained that "many of the subscribers have failed to make good."[69] The *Post* chastised the city: "Washington has not covered itself with glory in its treatment of the Symphony Orchestra."[70] The ensemble gave what appears to have been its last regular concert on February 5, 1905. Because of an illness, de Koven did not conduct, and his wife later remembered the events: "My husband struggled heroically to save the cause of the orchestra.... The effort to continue the orchestra without the promised financial subsidy was finally very harmful to my husband's health and diminished the vitality necessary for the writing of his operas."[71]

With the orchestra collapsing and de Koven in despair, blame could now be assigned. Reviews indicate that the ensemble had its fair share of problems. Without a dedicated hall in Washington, regular concerts had to be held in theaters, which required afternoon performances.[72] It took de Koven some time to realize that he must keep programs short "in order to permit hungry people to reach home at a reasonable dinner hour." Afternoon concerts conflicted with the "social duties demanding the attention of so many of the patronesses," which further complicated fund-raising.[73]

But the real culprit was the American Federation of Musicians. In an effort to protect its members, the union had effectively bankrupted the orchestra, a fact not lost on critic Berenice Thompson. Forcing the orchestra to import civilian players from other cities when Washington already had a wealth of Marine Band musicians placed the ensemble in a position of "water, water everywhere, nor any drop to drink." As Thompson explained, "With all due consideration for a certain few orchestral players in town who want to earn as large a livelihood as possible," the orchestra should not endure losses "caused by the weak subservience of union dictation."[74]

ton *Post*, January 30, 1905, 2; Jno. Pool, "Symphony Orchestra Music," *Washington Post*, January 30, 1905, 9; "Marine Band Will Play," Washington Post, February 4, 1905, 2; "Inaugural Sky Clear," *Washington Post*, February 5, 1905, 2.

69 · "The Symphony Concert," *Washington Post*, January 28, 1905, 3.
70 · Ibid.
71 · Anna Farwell de Koven, *A Musician and His Wife* (1926), 204.
72 · The *Musical Courier* stated bluntly: "The lack of a hall in which to give concerts is the basic cause of the suspension of the Washington Symphony Orchestra." See "Washington Symphony Orchestra," *Musical Courier* 50 (February 1, 1905): 41.
73 · "News and Gossip," *Washington Post*, January 18, 1903, 34.
74 · "Case of the Marine Band," *Washington Post*, June 25, 1905, S9.

Epilogue: The Marine Band, Washington, and the Possibility of a Local Orchestra

Oscar Sonneck noted the "threatened disbandment of the Washington Symphony Orchestra with extreme regret," but the ensemble's rapid disintegration was guaranteed almost from the start.[75] Despite Jeannette Thurber's efforts, the city still lacked a dedicated concert hall, a vacuum that forced ensembles such as the Washington Symphony to hold afternoon performances when the theaters were otherwise unoccupied. De Koven quickly discovered that such scheduling interfered with his patrons' social obligations and severely limited his efforts to build an audience or engage in fund-raising. Even more detrimental to the success of any professional orchestra was the presence of the United States Marine Band. This group, which did not require indoor performance space, provided Washingtonians with free outdoor concerts. During summer afternoons these occurred Wednesdays at the Capitol, Thursdays at the Marine Barracks, and Saturdays at the White House. On winter Sundays the band often presented sacred concerts of light orchestral music at the National Theatre.

The Marine Band's presence had two effects. First, it served as the professional ensemble Washington was otherwise lacking. Much of the band's repertory consisted of the Italian opera selections and light dance pieces so popular with nineteenth-century audiences. The band also performed more serious numbers, including overtures and selections from Wagner's *Tannhäuser, Rienzi, Lohengrin,* and *Der fliegende Holländer.* Thanks to the Marine Band, Washingtonians may well have been the first Americans to hear selections from Pietro Mascagni's *Cavalleria rusticana.*[76] But the Marine Band was important for a second reason: many of Washington's professional musicians were members of the ensemble, members eager to both supplement their military pay and heighten their musical experiences. This limited the opportunities available for civilian professional musicians to find work within the District of Columbia.

As de Koven discovered, any publically ambitious effort to combine

75 · Sonneck, "Views of People," *Washington Post,* January 30, 1905, 9.
76 · The Marine Band performed selections from Mascagni's opera in early 1891. See Kirk, *Music at the White House,* 129. Sousa had a catalog of the band's library prepared and published as *Catalogue of Music: Band, U. S. Marine Corps* (1885). It includes operatic and concert overtures, a large number of opera selections, as well as songs, various dances, and some orchestral music. The most frequently listed composers, in order, are Giuseppe Verdi, Johann Strauss, Emile Waldteufel, Arthur Sullivan, Fred Godfrey, Jacques Offenbach, Franz von Suppé, Gioachino Rossini, Gaetano Donizetti, Charles Gounod, Felix Mendelssohn, Adolphe Adam, Giacomo Meyerbeer, and Richard Wagner.

Marine Band players with their handful of civilian counterparts could run afoul of union rules. These rules forced de Koven to bring in musicians from other cities, musicians toward whom Washington audiences felt little loyalty. The city's many amateur ensembles, on the other hand, relied on native talent, which helped them to foster a sense of community that imported professionals could not match. The players brought in by de Koven or promised by Thurber were strangers; the amateurs were friends, neighbors, and colleagues. Because union rules did not apply, these amateurs were free to supplement whatever talent they might have with the skills of professional musicians borrowed from the Marine Band.[77]

The longest running of these ensembles was the Georgetown Amateur Orchestra, which began entertaining Washington audiences in January of 1882. It had largely ceased operations in the summer of 1895, and when the *Washington Post* first heard of de Koven's efforts seven years later, it decried Washington's lack of a permanent orchestra. There was only the Marine Band, "splendid in its way, but not an orchestra," and touring ensembles, "uncertain, vagrant, and not always satisfactory."[78] The Georgetown amateurs had made a second, tentative debut in May of 1900, and, provoked by this newspaper article, the orchestra's president, Brainard H. Warner, wrote to the *Post*, calling the city's attention "not only to our existence, but to the fact that we think we have a brilliant future." He continued: "For more than twenty years we have had an organization in this city in which several hundred Washington artists, young and old, combining our best professional and amateur talent, have given concerts to the satisfaction of the music-loving public."[79] The ensemble's vice president, Frank B. Metzerott, published a letter in the same issue of the paper in which he praised the Georgetown Amateur Orchestra and went on to express doubts about the viability of de Koven's enterprise: "We have an orchestra which has been in existence for many years, giving concerts of a very high order, so fine, in fact, that it will be a long time before the new organization will be able to equal them.... Why not encourage what we have instead of chasing rainbows, something that seems to be chronic in our city?"[80]

77 · Programs demonstrating the Marine Band's collaborations with various amateur ensembles can be found in the Fowles Scrapbook (Marine Band Library), as well as in the endless requests for the ensemble in Record Group 127, National Archives and Records Administration, Washington, D.C.

78 · "Artistic Prospects at This Capital," *Washington Post*, February 25, 1902, 6.

79 · Brainard H. Warner, "The Georgetown Orchestra," *Washington Post*, February 28, 1902, 4. On the orchestra's 1900 debut, see "Musical Notes," *Washington Post*, January 21, 1900, 17; "Georgetown Orchestra," *Washington Star*, May 4, 1900, 16.

80 · Frank B. Metzerott, letter to the editor, *Washington Post*, February 28, 1902, 4. The paper responded in "A Really Local Orchestra" on March 1, 1902, 6, to say that it merely meant

Whatever the musical value of de Koven's orchestra, its makeup prevented Washington audiences from seeing it as a local ensemble. The same cannot be said for the Georgetown Amateur Orchestra. It may have begun as a casual pastime, but after spending some two decades before Washington audiences, it could take credit for elevating the public taste: "Washington is becoming more and more a musical center. Of all the factors in the city's musical life there is none that excites more widespread interest than the Georgetown Orchestra. For over a quarter of a century it has united the amateurs and professionals of the city, and afforded a school for the younger generation of musicians. Most of the younger members of the orchestra—and they are in the majority—heard their first symphony at the concerts of the organization they are helping to perpetuate."[81] There can be little doubt that the personal connection felt between the Georgetown players, their audience, and the city's press led to many overly flattering reviews. However, the ensemble was also seen as contributing to Washington's musical edification: "The Georgetown Orchestra is a whole musical education in itself for those who are fortunate enough to possess the requirements necessary for membership in it. When a student in any of the musical institutions in this city becomes far advanced enough to be able to keep up with the playing of the orchestra, he is taken in and given a thorough course of instruction, for no better instruction can be obtained than that which is given in this practical way. The only requirement is that he be able, through practice and study, to play his part as well as the rest."[82]

Washington would see other orchestras come and go, some of which were made up of professional musicians. In October of 1906, Hermann Rakemann announced plans for a Rakemann Concert Orchestra, drawn from members of the Washington Symphony.[83] An orchestra formed by German-born conductor and composer Heinrich Hammer undertook a Beethoven cycle in 1909–10. In 1925 Kurt Hetzel proposed a professional orchestra, and the next year he pulled together "eighty-one musicians chosen from the theatres and cinema houses of Washington."[84] Such efforts kept professional orchestral music alive until Hans Kindler conducted the first concerts of the National Symphony in 1931.[85] Amateur ensembles also continued to exist. These in-

Washington needed an orchestra that would present concerts "thirty or forty times during a season."

81 · "Last Concert of the Georgetown Orchestra," *Washington Post*, May 21, 1901, 6.

82 · "Georgetown Orchestra's Fiftieth Concert," *Washington Post*, April 22, 1900, 26.

83 · See "New Orchestra Pleases," *Washington Post*, October 29, 1906, 12; "Under Director Rakemann," *Washington Post*, May 2, 1909, ES3.

84 · "In Washington," *Time*, May 3, 1926, 15.

85 · The National Symphony's early rosters reveal several musicians borrowed from its predecessors, including Minster, Arth, and Rakemann. My thanks to David Bragunier, princi-

cluded the Rebew Orchestra, put together in 1900 by H. W. Weber; the Government Printing Office Orchestra, which could be heard between 1900 and 1940, and the Agriculture Orchestra, which performed sporadically between the 1930s and 1960s.[86]

Modern scholarship often privileges professional ensembles, and it seems only fair to seek the roots of the National Symphony Orchestra in de Koven's turn-of-the-century efforts. Indeed, the first history of the National Symphony begins by noting that de Koven's ensemble "seems to have been the first organized attempt to form" a serious orchestra in the capital.[87] But focusing on professional musicians too easily dismisses the efforts of Washington's amateur musicians who during the late nineteenth century "devoted themselves, heart and soul, to the cult and gospel of the best music rendered by the best methods."[88] By the time it gave its last concert on May 17, 1905, the Georgetown Amateur Orchestra had managed to play fifty-seven "public rehearsals," as well as many benefit and joint concerts. Lasting more than a quarter century, this was, in many ways, Washington's first permanent orchestra.

---

pal tuba (emeritus) of the orchestra, for sharing his early rosters. The orchestra gave its first performances in Constitution Hall, where it often played before making its home at the Kennedy Center.

86 · Very little is known about the various government office orchestras, although some—such as the National Institutes of Health Philharmonia—continue to exist. Washington's most important amateur organization continues to be the Friday Morning Music Club. Its history is told in Charlotte Shear, The First Hundred Years of the Friday Morning Music Club of Washington, D.C. (1987).

87 · *A Short History of the National Symphony Orchestra* (1949), 1.

88 · "Good Amateur Music," *Washington Post*, January 31, 1891, 5.

PART III

Conductors, Promoters, Patrons

Marketing the American Orchestra

JOHN SPITZER

Nineteenth-century American orchestras supported themselves almost entirely at the box office, selling their performances to the public. This was a marked contrast to many European orchestras of the time, which enjoyed significant state patronage. It is also a contrast to today's American orchestras, most of which derive only about one-third of their income from ticket sales.[1] Several other income sources that modern orchestras enjoy—private contributions, recording royalties, and government grants, for example—were not available to nineteenth-century American orchestras. The public was their only patron, and orchestras lived and died in the marketplace, competing (or in some cases cooperating) with other forms of entertainment for the public's dollar.

Most orchestral performances in nineteenth-century America were sold in a package with another form of entertainment, most often in the theater, where the orchestra accompanied operas, ballets, or vaudeville acts and played incidental music for spoken dramas. Orchestras also accompanied performances by singers, instrumental soloists, and choruses; at restaurants and beer gardens they enlivened drinking, dining, dancing, and other entertainment. The public paid its money at the ticket booth to hear the singer, to see the play, or to be entertained by ventriloquists and trained dogs. It patronized the orchestra only indirectly.

In orchestral concerts, however, which became more frequent in the 1840s, the orchestra became the principal attraction. Such concerts were usually organized by the musicians themselves or by a conductor. Even though there was usually a singer or an instrumental soloist (often both), the bulk of the

---

1 · League of American Orchestras, "Quick Orchestra Facts, 2007–8 Revenue Breakdown," http://www.americanorchestras.org/images/stories/knowledge_pdf/Quick_Orch_Facts_2010.pdf.

program consisted of orchestral music, and the focus was on the orchestra itself. How could such a concert be marketed to the public? There were a number of possible strategies.

Selling spectacle was one of the earliest marketing strategies, following the pattern established by such showmen as P. T Barnum, who had sold the American public the "Feejee Mermaid" and "General Tom Thumb" in the 1840s and then Jenny Lind in the 1850s. The classic example of an orchestral spectacle was Louis Antoine Jullien's tour of 1853–54. Jullien came to America with a group of "unrivaled" European solo players to which he added some sixty American instrumentalists to make the largest orchestra that had ever been heard in the United States.[2] Americans flocked to hear Jullien and his orchestra—first in New York, then in Boston, Philadelphia, and Baltimore, and then on a tour that took him to more than twenty American cities. The success of Jullien's American tour demonstrated that an orchestra could be marketed to the public as a spectacle, independent of any other entertainment. Bernard Ullman ran a similar campaign in 1858, also selling orchestral concerts as spectacle. He brought Alfred Musard to New York, where the French conductor led a "MONSTER ORCHESTRA" of 120 instrumentalists for a five-week season.[3] Ullman's venture was a financial success, but it did not create as much of a sensation as Jullien had five years earlier, perhaps because Musard was judged to be considerably less charismatic than Jullien, perhaps because, as spectacle, an orchestra was already beginning to seem rather ordinary to the American public. Later attempts to market orchestra concerts as spectacle—for example, Theodore Thomas's concerts at the Centennial Exhibition in Philadelphia in 1876—were much less successful.[4] In general, orchestras found it hard to compete with other spectacles: they offered little visual interest, a relatively static repertory, and little by way of sex or scandal. Spectacle was a viable marketing strategy in the earliest days of American orchestras, but it was not promising for the long run.

A second strategy was *selling the soloist*. American orchestras tried to induce the public to buy tickets by presenting vocal or instrumental soloists at almost every one of their concerts. The Germania Musical Society in the late 1840s and early 1850s offered (among others) singers Fortunata Tedesco and Adelaide Phillips, violinists Ole Bull and Camilla Urso, and pianists Otto Dresel and Alfred Jaëll. While Tedesco, Bull, and Dresel were well-known soloists, whose international reputations attracted listeners to Germania

2 · For Jullien's tour, see chapter IV.1 in this volume.
3 · For Ullman and Musard, see chapter III.1 in this volume. Most of the members of Musard's orchestra were American musicians.
4 · See Ezra Schabas, *Theodore Thomas: America's Conductor and Builder of Orchestras, 1835–1905* (1989), 69–78.

concerts, Phillips, Urso, and Jaëll were young performers with compelling personal narratives.[5] The New York Philharmonic featured either singers or instrumental soloists (or both) on every single program from its founding in 1842 until 1878.[6]

Selling the soloist was a generally successful strategy for nineteenth-century American orchestras, but it created a financial problem. Soloists' fees were often high (especially those of singers), and they had to be guaranteed in advance of the concert. Before the orchestra could begin to make a profit, the soloist would have to attract enough additional listeners to cover his or her fee. The New York Philharmonic lost this wager several times, particularly during the depressions of 1857 and 1873. The Harvard Musical Association Orchestra in Boston usually avoided the problem by limiting itself to local soloists who would play for free. But these semi-anonymous soloists were harder to market and did not draw as many new listeners to concerts as did international stars.

Another marketing strategy, *selling the conductor*, was much less common in the nineteenth century than it is today. Jullien, with his raven locks, his white kid gloves, and his jewel-encrusted baton, made himself into a spectacle along with his orchestra. But most of the men who led American orchestras were not conducting specialists: they were all-around musicians who often played in the orchestras they led. At the New York Philharmonic, the conductorship rotated from concert to concert or from season to season until 1866. The Cincinnati Philharmonic in the 1880s was conducted in successive seasons by a cellist, a flutist, and a violinist.[7] Theodore Thomas was an effective and much-respected conductor, but he was far from charismatic. Rather than selling himself, he marketed his orchestra, his repertory, his soloists, and his mission. The first men after Jullien to capitalize on their personalities and their special prowess as conductors before American audiences were Anton Seidl in New York (1885–98) and Arthur Nikisch in Boston (1889–93). Young, handsome, and charismatic, Seidl and Nikisch became the focus of personality cults. People bought tickets to their concerts not just to hear the Boston Symphony or the Brooklyn Philharmonic but to see and hear Nikisch or Seidl conduct.[8]

5 · The Germanians also performed with yet more famous singers, Jenny Lind and Henriette Sontag, but as accompanists rather than at their own concerts. See chapter III.4 in this volume.
6 · The Philharmonic gave its first concert with exclusively orchestral music on February 9, 1878. A few earlier Philharmonic programs featured choruses rather than solo singers. See chapter V.3 in this volume.
7 · See chapter II.3 in this volume.
8 · On the Seidl cult, see Joseph Horowitz, *Wagner Nights: An American History* (1994).

Selling novelty was another way to market orchestras. For American audiences of the 1840s and 1850s, an orchestra was a novelty in and of itself. Many of the people who came to hear the Germania Musical Society or Jullien's orchestra on tour had never heard an orchestra play a concert. According to a reporter at Jullien's concert in Louisville, Kentucky, "Our citizens acquired altogether new ideas last evening as to the powers which a combination of musical instruments may possess."[9] The New York Philharmonic, the Harvard Musical Association Orchestra, the Chicago Philharmonic, and the Cincinnati Orchestra enjoyed similar success as fashionable novelties during their first few seasons. But as audiences became more familiar with orchestras and orchestral repertory, the novelty tended to fade, and box office receipts began to fall. For an orchestra to market itself as a novelty, it soon had to offer more than just a concert. Thus Alfred Musard's 1858 concerts in New York advertised "DISTINGUISHED SOLO PLAYERS FROM PARIS" and "YOUNG LADIES of prepossessing appearance" serving tea and coffee.[10] By the 1870s the bar for orchestral novelty had been raised yet further. Now the young ladies had taken their place in the orchestra itself. "LADY ORCHESTRA! LADY VIOLINISTS! LADY CORNET PLAYERS!" screamed an ad for Lina Edwin's New York Theater in 1871.[11] As a marketing strategy, novelty was inherently short-lived. By the last quarter of the century, the residents of most American cities were familiar enough with orchestral concerts that an orchestra (even a lady orchestra) was no longer much of a novelty at all.

Yet another strategy was *selling quality*. Marketing orchestras by emphasizing the quality of their performances was a promising long-range strategy because it allowed for both improvement and competition. The Germania Musical Society, introduced in 1848 as "the best band of instrumental performers ever in the country," astonished audiences with its precise ensemble, nuanced dynamics, and accomplished soloists. The tour five years later of Jullien's orchestra eclipsed the Germanians even in their home city of Boston, where a critic wrote that Jullien had provided "such music as has never before been given in this city and such as cannot be soon expected in the future."[12] The tours of the Theodore Thomas Orchestra, beginning in 1869, had a similar effect: audiences in Chicago, Cincinnati, St. Louis, and elsewhere came to hear the Thomas Orchestra because it was widely acknowledged to be "the finest organization of its kind in America."[13] Marketing an orchestra as "the best" gave ticket buyers the feeling that they were purchas-

9 · See chapter IV.1, note 58, in this volume.
10 · See chapter III.1, note 25, in this volume.
11 · See chapter I.2, note 25, in this volume.
12 · See chapter IV.1, note 48, in this volume.
13 · See chapter II.2, note 53, in this volume.

ing not just an evening's entertainment but a product of superior quality, and if this product seemed scarce enough, they might be convinced to buy season subscriptions rather than single tickets in order to demonstrate their discerning taste and guarantee themselves seats.

Most of the strategies reviewed above—selling spectacle, selling the soloist, and so forth—were successful in that they persuaded Americans, at least sometimes, to buy tickets to concert performances by orchestras. But none of these strategies enabled American orchestras to sustain themselves year after year at the box office. The Theodore Thomas Orchestra came closest, but only by means of incessant touring. Orchestras thrived in theaters, at the opera house, in beer gardens, and other venues where they accompanied other entertainment. But as concert performers, orchestras found it hard to compete for the patronage of the ticket-buying public.

Performances, however, were not the only thing that orchestras had to offer. Orchestras could also be marketed by *selling culture*. Nineteenth-century American orchestras overcame their shortcomings at the box office by creating patronage outside the marketplace—contributions from wealthy individuals, who made up the difference between ticket sales and the orchestra's expenses. Orchestras gained this patronage through a strategy that marketed the orchestra as cultural uplift and civic improvement.

Uplift was an important component of the New York Philharmonic's mission when the orchestra was founded in 1842. Its early annual reports appealed to "enjoyment of the highest intellectual character" and "refinement of the human heart."[14] The Harvard Musical Association saw its mission in even more idealistic terms: to offer the public "refined pleasure, instruction, and good to all concerned."[15] Music critics told the American public that orchestra concerts were an essential part of general culture and a vital ingredient of civic life. As one Chicago journalist put it: "That refined communities prosper, in a material point of view, more than those where the refining influence of music and education are less regarded, is a well-conceded fact."[16] Marketing orchestras as cultural uplift had at least two results: it broadened the market for orchestral music, and it persuaded civic leaders and wealthy elites to support orchestras as an investment in civic progress.

John Sullivan Dwight in Boston was a pioneer of uplift, both as editor of *Dwight's Journal of Music* and as manager of the Harvard Musical Association Orchestra.[17] Setting out from the premise that "the finer the kind of music

14 · See chapter V.3, note 5, in this volume.
15 · See chapter III.2, note 29, in this volume.
16 · See chapter II.4, note 21, in this volume.
17 · On Dwight, see chapter III.2 in this volume.

made or heard together, the finer the society,"[18] Dwight believed that orchestral concerts with "pure" programs of works by acknowledged masters
would raise the cultural level of listeners and that a "reliable nucleus of a musical public" would support the orchestra at the box office. The concerts were
initially successful, but in the longer run box office receipts could not pay
for top-level players or adequate rehearsal time, and the enterprise incurred
increasing deficits. Dwight's orchestra folded in 1882 and was replaced by
the Boston Symphony Orchestra, similarly committed to "good music" and
cultural uplift, but whose yearly deficits were covered by a wealthy patron,
Henry Lee Higginson.

The Boston model of an orchestra playing "pure repertory" and supported
by a combination of ticket sales and private patronage was soon imitated in
other American cities, with the difference that elsewhere the patrons tended
to be a group of wealthy music lovers rather than a single individual. The
Chicago Symphony was underwritten in its early years by an association of
more than fifty donors who contributed $1,000 apiece to cover the deficits.[19]
The Cincinnati Symphony was supported by the Ladies Musical Club, which
both raised money and provided administrative services.[20] These groups of
elite patrons were motivated by their desire to provide themselves with a
cultural amenity, to raise the cultural profile of their city, and to bring the
perceived benefits of "good music" to the American public. Marketing the
orchestra as cultural uplift did not replace the earlier strategies of selling
spectacle, selling the soloist, and others. But selling the orchestra as culture
gave American orchestras an ongoing source of support alongside the marketplace. When in the twentieth century the role of orchestras in entertainment was curtailed—by dance bands and by recordings—and then pretty
much eliminated by talking pictures, the orchestra became almost exclusively a vehicle of cultural uplift.

18 · John Sullivan Dwight, "Music as a Means of Culture," *Atlantic Monthly*, September
1870, 329.
19 · See chapter I.1 in this volume.
20 · See chapter II.3 in this volume.

[III.1] Bernard Ullman and the Business of Orchestras in Mid-Nineteenth-Century New York

BETHANY S. GOLDBERG

On the evening of April 24, 1858, a crowd began amassing outside the Academy of Music for the final subscription concert of the New York Philharmonic Society's season. At seven o'clock—the appointed time for the doors to open—the entrances to the theater remained barred shut. Inside, Bernard Ullman, the impresario and entrepreneur who held the lease and managed the Academy, refused to open the house until the Philharmonic directors, his subletting tenants, paid their rental fee in full and in cash.[1] His unprecedented demand (the payment was normally turned over to Ullman during intermission) was the culmination of tensions between Ullman and the Philharmonic Society that had escalated over the course of the 1857–58 season. The dispute was resolved at the last moment, the money was accepted, the doors were opened, and the concert went off as planned. But the relationship between the Philharmonic and its landlord was destroyed, and at the end of the season the Philharmonic began looking for a new venue. The immediate cause of the deteriorating relationship was the competing spring series of orchestral programs that Ullman had produced at the Academy featuring the famous French conductor Alfred Musard leading promenade concerts of dance music and virtuosic showpieces. More broadly, the dispute was about who would control orchestral music in New York City, how that music would be organized, and how it would be presented to the public.

The conflict that came to a head on that April evening highlights two contrasting models of the mid-nineteenth-century orchestra. The New York Philharmonic Society was locally based and self-governing. It defined its mission in simple but inspiring terms: "to elevate the Art, improve musical taste, and

---

1 · For a full account of the day's events, see Vera Brodsky Lawrence, *Strong on Music*, vol. 3, *Repercussions, 1857–1862* (1999), 125–26.

gratify those already acquainted with classic musical compositions."[2] Ullman, on the other hand, combined an imported showman with a large orchestra hired for the occasion to present a mixed repertory to mass audiences in a hall that he managed. Neither model was new, but the confrontation of these two ensembles in New York City during the spring of 1858 offers a fresh perspective on the growing presence of orchestral music in mid-nineteenth-century America, its increasing marketability, and the changing preferences of American audiences in entertainment and music.

Ullman and the Academy of Music

By the 1850s, Bernard Ullman (1817?–85) was one of the most successful musical managers in the United States. The Hungarian-born entrepreneur with no known musical background crossed the Atlantic probably around 1842 and soon thereafter entered the field of artist management.[3] During the first years of his career, Ullman managed the lucrative American tours of Austrian pianist Henri Herz (1846–49), Italian violinist Camillo Sivori (1847–48), German soprano Henriette Sontag (1852–54), German pianist Sigismond Thalberg (1856–58), and Belgian violinist Henri Vieuxtemps (1857–58). Thanks to America's expanding rail system, he was able to craft strenuous but highly profitable schedules for his artists. Ullman's performers made more appearances in less time than touring musicians had ever achieved before.

During Henri Herz's tours in the 1840s, Ullman nicknamed his management methods "financial music," highlighting the commercial success that his management tactics brought.[4] To magnify the musical display, Ullman coordinated the appearances of multiple performers, most of whom were under his management. Thalberg, during his 1856–57 tour, was frequently joined onstage by contralto Elena D'Angri and American pianist Louis Moreau Gottschalk, as well as Vieuxtemps, whose own touring route conve-

2 · Quoted from the first prospectus of the Philharmonic Society of New York, issued in the summer of 1842. The prospectus is reproduced in Howard Shanet, *Philharmonic: A History of New York's Orchestra* (1975), 85, 91–92. For more Philharmonic mission statements, see chapter V.3 in this volume.

3 · For an examination of Ullman's American career, see Laurence Marton Lerner, "The Rise of the Impresario: Bernard Ullman and the Transformation of Musical Culture in Nineteenth Century America" (Ph.D. diss., 1970). R. Allen Lott offers an account of the Herz and Thalberg tours in *From Paris to Peoria: How European Piano Virtuosos Brought Classical Music to the American Heartland* (2003).

4 · Henri Herz, *Mes voyages en Amérique* (1866), 299–300; Laure Schnapper, "Bernard Ullman-Henri Herz: An Example of Financial and Artistic Partnership, 1846–1849," in *The Musician as Entrepreneur*, ed. W. Weber (2004), 135.

niently crossed Thalberg's on several occasions.[5] Each night Ullman would change his programs and rotate his artists to feature a variety of pieces, played by different combinations of stars and supporting ensembles. Because audience members had an incentive to return again and again, multiple performances in the same city became more profitable. The creative entrepreneurial spirit Ullman exhibited early in his career opened doors to more favorable opportunities.

In 1857 Ullman secured the lease at the Academy of Music, a permanent home for Italian opera in New York since its construction in 1854. Located at Fourteenth Street and Irving Place, the Academy was built and overseen by a group of investors from the highest ranks of New York society who made up the governing board of stockholders and who cultivated an elite image for the theater.[6] The stockholders' primary responsibility was to select a manager who would hold the lease of the Academy and run its day-to-day operations. The leaseholder and the board agreed on the price and length of the lease. According to an announcement from the board immediately following the Academy's incorporation in 1852, the lessee was obligated to stage Italian opera and present at least seventy-five opera performances each year; after that he was free to schedule other musical entertainment as he chose.[7] The leaseholder's profit was whatever was left from ticket sales after he paid the rent, his administrative assistants, and production expenses, which included contracts with performers, advertisements, and all the costs associated with sets, costumes, and music. With 4,600 seats, the Academy was by far the largest music venue in the city. The sizable house provided the opportunity for generous financial returns but even greater odds for substantial losses.[8] In the first three years of the Academy's existence (1854–57), five different managers had tried their hands at managing the hall. Each either went bankrupt or broke off his lease at a considerable loss.[9]

5 · Lott, *From Paris to Peoria*, 128–31, 147–49; Lerner, "Rise of the Impresario," 110–11, 133.

6 · Vera Brodsky Lawrence, *Strong on Music*, vol. 2, *Reverberations: 1850–1856* (1995), 527–29.

7 · No original lease documents for the Academy of Music are extant. The Academy charter, the initial public announcement by the board of directors, and the organization's by-laws were printed together for distribution at a later date. A copy of this document can be found in the Museum of the City of New York, Theater Collection.

8 · See Karen Ahlquist, *Democracy at the Opera: Music, Theatre, and Culture in New York City, 1815–60* (1997), 116–59.

9 · The prior leaseholders included the well-known Shakespearean actor James H. Hackett, the Norwegian violinist Ole Bull, the conductor and impresario Max Maretzek, and two of the Academy's stockholders who stepped in to run the theater when others failed. For a brief account of the early years of opera at the Academy of Music, see Frédéric Louis Ritter, *Music in America* (1890), 313–18. See also Lawrence, *Strong on Music*, vol. 2, 507–8, 529–37,

To offset the losses incurred in producing opera, Ullman's predecessors at the Academy developed a strategy of subletting the hall to other organizations. In this way some of the financial risk was passed on to the organization that paid the leaseholder for the use of the hall. Subleases often were for one-time events, such as balls and lectures, but in some cases a series of appearances was booked over an extended period. In September 1856, the Philharmonic Society of New York arranged to sublet the hall for its 1856–57 season. The contract provided the orchestra with time in the hall for public and private rehearsals and four concerts per year. For the following year (1857–58 season), the Philharmonic negotiated a renewal of their contract with Ullman, who had recently secured the Academy lease.[10] Subletting the large hall was good business for both the Academy leaseholder and the orchestra. The leaseholder profited from the rental fees and the prestige brought to the venue by the Philharmonic's growing esteem and devoted audiences. Likewise, the Philharmonic capitalized on the hall's large seating capacity to earn record-breaking revenues during its first season at the Academy.[11]

When Ullman opened the academy in September 1857 as its leaseholder, he arranged for a series of short seasons of foreign operas with mostly foreign stars.[12] To compensate for the losses that opera would likely bring, Ullman applied his proven strategy of varied programming to the Academy's calendar. Between and during the opera seasons, he interspersed Sunday sacred concerts and performances by visiting virtuosos that showcased top performers and drew large audiences at a fraction of the cost of opera. Despite his careful planning, Ullman could not predict the most serious setback of his opening months at the Academy. After the collapse of the Ohio Life Insurance and Trust Company in August, the United States descended into economic turmoil. Banks failed, the stock market plummeted, bankruptcies and unemployment soared, and a negative economic outlook set in that lingered for several years. The panic of 1857 cast a pall over Ullman's triumphant arrival at the Academy of Music. Given the uncertainties the stormy economic climate brought, the manager began to lay the foundations for a new business model.

The Academy of Music's winter opera season had been an extraordinary

---

580–84, 591–94, 631–34, 680–85, 691–92, and 706–7; Lawrence, *Strong on Music*, vol. 3, 11–12, 18–20, and 43–44.

10 · No lease documents between the Philharmonic Society and Academy of Music leaseholders are extant. The minutes of the Philharmonic's board of directors meetings document discussions and actions taken to secure the season's venue typically in August and September of each year (New York Philharmonic Archives).

11 · Shanet, *Philharmonic*, 123, 125, 130 (graph).

12 · During this period, several short seasons of opera were organized over the course of a year. Companies would often take brief tours between seasons in their home opera house or city.

musical success but failed to meet monetary expectations. Ullman was determined to not just make ends meet but also turn a profit.[13] In the first months of 1858, he crafted a plan to safeguard against both the volatility of opera management and the unstable economy by scheduling less opera and personally producing a variety of other types of events at the Academy. The large returns Ullman enjoyed while managing tours of solo musicians probably served as the impetus for him to take more direct control of his venue's offerings. He bargained that he could make more money on events he planned and produced himself than from the fees accrued from subletting the Academy. And should an opera season flop, he could fall back on the less expensive and more profitable "financial music" events that had served him so well in the past. Ullman felt confident enough in this plan and in his own abilities that in February 1858 he negotiated a multiyear lease for the Academy of Music, lasting until September 1861, with an option to renew.[14]

Musard at the Academy

The day after Ullman was awarded the long-term lease for the Academy, he officially announced that he had engaged the showman-conductor Alfred Musard for a four-week season of promenade concerts.[15] Alfred Musard (1828–81) came to New York City from Paris, where he had succeeded his father, Philippe, as the conductor of the Opéra balls and led his own series of promenade concerts at the Hôtel d'Osmond.[16] Philippe Musard had made a small fortune as one of the first "entrepreneur-conductors," creating, conducting, and managing an orchestra that gave concerts and played for dancing.[17] The elder Musard's concerts served as the model for imitators across Europe and America, including those led by Alfred on both sides of the Atlantic.[18] Both Philippe and Alfred were prominent composers of the types of works fea-

13 · *New York Herald*, February 23, 1858, 4.

14 · Ibid., February 22, 1858, 5.

15 · Several New York daily newspapers announced the concert series on February 23, 1858, including the *New York Times* and the *New York Herald*. A later account in the *Spirit of the Times* (March 20, 1858, 72) paraphrases the Parisian *Courrier Franco-Italien* to the effect that Musard had "been engaged by Ullman at a salary of 40,000 francs and four half benefits (we presume for one year)."

16 · Biographical sketch, *Frank Leslie's Illustrated Newspaper*, April 10, 1858, 290.

17 · See John Spitzer, "The Entrepreneur-Conductors and Their Orchestras" *Nineteenth-Century Music Review* 5 (2008); see also William Weber, *The Great Transformation of Musical Taste: Concert Programming from Haydn to Brahms* (2008).

18 · Ullman was accused by a correspondent to the *New York Times* (April 1, 1858, 5) of misrepresenting Alfred Musard as his more famous father, a charge that Ullman vehemently denied.

tured on promenade concerts—mainly quadrilles, potpourris, waltzes, and other characteristic dance pieces.

This type of popular entertainment was already familiar in the United States by midcentury. As early as 1841, several "Concerts d'Hiver à la Musard" were presented at the Park Theatre in New York.[19] Over the next decade, similar productions also appeared at Niblo's Garden and Palmo's Saloon. All of these efforts were short-lived, however, lasting only a few nights each. This pattern of limited ventures was interrupted in 1853 and 1854 by the extremely successful American tour of Louis Antoine Jullien and his orchestra.[20] Assisted by a group of virtuoso instrumentalists that he brought with him from Europe and bolstered by his own extravagant showmanship, the renowned conductor established a new standard for orchestral concerts in America. With this model in mind, along with the experience of his conductor, Alfred Musard, Ullman set about planning his own season of promenade concerts for the Academy of Music.

Just as Jullien had done, Musard brought with him to New York several first-rate instrumentalists—five wind players recruited from Musard's own orchestra and other Parisian musical institutions, including the Opéra, the Garde Impériale, and the Musique des Guides.[21] This was far fewer than the twenty-seven performers whom Jullien had brought with him, but Ullman advertised them in characteristic capital letters as "DISTINGUISHED SOLO PLAYERS FROM PARIS."[22] These soloists were backed up by a "MONSTER ORCHESTRA" of 120 instrumentalists recruited in New York, comprising "the best professors of the City." Many of these players were members of the Philharmonic Society and filled seats in Ullman's opera orchestra.[23] Musard's orchestra, Ullman's ad continued, "will be the GRANDEST, COMPLETEST AND MOST COLOSSAL that has ever been brought before the American public." Although his soloists paled in comparison to Jullien's, Ullman did not hesitate to proclaim what he perceived to be the excellence of his ensemble as a whole: "It will exceed, both in numbers and quality, the orchestra of the New York Philharmonic Society and of Jullien's concerts."[24]

19 · George C. D. Odell, *Annals of the New York Stage* (1928), 4:452.
20 · For Jullien's 1853–54 American tour, see chapter IV.1 in this volume.
21 · The French soloists were Legendre (cornet), Demersmann (flute and piccolo), Moreau (ophicleide), Hubens (oboe), and Artus (bassoon). The soloists and their credentials are listed in an advertisement that appeared in the *New York Times* (March 17, 1858, 3).
22 · This and the following quotations appear in Ullman's advertisement in the *New York Times*, April 6, 1858, 2.
23 · *New York Times*, April 26, 1858, 4.
24 · Jullien's 1853–54 orchestra numbered just over one hundred players at its largest (see chapter IV.1 in this volume). The number of "Actual Members" of the Philharmonic Society—a figure that included some nonperforming members—stood at ninety-seven for the

In the wake of this seven-week publicity campaign, Musard's orchestra opened on April 12 at the Academy of Music. The repertory on opening night was similar to the programs that Musard offered his Parisian public:

Program 1. Program of the First Musard Concert at the Academy of Music, April 12, 1858

PART ONE
Rossini, Overture to *William Tell*
P. Musard, *Le Cent. Suisse Quadrille*
    (with solos for Legendre and Moreau)
Meyerbeer, Air of the Page from *Les Huguenots*
    (sung by Mme. D'Angri)
A. Musard, *The Express Train Gallop*
Legendre, *Celestine* (polka ronda for cornet)
    (solo by Legendre)
A. Musard, *Les Zouaves on the Malakoff: Grand Battle Quadrille*

PART TWO
Auber, Overture to *Fra Diavolo*
Strauss, *Ocean Breezes*
Thalberg, Fantasia on *Elisir d'amore*
    (solo by Thalberg)
A. Musard, *The Cattle Show: or, Beef and Mutton Comic Quadrille*
Malibran, *The Rataplan*
    (sung by Mme. D'Angri)
Morceau, Variations (for ophicleide)
    (solo by Morceau)
A. Musard, *The Military Polka*

As can be seen, the concert featured opera overtures to open each half, descriptive and comic quadrilles, polkas, and galops, and several pieces (many based on opera themes) that showcased the imported soloists. Musard's programmatic quadrilles, such as *Beef and Mutton Quadrille* and *Gotham: or, the Electric Telegraph Quadrille*, which he programmed on other concerts, earned special attention for their creative use of the monster orchestra to achieve

1856–57 season (Shanet, *Philharmonic*, 434n70.) The *New York Times* ad of April 6, 1858, describes Musard's orchestra as an ensemble of 60 violins, 30 contrabasses and cellos, 9 trombones, and 20 drums—which makes 119 players already—plus "the usual number of wind and brass instruments." This is evidently an exaggeration, a common feature of Ullman's promotional style.

unusual sound effects. Ullman and Musard emphasized entertainment: light operatic works, amusing programmatic pieces, and showpieces for virtuoso instrumentalists. Unlike Jullien's mixed programs of symphonic works and dance pieces, and even further from the Philharmonic Society's mission to promote serious concert music at every performance, Ullman's original plan for the Musard concerts had no edifying aspirations. Reflecting his entrepreneurial spirit, Ullman played to his conductor's strengths and reckoned that the lowest common musical denominator would attract the largest audiences.

Ullman's enticements went beyond the orchestra and its repertory. For the Musard season, the manager crafted a resident form of "financial music," using the Academy of Music to create a spectacle like none America had ever seen. The Academy was completely renovated, with lush carpet in the lobbies, one hundred sofas in the corridors, twenty-five candelabras, and new chandeliers. The audience was invited to stroll about the opulent theater and mingle during the performance and extended intermissions. Additional amenities were described in detail in Ullman's advertisements: "TWENTY WAITERS IN LIVERY" delivered refreshments to guests' seats, "YOUNG LADIES, of prepossessing appearance," served in the tea and coffee rooms, and twenty boys wearing "fancy uniforms" sold the evening newspapers during the concerts.[25] Ullman's business model depended on the same people coming back to the Academy night after night, and the luxury of the furnishings, refreshments, and individual service encouraged them to do so.

All this was available at the Academy every evening (save Sundays) for the rock-bottom price of "FIFTY CENTS ONLY to any part of the Academy."[26] This was one-third of what it cost to attend a Philharmonic Society concert in the same hall.[27] Henry Cood Watson, writing in *Frank Leslie's Illustrated Newspaper*, deemed the cost of a ticket for the Musard series "the true democratic standard" that made the "aristocratic" styling of the refurbished academy available to all the American public.[28]

---

25 · Details are taken from various ads: *New York Times*, April 1, 1858, 5; ibid., April 6, 1858, 2. Ullman had previously served refreshments at a high-priced series of matinee recitals by Thalberg (see Lott, *From Paris to Peoria*, 135).

26 · *New York Times*, April 6, 1858, 2.

27 · Tickets sold at the door on the evening of Philharmonic concerts during the 1857–58 season cost $1.50 (advertisement, *New York Times*, April 20, 1858). Subscribing members received tickets at a slightly reduced cost. The ticket price of fifty cents for the Musard concerts matches the cost of a general admission/promenade ticket for Jullien's Manhattan concerts in 1853. Reserved seats for the Musard concerts, when available, cost $1.00 — the same price of a balcony seat at Jullien's Castle Garden concerts (see Adam Carse, *The Life of Jullien* [1951], 74).

28 · *Frank Leslie's Illustrated Newspaper*, April 17, 1858, 315.

Adopting a practice from earlier in his career, Ullman relied on other solo performers under his management to enhance the musical offerings of the Musard series. Sigismond Thalberg, who had recently returned from a southern tour, and Elena D'Angri, Ullman's star contralto, both performed with the orchestra during a large portion of Musard's season. Their contributions emphasized well-known operas. In the first week of concerts, for example, D'Angri sang excerpts from *Les Huguenots*, *La Cenerentola*, and *Lucrezia Borgia*, and Thalberg played fantasias based on *L'elisir d'amore* and *La muette de Portici*.

Ullman introduced new artists across the month of concerts as a way to refresh the programs. In the second week Henri Vieuxtemps joined the production, playing at least one virtuosic show piece most nights. When Thalberg and Vieuxtemps left New York for a tour at the beginning of the fourth week, Carl Formes, the star of Ullman's opera company, stepped into the headliner's role.[29] By adding these well-known musicians to the lineup of his orchestra programs, Ullman was creating something of a new business model. An entrepreneur-conductor, famous singers, virtuoso instrumentalists, and a large orchestra, all under contract to the same manager, were mixed and matched in a kaleidoscope of combinations to attract large audiences to a hall leased by that same manager.

Mixed Reviews for Musard

At the end of the first week of six performances by the monster orchestra and Ullman's star artists, there was little consensus among the New York press. Most critics found positive aspects to emphasize in their first comments on what was to be a lengthy season. William Henry Fry, the composer and writer for the *New York Tribune*, tempered his usually high musical standards to critique the monster concerts on their own terms: "This entertainment, in a word, was generous and splendid, and merits every support. If the public will ever sustain concerts, it will be such gigantic ones as these."[30] The one aspect of the opening-week performances reviewers almost unanimously agreed on

29 · Four other artists under Ullman's management appeared as well: soprano Juliana May substituted for D'Angri during the third week; tenor Mario Tiberini appeared once on a Musard program and also during sacred concerts; the English violinist Henry Cooper replaced Vieuxtemps; and Madeleine Graever-Johnson appeared as piano soloist during the final week of the season.

30 · *New York Tribune*, April 13, 1858, 5. Fry's positive review should be read in the context of his relationship with Ullman. The manager had produced Fry's full-length opera, *Leonora*, at the Academy of Music just prior to the Musard season, and the composer's gratitude to Ullman may have guided his pen.

was that the abundance of entertaining features at the Musard concerts was a tremendous bargain at such a low price. Charles Bailey Seymour, in his review for the *New York Times*, noted some musical inadequacies, but continued: "Nothing of their kind can be better than these concerts, and what can be cheaper than Musard with a superb orchestra of one hundred and twenty performers, and Madame D'Angri and Mr. Thalberg, all for fifty cents?"[31]

As the primary attraction and foreign novelty, Alfred Musard received a lot of attention in the early reviews. The most common approach was to compare Musard to the promenade conductor most familiar to Americans, Louis Antoine Jullien. Musard did not fare well. Of all the conductors ever observed by the writer for the *New York Courier and Enquirer*, Musard was "the most unexceptional in manner and appearance."[32] The flair of Jullien's appearance and conducting antics, with white kid gloves and bejeweled baton, was nowhere to be seen at the Academy. "Unlike his celebrated contemporary, Jullien," the *Spirit of the Times* noted, "simplicity of dress and a quiet earnestness of manner are [Musard's] characteristics.... He seems to possess complete control over his mighty orchestra, never seeming to wish to draw attention to himself by oddity or extravagance of gesticulation, but with quiet precision of appropriate energy."[33] This simplicity and reserved nature are preserved in a portrait published on the cover of *Frank Leslie's Illustrated Newspaper* during Musard's first week at the Academy (fig. III.1.1). The conductor's detached facial expression and nonchalant posture, with one hand in his pocket, capture what some viewed as the conductor's blasé manner.

William Henry Fry preferred Musard's style to that of showier conductors. He described it as "simple and graceful ... without trick or dazzling expedients." Fry continued, "His great object appears to be to produce the best effect with the least display of manner. Such taste should be handsomely recognized."[34] In perhaps the most nuanced assessment of Musard's abilities, Charles Bailey Seymour in the *Times* complimented the conductor's mastery of orchestral control, but added that Musard was "not great in anything save the dance."[35] The varying perspectives among the press on Musard's conducting depended on whether the reviewer assessed the conductor in relationship to promenade-concert norms or considered him outside that tradition. In the latter case—removed from expectations of flashy display and

31 · *New York Times*, April 13, 1858, 4.
32 · *New York Courier and Enquirer*, April 13, 1858; reprinted in *Dwight's Journal of Music* 13 (April 24, 1858): 26.
33 · *Spirit of the Times*, April 17, 1858, 120.
34 · *New York Tribune*, April 13, 1858, 5.
35 · *New York Times*, April 13, 1858, 4.

FIGURE III.1.1.
Portrait of Musard in *Frank Leslie's Illustrated Newspaper.*

pretentious stardom—Musard received high marks for his command of the large orchestra.

The enormous ensemble garnered almost entirely positive reviews. Several reviewers called the orchestra the best ever heard in New York.[36] Others complimented the group's fine balance, accuracy, and power, as well as its delicacy in rendering a variety of dynamics and colors. Seymour, in particular, drew comparisons with New York's other famous orchestra: "[Musard's] band ... is something to be remembered. It is not a mixture of decrepid [*sic*] pensioners and good players like the Philharmonic, but a selection of the very best performers in America, reinforced by some admirable solo players brought by M. Musard from France. We have had good orchestras before, but nothing in point of general strength to compare with this."[37]

The orchestra's repertory, however, came in for many complaints. Several reviewers ridiculed the dance pieces and programmatic works. Raimond, in the *Albion*, went so far as to compare the cheap thrills of Musard's *Beef and Mutton Quadrille*—replete with instrumental "moos" and "baas"—to seeing the India rubber man at Barnum's American Museum fold himself into a box.[38] Fry called the dance pieces "grotesque": their "noise and mere mecha-

36 · Ibid., April 12, 1858, 4; *Spirit of the Times*, April 17, 1858, 120; *New York Courier and Enquirer*, April 13, 1858, reprinted in *Dwight's Journal of Music* 13 (April 24, 1858): 26.
37 · *New York Times*, April 13, 1858, 4.
38 · *Albion*, April 17, 1858, 105.

nism" hardly made them music at all.[39] On the other hand, Fry praised the fine execution of the *William Tell* overture and commented that "our public indeed have much to learn of High Art," but first-rate performances of these "classics" would encourage listeners to set aside the "noisy pieces" in favor of "the purer music."[40]

Raimond observed that the behavior of the listeners at the academy seemed curiously inappropriate to a promenade concert. The audience seemed to sit quietly and listen with no outward signs of excitement, whether they were hearing a moving aria sung by D'Angri or Musard's thundering *Express Train Gallop*.[41] The program's galops, waltzes, and quadrilles were never intended to be taken sitting down, let alone solemnly. But that is how the New York audience listened to them. The listeners' limited experience of different types of orchestral music, particularly in the austere Academy of Music, directly affected how the audiences received Musard's monster orchestra.

Although the reviewers by and large applauded the enterprise, they generally hoped that, as in Jullien's programs, some of the dance pieces would be replaced with the more meaningful music that New York audiences evidently preferred.[42] Charles Bailey Seymour made a direct appeal to management regarding the programming: "Mr. Ullman must give us some classical music—not old works but the latest and fullest. Here is the orchestra to interpret them."[43] Not only would the programs quickly become stale if the pattern of the first week was maintained, Seymour argued, but it would be a great shame to waste the talents of this tremendous orchestra on only popular music. Henry Cood Watson made the same case in *Frank Leslie's Illustrated Newspaper*, imploring, "We hope that evenings of classical music will be embraced in the month's programme of Mr. Musard's concerts. They will pay well, for the majority of our concert visitors really like the higher class of music."[44]

Midseason Modifications

Bernard Ullman was not one to stand by and watch as the newness of the monster concerts wore off, as the complaints by the critics piled up, and as

39 · *New York Tribune*, April 13, 1858, 5.

40 · Ibid., April 15, 1858, 6.

41 · *Albion*, April 17, 1858, 187.

42 · Lawrence, *Strong on Music*, vol. 3, 123.

43 · *New York Times*, April 13, 1858, 4.

44 · *Frank Leslie's Illustrated Newspaper*, April 24, 1858, 330. Because of the production schedule for the weekly newspaper, the publication date of Watson's comments postdates Ullman's announcement regarding this matter. Watson presumably penned his opinions earlier.

ticket sales dropped. Absorbing the reactions of his audiences from week one, Ullman went to work to make the remainder of the orchestral engagement a success. Relying on his proven strategy of varying programs and personnel to refresh his musical offerings, the manager announced that his well-respected opera conductor, Carl Anschütz, would lead a more serious "Grand Classical" portion of most concerts starting in the second week of the season.[45] Ullman's advertisement in the *Times* explained his reasons for the change.

> In organizing the "Musard" concerts the Director ... aimed at something more than to afford the public a few pleasant hours of amusement. Stimulated by the undivided appreciation he has met with as Director of the late opera season, his ambition has been roused and he will not spare any pains or expense in establishing in New-York a cheap and first-class permanent entertainment, which ultimately must greatly contribute towards the full development of the musical taste which, in an incredibly short time, has made such rapid progress....
>
> To be able to carry out his views he has entered into a fresh engagement with MR. CARL ANSCHUTZ, who will divide the conductorship with M. Musard. THE PROGRAMMES, commencing from to-day, will comprise *every species of standard music, classical and light,* and Mr. Ullman pledges himself that every concert will present many interesting features, and that all his promises, however great they may appear, will be fulfilled to the letter.[46]

On April 19, the Musard concerts presented a new three-part format that would remain the most common structure of programs for the remainder of the season. The first two parts of the program were conducted by Anschütz and included more serious orchestral works, such as symphonies and concert overtures, along with solo performances by Ullman's artists. The third part was led by Musard, and it featured virtuosic works showcasing his soloists and his celebrated dance music. In the fourth week of concerts, the distribution shifted slightly: now Musard conducted light music during the first and third portions, and Anschütz presented classical works during the program's middle section.[47]

The revised Musard programs brought together two styles of orchestral

45 · Anschütz came to the United States in September 1857 under Ullman's management to conduct opera at the Academy of Music.

46 · *New York Times,* April 15, 1858, 8; emphasis added.

47 · This three-part "arch-shaped" program resembled the programs of the Theodore Thomas Orchestra in the 1860s and later. On Thomas's programs, see chapters II.2 and V.2 in this volume.

music that by the middle of the nineteenth century were increasingly presented separately. As Ullman wrote in one of his advertisements, he was "devoting one-half of the concert to the perfect rendering of the CLASSICAL WORKS OF GREAT COMPOSERS, and reserving the other for the lighter and amusing pieces."[48] The divisions between lighter promenade programming and the self-consciously serious programs common to professional orchestral societies were still sometimes blurred. Opera overtures and virtuoso solo pieces, for example, could appear in either or both sections of the program. Nevertheless, Ullman strove to capitalize on a musical distinction that must have resonated with his public.

The first full two-conductor program of the season on April 19 was advertised as a "Grand Classical Night," featuring the compositions of Hector Berlioz. Program 2 illustrates how Anschütz and Musard divided their efforts in this three-part concert:

Program 2. Program for Musard's First "Grand Classical" Night (April 19, 1858), Featuring the Works of Hector Berlioz

"First Grand Classical Festival. The Hector Berlioz Night"

PART ONE (CONDUCTED BY ANSCHÜTZ)
Berlioz, Overture to *Les francs-juges*
Rossini, Aria from *Tancredi*
   (sung by Mme. D'Angri)
Weber, *Invitation to the Dance* (arranged by Berlioz)
Thalberg, Fantasia on *Lucretia Borgia*
   (solo by Thalberg)

PART TWO (CONDUCTED BY ANSCHÜTZ)
Berlioz, *Le carnaval romain,* concert overture
Beriot, *Le Tremolo*
   (solo by Vieuxtemps)
Traditional, Rakotzky March (arranged by Berlioz; used in *La damnation de Faust*)

PART THREE (CONDUCTED BY MUSARD)
Rossini, Overture to *Semiramide*
Legendre, *Nella Polka*
   (solo by Legendre)

48 · *New York Times,* April 20, 1858, 2.

A Spanish song
  (sung by Mme. D'Angri)
Musard, *Les Echos Quadrille*
Moreau, Ophicleide solo
  (solo by Moreau)
Musard, *The Express Train Gallop*
Musard, *Les Zouaves, with the Marsellaise*

As shown above, Anschütz led the first two parts of the program, which included four works composed or arranged by the featured composer and solo performances by D'Angri, Thalberg, and Vieuxtemps. In the final part, Musard conducted the orchestra in an overture by Rossini, more solo performances—two by stars of Musard's ensemble—and several of the conductor's popular quadrilles. Ullman capped the night off with the announcement that Berlioz planned to accept an invitation to conduct concerts in the United States during the following year.[49] The composer's music was "applauded vehemently," and Ullman repeated the program for three additional nights.[50] The new two-conductor format was an immense success. Critical commentary cheered the new direction the programs had taken; attendance numbers, though uneven at times, remained solid; and Ullman announced in May that he was adding a fifth week to the season.[51]

Ullman scheduled two more "Composer Night" programs during the season but highlighted less modern composers: Beethoven and Mendelssohn. The first Beethoven night, on April 27, presented the entire Fifth Symphony, a movement each of the Violin Concerto and a piano concerto, played by Vieuxtemps and Thalberg, respectively, and two overtures (one from the incidental music to *König Stephan* and the concert overture *Namensfeier*). When the program was repeated the following evening, the Sixth Symphony replaced the Fifth. A Mendelssohn night on May 12 featured the complete music to *A Midsummer Night's Dream* and selections from violin and piano concertos. It was coordinated with a performance, accompanied by Musard's orchestra, of the composer's *Elijah* at the academy during the same week. The "Composer Nights" were by far the most favorably reviewed of the two-conductor programs, which were already familiar to New York audiences. Ullman, again, was following Jullien's example. Jullien began programming concerts of works mostly by a single composer in 1846, and his

---

49 · *Porter's Spirit of the Times*, April 24, 1858, 128; R. Allen Lott, "Bernard Ullman: Nineteenth-Century American Impresario," in *A Celebration of American Music: Words and Music in Honor of H. Wiley Hitchcock*, ed. R. Crawford, R. A. Lott, and C. J. Oja (1991), 185.
50 · *New York Times*, April 20, 1858, 4.
51 · Ibid., May 8, 1858, 3.

1853–54 American tour included nights devoted to Beethoven, Mendelssohn, and Mozart.[52]

Ullman's new entrepreneurial strategy blended the entertaining aspects of Musard's promenade concerts with the more edifying elements of serious orchestral programs in individual programs and across the entire season. New York's music press rhapsodized about the opportunity to hear classical music several nights a week for a month. In the *Times*, Seymour again drew a stark comparison to the other orchestra in town: "A few highly respectable works by the best composers have been offered to us by the Philharmonic Society, but a miserable routine of four concerts a year can accomplish nothing. In a single week, Mr. Ullman's orchestra will give us a greater insight into modern music than the Philharmonic Society has afforded us in half the period of its existence."[53] Ullman's Berlioz program elicited further complaints about the Philharmonic, this time in the *New York Herald*, which chided the "old fogy" ensemble for requiring that "a piece of music should be at least fifty years old before it attained to a respectable performing age."[54]

Ullman engaged Musard and his "monster" orchestra at the Academy of Music in response to the difficult economic times and a hunger he perceived among New Yorkers for more orchestral music. In his attempt to satisfy those in attendance, Ullman revised his programs to fit the musical tastes he observed. New York audiences seemed to prefer more serious orchestral music to light, entertaining fare, and Ullman adjusted his offerings accordingly. Because he had such a large number of artists under his management, Ullman was able to adapt quickly. The two-conductor format that he adopted midway through the season simultaneously satisfied the artistic desires of the more seriously minded listeners and the desire for novelty and spectacle among the larger public. That Ullman was treading on the Philharmonic Society's long-held turf brought to the public's attention the increasingly complex relationship that existed between Ullman's orchestral ambitions and New York's oldest professional orchestra.

Two Orchestras, One Academy

The conflict that arose between the Philharmonic Society of New York and Bernard Ullman stemmed from the manager's profit-maximizing efforts to produce most of the Academy's events himself. All evidence suggests that

52 · Carse, *Life of Jullien*, 49; see also chapter IV.1, figure IV.1.2, in this volume. In contrast to Jullien's typical practice of presenting only single or select movements from symphonic works, Anschütz, during this concert series, always conducted complete symphonies.

53 · *New York Times*, April 19, 1858, 4.

54 · *New York Herald*, April 20, 1858, 3.

Ullman sought to squeeze the Philharmonic Society out of his theater so he could produce his own orchestral performances free of direct competition. Amid the financial panic of his first season at the academy, Ullman's managerial instincts seem to have told him that there was room for only one orchestra in New York and that his success depended on the eclipse of rival ensembles. Tensions mounted for months, until the orchestra and the manager came to blows during the Musard series.

The 1856–57 season, the year before Ullman took over management, was the Philharmonic Society's first at the Academy. Thanks to the new and more spacious accommodations, subscriptions and individual ticket sales soared, and the Society brought in a record amount of revenue.[55] Ullman, the new lessee, took advantage of this good news to negotiate a considerable increase in what he charged the orchestra for using the Academy. He increased the fee more than 55 percent, from $1,600 in 1856–57 to $2,500 for the 1857–58 season.[56]

Raising the rent could be passed off as smart business sense on Ullman's part, but once the manager set his mind to producing his own orchestral events he began to exploit his tenants by linking his own events at the Academy to the Philharmonic Society, thus taking advantage of the society's reputation. A performance by Ullman's opera orchestra at the conclusion of his day-long Sigismond Thalberg testimonial on January 2, 1858, was advertised as a "Grand Philharmonic Concert."[57] The Philharmonic Society complained that the manager was not only capitalizing on its name for an event in the same hall where it played but doing so only a week before the society's next subscription concert.[58] Indeed, a review of the week's events in the *Spirit of the Times* made no distinction between the two ensembles; each event, described only a few lines apart, was identified as a "grand Philharmonic concert."[59]

Ullman borrowed the society's name again to tout Musard's monster orchestra when he advertised the new "Grand Classical" component of the Musard programs as "a truly PHILHARMONIC CONCERT."[60] In adopting the Philharmonic name, Ullman highlighted his new effort to balance spectacle

---

55 · Shanet, *Philharmonic*, 125.

56 · Ibid., 127. Shanet notes that the Philharmonic's rent at the Apollo Rooms during its early seasons ranged from $100 to $250 for the entire season. These figures are recorded in the Philharmonic Society's annual financial reports (New York Philharmonic Archives).

57 · *New York Times*, January 1, 1858, 5.

58 · This grievance was logged in the society's annual report that year (reprinted in *Dwight's Journal of Music* 14 [October 9, 1858]: 219). The Philharmonic Society concert was held on Saturday, January 9, 1858, at the Academy.

59 · *Spirit of the Times*, January 2, 1858, 564.

60 · *New York Times*, April 20, 1858, 2.

with more refined music. And his advertised goal of contributing "towards the full development of the musical taste" echoed the Philharmonic Society's mission to promote higher musical standards. Ullman's announcement that the Musard series would offer "every opportunity ... to resident composers to establish their just claims" was another swipe at the Philharmonic, coming just four years after the upheaval within the Philharmonic Society over performing American works, some of which were read during rehearsals but not deemed worthy of concert performance.[61] Ultimately, the proposed consideration fell flat; no works by American composers appeared on the Musard programs. Adding injury to insult, Ullman barred his star performers—Vieuxtemps, Thalberg, and Formes—from appearing as soloists with the Philharmonic during the 1857–58 season.[62] The Philharmonic typically arranged solo appearances directly with the artists, many of whom reduced or waived their fees in support of the ensemble's work, but the obstinate Ullman required that the Philharmonic communicate with his artists only through him. Ullman did allow Elena D'Angri to appear, but in response to other requests he offered only his second-tier artists, including soprano Annie Milner, violinist Henry C. Cooper, and baritone Edouard Gassier, to perform with the Philharmonic. The biggest names were consistently withheld.

The Philharmonic Society directors believed they could not overlook what they considered an attack on their organization. They used an unforeseen opportunity to retaliate. Their lease at the Academy stipulated that the orchestra had full use of the hall for the entire day of their concerts—from their final rehearsal in the morning to the end of the evening's performance. When Ullman requested permission to present a Musard matinee concert at three o'clock in the afternoon on Saturday, April 24, the day of their final concert of the season, the society refused.[63] Much to their chagrin, an undeterred Ullman went on with his performance anyway.[64] When the time

61 · See Shanet, *Philharmonic*, 111–21.

62 · The minutes of the board of directors meetings from November 1857 to April 1858 show that negotiations with Ullman for the use of his artists were drawn out over the entire season (New York Philharmonic Archives).

63 · The minutes to the board of directors meeting on April 20, 1858, read, "Secretary instructed to inform Mr. Ulman [*sic*], in reply to his application of giving an afternoon Matinee on the day of the last Concert, that the B[oard] of D[irectors] consider it detrimental to the interest of the Society & therefore do not feel at liberty to comply with his wishes." Ullman's request to borrow scores and parts from the Philharmonic Society was similarly refused in the same meeting (New York Philharmonic Archives).

64 · Charles Bailey Seymour's comments on the day's events—which begin, "The poor fiddlers had a hard time of it on Saturday—almost twelve hours of constant sawing"—document the overlap of personnel between the two ensembles. See *New York Times*, April 26, 1858, 4.

came for that evening's Philharmonic concert, Ullman barred the doors of the Academy, resulting in the standoff described at the beginning of this chapter. The impasse was resolved, and the concert went on as planned that evening, but this day's events opened an insurmountable rift between the lessee and his tenant.[65]

In a hastily called board meeting the following week, the Philharmonic directors agreed to air their grievances against Ullman in the form of a public statement; that communication was published on May 1 and discussed extensively in the New York press.[66] All the music writers who weighed in on the issue exonerated the Philharmonic and chastised Ullman for his disregard of the contract stipulations and his poor treatment of a revered, local musical institution. Henry Cood Watson in *Frank Leslie's* pinpointed the larger issue: "It is very evident to all that Mr. Ullman is desirous to kill off all musical entertainments but those emanating from his bureau of management."[67] The Philharmonic directors must surely have expected what came next. Minutes from the Philharmonic board meetings and a notice for a trial rehearsal in a new venue confirm that sometime between early May and mid-July, Ullman refused to renew the Philharmonic's sublease at the Academy of Music for the 1858–59 season.[68]

From Ullman's perspective, canceling the Philharmonic's lease would not only rid him of orchestral competition in his own house but also free Saturday afternoons for profitable matinee performances. As Musard's season came to a close, Ullman announced his future orchestral plans. For the fall season at the Academy, he intended to alternate "instrumental concerts of the highest class" with his regular seasons of opera.[69] Whether or not he brought another conductor-showman from Europe for the upcoming season, Ullman had evidently decided that presenting regular orchestral concerts at the Academy of Music would be in his best interest both financially and artistically. Continually varying the types of events on the Academy's calendar had benefited Ullman before, and he bargained that New Yorkers' enjoyment of orchestral music would help him once again.

---

65 · On this evening, the Philharmonic treasurer had the full amount in hand prior to the concert but was among the crowd locked outside, unable to gain entry to pay Ullman. None of the press accounts clearly explain how the standoff came to an end.

66 · See meeting minutes for April 28, 1858. *Porter's Spirit of the Times* reprinted the entire statement on May 15, 1858, 176.

67 · *Frank Leslie's Illustrated Newspaper*, May 15, 1858, 379.

68 · An advertisement published in several newspapers on July 19, 1858, announced that the Philharmonic rehearsal in Cooper Institute's hall would be open to subscribers and members.

69 · *New York Times*, May 8, 1858, 3.

Future Plans in a Changing Musical Scene

As it happened, Ullman's fall plans for alternating operatic and orchestral performances never materialized. During the summer, Ullman successfully negotiated a deal with Benjamin Lumley, the director of opera at Her Majesty's Theatre in London, to bring the prima donna Maria Piccolomini to America. The result was one of the most successful seasons of Italian opera New York had ever seen, lasting from October to early December. Ullman was consumed with opera and had no time—or need—for orchestral endeavors. Beginning in December, Ullman took his opera company on tour, leaving the Academy virtually empty during the winter months, aside from a few balls, lectures, and short New York stopovers of his opera troupe between appearances in other eastern cities. In the context of Ullman's busy musical calendar, orchestral music simply had no place. In addition, the plan to bring Hector Berlioz to New York never came to fruition because the composer stipulated that his visit could only occur after the Parisian premiere of the opera he had almost completed. Berlioz's much-delayed *Les Troyens* did not receive its first performance—and then only a partial one—until 1863.[70]

Despite the absence of regular orchestral engagements at the Academy in the 1858–59 season, several new instrumental endeavors that year reinforced Ullman's belief that New York could support more orchestral music. Carl Bergmann, who shared conducting duties at the Philharmonic Society, presented at the City Assembly Rooms a successful series of six orchestral programs that he called Grand Sunday Concerts.[71] A more ambitious plan was the proposed Metropolitan Musical Association, which presented its first concert at the Academy of Music in May 1859. Led by Maurice Strakosch, George Bristow, and Harvey Dodworth, the association announced plans for ten monthly concerts of orchestral, band, and choral music that would engage the city's most highly skilled musicians. Following the first concert, however, the series was truncated and then converted into a short season of promenade concerts at Palace Garden. The enterprise fizzled after a handful of mediocre performances.[72]

Expelled from the Academy of Music, the Philharmonic Society moved to Niblo's for its 1858–59 season. In the smaller venue, the society had to limit its membership rolls and cut off extra ticket sales for its concerts. To counter the setbacks, a fifth concert was added to its schedule, but the year's revenue losses were dramatic. Nevertheless, the society endured, and in September

70 · Lott, "Bernard Ullman," 185.
71 · Lawrence, *Strong on Music*, vol. 3, 197, 282–83.
72 · Ibid., 283–85.

1859 the directors finalized an agreement with Ullman to return to the Academy of Music for its eighteenth season. Because the Philharmonic directors refused to deal directly with Ullman, the lease negotiations were conducted with a representative of the Academy's stockholders. In return for this concession, the society agreed to move its Saturday public rehearsals to Wednesday afternoons, freeing the weekend slot for Ullman's matinees.[73]

Following his 1858 spring season at the Academy of Music, Alfred Musard, still under Ullman's management, took his promenade programs on the road. He spent part of the summer in Philadelphia, where he and two of his Parisian soloists, plus a locally recruited orchestra, were warmly received. Here, too, at least some of the programs were divided in two. The first part included Musard's lively dance music, followed by a "Formes Concert," featuring Ullman's star bass singing several concert pieces.[74] In July, Musard returned to New York and partnered with Anschütz again for a short series of *Jardin d'Eté* concerts at the Academy.[75] Unfortunately, the conductors and their now more modest orchestra of sixty players were in direct competition with nightly promenade concerts directed by Thomas Baker at a popular open-air venue, Palace Garden.[76] The season was canceled after one week. Musard remained in the United States, and toward the end of the year he reappeared in New York to conduct three nights of performances with Carl Bergmann— two concerts and a full-dress ball to benefit the Mount Vernon Association. After this, he found himself welcome in New Orleans, where he led masked balls throughout the carnival season.[77] Musard would never achieve greater success in America than his five weeks at the Academy of Music.

Although there was a growing appreciation of music for music's sake in mid-nineteenth-century New York, the business of music still had a profound effect on what kinds of events were planned and performed. The prospect of losing money on Italian opera initially propelled Bernard Ullman to diversify the Academy of Music programming in 1858. Ullman witnessed the rising popularity of orchestral music—demonstrated by the accomplishments of the New York Philharmonic Society and by Jullien's American tour—and he decided the timing was right to produce a season of Musard's promenade

73 · Minutes to board of directors meeting, September 3, 1859 (New York Philharmonic Archives).

74 · *Dwight's Journal of Music* 13 (June 5, 1858): 79, and 13 (June 12, 1858): 87.

75 · See announcement in *New York Times*, July 10, 1858, 5.

76 · Lawrence, *Strong on Music*, vol. 3, 138.

77 · *New York Herald*, November 18, 1858.

concerts. Unlike the Philharmonic, whose classical orchestral programming was mandated by lofty musical goals, Ullman chose to present popular orchestral music for the utilitarian reason that he relied on ticket sales to make ends meet. The low ticket prices and entertaining repertory would encourage attendance by masses of New Yorkers, not just the educated elite.

After a week of concerts, the manager questioned whether the demand for almost nightly promenade concerts was strong enough in postpanic New York. Ullman maintained his business model but combined contrasting musical styles in the two-conductor programs of light and classical works with the hope of drawing a broader and larger audience. With this format in place, four more weeks of orchestra concerts filled the Academy of Music's calendar. Ullman's ongoing disagreements with the Philharmonic Society were a sign that the market, still recovering from the economic downturn, was too limited for two orchestras now playing similar repertories.

Bernard Ullman's orchestral experiment in the spring of 1858 was short-lived, but the interest in orchestral music did not disappear. With Ullman's return to opera management, orchestral ambitions were taken up by others—performers, conductors, and managers. The best model for a New York orchestra—classical and elite, popular and enterprise, or any other combination of possible elements—would continue to be negotiated for decades to come. Like Ullman's venture, few would last for long, but with the growing audience base and the rise of more institutional support, a greater variety of orchestral music was able to flourish. Ullman's creative negotiations in managing Musard and his monster orchestra in 1858 showed that there were as many different kinds of orchestras as one could imagine. Given the exciting volatility of orchestral life and musical taste in midcentury New York, any one of them just might be the next big hit.

[III.2] John Sullivan Dwight and the Harvard Musical Association Orchestra

A Help or a Hindrance?

MARY WALLACE DAVIDSON

In an essay written in 1849, John Sullivan Dwight outlines in rhapsodic prose his vigorously held beliefs about music: "Music is both body and soul …. The material part, which is measured sound, is the embodiment and sensible representative, as well as the re-acting cause, of that which we call impulse, sentiment, feeling, the spring of all our action and expression. In a word, it is the language of the heart … a natural, invariable, pure type and correspondence."[1] In Dwight's view, there are "three elements of music, as well as of our lives." The first element is variously called feeling/sentiment/passion (soul); the second is science/principles/laws (intellect); and the third is "sensible creation and enjoyment" (body). Great music unites all three elements. The music of Bach, Handel, Haydn, Weber, Schubert, and especially Mozart and Beethoven embodies and exemplifies the unity of the three strands, knitting the human race into "one mutually conscious, undivided whole."[2] This transcendentalist construct lay behind Dwight's enduring belief in the absolute necessity of what he called "pure music," an operant phrase that for better or worse shaped his creation and management of the Harvard Musical Association Orchestra in Boston from 1865 to 1882.

Strictly speaking, the Harvard Musical Association (HMA) has nothing to do with Harvard University. In 1837 its founding members were all, like Dwight, Harvard graduates and former members of the Pierian Sodality, a musical and social club.[3] They were initially focused on raising the standard of musical taste at their alma mater, on fostering a music department (which took thirty years), and on developing a music library for the use of the stu-

---

1 · John Sullivan Dwight, "Music," in *Aesthetic Papers*, ed. E. P. Peabody (1849), 27.
2 · Ibid., 25–30.
3 · Founded in 1808, the Pierian Sodality is still extant as the Harvard Radcliffe Orchestra.

dents.[4] Today Boston's HMA is a private social and charitable organization devoted to music, with the philanthropic mission to improve local musical creativity and culture in various ways.[5]

By the middle of the nineteenth century, the association had established a significant music library (still extant), sponsored a series of public chamber music concerts (1844–49), and raised the princely sum of $100,000 within two months in 1850 to underwrite the costs of the new Boston Music Hall. After the Civil War the HMA organized what became known as the "Harvard Orchestra," which performed an annual series of concerts in that hall from 1865 to 1882. The life of this ensemble may be divided into three periods: early development (1865–68), rise to maturity (1869–73), and gradual decline (1874–82).

Dwight, the guiding spirit and day-to-day manager of the Harvard Orchestra, was not a professional musician. He is known today chiefly as a music critic, thanks to his *Journal of Music*, which was published in Boston from 1852 to 1881 and supported in part by the HMA.[6] Born in Boston in 1813, he died there in 1893, some dozen years after the demise of both his journal and his orchestra. The beautiful Mary Bullard, "of a most unselfish and winning character," whom he married in 1851, died unexpectedly during his only tour abroad in 1860. After living with relatives and in studio apartments for a few years, he moved into the association's quarters in 1873, the same year that he became its president, and remained ensconced in both the office and the apartment until his death.[7]

Dwight's biographers note that he had no special talents as a child and was an impractical adult. He learned to play the flute and piano, but by his own admission, he could read a score only with great difficulty and preferred to explore a symphony through its piano reduction.[8] He graduated from the Boston Latin School and Harvard University and played the clarinet in the Pierian Sodality. During his senior year (1831–32) at Harvard he lectured on

4 · "Report Made at a Meeting … of the Pierian Sodality … August 30th, 1837," *Boston Musical Gazette*, June 27 and July 11, 1838, [33]–34, [41]–43.

5 · See the association's website, www.hmaboston.org.

6 · *Dwight's Journal of Music* was published in Boston by E. L. Balch from 1852 to 1858; O. Ditson published it from 1858 to 1878, Houghton Osgood from 1879 to 1880, and Houghton Mifflin from 1880 to 1881. It was reprinted by Johnson Reprint in 1968.

7 · On Mary Bullard, see George William Curtis, *Early Letters of George Wm. Curtis to John S. Dwight; Brook Farm and Concord* (1898), 49.

8 · John Sullivan Dwight, "Music as a Means of Culture," *Atlantic Monthly* 26 (1870): 330; Ora Frishberg Saloman, "John Sullivan Dwight," in *The American Renaissance in New England: Third Series*, ed. W. T. Mott, (2001); Edward Waters, "John Sullivan Dwight: First American Critic of Music," *Musical Quarterly* 21 (1935): 69–70.

music at the Northborough Lyceum and taught at the Northborough School, introducing music into his courses.[9] He may also have continued his private music studies, but otherwise his musical education was achieved mainly by going to concerts and later through close friendships with composers and pianists.

Dwight earned a degree from the Harvard Divinity School in 1836; his dissertation was titled "The Proper Character of Poetry and Music for Public Worship."[10] His career in the ministry was brief. Ralph Waldo Emerson recommended his friend Dwight to be his successor at a parish in Lexington in 1837, but Dwight failed to "settle" there, and later he left his parish in Northampton, also after a year.

Dwight returned to Boston in 1841 and joined Brook Farm in West Roxbury, remaining until it closed in 1847. There he taught music and Latin, arranged musicales, and walked seven miles to Boston to hear concerts that he reviewed for the *Harbinger* (1843–49), an associationist periodical, which he also coedited. Thus he began his career as a journalist and as a translator (mostly of German poetry and vocal works), leaving a long list of publications, most famously his *Journal of Music.*

These activities were his only source of income except for a small stipend as HMA librarian from 1871 and the salary he paid himself as manager of the HMA Orchestra. In its first season, Dwight paid himself $50 per concert as manager (the same as the conductor), but by the sixth season (1870–71), he was paying himself more than the conductor ($60 per concert).[11] As librarian, he earned $300 per year starting in 1871, reduced to $200 in 1881, about half of which he paid back to the HMA in the form of rent.[12] Dwight's biographer, George Willis Cooke, notes that Dwight "had no faculty for making money, had little appreciation of its value, was all his life poor, and was not capable of getting on in a thrifty and saving way of life."[13] Thus, although he was certainly part of Boston's social and cultural elite, especially among the transcendentalists, he was not a member of the financial elite to which many of his colleagues in the HMA belonged.

9 · William Foster Apthorp, "John Sullivan Dwight" [obituary], *Boston Evening Transcript,* September 5, 1893 (reprinted in his *Musicians and Music-Lovers, and Other Essays* [1894]), 280; George Willis Cooke, *John Sullivan Dwight, Brook-Farmer, Editor, and Critic of Music; A Biography* (1898), 7–8.

10 · Published in part as John Sullivan Dwight, "The Proper Character of Poetry and Music for Public Worship," *Christian Examiner* 21 (1836).

11 · Detailed records lacking after 1871.

12 · John Sullivan Dwight, "Reports on the Harvard Orchestra Concerts, 1865 to 1882," Harvard Musical Association Archives, 033.

13 · Cooke, *John Sullivan Dwight,* 266.

The Predecessors

The HMA Orchestra had several forerunners in Boston, beginning with the Philharmonic Society in 1810 or 1811.[14] The Handel and Haydn Society, founded in 1815, regularly assembled orchestras of local theater musicians to accompany its oratorio performances. The Boston Academy of Music, which focused on choral music, sponsored an orchestra intermittently from 1841 to 1847.[15] In 1847 the Musical Fund Society formed an orchestra, the first in Boston to be organized entirely by professional players (about sixty in 1852), all of whom shared in the profits.[16] The first two seasons' concerts were given in the nine-hundred-seat Melodeon Hall; the performances then moved into the Tremont Theatre, which seated about fifteen hundred. Particularly under conductor George Webb, the orchestra attempted to play the "best" music: the symphonies of Pleyel, Haydn, Mozart, and early Beethoven. But the concerts lost audiences to the better concerts of the Germania Orchestra (see below), and on an icy night in 1855 a fire destroyed all the musicians' instruments, which they had left in the theater, fearing to take them home because of the slippery streets. The society distributed its funds to needy musicians and disbanded.[17]

Meanwhile, the Germania Musical Society had immigrated to America in 1848, settling in Boston in 1851 until its dissolution in 1854.[18] That year, one of the Germanians, and future conductor of the Harvard Orchestra, flutist Carl Zerrahn (1826–1909), became the conductor of the Handel and Haydn Society. In 1855 he founded his own Philharmonic Orchestra, which failed in its turn during the Civil War. Zerrahn was an ambitious and influential musician who had an active conducting career in Massachusetts through the end of the century. Opinions about Zerrahn varied widely. According to one critic in 1872, "His style of conducting is exceedingly faulty and inelegant. He disdains to mark the divisions of a bar, even when the movement imperatively demands it, with anything like clearness or precision; but, on the contrary thrashes the air in the most unintelligible manner. His idea of tempo is not correct, and this often results in great damage to the composer's work

14 · John Sullivan Dwight, "History of Music in Boston," in *A Memorial History of Boston*, ed. J. Windsor (1881), 417.

15 · On the Academy of Music and other Boston orchestras, see chapter V.1 in this volume.

16 · Frédéric Louis Ritter, *Music in America* (1883), 239.

17 · Thomas Ryan, *Recollections of an Old Musician* (1899), 49–55. Ryan was a member of the Musical Fund orchestra. His anecdotal descriptions, written years after the fact, are colorful but not always accurate.

18 · Nancy Newman, "Good Music for a Free People: The Germania Musical Society and Transatlantic Musical Culture of the Mid-Nineteenth Century" (Ph.D. diss., 2002), chaps. 3 and 5.

he is conducting, and for which there is, as yet, no redress."[19] On the other hand, Thomas Ryan, who had played with various orchestras conducted by Zerrahn, praised the conductor for his ability to get the most out of his musicians: "He was … very firm and earnest in action, amiable in temper, and considerate of the shortcomings of the many inexperienced performers who came under his baton. He was never known to show up the weakness of an artist to the public; neither the highest or the humblest assistant ever received a discourteous word from him. He was and still is a rare man indeed; and unquestionably is enthroned in the hearts of very large numbers of those who came under his direction."[20]

In any case, the critic W. F. Apthorp recalled that the orchestral resources of Boston before the founding of the HMA Orchestra in 1865 "had never been conspicuous" and doubted that any Bostonians of the time had ever heard a well-balanced orchestra, referring to a "ridiculously small mass of strings."[21] The winds generally predominated, apparently being incapable of playing softly.

Early Development (1865–68)

The Harvard Orchestra was initiated by a discussion over supper before the annual meeting of the Harvard Musical Association on April 30, 1865, when someone (no doubt Dwight) suggested that Boston needed a "sure and permanent provision for orchestral music of the highest order." Boston still lacked a philharmonic society such as those in New York, London, and Leipzig that would similarly raise the level of musical taste. Currently, the only orchestral music to be heard in Boston was "dependent on private enterprise," the capriciousness of public taste, and uncertain subscriptions. "Was there not here a problem which the Association, with its combined intelligence, & musical zeal, & social influence, might undertake to solve?"[22] Dwight's initial goals, though grounded in a certain kind of practical reality, were thus ultimately idealistic: a permanent orchestra financed by assured subscriptions and free of the need to earn a profit, playing (only) music of the "highest order" (i.e., Bach, Handel, Haydn, Mozart, and Beethoven) that would automatically "raise the level of cultural taste." Such an orchestra

19 · "World's Peace Jubilee and International Musical Festival," *Metronome*, July 1872, 39–40.
20 · Ryan, *Recollections*, 82.
21 · William Foster Apthorp, "Musical Reminiscences of Boston Thirty Years Ago," in *By the Way* (1898), 68–69.
22 · John Sullivan Dwight, "H.M.A. Symphony Concerts: Report of the First Season (1865–1866)," presented to a special meeting of the association, May 2, 1866, in Dwight, "Reports," 033-C:26–32.

would presumably create a demand for more music of the same "high order" if not through musical influence, then through social pressure from those whose tastes had been "improved."

Dwight's means of achieving his goals and ensuring the new orchestra's success were even more idealistic. In his report on the meeting he describes "proper guarantees," typically leaving any concern for financial support until the end:

> 1. *Pure programmes....* The *real* music-lovers, the cultivated members of the musical public, had long ago lost confidence in concert enterprises, because with all the claims to "classicality," &c., the programmes commonly turned out to be medleys of good, bad, and indifferent. Concerts were given to make money; and programmes ... lost all unity, and so all hold upon ... the reliable nucleus of a musical public. To secure any permanence, we must secure that class; to secure them, the programmes must be pure. Now this was a condition within easy reach, if the control were placed in the right hands.... There is intelligence enough here to make good programmes; & one needed not to look beyond that supper table to find it.

> 2. The condition of *good performance* was not quite so easy. Good musicians were comparatively few in Boston, & the occupations of most ... were not so favorable to the artistic tone & temper of symphony interpreters as could be wished.... [These musicians] could be collected & with more attention to rehearsal could undoubtedly give us symphonies in a style enjoyable by persons of taste. Good programmes, too, would help to educate the orchestra.

> 3. The *audience* is as much a part of a good concert as the performers & the composer.... The audience must mutually enjoy *itself*; each must feel the music in his neighbor.... This, too, is only possible with pure programmes; these ... alone can ... set the tone of manners, if not of feeling, for all the rest.... Now, did not the members of the H.M.A., with their friends, afford just the nucleus of such an audience?

> 4. The guaranty of *means*. Let the members of this society pledge themselves in various sums to a guaranty program.... This nucleus audience at once inspires confidence in the like-minded, & exerts a social attraction which may double or treble the number of subscribers. The name H.M.A. has always proved a good name to conjure by.[23]

---

23 · All HMA Orchestra reports quoted are originally in Dwight's hand, and the emphasis is his.

Here again "unity" is an imperative for Dwight: the unity of the three strands in life, the unity of music, the unity of items on a program. For Dwight, "pure programmes" are not only an end in themselves; they will also "educate" the orchestra musicians and bring "mutual" enjoyment to the listeners. Dwight's concept of the "nucleus audience" as one where each member "must feel the music in his neighbor" and inspire "confidence in the like-minded," stems, like his notion of "unity," from his experiences at Brook Farm in the 1840s, as both a spiritual and a practical principle.[24]

To ensure that "control" of the orchestra would be "in the right hands," the association appointed a Concert Committee of seven members to consider the details of forming a "Philharmonic Society." In addition to Dwight, the committee included HMA treasurer James Sturgis, future Harvard Orchestra conductor Carl Zerrahn, pianist-conductor B. J. Lang, and piano manufacturer George Chickering, who supplied all pianos needed for the concerts.

It was too late to launch a full concert series that season, but a reserve of $2,000 was set aside from the association's funds. Composer-pianists Otto Dresel and J. C. D. Parker were added to the committee, which proceeded to perpetuate itself, with few changes, throughout the life of the orchestra.

For the first season of six programs, more than one thousand season tickets were sold for the twenty-seven-hundred-seat Boston Music Hall. These tickets were sold in advance at $5 each to HMA members, who were expected to buy more than they needed and sell the remainder to musically literate friends. Unreserved single seats were sold first to members at $1 each. The remaining seats were made available later to the public. In this way the HMA members themselves provided the guaranty of "audience" as well as "means." A letter to the *Boston Daily Advertiser* in 1871 complained that the "public, i.e. those who would like to patronize music now that it is fashionable, cannot get all the best seats in the hall and are wroth."[25] This ticket policy, with the exception of one financially unsuccessful season, remained firm despite frequent discussion in both the committee and the press.

The first program, on December 28, 1865, comprised the following works:

24 · For a fuller discussion of Dwight's "nucleus" idea, see Ralph P. Locke, "Music Lovers, Patrons, and the 'Sacralization' of Culture in America," *19th-Century Music* 17 (1993): 157–58.

25 · Upsilon [pseud.], letter to the editor, *Boston Daily Advertiser,* undated; pasted into HMA Orchestra criticisms at the end of the sixth season, March 1871, Harvard Musical Association, "Criticisms of HMA Symphony Concerts—1865 to 1881, Vol. 1," HMA Archives, 003-A:47.

Overture to *Euryanthe*	Carl Maria von Weber
Violin Concerto, E Minor	Felix Mendelssohn-Bartholdy
Carl Rosa, violin soloist	

INTERMISSION

Overture to *Lenora*, no. 3	Ludwig van Beethoven
Chaconne, for solo violin	J. S. Bach,
with piano accompaniment by	Felix Mendelssohn-Bartholdy
Am Springquell	Ferdinand David
Hungarian Air	Ferdinand David
Abendlied	Robert Schumann, arr. Joseph Joachim
Carl Rosa, violin	
Otto Dresel, piano	
Symphony in G Minor [K. 550]	W. A. Mozart[26]

The concert adopted a format that Dwight devised and that was to remain generally consistent throughout the seventeen seasons: an opening overture that usually had to absorb the noise of latecomers, followed by a concerted work, instrumental or vocal, as the centerpiece. The second half opened with another overture. The soloist then performed a number of shorter works, usually accompanied by a pianist, who was unnamed in the programs, but most often reviewers mentioned Otto Dresel, B. J. Lang, Hugo Leonhard, J. C. D. Parker, or the young Ernst Perabo. The final work was most often a symphony. Such "musical idealism," concentrating on "pure" (i.e., sonata) forms and generally eschewing vocal music, was not unique, but rare enough, and it was certainly new to Boston.[27]

All concerts were given on Thursday afternoons, from 4:00 to 6:00 p.m., thus attracting mostly women. Reviewers noticed the size of the audience and its social characteristics. For example, the *Boston Sunday Times* of November 16, 1868, reported, "A fair day … favored the fair sex, who consider the symphony concerts under their especial patronage and protection, and all amusement-seeking-and-finding-people in Boston were present—to a woman. Such room as the ladies left was gladly occupied by the deserving brave. The city's best, that may absent themselves—surreptitiously or other-

26 · The first printed program is not extant in the HMA Archives; information here is reconstructed chiefly from reviews in HMA Archives, 003-A:4–5, and lists of repertory and personnel from HMA Archives, 101:1–48. The order of solo works by Bach, David, and Schumann is uncertain.

27 · On "musical idealism" in concerts of the Philharmonic Society of New York, see chapter V.3 in this volume.

wise—from duty elsewhere, would have been found upon a roll call."[28] Many critics called for evening concerts, as did ultimately members of the Concert Committee, but Dwight remained rigidly opposed. The musicians' evenings were taken up by theater jobs.

Dwight's report of the concerts at the end of the first season summarized the orchestra's achievements as justifying continuation of "pure" programming:

1. A great deal of refined pleasure, instruction, and good to all concerned ... as audience, as performers, or as managers. A higher standard has been set, & taste was purified & elevated. Many *new* works have been introduced to us.

2. They leave a clear surplus of $1,385.00 ... in the hands of the A[ssociation], as a basis for the continuance of the good work.

3. They have added some $300.00 worth of music to the Library, consisting of orchestral scores & parts.

4. They have given the most signal demonstration that there is no need of descending from the highest standard in the composition of programmes, to secure a large and paying audience of the highest character.[29]

In the second season the number of concerts was increased to eight and two years later expanded to ten. During that fourth season (1868–69), the concert of February 18, 1869, coincided with the first concert in Boston of Theodore Thomas's orchestra, whose impact was enormous. Here was a touring orchestra that rehearsed every day, played a variety of music as a flexible ensemble under an inspired and intelligent conductor, and performed on several consecutive evenings when it was in town. Audiences flocked to listen. To its credit, the HMA Orchestra rose to the challenge in its next season with noticeably improved performances, as reported by the *Daily Advertiser*'s critic: "It is evident that the increase of time and care bestowed upon the preparation of these concerts has begun to bear fruit directly.... Improvement in vigor and vitality of style, in clearness and precision, and in that di-

28 · HMA, "Criticisms," HMA Archives, 003-A:34. On women as an audience for orchestral concerts in Boston and elsewhere, see chapter III.4 in this volume.

29 · Dwight, "Reports," HMA Archives, 033-C:33–34, continuing through 38, in the same self-congratulatory mode. During the early years, the surpluses, after deductions for the library, were deposited in the Concert Fund. Despite substantial losses during the last seasons, $1,000 remained in the Concert Fund when the orchestra was dissolved.

rectness of 'attack' which was so peculiarly characteristic of the New York artists, is already to be perceived."[30]

In the same season, the HMA Orchestra expanded to sixty-four players, including forty-six strings. It is impossible to determine just who played in the orchestra from year to year. Almost all the musicians were German or of German descent. A few had studied with well-known teachers before emigrating, and these musicians tended to find appointments in the new conservatories in Boston in the late 1860s. Most of the other players were recruited from Boston's theater orchestras.[31] The appendix to this chapter gives the rosters at six different moments in the orchestra's life. From the general account books, we know that they were well paid: $2 per rehearsal and $6 per concert.

Their organization and "Rules for Rehearsal" were specified in an undated document, probably from 1868.[32] The HMA's Concert Committee appointed three "officers": Carl Zerrahn, conductor; concertmaster Julius Eichberg, vice conductor; and violinist William Schultze, leader, that is, the person responsible for contracting the other orchestra players. The members of the orchestra met on October 11, 1868, and elected the following Executive Committee: Luke Murphy (horn), William Schultze, and Charles Eichler (principal second violin). The Executive Committee was empowered to (1) represent the orchestra to the Concert Committee and specify the placement of players; (2) keep track of attendance; and (3) receive and disburse all payments to individual members. According to the account books, principals, especially strings, were usually paid more than $6. The "Rules for Rehearsal" reveal that a grace period of five minutes was allowed for a musician's presence at the start of a rehearsal and that fifteen minutes could be added at the end of a rehearsal to finish a piece already started. Standard rehearsals were two hours; lateness was prorated up to an hour, after which the entire $2 wage was forfeited.

Various attempts were made to improve the quality of the roster. The leader of the Mendelssohn Quintet Club, violist and clarinetist Thomas Ryan, played viola for the first year but then resigned.[33] He was replaced by Julius Eichberg, who also conducted whenever Zerrahn had not yet returned

30 · *Boston Daily Advertiser*, November 4, 1870, in HMA, "Criticisms," HMA Archives, 003-A:43.

31 · Charles Nutter, *HMA Library Bulletin* 16 (April 1948): [3].

32 · Dwight, "Reports," HMA Archives, 033-A:33–35 (duplicate images). The document refers to current events of 1868.

33 · Thomas Ryan to Dwight, A.L.S., February 12, 1866, Harvard Musical Association, "HMA Orchestra: Letters to Mr. Dwight," HMA Archives, 088-C:15. Ryan continued to play with the orchestra, however, at least on occasion.

from his summer sojourn in Europe. The other members of the Mendelssohn Quintet Club, violinists William Schultze and August Fries and Fries's brother, cellist Wulf Fries, also occupied first chairs in the orchestra from time to time, but when the club went on tour, they did not go along. On October 28, 1867, the Music Committee voted at a special meeting to send the president and one other member, in consultation with Zerrahn, to New York for the purpose of recruiting violinists. Bernhard and Fritz Listemann were probably recruited at this time but returned to New York after only a few seasons and joined the Thomas Orchestra. There were so many complaints about the winds and brasses that no critic dared to mention names. In 1870 Dwight tried hard to lure oboist Joseph Eller from New York, but Eller declined because there was not enough theater work in Boston.[34] As critics and audiences became more "educated," they grew less tolerant of dissonance and imbalance in the orchestra despite what the critics referred to as Zerrahn's competent drilling. Composer Arthur Foote (1853–1937) recalled: "The performance[s] [were] inadequate, the players as a rule not of the first rank, and the rehearsals insufficient through lack of funds. . . . Boston pianists, violinists, and singers were as a rule willing to serve [as soloists] without being paid, while naturally members of our Association were glad to help. . . . When a harp was needed in the orchestra, as there was no harp player in the town, one of us would do the best he could to replace it by playing the part on an upright piano. I remember [critic William Foster] Apthorp's performance with the cymbals when Saint Saëns' *Phaéton* was played for the first time."[35]

Rise to Maturity (1869–73)

Dwight's report of 1869–70 revealed his frustration with the state of the HMA Orchestra: "Orchestra improved, strings especially, by extra rehearsals. Much yet wanting, *oboes, brass,* &c. Difficulty here is threefold: (1) not enough good musicians; (2) want of hold on them because they get their living chiefly by playing in the street, balls, theatres, &c, which both unfits them for symphony work, & makes men uncertain of attendance at rehearsals; (3) the Protective Union League."[36] Item 3 is the only mention of the musicians' union in all of Dwight's reports. Boston lay claim to one of the earli-

34 · Joseph Eller to and from Dwight, A.L.S., July–September 1870, HMA, "HMA Orchestra: Letters to Mr. Dwight," HMA Archives, 088-D:7–14. Dwight offered him $100 more than the other first chairs and tried to secure employment for him under two different theater conductors, but with no success. Eller was a member of the Theodore Thomas Orchestra at that time, according to this correspondence.
35 · Nutter, *HMA Library Bulletin* 4 (December 1935): [2].
36 · Dwight, "Reports," HMA Archives, 033E:23–25.

est unions for professional musicians, the Boston Musical Union, founded in the 1860s. Dwight went on to suggest that if the HMA could turn itself into a full-time orchestra, it would no longer have to abide by union rules or compete with the theaters for players and that it could pay the musicians well and even offer benefits:

> What we need is: to offer *so much* of this higher kind of employment to the best musicians, that they may afford and prefer to keep out of the *bands*, &c. Could we afford to give 20 instead of 10 concerts, with 2 or 3 rehearsals every week, and pay them well; might we not make individual contracts with the musicians in spite of bands or Prot. Unions?
>
> Or, if the members of the Orch. should seek to carry out a plan of their own (which we heard they have been discussing), might we not lend our name and influence to it, letting them have all the profit,—& thereby kill another bird with the same stone, viz., meet the demand for *variety*, for *new works*, &c., by 10 more popular, mixed concerts in the alternate Thursdays, leaving the programming to the orchestra itself![37]

Dwight's assessment was brutally honest, and his solution might have served the orchestra well. But the idea remained buried in this report; it was not even proposed to the board as a resolution.

In the same report Dwight also characteristically mentioned the successes of the first five seasons: the steady increase in attendance, the improvement of the orchestra, and "the general satisfaction manifested in the concerts," notwithstanding the reviews.[38] The programming had been able to maintain high standards of "*purity*, variety, and interest."[39] As he noted, however, "It is natural that, the further we go on, the more difficult & complex becomes the problem of arranging 10 or 12 satisfactory programmes;—the problem being: how to keep up to our high standard, and yet gratify the desire for novelty which comes up after so long experience."[40]

Dwight's idea of allowing the musicians to give "more popular, mixed concerts" under the umbrella of the HMA never surfaced again because Dwight himself was so unswerving about programming. The orchestra's repertory embodied his definition of the "pure" in music, especially the many works in generic forms (e.g., overtures, symphonies, and concertos) by the European composers Bach, Handel, Haydn, Mozart, Beethoven, Schubert, Mendelssohn, and Schumann. The same report of 1869–70 summarizes the compos-

37 · Ibid.
38 · Ibid., 19.
39 · Ibid., 26.
40 · Ibid., 29.

ers performed; in addition to the above, they included Cherubini, Gluck, Spohr, Sterndale Bennett, Rossini, Weber, Gade, Chopin, Hummel, Liszt, and one work each by Moscheles, Spontini, Wagner, Adolf Henselt, and Norbert Bergmüller, all pointedly marked, "new" on Dwight's list.[41] Not until the last concert of the tenth season, in 1875, was anything heard by an American composer, namely, two excerpts from a set of a capella partsongs by J. C. D. Parker, sung by the Cecilia.[42] Only three American symphonic works, not surprisingly by HMA members Parker, John Knowles Paine, and George Chadwick, were ever performed, and these came during the last five seasons. On the other hand, as Apthorp said, "The public persistently cried for the new things, and turned up its nose when it got them."[43] The *Sunday Times* critic of November 1871, after noting the empty seats and general lackluster mood of the audience, broadened the point: "Surely we cannot be too familiar with the noblest works of Bach, Mozart and Beethoven, and we can possibly hear too much of the music of the future; but the former knowledge is not to be obtained by completely ignoring the works of the thoughtful composers of today. They have a right to be heard, and the healthy development of musical taste and culture likewise demands that we should have the opportunity of hearing them."[44]

The concerts of the first season had been reviewed by only one or two critics, but the number of reviews grew over the years to as many as ten per concert. Although generally favorable, many of the reviews were unremarkable and continued to refer in common parlance to "the band," and the "entertainment." Proper "shading" was much valued, but the term apparently referred only to dynamics. By the beginning of the eighth season (1872–73), the critical honeymoon was over. An experienced musician and sharp-tongued critic, B. E. Woolf, had become editor of the *Boston Saturday Evening Gazette* in 1871 and soon began quarreling with Dwight in print, heavy-handedly detailing Dwight's lack of professional music skills.[45] Dwight responded in the pages of his *Journal* that he had "never ... pretended to technical musicianship at all" but that "over long years of intercourse with music of the noblest

41 · Ibid., 26–33. Dwight gave a complete summary of the "large allowance of modern works" in his "History of Music in Boston," 449.

42 · J. C. D. Parker, *Seven Part Songs* (1875); Harvard Musical Association, "HMA Symphony Concerts" programs, HMA Archives, 006-A:39–40 (March 18, 1875).

43 · Apthorp, "Musical Reminiscences," 82.

44 · "The Second Symphony Concert," *Boston Sunday Times*, November 1871, in HMA, "Criticisms," HMA Archives, 003B:5.

45 · [B. E. Woolf], "Anent Musical Criticism," *Boston Saturday Evening Gazette*, January 16, 1876, in HMA, "Criticisms," HMA Archives, 003-B:39. Benjamin Edward Woolf (1836–1901) was an experienced theater orchestra conductor, composer, and librettist as well as a critic.

masters," he must have learned at least something.[46] Both argued with zeal, and both eventually retreated: Dwight decided to make some changes, and Woolf realized that the orchestra was worthy of support.

Gradual Decline (1874–82)

At a special meeting of the HMA board at the end of the ninth season in 1874, the first serious loss of proceeds was reported, in the amount of $1,206.52.[47] The board agreed to broaden the orchestra's appeal by offering some choral music. On November 19, 1874 (during the tenth season) a group of one hundred professional and amateur singers, unnamed in the program but referred to by the critics as the Cecilia Club, was presented for the first time.[48] Formed on a voluntary basis for this occasion and directed by B. J. Lang, they sang two numbers a capella (Mendelssohn's *The Lark* and a madrigal by Weelkes that none of the critics liked), followed by Mendelssohn's *Walpurgisnacht* with the orchestra. The chorus took up the whole stage, so a wide, narrow platform was built in front of the stage for the orchestra. This was fine for the chorus but not for the orchestra, the soloists, or the overall balance. Some reported a lag between the production of sounds on stage left and right. The chorus was noticeably nervous. The large audience was reported to be attentive but apathetic. Free tickets were offered to all the singers in lieu of pay, causing further loss of revenue. Musically and financially, the experiment was a disaster.

During the eleventh season (1875–76), the critics broke out of their polite cages in full force. Woolf called for an infusion of younger management among the HMA concert directors and an end to the "oppressive monotony" of the programming so limited in its range. The other Boston papers filled their pages with commentary on the dispute. They tended to agree with Woolf but urged him to tame his remarks for the sake of the enterprise. Critics were further agitated by the Theodore Thomas Orchestra's performance on January 26, 1876, of John Knowles Paine's First Symphony (1875). Several were appalled that a major work by a Boston composer was not premiered by a Boston orchestra; others casually mentioned that the HMA Orchestra was not good enough to perform it. Although some thought Dwight had refused to perform the piece, an anonymous letter to the editor in the *Boston Transcript* on February 2, 1876, confirmed that Paine had not offered it to the

46 · "Howling Wolves,—'Last Ditches,'—'Enraged Mouth-pieces,' [etc.]," *Dwight's Journal of Music* 35 (January 22, 1876): 165–67.

47 · Dwight, "Reports," HMA Archives, 033-B:42–44.

48 · The Cecilia Club continued to sing occasionally with the HMA Orchestra and is still in existence as the Boston Cecilia.

HMA even though he was a member.[49] Several critics noted that the Thomas Orchestra had the advantage because of its daily rehearsals. Furthermore, the HMA Orchestra suffered from lack of leadership, and, after all, the players could do only what they were told.

At the end of that season, in April 1876, Dwight prepared a long report on behalf of the Concert Committee. The losses for the ninth through the eleventh seasons had grown progressively worse, totaling about $5,400, although the initial $2,000 still remained in the Concert Fund.[50] Dwight and the committee analyzed the causes for the losses quite fairly. The severe economic depression after the panic of 1873 had negatively affected the number of available subscribers (HMA members) and their purchasing ability; single-ticket buyers were no doubt similarly affected. Apparently subscribers, who as an inducement were allowed to attend the last rehearsal of each concert for free, were giving away these privileges, thus further reducing single-ticket sales. There was lingering public resentment about the method by which the best seats were distributed to subscribers.[51] The Cecilia debacle was mentioned, as was the old question of afternoon versus evening concerts. The final point concerned the presence of the Theodore Thomas Orchestra in Boston, which led Dwight to a frank self-examination of the HMA and its orchestra: "Doubtless our concerts have suffered most through the comparison ... between the execution of our own imperfect orchestra, made up every winter for these few occasions, & the remarkably brilliant and thoroughly trained orchestra of Mr. Thomas." The Thomas Orchestra, in his view, had divided both taste and opinion among the HMA members and had eroded support for HMA concerts by other Bostonians.

Against these "discouragements," Dwight posited "encouragements": the HMA Orchestra had improved during the last part of the season, and its members had volunteered one extra rehearsal for each concert. They had also rehired, at their own expense, musicians previously laid off to reduce costs. Finally, Dwight asked rhetorically, "What if we let the concerts die?" First, there would be no regular orchestra in Boston, causing a ripple effect for other performance organizations, and, second, "it would strip the H.M.A. of

---

49 · From reviews in HMA, "Criticisms," HMA Archives, 003-B:36, 003-C:4. Paine later offered his *Spring* Symphony to Dwight, although not as a premiere. It was performed by the HMA Orchestra in March 1880 to a long standing ovation. J. K. Paine, A.L.S., to Dwight, February 2, 1880, "HMA Orchestra: Letters to Mr. Dwight," HMA Archives, 101:10; "HMA Orchestra—1865 to 1882—Repertoire and Personnel," HMA Archives, 088-K:36.

50 · Losses in the ninth season were $1,206; in the tenth they were $1,750; and in the eleventh they were $2,414.05.

51 · In the beginning, when subscribers sent in their money, the Concert Committee determined who should have the best seats; later the determination was made by lottery.

nearly all its prestige & its power of usefulness. . . . And whence will come our power to help to build up Music in our University [i.e., Harvard], if we abandon our chief source of power, disheartened by a few unfavorable seasons?"[52] Dwight used the word "power" in his reports noticeably often, and this may be the key to his stubbornness about the management of the orchestra: he was afraid of losing his power, as would be natural for someone who was as impecunious and inexperienced in the "real" world as he was and who had risen to his social status by virtue of his official duties. Now that he was the HMA's president, the "we" and "our" very possibly stood for "I" and "my."

The twelfth and thirteenth seasons limped along with faint praise from the critics—stating the orchestra was "sounding better than ever" but also reporting "disagreeable disagreements" between the winds and the rest of the instruments.[53] The twelfth season suffered no loss for the first time in four years, so the Concert Committee was encouraged to keep going. They waited, however, until October of the next season (1877) to canvass the members for subscriptions. These had usually averaged between thirteen hundred and fourteen hundred, and the committee needed only six hundred to guarantee the season. When they received only 450, they "unwisely" (Dwight's later adverb) decided they could make it up by single-ticket sales and announced the full calendar of ten concerts. By midseason, they realized their losses would be heavy. The committee cut the number of rehearsals per concert from three to two, reducing the season's cost from the usual $10,000 to $7,000 but still leaving a deficit of more than $1,500. Dwight's report for the Concert Committee that year (1877–78), the last extant, included many good suggestions that the critics had long been demanding: evening and Sunday concerts, cheap concerts, lighter music, more young men on the committee, and a permanent fund of $100,000.[54] The board barely discussed the situation in January 1878, noting that the Concert Fund reserve would probably be spent by the end of the season. Once again, however, Dwight concluded that "the time to consider the Concert question . . . has not yet come."[55] In the board of directors' report for 1880, the rubric for the concerts was left bare and never mentioned again.

The fourteenth and fifteenth seasons (1878–80) did not begin until December and then were reduced to eight concerts. Violinist Bernhard Listemann was reengaged as concertmaster in late 1879, but in 1880 he started his own philharmonic, drawing off the HMA's already scanty audiences.

In December 1880, the Harvard Musical Association presented a testimo-

52 · Dwight, "Reports," HMA Archives, 033-H:1–12.
53 · Reviews of the twelfth season, fourth concert, in HMA, "Criticisms," 003-C:6–7.
54 · Dwight, "Reports," HMA Archives, 033-H:13–30. The deficit was $1,534.41.
55 · HMA, "Reports of Board of Directors, 1875–1879," HMA Archives, 031:3–40.

nial concert for Dwight, comprising works by his favorite composers. The invitation of November 15, signed by fifty of his colleagues (including B. E. Woolf), seems written in recognition of the pain that the signs of imminent failure of both the orchestra and his journal must have been causing Dwight: "A number of your friends, who remember your long and faithful services in behalf of the cause of music, and who are deeply grateful that it has been permitted to you to accomplish so much in elevating the standard of public performances and in refining the public taste, have determined to offer you a Testimonial Concert, to be offered on a fitting scale.... They respectfully ask your acceptance of the compliment, with their united good will and affection, and with best wishes for your continued health and usefulness." Dwight responded the following day with sincerest gratitude, noting that he had "simply preached the faith that was in me" about the true worth of music and that "after many periods of misgiving," this tribute gave him, "as it were, the sense of a new life."[56]

The Harvard Orchestra's seventeenth and last season, presented at the smaller Boston Museum rather than the Boston Music Hall, did not get under way until January 1882, and it ended after the fifth concert on March 9. The final program comprised the following:

Symphony no. 4	Robert Schumann
Piano Concerto no. 4	Ludwig van Beethoven
Carl Bergmann, pianist	

INTERMISSION

Serenade for Strings, D Major, op. 9	Robert Fuchs
Berceuse, op. 57	Frédéric Chopin
Scherzo no. 3, op. 39	Frédéric Chopin
Carl Bergmann, pianist	
Overture to *Ruy Blas*	Felix Mendelssohn-Bartholdy[57]

A Help or a Hindrance?

Clearly, Dwight was both a help and a hindrance to the development of Boston's orchestral and concert life. He created and managed an orchestra that survived for seventeen years—from 1865 to 1882—the longest of any in Bos-

56. "The Complimentary Concert to Mr. John S. Dwight," in HMA, "HMA Symphony Concerts," HMA Archives, 006-D:16–18 (program) and 40 (invitation and response).

57. This was the first Boston performance of the *Serenade* by the young Robert Fuchs; it had been given its first performance in Leipzig in 1874. Dwight did not retain reviews of this final concert in his scrapbooks.

ton to that date. He steadfastly guided both musicians and audiences through a transition from the miscellaneous programming that characterized orchestra concerts before the Civil War to programs consisting exclusively of what were in his view the finest symphonic works available. Through his control of programming and the mechanics of the performances (ticket sales, hall rental, and music purchasing and copying), Dwight set standards for orchestra managers of the next generation.

In the meantime, though, the forms of music by European composers had moved on to more chromatic and programmatic works, about which the audiences were increasingly curious, but which Dwight found both distasteful and antithetical to his principles. True, the HMA Orchestra probably could not have performed these more complex works with as little rehearsal as its schedule and its finances permitted. Although he almost invariably was forthright in his annual assessments to the board of both the successes and failures of the orchestra and reported many suggestions for change, he stubbornly refused to act on them.

From the beginning to the end of his career with the HMA Orchestra, Dwight maintained what had been his initial principle: that the works of the masters possessed intrinsic moral power because they embodied body, soul, and intellect in music. In themselves they could overcome all obstacles. "Pure programmes" would improve public taste, raise the playing standards of orchestra musicians, and unite the community to feel as one. The critics, the union, and the finances would necessarily follow. Dwight never lost his optimism and almost blind persistence about what could be (and eventually was) accomplished in Boston.

During the HMA Orchestra's last season (1881–82), the Boston Symphony Orchestra was founded by Henry Lee Higginson, a wealthy Boston banker and member of the HMA since 1869.[58] The HMA Orchestra supplied many members of the Boston Symphony's roster, even in that first simultaneous season.[59] We can now see that Higginson's initial policies for the new orchestra were based on a thorough understanding of what had *not* worked for the HMA Orchestra. At the Boston Symphony Orchestra, Higginson was able to schedule enough evening concerts and rehearsals, plus a summer season of light music, to ensure the livelihood of the musicians without recourse to other employment. He also instituted ticket sales to the entire public at reasonable prices. Conductors, although chosen by him, were given free rein over choice of musicians and of repertory. Higginson himself, as the corpo-

58 · Higginson was proposed for membership (by Dwight) in 1857 (HMA Archives, 018-B:1) but was not admitted until 1869 (HMA Archives, 060-A:41).
59 · Henry Lee Higginson, *Life and Letters of Henry Lee Higginson* (1921); M. A. De Wolfe Howe, *The Boston Symphony Orchestra: An Historical Sketch* (1914).

rate backer, covered the orchestra's yearly deficits, but it was also possible to appeal for public support because the orchestra was no longer sponsored by a private club. That Dwight foresaw many of these solutions is evident in his reports. However, he lacked not only Higginson's wealth but also the younger man's vision of goals beyond the transcendental ideals that he had initially defined for the HMA's orchestra.

Higginson was also well aware of what *had* worked for the Harvard Orchestra, and he probably could not have founded "his" orchestra before Dwight's accomplishments. Dwight's insistence on "pure" music and his belief in its effects on society impelled him to present many "classical" works in Boston for the first time. In so doing, he not only broadened the knowledge and taste of the audience but also increased the skills and understanding of at least some of Boston's professional musicians and made them ready for Higginson's next step.

APPENDIX III.2.1 *Membership of the Harvard Orchestra*

Information in the table below is compiled from extant rosters in the hand of either John Sullivan Dwight or hornist Luke Murphy, an Executive Committee member. The first column represents players' attendance for the first four concerts of that season only. The second, third, and last columns are records of rehearsals and performances of a single concert. The fourth and fifth columns appear to represent a summary of players contracted for the entire seasons before they began. In any case, these lists serve to demonstrate the instability of the ensemble during these years.

Those players shown in italics are identified in a card file not in Dwight's hand.[60] The indexer apparently had some sense of which players were more permanent and clearly had access to the list, the only one ever printed, in the program of December 10, 1879. The other names appear only in the manuscript rosters. Where similar names played different instruments, they may be the same or related performers. For example, E. Beyer, violin, is probably the same person as Edward Beyer, viola. Frequently the same person played different instruments, even of different instrument families, suggesting perhaps a lower level of proficiency on both, although not necessarily, as in the case of Ryan and Schlimper. A close study of the original charts reveals information about absences and substitutions.

Biographical information about these players is scarce. Many of them are mentioned briefly in Ryan's *Recollections*. Ryan played with the HMA Orchestra, but his memories, though charming, are not always reliable. Newman's dissertation serves as a corrective for those who had been members of the Germania Musical Society.[61] Many of the players performed with the Boston Symphony Orchestra during its first season (1881–82), and a few continued for several years.[62]

---

60 · "HMA Orchestra—1865 to 1882—Repertoire and Personnel," HMA Archives, 101, frames 49–65.

61 · Newman, "Good Music for a Free People," 553–71.

62 · Howe, *Boston Symphony Orchestra*, 242–51.

APPENDIX TABLE III.2.1. Harvard Orchestra membership

1867–1868[a]	Nov. 3, 1870[b]	Undated[c]	1871–1872[d]	1872–1873[e]	Dec. 11, 1879[f]
First violin	[*First violin*]	[*First violin*]	[*First violin*]	[*First violin*]	*First violin*
__Schmidt	B. Listemann	W. Fries	[Wm. Schultze]	J. Eichberg	Bernard Listemann
__Eichberg	Wm. Schultze	A. Suck	[Meisel]	Hassam	C. N. Allen
__Meisel	C. Meisel	Verron, Jr.	H. Suck	H. Suck	Julius Ackeroyd
Weinz	H. Suck	Rietzel	Ford	Wm. Schultze	Theodore Human
H. Suck	Lösch	A. Heindl	Lothian	F. F. Ford	F. Listemann
J. Schutz	Ford[new]	E. Regestein	*Mullaly*	N. Lothian	Carl Meisel
Lothian	Lothian	Hoffmann[n[ew]]	Allen	J. C. Mullaly	John C. Mullaly
Lösch	F. Listemann	Kaltenborn[n[ew]]	Torrington	C. N. Allen	Henry Suck
Van Olcker	Van Olcker		[Illegible][n[ew]]	F. H. Torrington	
Trautmann	Torrington		Lösch		
__Müller	*Allen*				
__Heindl					
__Lautenschlüger					
Second violin	[*Second violin*]	[*Second violin*]	[*Second violin*]	*Second violin*	*Second violin*
C. Eichler	C. Eichler	Stein	C. Eichler	C. Eichler	Vincent Ackeroyd
J. Eichler	J. Eichler	Friese	Van Olcker	J. Eichler	Carl Eichler
Schneider	J. Mullaly	Steinmann	*Schneider*	A. Schneider	Julius Eichler
Ford	Kuntzmann	Bapp	J. Eichler	G. H. Kuntzman	Richard Eltz
Beyer	*Schneider*	Messerschmidt[n[ew]]	Kellner[n[ew]]	F. Van Olker	Henry Strauss
Kuntzmann	Beyer	Brand[n[ew]]	A. Schultze	E. Beyer	Carl Trautmann
Mullaly	*Eltz*		Eltz, 2nd	R. Eltz	
Göring	*Patz*		Kuntzmann	"Substitute[s]:	
	Trautmann			Mr. Braham,	
	Aug. Schultze			Mr.Blodgett—	
				good"	
Viola	[*Viola*]		[*Viola*]	*Viola*	*Viola*
F. Zöhler, II	H. Heindl		*Weinz*	Heindl	Edward Beyer
__Ryan	Weinz		[Ryan]	C. Weinz	Henry Heindl
Keller	T. Ryan		[Heindl]	F. W. Schlimper	Aug. Schneider
Bauer	M. Heindl		*Schlimper*	C. Trautmann	E. Strasser
__G. Krebs	Verron (Sen.)		*Trautmann*	Thos. Verron	Carl Weinz
Schlimper	Bauer			Thos. Ryan	
Endres	*Schlimper*			E. M. Heindl	
Wiesel	*Endres*			"Subst[itutes]:	
Heindl				Mr. Bauer,	
				Dietz—good"	
Violoncello			*Violoncello*	*Violoncello*	*Violoncello*
__W. Fries			[W. Fries]	W. Fries	Wulf Fries
A. Suck			Hartdein	A. Hennig	Carl Behr
__Rietzel			*Heindl*	A. Suck	Alex. Heindl
Moorehouse			A. Suck	Wm. Rietzel	Wilhelm Rietzel
__Regestein III			*Rietzel*	A. Heindl	Aug. Suck
__McDonald			Verron	J. Hoffman	
Contrabass			*Contrabass*	*Contrabass*	*Contrabass*
Stein			Stein	A. Stein	H. A. Greene
Friese			Steinmann	H. Steinmann	L. Jennewein
Steinmann			Regestein (or	F. Friese	Aug. Stein
Kümmerling			Tremke)	A. Regestein	H. Steinmann
Kehrhuhn			Friese	P. Bapp	
Regestein II			Bapp	L. Lemmancier[?]	
			Messerschmidt		
			Brandt		
Flute		*Flute*	*Flute*	*Flute*	*Flute*
Zöhler		Göring	Göring	L. R. Georing	Edward Heindl
Rumetti		Zöhler	Zöhler	[i.e., Göring]	F. W. Schlimper
		Koppitz, 2nd		F. Zoehler	

continued

1867–1868[a]	Nov. 3, 1870[b]	Undated[c]	1871–1872[d]	1872–1873[e]	Dec. 11, 1879[f]
Oboe		*Oboe*	*Oboe*	*Oboe*	*Oboe*
Ribas	Newmann[n[ew]]	Kutzleben[n[ew]]	Mr. Kutzleb	A. L. De Ribas
Faulwasser	Faulwasser	Ribas (?)	C. Faulwasser	Carl Faulwasser
Clarinet		*Clarinet*	*Clarinet*	*Clarinet*	*Clarinet*
__Weber	Weber	Weber	E. Weber	Ernst Weber
__Liebsch.[g]	Kalkmann	Schülten[n[ew]]	P. Kalkman	O. A. Whitmore
Bassoon		*Bassoon*	*Bassoon*	*Bassoon*	*Bassoon*
Eltz	Eltz	Becker	Eltz	Paul Eltz
__Kalkmann	Becker	Regestein	F. Becker	E. Regestein
Horn		*Horn*	*Horn*	*Horn*	*Horn*
__Wack	Hamann	Hamann	A. Hamann	Edward Schormann
Regestein I	Murphy	Murphy	L. Murphy	Carl Schumann
Murphy	Schörmann	Schörmann	E. Schorman	L. Lippoldt
__Kluge	Kluge	Kluge	A. Kluge	A. Gumpricht
Trumpet		*Trumpet*	*Trumpet*	*Trumpet*	*Trumpet*
Heinicke	Arbuckle	Arbuckle	M. Arbuckle	E. M. Bagley
Pinter	Heinecke	Heinecke	A. Heinecke	B. Bowron
Trombone		*Trombone*	*Trombone*	*Trombone*	*Trombone*
Arbuckle	Brückner	*Paltz*	Wm. Brückner	G. A. Patz
Stöhr I	Regestein	[Regestein]	A. Rigg	A. Rigg
__Saul	Saul	Brückner	G. A. Paltz	G. W. Stewart
					Tuba
					W. C. Nichols
Timpani		*Timpani*	*Timpani*	*Timpani*	*Timpani*
Stöhr II	W. Stöhr	Simpson[n[ew]]	H. Simpson	H. D. Simpson
Librarian		*Librarian*			
[A. L. de Ribas]	Nichols[h]				

a. John Sullivan Dwight, "Reports," HMA Archives, 033-D, frames 26–28. Another representation of this chart summarized the number of players as strings (42) plus winds (18) for a total of 60 (ibid., frames 47–48). There were three rehearsals of two hours each, and a fourth of two and one-quarter hours, before the first concert on November 7. There were only two rehearsals, generally a week apart, prior to the other three concerts, although for some instruments none were recorded for the second or third concert. Those whose names are preceded with "__" (a designation in the source) missed several rehearsals, concerts, or both.

b. Dwight, "Reports," HMA Archives, 033-A, frame 18. Instruments are not identified, but have been suggested on the basis of prior lists. Only the violin and viola sections are shown. For this concert there were five rehearsals (including one that was public).

c. "Dwight, "Reports," HMA Archives, 033-A, frame 19. Because of adjacency in the file, it is possible (but not certain) that this concert appeared during the same season. Instruments are not identified, but have been suggested on the basis of prior lists.

d. "As agreed at conference, June 6, 1871, among Zerrahn, Dwight, Leonhard, and Thorndike (members of the Music Committee)," Dwight, "Reports," HMA Archives, 033-A, frame 44. There is no explanation for the brackets around some of the names; because they were the most well-known performers, they may have been on tour during some of the rehearsals or concerts.

e. Dwight, "Reports," HMA Archives, 033-A, frame 47, 49, both in the hand of, and signed by, hornist L. Murphy.

f. Printed in the program for this concert, "HMA Symphony Concerts," HMA Archives, 006-C, frame 49. Bernhard Listemann, as concertmaster, was given typographical prominence. Members of the Program Committee were J. S. Dwight, C. C. Perkins, J. C. D. Parker, B. J. Lang, W. F. Apthorp, and Arthur Foote, as also printed here.

g. Possibly an abbreviated name.

h. "Nichols" is probably W. C. Nichols, the tuba player, who was paid as a librarian for each rehearsal as well as for each concert. Accounting records show that oboist A. L. de Ribas, who preceded Nichols as librarian, was paid $5 for each concert only.

[III.3] The Leopold Damrosch Orchestra, 1877–78

Background, Instrumentation, Programming, and Critical Reception

ORA FRISHBERG SALOMAN

Before 1877 two main professional concert orchestras in New York City invigorated cultural activity and competed for audiences as well as press attention: the Philharmonic Society of New York's orchestra, which had been established permanently in 1842, and a younger challenger, the Theodore Thomas Orchestra. Thomas, a respected leader, founded his orchestra soon after beginning his orchestral conducting career in 1862 and subsequently transformed concert life through notable instrumental series presented in various locations.

A little remembered but highly consequential event in the history of music in New York City was Leopold Damrosch's successful creation of a transitional orchestra in 1877 which bore his name and emerged following an adverse professional circumstance. Histories of music have remained silent about Damrosch's formation of that orchestra or else have conflated it with his 1878 founding of the successor organization, the Symphony Society of New York, sponsor of the New York Symphony Orchestra as a third major instrumental ensemble in the city.[1] A regrettable absence of documents pertaining to the creation of Leopold Damrosch's original orchestra may stem

For granting access to materials in the New York Philharmonic Archives, I thank Barbara Haws, archivist, and Richard Wandel, associate archivist; for permitting access to information in the Archives of the Oratorio Society of New York, I thank Marie Gangemi, archivist.

1 · See, for example, Frédéric Louis Ritter, *Music in America* (1890), 452; F. H. M.[artens], "Damrosch, Leopold," in *Dictionary of American Biography* (1930), vol. 5; H. E. Krehbiel, *Notes on the Cultivation of Choral Music and the Oratorio Society of New York* (1884), 72; John Erskine, *The Philharmonic-Symphony Society of New York: Its First Hundred Years* (1943), 22–23; Walter Damrosch, *My Musical Life* (1923), 23–24; James Deaville, "Damrosch, Leopold" in *Die Musik in Geschichte und Gegenwart, Personenteil* (2001), 5:347–49; John Spitzer and Neal Zaslaw, "Orchestra," in *The New Grove Dictionary of Music and Musicians*, 2nd ed. (2001).

from a fire in 1887 that destroyed many of his valuable papers.[2] Despite that lacuna, I have reconstructed contextual information about events preceding the organization of the group in 1877, as well as its instrumentation, programming, and critical reception.

Background

Leopold Damrosch (1832–85) was almost thirty-nine years old when he arrived in America from Breslau in 1871 to conduct the Arion Society, a men's chorus consisting of German immigrants.[3] The society had invited him on the recommendation of music publisher Edward Schuberth, who had retained close connections to music circles in Germany.[4] Damrosch had built a prominent reputation particularly in German cities as an orchestral and choral conductor, concert violinist, and composer. In 1873, just two years after his arrival in the New World, Damrosch founded the Oratorio Society of New York, a mixed chorus performing sacred and secular music. With this organization he increased his musical responsibilities yet still remained within a largely German American environment. Damrosch retained close bonds of music making, friendship, and "paternal affection" with this group for the remaining twelve years of his life.[5] From 1873 to 1876, Damrosch gained the admiration of audiences in New York for his leadership of choral music and for an occasional appearance as violin soloist or participant in public chamber music events. Damrosch did not then have his own orchestra; his Oratorio Society collaborated during the 1875–76 season with the Theodore Thomas Orchestra, Damrosch conducting.[6]

Leopold Damrosch was an ardent and knowledgeable advocate of Richard Wagner's music as well as a former leading member of Franz Liszt's inner circle at Weimar. In the summer of 1876, with the help of a loan of five hundred dollars from a friend, music publisher Gustav Schirmer, he was able to travel to Bayreuth to attend the first cyclic performances of Wagner's *Ring*.

2 · Wilda Heiss and Margaret Collins, "Scope and Content Note," Damrosch-Tee Van Collection, Guide to Special Collections in the Music Division of the Library of Congress (1994), v.

3 · Frank Damrosch, "Biography of Leopold Damrosch," typescript, 5, in Papers of Leopold Damrosch, box 1, folder 11, Damrosch-Tee Van Collection, Music Division, Library of Congress.

4 · George Martin, *The Damrosch Dynasty: America's First Family of Music* (1983), 11.

5 · [Frederick A. Schwab], "A Talk with Dr. Damrosch: Will He Succeed Thomas as Conductor of the Philharmonic?" *New York Times*, August 31, 1878, 8.

6 · Oratorio Society of New York, broadside for February 28, 1876, MARC21 Display, New-York Historical Society; see also "Music: Oratorio Society, 'Paradise and the Peri,'" *Arcadian*, May 6, 1876, 5.

Damrosch quickly repaid Schirmer with an equal sum earned by writing a series of detailed articles commissioned by Charles Dana, editor of the *New York Sun*, about the Bayreuth *Ring* performances.[7] Dana's musical interests had been nurtured years before when he lived from 1841 to 1846 at the utopian community Brook Farm, where he sang bass in the choir, taught German and Greek, and wrote for the *Dial* and the *Harbinger.*[8] This brief summary of highlights from Damrosch's initial years in New York indicates that his eminent early supporters included music publishers Schuberth and Schirmer, newspaper editor Dana, and Dr. Frederick A. P. Barnard, first president of the Oratorio Society of New York as well as president of Columbia College.

Just before his departure for Bayreuth in July 1876, Damrosch learned that he had been elected to become the conductor of the New York Philharmonic for the 1876–77 season. Theodore Thomas had been asked to accept that post, but he had declined because the Philharmonic's directors had asked him to give up his competing Theodore Thomas Orchestra.[9] The honor thus went to Damrosch, regarded since his first concert with the Oratorio Society as "a valuable conductor—a man of culture, sound scholarship, energy, and personal magnetism."[10] On the podium, Damrosch, as a disciple of Liszt and Wagner, approached tempi flexibly, with an elasticity of the beat, emphatic gestures, and energetic ardor that remained characteristic, along with his progressive championing of new music.[11] During his one season with the Philharmonic, Damrosch fostered collaboration between it and his Oratorio Society.

Damrosch's appointment with the New York Philharmonic occurred during the widespread economic depression created after the financial panic of 1873, which lasted for five years and produced sharply increased unemploy-

7 · Martin, *Damrosch Dynasty*, 42–43. Copies of the articles dated August 23, August 26, and September 3, 1876, in the *New York Sun* can be located in the Papers of Leopold Damrosch, box 7, Damrosch-Tee Van Collection, Music Division, Library of Congress; additional articles in the series appeared on August 13 and August 18.

8 · See A. [Ilan] N. [evins], "Dana, Charles Anderson," in *Dictionary of American Biography*, 5:49–52, and Lindsay Swift, *Brook Farm: Its Members, Scholars, and Visitors* (1900), 145–52. For further recent discussion of the symphony as genre and related orchestral information in early critical writings emanating from Brook Farm, see Ora Frishberg Saloman, *Beethoven's Symphonies and J. S. Dwight: The Birth of American Music Criticism* (1995), esp. 81–180.

9 · Theodore Thomas, *Theodore Thomas: A Musical Autobiography* (1905), 1:74.

10 · [John Rose Green Hassard], *New-York Daily Tribune*, quoted in Krehbiel, *Notes on the Cultivation of Choral Music*, 64.

11 · For further information about Damrosch as conductor of Berlioz's music in New York, see Ora Frishberg Saloman, "Presenting Berlioz's Music in New York: Carl Bergmann, Theodore Thomas, Leopold Damrosch," in *European Music and Musicians in New York City, 1840–1900*, ed. John Graziano (2006).

ment, bank failures, and ruined personal fortunes.[12] The Philharmonic had been experiencing the effects of these difficulties in low levels of ticket sales, exacerbated by the dramatic decline of conductor Carl Bergmann's health in 1876 and poor morale among the musicians. In this climate Damrosch needed to achieve a double financial and artistic reversal that could restore the Philharmonic to its former prestige. His programs for the 1876–77 season were highly challenging; the critical reviews of his artistic results were very favorable.[13] That ticket receipts amounted to only $8,291 reflected the economic downturn and the competition posed by the Thomas Orchestra as well as Damrosch's emphasis on new music by composers including Wagner and Berlioz, choices that did not match the traditional preferences of the wider public comprising the Philharmonic's audience.[14] Just as important, each player's individual dividend amounted to the low figure of $18, realized after expenses, for the season of six concerts supplemented by eighteen public and twelve private rehearsals.[15] One contemporaneous periodical, the *Orpheus*, published a slightly higher estimate of profit to each member, $24.[16] In an orchestra organized as a cooperative venture such as the Philharmonic, in which performing members shared profits, that disappointing financial outcome seriously threatened Damrosch's prospects for reappointment.

At the final concert of the Philharmonic under his leadership, Damrosch appeared as conductor and violin soloist in a program consisting of Christoph Willibald Gluck's Overture to *Iphigenia in Aulis* with Wagner's ending, Ludwig van Beethoven's Violin Concerto in D, and Beethoven's Ninth Symphony with the participation of the Oratorio Society. The review in *Dwight's Journal of Music* commented that the program had been "unusually interesting, and the fact that the house was not filled is not creditable to musical New York."[17] The minutes of the directors' meeting of the New York Philharmonic Society for May 4, 1877, assert that after the financial statement had been read and accepted, those in attendance tendered votes of thanks to Damrosch for

12 · "The Panic: Excitement in Wall Street," *New York Times,* September 19, 1873, 1.

13 · For Leopold Damrosch's programs during his season as conductor of the New York Philharmonic, see "The Philharmonic Society of New York Founded 1842, 34th to 37th Season, 1875 to 1879," bound book of printed programs, 35th Season (1876–77), New York Philharmonic Archives; and H. E. Krehbiel, *The Philharmonic Society of New York: A Memorial* (1892), 143–44.

14 · This figure is drawn from Howard Shanet, *Philharmonic: A History of New York's Orchestra* (1975), 158–60. Shanet states that in the following year with Thomas as conductor, receipts rose to $12,499.

15 · Ibid., 158. According to Shanet, each player's dividend rose to $82 with Thomas at the helm in the next year (ibid., 160).

16 · "N.Y. Philharmonic Society," *Orpheus* 13 (July 1, 1877): 1–2.

17 · A. A. C., "Music in New York," *Dwight's Journal of Music* 37 (May 26, 1877): 29–30.

his "superb performance on the violin" and to the Oratorio Society for its "valuable assistance."[18]

According to the minutes of the directors' meeting for May 25, 1877, Damrosch was elected "an honorary member by acclamation." Also discussed at this meeting was Theodore Thomas's proposal to form a newly consolidated orchestra under his direction. Its nucleus, when expanded, would constitute the orchestra of the Philharmonic Society for its concerts. On other occasions it would be the Theodore Thomas Orchestra, with vacancies in the group to be filled by members selected from Thomas's "present orchestra."[19] Philharmonic musicians would gain considerable financial profit by playing in the Philharmonic Society's series as well as in the continuing Thomas symphony concerts and on tours with Thomas. The Philharmonic's concerts and programs would no longer conflict, as they had until then, with those of the more popular Theodore Thomas Orchestra. After further considering Thomas's proposal, those present elected the next season's conductor: of fifty votes cast, thirty-seven went to Thomas, nine favored Damrosch, and four were blank. In 1927 Walter Damrosch, Leopold's son, offered a subjective version of the election result. He believed that his father's Philharmonic concerts had created a sensational response among music lovers but that Thomas's promise to use the Philharmonic musicians in his own orchestra in a schedule that would not compete with the lucrative out-of-town touring engagements had been "bait ... too tempting to resist."[20]

The Philharmonic's decision against Leopold Damrosch most likely took him by surprise. He had received a note signed "S." from a Philharmonic musician, possibly its secretary, David Schaad. It read in part: "The Conductor Damrosch has not a solitary opponent in the Society. He has killed them all.... The Society has gained courage and is sure ... that with their present General she will conquer all difficulties in its way. Three times three for the hero who in one short season raised the Philharmonic up to its proper standing."[21]

Press assessments differentiated between the excellent artistic results that Damrosch had obtained and the problematic financial returns the society had garnered. As the weekly periodical the *Orpheus* expressed it: "No artistic victories will save from decapitation the unfortunate leader of a cam-

18 · Minutes of Directors' Meetings of the New York Philharmonic Society, May 4, 1877, 204–6, New York Philharmonic Archives.

19 · Ibid., May 25, 1877, 209–13. See also ibid., June 13, 1877, 1–3.

20 · Walter Damrosch, "Listening Backward: Fifty Years of Music with Grace-Notes on To-Day," *Century Magazine*, November 1927: Reprint 3–7, here 4.

21 · S., "Private Confidential," in "Philharmonic Symphony of New York," 2 pp., ink, Papers of Leopold Damrosch, box 1, folder 23, Damrosch-Tee Van Collection, Music Division, Library of Congress.

paign ending with meagre financial results."[22] It conjectured that the venerable Philharmonic's current membership and method of organization were "superannuated"; there were not equally competent performers on every instrument to cope with the technical difficulties of modern orchestral scores. In both areas, the writer believed, the Philharmonic under Thomas's direction could be reorganized to achieve results similar to those of the profitable Thomas Orchestra, which had acquired the best musicians who participated in disciplined regular rehearsals.

The *Music Trade Review* expressed indignation at Damrosch's treatment by an orchestra that he had brought "back to respectability, and an honest artistic name" within one year. It noted that Damrosch had "rehearsed carefully, made programmes which brought the best the publishing market in Europe offered, refused any remuneration for his services; and for all that he has done he gets an honorary membership of the Society, which elects another conductor."[23] It was widely believed that the Philharmonic musicians had hastened, as the weekly *Arcadian* put it, "to secure a leader who would be likely to bring them receipts, for it is the only thing clearly that Dr. Damrosch, to whom they owe so much, artistically speaking, could not do for them."[24]

Instrumentation

When Leopold Damrosch found himself involuntarily free to form an orchestra in 1877, he was motivated to choose a different structure from that of the Philharmonic. Rather than allowing the musicians to manage the orchestra themselves in a cooperative plan with all its risks, the conductor would select the players, who would be paid fixed salaries regularly.[25] Walter Damrosch asserted that after the Philharmonic musicians decided not to reappoint his father, there was great indignation among "a certain group of music lovers," but he does not name those who decided to help his father in establishing a new orchestra.[26]

22 · "New York Philharmonic Society," *Orpheus* 13 (July 1, 1877): 1–2.
23 · H. D., "Gratitude: Election of Theodore Thomas as Conductor of the Philharmonic Society," *Music Trade Review* 4 (June 3, 1877): 42–43.
24 · "Amusements," *Arcadian*, September 6, 1877, 5.
25 · Damrosch initially replaced the cooperative orchestral model with an entrepreneurial one. In an entrepreneurial model, as Mark Clague has described it, "an individual, often a charismatic impresario or conductor, assumed complete economic authority over an ensemble, receiving full benefit of the endeavor's success and accepting full liability for its failures" (see chapter I.1 in this volume).
26 · Walter Damrosch, "Listening Backward," reprint, 4. In this article Walter Damrosch conflates the new orchestra of 1877 with the formation of the Symphony Society of New York a year later.

The greatest obstacle confronting Leopold Damrosch in organizing his group was that the best orchestral musicians had already been chosen by Thomas to play in his combined orchestra. The Oratorio Society's treasurer Morris Reno recalled in an interview some years later that Damrosch "often found it impossible to get the material for a good orchestra. The good players generally accepted engagements from those who had more work to offer them, and he was obliged to take whatever he could get and make the best of it, which he did."[27]

A contemporaneous source lists the instruments and musicians in Damrosch's orchestra (see fig. III.3.1).[28] This article in the *Arcadian* declares successful the first of Damrosch's concerts presented on October 27, 1877, thanks him for introducing Joachim Raff's Symphony no. 8 in A to the New York public, and particularly praises the performances of *Hungarian Dances* by Johannes Brahms, as well as of a Gavotte by J. S. Bach in an orchestration by Damrosch. Based on the *Arcadian* article, its reprint in *Dwight's Journal of Music*, and a supplementary modern source, I believe that Dr. Leopold Damrosch's orchestra originally comprised fifty-three musicians as of October 18, 1877.[29] A total of thirty-three string players included ten first violinists, eight second violinists, five violists, five cellists, and five double bassists. The woodwind section comprised three flutists, two oboists (of whom one also played English horn as required), two clarinetists, and two bassoonists. Among the brass were four French horn players, two trumpeters, and three trombonists. The tuba player was drafted as needed from the double bass section. There was a timpanist, but one second violinist doubled on small drum, and another second violinist filled needs for grand cassa and cymbals. The harpist was the only woman in the group. A total of twenty people played instruments other than strings. The names are primarily German in national origin, as expected and especially given Damrosch's propensity to conduct rehearsals in German.[30]

27 · "Carnegie Music Hall: Some Account of the Labors of the New York Oratorio and Symphony Societies," *American Musician* 17 (June 14, 1890): 7. Reno makes no specific mention of the orchestra in the year before 1878, the date when the Symphony Society of New York was officially founded.

28 · "Dr. Damrosch's Saturday Matinees: First Matinee, October 27th," *Arcadian*, November 1, 1877, 5.

29 · See "Music in New York (from the *Arcadian*): Dr. Damrosch's First Saturday Matinee," reprinted in *Dwight's Journal of Music* 37 (November 10, 1877): 127–28. See also Norman Schweikert, comp., "The Personnel of the New York Philharmonic and Those Orchestras Merging with That Organization, 1842–2001," comprising sec. 2, "New York Symphony Orchestra, 1877–1928," 20 pp., unpaginated typescript, New York Philharmonic Archives.

30 · Edwin T. Rice, "Personal Recollections of Leopold Damrosch," *Musical Quarterly* 28 (1942): 271. Rice had attended rehearsals of the Symphony Society of New York and remem-

◆·◆

DR. DAMROSCH'S SATURDAY MAT-INEES.

FIRST MATINEE, OCTOBER 27TH.

MAGNIFICENT is the only word that expresses the wonderful ensemble, the vigorous sonority, the ener-getic entrain, of Dr. Damrosch's new orchestra. It is for the greatest part the orchestra dismissed by Theo-dore Thomas, therefore well accustomed to play to-gether; but since there are, nevertheless, some new elements, the remarkable ensemble is not the less meritorious.

THIS IS DR. DAMROSCH'S ORCHESTRA.

Ten 1st violins: Richter; Schüssel; Mollenhauer; Danz; S. Laendner; Christ; Arnold; Gantzberg; Fininger; Herfort.
Eight 2d violins: Habes; Schreiber; Risch; Jordan; J. Laend-ner; Neyer; Kühan; Heller.
Five violas: Schwarz; Reinboth; Wigand; Stockmar; Ringk.
Five violoncellos: Popper; Dragone; J. Barreither; Kalten-born; Hausknecht.
Five double-basses: Ch. Barreither; Gebhardt; Bartels; No-wack; Siebert
Harp: Miss E. Sloman.
Three flutes: Wehner; Wenzel; Werner.
Two oboes and English horn: Stohwasser; Hantel.
Two clarionets: Kayser; Stoberran.
Two bassoons: Hochstein: Neitz.
Four horns: Küstenmacher; Bremer; Hoffmann; A. Eller.
Two trumpets: Miller; Reuter.
Three trombones: Voss; Boeper; Groebler.
Tuba: L. Nowack.
Timpani: Bernstein.
Small drum: Jordan.
Grand cassa and cymbals: T. Heller.

FIGURE III.3.1. Dr. Damrosch's Saturday Matinees. *Arcadian*, November 1, 1877, 5.

The *Arcadian* asserted that many in Damrosch's group had been previ-ously dismissed by Thomas and were "therefore well accustomed to play to-gether; but since there are, nevertheless, some new elements, the remark-able ensemble is not the less meritorious."[31] The *Arcadian* was among several sources to report specifically that Damrosch's ensemble included thirty

bered that they were "then conducted in the German language for the musicians were pre-dominantly German in nationality."

31 · "Dr. Damrosch's Saturday Matinees: First Matinee, October 27th," *Arcadian*, Novem-ber 1, 1877, 5.

members of the most recent Thomas Orchestra who had been released when he assumed control of the New York Philharmonic.[32] Thomas often remodeled his orchestra by removing players whom he considered less capable. The *Springfield Republican* declared that under Thomas's "autocratic" leadership, his orchestra had been "made over repeatedly since he first organized it," with the result that most of the "leading performers" of the previous year had left him.[33] A comparison of detailed articles containing musicians' names indicates that the core nucleus of fifty musicians in Thomas's new orchestra of 1877 did not overlap with the newly formed Damrosch Orchestra. [34]

The Damrosch Orchestra of 1877 also included twelve musicians from the New York Philharmonic who had performed in it under Damrosch's leadership in the previous season. Checking the names on a Philharmonic roster for Saturday evening, November 4, 1876, I found that those involved were predominantly string players. The instrumentalists comprised six violinists, one violist, one cellist, two double bassists, one bassoonist, and the timpanist.[35] These musicians had been removed by the Philharmonic with Thomas at the helm, thus becoming available for Damrosch to hire for his new ensemble. Therefore, with thirty players drawn from the most recent Thomas Orchestra and twelve from the previous Philharmonic, forty-two musicians in Damrosch's new group were experienced orchestral players with a knowledge of the repertory. This estimate suggests that Damrosch secured the services of eleven additional instrumentalists from other sources (opera orchestras, for example) to fill out the roster for the initial debut of his new orchestra.

32 · See also unsigned and untitled clippings: "Thirty members of Mr. Thomas's orchestra, whose places will be taken by members of the Philharmonic Society, have been engaged by Dr. Damrosch, and he has selected several eminent players besides," *World*, October 7, 1877, unpaginated, in *Reviews Symphony Society of New-York, 1877–78*, 3, Oratorio Society of New York, Archives, and "first class performers, thirty of whom were members of the old Thomas Orchestra," *Jersey City Evening Journal*, October 29, 1877, unpaginated, in *Reviews Symphony Society of New-York, 1877–78*, 14, Oratorio Society of New York, Archives.
33 · "Thomas and His Orchestras," *Springfield Republican*, reprinted in *Dwight's Journal of Music* 37 (October 27, 1877): 120.
34 · "The New Orchestra (From the *New York Tribune*, Oct. 30)," reprinted in *Dwight's Journal of Music* 37 (November 10, 1877): 123–24. The Thomas Orchestra was enlarged to about eighty for his symphony concerts in Steinway Hall and to well over ninety for the New York Philharmonic Orchestra's performances in the larger Academy of Music.
35 · The Philharmonic players were E. Mollenhauer, F. Danz, and J. Gantzberg, who joined Damrosch's first violin section; G. Habes, J. Risch, and L. F. Heller, who played in his second violin section; M. Schwarz, viola; L. Hausknecht, cello; C. Gebhardt and L. Siebert, double bass; J. Neitz, bassoon; and S. Bernstein, timpani. See "The Philharmonic Society of New York Founded 1842, 34th to 37th Season, 1875 to 1879," bound book of printed programs, 35th Season (1876–77), New York Philharmonic Archives.

Programming and Critical Reception

Damrosch originally planned six Saturday afternoon matinees, but their success encouraged him to present a second series for a total of twelve weekly matinees from October 27, 1877, through January 12, 1878. Damrosch fixed the concert time from two o'clock to four o'clock in the afternoon for two avowed reasons. First, he wanted to avoid conflict with the Philharmonic and the Theodore Thomas concerts, both of which scheduled their formal presentations in the evenings. Indeed, Thomas had already begun a series of six symphony concerts on Saturday evenings in Steinway Hall when Damrosch audaciously decided to offer his orchestral events in the same location every Saturday afternoon. Musicians, audiences, and a fine hall were available then. Second, he desired to attract concertgoers by choosing a time during the day that would facilitate convenient travel and thus encourage the attendance of "suburban residents."[36] Damrosch's decision increased opportunities for women to attend these concerts.[37] The series of six matinees cost five dollars, a popular price that included a reserved seat.

After the first concert, Hassard of the *New-York Daily Tribune* pronounced Damrosch's orchestra to be "an excellent band" and noted the presence of well-regarded instrumentalists familiar to frequenters of Thomas's past concerts: "Arnold and other prominent musicians are among his violins; Wehner, the excellent first flute of the old Thomas orchestra, holds a corresponding position under Dr. Damrosch; and that fine player, Kayser, is the first clarinet. The brass is particularly strong and smooth."[38] Multiple press references described the "sonorousness" or "vigorous sonority" and "spirit" of Damrosch's group.[39] The woodwinds garnered praise for the splendor of their fortissimo passages. However, Hassard, accused with apparent justification by the *Music Trade Review* of glorifying Thomas, sounded more strident than others in declaring the special merit of Damrosch's group to be in its "force rather than in the softer graces of expression," possibly an oblique reference to Thomas.[40]

Damrosch's programming for his new orchestra can be situated briefly with respect to continuing critical and aesthetic tensions centering around

36 · "Music: Orchestral Matinees," *New-York Daily Tribune*, October 5, 1877, 4.
37 · On the relationship of matinee rehearsals and performances to the greater participation of women in concert life, see Adrienne Fried Block, "Matinee Mania, or the Regendering of Nineteenth-Century Audiences in New York City," *Nineteenth-Century Music* 31 (2008).
38 · "Music: Dr. Damrosch's Concert," *New-York Daily Tribune*, October 29, 1877, 5.
39 · As examples, see ibid. and "Saturday Symphony Concerts," *Arcadian*, January 5, 1878, 4.
40 · See, for example, "Editorial," *Music Trade Review* 4 (July 3, 1877): 65; "Music: Dr. Damrosch's Concert," *New-York Daily Tribune*, October 29, 1877, 5.

two important issues in nineteenth-century America: how best to cultivate an educated taste for so-called classical music as well as popular or light pieces and how to increase informed acceptance of abstract instrumental music while also welcoming newer kinds of programmatic works. Leopold Damrosch responded to both of these issues by favoring the musical enlightenment of large, broadly constituted audiences through the building of well-constructed programs that maintained high artistic standards. Although he did not overtly proclaim an aim "to make good music popular,"[41] as did Thomas, Damrosch embodied in his artistic ideals as in his actions a strong desire to communicate the aesthetic richness of a sweeping array of compositions. Moreover, there is no doubt that Damrosch believed in the social usefulness of music for its uplifting and ennobling effects. He has been considered a meliorist who advanced the musical education of audiences.[42]

Both orchestral leaders shared the desire to elevate the musical taste of the public, but the *Arcadian* suggested to them early in the season that in order to do so, it would be necessary first to attract people rather than to frighten them away by playing "too long, too severe, too much one-styled programmes."[43] That Damrosch succeeded in achieving an appropriate balance in his symphony matinees was approvingly asserted by Frederick A. Schwab of the *New York Times,* who declared that those programs contained severe and light elements sufficient "to delight the purist" while also addressing "more miscellaneous audiences."[44]

In Europe and then in America, Damrosch was particularly well known for having introduced challenging new works that were often programmatic in character, although he did not publicly debate their relative merit in contrast to abstract works. Nonetheless, he built his eminent reputation by leading both kinds of music in performance without detriment to one or the other. During the season of concerts with his new orchestra, for example, he frequently conducted music by Beethoven and Schubert as well as by Liszt and Wagner.

To understand why and how Damrosch chose pieces for performance during this transitional season, one needs to know what he proposed to accomplish. The periodical the *Independent* carried Damrosch's announcement that a "large and well-chosen orchestra" would perform, as would vocal and instrumental soloists along with two choral groups that Damrosch continued

41 · Thomas, *Autobiography*, 3.

42 · See Joseph A. Mussulman, *Music in the Cultured Generation: A Social History of Music in America, 1870–1900* (1971), esp. 51, 85.

43 · "The Coming Musical Season," *Arcadian,* October 4, 1877, 4.

44 · "Amusements: Musical and Dramatic, Saturday Symphony Matinees," *New York Times,* November 11, 1877, 7.

to lead, the Arion and the Oratorio Societies. Orchestral programs would include "standard works of ancient and modern masters, without excluding works of a more popular character, as far as they do not interfere with the high artistic aim to be followed. At least one novelty will be produced at each matinee."[45] The statement indicates Damrosch's recognition that this venture would have a greater chance to succeed if varied offerings included new, unusual, and lighter pieces.

Despite that acknowledgment, every Damrosch matinee concert but one presented a complete symphony as well as at least one overture and a few vocal solos; to that extent the concerts resembled earlier Philharmonic norms. The Damrosch programs included symphonies by Wolfgang Amadeus Mozart, Beethoven (the Fifth, Eighth, and Third in that order), Franz Schubert, Felix Mendelssohn, Robert Schumann, Brahms (the First twice), and Raff (the Eighth twice). During this season Damrosch did not present historically organized events.

Damrosch planned distinctive programs that introduced performances of new or rarely heard works while also utilizing four strategies that underscored his musical gifts. First, he chose pieces calling for a union of vocal and instrumental forces to provide variety as well as additional opportunities to present his two choral groups in combination with the orchestra. Second, he advanced his American reputation as a composer by placing on the programs a number of his own well-received works.[46] Third, he projected a greatly appreciated skill as orchestrator of short pieces or movements by Johann Sebastian Bach, Mozart, Luigi Cherubini, and Schubert, among others. He based several transcriptions on little-known movements from string quartets, which he enlarged for string orchestra, and these proved to be audience favorites that sometimes inspired encores. Fourth, he won acclaim when he performed as violin soloist in his own compositions, although those occasions were very infrequent. Damrosch's multiple musical assets enhanced the programs, brought widespread praise for his successful combination of vocal with orchestral forces, and increased respect for his "scholarly" compositional achievements.[47]

Notices in the press frequently named only the major orchestral works

---

45 · "Publisher's Department, Dr. Leopold Damrosch," *Independent* 29 (November 8, 1877): 17.

46 · For the compositional aspect of his career, see the valuable study by Wayne D. Shirley, "Leopold Damrosch as Composer," in *European Music and Musicians in New York City, 1840–1900*, ed. John Graziano (2006). See also the critical edition of Leopold Damrosch, *Symphony in A Major* (2005).

47 · As examples, see "Musical Notes," *Christian Union* 16 (November 28, 1877): 464 and "Dr. Damrosch's Matinee," *New-York Daily Tribune*, January 7, 1878. 5.

Damrosch had selected but rarely printed his actual programs. One news-paper that considered programming specifically in relation to time of day and expected audience was the *New-Yorker Staats-Zeitung*, which asked whether a need existed for programs of strictly classical music at Saturday matinee con-certs in New York. If such a need was perceived, the paper asserted, Dr. Dam-rosch was certainly in a position to fill it. The reviewer speculated that Dam-rosch must have been very happy with the results of his first concert played by an orchestra comprising "a number of capable musicians, even those of the first rank."[48] After the next matinee, the *Staats-Zeitung*'s critic clarified his position that it was important to strike a suitable tone when presenting after-noon programs lasting two or more hours to an audience that he estimated to consist primarily of women. That condescension was not appropriate in view of the well-documented musical literacy and participation of girls and women in amateur music-making as well as in professional study.[49] Still, the *Staats-Zeitung*'s critic believed that whereas the first concert had included two challenging instrumental works, Liszt's *Les Préludes* and Raff's Sym-phony no. 8, the second program possessed more fitting variety and interest by including Edvard Grieg's new "At the Cloister Gate" for soloists, women's voices, and orchestra as well as Mendelssohn's entire Incidental Music to *A Midsummer Night's Dream,* with vocal and instrumental forces again per-forming (see appendix). Although the second program's content "was not in as severe classical colors" as the first, it marked, from that writer's perspec-tive, "to some extent a progress."[50]

A consequential American premiere presented by Damrosch during that season was Brahms's Symphony no. 1 in C Minor, op. 68. Damrosch accom-plished this milestone in advance of Thomas, who had expected to lead the debut. Damrosch's orchestra introduced it on the eighth program and re-peated it at the ninth concert. Brahms's work initially received mixed reviews. Efforts to compare it favorably to Beethoven's symphonies in originality and form worked to its detriment.[51] Only Hassard recognized the significance of Brahms's innovation of an intimate kind of third movement, Un poco Alle-

48 · "Eine Anzahl tüchtiger Musiker sogar Musiker ersten Ranges," in "Theater, Musik und Kunst," *Sonntagsblatt der New-Yorker Staats-Zeitung*, October 28, 1877, 4.

49 · See Ruth A. Solie, "'Girling' at the Parlor Piano," in *Music in Other Words: Victorian Con-versations* (2004), and Block, "Matinee Mania," esp. 195–96, 201–2, and 212–14.

50 · "Nicht in so streng Klassischer Färbung gehalten, wie das des ersten Concertes ... das Programm des zweiten Concertes gewissermassen als einen Fortschritt bezeichnen," in "Theater, Musik und Kunst," *Sonntagsblatt der New-Yorker Staats-Zeitung*, November 4, 1877, 4.

51 · "Fine Arts," *Independent* 29 (December 27, 1877): 9; see also [Schwab], "Amusements: Musical and Dramatic, Saturday Symphony Matinee," *New York Times*, December 16, 1877, 6.

gretto e grazioso, instead of the characteristic Scherzo.[52] Neither Damrosch nor Thomas responded to the music of Brahms with Wagnerian partisanship despite the European controversy that flared between advocates of both composers.[53] The two conductors lavished attention on Brahms's symphony. By the end of one week they had led four closely spaced performances of it to its advantage. One critic attempted to divide the performance honors equally by declaring that although each conductor's approach had been meritorious, the first and second movements had been better communicated by Thomas's orchestra, whereas the third and fourth had been superior under Damrosch's leadership.[54]

The critical reception that greeted Damrosch's new orchestra in 1877–78 was generally favorable. On occasion during the season, a few questioned whether he had undertaken too many concerts in a demanding weekly schedule without allowing for sufficient rehearsals.[55] Despite these qualms the predominant view was that Damrosch, whose conducting movements had "grown much calmer, although equally determined," had achieved success in organizing and directing concerts that met the criteria of being both "agreeable and instructive."[56] The audiences, which included members of both German-speaking and English-speaking communities, were "large, intelligent, and enthusiastic."[57]

These observations suggest that Leopold Damrosch readily overcame the unexpected setback to his career resulting from his non-reappointment by the Philharmonic. He revealed an exceptional ability to adapt to changing

52 · [Hassard], "Music: The Brahms Symphony," New-York Daily Tribune, December 1, 1877, 5; see also [Hassard], "Music and the Drama: New York Philharmonic Society," New-York Daily Tribune, December 24, 1877, 5.

53 · On this point, see John H. Mueller, The American Symphony Orchestra: A Social History of Musical Taste (1951), 189. Walter Damrosch refers to his father's "wonderful liberal attitude" and states that the older Damrosch "did not share the narrow attitude of other Wagnerians who hated Brahms" (My Musical Life, 86).

54 · "Music in New York (From The World, Dec. 23.) Second Concert of the New York Philharmonic Society.—Brahms's Symphony," reprinted in Dwight's Journal of Music 37 (January 5, 1878): 160.

55 · H. D., "Dr. Damrosch's Matinees," Music Trade Review 5 (November 18, 1877): 18, and H. D., "Dr. Damrosch's Twelfth Symphony Matinee," Music Trade Review 5 (January 18, 1878): 90; [Hassard], "Music and the Drama: Dr. Damrosch's Matinee," New-York Daily Tribune, December 3, 1877, 5, and [Hassard],"Musical Notes," New-York Daily Tribune, January 14, 1878, 5.

56 · "Dr. Damrosch's Saturday Matinees: First Matinee, October 27th," Arcadian, November 1, 1877, 5; [Schwab], "Amusements: Musical and Dramatic, Saturday Symphony Matinees," New York Times, January 13, 1878, 7.

57 · [Hassard], "Music: Dr. Damrosch's Concert," New-York Daily Tribune, October 29, 1877, 5.

circumstances in the competitive musical life of New York City by recognizing the existence of public interest in instrumental music sufficient to sustain an increase in the number of orchestral concerts. The versatile and resourceful Damrosch was quickly able to shape varied programs that drew on his well-honed musical gifts. He also evinced positive organizational and personal skills that enabled him first to achieve distinction within and beyond the predominantly German-speaking choral realm and then to establish an additional orchestral series free of the problems inherent in the Philharmonic's cooperative model.

Damrosch envisioned, created, and conducted an orchestra whose competent instrumentalists offered varied programs of high quality to large and eager audiences. To have accomplished that worthy objective within one season would have constituted, in itself, an important achievement. However, Leopold Damrosch exceeded that goal by building an orchestra that led directly to his formation in 1878 of the highly successful Symphony Society of New York. Instrumentalists in Damrosch's orchestra of 1877–78 formed the nucleus of its successor group, the New York Symphony Orchestra sponsored by the Symphony Society. Its establishment lent welcome added vitality to concert activity in New York City, whose audiences amply supported three orchestras playing symphonic music during the later nineteenth century: the New York Philharmonic, the Theodore Thomas Orchestra, and the New York Symphony Orchestra created by Leopold Damrosch. After fifty years the New York Symphony Orchestra merged in 1928 with the rival New York Philharmonic, and the new organization became the Philharmonic-Symphony Society of New York.[58] Therefore, the contextual evidence supports the striking conclusion that although the Leopold Damrosch Orchestra has been little heralded in current accounts, it contributed significantly to the expansion and flourishing of professional orchestral activity in New York City during the nineteenth as well as the twentieth centuries.

58 · Martin, *Damrosch Dynasty*, 47–48.

APPENDIX III.3.1 *Concert Programs for the Saturday Symphony Matinees*

Placement of arias and short pieces has not been established definitively for certain programs; symphonies and overtures appear, as reported, at the opening and closing of concerts. The exact order of complete programs has been verified only for the second, fourth, ninth, and twelfth concerts. Main sources for these listings include the *Arcadian, Dwight's Journal of Music,* the *Music Trade Review,* the *New-York Daily Tribune,* the *New York Times,* and the *Sonntagsblatt der New-Yorker Staats-Zeitung.*

First Series

FIRST CONCERT: OCTOBER 27, 1877

Les Préludes, Symphonic Poem no. 3	Liszt
"Abendstern" from *Tannhäuser*	Wagner
Mr. Franz Remmertz	
Gavotte, Sixth [Sonata] Suite in D for Cello	Bach-Damrosch
String Orchestra	
Two Hungarian Dances (new composition)	Brahms
Grand Orchestra	
"Zwei Grenadiere"	Schumann
Mr. F. Remmertz	
Symphony no. 8 in A, *Frühlingsklänge (Sounds of Spring)*	Raff
(first time in New York)	
Grand Orchestra	

SECOND CONCERT: NOVEMBER 3, 1877

Allegro from Symphony no. 8 in B Minor	Schubert
"Kennst du das Land" from *Mignons Lied*	Liszt
Miss Antonia Henne	
Overture to *Oberon*	Weber
"At the Cloister Gate." For Soli, Chorus and Orchestra	
(new composition)	Grieg
Misses A. Henne and E. Urchs, the ladies of the	
Oratorio Society, and Grand Orchestra	
Air, "The King of Thulé" and "Jewel Song" from *Faust*	Gounod
Mrs. Imogene Brown	

The entire music to Shakespeare's *A Midsummer*
    Night's Dream   Mendelssohn
      For Soli, Chorus and Orchestra
      Mrs. I. Brown, Miss A. Henne, the ladies of the
        Oratorio Society, and Grand Orchestra

THIRD CONCERT: NOVEMBER 10, 1877

Symphony no. 5 in C Minor   Beethoven
    Grand Orchestra
"Heidenröslein" and "Gretchen am Spinnrade"   Schubert
    Miss Lillian Bailey
Marche Militaire [D. 733] (novelty as arranged)   Schubert-Damrosch
Two Hungarian Dances   Brahms
Overture to *Sakuntala*   Goldmark
    Grand Orchestra
"Cradle Song" from *Dinorah*   Meyerbeer
    Miss L. Bailey
Vorspiel, *Lohengrin*   Wagner
    Grand Orchestra

FOURTH CONCERT: NOVEMBER 17, 1877

Overture to *Coriolan*   Beethoven
    Grand Orchestra
Recitative and Aria ("Hai già vinta la causa"),
    Le Nozze di Figaro   Mozart
    Mr. A. E. Stoddard
Scherzo from a Quartet (first time in New York)   Cherubini-Damrosch
Menuet from Quartet in D Minor (first time
      in New York)   Mozart-Damrosch
    The String Orchestra
Adagio for Violin (new composition, manuscript)   Damrosch
Capricietto for Violin (new composition)   Damrosch
    Dr. L. Damrosch with Grand Orchestra
Symphony no. 1 in B-flat   Schumann
    Grand Orchestra
Overture, *Tannhäuser*   Wagner
    Grand Orchestra

FIFTH CONCERT: NOVEMBER 24, 1877

Symphony no. 9 in C	Schubert
Grand Orchestra	
Serenade for Piano, Organ, and Strings	
(new composition)	Saint-Saëns
String Orchestra	
Introduction and Gavotte (new composition)	Ries
"Procession of the Mastersingers" from *Die*	
Meistersinger von Nürnberg	Wagner
Grand Orchestra	
"Preislied" from *Die Meistersinger von Nürnberg*	Wagner
Mr. Bischoff	
"Siegfried's Sword"	Damrosch
Mr. Bischoff	
Overture to *Euryanthe*	Weber
Grand Orchestra	

SIXTH CONCERT: DECEMBER 1, 1877

Overture to *Anacreon*	Cherubini
Symphony [no. 40] in G Minor	Mozart
Grand Orchestra	
Two Songs	Schubert
Miss Lucy A. Homer	
Two Scandinavian Melodies	Svendsen
String Orchestra	
"Una voce poco fa" from *Il barbiere di Siviglia*	Rossini
Miss L. A. Homer	
"Danse Macabre" for Piano and Orchestra	Liszt
Mr. Bernard Boekelmann	
Leonore Overture, no. 3	Beethoven
Grand Orchestra	

Second Series

SEVENTH CONCERT: DECEMBER 8, 1877

Ruy Blas Overture	Mendelssohn
Intermezzo (new composition)	Speidel
Aria, "Dove sono" from *Le Nozze di Figaro*	Mozart

Mrs. Emma B. Dexter
Concerto in A Minor for Piano and Orchestra   Schumann
   Mr. Sebastian B. Mills
Air and Variations   Rode
   Mrs. E. B. Dexter
March in B Minor   Schubert-Liszt
Symphony no. 8 in F   Beethoven
   Grand Orchestra

EIGHTH CONCERT: DECEMBER 15, 1877

Overture to *Jessonda*   Spohr
Gavotte, Sixth Suite in D for Cello   Bach-Damrosch
   String Orchestra
Marche Militaire [D. 733] (novelty as arranged)   Schubert-Damrosch
Two Songs   Unidentified
   Mr. A. E. Stoddard
Overture to *Egmont*   Beethoven
Symphony no. 1 in C Minor (new composition,
     first time in America)   Brahms
   Grand Orchestra

NINTH CONCERT: DECEMBER 22, 1877

Part One
Symphony no. 1 in C Minor (repeated)   Brahms
   Grand Orchestra
Part Two
La fuite en Égypte from *L'enfance du Christ*
     (first time in America)   Berlioz
   Arion and Oratorio Societies, Mr. George Simpson,
     and Grand Orchestra
Christmas Chorus   Palestrina
Christmas Chorus   Praetorius
   Choruses of the Arion and Oratorio Societies
"Pastoral" and "March of the Kings of the East"
     from *Christus*   Liszt
   Grand Orchestra

TENTH CONCERT: DECEMBER 29, 1877

Symphony no. 8 in A, *Frühlingsklänge* (*Sounds of Spring*)	Raff
Grand Orchestra	
German War Song	Rietz
Arion Chorus and Orchestra	
"Nachthelle" for Tenor Solo, Male Chorus, and Piano	[Schubert]
Mr. Jacob Graf, Arion Chorus, Mr. Walter Damrosch	
Romance	D. Popper
Mr. William Popper, cello	
Air from *Jessonda*	Spohr
Mr. J. Graf	
"Kaisermarsch" with Final Chorus	
(first time in New York)	Wagner
Arion Chorus and Grand Orchestra	

ELEVENTH CONCERT: JANUARY 5, 1878

Symphony no. 4 in A	Mendelssohn
Grand Orchestra	
"In questa tomba oscura"	Beethoven
Mr. A. E. Stoddard	
Pastorale (first time)	Boccherini
String Orchestra	
"Dance of the Happy Spirits" from *Orfeo ed Euridice*	Gluck
Flute and String Orchestra	
Romanza from *Dinorah*	Meyerbeer
Mr. A. E. Stoddard	
Festival Overture	Damrosch
Grand Orchestra	

TWELFTH CONCERT: JANUARY 12, 1878

Overture to *Iphigenia in Aulis*	Gluck
Concerto in D [BWV 1054] (first time in New York)	J. S. Bach
Mr. Bernard Boekelmann, piano,	
with String Orchestra	
Octet for Strings (first time in New York)	Bargiel
String Orchestra	
Symphony no. 3 in E flat	Beethoven
Grand Orchestra	

[III.4] Gender and the Germanians

"Art-Loving Ladies" in Nineteenth-Century Concert Life

NANCY NEWMAN

"Took Hattie to the Germania rehearsal," wrote Henry Wadsworth Longfellow in his journal about the orchestra's appearance in Boston's Music Hall on March 2, 1853. "A pleasant concert; and we were quietly seated in the background, with an audience of thousands before us. Lovers of music the Americans certainly are, if not musicians; for two or three times a week this hall is thus filled with more than two thousand listeners!"[1]

"Hattie" was Harriot Appleton, the young half-sister of Longfellow's wife, Fanny Appleton. The poet's observations reflect the interest men and women took in the Germania Musical Society's weekly midafternoon concerts, which were called "public rehearsals." The orchestra had announced the opening of its rehearsals to Boston-area residents in December 1851, and their popularity far exceeded expectations. They certainly represented a bargain; tickets were as little as twelve and one-half cents each, whereas a ticket to an evening concert cost four times as much. The success of the afternoon performances was so great that a writer for *Scribner's Monthly* later reminisced that "at one time there were more than ten thousand tickets issued and in the hands of the public, while their use was so general that they have frequently been given and taken in 'making change.' Occasionally afternoon and evening concerts were given on the same day, but the crowds continued undiminished."[2]

According to Germania clarinetist Henry Albrecht, the orchestra gave as many as ninety public rehearsals from 1852 through 1854, its final three seasons. These performances "were principally attended by young ladies," he

1 · Henry Wadsworth Longfellow Papers, MS Am 1340 (205), Houghton Library, Harvard University.

2 · J. Bunting, "The Old Germania Orchestra," *Scribner's Monthly* 11, no. 1 (1875): 104.

noted in his memoir of the orchestra.[3] The predominance of young women is curious, as the programs were virtually identical to those offered in the evening. What made these events particularly attractive to women, and what significance does this have for the history of orchestral performance? The rehearsal heard by Longfellow and Hattie Appleton anticipated the orchestra's subscription concert three days later featuring violin prodigy Camilla Urso and local soprano Anna Stone (see fig. III.4.1). What was the relationship between the women in the audience and the accomplished women who shared the Germania's stage? This chapter addresses these questions by examining female participation in the Germania Musical Society's activities in the broader context of women's social condition and the democratization of concert life during the nineteenth century.

The starting point for this inquiry is Adrienne Fried Block's innovative essay titled "Matinee Mania, or The Regendering of Nineteenth-Century Audiences in New York City."[4] Block argues that afternoon concerts, which flourished from the 1850s on, were especially important opportunities for women to expand their knowledge and understanding of musical works. Their enthusiastic attendance at these daytime events had a lasting effect not only on New York concert life but on social relations generally. For women of the mid-nineteenth century, "leaving home to hear music, while minimally threatening to patriarchal control, can be considered an anticipation of other, more challenging claims for equity in public life."[5] Women were hampered in their recognition as full citizens on multiple fronts, including lack of the franchise, the legal doctrine of coverture, limited access to higher education, and discouragement from public speaking.[6] Participation in musical activities was a gentle, genteel, and seemingly nonpolitical way of positioning oneself in a not-altogether-receptive world.

Block proposes that a continuum of female activity, from audiences and patrons to teachers and performers, was the mechanism through which

3 · Henry Albrecht, *Skizzen aus dem Leben der Musik-Gesellschaft Germania (Germania Musical Society)* (1869), 18. A complete translation appears in my book, *Good Music for a Free People* (2010).

4 · Adrienne Fried Block, "Matinee Mania, or the Regendering of Nineteenth-Century Audiences in New York City," *19th–Century Music* 31 (2008). I am grateful to Block for allowing me to see an early version of her paper, which she presented at the Feminist Theory and Music 8 Conference, New York University, June 2005.

5 · Ibid., 195.

6 · Seminal works on these issues in feminist history include Mary Kelley, *Learning to Stand and Speak: Women, Education, and Public Life in America's Republic* (2006); Linda Kerber, *No Constitutional Right to Be Ladies: Women and the Obligations of Citizenship* (1998); and Ellen Carol DuBois, *Feminism and Suffrage: The Emergence of an Independent Women's Movement in America, 1848–1869* (1978).

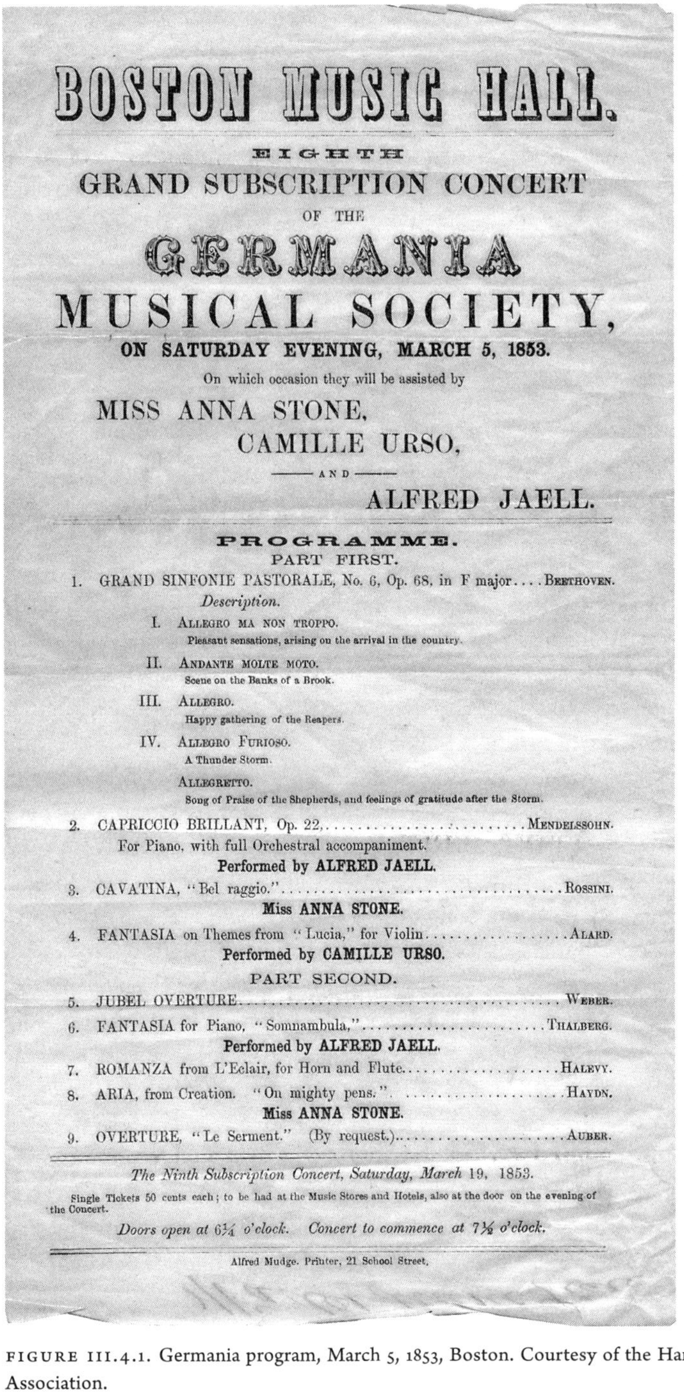

BOSTON MUSIC HALL.

EIGHTH

GRAND SUBSCRIPTION CONCERT

OF THE

GERMANIA

MUSICAL SOCIETY,

ON SATURDAY EVENING, MARCH 5, 1853.

On which occasion they will be assisted by

MISS ANNA STONE,

CAMILLE URSO,

AND

ALFRED JAELL.

PROGRAMME.

PART FIRST.

1. GRAND SINFONIE PASTORALE, No. 6, Op. 68, in F major.... BEETHOVEN.

Description.

I. ALLEGRO MA NON TROPPO.
Pleasant sensations, arising on the arrival in the country.

II. ANDANTE MOLTE MOTO.
Scene on the Banks of a Brook.

III. ALLEGRO.
Happy gathering of the Reapers.

IV. ALLEGRO FURIOSO.
A Thunder Storm.

ALLEGRETTO.
Song of Praise of the Shepherds, and feelings of gratitude after the Storm.

2. CAPRICCIO BRILLANT, Op. 22,............................ MENDELSSOHN.
For Piano, with full Orchestral accompaniment.
Performed by ALFRED JAELL.

3. CAVATINA, "Bel raggio."...................................... ROSSINI.
Miss ANNA STONE.

4. FANTASIA on Themes from "Lucia," for Violin.................. ALARD.
Performed by CAMILLE URSO.

PART SECOND.

5. JUBEL OVERTURE.. WEBER.

6. FANTASIA for Piano, "Somnambula,"...................... THALBERG.
Performed by ALFRED JAELL.

7. ROMANZA from L'Eclair, for Horn and Flute.................... HALEVY.

8. ARIA, from Creation. "On mighty pens."..................... HAYDN.
Miss ANNA STONE.

9. OVERTURE, "Le Serment." (By request.)...................... AUBER.

The Ninth Subscription Concert, Saturday, March 19, 1853.

Single Tickets 50 cents each; to be had at the Music Stores and Hotels, also at the door on the evening of the Concert.

Doors open at 6¼ o'clock. Concert to commence at 7½ o'clock.

Alfred Mudge, Printer, 21 School Street.

FIGURE III.4.1. Germania program, March 5, 1853, Boston. Courtesy of the Harvard Musical Association.

American women became incorporated into public musical life. This chapter applies her perspective to the situation of the Germania Musical Society. The members solicited women's interest in multiple ways, offering matinees, engaging accomplished female artists, and publishing sheet music. The picture that emerges is that the Germanians recognized that women were essential to their corporate, commercial, and musical success. They also seem to have found their dealings with the opposite sex personally rewarding. This combination of professional and personal motives offers insights into the American orchestra's role in the evolving gender relations of modern urban life.

The Orchestra

In many ways, the Germania Musical Society was typical of the new "private orchestras" that proliferated in Europe during the 1840s on the model of Johann Strauss's ensemble. The original members were young men who emigrated from Berlin during the 1848 revolutions. Many of them had worked with Joseph Gungl, the "Berlin Strauss," who also visited the United States that year.[7] The Germanians made their New York debut in October, quickly establishing relationships with members of the Philharmonic and other highly regarded musicians. In December they went to Philadelphia, where they had difficulty attracting audiences. A request to play for the inauguration of President Zachary Taylor in Washington, D.C., revived the group, and concerts in Baltimore were so successful that they decided to make that city their base. Lengthy subscription series during the next two years were supplemented by substantial engagements in New England, upstate New York, and eastern Canada. In autumn 1851, the Germanians relocated to Boston, where they offered an astonishing array of concerts. Notable Boston premieres included Mendelssohn's complete music for *A Midsummer Night's Dream* and Beethoven's Ninth Symphony. They also gave the first performances in the United States of Wagner's music, presenting selections from *Tannhäuser, Lohengrin*, and *Rienzi*. The Germania regularly accompanied the Handel and Haydn Society and touring virtuosos such as pianist Alfred Jaëll and violinists Ole Bull and Miska Hauser. Two extensive western trips included concerts in Pittsburgh, Cincinnati, Louisville, and Chicago. Summers were spent in Newport, Rhode Island, where members provided music both informally and formally at the large hotels that served the resort community. All told, the Germania gave upward of nine hundred concerts before it dis-

7 · See Roger Beck and Richard Hansen, "Joseph Gungl and His Celebrated American Tour: November 1848 to May 1849," *Studia Musicologica Academiae Scientiarum Hungaricae* 36 (1995).

solved in September 1854. As Albrecht put it, the orchestra had "stirred the souls of over one million people through [its] magic sounds" during its six-year existence.[8]

The Germania Musical Society, like almost every other nineteenth-century orchestra, was an all-male ensemble. Historian Jessica Gienow-Hecht characterizes it as a "boy band, replete with solidarity, friendship, and sex appeal."[9] The assertion of harmonious male identity can be seen in the Germania's lithograph portrait (see fig. III.4.2). Although the faces are highly individualized, the bodies are all of a type—svelte and graceful. The poses are collegial rather than stiff and formal, projecting congeniality. *Scribner's Monthly* later reported that it was widely believed that members of the orchestra had vowed in the interests of fraternity not to marry. Apparently this was not literally true, "but recognizing the difficulties of maintaining domestic ties in a life necessarily so nomadic, the members, for a long time, refrained from such ties."[10] Although contemporary gender relations made it almost inevitable that an ensemble such as the Germania would be homosocial, the members used that feature strategically to cultivate and build rapport with female audiences.

Listeners

Among the earliest performances that the Germanians gave after their arrival in New York were five concerts at the Brooklyn Female Academy (today the Packer Collegiate Institute). The programs included overtures by Mendelssohn, Rossini, and Mozart, as well as the Brooklyn premiere of Beethoven's Symphony no. 2.[11] Female academies and seminaries, newly founded in the mid-nineteenth century, aimed at providing an education on a par with the established male colleges and at giving women a place where they could "learn to stand and speak," as the abolitionist and feminist Lucy Stone put it.[12] They were one important way that American women gained the confidence and skills to address issues of public interest. That the Germanians recognized the pedagogic dimension of their performances is indicated by

8 · Albrecht, *Skizzen*, 19.
9 · Jessica Gienow-Hecht, *Sound Diplomacy: Music and Emotions in Transatlantic Relations, 1850–1920* (2009), 69–70.
10 · Bunting, "Old Germania Orchestra," 103.
11 · See *New York Tribune*, October 21–November 3, 1848. On music at female academies, see Jewel Smith, *Music, Women, and Pianos in Antebellum Bethlehem, Pennsylvania: The Moravian Young Ladies' Seminary* (2008), and Judith Tick, *American Women Composers before 1870* (1983), 33–56.
12 · As quoted in Kelley, *Learning to Stand and Speak*, 132.

FIGURE III.4.2. Germania Musical Society, 1852. Gift of Patricia Frederick to author.

Albrecht's later contention that their afternoon rehearsals, such as the one Hattie Appleton attended, had "exerted a significant influence over the musical education of Boston's youth" during the early 1850s.[13]

Among American musical organizations, one of the most momentous gestures toward inclusiveness was the New York Philharmonic's 1847 decision to open its rehearsals to female associate members. Within a few years, several hundred women regularly attended these daytime events.[14] In important respects, the Germania's Boston matinees surpassed developments in New York. In contrast to the Philharmonic, which admitted only associate members, the Germanians offered midafternoon concerts that were truly mass public events. Tickets were much less expensive than at the Philharmonic, which required an investment of $5 for the season (twelve rehearsals and four concerts). For the Germania rehearsals, $1 bought eight tickets, 50 cents purchased four, and a single ticket cost 25 cents. Low prices were especially attractive to women, as wages for single working women were meager, and married women did not have legal control over the family finances. The Germania's rehearsals in Boston's Music Hall could also accommodate many more than the Philharmonic's Apollo Room, which seated a thousand at best. Longfellow may have even underestimated the audience he observed. Albrecht states that attendance averaged twenty-five hundred, and John Sullivan Dwight reported that attendance at a single rehearsal amounted "by actual count of tickets to *three thousand and fifty-seven* persons, ... filling every seat and standing place in the new Music Hall, so that many sought admission in vain.... This was only a little more than what we behold every week."[15]

The Germanians occasionally gave afternoon concerts in smaller towns, too. A Providence, Rhode Island, playbill of January 27, 1852, explains their desire to accommodate "children and persons who are unable to attend the Concert in the evening," that is, women without escorts. The following month they held a "Grand Musical Festival, Exclusively for Children and Schools, accompanied by their Teachers," in Worcester, Massachusetts.[16]

Everywhere it was adopted, the matinee was crucial to increasing female opportunities for education and entertainment outside the home. A year after the Germanians disbanded, the pianist William Mason approached their conductor, Carl Bergmann, about offering chamber music concerts in New York. The Mason-Bergmann "Classical Musical Matinées" specifically

13 · Albrecht, *Skizzen*, 18.
14 · Block, "Matinee Mania," 198–99; Henry Krehbiel, *The Philharmonic Society of New York: A Memorial* (1892), 61–64.
15 · *Dwight's Journal of Music* 2 (January 29, 1853): 133.
16 · Scrapbook, "Concert Programs, 1847–1854," Providence Athenaeum; Festival notice on program of February 6, 1852, Broadside Collection, American Antiquarian Society.

targeted women by advertising that their early hour would "enable lady amateurs and students to be present without escort." This freed women from the
necessity of finding male companions, who helped ensure personal safety.
The historic first program of this series actually attracted more women than
men and was so successful that many had to stand. Such events represent an
early step toward women's taking for granted that they "could go unescorted
to public performances, choose their own sources of pleasure and edification, and enhance their lives as amateur musicians," as Block has observed.[17]

One early representative of such amateurs was Ann Elizabeth Jennison
(1827–69), youngest daughter of a prominent Worcester family, who left
visible traces of the orchestra's significance in a diary and in the margins of
broadsides. On a program for the Germania's earliest known performance
in New England, a Grand Sacred Concert in Worcester on April 8, 1849, she
wrote, "With my husband for the *first* time." Ann Elizabeth had married the
promising William Sumner Barton just a few days earlier. "Our first Sunday
together!!" she recorded in her diary breathlessly. "Went to a concert given
by the Germania Band. 25 in number! Magnificent—dignified—splendid
music! All things conspired to make our first Sunday together *most delightful*.
May all be as happy! Though they be not as *bright*!"[18] When the Germanians
returned to Worcester in early June, she wrote, "In the evening we attended
(with Kate) the first concert of the Germanians! An elegant night. They ser-
enaded Mr. Chapin. And *we* went out to hear them!" Ann Elizabeth meticulously noted on both programs that her older sister Kate accompanied the
newlyweds (see fig. III.4.3).

It is rare to find such ephemeral remarks about the orchestra's appearances
preserved. Ann Elizabeth's brief comments suggest a great deal about what
the Germania's performances meant to women. Henry Chapin was Worcester's first mayor, and Ann Elizabeth's presence at the serenade, as well as her
attendance three months earlier at an inaugural ball in Worcester to celebrate
Zachary Taylor's victory, shows her awareness of local and national politics.[19]
Ann Elizabeth took an active interest in a range of cultural affairs; her diary,
for example, indicates attendance at lectures by Emerson and Longfellow.

17 · Vera Brodsky Lawrence, *Strong on Music*, vol. 2, *Reverberations: 1850–1856* (1995), 657–
60; Block, "Matinee Mania," 204–6, 213.
18 · Germania Musical Society broadside, "Sacred Concert," April 8, 1849, and A. E. J. Barton Diary, Jennison Family Papers, American Antiquarian Society. Many thanks to Caroline
Wood Stoffel for sharing with me her extensive research on the Jennisons' cultural activities.
19 · "Record Book of Women Invited to the Inauguration Ball 'In Honor of the Great and
Good Zachary Taylor,'" Worcester (Mass.) Collection, 1686–1941, American Antiquarian
Society. For a provocative analysis of female political participation, see Ronald Zboray and
Mary Saracino Zboray, "Whig Women, Politics, and Culture in the Campaign of 1840: Three
Perspectives from Massachusetts," *Journal of the Early Republic* 17 (1997).

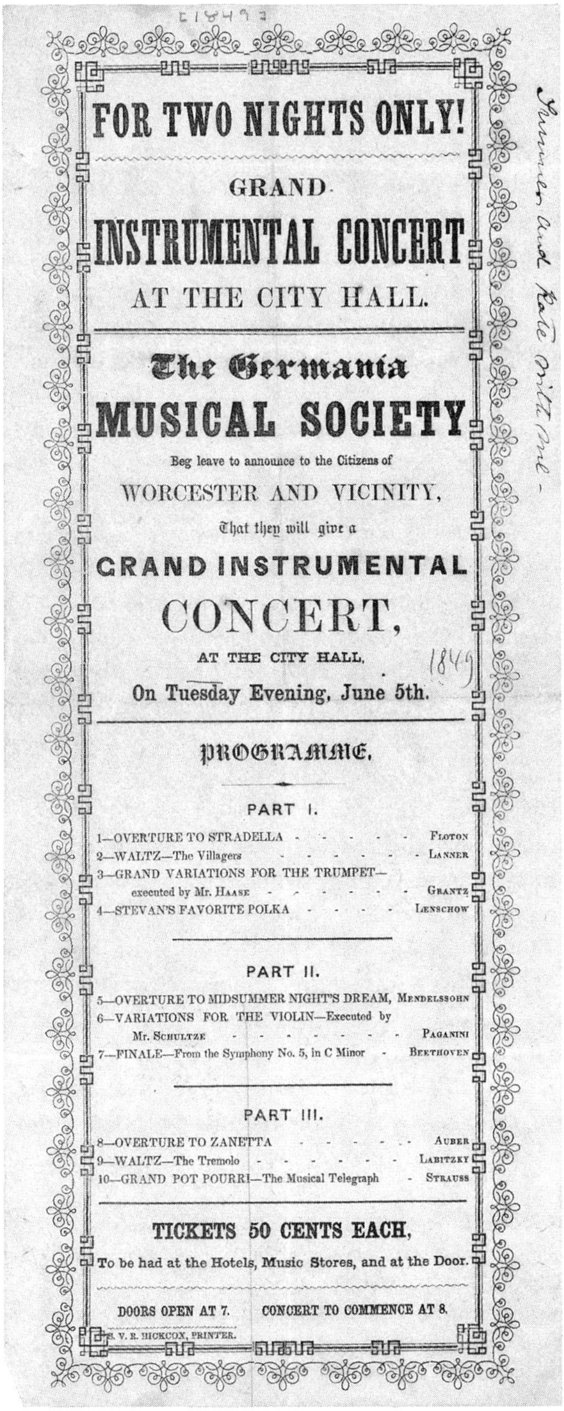

FOR TWO NIGHTS ONLY!

GRAND
INSTRUMENTAL CONCERT
AT THE CITY HALL.

The Germania
MUSICAL SOCIETY

Beg leave to announce to the Citizens of

WORCESTER AND VICINITY,

That they will give a

GRAND INSTRUMENTAL
CONCERT,
AT THE CITY HALL.

1849

On Tuesday Evening, June 5th.

PROGRAMME.

PART I.

1—OVERTURE TO STRADELLA		Floton
2—WALTZ—The Villagers		Lanner
3—GRAND VARIATIONS FOR THE TRUMPET—		
executed by Mr. Haase		Grantz
4—STEVAN'S FAVORITE POLKA		Lenschow

PART II.

5—OVERTURE TO MIDSUMMER NIGHT'S DREAM,		Mendelssohn
6—VARIATIONS FOR THE VIOLIN—Executed by		
Mr. Schultze		Paganini
7—FINALE—From the Symphony No. 5, in C Minor		Beethoven

PART III.

8—OVERTURE TO ZANETTA		Auber
9—WALTZ—The Tremolo		Labitzky
10—GRAND POT POURRI—The Musical Telegraph		Strauss

TICKETS 50 CENTS EACH,

To be had at the Hotels, Music Stores, and at the Door.

DOORS OPEN AT 7.   CONCERT TO COMMENCE AT 8.

S. V. R. HICKCOX, PRINTER.

FIGURE III.4.3.
Germania program,
June 5, 1849, Worcester,
Massachusetts. Cour-
tesy of the American
Antiquarian Society.

She was also an amateur musician and was publicly praised for her hymn singing and execution of piano compositions by Mozart and Beethoven.[20]

Performers

The women who formed such an important part of the Germania's audience saw themselves reflected onstage by the many women who appeared with the orchestra as performers. The Germania collaborated with female musicians from novices such as Camilla Urso (1842–1902) and Adelaide Phillips (1833–82) to established stars Jenny Lind (1820–87) and Henriette Sontag (1806–54). The inclusion of such musicians on Germania programs provided female audience members exposure to diverse repertory and high levels of artistry. It also encouraged them to imagine occupying similarly visible positions.

A few statistics give an idea of how important female guest artists were to the Germania's concerts. Of the 525 programs I have located, nearly half include assisting artists (251). About 70 percent of these performances (175) feature at least one woman, most often a singer. Nearly one-third of the performances involved Lind, Sontag, and Fortunata Tedesco (1826–after 1866). Other featured singers included Caroline Lehmann, Adelaide Phillips, Caroline Pintard, Elise Hensler, Marietta Alboni, Eliza Ostinelli Biscaccianti, Catherine Hayes, Teresa Parodi, and Amalia Patti (older sister of Adelina). All told, singers account for almost two-thirds of Germania performances with women; the remaining third included violinists and pianists.

As William Weber has shown, the inclusion of singers in "mixed repertory" concerts was conventional in the first half of the nineteenth century.[21] Programs in the United States, as in Europe, were miscellanies of vocal and instrumental works that offered variety to listeners. For example, during the New York Philharmonic's first six seasons (1842–48), one or more female vocalists were featured on nearly two-thirds of its programs (sixteen of twenty-five concerts).[22] Two of the Philharmonic's regular performers, Mary Ann Horton and Antoinette Otto, sang with the Germania during its first season. They had both been part of the Park Theatre's "operatic corps" in the early 1840s, and Otto was one of the soloists in the Philharmonic's 1846 American premiere of Beethoven's Ninth Symphony.[23] They sang at the Germania's

20 · Unidentified source, Newspaper Clippings File, American Antiquarian Society.

21 · See chapter V.1 in this volume. Also see William Weber, *The Great Transformation of Musical Taste: Concert Programming from Haydn to Brahms* (2008), 13–29.

22 · "New York Philharmonic Performance History Search," http://history.nyphil.org/nypwcpub/dbweb.asp?ac=a1; cf. Krehbiel, *Philharmonic Society*, 95–102.

23 · Vera Brodsky Lawrence, *Strong on Music*, vol. 1, *Resonances, 1836–1849* (1988), 36, 367. Horton was an English actress and contralto who had toured the United States with her hus-

benefit (November 11, 1848), and Otto sang a Cavatina and Grand Aria (both unspecified) at their farewell concert on November 29. Because opera selections were an integral part of early nineteenth-century instrumental concerts, professional women musicians were essential to concert life.

The Germania's first extended series with a female singer took place in Boston, where they engaged the Italian contralto Fortunata Tedesco. The orchestra gave top billing to the Havana Opera Company's prima donna, who had created a sensation in Boston in 1847. Ticket buyers were alerted that Tedesco, along with the recently arrived tenor Adelindo Vietti and Rosina Pico-Vietti, had been "secured at an immense expense." This was no doubt true, as Rosina Pico had been one of the reigning singers in New York City since mid-decade and Tedesco's Boston opera performances had commanded as much as $5 per ticket. In order to keep tickets at their usual fifty cents, the Germanians suspended the free list "with the exception of the Public Press."[24] Together, Tedesco and the Viettis assisted the Germanians for seven performances in Boston (May 1849). Tedesco joined the Germanians again in Baltimore and Richmond for at least five performances (November 1849 and April 1851). Her repertory included works by Rossini, Bellini, Donizetti, Verdi, and Meyerbeer. The Spanish songs "El Churru" and "La Colasa" were among the specialty numbers Tedesco performed in costume.

Notwithstanding the exotic tinge of Tedesco's repertory, "the delicious quality of her voice, its graceful production, and the flood of melody she could pour out ... overcame even Puritan reserve," wrote William Clapp in 1853.[25] The hint of religious and moral disapproval underlying his praise is typical of responses to nineteenth-century female musicians. Complex historical factors are at work here, including Calvinistic disdain for secular music-making, expectations of female modesty, and the association between theaters and prostitution.[26] Adrienne Fried Block has singled out Jenny Lind and Camilla Urso as particularly important in this regard, as they overcame conventional prejudices against women on stage through their restrained comportment, dedication to artistic goals, and flawless technique.[27] Lind's and Urso's per-

band, Charles E. Horn; Otto was married to Philharmonic violinist Henry Otto. On opera's pervasiveness, see Katherine Preston, *Opera on the Road: Traveling Opera Troupes in the United States, 1825–60* (1993).

24 · Scrapbook, "Programs of Concerts in Boston from 1817–1863," Music Collection, Boston Public Library.

25 · William Clapp, *Record of the Boston Stage* (1853), 446.

26 · On Puritanism in Boston, see Michael Broyles, *"Music of the Highest Class": Elitism and Populism in Antebellum Boston* (1992), 103–5; on prostitution, see Block, "Matinee Mania," 193–97.

27 · Adrienne Fried Block, "Two Virtuoso Performers in Boston: Jenny Lind and Camilla Urso," in *New Perspectives on Music: Essays in Honor of Eileen Southern*, ed. J. Wright (1992).

formances can be seen as offering an "acoustic mirror" to women in the audience, inviting them to imagine leading lives as professional musicians.[28] The Germanians' extended engagements with these artists helped define new paths for female participation in the concert world.

The Germanians first encountered Jenny Lind in Baltimore, where she paused from her tour of the East Coast to attend one of their concerts in December 1850. The orchestra for her tour consisted of a core group of instrumentalists brought from New York that was augmented with local musicians at each new location. After hearing the Germanians perform, Lind engaged them en masse for her concerts in Baltimore and also in Washington, D.C., the following week. Despite accolades from the press, the orchestra clearly occupied a supporting role in Lind's concerts, even more than they had with Tedesco. The Germanians assisted Lind, rather than the reverse. Having promised a twice-weekly subscription series to Baltimore residents, the Germanians remained in the area, while Lind resumed a circuit that took her through the south, Havana, and the lower midwest that winter. When she returned to Baltimore in late April 1851, the Germanians assisted her again, then intermittently in New York and Boston, for a total of about thirty performances together.

Lind's impeccable reputation countered widespread assumptions that women performers led dissolute lives. A "natural Puritan," as Block calls her, she "succeeded almost single–handedly in convincing the American public that a woman could go on stage and still retain her virtue."[29] Lind arrived in the United States just as women were beginning to advocate for a voice in public affairs, politicizing the respectability of appearing in public. The cause of abolition—the nation's chief moral issue—had become linked to questions of equal rights for women, a link that resulted in the 1848 Seneca Falls Convention and the first National Women's Rights Convention, which took place in October 1850. Women such as Harriet Beecher Stowe found it thrilling to hear Lind's voice—not only for its qualities but also for what it represented. Listening to her was "a bewildering dream of sweetness and beauty.... I am most happy to have seen her, for she is a noble creature."[30] As a correspondent for *Dwight's Journal* wrote, "Lind moves our hearts to better thoughts and deeds."[31] What better arguments could there be for

28 · "Acoustic mirror" alludes to Jacques Lacan's concept of the "mirror stage" as developed by Kaja Silverman in *The Acoustic Mirror: The Female Voice in Psychoanalysis and Cinema* (1988).

29 · Block, "Two Virtuoso Performers," 358.

30 · *Life of Harriet Beecher Stowe: Compiled from Her Letters and Journals by her Son, Charles E. Stowe* (1889), 182–83.

31 · "Philadelphia Correspondence" from Omega, *Dwight's Journal of Music* 2 (November 6, 1852): 38.

the inclusion of women's voices in matters of social and political signifi-cance?

Lind's success in the United States was also a direct inspiration for the visits of several European singers who subsequently worked with the Ger-mania, including Teresa Parodi, Catherine Hayes, Marietta Alboni, and the legendary German soprano Henriette Sontag. The Germanians assisted Son-tag in at least eight concerts in Philadelphia (October 1852) and ten in Bos-ton (November 1852 and December 1853), again playing a supporting role for a performer whose reputation exceeded their own. Her performances resembled Lind's in their inclusion of diverse genres calculated to appeal to a diversity of listeners. In addition to arias and ensembles from bel canto and grand opera, Sontag's repertory included folksy pieces, such as Rob-ert Burns's ballads; virtuoso works, such as Adam's variations on "Ah! vous dirai-je, maman"; and oratorio selections.

On her American tour, Sontag emulated the model established by Lind of the self-sacrificing and charitable artist. But she was also a musician whose status as a paid professional was publicly acknowledged to have been hard won. Sontag emerged from a modest background to become one of Europe's most celebrated singers. She married a Sardinian noble, Count Carlo Rossi, over the strenuous objections of his family and retired from the stage to ac-commodate his diplomatic career. When the 1848 revolutions caused the loss of his position, Sontag returned to public performance in order to reestab-lish the family finances and secure the education of their four children.[32] Sontag's public statements regarding her decision to tour America empha-sized the dignity and the demands of paid work, recalling the battle she had fought with her husband's aristocratic family: "I would not undertake such an enterprise were it not for the sake of my children, but for them I will under-take anything honorable, however arduous it may be."[33] Her determination to combine the roles of mother and artist respectably appears as a strikingly modern goal.

Both Lind and Sontag included young musicians on their programs as guest artists, giving them performing experience, exposure, and financial support.[34] Their efforts overlapped with that of the Germanians in interest-ing ways. For example, Boston teenagers Adelaide Phillips and Elise Hensler were showcased by the orchestra prior to their departure for study in Europe.

32 · *Dwight's Journal of Music* 1 (August 7, 1852): 137–38; Frank Russell, *Queen of Song: The Life of Henrietta Sontag* (1964).

33 · From the *Musical World*, as reprinted in *Dwight's Journal of Music* 1 (May 22, 1852): 55.

34 · Sontag hired the eleven-year-old violin prodigy Paul Julien on her arrival in New York in 1852. When he fell ill the following year, she replaced him with Camilla Urso for an ex-tended southern tour.

Phillips became a protégé of Jenny Lind, who gave her funds to study with Manuel Garcia, Lind's former teacher. Hensler made her public debut with the Germanians in December 1852, and a month later they held a benefit for her. Hensler and Phillips returned to the United States as finished artists and made notable contributions to the expanding opera and concert scene.[35]

In this context, it is not surprising that the Germanians embraced the opportunity to work with a prize-winning ten-year-old violinist shortly after her New York debut.[36] Camilla Urso made more than two dozen appearances with the Germanians in Boston and other New England towns between December 1852 and April 1853. She then went on tour with the orchestra and the pianist Alfred Jaëll to Philadelphia, Cincinnati, Louisville, and St. Louis. Her repertory included variation sets and fantasies typical of instrumental virtuosos, as well as concertos by Viotti, Bériot, and Vieuxtemps. Performing with an orchestra of the Germania's caliber and experience was undoubtedly important to Urso's development into one of the premiere violinists of the late nineteenth century. Their concerts together also provided welcome financial support, her family having sacrificed their savings to foster her talent.[37]

Despite her youth, Urso already exhibited the solemnity and dignity that was associated with Jenny Lind. The young violinist's portrait, which captures the earnest countenance described by contemporaries, appears on the cover of Caroline Bandt's *Urso Polka* (fig. III.4.4). Her transition to mature artist during the 1860s was aided by Germanians Carl Zerrahn and Carl Bergmann in their roles as conductors of the Harvard Musical Association Orchestra and New York Philharmonic, respectively. With the high caliber of Urso's playing as a model, the newly founded Boston Conservatory opened its string department to female students later that decade.[38] Not only did this break new ground in the acceptance of girls playing the violin but it also acknowledged a continuum between star performers (no longer a class apart) and the musical aspirations of young women.

It is particularly interesting to consider the Germania's effects in Boston in the broader context of the emerging women's movement. The decade before

35 · *Dwight's Journal of Music* 2 (February 5, 1853): 142. Also see Lawrence, *Strong on Music*, vol. 2, 614 (Hensler) and 681 (Phillips).

36 · A biographical sketch of Urso from *La France Musicale* was translated for *Dwight's Journal of Music* 2 (January 15, 1853): 115–16. See also Susan Kagan, "Camilla Urso: A Nineteenth-Century Violinist's View," *Signs* 2 (1977), which includes a reprint of Urso's 1893 lecture arguing that women should be allowed to work as theater musicians and in major orchestras.

37 · Charles Barnard, *Camilla: A Tale of a Violin* (1874), 84–89.

38 · Block, "Two Virtuoso Performers," 365–68; also see Christine Ammer, *Unsung: A History of Women in American Music* (1980), 21–31.

FIGURE III.4.4. Caroline Bandt's "Urso Polka," 1853. Courtesy of the American Antiquarian Society.

the orchestra's arrival, the city had been the launching ground for several outspoken activists, including Angelina and Sarah Grimké, Lydia Maria Child, Margaret Fuller, and Elizabeth Peabody. The Grimké sisters and Child argued for women's right to address mixed audiences on the evils of slavery; Fuller and Peabody sponsored "Conversations" that provided women with a forum to articulate and refine their ideas. Another local intellectual, Thomas Wentworth Higginson, made the connection between public expression and singing explicit. In his 1859 essay, "Ought Women to Learn the Alphabet?" Higginson argued that with adequate training and opportunity, women on the stage had already proved themselves the equal of men. His example par excellence was the prima donna Anna de LaGrange, who "after years of costly musical instruction, wins the zenith of professional success.... On the stage there is no deduction for sex, and, therefore, woman has shown in that sphere an equal genius." How can society continue to claim, he asked ironically, "that it is right to admit girls to common schools, and equally right to exclude them from colleges; that it is proper for a woman to sing in public, but indelicate for her to speak in public; that a post-office box is an unexceptionable place to drop a bit of paper into, but a ballot-box terribly dangerous?"[39] Here is a further dimension of the acoustic mirror that star female musicians offered audiences. American women were at an early developmental stage of becoming political beings, and accomplished performers provided an aural image of potential future autonomy. For their part, the Germanians helped make this possible by welcoming women into the concert hall as both performers and listeners.

Repertory and Printed Music

As suggested above, Sontag and Lind created a bridge to their listeners through the diversity of their programs. The Germanians created an analogous bridge through their mixed repertory, which included symphonies, overtures, opera selections, variation sets, polkas, waltzes, and marches. Their approach to programming was typical of European ensembles of the period, especially the "private" orchestras of Strauss, Gungl, and Jullien. These ensembles expanded the audience for orchestral music from the hundreds to the thousands by offering frequent concerts of "good music" at low prices in accessible venues. Their success demonstrated the orchestra's cultural and commercial potential, laying the foundation for the major symphony orchestras of the late nineteenth century.

---

39 · Thomas Wentworth Higginson, "Ought Women to Learn the Alphabet?" in *Women and the Alphabet: A Series of Essays* (1900), 14, 33. On LaGrange, see Lawrence, *Strong on Music*, vol. 2, 605–8.

During their six years together, the Germanians employed various strategies to appeal to audiences.[40] A typical early program is represented by the concert Ann Elizabeth Jennison heard in June 1849 (see fig. III.4.3). It included overtures, a symphony movement, virtuoso variation sets, a popular Strauss potpourri, and three dances. One of the dances was Lenschow's own *Stevan's Favorite Polka*. Like Strauss and Gungl, the Germania's conductors used their compositions as publicity for the ensemble. And like them, many of Carl Lenschow's and Bergmann's compositions were subsequently published in piano arrangements, extending the experience of hearing the orchestra into listeners' homes.[41] Occasionally, the orchestra gave sheet music away as a memento, another practice with European precedents. Lenschow's *Bachelor's Polka* and *Maiden Polka* were distributed after the orchestra's Philadelphia debut by the Junior Bachelor's Association, for which they were written.[42]

The Germania also used sheet music as advance publicity. When the orchestra was asked to play for President Taylor's inauguration, Lenschow lost no time in advertising the Germania to the capital city. His *Indian Polka* could be purchased at Wm. Fischer's music store several days before the orchestra's Washington appearance.[43] The publication of this piece had been encouraged by the *New York Herald* the previous October in a review that also noted there were "many very pretty ladies" at the concert.[44] Indeed, Lenschow's *Indian Polka* was "respectfully dedicated to the Ladies of Philadelphia" when it was published by Lee and Walker that spring.

Carl Bergmann, who led the orchestra after Lenschow, published twelve pieces in the series "A Choice Collection of Waltzes and Polkas," specifying on the title pages "as performed by the Germania Musical Society."[45] More than two dozen single titles by Bergmann and other Germanians, such as flut-

---

40 · See my *Good Music for a Free People* for a detailed analysis of the Germania's repertory.

41 · See Thomas Christensen, "Four-Hand Piano Transcription and Geographies of Nineteenth-Century Musical Reception," *Journal of the American Musicological Society* 52 (1999). Although this article is largely based on European sources, it is interesting to consider a parallel development in nineteenth-century America. More research is needed to establish the extent of what was undoubtedly a transatlantic phenomenon.

42 · *Bachelor's Polka* (Philadelphia: Lee and Walker, 1849) and *Maiden Polka* (Philadelphia: Lee and Walker, 1850). These and many other Germanian compositions are available online in the Library of Congress American Memory: Performing Arts, Music database "Music for the Nation: American Sheet Music," http://memory.loc.gov/ammem/mussmhtml/mussm home.html.

43 · *National Intelligencer*, March 2, 1849.

44 · *New York Herald*, October 21, 1848.

45 · The series was published by G. P. Reed in Boston in 1851–52 and included both original works and arrangements by Bergmann.

ist Carl Zerrahn, violinist William Schultze, trumpeter Friedrich Haase, and bassoon player Ferdinand Thiede, include a similar epithet. The Germanians' agent, F. B. Helmsmuller, was particularly astute about the advertising potential of sheet music, whether it was by members of the orchestra or not. Helmsmuller made piano arrangements of items from the Germania's repertory and found publishers for several series that promoted the ensemble.[46] The full name of each series contained a phrase that alluded to the experience of hearing the orchestra, and some titles, such as "Homage to American Ladies: Waltzes," aimed explicitly at the Germania's audience of women pianists at home.

Several pieces, such as Lenschow's *Indian Polka,* were dedicated to the ladies of particular cities. Those of Baltimore were honored with Helmsmuller's *Ladies Souvenir Polka* and Zerrahn's *Nameless Polka.*[47] Buchheister's *Bell Polka: Remembrance of the Germania,* published with the ensemble's portrait on the cover a year after the orchestra disbanded, was dedicated to the ladies of Detroit.[48] Many pieces were dedicated to individual women. Sometimes both title and dedication had female addressees, as with Lenschow's *Anna Polka,* dedicated to Miss Anna Isabella Stevens of New York, and Bergmann's *Mary Polka Redowa,* dedicated to Mrs. Mary E. Hart of Troy, New York, and *Joanna Schottisch,* dedicated to Miss Joanna Behrends of St. Louis.[49]

Another composition that named a woman in both the title and the dedication was Lenschow's *Betty Polka,* written in honor of Zachary Taylor's daughter, Mrs. Colonel William Bliss. Both elements reminded the public that the orchestra had performed this piece at the inaugural festivities. The *Betty Polka* is unusual among the Germanians' compositions in that it was dedicated to a well–known female figure. In most cases, finding information on their subjects is extremely difficult. But thirty of Lenschow's fifty-five extant publications were dedicated to women, as compared to the four dedicated to men. (Another eleven were to associations.) Bergmann also dedicated his publications primarily to women, such as his *Fancy Ball Polka Redowa* and *Love Polka (Ach und Krach),* for Lucia Holbrook and Marie Hyslop, respectively.[50] Like many of Bergmann's dances, the covers of these

46 · Benteen in Baltimore published "Souvenir de Germania: A Choice Collection of Favorite Pieces" and "Gems of the Germania: A Selection of Favorite Waltzes, Polkas, etc." E. H. Wade (Boston) published "The Germanians in Boston: A Selection of the Most Favorite Pieces."

47 · Benteen, 1849, and Lee and Walker (Philadelphia), 1850, respectively.

48 · Stein and Buchheister (Detroit), 1855. Buchheister had played viola in the orchestra. The portrait is the same as figure III.4.2 above.

49 · *Anna Polka* was published by E. H. Wade in Boston in 1849; Bergmann's pieces were published in Boston by G. P. Reed in 1853.

50 · Both were published by Prentiss in Boston in 1851.

works reminded buyers that they had been heard at Newport, where the Germanians had especially warm relations with women, as we shall see. Bergmann's *Pensées Musicales,* a set of character pieces, was dedicated to Caroline Bandt, herself the composer of the *Urso Polka.*[51] Bandt was a pianist who appeared with the Germanians as a soloist, in duets with Alfred Jaëll, and as an accompanist for Urso. Henry Bandt (possibly Caroline's husband or blood relative) was the Germania's business manager during the orchestra's final years. The variety of roles Caroline Bandt held—pianist, composer, dedicatee—exemplifies the continuum of female participation in mid-nineteenth-century musical life. At the same time, her relative historical obscurity underscores that such participation has fallen largely under the radar of both preservation and scholarship.

Patronage and Personal Relations

We might consider ticket buying and sheet music collection as forms of patronage by the public. The Germanians had learned just how important cultivating a specifically female public could be shortly after their arrival in the United States. In the fall of 1849, the Germanians returned to Baltimore, where they gave sixteen concerts in five weeks. Encouraged by their reception, they proposed a thirty-concert series for the remainder of the season, but encountered considerable difficulty selling subscriptions. According to Henry Albrecht, it was "the devoted efforts of young female admirers of music" that made this substantial undertaking a success: "Lovely ladies from rich families, who proudly called themselves 'Friends of the Germania' went around for days with lists to gather the necessary subscribers. Certainly, this was the finest proof that the members fully enjoyed the favors of the praiseworthy ladies of Baltimore thanks to their personalities as well as to the power of the divine art of music. The affectionate reception that the members found here forms one of the loveliest memories of their lives."[52] Before they left Baltimore, the Germanians showed their gratitude by making four women "honorary members" of the orchestra and presenting each with a certificate containing the autograph signatures of all the members. Unfortunately, Albrecht does not record the names of these Baltimore women, pioneers in the organized female patronage of American orchestras.[53]

The hint of romance in Albrecht's description takes stronger form else-

51 · Published by Prentiss in 1850. Bandt's *Urso Polka* is shown in figure III.4.4 above.
52 · Albrecht's quoted recollections appear in *Skizzen,* 14–19. Trans. in Newman, *Good Music* (2010).
53 · Seminal work on this topic is found in Ralph P. Locke and Cyrilla Barr, *Cultivating Music in America: Women Patrons and Activists since 1850* (1997).

where. At their farewell concert in Baltimore, each of the members "received a lovely bouquet of flowers from the young ladies of the most respectable families." In Canada the following spring, the bouquets contained private messages: "Not rarely, a notecard lay hidden between the rosebuds of the tossed bouquets in order to make known in words the feelings that music had called forth in the hearts of the fair sex. The members would be literally covered with flowers on the stage each evening, so that big baskets were necessary to transport them." The Germanians were called back to Newport for two summers even after their official dissolution because they were "so much the darlings of the resort guests, especially of the fair sex." Albrecht reminisced: "Not only in Newport, but everywhere the Germania functioned as a concert orchestra, the opportunity to earn the respect and goodwill of the lovely and kind American ladies was offered almost daily. The magical effect of the sounds of the Germania Orchestra awakened not rarely in the hearts of art-loving ladies more than friendly affections. That frequently yearning glances met, and the words: 'Music is the language of the heart,' turned to action, requires scarcely a mention."

Albrecht spends ample time recounting the Germania's appeal to men as well. Everyone was equally susceptible to the allure of the ensemble: "In whose soul shall not the thought develop directly—upon listening to such splendid orchestral playing, which acts like an electrical shock on all hearts—of securing similar artistic enjoyments through imitation?" But one wonders whether, fifteen years after the Germania's breakup, Albrecht's perspective about his twenty-something self wasn't colored not only by nostalgia for his own youth but also by the rhetoric about matinee idols that was beginning to preoccupy the theatrical world.[54]

Conclusion

The Germania Musical Society welcomed women's participation in multiple ways: on the stage, in the audience, playing their compositions, selling subscriptions, and throwing rosebuds. The inclusion of female performers, the public rehearsals, the production of sheet music, and even the cultivation of the female gaze reached out to the women in the audience, some of whom would eventually aspire to the stage. Without doubt this outreach was partly motivated by self-interest, as it sustained the ensemble for six years. But a recognition that women had a stake in public musical life, and therefore in the life of the republic, seems inherent in their activities. Jürgen Habermas's idea

54 · Richard Butsch, "Bowery B'hoys and Matinee Ladies: The Re-gendering of Nineteenth-Century American Theater Audiences," *American Quarterly* 46 (1994).

that the European middle classes' participation, around 1800, in nonpolitical activities such as theater, choruses, and reading clubs was essentially a rehearsal for the formation of a new kind of public sphere based on individual autonomy is relevant here.[55] As we know, women's full participation in that public sphere was initially foreclosed. I would argue that the appearance of women in the concert hall at midcentury operated similarly, as a rehearsal in a nonpolitical domain pointing the way to women becoming autonomous political beings. The signs are still pointing.

55 · Jürgen Habermas, *The Structural Transformation of the Public Sphere: An Inquiry into a Category of Bourgeois Society* (1989), 26–51.

PART IV

America
& Europe

Orchestras: American and European

JOHN SPITZER

The orchestra as an institution came to America along with European immigrants. Because the majority of immigrants during colonial times came from the British Isles, American orchestras, when they began to appear in the second half of the eighteenth century, resembled those in the home country. The orchestras of ten or fifteen musicians that played in the theaters and at concerts in Philadelphia, New York, and Charleston were made up mainly of English immigrants, and they performed the same music as orchestras back home, much of it imported from London. Immigrants from France and Germany also played in colonial and federal-period orchestras, but in this too the orchestras resembled orchestras in the British Isles, where many of the musicians in the eighteenth and nineteenth centuries were immigrants from continental Europe.

The wave of German immigration that began in the 1840s and continued into the 1880s brought a significant reorientation of American orchestras. Immigrant German musicians made up an increasing proportion of the instrumentalists in American theaters and concert halls. German immigrants also constituted a growing proportion of the audiences for orchestras. Immigrant performers and listeners brought many aspects of German musical life to the United States: a repertory of overtures and symphonies, concerts in restaurants and beer gardens, choral societies with orchestral accompaniment, and more. By the 1880s the world of American orchestras had become a blend of German and English traditions, enriched by performers and repertory from France, Italy, and a few other European countries.

It would be a mistake, however, to view American orchestras as "imported" from Europe or as an "imitation" of European ensembles. More helpful is to see both American and European orchestras as part of what Michael

Broyles calls "a single, transatlantic musical culture."[1] When American violinist Ureli Corelli Hill visited Europe in the 1830s, he listened to and played in several orchestras, comparing them naturally to those ensembles in which he had performed in the United States.[2] Some he judged to be better than anything he had heard before — for example, the orchestras of the King's Theatre in London and the Concerts du Conservatoire in Paris. Other European orchestras — such as the one at the Drury Lane Theatre, where he played for several months — he judged inferior to orchestras he was familiar with at home. For Hill the differences between European and American orchestras were a matter of degree, not differences in kind. All belonged to the same transatlantic culture.

European and American orchestras were linked in the first instance by the movement of musicians across the Atlantic throughout the nineteenth century. The bulk of these players were Europeans, especially Germans, who had been trained in conservatories or military bands and had gained experience in several orchestras before deciding to try their luck in the United States. Many of these men remained in the United States and took American citizenship. A few American musicians, either native born, like U. C. Hill, or the children of immigrants, like Theodore Thomas, went to Europe for training, then returned to the United States, where they assumed leading roles in American orchestras. This flow of personnel from Europe to the United States and back again meant that the performance practices and the organizational structures of European and American orchestras remained similar or identical during most of the nineteenth century.

American and European orchestras were also linked in the nineteenth century by their audiences. European immigrants made up an important part of the audience for orchestral performance in nineteenth-century America. New York, Milwaukee, Chicago, St. Louis, Cincinnati, and Baltimore all had large populations of German immigrants who transplanted the culture of orchestral music that had blossomed in Germany in the 1830s and 1840s to America in the 1850s and 1860s. Just like Berlin or Vienna or Dresden, these American cities had beer gardens, choral societies, German-language theater, and Sunday concerts — all featuring orchestras of German immigrant musicians.[3] Anglo-American music lovers who attended these events sometimes felt out of place amid so much German language and German culture. George Templeton Strong, attending a New York concert in 1841,

---

1 · Michael Broyles, *"Music of the Highest Class": Elitism and Populism in Antebellum Boston* (1992), 11.

2 · On Hill's trip to Europe, see chapter IV.2 in this volume.

3 · See, in this volume, chapters II.2 (New York), II.3 (Cincinnati), and I.3 (Baltimore, St. Louis, and others).

complained that the hall was "jammed with Dutchmen" and that he "scarcely saw an Anglo-Saxon physiognomy in the whole gallery."[4] But he acknowledged that the orchestra and the repertory it played were both excellent. The wave of Italian immigrants that arrived in the United States in the 1880s and 1890s brought a new cadre of orchestra musicians and created another European audience for American orchestras, particularly at the opera.

The repertories of nineteenth-century American and European orchestras were, for practical purposes, identical. Orchestras on both sides of the Atlantic played the same operas, the same symphonies and overtures, the same waltzes and galops. Most of this repertory was by composers who had lived and died in Europe. Orchestras in America also performed music by American composers—especially pieces of a more "popular" or topical character. The Jullien Orchestra on its tour of 1853–54 played shorter pieces by several American composers, as well as symphonic works by George Frederick Bristow and William Henry Fry.[5] Orchestras in Europe played very few works by American composers during most of the nineteenth century. There were no American "classics," and when it came to modern music, German, French, and Italian audiences tended to prefer works in local or national traditions.

Over the course of the nineteenth century, European and American orchestras underwent many of the same developments in parallel and in ongoing interchange with each other. On both sides of the Atlantic, orchestras became ever more ubiquitous in entertainment and public life. In Berlin, London, and Paris, as in New York, Baltimore, and Cincinnati, orchestras played at public concerts, in restaurants and cafes, in resorts and public gardens, at skating rinks, and in theaters of every description—opera, musical theater, spoken theater, vaudeville, and, by the end of the century, movie theaters. In both Europe and the United States, orchestras began to give concerts for larger and more diverse audiences, in auditoriums that accommodated thousands of people, at ticket prices that middle- and even working-class people could afford. These "democratic" and "commercial" trends were apparent in Europe in the 1830s and in America by the 1850s. The nineteenth century also saw the rise of "enterprise" conductors, such as Louis Antoine Jullien and Johann Strauss in Europe and Theodore Thomas in the United States, who led full-time orchestras that supported themselves at the box office. On both sides of the Atlantic, enterprise orchestras were driven by similar commercial motivations to expand their audiences, to lower ticket prices, to tour outside the capital city, and to offer a mixed repertory of classical, popular,

4 · Quoted in chapter V.3 in this volume. Anglo-Americans also objected to the German tradition of serving food and particularly drink during orchestral concerts and even more to the practice of scheduling such concerts on Sundays. See chapter II.2 in this volume.
5 · For Jullien's repertory of American works, see appendix IV.1.2, in this volume.

and modern music that appealed to a broad spectrum of tastes. The last third of the century saw a campaign in Europe as in America for canonic repertory and the "improvement" of public taste in orchestral music. "Symphony" orchestras dedicated themselves to the performance of classical or "serious" repertory and eliminated vocal numbers and dance music from their programs, while "pops" and "salon" orchestras, as well as concert bands, continued the mixed programming of earlier times.

Permanent symphony orchestras were founded at about the same time on both sides of the Atlantic. The pioneer orchestras were European: the Leipzig Gewandhaus Orchestra in 1781, the Royal Philharmonic Society (London) in 1813, and the Paris Conservatoire in 1828. Thereafter, developments were parallel: the New York and Vienna Philharmonics in 1842; the Hallé Orchestra (Manchester), 1857; the Boston Symphony and Concert Lamoureux (Paris), 1881; the Berlin Philharmonic, 1882; the Concertgebouw (Amsterdam), 1888; the Chicago Symphony, 1891; the Munich Philharmonic (Kaim Orchestra), 1893; and the Cincinnati Symphony Orchestra, 1894. Another trend that proceeded in parallel on both sides of the Atlantic was the unionization of orchestra musicians. Instrumentalists in America as well as in Europe had formed mutual-assistance societies in the eighteenth century to pay for medical expenses and funerals. In the 1860s both German and American musicians began to organize themselves into unions that aimed to improve wages and working conditions.[6] Musicians' unions followed in France (1876), Austria (1892), England (1893), and Belgium (1893). European musicians' unions often pointed to the American unions as a model of how orchestra musicians could and should improve their lot.

Although they participated in the same transatlantic musical culture, there were important differences between American and European orchestras in the nineteenth century. The level of execution in the better European ensembles was clearly higher than that in American orchestras, as acknowledged by American musicians who visited Europe and by Americans who heard European orchestras on tour in the United States. Whether the average European dance or theater or cafe orchestra in 1860 or 1880 was better than its American counterpart is an open question. On the other hand, American orchestra musicians were on average considerably better paid than European musicians. In America the demand for orchestral music outstripped the supply of musicians, and there was a shortage of competent instrumentalists in almost every American city with the exception of New York. Jobs were

---

6 · For U.S. musicians' unions, see chapter I.3 in this volume; for Germany, see Martin Jacob Newhouse, "Artists, Artisans, or Workers? Orchestral Musicians in the German Empire" (Ph. D. diss., 1979).

plentiful and wages high. A German violist wrote home in 1873 to say that in New York he earned five times what he had made in Berlin and Hamburg—and that he was able to save three-quarters of his income.[7]

The primary employment for orchestra musicians, both in Europe and in the United States, was in the theater, but in many European cities one or more of these theaters was dedicated to the performance of opera, a more demanding repertory than the music that orchestras played for spoken theater or musical comedy. The opera house provided personnel for concert orchestras in London, Vienna, Paris, Turin, and many other European cities. Since most European opera houses were subsidized by the state—sometimes by a royal court, sometimes a national or local government—this amounted to a state subsidy for orchestras and their musicians. Of American cities only New York and New Orleans had resident opera companies during the nineteenth century, and these did not receive any government support.

The tradition of government support for European orchestras dated back to the court orchestras of the seventeenth and eighteenth centuries. In the nineteenth century there were still a few court orchestras—for example, the Meiningen orchestra—and many court-subsidized theaters. Cities, especially in Germany, sponsored civic orchestras, which received yearly subsidies from the city budget. Governments, national and local, also subsidized music conservatories, producing a stream of instrumentalists who staffed European orchestras or immigrated to America. In the United States, by contrast, orchestras supported themselves almost entirely through box office receipts, and when patronage finally materialized toward the end of the nineteenth century, it was private, not state, patronage—wealthy individuals who undertook to support orchestras as a civic duty.[8] Even in Europe, however, government patronage was not universal. Many nineteenth-century European orchestras—the Strauss orchestra, the Pasdeloup orchestra, the Bilse orchestra, the orchestras at the Covent Garden and Drury Lane theaters in London—supported themselves, like American orchestras, by selling music to the public.

The presence or absence of state subsidy was perhaps the most important difference between American and European orchestras in the nineteenth century, and the difference persists to this day. However, this and other differences were never decisive or divisive. The world of orchestras became transatlantic in the nineteenth century and remained so in the twentieth. In the twenty-first century, with the success of orchestras in Japan, Korea, and China, the world of orchestras has become global.

7 · *Deutsche Musikerzeitung* 4 (March 20, 1873): 99.
8 · See chapter I.1 in this volume.

[IV.1] "A Concentration of Talent on Our Musical Horizon"

The 1853–54 American Tour by Jullien's Extraordinary Orchestra

KATHERINE K. PRESTON

The *New York Daily Times*, on August 8, 1853, ran a short announcement under the heading "Musical Novelty":

> M. Jullien, the projector and leader of the celebrated promenade concerts in London, visits the United States with a view to a similar musical season in the great cities of this country. He arrived here yesterday in the *Baltic*, and is at the Clarenden Hotel. His corps of instrumental artists will come out in the next Collins' steamer, due two weeks hence. The great musician was to be greeted at an early hour this morning by a serenade at his Hotel, which we presume was given, according to appointment. His concerts, which begin at Castle Garden on the 29th inst, will be a novelty in the musical entertainments of the country.[1]

So began a visit to the United States of the largest and best orchestra ever before heard on the North American continent, led by one of the most famous and popular European conductors of the nineteenth century, Louis Antoine Jullien (1812–60). Jullien and his celebrated ensemble remained in the United States for ten months, giving more than two hundred concerts in twenty cities both large (New York, Boston, Philadelphia) and small (Buffalo, Rochester, Savannah, Augusta, Richmond) in front of tens of thousands of Americans, many of whom had never before heard an orchestra outside of a theater.[2] Although largely forgotten today, this whirlwind tour by a charismatic conductor and a fabulous orchestra—"a concentration of talent on

---

1 · *New York Daily Times*, August 8, 1853. The serenade, which was to be given by Dodsworth's band ("and others of the musical fraternity") did not occur because of inclement weather. See *New York Daily Times*, August 9, 1853.

2 · For a complete list of cities in which the Jullien Orchestra performed, as documented by newspaper advertisements and published programs, see appendix IV.1.1 in this chapter.

our musical horizon," as a contemporary critic put it—was both an important event and a huge musical influence in midcentury America.[3] A careful examination of this musical hurricane that blew through the United States in 1853–54 and speculation about its impact reveal much about American culture at the midpoint of the nineteenth century.

The mastermind behind the tour—and the man responsible for its success—was Louis Jullien himself. As the critic of the *New York Courier and Enquirer* wrote in August 1853, the conductor "not only rides the whirlwind and controls the storm, but ... furnishes the tempest, the thunder and the lightning"; another critic made a similar observation eight months later: "Jullien himself is the centre of attraction, and the monster concerts without the *'gran maestro'* would be considered by every body a confounded bore."[4] But while the charismatic conductor was unquestionably a major part of the appeal, Jullien's flamboyance and theatricality were by no means the entire story. A careful examination of the tour—based almost entirely on information published in contemporary journals and newspapers in the towns and cities that he visited—suggests that Americans were attracted to a combination of elements. The music, the orchestra's virtuoso instrumentalists, Jullien's conducting prowess, and a barrage of publicity worked collectively to create a midcentury musical *furore* that escaped the notice of no one.

Louis Antoine Jullien was well known to music lovers in New York when he arrived, for he had made a name for himself both on the continent and in the United Kingdom starting in the 1830s.[5] His concerts in England had been well covered in the American musical press, especially after he announced plans to visit the United States.[6] Jullien studied at the Paris Conservatoire in the 1830s, after which he presented a series of entertainments at the Jardin Turc in Paris, challenging the famous Concerts-Musard in popularity. In 1838 he migrated to England, where, in the 1840s and into the 1850s, he helped to establish the promenade concert as a popular style of entertainment both

3 · James Otis, "Jullien's Concerts," *Spirit of the Times*, September 3, 1853, 23, 29.
4 · "Jullien's First Concert," August 30, 1854, *New York Courier and Enquirer*, republished in *Dwight's Journal of Music* 3 (September 3, 1853): 172; *Washington Evening Star*, April 11, 1854.
5 · The standard works on Jullien are Adam Carse, *The Life of Jullien: Adventurer, Showman-Conductor and Establisher of the Promenade Concerts in England* (1951); Carse, *The Orchestra from Beethoven to Berlioz* (1949), 230–41 and 377–82; and Eugene Victor Frey, "Jullien in America" (master's thesis, 1943). See also John Graziano, "Jullien and His *Music for the Millions*," in *A Celebration of American Music*, ed. R. Crawford et al. (1990). A recent book by Michel Faul, *Louis Jullien: Musique, spectacle et folie au XIXe siècle* (2006), does not add new information about Jullien's American tour.
6 · On the barrage of publicity in New York that preceded Jullien's arrival there in August 1853, see Vera Brodsky Lawrence, *Strong on Music*, vol. 2, *Reverberations: 1850–1856* (1995), 361–62.

in London and in the "provinces." (These concerts continue today as the London Proms, performed every summer at Royal Albert Hall in Kensington.) Jullien's goal as a conductor-composer, according to the *Illustrated London News*, was "to ensure amusement as well as attempting instruction, by blending in the programmes the most sublime works with those of a lighter school."[7] To entertain the public he programmed quadrilles, waltzes, polkas, schottisches, potpourris, and other light and amusing compositions, which he conducted with charisma, showmanship, and flamboyance. To "educate" the same audience, he regularly programmed more "serious" works, sometimes offering entire programs by such composers as Beethoven, Mozart, and Mendelssohn.

The repertory of orchestral concerts in the mid-nineteenth century differed significantly from such concerts today; from our point of view, it was quite eclectic. The programs of concert-society orchestras such as the Philharmonic Society of London, the Vienna Philharmonic, the Paris Concerts du Conservatoire, the Leipzig Gewandhaus, and the Philharmonic Society of New York almost always included overtures (frequently operatic), vocal pieces (usually opera arias or scenes, but also popular tunes, Scottish or Irish songs, and less frequently lieder), chamber works, and symphonic compositions, sometimes performed in their entirely but often limited to individual movements. Jullien's concerts were similarly eclectic, but with the added dimension of "lighter" pieces, like potpourris, variations, and dances. Jullien's orchestra was an example of a type of ensemble, different and distinct from concert-society orchestras, that emerged in the 1830s and 1840s. These ensembles performed in a variety of venues (theaters, salons, pleasure gardens); they gave concerts much more frequently than the concert-society orchestras; some of them toured regularly; and they performed dances and narrative works (potpourris and quadrilles) in addition to the eclectic "classical" mixture already mentioned. Christoph-Hellmut Mahling calls these ensembles "private orchestras" or "salon orchestras"; John Spitzer has dubbed them "enterprise orchestras."[8] They were organized by conductors like Johann Strauss *père* and *fils* in Vienna, Philippe Musard in Paris, Josef Gungl and (later) Benjamin Bilse in Berlin, and (of course) Louis Antoine Jullien in England. Spitzer calls these men "entrepreneur-conductors," for in addition to conducting they also raised capital, hired musicians, and organized the activities of their ensembles.

7 · *Illustrated London News*, November 9, 1850, quoted in Carse, *Life of Jullien*, 66.
8 · Christoph-Hellmut Mahling, "Berlin, 'Music in the Air,'" in *The Early Romantic Era*, ed. A. Ringer (1991), 134; John Spitzer, "The Entrepreneur-Conductors and Their Orchestras," *Nineteenth-Century Music Review* 5 (2008).

Louis Jullien was one of these "entrepreneur-conductors." He perfected the art of showmanship through his appearance (see fig. IV.1.1). The press frequently commented on his "raven locks," his "plentitude of ringlet and whisker," and his "superb mustache"; he dressed carefully and deliberately, choosing impeccable waistcoats "of unparalleled whiteness," embroidered shirts, dark trousers, wristbands, and white kid gloves that he wore while conducting.[9] *Punch* caricatured him regularly with both pen-and-ink illustrations and prose descriptions: "Jullien, the elegant, the pantomimic Jullien," the paper reported in its first issue, "exhibit[s] his six-inch wristbands and exquisitely dressed head."[10] He conducted from a raised platform on which were carefully placed an elaborately decorated music stand and a chair "of crimson velvet and gold."[11] But there was much more to the conductor than mere bombast, for Jullien was a naturally charismatic performer. His conducting, in the words of his biographer Adam Carse, was "spectacular, demonstrative, illustrative, dynamic, emotional, and above all, commanding"; he could "inflame his orchestra … give it something that it lacked when he was not there, and … dominate it to a degree that gave him … mastery over it."[12] And the orchestra was the finest he could put together; he spared no expense in attracting the best musicians to his ensemble. The general public responded with enthusiasm. As James William Davison, the influential critic for the *Times*, observed in a tribute he wrote after the conductor's death, Jullien "was essentially and before all a man for the people. He loved to entertain the people; he loved to instruct the people; and the people were just as fond of being taught as of being amused by Jullien."[13]

Jullien's Musicians

Jullien brought all of this to the United States: the showmanship and charisma, conducting virtuosity, excellent performers, and the goal of attracting to his concerts both the general public and the more-discriminating lovers of the "classical" repertory. In mid-August, he was joined in New York by a prima donna, the soprano Anna Zerr (1822–81), and a core group of some of the best solo instrumental virtuosi of Europe, to which he added some seventy local musicians. This resulted in an orchestra that numbered around one hundred;

9 · Carse, *Life of Jullien*, 101–3. Carse points out that wearing kid gloves while conducting was the practice of all conductors who performed in London (with the exception of Wagner).
10 · *Punch*, July 17, 1841, quoted in Carse, *Life of Jullien*, 102.
11 · John Ross Dix, "Jullien: A Sketch from the Life," *Dwight's Journal of Music* 4 (November 5, 1853): 36.
12 · Carse, *Life of Jullien*, 115, 117.
13 · *London Musical World*, March 17, 1860, reprinted in Henry Davison, *From Mendelssohn to Wagner: Being the Memoirs of J. W. Davison, Forty Years Music Critic of the Times* (1912), 471.

MAYALL   221, Regent Street

FIGURE IV.1.1. Portrait of Louis Antoine Jullien by Mayall. *Albumen carte-de-visite*, ca 1860.
Photographs Division, National Portrait Gallery, London. Used with permission.

in contrast, the Philharmonic Society, in 1853, could muster only sixty-seven performers.[14] Jullien's first American concert took place on August 29, 1853, at the large pleasure resort Castle Garden, located off the Battery in lower Manhattan. According to a review that appeared in the *Daily Tribune* on September 2, "all [of] Jullien's solo players are unrivaled, and we have now at Castle Garden an orchestra certainly unsurpassed, and probably unequaled by any in Europe."[15] The accolade was probably written by William Henry Fry, who less than a year earlier had returned from a six-year sojourn abroad. In another review, Fry noted that Jullien had searched "Paris, London, Berlin, and other great European cities … for players indisputably preeminent for the orchestra"; the resulting ensemble comprised "such a combination [of virtuosi] as we have never heard before and may never hear again."[16]

The core group of European orchestral musicians who accompanied Jullien to America numbered twenty-seven and included some truly brilliant performers. Although most have been forgotten today, it is clear that these were performers the likes of which (especially in the aggregate) had never before been seen or heard in North America. Among the wind players were Mathieu-André Reichert (b. 1830, flute), Hubert Collinet (1797–1867, flageolet), Antoine-Joseph Lavigne (1816–86, oboe), and Henri Wuille (1822–71, clarinet). Reichert, a Belgian, was described by the *London Musical World* as "an executant of unrivalled ability, whose performances have been frequently the source of astonishment and delight to the musical public"; a correspondent writing from New York to *Dwight's Journal of Music* described his playing as "very brilliant and clear." Collinet, whose instrument (the flageolet) was widely used for the performance of dance music, was called "the little king of that little instrument"; Lavigne, according to a Boston critic, was "generally considered the first oboist in Europe; his execution is most exquisitely delicate and the tone very thin and cutting, as it were, like glass." Henri Wuille, dubbed by the *Musical World* "the Belgian Lazarus, an artist who has no superior on his instrument," was described in America as a performer with "a beautiful tone and most finished execution."[17] Jullien's

14 · Frey provides a list of ninety orchestra members and notes that the ensemble also included six side drums and three fifers. Lawrence also identifies a harpist named Hughes as "Jullien's harpist," which brings the total to one hundred. See Frey, "Jullien in America," 31–32, and Lawrence, *Strong on Music*, vol. 2, 420–21, 749, 826.

15 · *New York Daily-Tribune*, September 2, 1853.

16 · Ibid., December 15, 1853.

17 · Unless otherwise noted, the contemporary comments in this paragraph are from three sources: an article in the *London Musical World*, July 30, 1853, 476 (reprinted in *Dwight's Journal of Music* 3 [August 20, 1853]: 159; James Otis, "Jullien," *Spirit of the Times*, August 20, 1853, 23, 27; and An Artist, "Jullien's Concert," *Dwight's Journal of Music* 3 (September 24, 1853): 199.

imported wind and reed players also included performers on piccolo, clarinet, and bassoon.[18]

The brass and string sections were similarly based on a core of first-class European players. The most notable among the brass were William Winterbottom (ca. 1820–89, trombone), S. Hughes (dates unknown, ophicleide), Hippolyte-Jean Duhem (1828–1911, trumpet), and Hermann Koenig (dates unknown, cornet-à-pistons). Among the string players were concertmaster Thomas Baker (d. 1888), Henry Weist Hill (1828–91), and the Mollenhauer brothers Eduard (1827–1914) and Friedrich (1818–85), in addition to the double-bassist extraordinaire Giovanni Bottesini (1821–89). Winterbottom, who served for a time as the principal trombone of the London Philharmonic, was described in 1853 as "one of the finest players on that fine instrument"; also according to the *Musical World*, he had earlier that year "performed a solo ... at the Philharmonic Concerts ... with the greatest success."[19] The ophicleidist Hughes was "a well-known English player of ability"; according to *Dwight's Journal of Music* correspondent, he achieved "a most astonishing tone from his instrument.... It is large, round, and as mellow as anything I ever heard."[20] Duhem toured widely (in Denmark, Germany, England, Scotland, Ireland, and the Netherlands) as a trumpet performer before signing on with Jullien; a native of Paris, he later taught at the Royal Conservatory in Brussels and was described as "the greatest player on that difficult instrument in all Belgium and an equal proficient on the cornet-à-pistons."[21] The cornetist Koenig, according to James Otis (writing for the *Spirit of the Times*), had been praised "by the whole European press" and his name was "as familiar as 'household words,' even in the backwoods of America."[22]

The four European first violinists were all well known to the British concertgoing public, but the Mollenhauer brothers were the stars. As one former member of the Jullien Orchestra remembered in 1878, "I have heard many fine

18 · These musicians were identified by only their surnames: Charles (flute and piccolo), de Prins (second oboe, "another good player, also from Brussels"), Sonnenberg (second clarinet, "a player of the highest ability, who has frequently distinguished himself at the Drury Lane concerts"), and Hardy (first bassoon and "an English performer of eminence") (*London Musical World*, July 30, 1853, 476). Hardy was one of the few of Jullien's instrumentalists criticized in the American press (*Albion*, September 10, 1853, 12, 37).

19 · The quotations are from the *London Musical World*, July 30, 1853, 476. For Winterbottom, see "The Rise and Development of Military Music," http://www.traditionalmuisc.co .uk/military/military-music%20-%200249.htm.

20 · *London Musical World*, July 30, 1853, 476; *Dwight's Journal of Music* 3 (September 24, 1853): 199.

21 · *Archief Oostende*, http://archief.oostende.be/product/91/default.aspx?_vs=0_N&id =6371; the quotation is from the *London Musical World*, July 30, 1853, 476.

22 · *Spirit of the Times*, August 20, 1853, 23, 27.

violin players, but never two who played together with such oneness. A duet by them could not be as well played by any two other men in the world."[23] Jullien featured them regularly in duets throughout the tour. Thomas Baker, Jullien's concertmaster, remained in the United States after the orchestra returned to London and became a very successful theater orchestra director in New York.[24] Another major star was the celebrated double-bassist Giovanni Bottesini, dubbed "the Paganini of the double-bass." This acclaimed instrumentalist was so well known even in America that critics assumed that they need provide no further information about him; the comment by the correspondent to *Dwight's* was typical: "of course, Bottesini is too well known in Boston to need any praise from my hands."[25] Jullien also brought along two hornists, a second cornetist, one second violinist, one violist, first and second cellists, two additional double-bassists, and a percussionist.[26] Jullien's imported instrumentalists anchored their various sections and were also featured as soloists throughout the tour; almost all of them remained with the orchestra for the entire ten months.

The final star performer was the soprano Anna Zerr, who provided the vocal component that was such an essential aspect of most concerts during the period. Zerr was a German singer (born at Baden-Baden) whose voice, which was described as "fine, pure, and sympathetic ... [and] of full calibre," had a full three-octave range. Commentators pointedly observed that Zerr had three more notes in her range than did Jenny Lind, who had mesmerized Americans on her 1850 tour.[27] Overwhelmingly favorable comments about almost all of Jullien's virtuosi by American critics continued unabated throughout the orchestra's visit, suggesting that the soloists lived up to their reputations in the United States.

23 · Interview with Benjamin J. Deane, former violinist in Jullien's orchestra and longtime performer and theater orchestra conductor in New York: "Knight of Bow and Baton; Remembrances of Men and Music by a Veteran Leader," *New York Times*, October 6, 1878.
24 · Baker subsequently served as the musical director at Niblo's Theatre and at Laura Keene's Theatre in New York. See chapter II.1 in this volume.
25 · *Dwight's Journal of Music* 3 (September 24, 1853): 199.
26 · The additional European brass players were R. Hughes (horn), Steneberger (horn), and Holt (cornet-à-pistons). Among the string players were second violinist Louis Barque, violist (and viola d'amore) Schreus, first cellist Lütgen, second cellist Engelke, bassists H. Winterbottom and Bull, and percussionist F. Hughes. Most of the string players, according to the *London Musical World*, came from the orchestra of the Grand Opera at Brussels. See *London Musical World*, July 30, 1853, 476; Frey, "Jullien in America," 33.
27 · Zerr's first appearance in England was in 1851 in concert at the Hanover Square Rooms. She performed successfully in concerts and opera on the continent, in the United Kingdom, and in America with Jullien. She retired from the stage in 1857. See Alexis Chitty, "Zerr, Anna," *Grove's Dictionary of Music and Musicians*, 3rd ed. (1935).

Approximately half of the seventy-odd American musicians Jullien added to his orchestra in New York were members of the Philharmonic Society of New York: these included at least seventeen first and second violins, three violists, four cellists, and five string bassists.[28] Only a handful of the names are familiar, all of them first violinists: Ureli Corelli Hill (1802–75), Theodore Thomas (1835–1905), George Frederick Bristow (1825–98), and Charles Schmidt. The other thirty instrumentalists are unknowns but they probably worked in the orchestras of New York theaters.[29] The Jullien Orchestra concerts would not have interfered with Philharmonic Society work, since that ensemble gave but four concerts per year. But many of the Philharmonic musicians were also employed in the New York theaters, and they—like the non-Philharmonic musicians—would have had to take a leave of absence from their regular positions in order to accept the (presumably higher-paying) job with Jullien's orchestra. It is probable that the musicians simply engaged long-term substitutes for their regular theater-orchestra jobs.[30] No information exists about how much Jullien paid his American instrumentalists, but as already mentioned, he had a reputation in England of sparing no expense to attract superior musicians. Most likely he paid his New York musicians considerably more than the $12 per week that they made in most New York theaters.[31] Furthermore, any New York musician worth his salt would have leapt at the opportunity to perform in such an ensemble, with some of the best instrumentalists ever heard in North America. Benjamin Deane, a thirty-one-year-old violinist when he joined Jullien's band, was still in awe some twenty-five years later. "What an orchestra that was!" he remembered in 1878. "Never [was there] one in this country to match it before or since. Never anywhere so many great solo performers [who] traveled together."[32] Many of the Americans who played in the orchestra—including both George Bristow and Theodore Thomas—learned much about the performance of symphonic music while working under Jullien, both because of the superb quality of the orchestra itself and because of Jullien's dynamic conducting.[33]

---

28 · Frey provides a complete list of the personnel in Jullien's Orchestra for its opening season in New York ("Jullien in America," 32–33). See also Henry Edward Krehbiel, *The Philharmonic Society of New York: A Memorial* (1892).

29 · Deane interview, "Knight of Bow and Baton."

30 · This was the standard modus operandi, at least later in the century. See Katherine K. Preston, *Music for Hire: A Study of Professional Musicians in Washington, 1877–1900* (1992).

31 · On wages in New York theater orchestras, see chapters I.3 and II.1 in this volume.

32 · Deane interview, "Knight of Bow and Baton."

33 · Ezra Schabas, in his biography of Theodore Thomas, writes that Jullien influenced Thomas as a conductor "even if he was reluctant to acknowledge it." Schabas, *Theodore Thomas: America's Conductor and Builder of Orchestras, 1835–1905* (1989), 9–10.

In late August 1853, with his ensemble completely assembled, Jullien embarked on a series of forty-nine concerts in Manhattan, first at Castle Garden and later at Metropolitan Hall. After a fairly slow start, these events quickly caught the attention of both critics and audiences. By the end of the first week the critics were gushing about the caliber of the ensemble as a whole. "Jullien's orchestra—without mincing matters—is the most perfect and superb in the world," wrote James Otis in the *Spirit of the Times*. "Nothing like its individual and collective instrumental skill, precision, and wonderful discipline," he continued, "has ever been heard in America before."[34] Richard Grant White, reviewing the orchestra's first concert, noted that Jullien "obtains from fifty strings a *pianissimo* which is scarcely audible, and he makes one hundred instruments stop in the midst of a *fortissimo* which seems to lift the roof, as if an hundred men dropped dead at the movement of his hand."[35] And John Sullivan Dwight's New York correspondent, "An Artist," declared that "those who have not heard [Jullien] imagine he only excels in the lighter and volatile performances, but I heard the *Scherzo* of Mendelssohn's Third Symphony performed in a most exquisite manner."[36]

Jullien's Repertory

The repertory of the Jullien Orchestra was remarkably consistent during the New York engagement; it would, in fact, remain consistent throughout the entire ten months of the visit, regardless of location. A typical program commenced with an overture; there were generally three (occasionally four) vocal pieces, two to four chamber works that featured the instrumental virtuosi, two to four dances, one or two orchestral movements (usually from a symphony), and two to four quadrilles. The overtures were usually from operas, but occasionally Jullien programmed concert overtures, like Beethoven's *Egmont* or Berlioz's *Roman Carnival*. The vocal works included both songs and operatic arias (or scenes). Anna Zerr, who performed with the orchestra for the entire ten months, had some clear favorites; these included "Air with Variations" by Heinrich Proch, "I've Been Roaming" by Charles Edward Horn, and "Forget Me Not," a Tyrolienne by Carl Haas. She also occasionally sang "national" songs such as "Coming through the Rye" and Thomas Moore's "The Last Rose of Summer." The operatic selections that she performed most frequently were "Batti, batti" from *Don Giovanni*; "Where the Bee Sucks," from *The Tempest*, by the seventeenth-century British composer

34 · *Spirit of the Times*, September 3, 1853, 23, 29.
35 · *New York Courier and Enquirer*, August 30, 1853.
36 · *Dwight's Journal of Music* 3 (September 24, 1853): 199.

Matthew Locke; the Queen of the Night's aria from *The Magic Flute*; and various arias from Donizetti's *Lucia di Lammermoor* and Jullien's *Pietro il Grande* (1852). The chamber works were a mixed bag, generally duos, themes and variations, or adaptations from popular operas that were designed to showcase the virtuosic abilities of Jullien's soloists and frequently attributed to the virtuosi themselves. Giovanni Bottesini, for example, contributed four chamber works to the concert repertory: Duo for Clarinet and Contrabass, Duo for Violoncello and Contrabass, Tarantella for Contrabass Solo, and Contrabass Solo on Themes from *La Sonnambula*. The orchestra also performed his "Cerrito," a fantasia, apparently arranged for double bass and orchestra. Similar works were composed and performed by Hippolyte-Jean Duhem, Hermann Koenig, Antoine-Joseph Lavigne, the Mollenhauer brothers, Mathieu-André Reichert, William Winterbottom, and Henri Wuille, as well as by two less-renowned virtuosi, the hornist Steneberger and cellist Lütgen.

Beethoven and Mendelssohn were by far the most popular symphonic composers. Of Beethoven's orchestral works, Jullien regularly programmed individual movements from symphonies nos. 2, 3, 4, 5, 6, and 8, and occasionally performed Symphony no. 5 in its entirety. He also programmed several overtures (*Egmont, Leonora, Fidelio*) and the song "Adelaide" (op. 46) arranged for cornet. The most frequently performed of Mendelssohn's orchestral works were the *Incidental Music to a Midsummer Night's Dream* and the Symphony no. 3 (*Scottish*); again, Jullien sometimes programmed individual movements, sometimes the entire work. In addition, the orchestra performed Mendelssohn's Violin Concerto several times, with Henry Weist Hill as soloist. In New York and other large cities (Boston, Philadelphia, Baltimore, and New Orleans), Jullien occasionally gave concerts—a Grand Beethoven or a Grand Mendelssohn Night—that highlighted one of these two composers. At these concerts most of the works performed (except the dances and quadrilles) were by the featured composer; it was generally these events that included complete performances of multimovement compositions. Figure IV.1.2 shows the program for a Grand Beethoven Night that the orchestra gave in Boston on October 26, 1853.

Jullien, as is well known, also programmed symphonic works by several American composers and commissioned symphonic compositions by three: George Frederick Bristow (Symphony no. 2, *The Jullien*), William Henry Fry (*Santa Claus* [*The Christmas Symphony*] and the programmatic symphony *Childe Harold*), and the Philadelphian Karl Hohnstock (1828–89) (a "descriptive symphony" titled *The Sea Voyage*).[37] The principal beneficiaries

---

37 · I discuss Jullien's support for American composers and the reaction in the American press in the introduction to *George F. Bristow's Symphony No. 2 ("Jullien"): A Critical*

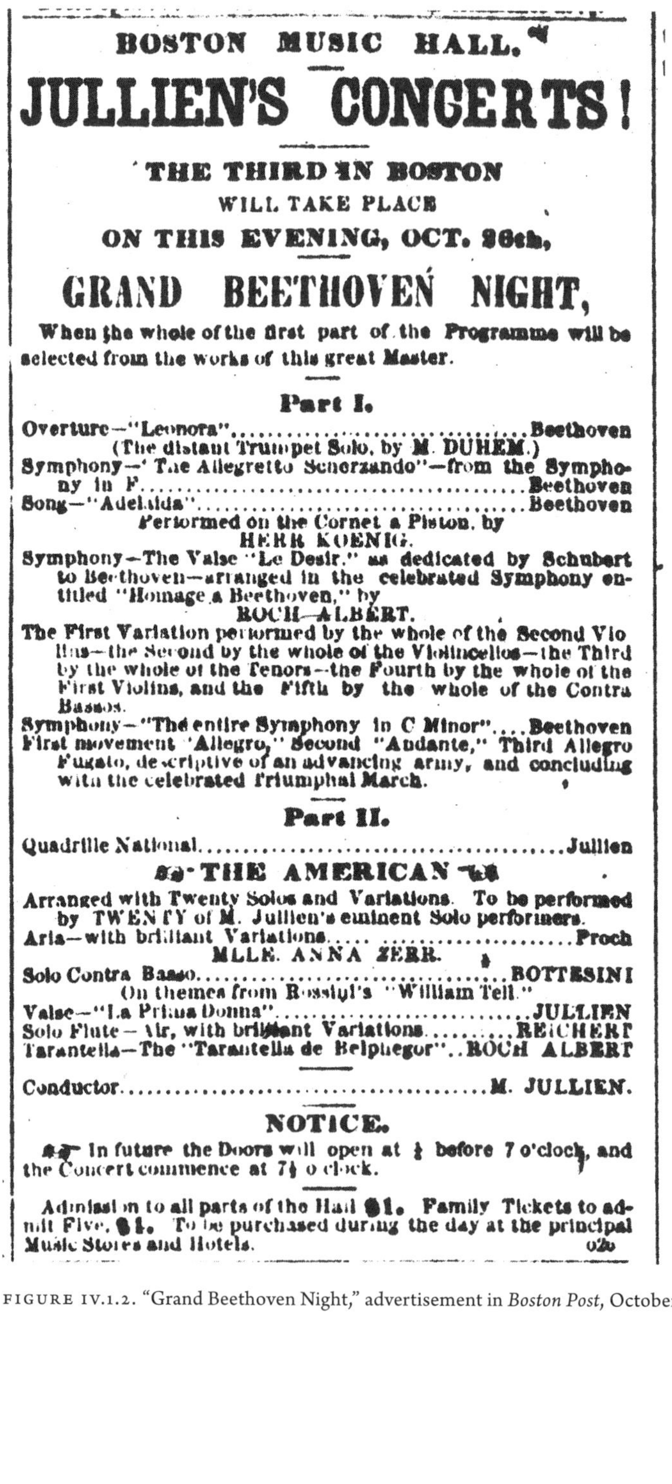

BOSTON MUSIC HALL.

JULLIEN'S CONCERTS!

THE THIRD IN BOSTON

WILL TAKE PLACE

ON THIS EVENING, OCT. 26th,

GRAND BEETHOVEN NIGHT,

When the whole of the first part of the Programme will be selected from the works of this great Master.

Part I.

Overture—"Leonora"...................................Beethoven
(The distant Trumpet Solo, by M. DUHEM.)
Symphony—' The Allegretto Scherzando"—from the Symphony in F..Beethoven
Song—"Adelaida"...................................Beethoven
Performed on the Cornet a Piston, by
HERR KOENIG.
Symphony—The Valse "Le Desir." as dedicated by Schubert to Beethoven—arranged in the celebrated Symphony entitled "Homage a Beethoven," by
ROCH ALBERT.
The First Variation performed by the whole of the Second Violins—the Second by the whole of the Violincellos—the Third by the whole of the Tenors—the Fourth by the whole of the First Violins, and the Fifth by the whole of the Contra Bassos.
Symphony—"The entire Symphony in C Minor"....Beethoven
First movement 'Allegro," Second "Andante," Third Allegro Fugato, descriptive of an advancing army, and concluding with the celebrated Triumphal March.

Part II.

Quadrille National...................................Jullien

THE AMERICAN

Arranged with Twenty Solos and Variations. To be performed by TWENTY of M. Jullien's eminent Solo performers.
Aria—with brilliant Variations....................Proch
MLLE. ANNA ZERR.
Solo Contra Basso...................................BOTTESINI
On themes from Rossini's "William Tell."
Valse—"La Prima Donna"...................................JULLIEN
Solo Flute—Air, with brilliant Variations..........REICHERT
Tarantella—The "Tarantella de Belphegor"..ROCH ALBERT

Conductor...................................M. JULLIEN.

NOTICE.

In future the Doors will open at ½ before 7 o'clock, and the Concert commence at 7½ o'clock.

Admission to all parts of the Hall $1. Family Tickets to admit Five, $4. To be purchased during the day at the principal Music Stores and Hotels.   o2t

FIGURE IV.1.2. "Grand Beethoven Night," advertisement in *Boston Post*, October 26, 1853.

of Jullien's attention were the two native-born composers Bristow and Fry. Jullien performed the Minuet movement from Bristow's Symphony no. 1 in New York, Boston, Philadelphia, Louisville, and New Orleans, and two movements from the *Jullien* symphony several times in New York. Of Fry's orchestral works, the orchestra performed four of the six programmatic symphonies (played thirty-nine times, in New York, Boston, Philadelphia, New Orleans, and Baltimore).[38] He also programmed symphonic works by several other Americans—or, at least, by composers who lived in America. These included Jean-Pierre Oscar Comettant (1819–98), Theodore Eisfeld (1816–82), Émile Girac (d. 1869), Charles Edward Horn (1786–1849), and William Vincent Wallace (1812–65). (For a complete list of American works performed by Jullien's orchestra, see appendix IV.1.2.) This overt support of composition in the United States (by native-born as well as immigrant composers) was arguably one of the most important legacies of Jullien's tour. Jullien made this commitment explicit near the beginning of his visit by programming a "Grand American Night" concert in New York on December 29, 1853. This support by Jullien for "native" composition was welcomed by both critics and composers active in New York. The unexpected encouragement by a European conductor was in marked contrast to the attitude of the Philharmonic Society, which (in the view of many in the New York musical community in the late 1840s and early 1850s) was neglecting an important means to foster the development of musical culture in America: the encouragement and performance of compositions by American composers.

The orchestral works by Beethoven, Mendelssohn, and the American composers were an important part of the Jullien Orchestra repertory. But by far the most frequently performed orchestral composer was Louis Antoine Jullien himself, whose quadrilles, in particular, were both "fashionable" and popular. Jullien made these sectional dance compositions into descriptive and sometimes quasi-narrative pieces, full of passages that showed off his skilled soloists.[39] Richard Storrs Willis, editor of the *New York Musical World*

Edition (2011). Jullien premiered the first movement of Bristow's symphony (which was described as written "expressly for the occasion") in New York on December 29, 1853 (*New York Times*, December 29, 1853, 5). Fry's *Christmas Symphony* (also "composed expressly for these Concerts") was premiered on December 24, 1853 (*New York Times*, January 2, 1854, 5). *The Sea Voyage*, by the German-born Hohnstock, was performed by the Jullien Orchestra in Philadelphia on January 24, 1854. See *Cummings' Evening Bulletin* (Philadelphia), January 24, 1854.

38 · This information comes from programs and other notices printed in local papers. See also William Treat Upton, *William Henry Fry: American Journalist and Composer-Critic* (1954), and Frey, "Jullien in America."

39 · According to J. W. Davison, Jullien had "elevated a set of quadrilles to unusual importance. Instead of being composed of five tunes following each other irrespectively, the qua-

and Times, suggested that Jullien's practice of highlighting his soloists in these quadrilles helped to sustain interest among audience members, especially the neophytes. "In arranging his music," Willis wrote, "[Jullien] can give, in one piece … each soloist an opportunity for display, subordinating the whole orchestra to him, for the time being. The resulting effect and variety of this, in a long instrumental piece, is of course very great. It also arrests the attention, and strikes the audience powerfully."[40] The extra-musical structure and the potpourri-like compositional technique of Jullien's quadrilles also helped maintain audience interest.

The work performed most frequently was a patriotic composition that Jullien wrote expressly for the tour titled the *American Quadrille*, a potpourri of familiar American tunes, including "Our Flag Is There," "The Land of Washington," "Hail to the Chief," Foster's "Old Folks at Home," "Yankee Doodle," the "Star Spangled Banner," and "Hail Columbia." The work was performed fifty-two times, and the effect on audiences all over the country was astonishingly consistent. One critic described the effect that the *American Quadrille* had on audiences in staid Boston:

> From a seeming momentary confusion comes the air of a national piece, and "Hail to the Chief" elicits a burst of applause. Scarcely is it ended before "The Star Spangled Banner" renews the testimonials of delight, and on goes Jullien, conquering and to conquer. The audience becomes almost frantic as the guns [timpani] boom, without as well as within the Hall, and … they leap to their feet and cheer and stamp and wave hats and handkerchiefs. The enthusiasm is prodigious, and when it is at its height, a shout bursts from the lips of the musicians themselves, which is echoed by all present, and amidst a hurricane of cheers Jullien flings himself gracefully in his gilded chair and enjoys his triumph.[41]

The *American Quadrille* reveals a great deal about antebellum American patriotism and the techniques that Jullien used to exploit this feeling among his auditors. Many of Jullien's quadrilles were nationalistic in orientation and included works that celebrated England, Ireland, Hungary, the Brit-

---

drille under M. Jullien's hands becomes a sort of symphony or fantasia, where all the subjects bear strict relation to each other, where nothing is disjointed, and all is harmony and order." *London Musical World*, December 2, 1854, 791.

40 · Richard Storrs Willis, "Jullien's Strong Points," *Musical World and Times*, September 17, 1853.

41 · John Ross Dix, "Jullien: A Sketch from the Life," *Dwight's Journal of Music* 4 (November 5, 1853): 36–37.

FIGURE IV.1.3. "Jullien's *American Quadrille*," sheet music cover (New York: S. C. Jollie, 1853). Lester S. Levy Collection of Sheet Music, Johns Hopkins University.

ish navy, California, and Naples. But the *American Quadrille* was easily the most popular during this tour, and it illustrates a shrewd strategy: to attract Americans by appealing to their love of country. The cover chosen for the sheet music publication of this piece illustrates this goal, for it is a three-color image of the American flag (fig. IV.1.3). A columnist for the New Orleans *Delta* in 1854 noted without irony that a French conductor and his European orchestra had made Americans aware of their national heritage. Jullien, he wrote, "has aroused patriotic feelings which seemed to slumber amongst us. He has done more [in] fifteen minutes … than all the orators, or writers, or artists of the world…. The oldest lady in the room rose to her feet from the same impulse that inspired the boys, and in the entire audience there was but one idea,—the martial glory of our nation."[42] The American composer George Root also recognized what Jullien was up to, and approved. "Ah, Monsieur Jullien," he wrote in a review of an *American Quadrille* performance, "you have hit the right chord, and wherever you go in America, you will be sure of a welcome."[43] The orchestra's appeal to Americans was clearcut: entertainment, enjoyment, and patriotism. Jullien was a master at this, and Root's prophecy proved correct, for audiences throughout the United States welcomed Jullien and his orchestra and thrilled to performances of this patriotic composition.

---

42 · "Jullien among the Filibusters," reprinted in *Dwight's Journal of Music* 5 (May 20, 1854): 55.
43 · George Root, "Sofa Scribblings at Jullien's," *Musical World and Times*, October 22, 1853, 57.

Jullien on Tour

After two months of astonishingly successful performances in New York City, Jullien took a pared-down ensemble on the road to Boston, Baltimore, Washington, D.C., and Philadelphia before returning to New York in December 1853.[44] The orchestra's itinerary is shown in appendix IV.1.1. As in New York, audiences in these cities were small at first but grew, almost with a sense of inevitability. The audiences in Boston, for example, were initially disappointing, but by the second week Jullien was "fast getting to be the fashion," and auditors were showing up in droves.[45] In Philadelphia the audiences were "very large," and the concert on November 22 in Baltimore was "the greatest musical triumph ever achieved" in that city, with an estimated three to four thousand auditors crammed into Institute Hall.[46] Audiences in some of these cities had been prepared for concerts of this nature by visits in the 1840s by several other itinerant European ensembles, including the Saxonian Band, the Steyermark Orchestra, Josef Gungl's Band, and the Germania Musical Society, which was still performing widely in 1853. At the beginning of Jullien's visit to Boston, in fact, a local critic pointed out that the orchestra's concerts would be "similar in form and materials to those with which we have so long been familiar."[47] But Americans even in the largest cities had never before been exposed to an orchestra the size of Jullien's, nor to musicians of the caliber of his performers. Even John Sullivan Dwight was won over. "To hear the great works of the masters brought out in the full proportions of so large an orchestra, where all the parts are played by perfect masters of their instruments," he wrote in October, "is a great privilege and great lesson."[48]

After another month of performances in Manhattan (December 5, 1853–January 3, 1854), Jullien undertook a second tour, with an ensemble of thirty to thirty-five and a much more ambitious itinerary than that of the previous trip.[49] Since the tour of 1853 had succeeded beyond Jullien's wildest

---

44 · In Boston the orchestra was made up of sixty-one performers (*Boston Herald*, October 25, 1853); in Philadelphia, however, the ensemble consisted of "thirty or more" musicians (*Cummings' Evening Bulletin*, November 10, 1853).

45 · *Boston Post*, November 4, 1853.

46 · *Cummings' Evening Bulletin*, November 18, 1853; *Baltimore American and Commercial Advertiser*, November 23, 1853.

47 · *Boston Post*, October 24, 1853.

48 · *Dwight's Journal of Music* 4 (October 29, 1853): 29–30. The critic for the *Boston Post* (November 4, 1853) provided an implicit comparison between Jullien's orchestra and the Germanians. He noted that Jullien provided "such music as has never before been given in this city and such as cannot be soon expected in the future" and in the next sentence pointed out that the Germanians would give a concert in Boston the following Saturday.

49 · A complete itinerary of the 1854 tour is given in appendix IV.1.1 in this chapter.

expectations, it made sense to take the ensemble on the road again. This was not only the well-established modus operandi he followed in England, but it would also maximize exposure of his ensemble to American audiences and help him to achieve his goal, which was, he stated at the end of the tour, "to popularize music; first in France, then in England, [and] lastly in America."[50] In early January 1854, Jullien and the orchestra paid another visit to Boston, gave single concerts in New York and Newark, New Jersey, then revisited Philadelphia and Baltimore before journeying west across the mountains to Wheeling, Virginia, on the Ohio River (see fig. IV.1.4). From this point they traveled downriver by steamer to Cincinnati and Louisville and ultimately down the Mississippi to New Orleans. They generally mounted between one and four concerts in each town, except in New Orleans, where the orchestra gave thirteen concerts and one ball. After leaving the Crescent City, they spent March, April, and part of May performing in the south: Mobile, Montgomery, Savannah, Charleston, Augusta, and—via Wilmington, North Carolina—Richmond.[51] After return visits to Washington, D.C., Baltimore, and Philadelphia, they embarked on yet a third tour (see fig. IV.1.5), this time west and north to Pittsburgh, Cleveland, Buffalo, Rochester, and Albany, before returning to the East Coast (Boston) and ultimately to New York.

The orchestra's repertory was consistent throughout the tour; Jullien regularly programmed the same quadrilles, dances, chamber works, arias, and symphonic compositions that he had performed on the East Coast. He did reduce the number of pieces performed over the course of the tour: because the orchestra was changing venues (and thus audiences) frequently, it was not necessary to offer such a varied repertory as had been required in New York, for example. But Jullien still made sure to introduce audiences in each town to orchestral compositions by Beethoven and Mendelssohn. The fifth movement of the *Pastoral* Symphony (Hirtengesang. Frohe und dankbare Gefühle nach dem Sturm) became a warhorse: it was performed in Augusta, Charleston, Cincinnati, Cleveland, Louisville, Mobile, New Orleans, Pittsburgh, Richmond, Rochester, Savannah, and Wheeling. The ensemble also performed movements from at least four other Beethoven symphonies (nos. 2, 3, 8, and 5), as well as Symphony no. 5 in its entirety in New Orleans. Mendelssohn's *Midsummer Night's Dream* and his *Scottish* Symphony were likewise well represented on programs throughout the tour. Many of these

---

50 · Review of final concert on June 26 in *New York Times*, June 27, 1854.

51 · It was possible for the orchestra to travel by land, as there were completed railroads connecting the various southern cities that the ensemble visited. See *Map of All the Railroads in the United States in Operation and Progress* (1854) in the American Memory collection of the Library of Congress (http://memory.loc.gov/ammem/browse/ListSome.php?category=Maps).

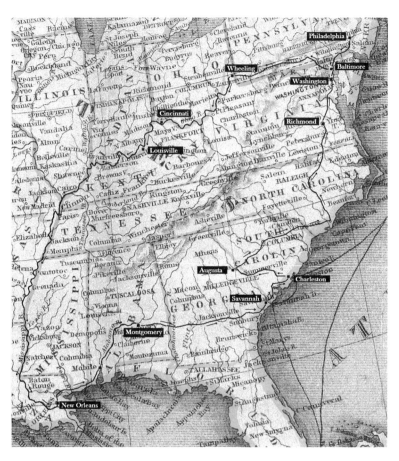

FIGURE IV.1.4.
Jullien's tour,
southern route
(January–April
1854). Detail
from *Map of the
United States, the
British Provinces,
Mexico, &c.* (New
York: J. H. Colton,
1849). David Rum-
sey Map Collec-
tion, www
.davidrumsey
.com. Used with
permission.

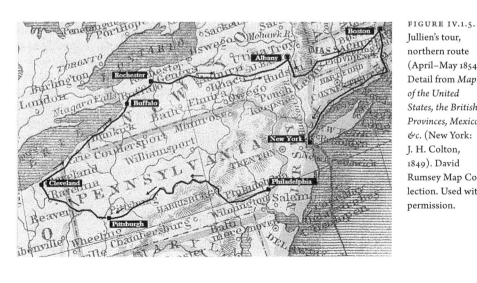

FIGURE IV.1.5.
Jullien's tour,
northern route
(April–May 1854).
Detail from *Map
of the United
States, the British
Provinces, Mexico,
&c.* (New York:
J. H. Colton,
1849). David
Rumsey Map Col-
lection. Used with
permission.

performances—especially in the southern cities that the Germanians had never visited—were local premieres.

Jullien's orchestra was much smaller on the tour than it had been initially, although only one critic—in Cleveland—complained about this.[52] But at thirty-five musicians, the orchestra was still larger than that of the Germanians, and Jullien's ensemble was probably the first non-theater orchestra that many of his auditors had ever heard. Furthermore, most of Jullien's original twenty-seven core instrumentalists remained with him for the entire tour, which guaranteed a high performance level by skilled musicians, who by this point had worked together playing much the same repertory since August. The size of the ensemble on this tour also suggests either that a handful of American performers were recruited in each city or, more likely, that six or eight of the New York musicians who had been part of the original hundred-man orchestra had agreed to participate in the tour. We know the identity of one: Ureli Corelli Hill apparently traveled with the orchestra, for his name appears on advertisements in a variety of cities. The identities of any other non-European members of the orchestra, however, are unknown.[53]

The critical reaction to the ensemble continued to be glowing. In Cincinnati, Jullien was described as "the monarch of sound—a Lord High Admiral on the ocean of melody," and a Wheeling critic portrayed him as "the presiding genius of a world of sweet sounds."[54] Louisville music lovers—some one thousand of whom packed Mozart Hall—enjoyed "by far the most superb concert of instrumental music ever given in this city," and in Savannah "the solos were exquisite—thrilling—whilst the combinations were grand and inspiring."[55]

Critics commented repeatedly on the effect of Jullien's programming, and this illustrates the other hard-to-measure but important impact of his tour: the introduction of orchestral music to large numbers of Americans. His scheme of mixing the repertory—dances, quadrilles, and patriotic compositions cheek-by-jowl with examples of more "elevated" works from the classical repertory—was clearly successful. Americans all over the country flocked to his concerts, frequently by the thousands. James Otis, writing in New York in September 1853, described this balance of entertainment and education: "He caters for the multitude nobly, but in his love for his art, and devotion to that which is great and beautiful appertaining

52 · *Cleveland Plain Dealer*, April 29, 1854.

53 · Programs published in local newspapers (as advertisements) list soloists who are scheduled to appear in the concert, and Hill's name shows up for concerts in Philadelphia, Boston, Louisville, Mobile, Washington, Pittsburgh, and Buffalo.

54 · *Musical World*, March 4, 1854, 152; *Wheeling Daily Intelligencer*, February 1, 1854.

55 ·*Louisville Daily Journal*, February 9, 1854; *Savannah Daily Morning News*, March 23, 1854.

to it, the educated musician perceives at once that Jullien is no charlatan, whose whole aim is popularity and dollars, but a high minded, deep thinking philosopher, who is bent not only on gratifying the public taste, but at the same time on *educating* and improving it."[56] In Wheeling, a critic noted that "M. Jullien has done much to elevate and refine the standard of musical taste in this country," and his counterpart in Charleston, South Carolina, wrote that "his programmes are both brilliant and varied, now awakening our emotions with the grand and martial strains of Meyerbeer's Huguenots, or a gentle symphony of the immortal Beethoven, and anon causing us to enter as it were involuntarily into all the spirit of the most voluptuous and exciting dance music in the world."[57] Critics also frequently mentioned that Jullien attracted newcomers to his concerts and lauded his efforts at educating "the masses." A critic in Louisville wrote in February that "our citizens acquired altogether new ideas last evening as to the powers which a combination of musical instruments may possess."[58] A commentator in Richmond likewise reassured potential audience members who feared that they might feel out of place at an orchestra concert, pointing out that although "a prejudice exists with some persons, who stay away from such concerts because as they imagine, they cannot understand, and therefore cannot enjoy such music," in fact, "these persons are mistaken, for while the compositions rendered night after night by Jullien are of the highest order, they cannot fail to impart pleasure to all classes who hear them. Go to Jullien's concerts all that you can."[59] To those connoisseurs who felt that letting in "the masses" somehow denigrated the performance of classical music, none other than John Sullivan Dwight himself responded, writing, "We are not of the opinion … that Jullien's triumphs in this country have done injury to the cause of music." He praised Jullien for "acquaint[ing] so many with the powers and glories of a mighty orchestra" and "educating the *musical sense*" of "multitudes."[60]

In retrospect it seems clear that the critics and auditors who were unfamiliar with the "classical" repertory were astonished by it, while those who turned up their noses at the more popular pieces were seduced by the performances. A commentator writing in the *Christian Inquirer* in September 1853 noted that people attended Jullien's concerts "not because it is the fashion, not because it is mortifying not to have heard a celebrity … but because the music is fascinating, and the whole entertainment charming. M. Jullien has

56 · "Jullien's Concerts," *Spirit of the Times*, September 3, 1853, 23, 29.
57 · *Wheeling Daily Intelligencer*, January 30, 1854; *Charleston Mercury*, March 29, 1854.
58 · *Louisville Daily Journal*, February 9, 1854.
59 · *Richmond Enquirer*, April 7, 1854.
60 · "Jullien and His Orchestra," *Dwight's Journal of Music* 5 (May 13, 1854): 40.

had the good sense to give to popular music the very best expression of which it is capable." This writer concluded, "His baton was made for democrats."[61]

Jullien's Legacy

In general, Americans bought the entire package. Jullien's showmanship and theatricality, the gilded chair, impeccable dress, kid gloves, and jeweled baton (for conducting Beethoven), along with his European celebrity, his undeniable conducting ability, and the skill of his virtuosi were irresistible to many Americans who had never attended an orchestral concert. Jullien was also savvy enough to use performances by his European ensemble to appeal to the patriotism of Americans. He did this both subtly—by commissioning and performing works by musicians living in the United States—and overtly: the *American Quadrille* was so phenomenally successful as a patriotic piece that he included it in almost 25 percent of his concerts. His dances and quadrilles appealed to the popular taste, and the skilled performances of some of the best "serious" compositions of the repertory attracted those who already knew and loved such music. Above all, the quality of performance by the ensemble, and its masterful guidance by a virtuoso conductor, seduced everyone and undoubtedly significantly raised the bar for performance of orchestral music in the United States.

The *New York Musical World and Times*, citing the *London Musical World*, reported on his arrival that a consortium of English backers had agreed to pay Jullien $15,000 per month for the six months of his American tour; the other artists were also paid handsomely (Bottesini was the highest paid, at $1,000 per month).[62] But the ensemble stayed in North America for ten months, and it is unclear whether Jullien's backers also paid salaries and transportation costs for the additional time.[63] Whether or not his tour was a financial success, however, Jullien was extremely pleased with the overall effect of his visit to America, for he had achieved his goal of "popularizing music." His orchestra had mounted more than two hundred concerts. (To put this into context, during this period the Germanians gave half that number and the

---

61 · "Jullien's Concerts," *Christian Enquirer*, September 24, 1853, 7, 51.

62 · According to the same source, three or four English gentlemen underwrote the tour with an investment of £40,000 ($200,000), which would presumably have covered players' wages and travel expenses as well as Jullien's salary. See "Julian-iana," *New York Musical World and Times*, September 3, 1853, 1.

63 · According to Vera Lawrence, Jullien's backers pocketed the proceeds from all but one of his benefit concerts (the exception was the final performance, on June 26, 1854, which attracted some forty-five thousand auditors). They had done so to "retrieve some of their losses on his tour." Lawrence, *Strong on Music*, vol. 2, 469.

340 KATHERINE K. PRESTON

Philharmonic Society mounted a grand total of four.) Furthermore, it was clear that the conductor had accurately estimated the tastes of American audiences. Richard Storrs Willis, toward the end of Jullien's visit, observed:

> Had we been told two months since that the works of Beethoven and Mendelssohn would have attracted enthusiastic applause and unanimous demands for repetition, we should have declared such a circumstance beyond the range of probability. Great is Jullien both in conceptions and execution, and greater still as an educator and refiner of universal taste. He first wins our willing sympathies by his inimitable light music ... [then] presents us with more refined and classic fare ... and in the end we are led to appreciate the surpassing excellencies of high art, developed by genius, and [are made] almost to loathe anything of an inferior character.[64]

Toward the end of his tour, Jullien announced that he intended to return to the United States to complete the work that he had started. His original plan, in fact, had been to make a series of visits, for he had assumed that true success would come only after five years of preliminary work.[65]

Perhaps if he had, the several nascent organizations devoted to the performance of American music that sprang up in New York in the mid-1850s would have survived or even thrived.[66] However, this was not to be. After the conductor returned to London in the summer of 1854, he suffered a series of serious financial setbacks, including the loss of all of his manuscript orchestral scores and parts in the fire that destroyed Covent Garden Theatre in 1856. The conductor's health was seriously affected, and he eventually suffered a nervous breakdown from which he never fully recovered. On March 14, 1860, Jullien, at the age of forty-eight, died in an asylum in Paris.[67]

Even without a return engagement to solidify his "outreach" to Americans, however, it is clear that Jullien and his orchestra had an impact on American musical culture at midcentury. The most obvious impression he made was on American composers. The conductor's open support for this

64 · *Musical World and Times*, March 4, 1854, quoted in Carse, *Life of Jullien*, 81.

65 · *Dwight's Journal of Music* 5 (July 8, 1854). During the summer of 1855, in fact, New Yorkers were eagerly awaiting a return visit by Jullien, which never materialized. See Lawrence, *Strong on Music*, vol. 2, 617.

66 · In 1854 Bristow announced his intention to establish a rival American Philharmonic Society, which apparently never came into being. Bristow also helped to found a number of other New York–based groups that promoted American music, including the New-York American Music Association (1855–58) and the Metropolitan Music Society (1859). See Lawrence, *Strong on Music*, vol. 2, 488, 749–56, and Vera Brodsky Lawrence, *Strong on Music*, vol. 3, *Repercussions: 1857–1862* (1999), 72–75, 203–5, 283–85.

67 · See Carse, *Life of Jullien*, 87–97.

small and struggling band of musicians gave them a much-needed dose of self-confidence. According to Vera Lawrence, the "most indebted to Jullien were the performance-starved American composers William Henry Fry and George Frederick Bristow, whose orchestral works Jullien had welcomed with open arms, adopting them into his repertory and performing them repeatedly in New York and on tour."[68] The most tangible effect, however, was Jullien's role as the catalyst for the angry public debate about support for American composition that erupted into the open after simmering beneath the surface in New York for almost a decade prior to his arrival. As music historian John Tasker Howard wrote, Jullien gave American composers "a hearing and at the same time crystallized the beginning of a controversy that has not yet ended"; in the 1850s, Howard continued, "a few of our composers began to be conscious of their nationality, and to feel slighted over the recognition they were not receiving."[69] Jullien's support for Bristow is a case in point. According to Delmer Rogers, Jullien's recognition represented "one of the few times in [Bristow's] life [that] ... he received unsolicited encouragement as a composer."[70] And the support continued after Jullien returned to Europe, for shortly after he left the United States the conductor wrote to Bristow, congratulating him on the success that his compositions were receiving in England and reminding him that he was "waiting for your Symphony in F# minor [which] you can send at your earliest convenience."[71] Furthermore—perhaps because of the public contretemps in which he had participated, or perhaps because of the success he saw in the reception of American-themed compositions performed by Jullien's orchestra—Bristow subsequently turned his compositional attention increasingly away from what Fry called the "classical style" and toward compositions (such as his opera *Rip van Winkle*) that were more clearly identifiable as Americanist in orientation.

Less quantifiable—but no less significant—is the impact that Jullien and his orchestra had on the American concertgoing public. Jullien and his orchestra enticed tens of thousands of Americans into the concert hall, where many of them heard for the first time the amazing sounds that could be pro-

68 · Lawrence, *Strong on Music*, vol. 2, 368.

69 · John Tasker Howard, *Our American Music* (1965), 224–25.

70 · Delmer Dalzell Rogers, "Nineteenth-Century Music in New York City as Reflected in the Career of George Frederick Bristow" (Ph. D. diss., 1967), 117, and *New York Times*, January 9, 1856.

71 · ALS [Jullien, via his secretary] to Bristow, December 14, 1854, Bristow Manuscript Collection, in the possession of Ms. Marion Edwards of East Hampton, Long Island. Ms. Edwards is the niece of Bristow's granddaughter, and I thank her for allowing me access to some of the materials in this collection. In 2010 the collection was acquired by the New York Public Library, where it is now part of the George Bristow Collection.

duced by a combination of instruments played by skilled and practiced musicians. Perhaps this exposure encouraged some Americans to think about music more seriously, to undertake the study of an instrument, or to encourage their children to do so. Although there was no sudden interest in establishing community orchestras in American towns following Jullien's visit, there was a remarkable growth in the number of local brass bands at mid-century. Certainly both the important role of bands in the Civil War and the increased numbers of German musicians coming to America after the late 1840s were catalysts for the American brass-band movement at midcentury. But Americans' newfound interest in the power of instrumental music, kindled perhaps by Jullien's performances, also played a role in this important development, as young and old alike turned their attention to a different — but available — type of performing ensemble. Finally, the techniques that Jullien used in choosing his repertory (combining "light" compositions with those that are "more elevated") and the goals that he articulated (to entertain and to educate) were successfully replicated by later conductors active in America, not the least of whom was Theodore Thomas, who learned the effectiveness of the technique under the baton of the master.

Whatever the long-term tangible or intangible effects of Louis Jullien's visit, there is no question that he was a force to be reckoned with in mid-century America. It is appropriate that one of Jullien's contemporaries, the American composer and critic William Henry Fry, should have the final word. He succinctly summarized Jullien's visit with the immediacy of someone who was there: "To say that M. Jullien has done more than any one in this country for music of a high order, is to say very little: he has done more than all others put together. He has given us all kinds of music, never wanting in perception as to its interpretation.... He has laid [High Art] before the people [and] he has opened the door of the exclusive concert-room to tens and twenties of thousands who would never have entered it otherwise."[72]

72 · *New-York Daily Tribune*, May 26, 1854, 7.

APPENDIX IV.1.1. *Jullien's Itinerary, 1853–54*

Dates	Location	Venue	Number of Concerts
1853			
Aug. 29–Sept. 24	New York City	Castle Garden	24[a]
Sept. 26–Oct. 21	New York City	Metropolitan Hall	25[b]
Oct. 24–Nov. 6	Boston	Boston Music Hall	13[c]
Nov. 8	New York City	Metropolitan Hall	1
Nov. 9–21	Philadelphia	Concert Hall, Chestnut Street	11
Nov. 22–23	Baltimore	Hall of the Maryland Institute	2
Nov. 24–26	Washington, DC	National Theatre	3
Nov. 28–30	Baltimore	Hall of the Maryland Institute	3
Dec. 1–3	Philadelphia	Concert Hall	3
Dec. 5–Jan. 3	New York City	Metropolitan Hall	26
1854			
Jan. 5–13	Boston	Music Hall	9[d]
Jan. 18	New York	Niblo's Theatre	1[e]
Jan. 19	Newark, NJ	Newark Theatre	1
First Extended Tour			
Jan. 20–24	Philadelphia	Concert Hall, Chestnut St.	4
Jan. 25–28	Baltimore	Hall of the Maryland Institute	4
Jan. 30	Wheeling, VA	Washington Hall	1
Feb. 2–6	Cincinnati	Smith and Nixon's Hall	4
Feb. 8–10	Louisville	Mozart Hall	3
Feb. 18	Steamer *Eclipse*	Concert on board	1
Feb. 20–26; Mar. 2–4, 6, 8, 10, 11	New Orleans	Odd Fellows' Hall	13
Mar. 9	New Orleans	Odd Fellows' Hall	Ball[f]
Mar. 13–15	Mobile	Odd Fellows' Hall	3
Mar. 18–20	Montgomery, AL?	?	3?[g]
Mar. 22–24	Savannah, Georgia	Athenaeum	3
Mar. 27–29	Charleston, SC	Military Hall	3
Mar. 30	Augusta, Georgia	Concert Hall	1
Apr. 3–7	Richmond, Virginia	Metropolitan Hall	4
Apr. 10–11	Washington, DC	National Theatre	2
Apr. 12–13	Baltimore	Hall of the Maryland Institute	2
Second Extended Tour			
1854			
Apr. 14–17	Philadelphia	Concert Hall, Chestnut Street	3
Apr. 19–20	Pittsburgh	Masonic Hall	2
Apr. 21–27	?	?	?[h]
Apr. 28	Cleveland	Melodeon Hall	1
Apr. 29–May1	Buffalo	Eagle Street Theatre	2
May 2	Rochester	Corinthian Hall	1

APPENDIX IV.1.1. *(continued)*

Dates	Location	Venue	Number of Concerts
May 4	Albany	Association Hall	1
May 8–12	Boston	Music Hall	4
Final Season in New York; Musical Congress			
May 15–June 5	New York City	Castle Garden	18
June 15–26	New York City	Musical Congress (Crystal Palace)	11
		TOTAL	213 (approximate)

a. Total includes one benefit concert on Sunday, September 11.

b. Total includes two Sunday "sacred concerts," October 2 and October 9.

c. Includes one "sacred concert" on Sunday, November 6.

d. Total includes two performances (matinee and evening) on Friday, January 13.

e. "Grand Concert" was given in lieu of the advertised *Grand bal paré*, which could not occur because of the destruction of Metropolitan Hall by fire on January 9, 1854.

f. Ball was postponed from February 28 because a gallery of the New Orleans Theatre collapsed on February 27, killing several individuals and closing the theater.

g. I have been unable to locate any extant newspapers from Montgomery, Alabama, for this week, but I assume that the company made a stop in the Alabama capital en route to Savannah. Supporting this assumption is an announcement in the *New Orleans Daily Picayune* (March 6, 1854), noting that the orchestra would not be able to extend its season there because the ensemble had engagements in Mobile and Montgomery, starting on March 13 and 18, respectively.

h. According to an advertisement, the concerts in Pittsburgh were the 188th and 189th of the tour. The concert in Cleveland was described as the 191st. Where the troupe might have performed between Pittsburgh and Cleveland, however, is unknown. The ensemble's manager, William Brough, arrived in Cleveland on Saturday, April 22. On the other hand, the concert in Rochester on May 2 was advertised as the 200th concert of the tour, which is clearly inaccurate. See *Pittsburgh Gazette*, April 19, 1854; *Daily Cleveland Herald*, April 22, 1854; and *Rochester Daily American*, April 29, 1854.

APPENDIX IV.1.2. *Performances of Works by American Composers by Jullien's Orchestra during Its American Tour*

Performances of works by composers either living in the United States during the period of Jullien's visit (August 1853–June 1854) or generally considered to be American (e.g., Charles Horn). Included are both native-born composers and Europeans who were resident in the United States around midcentury, whether or not they remained permanently in America. The list may be incomplete because there are no known extant programs for some of the Jullien Orchestra concerts.

BRISTOW, GEORGE FREDERICK (1825–98) (b. New York City)

Sinfonia (Symphony no. 1 in E-flat) (1848)

Minuet: New York: Oct. 12, 14, Dec. 8, 19, 28, 29, 1853; May 18, 1854; Boston: Nov. 4, 1853; Philadelphia: Dec. 3, 1854; Louisville: Feb. 10, 1854; New Orleans: Mar. 6, 1854

Complete work: Philadelphia: Nov. 21, 1853

Symphony no. 2 (*The Jullien*) (1853) (commissioned by Jullien)

Allegro moderato (recte Allegro appassionato) (first movement): New York: Dec. 29 (premiere), Dec. 31, 1853

Andante (recte Allegretto) (second movement): New York: May 24 (premiere), May 26, 31, 1854

COMETTANT, JEAN-PIERRE OSCAR (1819–98) (b. France; lived in United States 1852–55)

Galop du Bal Masque
New York: Oct. 10, 1853

New Galop
New York: May 23, 1854

Exhibition Galop
New York: Oct. 11, 12, 13, 14, 15, 17, 1853; Philadelphia: Nov. 18, 1853; Boston: Nov. 5, 1853

EISFELD, THEODORE (1816–82) (b. Germany; resided in United States 1848–66)

Romance Dramatique (also *Romanza and Dramatic Scena*) (solo for cornet-à-pistons); performed by Herbert Koenig

New York: Dec. 30, 1853; Jan. 2, 1854; Boston: Jan. 9, 1854

FOSTER, STEPHEN (1826–64) (b. Lawrenceville, PA)

"Old Folks at Home" (song) (1851)
Zerr sang this song numerous times as an encore

FRY, WILLIAM HENRY (1813–64) (b. Philadelphia)

A Day in the Country (1853)
New York: Sept. 20, 21, 24, 30, Oct. 3, 5, Dec. 11, 17, 19, 29, 1853; May 23, 1854; Boston: Oct. 29, 1853; Philadelphia: Nov. 12, 1853; Baltimore: Nov. 28, 1853

The Breaking Heart (1852) (either complete or individual movements)
Boston: Nov. 1, 3, 5, 1853; Philadelphia: Nov. 14, 18, Dec. 1, 1853; New York: Dec. 7, 10, 16, 29, 1853; May 17, 20, 30, June 19, 1854; New Orleans: Feb. 25, 1854

Childe Harold (symphony) (1854) (commissioned by Jullien)
New York: June 1, 1854 (premiere)

Christmas Symphony (1853) (commissioned by Jullien)
New York: Christmas Eve, 1853 (premiere); Dec. 27, 28, 31, 1853; Jan. 2, 1854; Boston: Jan. 12, 1854; Philadelphia: Jan. 21, 24, 1854; Baltimore: Jan. 28, 1854

GIRAC, ÉMILE (d. 1869) (b. France; emigrated to United States in early 1850s)

Military Symphony: The Life of a Hero (*The Washington Symphony*): Allegro finale
New York: Dec. 30, 1854

HOHNSTOCK, KARL (1828–89) (b. Germany; in United States 1848–60)

Sea Voyage (symphony) (commissioned by Jullien)
Philadelphia: Jan. 24, 1854

HORN, CHARLES EDWARD (1786–1849) (b. England; lived in United States 1827–30, 1832–42, 1847–49)

"I've Been Roaming" (song)
Sung thirty-two times by Zerr

WALLACE, WILLIAM VINCENT (1812–65) (b. Ireland; in United States 1841–44, 1850–54?, naturalized U.S. citizen 1854)

Maritana (1845)

Overture: New York: Dec. 15, 24, 30, 1853; May 23, 24, 27, June 3, 1854

"Scenes That Are Brightest" (aria): New York: May 24, 27, June 3, 17, 1854
Unidentified aria (male): New York: June 3, 1854

Cracovienne and Variations (Piano duo), performed by M/M Wallace
New York: June 19, 20, 21, 1854

Grand Duo for Two Pianos, on a romance from the opera *L'éclair* (Halévy)
New York: June 3, 15, 16, 1854

Romanza (cornet solo) (commissioned by Jullien, 1853); performed by Koenig
New York: Dec. 15 (premiere), 19, 24, 30, 1853; Boston: Jan. 10, 1854

Grand Polka de Concert, with orchestral accompaniment; performed by Mr. Wallace
New York: June 3, 1854

"The Flag of Our Union" national song
New York: June 3, 1854

"Happy Birdling" (song)
New York: May 25, 29, 30, 1854

[IV.2] Ureli Corelli Hill

An American Musician's European Travels and the Creation of the New York Philharmonic

BARBARA HAWS

On December 7, 1842, the Philharmonic Society of New York played its first concert.[1] The conductor of the first work, Beethoven's Fifth Symphony, was violinist Ureli Corelli Hill (1805?–75), who had organized the new orchestra and had been elected president of the society. The review of the concert in the *Albion* praised the "precision and care" with which the symphony was performed and complimented Hill, along with the conductors of the other pieces on the program, stating that they "did their duty carefully and well."[2]

Seven years before this concert, Ureli Corelli Hill had set out from New York on a "greatly wished for voyage across the Atlantic to Europe."[3] Hill, according to the *New York Evening Star* had the distinction of being "the first *American Musician* who has gone to Europe solely with the view of improvement in his profession." The newspaper continued: "It augurs well for the interests of the musical art to see its professors braving the dangers of the Atlantic, to obtain instruction from the great masters of Europe.... A similar course by the professors of the sister art of painting, has tended to raise that

I would like to thank Richard Wandel for his invaluable help in transcribing the U. C. Hill diary, Wolfram Boder for insights into the musical life of Kassel at the time of Hill's visit, and Gabe Smith for help with the orchestra diagrams.

1 · The Philharmonic of 1842 was the third New York orchestra to bear that name, being successor to the Philharmonics of 1799–1816 and of 1824–27. See Howard Shanet, *Philharmonic: A History of New York's Orchestra* (1975), 63–68. For the program of the first Philharmonic concert, see chapter V.3 in this volume.

2 · *Albion,* December 10, 1842, 591; quoted in Shanet, *Philharmonic*, 89.

3 · U. C. Hill, Diary, 1835–37 (manuscript), New York Philharmonic Archives, Box 500-01-01 ["Hill Diary"], page 4. The page numbering for the Hill diary was applied by me and reflects Hill's own order: pages 1 through 112 read left to right, beginning with the inside cover; then for unknown reasons Hill turned the diary upside down and took up writing from the back of the notebook forward; these pages are 113 [R] through 153 [R]. Finally, pages 154 through 170 are loose oversized sheets.

art to its present pre-emmence [*sic*] among us."[4] Hill left New York, accompanied by his wife, on June 10, 1835, and returned in the spring of 1837. He began his journey in London, traveled through Rotterdam to Kassel then Düsseldorf, back to London, and ended his trip in Paris. Among his many activities during the course of his journey, he took violin lessons from Louis Spohr in Kassel, played in the Drury Lane Theatre orchestra in London, and was invited by Felix Mendelssohn to participate in the orchestra at the 1836 Rhine Valley Music Festival in Düsseldorf.

While on his European journey, Hill kept a diary of his experiences and impressions, 154 bound pages plus additional notes written on concert programs and oversize loose-leaf pages.[5] Hill's diary documents concerts he attended, people he met, lessons he took, and orchestras he played in, in addition to the cost of food, lodging, travel, and concert tickets. The diary is a rich and illuminating American eyewitness account of European musical life in the mid-1830s, the time just preceding the major emigration of European, principally German, musicians to the United States after the upheavals of 1848.

U. C. Hill was at least a third-generation American, born in 1805 probably in Hartford, Connecticut. He was one of two sons of Uri K. Hill (1780–1844); the other was the well-known comedian and actor George Handel "Yankee" (1809–49) Hill.[6] Their grandfather, Frederick, was a lawyer and a fifer in the Revolutionary army. Hill's father, a music teacher and composer, was probably U. C.'s first violin teacher—a New York newspaper ad in 1810 billed Uri K. as the "first performer on violin in America."[7] The first record of U. C. Hill on the New York music scene is as a violinist in the "second" Philharmonic (1824–27) and as conductor of the Sacred Music Society, which gave the New York premiere of the complete *Messiah* under Hill's direction in 1831. By the time he set out for Europe, Hill was well known around New York as a violinist, teacher, chamber music player, and tireless concert organizer.

One of Hill's primary objectives on his journey was to improve his violin playing and musicianship by studying with Louis Spohr (1784–1859), the famous German violinist and composer. Spohr was Kapellmeister in the German principality of Kassel, and Hill took forty-six violin lessons with him at

4 · *New York Evening Star*, December 2, 1836.

5 · The Hill diary was acquired by Harold Lineback of St. Louis sometime in the 1940s. Lineback would not let scholars study the diary or allow any of its contents to be published. In 2001 the New York Philharmonic acquired Lineback's entire music collection, including the diary. It is now in the archives of the New York Philharmonic.

6 · Robert Stevenson and Betty Bandel, "Hill, Ureli Corelli," *The New Grove Dictionary of American Music* (1986).

7 · Ibid., 387.

$1 per lesson. The first lesson was on August 10, 1835, and Hill recorded the experience carefully in his diary:

> I attended and play'd him a piece. He play'd an accompaniment on his violin. He told me my left hand was excellent and very just in the intonation. My bow hand was good but my bow required more judicious distribution and it required a little more of a good school. I told him I was aware of it and had come all the way from America for this purpose.... Spohr look'd upon it as a very novel thing that a person should come from America, such a great distance, to him. He seem'd rather flattered and pleased by the idea. He might indeed consider it novel, as I am the first American artist in musick that ever undertook it. Had we had a good school for musick at home it would have saved me this great undertaking.[8]

In addition to violin lessons with Spohr, Hill also studied composition in Kassel with Moritz Hauptmann.[9]

Before he arrived in Kassel, Hill had already heard some of the greatest artists of the time perform during his brief sojourn in London. On July 3 he heard his first *Fidelio* at Covent Garden with none other than Maria Garcia Malibran singing the title role. "I shall never forget the effect produced by the music, the singing, and acting of Mad. Malibran which was incomparably excellent," he wrote in his diary. "Particularly where she as Fidelio makes herself known in the prison to her husband and the goaler [*sic*] etc. it was beyond measure effective. I tho't they would tear the house down which (by the by was cram'd) 800 £ being the receipts."[10] Also in London, Hill attended a concert by Malibran's husband, the Belgian violinist Charles de Bériot (1802–70) in the concert room at the King's Theatre. He confessed in his diary to being more impressed by Bériot's playing than by the violinist's stage presence:

> The violin being my favorite instrument, it was natural I should feel great interest in hearing De Beriot. Here I heard, for the first time, a man who is considered in Europe a first rate violinist, and by many is ranked the best. I perceived he was the greatest favorite in the concert. I was entirely disappointed in his appearance, it was most unbecoming. He look'd more like a modest Yankie than a Frenchman. He is slim, rather thin visage, dark eyes, light complexion, about 5 feet 9 ½ inches, 35 years old. He produces more sensation than any one has of late—Paganini excepted.... I heard him to my

---

8 · Hill, Diary, 161 [R].
9 · Moritz Hauptmann (1792–1868), composer, theorist, and teacher, was later appointed cantor of the Thomasschule in Leipzig on the recommendation of Spohr and Mendelssohn.
10 · Hill, Diary, 26.

hearts content. He performed three times in this concert. His 1st piece was an Adagio and Rondo Russe which he had play'd at the last spring Philharmonic concert. His tone is full, rich and thrilling. His style was melting, touching and charming. He made many a wet eye in his cantabile.[11]

During the course of his journey, Hill heard and also played in a wide variety of orchestras. The orchestra at the King's Theatre in London, where he heard Rossini's *La gazza ladra* in July 1835, impressed him a great deal in comparison with what he was used to in New York: "I attended with my wife the King's Theatre or Italian Opera.... Sometimes when all were playing it was like a whisper it was so piano. Each part could be heard distinctly. All the parts appeared properly balanced, a thing so rarely met with in our orchestras."[12]

On the other hand, the Drury Lane Theatre orchestra, which Hill joined as third viola when he returned to London in 1836, did not impress Hill at all. He played in the orchestra for eight months, and the experience sharpened his understanding of what made some orchestras better and others much worse. The descriptions in the diary are scathing: "Most of the principal instruments execute their solos in the orchestra in a very bad form. The violins come in out of time in the most careless manner. In fact through the whole orchestra the pianissimos are very much neglected as well as all other marks of expression. I really doubt sometimes whether they understand all the marks. In fact they play mechanically, that is they play as if they were mercenaries and not musicians with souls for their occupations."[13]

The orchestra at the Paris Concerts du Conservatoire was another matter altogether. On March 5, 1837, Hill attended a *Concert Extraordinaire* led by F. A. Habeneck that included works by Beethoven, Mozart, Méhul, and Weber. His description shows how, by the later stages of his trip, Hill had become a sophisticated critic of orchestral performance practices. Impressed though he was by what was widely acknowledged as the world's best orchestra, he still found room for improvement: "The playing of the [London] Philharmonic is nothing to compare to the Conservatoire at Paris, nor is there its superior in the world. The Academie Royal [de Musique] beats the Philharmonic. There were nearly 40 violins. Their united pianissimo when all playing was like a whisper. There were not violas enough, 8 or 10. This fault exists in almost all orchestras in the world. Some of the wind at times were a little too loud. It is, I think, the best band I ever heard. This alone was worth a voyage across the Atlantic."[14]

11 · Ibid., 33.
12 · Ibid., 28.
13 · Ibid., 75.
14 · Notes written on Hill's loose concert program, March 5, 1837.

Hill's diary contains a great deal of information about European orchestras in the 1830s, but, if we read between the lines, it can also tell us something about early nineteenth-century American orchestras. In particular, how similar was the 1842 New York Philharmonic to the orchestras that Hill encountered in Europe? In what respects did it differ from those European orchestras? Because Hill frequently compared his European experiences to his experiences at home, we can make inferences about the American music scene and about the motivations and models that lay behind the foundation of the New York Philharmonic.

Three themes run side by side through Hill's diary: (1) his documentation of the number of musicians in European orchestras and how the players were arrayed on stage or in the pit; (2) his judgments about the overall quality of European orchestras and their individual players; and (3) his comparison of European with American performers and practices. In addition to documenting the number and placement of the musicians, Hill writes often about the conductor's role and how he communicates with the musicians. It is clear that in 1830s Europe, the role of the conductor was not fixed or standardized even within a single country.

Hill's European Orchestras

Through Hill's descriptions we are able to compare several very different European orchestras: the Kassel orchestra of Louis Spohr, Mendelssohn's festival orchestra in Düsseldorf, London's Drury Lane Theatre orchestra as well as the Royal Philharmonic, and, in Paris, the orchestras of Philippe Musard and the Concerts du Conservatoire.

As a student of Spohr, Hill played in the Kapellmeister's orchestra, "a right which only his pupils have."[15] This gave him the opportunity to make detailed observations about the number of musicians and their proportions in the Kassel Kapelle: "The orchestra is efficient and large, it is composed of about 60 performers, viz. 16 violins, 8 firsts, 8 2nds, 4 violas, contra basses 3, violoncellos 3, clarinettes 3, flautos 3, faggotti 3, oboes 2, corni 4, trumpets 3, trombones 3, kettledrums or tympani, bass drum, cymballs, small drum and tryangles. They have, when required, an additional 6 which they call in at

---

15 · In German Kapellen, advanced students of Kapelle members were often enrolled as *Accessisten*, young musicians who played for free while they waited for a regular position to come open. See Christoph-Hellmut Mahling, "The Origin and Social Status of the Court Orchestral Musician in the 18th and Early 19th Century in Germany," in *The Social Status of the Professional Musician*, ed. W. Salmen (1983), 242–43.

pleasure, mostly for strengthening the string'd instruments."[16] Hill also comments on the seating plan and performance practices of Spohr's orchestra, both in the opera house and in concert:

> The way Spohr has disposed his orchestra [for opera] is very good. He himself is in the center with his short stick to make the time always by motion, not noise. His string'd instruments are all together, the 1st violoncello player Mr. Housemann [Nikolaus Hasemann (1788–1842)] directly at his right side, a little back the other violoncellos and double basses in his rear, the 1st violins with Mr. Weile [Adolf Wiele (1794–1845 or 1853)] and Baldwein [Johann Christoph Baldewein (1784–1848)] on the 1st desk very near him to his left, the other 1st violins are strung out next to the pit. The second violins are next strung out in the same manner. The leader of the second violins comes up even with the 1st violin stand to his left, still farther to his left come the altos [violas], 4 deep from the stage. 2 string instruments play from one stand. In the rear again of the altos to his extreme left comes the bass drum, side drum, cymballs and tryangles, so it will be observed that all his string'd instruments are together. To his right he has his wind instruments, the oboes, clarinets and flutes nearest him. After the bassoons, horns, trumpets, trombones and last the kettle drums on his extreme right. All facing him so he may look any one of them in the face.[17]

Figure IV.2.1 shows the configuration that Hill describes. "Violoncellos and double basses in his rear" seems to contradict the statement that the conductor could "look any one of them in the face," but perhaps Hill means that when Spohr turned away from the stage to cue the orchestra, he would face all the musicians, thanks to his central position.[18]

For a concert in Kassel that included a performance of Haydn's *The Seasons*, Hill describes a different arrangement of Spohr's orchestra, now on the stage (see fig. IV.2.2): "The singers were placed in the front in 2 sloping lines from the centre. The position of the orchestra was thus the conductor Spohr in centre of the front by the piano, which was beside him, the basses all in the centre behind him the 1st violins a little farther forward to the right hand of the basses. The 2nd violins in the same position to their left. The altos little to the right, rear of the basses. The clarinetts, flutes, horns, and bassoons in a line behind the strings and the heavy brass trombones, trumpets, drums, etc.

16 · Hill, Diary, 164 [loose leaf].
17 · Ibid. By "pit" Hill means the parterre, where the audience sat or stood.
18 · I thank Kurt Masur for this insight.

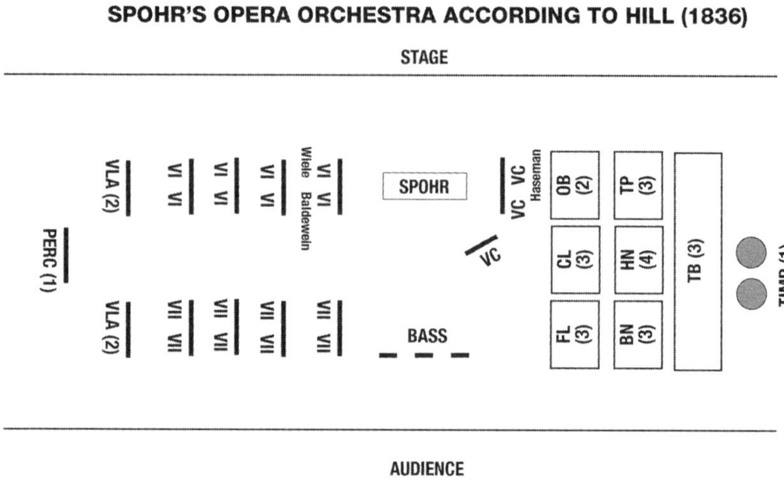

SPOHR'S OPERA ORCHESTRA ACCORDING TO HILL (1836)

STAGE

AUDIENCE

FIGURE IV.2.1. Spohr's opera orchestra at Kassel, 1836, according to Hill.

still further in the rear."[19] Hill's comment that the basses are "behind" Spohr suggests that the conductor may have faced the audience rather than the orchestra, a common practice in the early nineteenth century.[20]

At Bériot's concert in London with the Philharmonic Society, Hill noted the size of the orchestra, which was larger than Spohr's: "The numbers are 14 1st violins, 12 seconds, 8 violas (too small in every orchestra—should be as many as there are first violins), 8 cellos, 6 double basses, 2 flutes, 2 oboes, 2 clarinetts, 2 bassoons, 4 horns, 2 trumpets, sometimes 3, 3 trombones and drums, with small drums, cymballs, triangles etc. etc. It will number 70 about."[21] Hill's notion about the size of the viola section is unusual. No European orchestra of the time had equal numbers of violas and first violins.[22] The New York Philharmonic, in its first season, counted six violas against eleven first violins, a more usual proportion.[23]

After his time in Kassel, Hill traveled next to Düsseldorf, arriving on May 19, 1836. He introduced himself to Felix Mendelssohn, who had recently resigned as Music Director of the city but had returned to lead the annual

19 · Hill, Diary, 131 [R].

20 · See Daniel J. Koury, *Orchestral Performances in the Nineteenth Century: Size, Proportions, and Seating* (1986), 79–80.

21 · Hill, Diary, 39.

22 · See *The Opera Orchestra in 18th- and 19th-Century Europe I: The Orchestra in Society*, ed. N. M. Jensen and F. Piperno (2008), especially pp. 48–49 (Italy), 93–95 (Vienna), 232 (Paris), 351 (Dresden), 432–33 (Madrid), 590–93 (Copenhagen).

23 · Shanet, *Philharmonic*, 91.

SPOHR'S CONCERT ORCHESTRA WITH CHORUS ACCORDING TO HILL (1836)

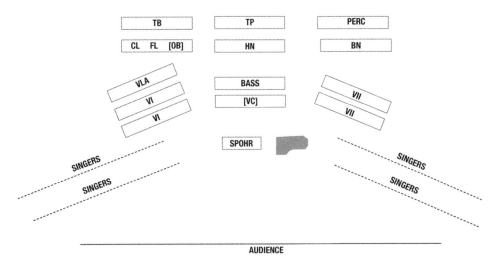

FIGURE IV.2.2. Spohr's concert orchestra with chorus at Kassel, 1836, according to Hill.

Rhine Valley Music Festival. Hill found Mendelssohn to be "a very affable man, about 40 years old, speaking perfect English," and was "invited to assist at his performances" at the Festival, where Mendelssohn was premiering his oratorio *St. Paul.*[24] "We rehearsed 12 hours a day," Hill wrote in his diary. He went on to give detailed and valuable information about arrangements and performance practices:

> There were to be two grand performances—the 1st day was Paulus—the following day Monday, the performance was composed of the Sinfonie No. 9 in D minor of Beethoven.... There were 366 vocal performers and 174 instrumental, 74 violins alone, total 539. The orchestra came in with the chords when accompanying the recitative like one instrument. There was no organ. The chorus director had a piano-forte. I will give a little idea of the situation of the performers in the orchestra. The singers were all directly in front. Mr. Mendelssohn was in the centre of the front. The ladies in the 1st lines—director in centre of the front—chorus director with his piano near the front—the solo singers front—all the chorus singers were very nearly on a level area. The instruments were all in the rear of the singers. Each platform was put at an elevation of perhaps 10 inches, so that in the very rear the heads of the wind instruments come near the ceiling. There was a line of violins and

contra basses running right up thro' the centre of the orchestra. The 3 kettle drums in the centre of the very rear. Some double basses were near the two back corners of the orchestra. The contra fagotto and all the brass instruments were all in the very rear. The fagotto and flutes, clarionetts, etc. back of the violins. The violins were directly back of the singers. The instrumental leader was in the centre. The 1st violins to his right, the 2nd to his left, the tenors [violas] were near the violins, a little to the right of the centre etc. etc.[25]

The diagram in figure IV.2.3 shows the approximate layout of Mendelssohn's orchestra according to this report. Hill went on to describe the setting and the audience: "This performance was given in a spacious hall in the Court Gardens, which are more extensive and beautiful than anything of the kind to be found about London. Tickets were sold at $3.00 a piece. One of the tickets admitted to the 2 days and the last rehearsal, which was full—or, tickets could be had to admit to the last rehearsal alone or either of the performances separate. The room was completely filled in every part. But a small proportion of the musicians are paid for services. A great number that come from a distance have their traveling expenses paid, etc."[26]

Hill took advantage of his access to Mendelssohn to suggest an idea for a new composition: "While in Germany I spoke to Mendelssohn about writing on an American subject. He liked the idea."[27] Whether at this time the "affable" composer was answering out of politeness or whether Mendelssohn actually contemplated a work with an American theme is not known, although there is a good chance that he was genuinely interested, as seen in his apologetic rejection of the Philharmonic's 1845 invitation to lead a music festival in New York. His warm reply of regret and gratitude to Hill was confirmed in a letter to his brother Paul, whom he told of how "flattered" he was to have received the invitation.[28]

Following his return to London in 1836, Hill joined the orchestra at Drury Lane Theater, an ensemble for which he had nothing but criticism:

The "Tout Ensembles" is bad in this orchestra. They don't blend well together. The solo instruments often botch their parts. The movements [tempos] are often very badly judged. [Thomas S.] Cooke's baton seems to bother him. It seems to confuse him and others. His baton is about 12 inches long. He has a very faulty way of following singers, when they should be taught by him at the rehearsals to follow his true time and that of the orchestra. But his

25 · Ibid., 153 [R].
26 · Ibid.
27 · Ibid., 45.
28 · Quoted in Shanet, *Philharmonic*, 429–30.

MENDELSSOHN'S FESTIVAL ORCHESTRA ACCORDING TO HILL (1836)

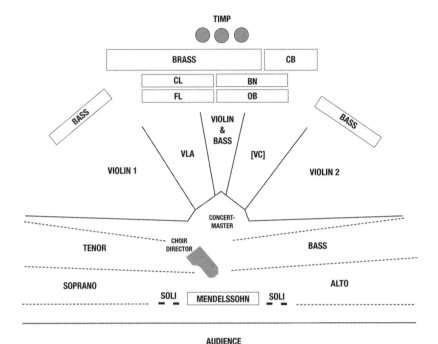

FIGURE IV.2.3. Mendelssohn's festival orchestra for *St. Paul*, Düsseldorf, 1836, according to Hill.

manner is very much to allow bad singers and musicians their own whims in time, by which consequence the ensemble of the orchestra is ever destroyed and the music is marred. He seems to lack decision not knowing who to follow, or he seems to lack stamina to take a stand of his own. Like most of the English, he permits singers to take a start and the orchestra runs after.[29]

In Paris, on the other hand, where Hill traveled in spring, 1837, he found the standard of performance much higher than that at Drury Lane. Even before he heard the renowned orchestra at the Conservatoire, he attended Musard's concerts in the Rue Neuve Vivienne. He noted the fine playing of the musicians, the mixed repertory, and the low price of admission. He was also impressed by how well paid the musicians were:

> The room was very tastefully decorated and his band was composed of 90 musicians.... Colinet was the flageolet and many of the instruments were very well play'd. Musard—conductor, composer, etc. The pistons trumpet

was [played] very well. They performed overtures and had a small chorus and an organ with them. Also they play'd Cotillions and Quadrilles. Musard gets about £700 per annum by this, and some of the principal performers receive 2 and 300 pounds per annum. They play every night all the year round. There [are] other establishments similar to this, but I believe not so good. These sort of amusements took their origin from the miserable pay musicians rec'd at the theatres. Good performers not getting more than 40 pounds per annum in the *best* theatres such as some of the principal instruments. This place is thronged every evening and they play really so well that they might well shame the Drury Lane Band. The precision and ensemble was really fine and all the marks well observed and they went like machinery together. The price of admission *is only one franc*.[30]

Comparisons between the United States and Europe

We can compare what Hill says in his diary about European orchestras with what we know about the initial composition and organization of the 1842 New York Philharmonic. The total number of players that Hill was able to muster in New York could not match what he had seen abroad (except for Drury Lane, which was a theater rather than a concert orchestra). The Philharmonic's founding constitution limited the number of members to seventy "professors of music" with the orchestral forces specifically defined, totaling fifty-three players. The remaining seventeen members, according to the constitution, were "pianists and professors of instruments not specified," who, like the members of Spohr's orchestra, could be called upon to fill in at any concert. One of the most significant departures of the 1842 Philharmonic from its predecessor New York orchestras was the insistence on regular rehearsals, two hours in length on alternate Saturday afternoons. Not only were the members required by the constitution to appear at these rehearsals, but they were penalized for not attending. This emphasis on rehearsal may have come from Hill's memory of Spohr's rehearsal schedule in Kassel. It might also be attributed to Hill's exposure to a high standard of ensemble playing in the best European orchestras—or from his dismay at the low standard in the

30 · Ibid., 111–12. Musard's income of £700 per year is equivalent to roughly £36,600 or $57,000 in modern (2010) money, according to the National Archives, "Currency Converter," www .nationalarchives.gov.uk/currency/. On the good wages that Musard paid his musicians in comparison to the Opéra and other Paris theaters, see Antoine Elwart, "Quelques mots sur la position des musiciens d'orchestre de nos trois scenes lyriques," *Revue et Gazette Musicale,* February 14, 1839, 53; quoted in John Spitzer, "The Entrepreneur-Conductors and Their Orchestras," *Nineteenth-Century Music Review* 5 (2008): 5–6.

Drury Lane orchestra, which almost never rehearsed. Hill's high standards, especially his expectation of fine ensemble playing, were ahead of their time for American orchestras in the early nineteenth century and demonstrated a level of musical sophistication that most likely was honed by his European travels.

Hill's comparisons with New York provide insights into the quality of the musicianship in the city. Although we have other firsthand American descriptions of New York events, such as those by George Templeton Strong and Philip Hone, these observers were not musicians, and their opinions lack the critical insight of a broad musical and specifically orchestral experience. Hill's travels increased his confidence in his own ability to judge what was or was not good. Hill says nothing direct in his diary about the playing standard of the second Philharmonic (1824–27) or the Sacred Music Society or other American orchestras that he led or played in. But his astonishment at the ensemble and the dynamics of the best orchestras he heard—the Paris Conservatoire, the London Philharmonic, Musard's orchestra—suggests that their standard was considerably higher than anything he had experienced in New York. At the same time, his descriptions of inadequate playing and conducting at Drury Lane and elsewhere reveal a developed critical ability. The traits that Hill valued were firm leadership, unity of execution, attention to dynamics (especially the ability to play softly), and the commitment of the musicians to the music and the performance.

In his diary Hill is both astute and fair about general standards of musical performance in America versus Europe. In general he tries to defend the New York music scene against the chauvinistic attitudes that touring performers and recent European immigrants often brought with them to the New World. He acknowledges European performances, solo and orchestral, that surpass anything he has heard in New York. But not infrequently he asserts that the American product is equal to or better than a European performance he has just witnessed. For example, after the Covent Garden performance of *Fidelio* in 1835, Hill commented on John Templeton, who sang the role of Florestan: "Templeton's voice is against him. I have not heard any of their English singers equal to Jones of the Park Theatre, N.Y." Malibran, on the other hand, he thought sublime, but here too he found cause to defend American standards: "I have not forgotten what the foreign musicians were wont to tell me and others when she [Malibran] was delighting every one [in New York], that we in America might think her 1st rate because we knew no better singer but let us hear their singers in Europe and we should then know the difference. Mark the difference! She left us after delighting us for one year and a half. She returns to Europe, is the rival of [Giuditta] Pasta and [Henriette]

Sontag. By most of the 1st musical artists and diletanti she is rank'd above her compeers. So by the general opinion there is but *one Malibran*."[31] Similarly, after a Kassel performance of Mozart's *Don Giovanni* he comments: "I could but remark the pausity [*sic*] of the principal singers on the stage, when compared with the Garcia Co. in N.Y. We never had so poor a company as to the principal singers in N. York but Spohr's orchestra makes up in a measure."[32]

On the other hand, in the diary entry quoted above on the London performance of *La gazza ladra*, Hill acknowledges a characteristic failing of American orchestras. At the King's Theatre, says Hill, "Each part could be heard distinctly. All the parts appeared properly balanced, a thing so rarely met with in our orchestras. The violins and stringed instruments were never obscured by the wind instruments. This orchestra did not obscure the solo singers in even one instance. What should be heard they let be heard. Our late Italian Opera Band persued [*sic*] a very different course. They were determined to make themselves heard at all events. This is a crying fault in most all cases in the U.S."[33]

The issue of American versus European expectations about performance comes up again in the diary entry about Bériot's concert in London: "As great as he was he was a mortal. He entirely missed one of his *traits* when ascending to the upper part of his instrument, I have been told in America that accidents *never* occurred to great performers in Europe, but at the same time I did not believe it.... He finished the performance with recollections on the *Somnambula* for piano and violin, himself and Julius Benedict playing. During this piece the audience were constantly leaving the room to the great discomfiture of those that desir'd to listen, but the fashionables could not wait as it was the last piece."[34] As well as confirming that violinists missed notes in Europe just as they did in America, Hill's critique demonstrates a fairly sophisticated knowledge of violin technique and performance style, plus a musician's irritation with rude audience behavior.

Hill's knowledge of musical standards and performance practices emerges even more vividly in his description of a chamber concert that he attended in London soon after he arrived:

July 13th. Heard a quartett for the first time in Europe. This reminded us of our own Bocherini parties. They play'd the Quartett in D of Mozart and the one in C minor of Beethoven. Quartetts of this description do not at present

31 · Hill, Diary, 23–24. Hill was a member of the pit orchestra that performed for the Garcia Opera Company when Maria Garcia, later Malibran, made her New York debut.
32 · Ibid., 163 (loose leaf).
33 · Ibid., 29.
34 · Ibid., 33. By "trait" Hill means a rapid and difficult passage.

appear very regularly established in this metropolis. The tone of the instrument of the 1st violin was thin and ruff. His playing was more like coarse orchestra playing than the smooth and finish'd quartett style. The pianos were not sufficiently attended to. The cello was a young man of 25 and master of his instrument. His position of the left hand like that of Herr George Knoops resembled more the violin position than that of the French school which I have been used to seeing. The thumb was rather thrown back towards the mute on the side of the neck which I did not like. I tho't the movements [tempos] were entirely mistaken in Beethoven's Quartet. The 3/8 movement was entirely too fast, it lost its effect and in this movement particularly they play'd too strong. I think the lst violin the main cause of it. The last movement which begins allegretto and finished prestissimo, was begun full presto. This quartet made me feel proud of *our* humble quartet parties. I think our *judgments* of the matter was better, and that we have at times play'd more effectively together. But they were more perfect in the execution of the passages than we were generally.[35]

Hill was often a keen observer of different performance practices of works with which he was already familiar. For example, Weber's *Freischütz* in Kassel was "quite a different sort of thing from what it is in America or England. With us there is much fine music omitted and the scenery, machinery, etc. is far preferable here. The music of the incantation scene was admirably executed. What I never heard in any Anglo' American Orchestra."[36]

Most of Beethoven's symphonies had yet to be performed in the United States in their entirety. Hill first heard the Ninth Symphony performed at the Rhine Valley Music Festival under Mendelssohn's direction and described it in rhapsodic terms: "The majesty vigor, genius, originality and the lyric effects of the Sinfonie of Beethoven on the 2nd day was indescribably fine. It surpassed everything I heard by far. To perform this production it occupied nearly an hour." It would be a hundred years, Hill declared, "before the like can possibly be hoped to be heard in the United States."[37] In fact, it was just ten years. In May 1846, Hill, as the orchestra's president, arranged for the U.S. premiere of the Ninth Symphony performed by the Philharmonic at Castle Garden, now in Battery Park. Conducted by George Loder, the chorus sang the "Ode to Joy" in the first English translation of the work.

35 · Ibid., 30–31. The Beethoven quartet Hill heard was Op. 18, no. 4. George Knoop, a German immigrant, was New York's foremost cellist from the early 1830s until his death in 1849. See Vera Brodsky Lawrence, *Strong on Music*, vol. 1, *Resonances, 1836–1849* (1988), 118–19 and passim.
36 · Hill, Diary, 67.
37 · Ibid., 154 [R].

At frequent reprises in the course of his diary, Hill captures the political undercurrents and dissatisfaction of European musicians with the conditions under which they worked—a sentiment that would soon drive many of them to immigrate to the United States. Hill presciently foresaw that this would be a great challenge to those musicians, like himself, who were already employed in the American orchestras. In Darmstadt, Hill met Wilhelm Mangold (1796–1875), the city's Kapellmeister, and his orchestra. "The musicians treated me with the best marked respect and attention," writes Hill. "They, like all the rest of the musicians complained bitterly of the profession in Germany. Mangold said if the sea was not between, he should go immediately to America.... Thousands of musicians will come to America if they can get there. So our musicians must study to compete with them."[38]

How American Was the Philharmonic?

How *American* was the 1842 New York Philharmonic? Was the early nineteenth-century American orchestra simply a German or English orchestra transplanted? From comparisons with previous New York orchestras and from Hill's diary there are some striking differences between the 1842 Philharmonic and the European orchestras that Hill encountered abroad. To evaluate these differences, we need to (1) examine the national origins of the musicians in leadership positions, not just the national origins of every player, and (2) analyze the structure and governance of the New York Philharmonic.

Ureli Corelli Hill, who was elected president at the April 1842 Philharmonic organizing meeting, was American born. Vice President Anthony Reiff was born in Germany and had been in the United States for nearly twenty years; George Loder (conductor), English, arrived in 1836; Denis G. Etienne (conductor), French, arrived in 1814; F. W. Rosier (secretary) was French or English; Allen Dodworth (treasurer), English, arrived as a young boy; and Henry Christian Timm (conductor), German, arrived in 1836. So although German musicians were involved with the founding of the Philharmonic, English, French, and American musicians were also significant leaders. Many of the immigrants were long-time residents and well established in America. The Philharmonic's organizational structure, as an independent association with a constitution and bylaws, had no precedent in Germany but was similar to not only the 1813 London Philharmonic but also the second New York Philharmonic (1824–27), of which Hill was a member. What was distinctive to both American Philharmonics in contrast to the English

38 · Ibid., 145 [R].

was the way they were governed. Whereas the English appointed or elected "Directors," both of the New York Philharmonics mandated the election of a president and vice president, most likely modeling themselves on English and American fraternal organizations, as well as on the recently established American Republic. The 1842 Philharmonic took the American ideal of self-governance or full representation one step further than its 1824 counterpart by making any changes to the orchestra's constitution dependent on a vote of the entire membership, giving each member a say.[39]

On the basis of what we know from Hill's diary and what we know about the structure of earlier Philharmonics in New York, the 1842 Philharmonic was not simply a transplanted European orchestra landing on American shores. The 1842 Philharmonic was a hybrid of wide-ranging experiences and traditions, like the United States itself, influenced not only by those who led it but by the place in which it was organized and also by the experiences of U. C. Hill, in both his travels abroad and his experience at home.

The leadership of the Philharmonic and the conducting duties did change dramatically when the 1848 German immigrants began to arrive. From 1842 to 1848 the conducting duties of the orchestra were shared among the players. At the first concert, the program was led by no less than three conductors: U. C. Hill (American) conducted Beethoven's Fifth Symphony, H. C. Timm (German) led all the vocal music and the Kalliwoda Overture, and D. G. Etienne (French) led the overture to Weber's *Oberon*. However, the practice of multiple conductors leading a single concert did not last long. By the early 1850s, it had become the Philharmonic's practice to choose a single conductor per concert and soon after, for an entire season.

The 1842 Philharmonic was a truly American institution made up of and led by musicians of various nationalities, in most cases immigrants, but often longtime residents of the United States. It is important to make this distinction between the 1842 Philharmonic and the Philharmonic of the 1850s, because this delineation establishes the orchestra as a uniquely American institution and not merely a German transplant.

Earlier historians of the Philharmonic tended to dismiss the New York music scene prior to the German immigration of 1848 as being dominated by amateur or less-than-competent players with little sophistication and knowledge of music.[40] Hill's diary shows a critical and exacting high standard of expectation. Whether Hill's own playing was at the level of his expectations

39 · Shanet, *Philharmonic*, 48–49.
40 · See, for example, Frédéric Louis Ritter, *Music in America* (1890), 270–94; Henry Edward Krehbiel, *The Philharmonic Society of New York* (1892), 23–32. Howard Shanet (*Philharmonic*, 54–68) recognizes that New York's musical life became much more cosmopolitan between 1825 and 1842, but his book was not published until 1975.

is not relevant; his critical assessments of the "stars" of the European music stage demonstrate a sophistication and expectation on the New York music scene that has often been overlooked. Whatever talent and skill Hill and his compatriots possessed, they knew what a good orchestra should sound like, and they understood the performance practices that could achieve that level of quality.

PART V

Orchestral Repertory

Orchestral Repertory: Highbrow and Lowbrow

JOHN SPITZER

The programs of a few orchestra concerts given in New York in the 1850s and 1860s illustrate a great diversity of orchestral repertory in the mid-nineteenth century:

- The New York Philharmonic at its subscription concert on April 19, 1856, began the program with Beethoven's Fourth Symphony. Then it accompanied arias from operas by Verdi and Mercadante and played one movement of a Vieuxtemps violin concerto, as well as overtures by Mendelssohn and Märschner and a "Grand Duo" for two violins by Edward Mollenhauer, a local virtuoso.[1]
- At the New York Academy of Music in April 1858, the impresario Bernard Ullman presented the first of a series of promenade concerts by Alfred Musard and his orchestra. The program featured overtures by Berlioz, Rossini, and Auber; arias by Rossini and Meyerbeer; virtuoso variations for soloists on cornet and ophicleide; and polkas, quadrilles, and other dances by Musard himself, including "The Cattle Show: or, Beef and Mutton Comic Quadrille"[2]
- At Wallack's Theatre in New York in 1863, before the show and between the acts, the orchestra played the overture to Flotow's opera *Alessandro Stradella*, instrumental selections from a recent opera by Petrella, a quadrille on themes from Weber's *Jubel Overture,* and a polka by Mollenhauer.[3]
- At the Terrace Garden in 1867 the Theodore Thomas Orchestra played a three-part program that included overtures by Rossini, Spohr, and Wag-

---

1 · New York Philharmonic Archives, http://nyphil.org/about/archives.cfm.
2 · See program 1 in chapter III.1 of this volume.
3 · See chapter II.1 in this volume.

ner; single movements from two Beethoven symphonies (the Third and
the Fifth); a "fantasie" of tunes from *Don Giovanni;* plus waltzes, polkas, a galop, and a Ländler by Johann Strauss Jr., Joseph Lanner, George
Matzka, and Carl Müller.[4]

These programs by orchestras in various venues during the 1850s and
1860s have several common elements. They contain a great deal of opera-
derived music: overtures, arias, instrumental excerpts, and quadrilles and
fantasies on opera melodies. Most of the programs feature a singer and/or
one or more instrumental soloists. Overtures are common, but symphonies
are rare: only the Philharmonic performed a symphony from beginning to
end; the Thomas orchestra instead played individual movements. Finally, the
programs of the 1850s and 1860s are striking in the way they mix "serious"
with "light" repertory. Symphonies, overtures, and concertos by composers
like Beethoven, Weber, and Mendelssohn are programmed side by side with
opera potpourris, virtuoso variations for solo instruments, polkas, waltzes,
and galops. This mixture of "classical" and "popular" seems very far from the
programming practices of modern orchestras, which, if they play "popular"
repertory at all, confine it to summer "pops" concerts. Equally striking is the
way that the same composers and some of the same pieces—especially overtures and opera arias—turn up in all of the venues. From the Philharmonic
to the theater to the beer garden, American orchestras of the mid-nineteenth
century shared more or less the same repertory.

By the 1880s and 1890s, mixed programming and repertory sharing had
become somewhat less pronounced. Theodore Thomas's Summer Night
Garden concerts in Chicago, for example, offered a repertory that was considerably less mixed than that of his New York Terrace Garden concerts of
the 1860s. An August 1881 program was typical. It featured the *Academic Festival Overture* by Brahms (new that year), orchestral selections from Wagner's
Ring cycle, the march from Mendelssohn's *Midsummer Night's Dream,* the
finale of Beethoven's *Creatures of Prometheus,* Liszt's Hungarian Rhapsody
no. 2, and a waltz by Johann Strauss Jr. ("Wine, Woman and Song").[5] No
arias from Italian operas, no virtuoso turns, and only one dance number appeared on the program. Leopold Damrosch's Saturday Symphony Matinees
at Steinway Hall in 1877–78 offered New York audiences yet more classical

4 · See chapter II.2 in this volume. American composers George Matzka and Carl Müller
both played in the Thomas Orchestra.
5 · Theodore Thomas, *Theodore Thomas: A Musical Autobiography* (1905), 2:199. Also on
this 1881 Summer Night Garden program were Wagner's *Faust* overture and an instrumental arrangement of "The Evening Star" from *Tannhäuser,* an arrangement of Schubert's "Ave
Maria," and the Rakoczy March from Berlioz, *Damnation of Faust.*

programs—symphonies by Beethoven, Schumann, Raff, Mendelssohn, and Brahms; overtures by Beethoven, Weber, and Wagner; songs by Schumann and Schubert; and arias from the operas of Mozart, Gounod, and Wagner.[6] The New York Philharmonic in the 1880s programmed much less vocal music than it had in the 1860s and fewer instrumental solos, but more symphonies and tone poems.[7] Conversely, programs at other venues moved toward more popular repertory. Where concerts by the "Lady Orchestra" at the Atlantic Gardens in the 1870s had offered the same mixed repertory as the Theodore Thomas concerts of the same period, a program from 1896 shows the orchestra playing novelty numbers and also accompanying the popular singer Imogene Comer.[8] And in Daly's Theater in 1892 the orchestra no longer played Beethoven between the acts of a Shakespeare play, but rather "Sally in Our Alley."[9] Other orchestras in the 1880s and 1890s still mixed classical and popular numbers. Summer Night concerts by the Cincinnati Grand Orchestra in the 1880s combined complete symphonies by Haydn and Beethoven with overtures by Rossini and Weber and waltzes and galops by Strauss and Gungl.[10] The programs of the all-woman Boston Fadettes orchestra in the 1890s mixed symphony movements with overtures and shorter light classics. When the Fadettes joined the Keith vaudeville circuit in 1903, however, they altered their repertory to emphasize popular tunes and novelty numbers.[11] By the end of the nineteenth century, mixed repertory programming had begun to seem slightly old-fashioned.

This account of a shared orchestral repertory being replaced by separate "classical" and "popular" repertories seems to correspond to the narrative offered by American historian Lawrence Levine, in which Americans "shared culture" during the first two-thirds of the nineteenth century, then developed a "cultural hierarchy" after the Civil War.[12] In the early nineteenth century, asserts Levine, Americans of different social classes read the same books, attended the same theaters, and listened to the same music. During the second half of the century, by contrast, opera, symphonic music, and "legitimate" theater came to be designated as "high" culture, while band music, sentimental songs, and vaudeville became "popular" culture. The plays of Shakespeare, the symphonies of Beethoven, and paintings by European masters were "sa-

6 · See chapter III.3 in this volume.
7 · See chapter V.3 in this volume.
8 · See chapter II.2 in this volume.
9 · See chapter II.1 in this volume.
10 · See chapter II.3 in this volume.
11 · See chapter I.2 in this volume.
12 · Lawrence W. Levine, *Highbrow/Lowbrow: The Emergence of Cultural Hierarchy in America* (1988).

cralized," becoming more like objects of worship than entertainment. Levine cites orchestral repertory as one of his primary examples of sacralization and cultural hierarchy.

While Levine's framework helps explain the changes in repertory of American orchestras during the nineteenth century, it needs to be tempered by at least two caveats. First, nineteenth-century culture sharing was not an idyllic, pre-lapsarian state of American nature. Americans of different classes shared culture because cultural commodities were relatively scarce. American orchestras in the 1850s and 1860s programmed a mixed repertory and played the same pieces in diverse venues because the audience for orchestral music was small, because orchestral musicians were few and their abilities often modest, because dedicated venues for orchestral music were rare, and because the available orchestral repertory was limited. With the rapid growth of urban populations in the second half of the century, the immigration of German and then Italian musicians, and the construction of a network of railways, these conditions of scarcity began to abate. Equally important was the flowering of American popular music: minstrel songs, Tin Pan Alley, musical theater, marches, and ragtime. Here was an abundant repertory of music specifically aimed at distribution and sale to a large, diverse audience. By the end of the century, there was plenty of music to go around. Americans were no longer obliged to share culture with one another, and to a considerable extent they no longer did.

The second caveat is that the separation of "classical" from "popular" orchestral repertories should not be seen as a plot by newly emerging American elites to appropriate for themselves the culture that they had previously shared with the rest of society.[13] The vanguard in the creation of hierarchical repertories was not robber barons (and their wives) but the musicians themselves. Orchestral players preferred symphonies to polkas and quadrilles, and they did everything in their power to create opportunities to perform the music that they loved. From the 1840s on, orchestra musicians campaigned to "improve" orchestral repertory by ending the mixture of "serious" with "light" music. The musicians of the New York Philharmonic, in the annual reports they wrote during the 1840s and 1850s, articulated their goal as playing music that offered "enjoyment of the highest intellectual character."[14] The members of the Chicago Philharmonic Society of 1860 stated that their mission was to "promote and cultivate a taste for the higher branches of music."[15]

Supporting the musicians' campaign were the musical press, music educa-

---

13 · See Ralph P. Locke, "Music Lovers, Patrons, and the 'Sacralization' of Culture in America," *19th-Century Music* 17 (1993).

14 · See chapter V.3 in this volume.

15 · See chapter I.1 in this volume.

tors, and intellectuals. John Sullivan Dwight, who managed the Harvard Musical Association orchestra, complained about programs that were "medleys of good, bad, and indifferent," and insisted that in order to appeal to the "reliable nucleus of a musical public," the orchestra's programs must be "pure."[16] Critics such as Theodore Hagen and Henry Cood Watson in New York and W. S. B. Mathews and George P. Upton in Chicago, as well as Dwight in Boston, condemned "light" music on concert programs and exhorted orchestras to play more "serious" music.

Mixed programming and repertory sharing between orchestras in different venues persisted well into the twentieth century, though, to World War I and beyond. The Cincinnati Symphony Orchestra started out in 1895 with a repertory of "classical" music in a high-class venue (Pike's Opera House). Soon, however, the orchestra began adding "popular" concerts to its schedule, in a larger auditorium, and offering a much more mixed repertory.[17] However, the orchestra did not give its popular concerts as the "Cincinnati Symphony" but rather as the "Cincinnati Orchestra." The name change tried to make it clear that a "symphony" orchestra did not play "popular" music. Similarly, members of the Boston Symphony began giving Promenade concerts in 1885, an enterprise that came to be known by 1901 as the "Boston Pops," distinct from the Boston Symphony, which played only "serious" music.[18] Evidently the *idea* of hierarchy had prevailed even if the repertory was still shared and the programs were still mixed. By the turn of the century, "classical" and "popular" were perceived as categorically different kinds of music, and orchestras were increasingly seen as belonging on the "classical" side of the fence. Popular repertories were taken over by other sorts of ensembles — concert bands, pit orchestras, dance bands, small combos, and studio orchestras. The concert hall belonged to Beethoven.

16 · See chapter III.2 in this volume. Dwight's comments date from 1865.
17 · See chapter II.3 in this volume.
18 · See Ayden Wren Adler, "Classical Music for People Who Hate Classical Music: Arthur Fiedler and the Boston Pops, 1930–1950" (Ph.D. diss., 2007), 27–30.

[v.1] Orchestral Programs in Boston, 1841–55, in European Perspective

WILLIAM WEBER

Historians now see a common Western culture spanning the Atlantic as a central feature of American history. American society was international at its creation; educated people in the United States and Canada remained deeply involved with European ideas and cultural activities. "The new account of American history," Karen Kupperman has suggested, "demonstrates that America was international before it became national."[1] Michael Broyles has argued along similar lines in his seminal book on Boston's musical life, contending that there existed "a single transatlantic musical culture" from which Boston's musical life departed as it shaped its own institutions and tastes.[2] To be sure, an infrastructure of musical institutions of the sort basic to modern musical culture did not develop in the United States until well into the nineteenth century. Opera companies did not take local root until the 1840s, and orchestral series arose from the 1840s to the 1880s. Yet when we look at musical life during the 1850s, we find that European cities differed among themselves musically as much as Boston or New York did from any one of them.

This chapter discusses orchestral programs performed in Boston between 1841 and 1855 by the Academy of Music (1841–47), the Musical Fund Society (1847–55), and the Philharmonic Society (1843–55). It compares these programs with those given in Birmingham, London, and New York in the same

---

1 · Karen Kupperman, "International at the Creation: Early Modern American History," in *Rethinking American History in a Global Age*, ed. Thomas Bender (2002), 105; see also Thomas Bender, "Introduction: Historians, the Nation, and the Plenitude of Narratives," in the same collection.

2 · Michael Broyles, *"Music of the Highest Class": Elitism and Populism in Antebellum Boston* (1992), 10–11.

period.[3] London and New York in the 1850s were the focal points musically of each of their nations, while Birmingham and Boston were important second-tier cities musically; musical activities were expanding rapidly in both places, and cultural interactions between cities were becoming much more extensive in both Europe and America.

We must think on several levels when analyzing how European and American musical life related to one another in the first half of the nineteenth century. In the first place, concert programming was highly international in America at the start. To be sure, in London or Paris programs always included pieces from a variety of countries. But an unusual number of countries were typically represented on programs in American cities, because a self-conscious composing profession did not emerge until after 1850. Second, British and American concerts developed in particularly close relationship with one another. The two countries shared similar kinds of tastes, programming, and entrepreneurship in musical life; concerts in both countries tended to be long, commercial, and eclectic in taste. Influence went in both directions. British musicians were the predominant group among immigrant musicians in America from colonial times until the 1830s, while demand for music in America had a strong influence in Britain on the dynamic growth of the ballad and the music that came to be called "popular song."

Finally, American musical life developed idiosyncratically in certain respects. The absence of a monarchy or nobility and the recent development of musical institutions brought an unusually vigorous entrepreneurism to American musical life. Musicians did not face as strong traditional and legal limitations as did their European colleagues; in the United States experimentation developed more freely in programming. European musicians who immigrated to America embraced New World capitalism; even though they sometimes inveighed against it, they found it very much in their interests.

Concert programming in this period, whether in Europe or in America, followed principles quite different from those we take for granted today. Almost every concert included voices as well as instruments, most often being advertised as a "vocal and instrumental concert." Such concerts grew from the assumption that virtuosity of a solo voice and virtuosity of a solo instrument were interdependent. As Rodolfo Celletti argues, their relationship amounted to a "love duet" inherent in the bel canto tradition of cultured music-making.[4] Strict practices governed how this tradition was applied in

3 · I discuss programming in London, Birmingham, and other European cities in William Weber, *The Great Transformation of Musical Taste: Concert Programming from Haydn to Brahms* (2008).
4 · Rodolfo Celletti, *A History of Bel Canto* (1991), 3.

a program. Because the number of concerts was limited in the small musical world of the 1700s, diverse genres and kinds of taste had to cohabit on the same programs. Opera selections—variously overtures, arias, choruses, and ensemble numbers—appeared on the great majority of programs. In public concerts it was deemed necessary to alternate between vocal and instrumental pieces and, when exceptions did occur, to avoid putting two examples of a genre or a certain tessitura back-to-back. A multitude of other rules and expectations guided musicians as they designed programs. What can look like heterogeneity to us in reality possessed musical and social coherence.

Programs in America and England were usually quite similar, as is evident in a pair of programs given in Salem, Massachusetts, in 1799 and in Birmingham, England, two years later (see appendix V.1.1, programs 1 and 2). The Salem concert was organized by two of Boston's most prominent musicians, Catherine Graupner (an English actress married to a German musician) and Peter Van Hagen (the son of a Dutch musician born in Charleston, South Carolina).[5] The Private Concerts of Birmingham, begun in 1799, served as the city's central series for fifty years.[6] The two programs included the same genres—concerto, song or glee, and overture—and both alternated strictly between vocal and instrumental numbers. Indeed, the two halves of both concerts opened with instrumental pieces by Ignace Pleyel and Joseph Haydn. Virtually the same proportion of British-American composers or genres (as opposed to continental) appears in the two programs—five out of thirteen pieces in Boston and three out of ten in Birmingham. Each meeting of Birmingham's Triennial Festival usually included two "miscellaneous concerts" of similar design.[7]

The British-American character of the programs is also evident in the central role of the glee in the two concerts. Normally set for three or four unaccompanied male solo voices, glees were performed in a wide range of contexts—at men's clubs and local music societies, in English opera productions, and at the pleasure gardens.[8] The solo songs on the programs "Columbia's Bold Eagle" in Boston and "In April When Primroses Grow" in Birmingham—also represented an important British-American practice. With

---

5 · On Van Hagen's song, see William J. Murdoch, "Graupner Became a Papa, Too!" *Music Educators Journal* 35 (1948); and Richard Crawford, *America's Musical Life: A History* (2001), 89–90.

6 · See Antje Pieper, *Music and the Making of Middle-Class Culture: A Comparative History of Nineteenth-Century Leipzig and Birmingham* (2008); and Margaret Handford, *Sounds Unlikely: 600 Years of Music in Birmingham, 1392–1992* (1992), 77, 79.

7 · Programmes of the Triennial Festival, British Library 7894.s.1, London.

8 · Brian Robins, *Catch and Glee Culture in Eighteenth-Century England* (2006).

such a repertory, Britain and the United States led in the development of the "popular song" rooted in the theater and the parlor.

The Salem and Birmingham programs illustrate how canonic repertory was less significant in America than in Britain. The pieces by G. F. Handel and Francesco Geminiani on the Birmingham program illustrate the special canonic tradition that had been developing in Britain since the early seventeenth century.[9] The persistence of a piece in repertory implied canonic respect, and the presence on concert programs of music by deceased composers serves as a convenient indicator of the growth of canonic programming. The dead composers on the 1799 Salem program, Stephen Storace and J. C. Vogel, were recently deceased and they did not acquire canonic reputations in the early nineteenth century. Moreover, the American program was even more international than the British one, representing some eight countries as compared to five in Birmingham.

Breakdown of the Old Musical Order

The framework of values, repertories, and social relationships basic to musical culture came into crisis almost everywhere in Europe under the pressure of economic change and political crises after the turn of the nineteenth century. Similar economic and social changes came about in the United States two decades or so later. In Europe the sequence of political upheavals that reached from 1789 to 1848 went far beyond governmental matters, affecting the exercise of authority in many areas of society. The instability of the European political order opened the way for efforts to reshape cultural life, either by challenging hegemonic institutions or setting up new ones. In America as well as Europe, musicians began taking advantage of this cultural instability to set up new kinds of concerts or theatrical institutions that took musical life in new directions.

The growth in publishing and cultural capitalism as a whole stimulated so many new musical genres that the miscellaneous concert no longer could function in traditional fashion. Conflict over musical values arose between proponents of the more commercial versus the more learned tastes. On the one hand, around 1815, leaders of string quartets in Vienna and Paris broke fundamentally from the tradition of the "miscellaneous" concert by removing vocal music completely from their programs. Orchestral series began performing many more "classical" works by revered deceased composers. In the 1840s a few pianists began performing classical repertory at their benefit concerts, eventually bringing about the solo recital focused on such music. On

---

9 · William Weber, *The Rise of Musical Classics in Eighteenth Century England* (1992).

the other hand, in the 1840s singers began putting on concerts aimed at the broad general public. Such concerts were made up of opera selections, developing a canonic vocal repertory distinct from that of orchestral or chamber-music concerts. The most "popular" repertory emerged in venues called music halls in Britain and *cafés-concerts* in Paris during the 1850s, places that offered songs, opera excerpts, and musical character sketches.[10] The musical world had begun to break apart into separate spheres ruled by different tastes. By 1870 a new order in musical culture was in place in both Europe and America.

Michael Broyles and I have used the term "musical idealism" to define the movement that called for a higher order of taste and performance practices in orchestral and chamber-music concerts. As Broyles has demonstrated, the repertories performed in Europe and America were basically the same, originating in the transatlantic movement of performers and musical commentary. Since the founding of the Handel and Haydn Society in Boston around 1815, according to Broyles, "musical idealism served the principles of high culture for much of its history in the United States."[11] The values propounded by writers such as John Sullivan Dwight did not differ in many respects from those circulated in London.[12]

What distinguished the early classical-music world in Boston from that in London, Broyles says, was the deep conflict that went on in such concerts regarding religion and social class. Proponents of Boston's orchestral concerts of the 1840s came from upper-class families who were discarding the theology and social values of traditional Puritanism and moving from Evangelical to Unitarian or Episcopal churches. Rich or influential families were involving themselves in musical life deeply for the first time, activities that had long been conventional for such people in London. In Boston, going to the most respectable churches or concerts was making class lines deeper and more rigid.

The movement of musical idealism flourished to a striking extent in Boston, bringing what Broyles calls "a hierarchical attitude toward music in which aesthetic value was subordinated to moral value."[13] The 1843 Annual Report of the Boston Academy of Music defended its orchestral concerts as providing music "capable of something better and higher than producing a

10 · Weber, *Great Transformation of Musical Taste*, 273–78, 288–93.

11 · Broyles, *"Music of the Highest Class."* See also Ora Frishberg Saloman, *Listening Well: On Beethoven, Berlioz, and Other Music Criticism in Paris, Boston, and New York, 1764–1890* (2009), 137–49.

12 · See Ora Frishberg Saloman, *Beethoven's Symphonies and J. S. Dwight: The Birth of American Music Criticism* (1995).

13 · Broyles, *"Music of the Highest Class,"* 11; see also Broyles's chapter 6.

dry, unprofitable astonishment."[14] A tough-minded version of such thinking was regularly published in Boston's Fourierist magazine *The Harbinger, devoted to Social and Political Progress,* written chiefly by John Sullivan Dwight. the *Harbinger* brought the utopianism of the Brook Farm community to a critique of the city's emerging musical life. In 1846 one of its writers (Dwight?) attacked the academy's directors for "pandering to a medium and uneducated taste" after initially trying to elevate standards.[15] Later, in the pages of his *Journal of Music,* Dwight took a more accommodating stance. Asking why a singer offered a song by so imposing a composer as Louis Spohr in the midst of less serious fare, he declared: "Miscellaneous programme-making should be more a work of art."[16] Such an argument broke with the traditional principle that a program would balance contrasting genres and tastes and serve a variety of publics. The notion of programming as a "work of art" excluded those who wanted to be entertained and divided musical culture into separate regions in programming and aesthetics.

The Rise of Orchestral Concerts in Boston

Bostonians could attend orchestral concerts by three different ensembles during the 1840s and early 1850s.[17] The Boston Academy of Music gave its original series of orchestral concerts in 1841, offering the first extensive performance of the Beethoven symphonies in America. The Musical Fund Society, employing only professional players, began giving similar concerts in the spring of 1847, just as the academy performed its last series. Fire loss of the instruments led the Musical Fund Society to disband in 1855. The Philharmonic Society, begun as an amateur ensemble in 1843, began hiring some professional players around 1848 and gave concerts of contrasting kinds through 1855. In addition, chamber-music concerts began in Boston in 1844, sponsored by the Harvard Musical Association and from 1850 by the Mendelssohn Quintet Club. Thus did Bostonians enjoy rich and varied musical fare during a crucial period in the development of the city's musical life.

   That no central orchestra developed in Boston at this time, as did occur in New York, came chiefly from the slower development of opera in the New England city. All the principal orchestras in Europe—the Gewandhaus, the Philharmonic Society of London, and the Conservatoire Concerts in Paris—

---

14 · Boston Academy of Music, *11th Annual Report of the Boston Academy of Music* (1843), 4–5.

15 · "Sixth Concert of the Boston Academy," *Harbinger,* March 7, 1846, 204. The magazine was sponsored by the American Union of Associationists.

16 · *Dwight's Journal of Music* 5 (January 21, 1854): 127.

17 · See also chapter III.2 in this volume.

were drawn almost entirely from the opera orchestra in each city, providing a collegial base of high-level players. Members of the New York Philharmonic likewise played in the opera orchestra, although there was no public subsidy for the city's entrepreneurial opera company.

Orchestral concerts took considerably different characters in Protestant and Catholic cities, a pattern that helps illuminate what happened in Boston. The two European series that went the farthest toward classical repertories—drawing small audiences—were in the Catholic court cities of Paris and Vienna. A series called the Concert Spirituel, begun in Vienna in 1819, established the earliest and most systematic classical-music repertory, a sacred piece on every program. Likewise, the Société de Concerts du Conservatoire in Paris offered sacred works at two out of three of its concerts from its start in 1828. At both series three-quarters of the pieces performed were by dead, and in most cases canonic, composers by the mid-1840s. Catholicism thus provided a firmer set of traditions for defining musical classics than did Protestantism. In Protestant Boston, sacred music and secular music interacted uneasily in orchestra concerts. Boston's three orchestral series offered only occasional short selections from Handel's oratorios: sacred works remained the province of the Handel and Haydn Society and occasional events called "Concert of Sacred Music."

The countervailing strength of religion and musical idealism complicated the establishment of a long-term set of orchestral concerts in Boston. The Academy of Music, formed in 1833, originally drew members to a great extent from ministers and church musicians. The list of subscribers to the academy in 1842 included clergymen from a wide range of denominations, evangelical Congregationalists prominent among them.[18] The academy's main initial project was building separate choruses for adults and children, with sacred music central to both repertories.[19] The concerts offered selections from sacred works by Handel, W. A. Mozart, Joseph Haydn, Carl Heinrich Graun, Giovanni Paisiello, Louis Spohr, and Rossini.[20]

The project in the early 1840s of developing a series of orchestral concerts brought to the fore a serious disagreement in the goals held by the academy's leaders. The influential civic leader Samuel A. Eliot, who served as the academy's president, wanted an orchestral series focused on secular music, but Lowell Mason, the original music director, was intent on building choirs and

18 · Boston Academy of Music, *Annual Report of the Boston Academy of Music* (1842), 10–11. See also Martin Moore, *Boston Revival, 1842: A Brief History of the Evangelical Churches of Boston* (1842); Justin Winsor, ed., *Memorial History of Boston* (1881), vol. 3.

19 · Broyles, *"Music of the Highest Class,"* 182–214; Boston Academy of Music, *Annual Report of the Boston Academy of Music* (1835), 3–18.

20 · "Programs of Concerts in Boston, 1817–63" (microfilm), Boston Public Library.

training church musicians. Mason was a Congregational Evangelical, whereas Eliot tended toward the Unitarianism of the city's upper classes. After Eliot worked out a tenuous compromise that involved the two alternatives, Mason departed to form his own teaching institute. The inauguration of orchestral concerts in the fall of 1841 was related to the relaxation of moral bans on entertainment developing among liberal theologians. Henry Ward Beecher, for example, wrote against "those who, confounding amusement with pleasure, reject both as not only frivolous, but absolutely wicked."[21] Yet opposition to public concerts persisted, and religious tensions remained strong in the Commonwealth of Massachusetts.

Programming in Orchestral Concerts

The Academy of Music set a high standard for adherence to idealistic principles. Some kind of compromise among different avenues of taste was necessary at almost any series of concerts in 1840s Boston, but the programs Eliot and his colleagues designed for the Academy of Music orchestra conformed to a considerable extent to practices that were deemed serious in European musical life. Most important, a Beethoven symphony was offered alone after intermission in at least half of the concerts. One concert given in 1845 (appendix, program 3) followed tradition in offering a conventional sequence of vocal and instrumental pieces in the first half but then took a new direction in making Beethoven's Fifth Symphony the only piece in the second half. The practice of performing an instrumental work alone after intermission constituted a fundamental change in concert programming. Initiated at the Gewandhaus concerts with the "Eroica" Symphony in 1807, the practice endowed the featured work with a special, in this case iconic, status. The Philharmonic Society of London performed the Ninth Symphony in a similar format in 1825 but played the other Beethoven symphonies in the traditional position as the first piece on a program.

The seven pieces in the first half of the 1845 Boston Academy of Music concert balanced the needs of general and learned taste carefully. Three opera overtures by Daniel Auber popular with the general public framed the half; an aria from a Handel opera was standard repertory in many English and American concerts. By the 1840s, however, the glee had become a specialized taste; the two examples here were by composers deemed canonic in the genre, Thomas Attwood and Reginald Spofforth. The violin solo by the

21 · "Interesting and Useful Lecture," *Boston Evening Transcript*, December 30, 1848, 67; Robert Lewis, "'Rational Recreation': Reforming Leisure in Antebellum America," in *Religious and Secular Reform in America: Ideas, Beliefs, and Social Change*, ed. D. K. Adams and C. A. Van Minnen (1999).

Viennese Joseph Mayseder likewise suited a conservative taste for instrumental virtuosity; his well-crafted style was still respected among connoisseurs as the opera *fantaisie* began to dominate programs.

Comments in the Boston press reflect how tastes competed among the Boston orchestra's public. The writer for the *Harbinger* complained that "they who can appreciate good music are the most dissatisfied part of the audience [since] the high rank, which the society bid fair to take, has not been realized." The level of composers chosen had supposedly declined: "The directors of the Academy began with the design of elevating the standard of musical taste, but … from Mozart and Haydn and Spohr they fell down to Auber, and then slipped a stage lower in wearisome solos by second-rate performers."[22] A reviewer in the *Musical Cabinet* was kinder, saying that these "miscellaneous concerts" were thought to "consist largely of the more elaborate instrumental pieces of a high order," that is, pieces by Mayseder rather than the commercialized music of Henri Herz.[23]

By contrast, programs given by the Philharmonic Society of London were suffused with opera, as we can see in one performed in 1845 (appendix, program 4). This concert was focused on selections by Rossini, Spohr, and Giacomo Meyerbeer and included a fantasia for harp on airs from *Robert le Diable*. The absence of a local opera company in Boston meant that the Academy of Music could not offer as many opera selections as the London Philharmonic or indeed (as we will see below) the one in New York. Some programs did offer several opera selections; one given in 1846, for example, included arias by Gaetano Donizetti and Vincenzo Bellini.[24]

The Boston Academy programs also differed from those of the London Philharmonic Society in the continuing strong presence of glees and in the continuing representation of music by British composers. The ideology propounded for classical music made the glee outmoded at "serious" concerts in Britain, even though such pieces were still sung widely in clubs and local concerts. The London Philharmonic Society excluded them from the start and performed a minimum number of pieces by British composers. Music by living, indigenous composers was becoming less central to the repertory of most of the premier orchestral concerts in Europe. The same was already happening with the New York Philharmonic Orchestra, as Adrienne Fried Block has shown.[25]

22 · "Sixth Concert of the Boston Academy," *Harbinger*, March 7, 1846, 204.
23 · "Boston Academy of Music," *Musical Cabinet*, February 1, 1842, 115.
24 · "Programs of Concerts in Boston, 1817–63," December 14, 1844.
25 · See chapter V.3 in this volume; also see Adrienne Fried Block, "New York's Orchestras and the 'American' Composer: A Nineteenth-Century View," in *European Music and Musicians in New York City, 1840-1900*, ed. John Graziano (2006).

Considering the limited exposure to classical music among the Boston public in 1840, we must be impressed by the idealism with which the academy defined its programming. Yet a repertory such as this one could not last long where the musical world was still in process of formation. The last of the academy's orchestral concerts occurred in the spring of 1847, faced with competition from the Musical Fund Society and the Philharmonic Society. It seems likely that Eliot did not succeed in obtaining a dependable enough public to pay many professional players, and as a consequence the performing standards seem to have been rather low. A reviewer in the *Harbinger* complained that William Kayser showed "the want of an efficient leader," giving the performance "all the faults incident to a *democratic* orchestra, when the leader is only one of the people."[26]

The purest ideal for a concert emerged in chamber-music concerts rather than orchestral series, in both Europe and America. A series focused on string quartets, begun by the Harvard Musical Association in 1844, avoided vocal music almost entirely, for the programs offered two or three quartets, trios, or quintets, plus an instrumental virtuoso piece in the middle. The format stood closer to those of the Parisian chamber-music concerts than those in London in excluding vocal music. Arguably that is where listeners went for what they took to be the most serious kind of music-making. The Mendelssohn Quintet Club began giving chamber-music concerts in Boston around 1850.[27]

The concerts of the Musical Fund Society served a broader purpose than did the academy's orchestral concerts—to raise funds for infirm musicians in Boston generally. Made up of fifty professional players, most from the theaters, the Musical Fund's ensemble established a strong presence in public life.[28] The words "Charitable Fund" on advertisements gave the series a more familiar goal than the idealism claimed by the academy. The collegial body that ran the concerts resembled that of the London Philharmonic Society; thirty years later Dwight characterized the organization as "a league of interest."[29] The high professional level of the players set a new standard for orchestral concerts. In 1848 the *Evening Transcript* said the series involved "the best musicians in the city" and declared that "[t]his is properly the Boston Orchestra."[30]

26 · *Harbinger*, March 7, 1846, 204; Broyles, *"Music of the Highest Class,"* 241.

27 · Weber, *Great Transformation of Musical Taste*, 139; programs in the Boston Public Library and the Harvard Musical Association. For the later history of the Harvard Musical Association, see chapter III.2 in this volume.

28 · Broyles, *"Music of the Highest Class,"* 331–32. Thomas Ryan discusses the concerts in *Recollections of an Old Musician* (1899), 50–51.

29 · John Sullivan Dwight, "History of Music in Boston" (1881), 425.

30 · *Boston Evening Transcript*, December 9, 1848, 3; January 6, 1849, 79.

The Musical Fund attracted a broader public than its predecessor, eventually performing in Tremont Temple, which held fifteen hundred people. The advertisements for its concerts had a commercial ring, making claims for the vocal and instrumental soloists performing each week. As one notice put it, Madam Annetta Stephani "will perform some of her most popular pieces, making her first appearance in Boston."[31] Indeed, the series offered twice as many vocal pieces as did the academy concerts. Major singers came to the Musical Fund concerts from Britain—for example, Anna Bishop and John Hatton, famous for performing both oratorios and ballads, as well as opera selections. In 1848 Signora Valtellina sang the cavatina from Bellini's *I Capuleti e i Montecchi* and collaborated with one of her students in the duet from *Linda di Chamounix*. Yet some pieces on the Boston programs must have appealed mainly to the cognoscenti. For example, Miss Anna Stone, a leading local singer, performed "The Mermaid," a canzonet Haydn wrote while in England, and a setting of "Gratia agimus tibi" from a mass by Pietro Carlo Guglielmi, who had died in 1817.

A Music Fund concert in 1848 (appendix, program 5) illustrates how its leaders accommodated contrasting tastes. The program opened with what the *Evening Transcript* called "the solid half of the banquet"—Beethoven's Seventh Symphony and Mendelssohn's Piano Concerto in G minor. The second half was oriented toward the general public: a violinist played a *fantaisie* on Bellini's *Norma,* and the Spanish oboist J. M. de Carmen Ribas varied themes from Auber's *Gustave III.* Ribas, resident in Boston that season, had played previously as soloist and ensemble member at Covent Garden and the Gewandhaus.

The orchestras of the Boston Academy and the Musical Fund contrasted significantly with the major European ensembles in performing little vocal music on many of their programs. The American practice focused attention on overtures, virtuoso pieces, and the Beethoven symphonies. For example, in March 1846 the Academy of Music orchestra offered three overtures by Auber, a pair of accompanied virtuoso solos, and Beethoven's Second Symphony.[32] Two years later a concert by the Musical Fund Society included one concerto, three solo pieces (potpourri, variations, and fantasia), a quartet for four flutes, and three overtures.[33] It is striking that neither program included a glee or a selection from an oratorio to fulfill traditional expectations. It is almost impossible to find any orchestral concerts without vocal pieces in Europe in the 1840s; a concert without singing was a non sequitur. Songs

31 · Ibid., February 22, 1851, 3.
32 · *Harbinger*, March 7, 1846, 204.
33 · *Boston Evening Transcript*, March 25, 1848, 3.

and excerpts from operas or oratorios remained standard repertory in most orchestral series for the rest of the century.[34]

The early programs of the New York Philharmonic Society were similar to those of the two Boston series, both in format and in frequent departures from convention. An all-instrumental program in January 1848 included Mendelssohn's Third Symphony, overtures by Weber (*Euryanthe*) and Peter Lindpaintner (*Der Vampyr*), and a concerto for two pianos by František Xaver Dušek.[35] The strength of opera in New York also made for more vocal music than in Boston's orchestral concerts. For example, a typical New York program in 1848 (appendix, program 6) included "Dies Bildnis ist bezaubernd schön" from *The Magic Flute* (translated into Italian), a duet from Spohr's *Jessonda*, and a song by Franz Lachner.

A program for Birmingham's Private Concerts in 1842 (appendix, program 7) contains even more vocal pieces than were usually found in either Boston or New York. Diverse vocal genres were performed on this program: Italian opera selections by Bellini, Mozart, and C. W. Gluck; four songs by the famed Henry Russell (who appeared in person); and in addition a glee, a ballad, and a comic song by Londoner John Parry. Works by classical composers served as bookends for each half, with a song by Johann Pepusch from the *Beggar's Opera* representing the canon of British opera. Russell's tours to America, and the editions of his songs, served as an important conduit of music between the two countries.

Entrepreneurial Experimentation

Boston's orchestral concerts underwent considerable experimentation from the late 1840s, influenced by the expansion of opera production in Boston and the arrival of diverse touring ensembles. Traveling opera companies or groups of singers had for decades given concerts in Boston. Such programs usually contained little if any instrumental music, a practice that was unusual in England or on the Continent until the 1850s. In 1833, for example, Sophie Hewett, a pianist married to the promoter Louis Ostinelli, organized a "Concert of Vocal Music" for four Italian singers whose pieces involved a sophisticated range of composers: Vincenzo Fioravanti and Francesco Morlacchi as well as Rossini, Bellini, and Donizetti.[36] Local singers also often put on benefit concerts made up almost entirely of vocal selections. The promi-

34 · The leading exception was the Prussian Court Orchestra in Berlin; see Weber, *Great Transformation of Musical Taste*, 251–78.

35 · Concert of January 15, 1848; program at http://history.nyphil.org/.

36 · "Programs of Concerts in Boston, 1817–63"; Broyles, *"Music of the Highest Class,"* 106–14, 319–20.

nence of such concerts, and the cost of paying high-level singers, may have discouraged both the Academy of Music and the Music Fund from putting many vocal selections on their programs.

The Philharmonic Society of Boston was founded in 1843 by a group of amateurs who gave as their aim "the elevation of musical taste and the performance of the best works of the great composers."[37] Yet the ambitious directors of the society steered their programs closer to the opera world than had the leaders of the Academy of Music or the Musical Fund Society. A succession of music directors, supported by a board of prosperous laymen, kept the society's expenses manageable by balancing the cost of professional singers with a still largely amateur ensemble. As Michael Broyles suggests, leaders of the Philharmonic Society strove to "meet the public on its own terms."[38] The *Harbinger* noted in 1847 that the concerts "struck at once for popularity" because they offered selections of vocal music thought accessible to the general public.[39] At this point the word "popular" meant simply "favorite"; it did not have strong ideological implications such as arose after 1870.[40] An 1843 Philharmonic program resembled what the Music Fund offered in its combination of glees, opera selections, instrumental pieces, and overtures. Another Philharmonic Society concert featured Beethoven's Fifth Symphony with Thomas Balfe's "I Dreamt I Dwelt in Marble Halls" and Thomas Moore's "Believe Me, If All These Endearing Young Charms" inserted between the movements.[41]

But the society's repertory tended increasingly toward opera. A concert in the first season (appendix, program 8) was opera-rich: four selections by Bellini, one by Rossini, and one by the Irishman William Rooke (from *Amile, or the Love Test*), interspersed with four instrumental solos accompanied by piano (one written by the conductor J. G. Jones). The only purely orchestral number was a "finale," unidentified in the announcement, perhaps because it had not yet been chosen. As was suggested above, it was not seen as odd for a "philharmonic" concert to present so little of what we would call "orchestral" music.

In 1848 the directors of the Philharmonic Society began bringing touring ensembles—both instrumental and operatic—into their concerts. The first such effort was a concert in December performed by the ensemble of Josef

---

37 · *Boston Courier*, December 7, 1843, 1.

38 · Broyles, *"Music of the Highest Class,"* 236.

39 · *Harbinger*, January 9, 1847, 77. See also Ryan, *Recollections of an Old Musician*, 49–50.

40 · Weber, *Great Transformation of Musical Taste*, 34–36, 274–76; Derek Scott, *Sounds of the Metropolis: The 19th-Century Popular Music Revolution in London, New York, Paris, and Vienna* (2008), 85–113.

41 · *Harbinger*, February 27, 1847, 185–86.

Gungl, featuring English soprano Anna Bishop, also on tour in America, and seventeen-year-old pianist Richard Hoffmann. The Philharmonic Society called the event its "First Musical Festival." Mme. Bishop sang four numbers, two from the operatic repertory, two of a more "popular" character; Hoffmann played Thalberg's fantasy on *Sonnambula* and Liszt's on *Lucia di Lammermoor*; and the Gungl orchestra played Gungl's *Alpine Spring Jubilee*, *News Boy Potpourri*, and *Farewell to Berlin*, plus Mendelssohn's overture to *Midsummer Night's Dream*, which opened the concert.[42] This program differed from earlier programs by the Academy of Music and the Philharmonic Society in the prominence of opera solos, the absence of "classical" repertory, and the orchestral novelty numbers.

In 1850 the Philharmonic Society began collaborating with Max Maretzek, whose Astor Place Opera House Company was bringing Boston its first full productions of Italian opera.[43] A program given on February 16, 1850 (appendix, program 9) offered well-known selections from Donizetti's *Elisir d'amore* and *La Favorita*, Rossini's *Semiramide*, Bellini's *Norma*, and Verdi's *Linda di Chamounix*, along with the overtures to Rossini's *La gazza ladra* and Auber's *Masaniello*. But each half concluded with pieces that Maretzek had composed for "promenade" concerts—*Tip Top Polka* and variations on themes from Donizetti's *Lucrezia Borgia*.

In 1853 and 1854 Boston concertgoers experienced the premier entrepreneur of the "promenade" concert, Louis Antoine Jullien, on tour in the United States.[44] Jullien had refined the promenade format—casual surroundings, frequent performances, large audiences, low ticket prices, and a first-rate orchestra—at the Jardin Turc in Paris and then at several venues in England.[45] Promenade programs typically featured overtures, virtuoso instrumental pieces, opera potpourris, and dance numbers. Jullien's performances in Boston featured the extreme points of his repertory. On the one hand, Jullien brought Hermann Koenig, the internationally known cornet

42 · *Boston Evening Transcript*, December 16, 1848, 3.

43 · Katherine K. Preston, *Opera on the Road: Traveling Opera Troupes in the United States, 1825–60* (1993); Ruth Henderson, "A Confluence of Impresarios: Max Maretzek, the Strakosches, and the Graus," in *European Music and Musicians in New York, 1840–1900*, ed. John Graziano (2006).

44 · On Jullien, see chapter IV.1 in this volume.

45 · See Adam Carse, *The Life of Jullien: Adventurer, Showman-Conductor and Establisher of the Promenade Concerts in England* (1951); also John Spitzer, "The Entrepreneur-Conductors and Their Orchestras," *Nineteenth-Century Music Review* 5 (2007); and Simon McVeigh, "Concert Promoters and Entrepreneurs in Late-Nineteenth-Century London," in *The Musician as Entrepreneur, 1700-1914: Managers, Charlatans, and Idealists*, ed. William Weber (2004).

virtuoso, to play solos that were the high point of his concerts for many listeners. On the other hand, Jullien held a "Grand Beethoven Night," whose
first half included the song "Adelaide" played by Koenig, the Fifth Symphony
complete, a movement from the Eighth, and "*Le Désir,*" an arrangement of
a waltz by Franz Schubert published under Beethoven's name.[46] The second half of the concert focused on Jullien's dance pieces—the *Prima Donna
Waltz* and the *American Quadrille,* the latter with twenty solos and variations
by members of the orchestra.

Several other musical entrepreneurs and enterprises produced concerts
in Boston during the 1840s and 1850s. The Steyermark Musical Company
visited Boston in October and November 1848, giving "Grand Promenade
Concerts" that included overtures, solos, duets, marches, quadrilles, polkas,
and other numbers.[47] In some venues a caller was provided so that the audience could dance.[48] On Sundays the Steyermarkers evaded the blue laws
by staging "Grand Sacred Concerts."[49] One of these (appendix, program 10)
opened and closed with orchestrated chorales and offered selections from
Verdi's *Nabucco* (1836) and Rossini's *Stabat Mater.* Instrumental solos from
slow movements by Beethoven and Mendelssohn were performed under religious titles.[50]

The Germania Musical Society, which had visited Boston several times
since its arrival in the United States in 1848, settled down and made Boston
its base of operations in 1851.[51] Some of its programs were typical promenade combinations of overtures, solo turns, and dances, while others combined classical works with instrumental solos and vocal numbers. Its repertory often included opera selections; the program on January 8, 1852, for
example, began with Beethoven's Second Symphony (probably one or two
movements) and then offered the overture from Spohr's *Jessonda,* the cavatina from Meyerbeer's *Robert le Diable,* and the finale from the second act of

---

46 · This program is given in chapter IV.1 of this volume, figure IV.1.2.

47 · *Boston Evening Transcript,* October 28, 1848, 3; November 11, 1848, 2.

48 · *Boston Daily Atlas,* November 17, 1848, 3.

49 · *Boston Evening Transcript,* October 21, 1848, 3. See also Ryan, *Recollections of an Old
Musician,* 56–57. For similar "sacred concerts" in New York, see chapter II.2 in this volume.

50 · *Boston Evening Transcript,* October 21, 1848, 3.

51 · On earlier visits of the Germania Musical Society to Boston, see chapter III.4 in this volume. See also Nancy Newman, *Good Music for a Free People: The Germania Musical Society
in Nineteenth-Century America* (2010); and Newman's "Gleiche Rechte, gleiche Pflichten,
und gleiche Genüsse: Henry Albrecht's Utopian Vision of the Germania Musical Society,"
Yearbook of German-American Studies 34 (1999). See also Ryan, *Recollections of an Old Musician,* 58–59.

Friedrich Flotow's *Martha,* the latter two sung by Madame Eckhardt.[52] In December 1853 the Germanians attempted to present a series of four concerts devoted entirely to classical music, something that had never been attempted before in Boston.[53] They advertised for subscribers with the promise of symphonies by Haydn, Beethoven, Spohr, and Mendelssohn, plus overtures by Gluck, Weber, Berlioz, and Wagner. Neither vocal music nor instrumental solos were proposed.[54] Not nearly enough subscribers stepped forward, so the series was cancelled and replaced by concerts that offered a few overtures and symphony movements, lightened with operatic excerpts, waltzes, quadrilles, and galops.

The failure of the Germanians' project illustrates how Boston's music public was not ready for "pure" classical music without vocal pieces, as was also the case with concertgoers in most European cities. Still, when the Germania Musical Society disbanded in 1854, flautist Carl Zerrahn led the way toward a workable compromise between tastes in orchestral music. Having become music director of the Handel and Haydn Society in 1854, he also started an ensemble called the Philharmonic Orchestra (at points referred to as the Orchestral Union), which became the focus of orchestral music in the city for almost a decade. Where the Philharmonic Society of 1843 had been organized and managed by a committee of amateurs, Zerrahn's Philharmonic Orchestra seems to have been composed of professional musicians and managed by himself. Some of the concerts offered an unusually high proportion of pieces by classical composers, though always with opera selections involved. An 1855 concert (appendix, program 11) had only one piece by a living composer. It opened and closed with well-known pieces by Beethoven and Mendelssohn and featured "Batti, batti" from Mozart's *Don Giovanni* and a piece from *Il giuramento,* an opera by Saverio Mercandante well known to connoisseurs. The overture to Cherubini's *Médée* was a mainstay at classical-music concerts; Weber's *Concert-Stück* for piano and orchestra was performed equally often. Thus vocal music was retained, but ballads and glees were replaced by pieces from the emerging operatic canon. In 1865 Zerrahn helped begin the orchestral concerts of the Harvard Musical Association, one of the many contributions in his long career.

52 · Germania Musical Society Programs, 1851–53, Harvard Musical Association Archives, Boston. Madame Eckhardt appears to have been the wife of Herman Eckhardt, who published numerous songs in Boston in this period.
53 · Newman, "Good Music for a Free People," 347–52.
54 · *Dwight's Journal of Music* 5 (December 10, 1853): 79.

The Vitality of Change

In 1855 a hegemonic orchestral series focused on classical music had still not been established in Boston, and in this respect Boston differed from London, Paris, Leipzig, and New York. But is stability necessarily better than change in a musical community? It is much to Boston's credit that a variety of locally based orchestras competed for the public during this period. We have seen a gradual shift taking place between 1842 and 1855 away from ballads and glees and toward opera selections and classical repertory in orchestral concerts. Virtuoso pieces remained prominent in the programs during this time. To be sure, the absence of a hegemonic orchestral society in Boston limited the authority of classical music and the ideology that its proponents propounded. The arrival of staged Italian opera overshadowed the consolidation of orchestral music and the classical repertory, and the visits by touring orchestras tended to increase the mixture of tastes in any one repertory. The instability of the orchestras and concert productions as a whole brought freshness to musical life different from the rigid tastes and practices that evolved in Europe by the 1870s and '1880s and in the United States in the twentieth century. The entrepreneurial efforts in the period offered Bostonians the luxury of comparing their experiences hearing old and new works performed by a variety of different orchestral ensembles.

APPENDIX V.1.1. *Selected Orchestral Programs, 1799–1855*

(Note: Composers who performed their own works in a concert are designated by the symbol *; composers who were deceased on the date of the concert are designated by the symbol †.)

PROGRAM 1. CATHERINE GRAUPNER AND PETER VAN HAGEN, CONCERT HALL, SALEM, MASSACHUSETTS, JUNE 25, 1799[55]

Overture	Ignace Pleyel
Song	Samuel Arnold
Sonata for Pianoforte, 4 hands	Johann Kozeluch
"By My Tender Passion," *Haunted Tower* (1789)	Stephen Storace†
Solo for Clarinet	Johann Christoph Vogel†
Glee, 4v, "Lullaby," inserted in Storace's *The Pirates*	Samuel Harrison
Concerto for Violin (Van Hagen)	Giovanni Giornovichi
Concerto performed on the piano	Joseph Haydn
Patriotic Song, "Columbia's Bold Eagle"	Gottlieb Graupner
Concerto for Oboe	Jean Le Brun
Glee, "Play'd in Air," *Castle Spectre* (1798)	Michael Kelly
Vocal quartet	
Song, "To Arts, to Arms" (words Tom Paine)	P. A. Van Hagen*

PROGRAM 2. BIRMINGHAM PRIVATE CONCERT, STYLES HOTEL, NOVEMBER 30, 1801[56]

Overture	Ignace Pleyel
Glee [Scotch song], "In April When Primroses Grow"	Harmonized by James Corfe
Overture	G. F. Handel†
Song, "My Lodging Is on the Cold Ground, Love"	Robert Bochsa
Concerto for Flute	
Duet, "Se potesse un suono eguale," *Il Flauto Magico* (1791)	W. A. Mozart†
Overture	Haydn

55 · Oscar Sonneck, *Early Concert-Life in America (1731–1800)* (1907), 315–16.
56 · Local History Collection, Musical Archive, Birmingham Central Library.

Hunting Glee, "Hark! The Hollow Woods Resounding"	John Stafford Smith
Concerto	Francesco Geminiani†
Song, flute obbligato, "First and Chief on Golden Wing" and "Sweet Bird," *L'Allegro, il Penseroso ed il Moderato* (1740)	Handel†

PROGRAM 3. BOSTON ACADEMY OF MUSIC, ODEON, JANUARY 11, 1845[57]

Overture, *Masaniello* (*La muette de Portici, 1828*)	Daniel Auber
Glee, "Arise, My Fair One, Come Away!"	Reginald Spofforth†
Air, "Oh! Had I Jubal's Lyre," *Joshua* (1748)	Handel†
Overture, *Le dieu et la bayadère, ou La courtisane amoureuse* (1830)	Auber
Glee, "There Is a Mild and Tranquil Light"	Thomas Attwood†
Solo on the violin (Mr. Ketzer)	Joseph Mayseder
Overture, *Le Domino noir* (1837)	Auber
Symphony no. 5	L. van Beethoven†

PROGRAM 4. PHILHARMONIC SOCIETY, HANOVER SQUARE ROOMS, LONDON, MAY 26, 1845[58]

Symphony in A minor, "*Scotch*"	Felix Mendelssohn
Recitative, "Unglückseel'ge"; Aria, "Fahret wieder," *Elias* [Elijah]	Mendelssohn
Concerto for Pianoforte in C Minor	Mozart†
Recit., "Ils s'éloignent"; Air, "Sombre forêt," *William Tell* (1829)	Gioachino Rossini
Overture and duet, "In Sinnenlust," *Faust* (1813)	Louis Spohr
Symphony no. 8 in F	Beethoven†
Air, "En vain j'espère," *Robert le Diable* (1831)	Giacomo Meyerbeer
Fantasia for Harp on airs from *Robert le Diable*	Félix Godefroid
Aria, "Pro peccatis," *Stabat Mater*	Rossini
Overture, *Der Freischütz* (1821)	C. M. von Weber†

57 · "Programs of Concerts in Boston, 1817–63."
58 · Myles Birket Foster, *History of the Philharmonic Society of London: 1813–1912* (1912), 191.

PROGRAM 5. BOSTON MUSICAL FUND SOCIETY, MELODEON,
DECEMBER 9, 1848[59]

Symphony in A, no. 7	Beethoven†
Concerto for Piano in G Minor, op. 25	Mendelssohn†
Overture, *Le Roi de Yvetot* (1842)	Adolphe Adam
Fantaisie for Violin on Bellini's *Norma*	Delphin Alard
Recitative and air, "O ruddier Than the Cherry,"	
Acis and Galatea	Handel†
Fantaisie and Variation Brilliante for Oboe on a	
theme from Auber's *Gustave III, ou le*	
Bal Masqué	J. M. de Carmen Ribas*
Overture, *La Sirène* (1844)	Auber

PROGRAM 6. NEW YORK PHILHARMONIC ORCHESTRA,
APOLLO ROOMS, APRIL 29, 1848[60]

Symphony no. 2, op. 20	Louis Spohr
Aria, "O cara imagine," *Il Flauto Magico* (1791)	Mozart†
Concerto for Piano in G Minor, op. 58	Ignaz Moscheles
Hebrides Overture	Mendelssohn†
Song, "Weep Not for Sorrow"	Franz Lachner
Duetto, *Jessonda* (1823)	Spohr
Concert Overture, no. 11	Johann Kalliwoda

PROGRAM 7. BIRMINGHAM PRIVATE CONCERTS, DEE'S ROYAL
HOTEL, APRIL 14, 1842[61]

Overture	Beethoven†
Glee, 4v, "See the Chariot at Hand of Love"	William Horsley
Scena, *The Maniac*	Henry Russell*
Aria, "Come per me sereno," *La Sonnambula* (1831)	Vincenzo Bellini†
Variations for Violin	Kalliwoda
Song, "A Life on the Ocean Wave"	Russell*
Ballad, "Dermot astore," *Echoes of the Lakes*	F. Nicholls Crouch
Arietta à quartet, "Invano alcun desir," *Armide* (1777)	C. W. Gluck†

59 · "Programs of Concerts in Boston, 1817–63."
60 · Henry Edward Krehbiel, *The Philharmonic Society of New York: A Memorial* (1892), 102.
61 · Birmingham Private Concerts, Archive.

Overture, *Anacreon*	Luigi Cherubini†
Quartet, "Placido è il mar," *Idomeneo* (1781)	Mozart†
Scena, *The Ship on Fire*	Russell*
Concerto for Violin	Ludwig Maurer
Song, "The Last Adieu"	John Parry
Song, "The Old Arm Chair"	Russell*
Air with variations, "Cease Your Funning"	
[*Beggar's Opera*]	[Johann Pepusch†]
Finale [symphonic allegro]	Haydn†

PROGRAM 8. PHILHARMONIC SOCIETY OF BOSTON, TREMONT TEMPLE, DECEMBER 9, 1843[62]

Cavatina, "Tutto è sciolto," *La Sonnambula* (1831)	Vincenzo Bellini†
Song, "Thou Art Gone," *Amile, or the Love Test* (1818)	William Rooke
Solo for Clarinet	Herman Bender
Cavatina, "Casta diva," *Norma* (1831)	Bellini†
Solo for Bugle	J. G. Jones*
Cavatina, "Come per me sereno," *La Sonnambula*	Bellini†
Aria, "Un vago sembiante," *Il Turco in Italia* (1814)	Rossini
Solo for Violin	Ludwig Maurer
Polacco, "Son vergin vezzosa," *I Puritani* (1835)	Bellini†
Fantasia for Harp	Nicholas Bochsa
Finale for orchestra	

PROGRAM 9. PHILHARMONIC FESTIVAL OF THE PHILHARMONIC SOCIETY, TREMONT TEMPLE, BOSTON, FEBRUARY 16, 1850[63]

Overture, *La gazza ladra* (1817)	Gioachino Rossini
Duo from *Elisir d'amore* (1832)	Gaetano Donizetti†
Duo from *Semiramide* (1823)	Rossini
Cavatina, "Casta diva," *Norma* (1831)	Vincenzo Bellini†
Fantasia for Grand Orchestra on themes of *Lucrezia Borgia*, with solos and variations for trombone, flute, trumpet, clarinet	Max Maretzek

---

62 · Boston Philharmonic Orchestra, Programs, Harvard Musical Association Archives.

63 · *Boston Evening Transcript*, February 16, 1850, 3.

Overture, *Masaniello* (1828)   Daniel Auber
Duo from *Attila* (1846)   Giuseppe Verdi
Rondo Finale introduced in *Linda di Chamounix*   Maretzek
Romanza from *La Favorita* (1840)   Donizetti†
"Tip Top Polka" (by request)   Maretzek

PROGRAM 10. LAST GRAND SACRED CONCERT: THE
STEYERMARKISCHE MUSICAL COMPANY, MASONIC TEMPLE,
OCTOBER 22, 1848[64]

Chorale, "May the Lord Be Merciful to Us"   Martin Luther†
Sacred overture   Luigi Cherubini†
Adagio Religioso, solo for French horn   Beethoven†
Aria, no. 2, *Stabat Mater*   Rossini
Cavatina, *Nabucodonozar* (1842)   Verdi

Overture, *The Ruins of Babylon* (1812)   Karol Kurpiński
Andante Religioso, no. 2   Beethoven†
Solo for Trombone, "The Prayer"   Mendelssohn†
Chorale of the 15th century, "Come Holy Ghost"

PROGRAM 11. PHILHARMONIC ORCHESTRA OF BOSTON,
MUSIC HALL, DECEMBER 22, 1855[65]

"Pastorale" Symphony, op. 68   Beethoven†
Romanza, "Ma negli estremi istanti," *Il giuramento*
    (1837)   Saverio Mercandante
Overture, *Médée* (1797)   Cherubini†
Concert-Stück for Piano and Orchestra   Carl Maria von Weber†
Aria, "Batti, batti," *Don Giovanni* (1787)   Mozart†
Overture, *A Midsummer Night's Dream*   Mendelssohn†

64 · Ibid., October 21, 1848, 3.
65 · Boston Philharmonic Orchestra, Programs, Harvard Musical Association Archives.

[v.2] Theodore Thomas and the Cultivation of American Music

BRENDA NELSON-STRAUSS

Theodore Thomas (1835–1905) was one of America's most influential conductors and orchestra builders. He led the Brooklyn Philharmonic Society
from 1866 to 1891, the New York Philharmonic from 1877 to 1891, and the
Chicago Orchestra (later renamed the Chicago Symphony Orchestra) from
1891 until his death in January 1905. With his own Theodore Thomas Orchestra, based in New York, he toured throughout the United States, giving performances in more than two hundred cities—as far west as San Francisco,
north into Canada, and throughout the South. Many American cities heard
no symphonic music at all until Thomas began touring in 1869.[1]

For decades, Thomas's relationship with American composers and his
role in promoting and performing American works have been overlooked.
Interest in Thomas's career was rekindled in 1989 with the publication of the
landmark biography by Ezra Schabas, which offered a thorough reexami-
nation of the conductor and paved the way for other new perspectives on
Thomas.[2] Thus far, however, Adrienne Fried Block has been the only scholar
to acknowledge the important role that Thomas played in performing and
promoting the music of native-born and resident American composers.[3]

It has often been said or implied that Thomas was no great champion of
American composers. Howard Shanet, in his history of the New York Philharmonic, portrays Thomas as a proponent of European rather than American
music: "[Thomas] is usually said to have done more than anyone else to educate the American public to good music; this must be translated to mean that

---

1 · Philip Hart, *Orpheus in the New World* (1973), 7.

2 · Ezra Schabas, *Theodore Thomas: America's Conductor and Builder of Orchestras, 1835–
1905* (1989).

3 · Adrienne Fried Block, "New York's Orchestras and the 'American' Composer: A
Nineteenth-Century View," in *European Music and Musicians in New York City, 1840–1900*,
ed. John Graziano (2006).

he did more than anyone else to establish the German-serious style as the proper high-class style for music in America."[4] Regarding Thomas's performances of American works, Shanet goes on to say:

> In his thirteen years with the Philharmonic Thomas did only one American composition worth mentioning: John Knowles Paine's *An Island Symphony* in 1890. He played other American compositions in his Brooklyn Philharmonic programs and in some of the free-lance concerts that he conducted in New York, but he seemed to regard the Philharmonic as too conservative a forum for such music. The programs of his "light" summer concerts and matinees in New York and other cities had sometimes contained American names, but many of these did not represent real orchestral works but solo pieces interpolated in an orchestral program when the composer could be present as performer.... For the "serious" programs of his later years, whether in New York or elsewhere, the proportion of major American compositions that Thomas presented was not very large—perhaps 1 or 2 percent of the music he performed.[5]

John H. Mueller, in his study of the repertory of American orchestras, offers a similar view: "In his day ... Thomas had not only failed to make a reputation as a friend of American music, but was actually criticized for his apathy toward it. It can be said only that he played a moderate number of American 'classics' (Paine, Chadwick, MacDowell, Converse, etc.)."[6] Though one cannot dispute certain elements of this criticism, it places too much emphasis on New York performances, it does not fully take into account the fledgling nature of American music during the early years of Thomas's conducting career, and it overlooks key primary sources.

In his *Memoirs* Thomas offered what seems to be a clear statement of his views about performing music by American composers: "As for the American composers, the only way in which to develop composition in our own country is to play the works by American writers side by side with those of other nationalities, and let them stand or fall on their own merits. I do not believe in playing inferior works merely because they are American, nor rejecting good ones because they are foreign. Let our composers realize that there is a standard to be reached before they can be recognized, but that if they

4 · Howard Shanet, *Philharmonic: A History of New York's Orchestra* (1975), 167.
5 · Ibid., 169. In addition to Paine's symphony, Thomas also led the Philharmonic in a performance of Victor Herbert's Cello Concerto no. 1, op. 8.
6 · John H. Mueller, *The American Symphony Orchestra: A Social History of Musical Taste* (1951), 112.

do reach it, they will be certain of equal recognition with writers of other nations."[7] Though the recognition that Thomas gave to American composers was seldom equal to his recognition of European composers—both classics such as Mozart and Beethoven and contemporaries such as Liszt and Wagner—Thomas did, in fact, perform a good deal of American music. During his lifetime he programmed and/or conducted works by more than 150 American composers, including native-born composers as well as immigrants to the United States.[8] A list of American composers and works that Thomas performed is found in the appendix to this chapter.

Much of the critical analysis of Thomas's repertory seems to have been based on his posthumously published autobiography, which lists complete programs for his subscription concerts with the Brooklyn Philharmonic, New York Philharmonic, and Chicago Orchestra.[9] However, the autobiography gives only a sample of programs by the Theodore Thomas Orchestra. An estimated two thousand concerts were omitted, including more than one thousand New York Summer Garden Concerts as well as programs given by the Thomas Orchestra on its annual tours. These concerts are documented in the Theodore Thomas collection of concert programs at the Newberry Library.[10] Furthermore, Thomas amassed one of the largest private libraries of orchestral music in the world, with scores and parts to over thirty-five hundred works. On his death in 1905, several hundred scores and librettos were deposited in the Newberry Library by his widow, but the bulk of the music remained with the Chicago Orchestra. Though the scores in the Newberry Library have been widely used and cited by researchers, the Thomas collection in the Chicago Symphony Orchestra's Rosenthal Archives was only recently reassembled and cataloged. A thorough examination of Thomas's music library, as well as the unpublished portion of his concert programs, reveals a much broader range of repertory and sheds new light on his performances of American works and relationships with American composers.[11]

---

7 · Rose Fay Thomas, *Memoirs of Theodore Thomas* (1911), 67–68.

8 · This tally is based on a survey of Thomas's extant programs at the Newberry Library. For the purposes of this study, all composers who were confirmed as residents of the United States at the time their works were composed or performed have been included.

9 · Theodore Thomas, *Theodore Thomas: A Musical Autobiography* (1905). George P. Upton, the editor of Thomas's autobiography, selected for volume 2 what he considered to be a representative sample of Thomas's programs.

10 · The Newberry Library collection of Thomas programs is available on microfilm.

11 · I am in the process of compiling a catalog of Theodore Thomas's music library. Most of the music manuscripts have been cataloged and are accessible through the online catalog of the Rosenthal Archives, http://cso.org/About/History/Default.aspx.

The Formative Years: 1845–50s

Thomas, who was born in Germany in 1835, arrived in New York ten years later on the leading edge of a wave of German immigrants, including many musicians, whose number grew dramatically following the European revolutions of 1848. By the late 1850s, when Thomas was actively making a living as a violinist, nearly 25 percent of New York's population was of German descent. In the orchestras of New York—including those in the theaters, concert halls, beer gardens, and even the Philharmonic—the percentage rose as high as 80 percent.[12] The repertory of these orchestras, as one might expect, was heavily weighted toward Austro-German music.[13] Despite these demographics, Thomas gained considerable exposure to American composers. During the early years of his career, Thomas performed in various musical events organized by Harvey B. Dodworth and William Henry Fry, which featured performances of their works as well as those by other native-born composers. In 1853 he joined the touring orchestra of Louis Antoine Jullien, who profoundly influenced young Thomas in terms of repertory selection and programming. Jullien performed an unprecedented number of American orchestral works, including multiple performances of four of Fry's symphonies: *Santa Claus, A Day in the Country, Childe Harold,* and *A Breaking Heart*.[14] George Bristow, who also played in Jullien's orchestra, was rewarded with repeat performances of selections from three of his symphonies.[15] Jullien's magnanimity toward American composers led Fry and Bristow to publicly level "anti-American" charges against the Philharmonic the following year.[16] The Philharmonic capitulated by programming Bristow's Second (*Jullien*) and Third Symphonies (in 1856 and 1859, respectively), which Thomas, who had joined the orchestra in 1854, performed alongside Bristow (both were members of the first violin section). Thomas may also have been in the orchestra pit for the premieres of Bristow's *Rip*

12 · Block, "New York's Orchestras," 115–17.
13 · Shanet, *Philharmonic,* 109.
14 · On Jullien's performances of works by American composers, see chapter IV.1 in this volume. See also Gilbert Chase, *America's Music: From the Pilgrims to the Present* (1987), 311–12.
15 · On Jullien's support for Bristow, see Katherine K. Preston's introduction to *George F. Bristow's Symphony No. 2 ("Jullien"): A Critical Edition* (2011).
16 · Bristow was a member of the first violin section of the New York Philharmonic from 1843 to 1879. For a summary of Bristow's compositions performed in New York through 1859, see Vera Brodsky Lawrence, *Strong on Music,* vol. 2, *Reverberations: 1850–1856* (1995), 290. See also Chase, *America's Music,* 308–9; Joseph Horowitz, *Classical Music in America: A History of Its Rise and Fall* (2005), 211–15; Block, "New York's Orchestras," 114–34.

Van Winkle (the first opera on American themes) in 1855 and Fry's *Leonora* in 1858.[17]

Perhaps of equal significance, Thomas was occasionally associated with the New York American Music Association (NYAMA), whose stated purpose was to perform music by "native or naturalized American composers."[18] Formed in 1856 and presided over by Vermont native C. Jerome Hopkins, the association had performed fifty-seven American works by the end of 1857, the majority of which were songs, instrumental solos, and chamber works.[19] Thomas participated in at least a few of the NYAMA concerts and was well acquainted with most of the composers, including Bristow, Fry, Hopkins, J. N. Pychowski, William Mason, and Louis Gottschalk—all of whom found their way onto Thomas's concert programs in the ensuing years.[20] Though it would be two more decades before Thomas organized his own all-American concert, the programming during his formative years as a conductor suggests more than a passing influence from these various affiliations and events.

Early Years as a Conductor: 1860–75

Thomas gradually made the transition from violinist to conductor, beginning with a few miscellaneous concerts in 1858 and achieving his first major success shortly thereafter with Carl Anschütz's New York–based Italian opera company. From the very beginning of his conducting career, works by American composers were included on his programs. For example, Thomas's Irving Hall matinee series of 1862–63 featured sixteen American works, most of them instrumental solos rather than orchestral works. The bulk of these were American-born pianists playing their own works, including Louis Gottschalk, John Nelson Pattison, Sebastian Bach Mills, and Harry Sanderson. German immigrants to the United States were represented by violinist Edward Mollenhauer and composer Charles Fradel, who contributed two original orchestral works. By far the most significant American work of this period was Fry's opera *Notre Dame of Paris,* which Thomas conducted at the Philadelphia Academy of Music on May 4, 1864, as part of a "grand musical

17 · Shanet, *Philharmonic*, 125. See also Delmer Dalzell Rogers, "Nineteenth Century Music in New York City as Reflected in the Career of George Frederick Bristow" (Ph.D. diss., 1967), which cites various performances involving Thomas.
18 · Lawrence, *Strong on Music*, vol. 2, 72–75. See also E. Douglas Bomberger, "A Tidal Wave of Encouragement": American Composers' Concerts in the Gilded Age (2002), 2–3.
19 · Lawrence, *Strong on Music*, vol. 2, 75.
20 · Ibid.

festival inaugurating the National Fair for the benefit of wounded and ill soldiers and sailors of the United States Army and Navy."[21]

By 1865 Thomas had formed his own orchestra with the objective of cultivating the public taste for instrumental music, which in his opinion was not achievable through the severely limited number of concerts given by the New York Philharmonic.[22] His programming followed the model of European orchestras led by conductors like Jullien and Gungl, who interspersed the requisite dance music with meatier fare, including overtures and movements from symphonies.[23] This created an opportunity for Thomas to program orchestral works by local composers, mostly "novelties," which were better suited to less formal concerts. Over the next decade the majority of American works performed by Thomas were offered during his outdoor Summer Garden Concerts in New York—held at Belvedere Lion Park (1865), Koch's Terrace Garden (1866–67), and Central Park Garden (1868–75)—as well his popular concert series at Steinway Hall and the Academy of Music.[24]

An examination of Thomas's concert programs from this period reveals that he was constantly expanding his repertory of contemporary music. During the 1860s, the lion's share of new American works came from musicians who performed with the Mason-Thomas Quartet, the Philharmonic, or the Thomas Orchestra—Carl Bergmann, Frederic Bergner, William Dietrich, Joseph Eller, Emanuel Grill, Eduard Heindl, Frederick Letsch, Jacob Mallach, George Matzka, Joseph Mosenthal, Frederick Rietzel, and Henry Schmitz—and soloists, such as cornet virtuoso Jules Levy and violinist Julius Eichberg.[25] Most of these compositions were the dances and marches so popular in that era, but some interesting American themes were also presented, such as [J. D.?] Scholl's *Grand Fantasia Yankee Doodle* and *Grand Fantasie on a National Air*, Harvey Dodworth's *Union Medley*, Carl C. Müller's *Lafayette Galop,* Mallach's *Medley on American Airs*, and Charles Koppitz's *National Medley*. Local composers also supplied Thomas with a steady stream of polkas, galops, and marches commemorating the garden concerts, with Thomas himself contributing an *Opening March for the Central Park Garden* in 1868.

Though few substantial orchestral works by American composers were presented by Thomas during the 1860s and early 1870s (one could argue

21 · Printed program in the Theodore Thomas collection at the Newberry Library.
22 · Thomas, *Musical Autobiography,* 1:51.
23 · Ibid., 50–51; John Spitzer, "The Entrepreneur-Conductors and Their Orchestras," *Nineteenth-Century Music Review* 5 (2008).
24 · On Thomas's "garden" concerts in New York, see chapter II.2 in this volume.
25 · Block, "New York's Orchestras," 125–30. Norman Schweikert also kindly assisted by identifying Thomas Orchestra members.

that few existed), there were some notable exceptions. Popular favorites performed by the Thomas Orchestra on tour and at both the Summer Garden and Steinway Hall concert series were the overture *Hail Columbia!* by Karl Hohnstock and the *Nordishe Suite* no. 1, by Asger Hamerik, the Danish-born director of the Peabody Institute in Baltimore. Dudley Buck's Overture to *Don Munio*, Leopold Damrosch's *Festival* Overture, John Loretz's *Deborah* Overture, and Müller's *National* and *Union* overtures all received at least one hearing, as did overtures by Stoeckel, Koppitz, Matzka, Sobolewski, Joseph Noll, Andrew Nembach, and S. Austen Pearce, as well as James Deems's Grand Fantasie *Ione*. The only American symphony presented by the Thomas Orchestra during this period was the final movement of *Life* by Hopkins, given at Steinway Hall in 1866. Charles Converse's *Festival* Overture and Loretz's *Deborah* Overture were performed with the Brooklyn Philharmonic Society, along with several minor works, while the Thomas Orchestra and the Brooklyn Handel and Haydn Society combined forces in November 1875 for a Leopold Damrosch Benefit Concert, in which they presented his *Ruth and Naomi* and *Siegfried's Sword*.

Two New York–based composers who were featured prominently on Thomas's early programs have received scant mention in histories of American music, perhaps because few if any of their orchestral works appear to be extant. Carl Christian Müller was born in Germany in 1831 and studied harmony with Zöllner and piano with Heinrich Pfeifer before immigrating to New York in 1854, where he was active as a pianist, composer, and teacher until his death in 1914. Dudley Buck once referred to Müller as the "greatest expert in counterpoint in the country."[26] During the latter half of the 1860s he composed several works specifically for the Thomas Orchestra, including the *Terrace Garden Galop* and *Central Park Garden Galop*. In addition to the overtures previously mentioned, he contributed a Fantasia for Trombone as well as various dances and marches performed extensively by the Thomas Orchestra. His relationship with Thomas appears to have culminated in a Grand Orchestral Concert on January 5, 1877, apparently organized as a tribute to Müller. The orchestra premiered Müller's new symphony, the overture *Nathan the Wise*, a nocturne on *Hiawatha*, and a Romance for Horn and Harp (presumably with orchestra). For reasons that remain unclear, his works were seldom performed by Thomas following this event.

Just as Müller's popularity was beginning to wane, Alfred Humphreys Pease came to Thomas's attention. A native of Cleveland, Pease spent six years in Berlin studying piano with Hans von Bülow and Theodor Kullak, composition with Richard Wüerst, and orchestration with Wilhelm Wie-

26 · *New York Times*, July 21, 1914, 6.

precht (apparently during the same period that John Knowles Paine was his student). On his return to America in 1864, Pease began to achieve acclaim as a concert pianist and shortly thereafter made several appearances with the Thomas Orchestra performing his own works, including solo pieces as well as a Grand Concerto for Piano and Orchestra. For a few brief years between 1871 and 1876 he produced a steady stream of orchestral works for the Thomas Orchestra, practically serving as Thomas's composer-in-residence. By far the most popular was his *Japanese Galop*, completed in 1872 and performed at least fifty times over the course of the next decade. The *Red Cloud Galop*, composed just a month later, was also popular for a short time, as were his *Les Vivandieres* March, Piano Concerto in E, and other short concert pieces. Like Müller, Pease disappeared from the scene nearly as quickly as he had arrived. It seems likely that he left New York around 1877 to embark on a series of concert tours, thus ending his affiliation with the Thomas Orchestra. Overall, Pease is better known as a composer of art songs, having completed nearly one hundred before his untimely death at the age of forty-four.[27] Pease and Müller would soon be supplanted in the Thomas repertory by a new group of American composers, most notably John Knowles Paine and Dudley Buck, who had been Thomas's assistant conductor during the 1875 Central Park Garden concerts.

The Philadelphia Centennial Exposition of 1876

The celebration of the nation's centennial was scheduled for the spring of 1876, with a grand exposition to be held in Philadelphia. Thomas, now America's leading conductor, was contracted to be the director of music by the Women's Centennial Executive Committee, headed by his longtime friend Mrs. E. D. Gillespie.[28] Thomas received funding to commission works by two leading American composers (he chose Paine and Buck), and he also persuaded the committee to commission a work by Richard Wagner, who, in Thomas's opinion, was the world's greatest living composer.[29] President Grant officiated at the opening ceremonies on May 10, 1876, followed by the performance of the three newly commissioned works. Wagner's *Grand Centennial Inauguration March*, though praised by most of the critics, was at best a novelty, leaving Thomas bitterly disappointed and open to criticism that

27 · Carl Stanton Rogers, "The Songs of Alfred H. Pease (1838–1882)" (Ph.D. diss., 1980), 32. On Pease's death, see "Alfred H. Pease's Fate: The Body Found in the St. Louis Morgue, Death Caused by Intemperance," *New York Times*, July 16, 1882.

28 · Thomas, *Musical Autobiography*, 1:66.

29 · Schabas, *Theodore Thomas*, 71. See also Abram Loft, "Richard Wagner, Theodore Thomas, and the American Centennial," *Musical Quarterly* 37 (1951).

such an enormous commission (reputedly $5,000) had been offered to a German rather than an American composer. Dudley Buck's cantata, the *Centennial Meditation of Columbia*, and John Knowles Paine's *Centennial Hymn*, both set to texts by American poets (Sidney Lanier and John Greenleaf Whittier, respectively), were so well received that Thomas programmed them repeatedly throughout the summer.[30]

After the opening ceremonies, Summer Night concerts commenced at the Women's Centennial Music Hall, following a prospectus that laid out a plan for Thomas to "give a series of concerts in Philadelphia during the entire period of the Exposition, for the purpose of illustrating the musical progress of America."[31] Though not explicitly stated, the progress of the American composer was also to be on display, culminating in an "American Night" on July 19, 1876. Featured on the program were Buck's Overture to *Don Munio* as well as his *Concertstück* for Orchestra and Horn Quartet; Paine's Symphony no. 1 in C Minor (premiered earlier that year during Thomas's concerts in Boston and New York); Pease's Concerto for Piano in E-flat and his ever-popular *Japanese Galop*; Myron A. Ward's *Allemania Waltzes* for Orchestra; and William Henry Fry's symphony *A Day in the Country*.[32] Fry had passed away more than a decade earlier and his music was no longer fashionable, yet Thomas evidently wished to acknowledge this dean of American composers. A conspicuous omission from the American Night program was Bristow, arguably the most senior among the "native-born" composers, whose *Columbus* Overture would have been quite fitting for the occasion.[33]

Other works by American composers were sprinkled throughout the Summer Night concert series, including C. Baetens's *Night and Morning* Overture and Hamerik's first *Nordishe Suite*, along with galops and scherzos by Müller and Pease. Music of a more patriotic nature was provided by Philadelphia native A. H. Rosewig, whose nationalistic cantata *The Flag That Bears the Stripes and Stars* received its premiere on July 8, 1876. Interestingly, the only other work on American themes was offered by the German composer Heinrich Schulz-Beuthen, whose *Indian Corn Dance* was repeated throughout the summer. Though the Summer Night series was cancelled abruptly at the end of July due to poor attendance, leaving Thomas nearly bankrupt, Mrs. Gil-

---

30 · Schabas, *Theodore Thomas*, 73–74.

31 · Thomas, *Musical Autobiography*, 1:67.

32 · Though Fry's *A Day in the Country* was long thought to have been lost, a manuscript score and parts were found in Thomas's music library at the Chicago Symphony Orchestra's Rosenthal Archives.

33 · Over the course of his career, Thomas programmed only two or three of Bristow's works, none of which seems to have been repeated. No correspondence has been found that can shed further light on this issue.

lespie secured funding for an additional ten concerts to be given that fall at the Philadelphia Academy of Music.[34] There, Thomas continued to program music by American composers, regularly repeating the commissions by Buck and Paine and closing the series with three works composed and performed by New York native William H. Sherwood (all appear to have been for solo piano). This concluded Thomas's first major foray into the focused programming of American music. For American composers, the Philadelphia Centennial Exposition represented a major step forward, albeit one tempered by sparse attendance. For Thomas, this great venture, which had started out so full of promise and possibilities, pushed him to the brink of professional and financial disaster.[35]

The Middle Years: 1877–91

The next fourteen years were a period of remarkable growth for Thomas, who expanded his concert series in Chicago and Cincinnati, took over the helm of the New York Philharmonic, and continued a grueling tour schedule with the Thomas Orchestra. During this same period, the establishment of music conservatories and university music departments offered academic positions to a number of leading American composers, particularly those of the Second New England School, resulting in a growing quantity of serious American music available to Thomas.[36] Gradually Thomas's repertory shifted away from the lighter fare of dances and marches, and his summer concert series, in particular, began to incorporate a significant number of overtures and symphonies by this new generation of American composers.

The Central Park Garden venue closed following Thomas's 1875 concert series, and, after the debacle in Philadelphia, he desperately needed a summer engagement for his orchestra. Thomas decided to look west to Chicago, a city that had been extremely receptive since his first tour there with the Thomas Orchestra in 1869. A new series of Chicago Summer Night Garden concerts commenced in June 1877 at the enormous Exposition Building on Lake Michigan, which had been divided into a concert hall at one end and a beer garden at the other. According to Thomas, "it was the last place in the world one would have expected orchestral concerts to succeed. Neverthe-

34 · Charles Edward Russell, *The American Orchestra and Theodore Thomas* (1927), 101. See also Schabas, *Theodore Thomas*, 73–74.

35 · Schabas, *Theodore Thomas*, 69–84. Thomas's finances following the fair were so dire that his entire library was seized by the sheriff and sold at auction, only to be purchased by one of Thomas's friends and returned.

36 · Nicholas E. Tawa, *The Coming of Age of American Art Music: New England's Classical Romanticists* (1991).

less ... the programs, though popular in character, were always filled with good standard music, besides many novelties, and each week we gave one Symphony and one Composer's programme."[37] Because the Thomas Orchestra had been a fixture in the city for nearly ten years the audience was already well established, allowing Thomas considerable leeway to advance his ideas for programming. Though the initial season was short on American works, he did program Pease's *Japanese Galop* and a new work by Hamerik, and on the Fourth of July the entire inaugural program from the Philadelphia Exposition was repeated. Apparently satisfied with this new venue, he proclaimed at the close of the season, "Chicago is the only city on the continent, next to New York, where there is sufficient musical culture to enable me to give a series of fifty consecutive concerts."[38]

After a three-year hiatus, Thomas returned to Chicago in the summer of 1881 to resume his Summer Night Garden concerts, which continued through 1890, the year before he founded the Chicago Orchestra. Immediately his programs were more adventurous—the first season alone featured American works on nine out of the fifty concerts. Even more interesting is that Thomas chose Chicago, rather than New York, for the premieres of George E. Whiting's Overture to the *Tale of the Viking*, Frederick Grant Gleason's Introduction to *Otho Visconti*, Ernest Guiraud's *Danse Persane*, Silas Pratt's Antique Menuet and Pastorale, and two new works by Carl Koelling, who had recently emigrated from Germany.[39] Thomas must have considered the reception of these new works a success, for the following year he scheduled an American Composers' Night on August 2, 1882, featuring George Chadwick's Overture to *Rip van Winkle* and Andante for Strings, selections from Gleason's *Montezuma*, Paine's Second Symphony, and Whiting's Overture and March from the *Tale of the Viking,* among others. The following day a local critic noted that the "new and strange" works, though "replete with the charm of originality ... aroused but little enthusiasm."[40]

Undaunted, Thomas persevered with his promotion of American composers, and the repertory offered to Chicagoans over the next five summers followed a similar pattern. Of the seventeen new works introduced in 1883, more than a quarter were American, highlighted by Whiting's concert overture *The Princess*, Edgar S. Kelly's Overture to *MacBeth*, and George Templeton Strong's *Ein Märchen*. Taking a much-needed break, Thomas spent the summer of 1884 in Europe attending concerts and collecting a wide variety of new music, which he was eager to introduce. Consequently, in 1885 American

37 · Thomas, *Musical Autobiography,* 1:69.
38 · Schabas, *Theodore Thomas,* 83.
39 · Guiraud, though born in New Orleans, spent most of his life in Europe.
40 · Bomberger, "*Tidal Wave,*" 6. Unattributed quote from the *Chicago Inter-Ocean.*

works fared somewhat less well, as Thomas gave precedence to the latest compositions from Germany. He did, however, organize another American concert in August of that year with works by Müller, Gleason, and Louis Maas (a recent immigrant), although, interestingly, it was not designated or advertised as such. A performance of Paine's Symphonic Fantasie on Shakespeare's *Tempest* was scheduled the following night. By the next season, American works were sufficiently popular that they were added to "Request Programs," indicating that members of the audience had demanded additional performances. This honor went to Arthur Bird's *Carnival Scene*, Pratt's Court Minuet, and Rietzel's *Humoristic* Suite and *Eine Volksthümliche* Suite.[41]

Thomas's American concerts in his Chicago summer series were part of a trend. By the 1880s, the number of individuals and groups interested in promoting American composers had grown to the extent that American Composers' Concerts became widespread. The Music Teachers' National Association (MTNA), formed in 1876, was at the forefront of this movement: one of its stated missions was the "official recognition of the American composer."[42] The association's initial large-scale effort culminated in a three-day convention in Chicago in July 1884 (the summer that Thomas spent in Europe). Over the next three years the MTNA featured American Composers' Concerts during its conventions in New York, Boston, and Indianapolis, presenting many of the same works that Thomas had been including on his Summer Night Garden programs. When the convention returned to Chicago in 1888, Thomas was contracted to lead his orchestra in three Grand Festival Concerts. Sponsored by the MTNA, these were also billed as the opening concerts of Thomas's summer series, which no doubt had an impact on the size of the audience. Major American works presented under Thomas's baton included Gleason's cantata *Praise Song to Harmony*, Maas's *Will O'Wisps* for female chorus and orchestra, selections from Converse's 126th Psalm, Chadwick's Second Symphony, Pratt's *Elegy* for Chorus and Orchestra, MacDowell's Piano Concert no. 1 (with Teresa Carreño as soloist), and two movements from George Whiting's Symphony in C. Two years later in 1890, the MTNA staged a grandiose convention in Detroit and again contracted the Thomas Orchestra for three days. Douglas Bomberger points to these Detroit concerts as the high point of the MTNA's campaign to promote American music, based on the number of significant American works for orchestra and orchestra with chorus that were brought to public attention.[43]

Another significant event during this period was the American compos-

---

41 · Because some of these works appear to be new, it is possible that the composers' friends and colleagues stuffed the ballot box.

42 · Bomberger, "*Tidal Wave*," 11.

43 · Ibid., 18–19, 75–78.

ers' competition sponsored by the Cincinnati May Festival. Thomas was the director of sixteen biennial May Festivals held in Cincinnati from 1873 through 1904, where he presented German serious repertory that mirrored his New York Philharmonic programs and was equally well suited to this heavily Germanic city on the Ohio River.[44] George Ward Nichols, the manager of the festival, initially proposed the composer competition in 1878. Thomas strongly supported the idea since it would serve to advance the recognition of American composers.[45] The jury, chaired by Thomas, set strict rules, accepting only large-scale works for chorus and orchestra by native-born composers. Dudley Buck was the first recipient of the $1,000 cash prize for his *Scenes from Longfellow's Golden Legend*, performed during the 1880 festival.[46] The competition was extended for one additional festival, with the prize awarded to William Wallace Gilchrist in 1882 for his *Setting of the Forty-Sixth Psalm*. Apparently neither of these works lived up to Thomas's expectations and thereafter he dispensed with the competition altogether, preferring to take sole responsibility for the selection of new works.[47] Several years later he turned to his friend John Knowles Paine, whose cantata *Song of Promise* was premiered at the 1888 May Festival. Other American choral works performed at subsequent Cincinnati May Festivals include Horatio Parker's *Hora Novissima* (1894) and Hugo Kaun's *Festival March and Hymn to Liberty* (1898).

During much of this period Thomas also served as conductor of the New York Philharmonic (1877–78, 1879–90). There he carried on the conservative agenda that was well established prior to his tenure. In an interview given in 1882, he explained that his programming was subject to the parameters of what he called the Philharmonic Creed: "to endeavor always to form a refined musical taste among the people by the intelligent selection of music; to give, in order to accomplish the desired result, only standard works, both of the old and new masters; and to be thus conservative and not given to experimenting with the new musical sensations of the hour."[48] Obviously there were no "old" American masters, and, looking at the Philharmonic's repertory, it seems as though John Knowles Paine was the only American composer elevated to the stature of "new master."

44 · On orchestral music in Cincinnati, see chapter II.3 in this volume.

45 · Schabas, *Theodore Thomas*, 95–96.

46 · Ibid., 95. The vote was initially split between Buck and George Whiting, with Thomas breaking the tie. Whiting later accused Thomas of exercising undue influence, leading to bad publicity for the contest.

47 · Ibid., 118.

48 · Thomas, *Musical Autobiography*, 1:152. No print source is cited for this quote. See also Schabas, *Theodore Thomas*, 188, and Shanet, *Philharmonic*, 167–68.

At the Brooklyn Philharmonic Society, where he had been conductor since 1866, Thomas had greater control over programming, and here American composers received far more exposure. Between 1877 and 1888, the Brooklyn Philharmonic premiered Bristow's overture *The Great Republic*, and performed Paine's Second Symphony, Music to *Oedipus Tyrannus*, and *Tempest Fantasie* (the latter receiving two readings). Buck's cantata *Hymn to Music* and *Marmion* Overture were also introduced, as were two movements from E. C. Phelps *Hiawatha* Symphony and works by Harry Rowe Shelley and Robert Goldbeck.

Thomas continued to organize and participate in a wide range of concerts, most of them more eclectic than his offerings at the New York Philharmonic. At Steinway and Chickering Halls the Thomas Orchestra presented works by Florsheim, Pratt, Herbert, Gleason, Brandeis, Klein, and Foote and participated in testimonial concerts for the composers Caryl Florio and Henry C. Timm. Paine's *Oedipus Tyrannus* was given on three occasions between 1881 and 1882, twice with the New York Choral Society. The 1890–91 Lenox Lyceum series featured works by Aronson, Herbert, Paine, Rietzel, Gleason, Hamerik, and Shelley. On tours along the "Thomas Highway," the Thomas Orchestra also began to introduce audiences to works by Paine, Buck, Hamerik, and Guiraud, as well as lesser-known American composers such as Eduard Sobolewski.[49]

As Thomas's New York tenure drew to a close, his commitment to American music was firmly established. He was performing American works with much greater frequency, but it was in Chicago that his programming was the most adventurous. By the closing season of the Chicago Summer Night Garden concerts in 1890, nearly half of the twenty-five new works were by native-born or resident American composers. These Chicago summer concerts would prove crucial to Thomas's future success with the Chicago Orchestra, for he had developed an audience eager to hear orchestral music and, even more important to this story, receptive to new works.

The Chicago Years, 1891–1905

In 1891 Thomas was induced to leave New York by a group of wealthy citizens in Chicago, who promised him a permanent orchestra, a twenty-eight-week season, and a limited touring schedule. The annual salary offered by Chicago meant he would no longer be required to finance concerts out of

---

49 · Thomas's regular tour route between the Northeast and Chicago was commonly referred to as the Thomas Highway. In several instances, he selected works by local composers to perform in their respective cities. For example, Sobolewski's works were primarily performed in his home city of St. Louis.

his own pocket, yet he still maintained complete control over the orchestra and its repertory. Thomas's first season with the Chicago Orchestra was extremely ambitious and featured a wide variety of American works. Songs and instrumental solos, such as Ethelbert Nevin's "At Twilight" and harpist Edmund Schuecker's popular *Fantasie di Bravura*, were occasionally interspersed on the programs, especially during regional tours. Nonsubscription concerts teamed the Chicago Orchestra with the Germania Männerchor, and at these Thomas conducted his own Festival March and the *Suite Characteristique* for Strings by Henry Schoenefeld (the Männerchor's director). Toward the end of the 1891–92 season an American concert was scheduled, featuring works by Chadwick ("The Lament" and *Melpomene* Overture), Gleason (*Romanza* from *Otho Visconti*), Paine (Second Symphony and an aria from *St. Peter*), and Shelley (*Francesca di Rimini*). This program, however, was far from a critical success. Since many of the same works had already been heard at Thomas's Chicago Summer Night concerts, the conductor may have assumed that the public would relish a repeat performance. Filling the forty-five-hundred-seat Auditorium Theatre without benefit of a beer garden and a program interspersed with lighter works, however, proved an insurmountable obstacle. With box office receipts dwindling and trustees grumbling about deficits, Thomas was forced to confront reality—he would never be free to program whatever works he desired, even when someone else was picking up the tab.

The following season (1892–93) found the city in a frenzy of preparations for the World's Columbian Exhibition, planned as a celebration of the four-hundredth anniversary of the discovery of America by Columbus and constructed on a grandiose scale that would surpass the Philadelphia Centennial Exhibition. Thomas was appointed director of the Bureau of Music, and he issued a proclamation in the spring of 1892 setting forth many lofty goals, among them "the hearty support of American musicians, amateurs and societies, for participation on great festival occasions of popular music, and for the interpretation of the most advanced compositions, American and foreign."[50] Thomas commissioned two of America's leading composers to contribute blockbusters for the opening ceremony. Paine's *Columbus March and Hymn* for orchestra, military band, and chorus, and Chadwick's *Columbian Ode* (on a poem by Harriet Monroe) for chorus, solo voices, and orchestra were performed on October 21, 1892, with Thomas leading the Exposition Orchestra (an expanded Chicago Orchestra) and a chorus numbering more

---

50 · World's Columbian Exposition Bureau of Music handbill, June 30, 1892, Theodore Thomas Felsengarten Collection, Rosenthal Archives, Chicago Symphony Orchestra. Portions reprinted in Thomas, *Musical Autobiography*, 1:195.

than five thousand. For the opening ceremonies of the Woman's Building, Mrs. Potter Palmer, who served as director of the Board of Lady Managers, commissioned Amy Beach to write a *Festival Jubilate,* which Thomas premiered on May 1, 1893.[51]

In June 1892 Thomas issued a press release expressing the Bureau of Music's desire to include "representative choral, orchestral and chamber works by native American composers," and promised that favorable recommendations by a select committee would "be final and insure performance."[52] Twenty-one composers responded to the open call, submitting a total of thirty-one works, of which eight were selected for performance: John A. Broekhoven's *Suite Creole,* A. M. Foerster's Festival March, Margaret Ruthven Lang's overture *Witichis,* Hermann Wetzler's Concert Overture, George E. Whiting's cantata *Dream Pictures,* C. B. Rutenber's cantata *Divine Love,* and Lucius Hosmer's *Resouvenir du Ballet* and *The Satyr's Reveille.* Regrettably for Rutenber and Whiting, the plan to mount two new large-scale choral works was later abandoned, and the Hosmer pieces met the same fate. Thomas also invited Paine, Chadwick, MacDowell, Foote, Bristow, and Strong to "name such of their compositions as they desired to have performed at Exposition concerts."[53]

In the end, Thomas organized three American music concerts in connection with the World's Columbian Exposition, all as part of the ticketed Symphony Concert series geared toward the musical elite. The first was a relatively short program given on May 23, 1893, featuring Chadwick's Second Symphony, Foote's Serenade in E, and MacDowell's Suite op. 42. The second and third American programs were scheduled back-to-back during the first week of July, perhaps in an attempt to capitalize on the patriotic spirit surrounding Independence Day. Thomas dedicated the July 6 concert to the MTNA and repeated the Foote and MacDowell works, while adding Paine's *Island Fantasy,* Van der Stucken's Festival March, and Chadwick's *Melpomene* Overture. A more eclectic mix was offered the following day, with songs by Ethelbert Nevin and Helen Hood, Shelley's *Carnival* Overture, and relatively short works by Foerster, Schoenefeld, Gleason, and Bird. Though not quite

51 · Ann E. Feldman, "Women Composers at the 1893 World's Columbian Exposition," *Notes* 47 (1990): 12–13.

52 · World's Columbian Exposition Bureau of Music, *Announcement regarding American Music at the Exposition,* October 20, 1893, pamphlet in Theodore Thomas Felsengarten Collection, Rosenthal Archives. The selection committee included A. C. Mackenzie, Asger Hamerik, Carl Zerrahn, B. J. Lang, Wm. L. Tomlins, and Theodore Thomas. Saint-Saëns was also invited but declined.

53 · Ibid.

exclusively American, there was one additional program of great interest during the final week of the series, when compositions by Lang, Broekhoven, and Hermann Wetzler (a recent German immigrant) were paired with the Mendelssohn Violin Concerto, performed by America's foremost violinist, Maud Powell.

American works were also sprinkled liberally throughout the free Popular Concerts given by the Exposition Orchestra for the enlightenment and entertainment of the general public. Though a few novelties were added, such as Koelling's *World's Columbian Exposition Waltz*, Thomas repeated most of the American works performed during the Symphony series and even added a few more substantial works such as Bristow's overture *Jibbewainoske* and Shelley's *The Ruined Castle* suite. Popular concerts were more likely to feature one American work per concert, as opposed to the "serious" symphony concerts, which grouped compositions together on American-themed programs. All in all, more than thirty performances of works by twenty-two American composers were presented by the Exposition Orchestra under Thomas's baton, spread over eighty-eight concerts.[54] The majority of the works had been previously performed by Thomas, which was likely a contributing factor in their selection given the paucity of rehearsal time. Of the new works premiered at the Exposition, none were selected for a second hearing on Chicago Orchestra programs. By mid-August of 1893, distraught over poor attendance and mired in controversy, Thomas resigned as musical director.[55] The three American music concerts at the World's Columbian Exposition were the last all-American concerts that Theodore Thomas ever programmed. None had been very successful—in fact, they seemed to engender more bickering and criticism than goodwill.

During Thomas's remaining years with the Chicago Orchestra he dispensed with thematic programming almost entirely. The representation of American composers did not diminish, but their works were interspersed on programs throughout the season—certainly an idea whose time had come. Over the course of his fourteen and a half seasons with the Chicago Orchestra, Thomas presented American works approximately seventy-one times (including works repeated during different seasons), which is far more than the New York Philharmonic during the same period (1891–1905), but roughly equivalent to the Boston Symphony Orchestra. The Chicago and Boston orchestras performed many of the same compositions, since by this

---

54 · *Musical Yearbook of the United States, 1892–1893* (1893), xxiv–xxxii, 145–91. Thomas gave thirty-two symphony concerts, fifty-three free popular concerts, and three opening-ceremony concerts with the Exposition Orchestra.

55 · Schabas, *Theodore Thomas*, 202–6.

time a few works by native composers were beginning to form something of an American canon. However, the regional differences were distinct. Nearly three-quarters of the American repertory programmed by the Boston Symphony represented Boston-area composers, including Paine, Chadwick, Whiting, Foote, MacDowell, and Loeffler.[56] In Chicago, Thomas likewise promoted a number of composers with local ties, such as Henry Schoenefeld, W. C. E. Seeboeck, Wilhelm Middleschulte, Frederick Grant Gleason, A. D. Duvivier, Hugo Kaun, and orchestra members Edmund Schuecker, Adolf Weidig, and Frederick Stock.[57] Thomas's relationships with New England composers remained strong (he visited them frequently when traveling to and from his summer home in the mountains of New Hampshire), and he was particularly close to Paine, who was the only significant American composer from Thomas's generation still active. Paine even gave Thomas the opportunity to premiere his Prelude to the *Birds of Aristophanes* with the Chicago Orchestra prior to its presentation in Boston.[58]

Conclusion: "I Played All There Were"

Thomas did not grow more conservative in his later years. He kept pushing forward, always ready to perform the latest works from home and abroad. Toward the end of his life, when asked about music by American composers, Thomas claimed to have "played all there were."[59] Indeed, there were few American composers of any stature who were not represented on Thomas's programs, and dozens of minor composers, many long since forgotten, owed their initial exposure to the conductor. Though not a proselytizer for American music in the manner of composer-conductors such as Frank Van der Stucken and Frederick Stock, Thomas made much more of an effort to promote American composers than he is generally given credit for. Overall, he performed at least four hundred individual works by more than 150 composers who were either native-born or resident Americans — by no means an insignificant number.

After Thomas's death in 1905, George Chadwick wrote that of all the conductors in America, Thomas alone had treated American composition as a "dignified and serious effort … [producing] the works of American writers

56 · Richard Crawford, *America's Musical Life: A History* (2001), 353. See also Joseph Horowitz, "Reclaiming the Past: Musical Boston Remembered," *American Music* 19 (2001).

57 · Dena J. Epstein, "Frederick Stock and American Music," *American Music* 10 (1992). Stock succeeded Thomas as music director of the Chicago Symphony Orchestra and, as a composer-conductor, continued to advance the programming of American music.

58 · Crawford, *America's Musical Life*, 352.

59 · Mueller, *American Symphony Orchestra*, 112.

side by side with the classic, and also the modern masters, so that they could be compared with their contemporaries, and could stand or fall by their own intrinsic value—the only position a real artist cares to occupy."[60] One could not ask for a more fitting tribute to the man who for so many decades cultivated American music.

60 · Crawford, *America's Musical Life*, 313. See also Rose Fay Thomas, *Memoirs*, 67–68.

APPENDIX V.2.1 *Theodore Thomas's Performances of Works by American Composers*

Included in this list are works by native-born and resident American composers conducted by Thomas or, in the case of solos, programmed at Thomas concerts; arrangements by American composers of European works have not been
included. In addition, American works included in the Theodore Thomas Music
Library have been added if they bear performance markings. Because early programs typically list surnames only, some American composers may have inad-
vertently been omitted; likewise, though every effort has been made to confirm
the identities of the composers below, some errors may remain.[61]

Performing ensembles are abbreviated as follows: BPS = Brooklyn Philharmonic Society; CSO = Chicago Orchestra; NYP = New York Philharmonic;
TTO = Theodore Thomas Orchestra.

Venues for Thomas's major concert series with the Theodore Thomas Or-
chestra (except as indicated) are abbreviated as follows: BLP = Belvedere Lion
Park, NYC; CPG = Central Park Garden, NYC; CMF = Cincinnati May Festi-
val; CSNC = Chicago Summer Night concerts; GG = Gilmore Garden, NYC;
HHB = Highland House Belvedere, Cincinnati; IHM = Irving Hall Matinees,
NYC; LL = Lenox Lyceum, NYC; MTNA = Music Teachers National Associa-
tion conventions; PCE = Philadelphia Centennial Exposition; SH = Steinway
Hall, NYC; SS = Symphony Soirees, NYC[62]; TG = Terrace Garden, NYC; WCE
= World's Columbian Exposition, Chicago.

Composers who were members of the Theodore Thomas Orchestra, New
York Philharmonic, or Chicago Orchestra are indicated by the symbol §.

ARDITI, LUIGI. (b. Italy; to US 1854)
Leggero Invisibile-Bolero: (marked parts in Thomas Library)

ARONSON, RUDOLPH, 1856–95. (b. New York)
Alma Waltz: 3/16/1890 LL
Arcadian Waltz: 9/6, 9/13/1873 CPG
Martha Washington Gavotte: 3/1/1891 LL

---

61 · Sources for this research include the Theodore Thomas Concert Program Collection
at the Newberry Library in Chicago; the Theodore Thomas Felsengarten Collection, the
Theodore Thomas Music Library Collection, and Chicago Symphony Orchestra programs
at the Chicago Symphony Orchestra's Rosenthal Archives; and Theodore Thomas, *Theodore
Thomas: A Musical Autobiography* (1905), vol. 2. Additional biographical assistance regarding orchestra musicians was graciously provided by Norman Schweikert.
62 · After 1872 the Symphony Soirees given in New York City by Thomas were generally referred to as Symphonic Concerts.

BACH, CHRISTOPH, 1835–1927. (b. Germany; to US ca. 1855)
Amazon March: 5/25–9/17/1871 (5x); 6/5/1872 CPG
Diva March: 6/8, 6/9, 8/8, 9/6/1871; 7/3/1872 CPG
March: 9/6/1877 HHB
Wiegenlied: (marked score in Thomas Library)

BAETENS, CHARLES, M.§ (b. Holland; to US 1872)
Elegy: 9/17, 9/27/1878 GG
Overture, *Night and Morning:* 7/26, 7/27/1876 PCE; 8/15/1878? HHB; 8/19,
    8/26/1879 HHB
Tarantelle (flute solo): 6/23/1870 HHB

BALDWIN, SAMUEL A., 1862–1949. (b. Minnesota)
Overture in C Minor (*Norwegian*): 7/21/1888 CSNC

BEACH, AMY CHENEY, 1867–1944. (b. New Hampshire)
Festival Jubilate: 5/1/1893 WCE
Symphony in E Minor, op. 32: 4/8, 4/9/1898 CSO

BECK, JOHANN HEINRICH, 1856–1924. (b. Cleveland)
Symphonic Scherzo: 7/4/1890 MTNA
Skirnis-Mal (Elder Edda, 1st mvt.): 7/4/1888 CSNC/MTNA

BERGMANN, CARL, 1821–76. (b. Saxony; to US 1850)
Echo Galop: 6/11/1867 TG
Serenade, Horns (2), Trombone[63]: 6/24/1867 TG
Trio, Horns (2), Trombone: 1/25/1868 BPS; 11/3/1869 TTO

BERGNER, FREDERICK, 1827–1907.§ (b. Germany; to US 1847)
Reverie for Violoncello (solo): 12/14/1867 Lyric Hall

BERNSTEIN, [JULIUS?].[64]
White Roses Waltz: 11/10/1880 TTO

BIRD, ARTHUR H., 1856–1923. (b. Massachusetts)
Episodes: 7/3/1890 MTNA
Carnival Scene, op. 5: 7/26/1886 CSNC
Kleine Suite no. 3, op. 32: 6/12, 7/7/1893 WCE

63 · The latter two works might have been composed by Gustave Bergmann, a horn player
active in New York City from 1866 to 1876.
64 · Composer not confirmed; may not have been American, though there were many active
musicians in New York City with the surname Bernstein at that time.

BRANDEIS, FREDERICK, 1835–99. (b. Vienna; to US 1849)
Introduction and Capriccio: 8/18, 9/10/1875 CPG
Danse Heroique: 3/2/1888 SH

BRIDGMAN, FREDERICK A., 1847–1928. (b. US; emigrated to Paris 1866)
Minuet: 8/2/1890 CSNC

BRISTOW, GEORGE F., 1825–89.§ (b. New York)
Rip Van Winkle, Selection: 9/23/1878 TTO benefit concert
Great Republic Overture: 5/10/1879 BPS
Jibbewainoske Overture, op. 64: 7/24/1893 WCE

BROEKHOVEN, JOHN A., 1852–1930.§ (b. Holland; to US by 1889)
Suite Creole: 8/4/1893 WCE

BUCK, DUDLEY, 1839–1909. (b. Hartford, CT)
At Evening [Idylle, op. 52] (organ solo): 1/3/1880 CMF
Bugle Song: (marked parts in Thomas Library)
Centennial Meditation of Columbia: 5/10–11/7/1876 (7x) PCE; 10/16, 10/18,
    10/21/1876 SH; 11/15/1876 Boston; 11/16/1876 Springfield; 2/12/1877 Hart-
    ford; 7/4/1877 CSNC; 8/10/1877 St. Louis
Concertstück, horns (4), orchestra: 3/2/1876 Taunton; 3/3/1876 Providence;
    3/4/1876 Boston; 3/13/1876 Springfield; 3/21/76 Lincoln Hall [D.C.?];
    4/6/1876 Worchester; 7/19/1876 PCE
Don Munio, Overture: 5/15–5/23/1874 (5x) CPG; 10/3/1874 Chicago; 10/30/1874
    Providence; 11/4/1874 Hartford; 7/19/1876 PCE; 3/26/1878 Hartford
Hymn to Music: 12/15/1877 BPS
In Thy Dreams, Serenade, op. 67, no. 2 (vocal solo?): 12/29/1874 SS
Festival Hymn: 4/21/1874 Providence
Marmion Overture: 3/1, 3/13, 3/30/1878 BPS; 3/27/1878 New Haven
Romanze, Horn Quartet and Orchestra: 7/6–7/19/1875 (6x) CPG
Scenes from Longfellow's Golden Legend: 5/20/1880 CMF; 2/22/1883 Jersey City
Sunset, ballad, op. 76, no. 4 (vocal solo): 5/31/1877 CMF
"When the Heart Is Young," op. 67, no. 5 (vocal solo): 9/12/1878 GG

BUECHEL, [AUGUSTUS?]. (fl. US 1860s)[65]
Something for Everybody, Grand Potpourri: 8/3/1866 TG

65 · Presumably an American composer because his best-known work is the *Funeral March in Memory of Lincoln.*

BURMEISTER, RICHARD, 1860–1944. (b. Germany; to US ca. 1885; returned 1903)
Concerto for Piano, D Minor, op. 1: 12/21, 12/22/1900 CSO

BURR, WILLARD, 1852–?. (b. Ohio)
Andante and Scherzo for Strings: 7/6/1888 CSNC/MTNA

BUSCH, CARL, 1862–1943. (b. Denmark; to US 1887)
Reverie Pastorale: 7/4/1890 MTNA

BUSSMEYER, HUGO, 1842–1912. (b. Germany; fl. 1867–76 NYC)
Nocturne op. 12; Banjo (piano solo): 3/21/1869 SH
Hungaria (piano solo): 4/18/1869 SH

CHADWICK, GEORGE W., 1854–1931. (b. Massachusetts)
Andante for Strings: 8/2/1882 CSNC
Columbian Ode (for the Opening of the Chicago World's Fair): 5/26/1892 (last mvt.), 10/22/1892 WCE
Euterpe Overture: 1/27/1905 CSO (programmed by Thomas, performed posthumously)
Lament (Egyptian song from *Ben Hur*) (vocal): 1/19/1892 CSO
Lovely Rosabelle, Ballad for Soprano, Tenor, Chorus, Orchestra: 7/4/1890 MTNA
Melpomene Overture: 4/8, 4/9/1892 CSO; 7/6/1893 WCE
Pastoral Prelude: 1/25, 1/26/1895 CSO
Rip Van Winkle, Overture: 8/2/1882 CSNC
Symphony no. 2: 7/5/1888 CSNC/MTNA; 5/23/1893 WCE
Symphony no. 3: 1/8, 1/9/1897 CSO

CLARKE, HUGH ARCHIBALD, 1839–1927. (b. Ontario, Canada; to US ca. 1859)
Jerusalem, Selections: 7/2/1890 MTNA

CONVERSE, CHARLES, 1834–1918. (b. Massachusetts)
Endymion's Narrative: 1/27, 1/28/1905 CSO (programmed by Thomas, performed posthumously)
Festival, Overture: 1/25/1868 BPS
Hail Columbus, Overture: 7/4/1893 WCE
Im Frühling, Overture: 4/4/1889 Chickering Hall; 7/28/1890 CSNC
126th Psalm, Selections: 7/4/1888 CSNC/MTNA

COONEY, MYRON A., 1841–98. (b. Ireland; to US 1860)
Nautilus Waltz: 7/1–9/1/1874 (13x) CPG; 9/8/1875 CPG

CUTLER, H. S. (HENRY STEPHEN), 1825–1902. (b. Boston)
Anthem, for Soprano, Chorus, and Orchestra: 7/2/1890 MTNA

DAMROSCH, LEOPOLD, 1832–85. (b. Germany; to US 1871)
Fest-Ouverture, op. 15: 6/6, 6/12/1872 CPG
Ruth and Naomi, for Soli, Chorus, Orchestra: 11/30/1875 BPS/Handel and
    Haydn Society
Siegfried's Sword, Ballad for Tenor, Orchestra: 11/30/1875 BPS/Handel and
    Haydn Society
Young Siegfried, Ballad for Tenor: 1/12/1876 Baltimore

DANIELS, C. F. (b. US)
Concert Mazurka (piano solo): 2/14/1869 SH

DEEMS, JAMES M., 1818–1901. (b. Baltimore)
Grand Fantasie *Ione:* 10/12/1868 CPG

DIETRICH, WILLIAM G., 1836–1903?§ (b. US?)
L'Adieu Galop: 6/30, 7/2, 8/23/1875 CPG
Six in Hand Galop: 6/18, 6/29/1878 GG
Enchanting Galop: 6/20/1867 TG

DODWORTH, HARVEY B., 1822–91. (b. England; to US 1826)
Union Medley: 8/30, 9/2/1865 BLP (with Dodworth's Band)

DULCKEN, FERDINAND Q., 1837–1902. (b. England; to US 1876)
"Bonnie Wee Thing," Scotch ballad: 12/4/1877 Hartford
Humoreske (orch. by Dietrich): 9/18, 9/19, 9/22/1878 GG
"O Sweet Birdling" (vocal solo): 1/4/1883 SH
Padre Martini's Gavotte: 1/25/1879 Chickering Hall

DUVIVIER, A. D. (A. DEVIN). (b. Liverpool; fl. Chicago 1890s)
Triumph of Bacchus: 2/24, 2/25/1893 CSO
Marche Elegaic, Intermezzo Scherzando: 3/30, 3/31/1900 CSO
Dramatic Symphony, F Minor: 12/12, 12/13/1902 CSO

EICHBERG, JULIUS, 1824–93. (b. Germany; to US 1857)
Religious Meditations (solo violin?): 12/2/1866 SH

Fantasie de Concert on Themes from *Elisire d'Amore* (solo violin?): 12/5/
1866 SH

La Parane, Dance of the 17th Century (solo violin?): 12/5/1866 SH

ELLER, JOSEPH, 1838–?.§ (b. Germany; to US 1854)
Fantasia for Oboe (solo?): 1/16/1867 SH

FEININGER, KARL WILLIAM FREDERICK, 1844–1922. (b. Germany; to
US 1853)
Durch March: 7/31, 9/16/1878 GG
Theme and Variations, op. 2 (cornet solo?): 8/7/1878 GG

FLOERSHEIM, OTTO, 1853–1917. (b. Germany; to US 1875)
Concert Prelude and Fugue, op. 18: 1/25/1883 SH
Consolation, op. 21: 1/19/1886 Academy of Music NYC

FLORIO, CARYL, 1843–1920. (b. England; to US 1865)
Concerto for Piano, A-flat: 5/27/1888 SH
Nocturne: 7/22/1874 CPG
"St. Agnes Eve" (vocal solo?): 5/27/1888 SH
Symphony no. 1, G Major: 5/27/1888 SH
Symphony no. 2, C Minor: 5/27/1888 SH; 7/30/1889 CSNC
Syren's Charm: 5/27/1888 SH

FOERSTER, ADOLF M., 1854–1927. (b. Pittsburgh, PA)
Festival March: 7/7/1893 WCE
Love song, op. 23, for Soprano and Orchestra: 7/2/1890 MTNA
Thusnelda, op. 10: 5/13/1884 Pittsburgh

FOOTE, ARTHUR, 1853–1937. (b. Massachusetts)
Concerto for Violoncello, op. 33: 11/30, 12/1/1894 CSO
Serenade for Strings, E Major, op. 25: 7/4/1888 CSNC/MTNA; 5/23,
7/6/1893 WCE; 7/13/1893 WCE
Suite, op. 12, E Major: 2/14/1889 Chickering Hall; 7/30/1889 CSNC
Suite no. 2, op. 21, D Major: 7/2/1890 MTNA; 8/1/1890 CSNC; 3/31, 4/1/1899
CSO
Theme and Variations, op. 32: 4/25, 4/26/1902 CSO

FRADEL, CHARLES, d. 1880? (b. Germany; to US ca. 1860)
Christmas Polka: 12/19, 12/26/1863 IHM
Faust Quadrille: 12/26/1863 IHM

FRY, WILLIAM HENRY, 1813–64. (b. Pennsylvania)
A Day in the Country: 7/19/1876 PCE
Notre Dame of Paris: 5/4/1864 Philadelphia (repeated 7x May 1864?)

GILCHRIST, WILLIAM W., 1846–1916. (b. New Jersey)
46th Psalm, "God Is Our Refuge and Strength": 5/19/1882 CMF

GLEASON, FREDERIC G., 1848–1903. (b. Connecticut)
Auditorium Festival Ode: 7/28, 8/1/1890 CSNC; 7/4/1890 MTNA
Edris, Symphonic Poem: 4/17, 4/18/1896 CSO; 1/7, 1/8/1898 CSO
Montezuma, Introduction and March of the Priests: 8/2/1882 CSNC;
    2/15/1891 LL
Montezuma, Introduction to Act II: 8/11/1883 CSNC
Montezuma, Selections from Act III: 8/5/1885; 8/1/1886; 7/22/1889; 7/19,
    8/8/1890 CSNC
Otho Visconti, Vorspiel: 8/10/1881 CSNC; 7/21/1886 CSNC; 7/27/1887
    CSNC; 12/24/1887 SH; 7/28/1888 CSNC; 5/26/1893 WCE
Otho Visconti, Romance, "Deep in My Heart": 4/8, 4/9/1892 CSO
Praise Song to Harmony, Cantata: 7/4/1888 CSNC/MTNA; (Allegro mvt.):
    7/30/1889 CSNC
Procession of the Grail: 7/7/1893 WCE
Song of Life, Symphonic Poem: 11/30, 12/1/1900 CSO

GOLDBECK, ROBERT, 1839–1908. (b. Germany; to US 1857)
Forest Devotion; Leaping Minstrels; Two Mexican Dances: 12/7, 12/8/1894 CSO
String Quintette: 10/3/1874 Chicago
Tennyson's Bugle Song: 9/9/1866 IHM
"Three Fishers," Part song for male voices: 4/27/1878 BPS
Victoria Symphony: 3/21/1863 Academy of Music, NYC[66]

GORI, AMERICO. (fl. NYC 1890s)
Serenade: 7/26/1890 CSNC

GOTTSCHALK, LOUIS M., 1829–69. (b. New Orleans)
Cradle Song (piano solo): 11/7/1863 IHM
Last Hope Meditation (piano solo): 4/18/1869 TTO SH
Marche Funèbre (piano solo): 11/7/1863 IHM
Minuit à Séville (piano solo): 11/7/1863 IHM
Ojos Criollos (two pianos): 10/31/1863 IHM

---

66 · Thomas participated in this concert, but it is unclear whether he was the conductor.

Pastorale e Cavaliere (piano solo): 10/24/1863 IHM
The Union (piano solo): 10/31/1863 IHM

GREINER, [AMANDUS F.?]. (fl. Philadelphia 1850s)[67]
March of Victory 9/8/1873 CPG

GRILL, EMANUEL (ERNST). § (b. Austria; to US 1849)
Mephisto Polka: 6/18, 6/24/1867 TG
Steuben March: 7/25/1868 CPG
Teufels Polka: (marked parts in Thomas Library)

GUIRAUD, ERNEST, 1837–92. (b. New Orleans; emigrated to Paris)
Carnaval [from *Suite d'Orchestre?*]: 7/20/1877 CSNC; 10/20/1877 SH;
    11/5/1877 Philadelphia; 11/7/1877 Washington, DC; 11/12/1877 Brooklyn;
    11/14/1877 Boston; 11/15/1877 Providence; 11/17/1877 Harvard; 12/8/1877
    Melrose Lyceum (MA?); 2/21/1878 BPS; 5/20/1878 Cleveland
Chasse Fantastique, Symphonic poem: 12/15, 12/16/1893 CSO
Danse Persane, Air de Ballet: 7/14, 7/27/1881 CSNC; 7/7/1881 Cleveland;
    8/24/1881 Milwaukee; 8/31/1881 HHB
Gretna-Green Valse: (marked score and parts in Thomas Library)
Melodrame de Piccolino: (marked score and parts in Thomas Library)

HAAS, [CARL (CHARLES)?].[68]
Polka Gracioso: 5/17, 5/23/1872 CPG

HADLEY, HENRY KIMBALL, 1871–1937. (b. Massachusetts)
Symphony no. 2, op. 30, F Minor: 1/24, 1/25/1902 CSO

HAMERIK, ASGAR, 1843–1923. (b. Denmark; to US 1871; returned 1900)
Christian Trilogy: 5/1/1884 Baltimore City Musical Festival
Nordishe Suite, op. 22, no. 1: 9/3–9/17/1873 (6x) CPG; 10/6/1873 Chicago;
    10/21/1873 St. Louis; 11/1/1873 Cincinnati; 11/15/1873 Philadelphia;
    12/5/1873 Boston; 1/21/1874 Washington, DC; 2/14/1874 Pittsburgh;
    2/21/1874 Cleveland; 6/3–9/21/1874 (6x) CPG; 8/12, 8/22, 9/7/1874 CPG;
    7/23–9/10/1875 (5x) CPG; 5/22, 6/9, 6/24/1876 PCE; 2/20/1877 Bos-
    ton; 7/3/1877 CSNC; 7/18, 7/29, 8/12/1878 HHB; 8/6/1878 GG; 7/29,
    8/21/1879 HHB; 2/16/1882 Orange, NJ; 11/2/1890 LL; 2/10, 2/11/1893 CSO

---

67 · Not able to confirm whether this work was by Amandus Greiner or a German composer.
68 · Not able to confirm whether this work was by Carl Haas or a German composer.

Love Scene, "Evening in the Woods": 7/3, 7/18/1877 CSNC; 8/27, 8/29/1877
    HHB; 10/19/1877 SH; 11/15/1877 Providence; 11/16/1877 Worchester;
    11/17/1877 Harvard; 9/11/1877 (or 1878?) HHB; 9/12/1879 HHB
Swedish Folk Songs (for orchestra): 7/6/1881 Cleveland; 8/14/1882 HHB;
    7/16, 7/27/1889 CSNC; 7/19, 7/28/1890 CSNC; 7/11, 7/14, 7/25/1891 NY;
    7/25/1893 WCE

HANER, J. EDWARDS (b. US)
Reverie d'un Inventeur (piano solo): 1/24/1868 SH

HART, H. B. (fl. Philadelphia 1870s)
Quick Step, *Fête de L'Armée:* 9/13/1875 CPG

HATTON, JOHN LIPTROT, 1809–86. (b. England; to US 1848; returned
    1875)
"Goodbye Sweetheart" (vocal solo?): 1/9, 1/14/1867 Brooklyn
Evening Twilight: 6/6/1877 Chicago (with Apollo Club)

HEINDL, EDWARD MARTIN, 1838–1918? (b. Bavaria; to US ca. 1864)
Carnival of Venice (flute solo): 8/23/1866 TG; 10/14/1866 IHM; 11/20/1866
    Academy of Music NYC

HERBERT, VICTOR, 1859–1924. § (b. Ireland; to US 1886)
American Fantasie: 1/26/1890 LL (conducted by composer)
Concerto for Violoncello: 12/10/1887 NYP
Serenade for Strings, op. 12: 7/22, 7/27, 8/3/1889 CSNC; 5/22/1890 CMF

HILLBRECHT. (fl. NYC 1860s)
Central Park Garden Festival [March]: 8/18–10/13/1868 (5x) CPG; 8/31,
    9/25/1869 CPG

HOHNSTOCK, KARL, 1828–?. (b. Germany; to US 1848)
Overture, *Hail Columbia!:* 7/4/1866 TG; 7/4/1867 TG; 7/4/1868 CPG;
    7/5/1869 CPG

HOOD, HELEN, 1863–1949. (b. Massachusetts)
Summer Song: 7/7/1893 WCE

HOPKINS, JEROME, 1836–98. (b. Vermont)
Madcap Galop: 10/1/1868 CPG
Symphony, *Life* (last mvt.): 12/30/1866 SH

HUSS, HENRY HOLDEN, 1862–1953. (b. New Jersey)
Ave Maria, for Female Chorus, Soli and Strings, op. 4: 7/6/1888 CSNC/MTNA

KAUN, HUGO, 1863–1932. (b. Germany; to US 1887)
Fantasie and Fugue for Organ: 3/29, 3/30/1901 CSO
Festival March and Hymn to Liberty: 10/22, 10/23/1897 CSO; 3/16/1898 CSO
    (NY); 5/28/1898 CMF; 11/4, 11/5/1899 CSO; 4/22, 4/23/1904 CSO
Im Urwald, Symphonic Poem: No. 1 "Minnehaha"; No. 2 "Hiawatha": 2/6,
    2/7/1903 CSO
Der Maler von Antwerpen, Overture: 2/3, 2/4/1899 CSO; 4/6, 4/7/1900 CSO
Normannen-Abschied: 4/24/1900 CSO (Milwaukee)
Symphony no. 1, D Minor, op. 22: 1/14, 1/15/1898 CSO
Volkslied: 4/9/1901 CSO (Milwaukee)

KELLEY, EDGAR STILLMAN, 1857–1944. (b. Wisconsin)
Overture to *MacBeth,* op. 7: 8/3/1883 CSNC

KLEIN, BRUNO OSCAR, 1856–1911. (b. Germany; to US 1883)
Liebeslied; Hochzeitsklange: 4/14/1888 SH; 8/3/1888 CSNC

KLETZAN, [G.?]. (fl. NYC 1860s)
Terrace Garden Polka: 6/12, 6/14/1866 TG

KOELLING, CARL, 1831–1900. (b. Germany; to US 1878)
Amicitiae Fidelitas, Overture: 8/6/1881 CSNC
World's Columbian Exposition March [i.e., Waltz?]: 7/1, 7/25/1893 WCE
O! Maria, Romance: 8/15/1881 CSNC
Roman Pilgrim March: 8/3/1889 CSNC

KOPPITZ, CHARLES C., d. 1873. (b. US)
Fantime, Selections: 8/28/1866 TG
National Overture: 12/22/1866 Cooper Institute NYC; 7/4/1868 CPG
National Medley: 7/5/1869 CPG; 11/21/1866 Brooklyn; 10/1/1867 Brooklyn

KORBAY, FRANCIS A., 1846–1913. (b. Hungary; to US 1871; to London 1894)
Nuptiale: 6/11, 6/23/1875 CPG; 6/17/1878 GG
Prelude et Impromptu: 2/8/1883 SH
Three Hungarian Songs: 5/24/1894 CMF

KUNKEL, CHARLES, 1840–1923. (b. Germany; to US 1860s)
Alpine Storm, op. 105: (marked score and parts in Thomas library)
Butterfly Galop: 7/11–8/1/1871 (10x) CPG

LACHMUND, CARL V., 1853–1928. (b. Missouri)
Japanese Overture: 7/6/1888 CSNC/MTNA

LANG, MARGARET RUTHVEN, 1867–1972. (b. Massachusetts)
Witichis Overture: 7/29, 8/4/1893 WCE

LASSERVE, [H. B.?].[69]
Mathilde Waltz: 7/22/1868 CPG

LETSCH, FREDERICK, 1829–1919.§ (b. Saxony; to US ca. 1850s)
Fantasia for Trombone: 2/24/1867 SH

LEVY, JULES, 1838–1903. (b. England; to US 1860s)
Air Hongroise (cornet solo): 5/12–7/5/1869 (5x) CPG
Central Park Garden Polka: 9/17, 9/19/1869 CPG
Maud Waltz (cornet solo): 5/12–6/29/1869 (6x) CPG
Levy Athen Polka (cornet solo): 5/16–7/8/1869 (4x) CPG
Whirlwind Polka: 5/20–7/4/1869 (4x) CPG

LILIENTHAL, ABRAHAM W., 1859–1928. (b. New York)
Grand March: 7/26/1890 CSNC

LEUNING, EUGENE, 1852–1944. (b. Milwaukee)
Lustspiel Overture: 8/18/1883 Milwaukee

LOEFFLER, CHARLES M., 1861–1935. (b. Germany; to US 1881)
La Villanelle du Diable: 1/8, 1/9/1904 CSO

LORETZ, JOHN M., 1840–?.(b. Lorraine; to US ca. 1840s)
Deborah Overture: 7/28/1868 CPG; 2/11/1869 Brooklyn

MAAS, LOUIS, 1852–89. (b. Leipzig; to US 1880)
Concerto for Piano, C Minor, op. 12: 7/3/1890 MTNA
Concerto for Violin, op. 18: 7/5/1888 CSNC/MTNA
Three Characteristic Pieces (Norwegian): 8/5/1885 CSNC
Will O' Wisps, Female Chorus and Orchestra: 7/4/1888 CSNC/MTNA

---

69 · Composer not confirmed; possibly H. B. Lasserve, a pianist active in New York City in
the 1860s, or Ch. Henri Lasserve, composer of *The Snow Drop Schottisch*, published by Oliver Ditson around the 1850s.

MACDOWELL, EDWARD, 1860–1908. (b. New York State)
Concerto for Piano, no. 1, op. 15: 7/5/1888 CSNC/MTNA; 2/9, 2/10/1894 CSO
Concerto for Piano, no. 2, op. 23: 3/5/1889 Chickering Hall, NYC; 7/2/1890
    MTNA; 1/20, 1/21/1899 CSO
Lancelot and Eliane, Symphonic poem, op. 25: 12/15, 12/16/1899 CSO
Suite, no. 1, op. 42: 1/18/1892 CSO (Louisville); 3/18, 3/19/1892 CSO; 5/23,
    7/6/1893 WCE
Suite, no. 2 (*Indian*), op. 48: 11/12, 11/13/1897 CSO

MALLACH, JACOB [SR.?]. (fl. NYC)
Friendship Galop: 6/22/1871 CPG
March Grande [Amus?]: 9/29/1868 CPG
Medley on American Airs: 9/25/1869 CPG
New York Schützen March: 8/22, 8/25, 9/19/1868 CPG
Sweet Spirit March: 9/15/1868 CPG

MASON, WILLIAM, 1829–1908. (b. Massachusetts)
Silverspring (piano solo): 3/27/1878 New Haven

MATZKA, GEORGE, 1825–83.§ (b. Coburg; to US 1852)
Concert Overture: 9/16/1870 CPG
Josephine Waltz: 8/31–9/18/1866 (4x) TG; 8/2, 9/12/1867 TG; 6/21/1868
    CPG; 9/27/1868 CPG
Wedding March: 7/7, 9/22/1869 CPG

MIDDELSCHULTE, WILHELM, 1863–1943. (b. Germany; to US 1891)
Passacaglia for Organ: 2/3, 2/4/1899 CSO

MILLS, S. B. (SEBASTIAN BACH), 1839–98. (b. England; to US 1856)
Caprice Characteristic, "Fairy Fingers" (piano solo): 10/26/1868 SH
Caprice Galop (piano solo): 11/5, 11/9/1866 TTO; 2/10/1867 SH; 1/14/1867
    Brooklyn
Grand Fantasie for Piano: 12/26/1863 IHM; 3/16/1867 SH
Murmuring Fountain (piano solo): 11/2/1866 SH
Tarantella (piano solo): 11/10/1866 SH
Tarantella, no. 2 (piano solo): 2/3/1867 SH
Recollections of Home (piano solo): 2/6, 3/16/1867 SH; 4/2/1868 IHM

MOLLENHAUER, EDWARD, 1827–1914.§ (b. Germany; to US 1851)
La Sylphide, Fantasia for Violin (solo): 11/21/1863 IHM
Virtuosen Waltz: 7/12/1873 CPG (cond. by composer)

MORGAN, G. W. (GEORGE WASHBOURNE), 1823–92. (b. England; to
US 1850s)
National Airs (organ solo): 4/28, 5/12/1867 SH
Solo and Variations (organ solo): 4/28, 5/12/1867 SH

MOSENTHAL, JOSEPH, 1834–96. (b. Germany; to US 1853)
Terrace Garden Galop: 8/18, 9/15/1866 TG

MÜLLER, CARL C., 1831–1914. (b. Meiningen; to US 1854)
Central Park Garden Galop: 7/13, 9/4/1870; 9/7, 9/10/1871; 8/22/1868;
    9/9/1872 CPG
Fantasia for Trombone: 11/26/1866 Brooklyn; 11/13/1866 SH; 1/6, 1/7/1867 SH
Festival March for Orchestra: 6/15–7/23/1866 (4x) TG; 5/26/1867 SH;
    6/21/1867 TG
Galop (unidentified): 7/13/1876 PCE
German Song, "Tief Drunten" (vocal solo): 12/16/1866 SH
Grecian Bend Polka: 9/24, 9/26/1868 CPG
Idyl, op. 24 (after Longfellow's Hiawatha): 8/5/1885 CSNC
Introduction and Galop: 1/5/1877 NYC (Müller's Grand Orchestral Concert)
Irving Galop: 1/16/1867 SH; 2/25/1867 Brooklyn; 3/16/1867 SH; 2/23/1868 SH
Lafayette '67 Galop: 1/7, 1/9/1867 Brooklyn; 6/14–8/20/1867(6x) TG
Nathan the Wise, Overture: 1/5/1877 NYC (Müller's Grand Orchestral Concert)
National Overture: 7/4/1866 TG
Nocturne [on *Hiawatha*?]: 1/5/1877 NYC (Müller's Grand Orchestral Concert)
Pleasant Recollections (piano solo): 1/5/1877 NYC (Müller's Grand Orchestral
    Concert)
Romance (with horn and harp): 1/5/1877 NYC (Müller's Grand Orchestral
    Concert)
Symphony: 1/5/1877 NYC (Müller's Grand Orchestral Concert)
Terrace Garden Galop: 6/15–9/25/1866 (7x) TG; 8/19/1868 CPG
Under the Rhine March: 1/23, 1/26, 2/6, 5/19/1867 SH; 1/26/1867 Brooklyn
Union Overture: 7/5, 9/27/1866 TG; 1/5/1877 NYC (Müller's Grand Orches-
    tral Concert)

NEMBACH, ANDREW, 1839–?.(b. Germany; to US ca. 1860)
Overture: 9/25/1868 CPG

NEUENDORFF, ADOLF, 1843–97. (b. Germany; to US 1854)
Stiftungsfest Waltz: 9/1/1873 CPG

NEVIN, ETHELBERT WOODBRIDGE, 1862–1901. (b. Ohio)
"At Twilight" (vocal solo): 1/18–1/25/1892 (5x) CSO
"Before the Daybreak" (vocal solo): 7/7/1893 WCE

NICHOLL, HORACE WADHAM, 1848–1922. (b. England; to US 1871)
Romanze, March and Fugue: 5/29/1877 Pittsburgh

NOLL, JOSEPH.§ (b. Germany; to US ca. 1850s)
Concert Overture: 7/23/1873 CPG

OSGOOD, GEORGE L., 1844–?. (b. Massachusetts)
"Kiss Me Softly and Speak to Me Low" (vocal solo): 9/26/1872 Albany (and
    additional tour concerts)

PAINE, JOHN KNOWLES, 1839–1906. (b. Maine)
Centennial Hymn: 5/10–11/7/1876 (8x) PCE; 10/16, 10/18, 10/21/1876 SH;
    11/15/1876 Boston; 11/16/1876 Springfield; 2/12/1877 Hartford; 7/4/1877
    CSNC; 8/10/1877 St. Louis
Columbus March and Hymn: 10/22/1892 WCE; 1/20, 1/21/1893 CSO; 5/1–
    8/7/1893 (5x) WCE
Concert Variations on the Star-Spangled Banner (organ solo): 5/31/1878 CMF
Duo Concertante for Violin, Violoncello, Orchestra, op. 33: 4/23/1878 Cam-
    bridge
Island Fantasy, op. 45: 7/2/1890 MTNA; 1/11/1890 NYP; 7/25/1890 CSNC;
    6/2, 7/6/1893 WCE
Moorish Dances: Azara: 10/26, 10/27/1900 CSO
Nativity, cantata: 5/2/1883 Boston (with Handel and Haydn Society)
Oedipus Tyrannus, for Tenor, Male Chorus, Orchestra: 1/28/1881? with NY
    Choral Soc.; 3/18/1882 BPS; 6/24/1882 Milwaukee
Overture to Shakespeare's *As You Like It,* op. 28: 11/21/1876 Cambridge;
    1/8/1877 Albany; 2/20/1877 Boston; 7/26, 7/30/1889 CSNC
Prelude to the *Birds of Aristophanes:* 2/27, 2/28/1903 CSO
St. Peter: 5/9/1874 Boston (with Handel and Haydn Society)
St. Peter, Aria, "O God, My God, Forsake Me Not": 4/8, 4/9/1892 CSO
Song of Promise, op. 43: 5/22/1888 CMF
Symphony No. 1: 1/26, 2/19/1876 Boston; 2/5/1876 SH; 4/6/1876 (Adagio)
    Worcester; 7/19/1876 PCE; 2/27, 11/13/1877 Cambridge; 8/6/1885 CSNC
Symphony No. 2 (*Im Frühling*): 8/2/1882 CSNC; 3/31/1883 BPS; 8/6/1885
    CNSC; 4/8, 4/9/1892 CSO
Symphonic Fantasie on Shakespeare's *Tempest:* 10/19/1877 SH; 12/6/1877
    City Hall, NYC; 11/29/1884 BPS; 8/5/1885 CSNC; 4/7/1887 Philadelphia;

7/28/1887 CSNC; 11/17, 11/22/1887 SH; 12/14/1887 New Haven; 2/17/1888 BPS; 4/7/1888 Philadelphia; 12/30, 12/31/1898 CSO

PARKER, J. C. D., 1828–1916. (b. Massachusetts)
Hiawatha Overture: 9/4, 9/16/1878 GG
Day Break (vocal solo): 4/9/1877 Hartford

PARKER, HORATIO W., 1863–1919. (b. Massachusetts)
Concerto for Organ: 1/2, 1/3/1903 CSO
Count Robert of Paris, Overture: 12/1, 12/2/1893 CSO
Hora Novissima, op. 30: 5/23/1894 CMF
Northern Ballad, op. 46: 2/9, 2/10/1900 CSO; 5/12/1900 CMF

PATTISON, JOHN NELSON, 1845–1905. (b. Niagara Falls, NY)
Air Russe, Fantasia de Concert: 11/14/1866 SH
Concert Overture: 12/12/1863 IHM
Doctor of Alcantra, Grand Fantasia on Themes from Eichber's Opera (piano solo): 5/26/1867 SH
Faust, Grand Fantasia (piano solo): 10/28/1866 IHM; 1/10/1869 SH
Intro and Grand Polka de Concert (piano solo?): 6/5/1868 CPG
Faust, Paraphrase de Concert: 6/2/1867 SH
Martha, Fantaisie de Concert (piano solo): 12/5/1863 IHM
Russian Hymn, Variations de Concert (piano solo?): 12/12/1863 IHM; 6/5/1868 CPG
Soiree et Bal, Intro. and Grand Polka de Concert (piano solo): 1/3/1869 SH

PEARCE, S. AUSTEN (STEPHEN AUSTEN), 1836–1900. (b. England; to US 1872)
Allegro Agitato in D Minor: 6/16, 6/18/1875 CPG
Overture, D Minor: 9/8/1875 CPG

PEASE, ALFRED HUMPHREYS, 1838–82. (b. Ohio)
Andante and Scherzo: 9/13, 9/20/1872 CPG
"Bedouin Song" (vocal solo?): 4/11/1874 SH
Bolero de Concert: 4/26/1871 Chicago; 8/2/1871 CPG
"Break, Break, Break" (vocal solo): 1/16/1867 SH
Caprice Espagnol, Bolero: 12/19/1866 SH
Concerto for Piano, B Minor, Barcarola mvt.: 11/20/1869 St. James Hall (NYC?)
Concerto for Piano, E-flat: 7/19, 7/25/1876 PCE
Crispino, Grand Duet for piano: 11/26/1866 Brooklyn; 2/19/1867 SH
Crispino, Grand Duo, Sextette (voice/piano): 11/13/1866 SH

Dreamland, Reverie et Berceuse: 5/29/1872 CPG
Grand Concerto, Piano and Orchestra (two mvts.): 5/24/1868 SS
Grand Duo on Themes from Verdi's *Aida* (two pianos): 4/23/1874 SH Pease
   Concert
Huldigungs Marsch: 4/23/1874 SH Pease Concert; 6/17, 9/18/1874 CPG;
   9/26/1874 Buffalo; 10/20/1874 Cleveland
Japanese Galop: 6/16–9/18/1872 (20x) CPG; 10/9, 10/10/1872 Chicago;
   11/23/1872; Philadelphia; 5/15–7/18/1873 (7x) CPG; 6/16–9/9/1874 (6x)
   CPG; 6/15/1875 CPG; 5/12–7/19/1876 (5x) PCE; 7/19/1877 CSNC; 7/6,
   8/6/1878 GG; 8/13/1881 CSNC
Mignon: Polacca: 4/23/1874 SH Pease Concert
Scherzo: 4/23/1874 SH Pease Concert; 7/25/1876 PCE
Red Cloud Galop: 7/8–9/21/1872 (17x) CPG; 7/25, 7/28, 8/5/1873 CPG; 7/4,
   8/10/1874 CPG; 8/2/1882 CSNC
Romanze: 6/18, 7/7/1873 CPG
Spring Song: 8/13/1873 CPG
Vivandieres March: 8/20–9/6/1873 (8x) CPG; 7/30/1875 CPG

PEASE, FREDERICK H., 1839–1909. (b. Ohio)
"Remember Now Thy Creator" for Tenor and Orchestra: 7/3/1890 MTNA

PERRING, JAMES ERNEST, 1822–89. (b. England; to US ca. 1857)
Grand Exhibition March: 8/26/1878? HHB; 8/26/1879 HHB

PETRI, [J. F.?]. (fl. US 1830–60s)
Wedding March: 7/18/1870 CPG

PHELPS, ELLSWORTH C., 1827–?. (b. Connecticut)
Hiawatha Symphony, op. 36: (two mvts.): 5/10/1879 BPS
Selections (Song of Nokomis, Dance of Pau-puk-Keewis): 7/28/1890 CSNC

PRATT, SILAS G., 1846–1916. (b. Vermont)
Antique Minuet and Pastorale: 8/8/1881 CSNC
Court Minuet: 3/23/1886 TTO; 8/6/1886 CSNC
Elegy on the Death of General Grant, Chorus and Orchestra: 7/6/1888 CSNC/
   MTNA
Soliloquy: 7/26/1889 CSNC
Symphony, *The Prodigal Son:* 7/3/1890 MTNA

RIETZEL, [FREDERICK?].§ (fl. US 1848–95)
Aurelien Polka: 8/19/1865 BLP
March [*Lanciers?*]: 8/30/1865 BLP

RIETZEL, JOHN CHARLES. (b. New York)
Eine Volksthümliche Suite: 8/5/1887 CSNC; 12/24/1887 SH; 2/17/1888 BPS;
   7/21/1888 CSNC
Humoristic Suite: 8/6/1886 CSNC

RITTER, FANNY RAYMOND, 1840–90. (b. England?; to US 1850s)
Elfenliebe, Ballade (vocal solo): 12/9/1866 SH

RITTER, FREDERIC LOUIS, 1834–91..(b. France; to US 1856)
Introduction and Scherzo: 12/7/1872 Boston

RIVÉ-KING, JULIA, 1855–1937. (b. Ohio)
On Blooming Meadows, Waltz (piano solo?): 9/27/1878 GG

ROSEWIG, A. H. (ALBERT HENRY), 1846–1929. (b. Pennsylvania?)
The Flag That Bears the Stripes and Stars, Chorus and Orchestra: 7/8/1876 PCE

SANDERSON, HARRY. (b. US)
Bridal Eve Polka (piano solo): 10/3/1862 IHM
Electric Polka (two pianos): 10/24/1873 IHM

SCHARWENKA, XAVER. (b. Germany; to US 1891; returned 1898)
Concerto, Piano, No. 1, B Minor, op. 32: 3/24, 3/25/1893 CSO
Mataswintha, Vorspiel: 3/24, 3/25/1893 CSO

SCHMITZ, HENRY, 1827–1914.§ (b. Germany; to US 1845)
Fantasie for French Horn: 7/18, 8/12/1867 TG; 12/14/1867 Lyric Hall NYC;
   1/5/1869 Music Hall NYC; 1/6/1869 Allyn Hall (Hartford?); 4/14/1869
   SH; 7/13/1870 CPG

SCHOENEFELD, HENRY, 1857–1936. (b. Wisconsin)
Air, Gavotte, and Musette: 8/2/1889 CSNC
Impromptus for Strings: Meditation and Valse Noble: 12/22, 12/23/1899 CSO
Suite for String Orchestra, op. 15: 7/3/1890 MTNA; 7/25/1890 CSNC
Suite (unidentified): 7/7/1893 WCE
Suite Characteristique for Strings: 11/6, 11/7/1891 CSO
Symphony in G Major, op. 20, Pastorale: 4/13, 4/14/1894 CSO; two mvts.
   10/25/1894 Germania Männerchor/CSO

SCHOLL, [J. D.?]. (fl. NYC 1860s)
Grand Fantasie on a National Air: 12/22/1867 Trenor's Lyric Hall, NYC

Grand Fantasia Yankee Doodle: 12/14/1867 Trenor's Lyric Hall, NYC; 6/2/1868
CPG; 7/5/1869 CPG

SCHREIBER, LOUIS, 1827–1910.§ (b. Germany; to US 1856)
Campaign March for Orchestra: 6/3–9/15 /1872 (9x) CPG; 5/31–8/19/1873
(7x) CPG
Caprice de Concert (cornet solo): 3/21/1871 Syracuse
Song without Words (cornet solo): 6/22/1871 CPG; 10/2/1871 Troy; 10/6/1871
Cleveland; 10/18/1871 St. Louis

SCHUECKER, EDMUND, 1860–1911.§ (b. Austria; to US ca. 1890)
Fantasie di Bravura for Harp (solo?): 1/13/1892–2/10/1892 CSO tour (6x);
1/22, 1/23/1892 CSO; 12/28/1892–1/31/1893 CSO tour (5x); 3/11/1893 CSO
(Des Moines); 1/6/1894 CSO (Quincy, IL)
At the Fountain (harp solo): 3/31, 4/1/1893 CSO
March Miniature (harp solo): 1/5/1894 CSO (St. Louis)
Mazurka Brillante (harp solo): 6/17/1893 WCE
Nocturne (harp solo): 1/5/1894 CSO (St. Louis)

SEEBOECK, W. C. E., 1859–1907. (b. Vienna; to US 1880)
Concerto for Piano, D Minor: 1/25, 1/26/1895 CSO

SEIFERT, EMIL. (fl. NYC 1870s–80s)
Festival March: 6/15, 6/19/1875 CPG

SHELLEY, HARRY ROWE, 1858–1947. (b. Connecticut)
Ballet music (fragment): 7/30, 7/31/1889 CSNC
Carnival Overture: 7/7/1893 WCE
Francesca di Rimini, Symphonic Poem: 4/8, 4/9/1892 CSO
Grand Sonata for String Orchestra: 3/2/1888 BPS
Orientale Suite: 3/1/1891 LL (cond. by comp.)
Romance, Evening Prayer: 7/26/1890 CSNC
Ruined Castle, Suite: 7/19/1893 WCE

SHERWOOD, WM. H., 1854–1911. (b. New York)
Capriccio, op. 4 (piano solo): 10/21/1876 SH; 11/4/1876 PCE
Mazourka, Song without Words, op. 6 (piano solo): 11/3/1876 PCE

SILBERBERG, J. A. (J. ALEXANDER). (fl. NYC 1870s–90s)
Express Galop: 6/14–6/27/1872 (5x) CPG

SINGER, OTTO, 1863–93. (b. Leipzig; to US 1867)
Fantasia, Orchestra and Piano Obligato: 4/3/1869 SH
Festival Ode for Orchestra, Chorus and Organ: 5/14/1878 CMF
Grand March: 9/10, 9/12, 9/15/1869 CPG
Inauguration [Central Park Garden?] March: 7/2/1872 CPG; 7/5, 7/7/1873
    CPG; 7/23, 7/25/1874 CPG

SOBOLEWSKI, EDUARD, 1808–72. (b. Prussia; to US 1859)
Skating Feast in Scandinavia, or Overture to *Tialf:* 10/23/1871 St. Louis;
    6/4/1872 CPG
"Sweet Memories of Thee; Thoughts of Thee" (vocal): 8/18/1877 St. Louis

STETSON, NAHUM. (fl. NYC 1870s)
Musical Sketches: 7/30, 8/13/1878 GG

STOCK, FREDERICK, 1872–1942. (b. Germany; to US 1895)
Symphonic Variations: 2/26, 2/27/1904 CSO

STOCKTON, JOHN P., JR. (fl. NYC 1870s)
Good Night and Goodbye Galop (marked parts in Thomas library)

STOECKEL, GUSTAV JACOB, 1819–1907. (b. Germany; to US 1849)
Studenten Leben Overture: 10/23/1868 CPG

STRECK, V. (fl. US)
Grand Military Potpourri: 8/12/1865 BLP

STRONG, GEORGE TEMPLETON, 1820–75. (b. New York)
Ein Märchen: 8/9/1883 CSNC

THOMAS, THOMAS, 1835–1905. (b. Germany; to US 1845)
Carnival of Venice: 1/16/1867 SH
Central Park Garden Opening March: 5/25–8/24/1868 (ca. 15x) CPG;
    8/22/1871 CPG; 7/17, 7/18/1872 CPG
Concert Overture: 8/23–24/1871 CPG
Divertissement (viola solo): 11/2/1878 CMF
Festival March: 1/5/1889 Chickering Hall; 7/22, 7/26, 7/27/1889 CSNC;
    8/9/1890 CSNC; 11/7/1891 Chicago (with Germania Männerchor)
Inauguration March: 5/13/1870 CPG (many additional performances)
Introduction and Bolero for Viola: 9/30/1871 Tonkünstler Verein, NYC

TIMM, HENRY C., 1811–92. (b. Germany; to US 1835)
Inauguration March: 11/21/1885 SH (Timm Testimonial Concert)
Bededictus, for Four Voices and Orchestra: 11/21/1885 SH
Qui Tollis, for Four Voices and Winds: 11/21/1885 SH

TOULMIN, ALFRED F. § (b. England; to US ca. 1852)
Coliseum March: 7/16, 9/17/1873 CPG
Un Ballo in Maschera, Fantasia for Harp (solo): 10/27/1866 BPS

UNGER, JULIUS, 1818–?§ (b. Prussia; to US ca. 1850)
Musical Convention Grand Potpourri: 7/4/1870 CPG
Unser Vaterland (Marsch Potpourri): 8/2/1870 (many additional performances) CPG

VALENTINE, [A. E.?].[70]
Lucca Waltz: 9/10/1873 CPG

VAN DER STUCKEN, FRANK, 1858–1929. (b. Texas)
Festival March: 7/5/1888 CSNC/MTNA; 7/6/1893 WCE
Vlasda, Interlude: 7/5/1888 CSNC/MTNA

VOGRICH, MAX, 1852–1916. (b. Transylvania; to US 1880s?)
Diver, Ballad for Solos, Chorus and Orchestra: 7/3/1890 MTNA

WALLACE, WILLIAM VINCENT, 1812–65. (b. Ireland; to US 1850)
Desert Flower, Overture: 5/14/1872 CPG
Lurline, Fantasia: 5/12/1869 CPG
Lurline, Solo for French Horn: 5/9/1870 CPG; 10/8/1870 Boston
Lurline, Sweet Spirit, Hear My Prayer: 12/14/1867 BPS
Maritana, Finale: 11/7/1863 IHM
Maritana, Overture: 8/3, 8/15/1866 TG; 9/7/1875 CPG, 1/21/1871 Boston

WARD, MYRON A., 1844–1919. (b. New York)
Allemania Waltzes: 7/19/1876 PCE

WARREN, GEORGE W., 1828–1902. (b. New York)
Andes, Marche di Bravura (2 pianos): 12/8/1866 BPS

70 · Composer not confirmed; work was possibly composed in United States between 1872 and 1873 during the American tour of soprano Pauline Lucca.

WEIDIG, ADOLF, 1867–1931.§ (b. Germany; to US 1892)
Scherzo Capriccioso, op. 13: 1/5, 1/6/1900 CSO; 4/25, 4/26/1902 CSO

WETZLER, HERMANN H., 1870–1943. (b. Germany; to US ca. 1890)
Concert Overture: 8/4/1893 WCE

WHITING, ARTHUR, 1861–1936. (b. Massachusetts)
Fantasia for Piano and Orchestra, op. 11: 4/8, 4/9/1904 CSO

WHITING, GEORGE E. (GEORGE ELBRIDGE), 1842–1923. (b. Massa-
    chusetts)
Concert Overture in C Major, op. 3: 7/4/1890 MTNA
March of the Monks of Bangor: 2/7/1883 Brooklyn (with Amphion Musical
    Society)
Pastorals (organ solo): 3/19/1878 CMF
Princess, Concert Overture: 8/1/1883 CSNC
Symphony in C (two mvts.): 7/6/1888 CSNC/MTNA
Tale of the Viking, Overture: 7/20, 7/25/1881 CSNC; 9/2/1881 HHB
Tale of the Viking, Overture and March: 8/2/1882 CSNC; 8/25/1882 HHB

WIEGAND, DANIEL. (b. US?; fl. NYC 1860s–80s)
Beau Trompette Waltz: (marked parts in Thomas library)
Fantasy of Irish Airs: 10/23/1868 CPG
Fantasy on Scotch Airs: 12/13/1868 CPG; 2/11/1869 Brooklyn YMCA
March Rendezvous (military band): 6/20/1872 CPG
Minorca Waltz: (marked score and parts in Thomas library)
Marien Waltz: 8/18, 8/19/1871 CPG

WOLFSOHN, CARL, 1834–1907. (b. Germany; to US 1854)
I Wept While I Was Dreaming; The Water-Lily: 4/6/1867 NYC (Liederkranz
    Society and TTO)

WOLLENHAUPT, HERMANN A., 1827–63. (b. Germany; to US ca. 1850s)
La Gazelle Polka: 10/28/1863 IHM

ZÖLLNER, HEINRICH, 1854–1941. (b. Germany; to US 1890; returned
    1898)
Mitternacht zu Bei Sedan: 12/11, 12/12/1896 CSO
"Begrüssung"; "Indian Love Song"; "Die Heini von Steier" (vocal solo):
    7/5/1893 WCE (with German Liederkranz of NYC)

[v.3] Thinking about Serious Music in New York, 1842–82

ADRIENNE FRIED BLOCK

Lastly, it is contended that in performing or hearing such Instrumental Music as exists in the Symphonies, Overtures and the many pieces for smaller combinations of instruments, of Beethoven, Haydn, Mozart, Spohr, Weber, Mendelssohn, &c., is an enjoyment of the highest intellectual character.

Sixth Annual Report of the Philharmonic Society of New-York, September 9, 1848

When the Philharmonic Society of New York was founded in 1842, it stated its purpose as "the advancement of Instrumental Music." This phrase turns up in many of the 'society's early annual reports, along with the commitment to a short list of approved composers and the appeal to intellect as the source of enjoyment. All suggest an attitude toward music that was relatively new in the mid-nineteenth century and that has been characterized by recent scholars as "musical idealism."[1] By "Instrumental Music" the men who wrote the annual reports—and in most cases they were musicians who played in the orchestra—did not mean just any kind of music played by instruments. They

At the time of her death in April 2009, Adrienne Fried Block was working on her third revision of this chapter. It was finished by John Spitzer, working from Adrienne's drafts and notes with the assistance of Ora Frishberg Saloman.

1 · On musical idealism, see Mark Evan Bonds, "Idealism and the Aesthetics of Instrumental Music at the Turn of the Nineteenth Century," *Journal of the American Musicological Society* 50 (1997); David Gramit, *Cultivating Music: The Aspirations, Interests, and Limits of German Musical Culture, 1770–1848* (2002); William Weber, "Wagner, Wagnerism, and Musical Idealism," in *Wagnerism in European Culture and Politics,* ed. D. C. Large and W. Weber (1984); and Ora Frishberg Saloman, *Beethoven's Symphonies and J. S. Dwight: The Birth of American Music Criticism* (1995). Bonds emphasizes the underpinnings of musical idealism in German philosophy. Gramit discusses the genres considered appropriate for serious concerts and the conflicts that arose over the need to sell serious music to an audience. Weber links "musical idealism" with the rise of criticism and the "classical" repertory. Saloman investigates the transmission of idealism to America.

meant symphonies, overtures, and also concertos, whose formal structures grew out of the interaction of thematic elements, most typically in so-called sonata form. Other music—instrumental and vocal—was considered less worth performing or hearing and unlikely to produce "enjoyment of the highest intellectual character."

The musicians of the newly organized Philharmonic Society intended to create this intellectual enjoyment for themselves by playing the music of Beethoven, Haydn, Mozart, and others, but they also undertook to bring intellectual enjoyment to large numbers of New Yorkers—an audience large enough to support the activities of the society at the box office. In identifying their repertory the musicians pointedly ignored vocal music, especially Italian opera, and they also eschewed dance music, music emphasizing individual technical display, and any other music that conveyed strong physical sensations. They were determined to base their programs on the masterworks of symphonic literature, especially the symphonies, overtures, and concertos of Beethoven—music that required intellectual engagement and gave intellectual satisfaction. Although the musicians of the Philharmonic considered instrumental chamber music ("pieces for smaller combinations of instruments") of the masters to give similar intellectual satisfaction, their real mission was "the proper performance of great orchestral pieces," which, unlike chamber music, could reach audiences of thousands at each concert.[2]

I begin this chapter with a brief discussion of the ideology of musical idealism and how this ideology was transmitted from Europe to New York City. I analyze the New York Philharmonic's programs from 1842 to 1882 and consider the extent to which those programs embodied or implemented the tenets of idealism. Then I ask how the orchestra's organization affected programming. Finally, I discuss how the Philharmonic went about developing an audience for serious music in New York from 1842 to 1882. This study of programming and ideology in America's first permanent symphony orchestra will help to illuminate the history of American orchestras not just in the nineteenth but also in the twentieth century.

Musical Idealism in the New World

Musical idealism, according to Mark Evan Bonds, was a group of ideas that emerged in the late eighteenth and early nineteenth centuries based on the

2 · New York Philharmonic Society, *Tenth Annual Report of the New-York Philharmonic Society, Sept. 11, 1852,* 1.

proposition that "the aesthetic effect of an artwork resides in its ability to reflect a higher ideal."[3] For idealist writers such as Wackenroder, Tieck, and E. T. A. Hoffmann, instrumental music was superior to vocal music as a means of reflecting this world of the spirit. Instrumental music—at least the "higher" forms like symphonies and overtures—could evoke and communicate what could not be seen and could not be named. As articulated in the 1830s by Adolf Bernhard Marx, the structures of "serious" instrumental music—the music of Beethoven in particular—grew out of thematic elements rather than the harmonies defined by the bass line. Beethoven's instrumental music, especially the symphonies, became the standard against which other music was measured. The symphonies of Beethoven, except for the Ninth, contained no words, no virtuosic display, no singing bodies on stage to demand the attention of the audience, no waltzes or polkas to make people tap their toes—no undesirable distractions from the music's formal design and spiritual content. Free from the constraints of words and the distractions of vocal and instrumental gymnastics, symphonies, overtures, and concertos could carry the listener upward into a "spirit-realm," a "transcendent consciousness."[4]

This was the ideology that lay behind the effusive language of a series of New York Philharmonic Society Annual Reports, beginning with the sixth season in 1848 and continuing for at least ten years thereafter. "Advancement of instrumental music," "enjoyment of the highest intellectual character," "great orchestral pieces," "refinement of the human heart," and so on—these and other phrases echoed the ideas, the values, and the language of German idealism.[5] How were these ideas about serious music transmitted from European sources to the musicians in the New York Philharmonic in the 1840s as well as to their audience? The most obvious way was through the musicians themselves. Twenty-two of the fifty-nine musicians who founded the Philharmonic in 1842 were born in Germany, and several of the others were sons of German immigrants.[6] Many were well-educated men who brought ideas about music with them to America and kept up from a distance with the German musical press. Ureli Corelli Hill, the founder and first president of the Philharmonic, had studied violin in Germany with Spohr and brought back,

3 · Bonds, "Idealism," 392.
4 · Carl Dahlhaus, *The Idea of Absolute Music* (1978), 8; David Charlton, "Hoffmann as a Writer on Music," in *E. T. A. Hoffmann's Musical Writings,* ed. D. Charlton (1989), 7–8.
5 · The quoted phrases come from the sixth (1847–48), tenth (1851–52), and twelfth (1853–54) annual reports.
6 · See Henry Edward Krehbiel, *The Philharmonic Society of New York: A Memorial* (1892), 76; also see Howard Shanet, *Philharmonic: A History of New York's Orchestra* (1975), 109.

if not fully articulated musical idealism, at least idealist attitudes about the importance of instrumental music.[7]

Musical idealism was also transmitted to New York musicians and audiences by music teachers and critics such as Frédéric Louis Ritter. Born in Alsace and trained in both Germany and France, Ritter came to the United States in 1856 and to New York in 1861, where until 1870 he worked as a choral conductor. After his appointment as professor of music at Vassar in 1867, he remained in close touch with New York musical life. Ritter also kept up with German musical literature of the day and was a reliable and objective transmitter of the ideas he encountered there.[8] Critic Theodore Hagen arrived in New York in 1855, where he became editor of the *Musical Review and Musical World* and music reviewer for the *New-Yorker Staats-Zeitung* and the *Neue New Yorker Musik-Zeitung*. Writing alternately in English and German, he not only revealed the influence of German musical idealism in his writing but also quoted directly from German sources, especially A. B. Marx. Marx was also an important influence on John Sullivan Dwight, as Ora Saloman has shown.[9] Though based in Boston, Dwight covered the New York music scene closely, and many New Yorkers subscribed to his *Journal of Music*.

The ideas in the Philharmonic's annual reports—at once idealist and idealistic—were aimed at a broad audience of New York music lovers. European concert societies, such as the Gewandhaus concerts in Leipzig or the Paris Concerts du Conservatoire, could count on an audience of connoisseurs who had heard and patronized instrumental music for many years. In New York, however, there was no such cadre beyond the musicians themselves, a handful of musical amateurs, and a few critics. In order to advance instrumental music, the Philharmonic needed to create an audience that desired and would pay for enjoyment of the highest intellectual character. This they proposed to accomplish through programming, as one annual report explained: "The selections for the Concerts have always been made with a view of satisfying the demands of those hearers whose taste has been properly formed in Europe and to improve the taste of those whose advantages have been comparatively small."[10] Through repeated performances of orchestral masterworks, the Philharmonic aspired to educate its audience to musical idealism.

---

7 · On Hill's trip to Germany, see chapter IV.2 in this volume.

8 · Ritter owned one of the most extensive nineteenth-century American collections of German books and journals on music. His library is now in the collection at Tufts University.

9 · Saloman, *Beethoven's Symphonies and J. S. Dwight*. On Dwight, see also chapter III.2 in this volume.

10 · New York Philharmonic Society, *Sixth Annual Report*, 10.

New York Philharmonic Programs

One of the inducements for New York musicians to form a symphony orchestra had been the first complete performance in February 1841 of Beethoven's Fifth Symphony at the Broadway Tabernacle. The event generated considerable excitement among the performers, and among listeners it elicited, if not understanding, at least interest in hearing the work again. George Templeton Strong, for example, recorded in his diary the impact of Beethoven's symphony along with his prejudice against German immigrants, typical of the New York elite in his day: "Went to the German charitable concert at the Tabernacle, which was jammed with Dutchmen, like a barrel of Dutch herrings. I scarcely saw an Anglo-Saxon physiognomy in the whole gallery. The music was good, very well selected and excellently well performed, so far as I could judge. The crack piece, though, was the last, Beethoven's *Sinfonia* in C minor. It was generally unintelligible to me, except the Andante."[11] In a review of the performance Henry Cood Watson noted that "many people left before the symphony was over."[12] Some of the musicians decided that this problem could be solved by more frequent performances, an idea that bore fruit a year later at a meeting of New York's orchestral musicians in April 1842, at which it was agreed to establish the Philharmonic Society of New-York. Perhaps in an effort to better capture and hold the attention of the audience, the society did not close but opened its first program with the Beethoven Fifth Symphony.

Program 1. Inaugural Concert, December 7, 1842

PART I

Beethoven, Symphony no. 5

Weber, *Oberon*: Scena (Mme. Otto, soprano)

Hummel, Quintet in D Minor for piano, violin, viola, cello, double bass

PART II

Weber, Overture to *Oberon*

Rossini, *Armida*: duet (Mme. Otto, Mr. Horn)

Beethoven, *Fidelio:* Scena (Mr. Horn)

Mozart, *Belmont and Constance* [*The Abduction from the Seraglio*], Aria
    bravura (Mme. Otto)

Kalliwoda, New Overture in D

11 · Diary entry of February 11, 1841, quoted in Vera Brodsky Lawrence, *Strong on Music*, vol. 1, *Resonances, 1836–1849* (1988), 111. The program was a benefit for the German Society and included music by Mozart, Ries, and others besides the featured symphony.

12 · Lawrence, *Strong on Music*, vol. 1, 110.

This inaugural program did not restrict itself to instrumental music: rather it was a miscellany of instrumental and vocal music, mostly by German composers.

The Beethoven symphony that opened the concert and the overtures that began and ended the second half represented the kind of music that the Philharmonic had organized itself to play. The vocal selections were probably an effort to make the program more accessible to the New York audience, which had been enthusiastically attending opera since the 1820s.[13] The Hummel quintet, an instrumental work with symphony-like formal structures but not for orchestra, may have been a concession to lack of rehearsal time.[14] The choice of repertory for the inaugural concert—the types of pieces and the order in which they were presented—became a model for Philharmonic programs for the next thirty years or more.

Opening the program with a Beethoven symphony was a characteristic gesture. Some years later, a New York critic, writing in German in the *Neue New Yorker Musik-Zeitung*, waxed eloquent on the cultural significance of Beethoven's orchestral music: "With the arrival of a Beethoven sonata in a family's home, a better spirit, an increasing ambition commences there. How much more effect then, will an orchestral sonata have.... Fleeting [musical] images in their alternating hues inevitably move us more profoundly [in an orchestral setting] than when they are rendered by one instrument only."[15] The choice of the Fifth Symphony was equally telling. Not only was this the work that convinced New York musicians to form the Philharmonic, but also it was the subject of one of the most famous and influential musical essays of the nineteenth century: E. T. A. Hoffmann's 1810 review, which heard "the immeasurably magnificent and profound Symphony in C minor" as revealing a "spirit-realm," in which "the enraptured soul perceives an unknown language and understands all the most mysterious presentiments that hold it in thrall."[16]

If the new society's purpose was the advancement of instrumental music, what were an aria by Mozart, a duet by Rossini, and a scene from Beethoven's *Fidelio* doing on the inaugural program? The sixth annual report in 1848 belatedly explained the orchestra's reasoning: "Vocal Music has been introduced only to satisfy the demands of those who desired it as a relief from

13 · See Karen Ahlquist, *Democracy at the Opera: Music, Theatre, and Culture in New York City, 1815–60* (1997).

14 · This quintet was the composer's arrangement of his Septet, op. 74, originally for piano, flute, oboe, horn, viola, cello, and double bass.

15 · *Neue New Yorker Musik-Zeitung*, March 22, 1876, 65.

16 · E. T. A. Hoffman, "Beethoven's Instrumental Music," in *E. T. A. Hoffmann's Musical Writings* (1989), 98, 102.

that which they did not so well appreciate, and who could not, without it, perhaps, have been persuaded to contribute that support to the cause."[17] Some idealistic orchestra members evidently chafed at this concession to economic necessity and popular taste: "Expressions have been made from time to time at the business meetings of the Society, which show that it is a prevailing opinion or wish that no more vocal Music should be introduced at our Concerts, but that the cause of Instrumental Music should stand or fall on its own merits."[18] More practical heads prevailed, however. The Philharmonic's reading of public taste obliged it to forego—for decades—the presentation of purely instrumental programs. In a city where the favorite entertainments were opera and minstrel shows, the musicians were forced to concede that, contrary to their ideals, vocal music had to be included in their programs to satisfy a range of tastes. Despite their fear that vocal music might have a negative effect on audience tastes, the musicians hoped that many in their audiences, after listening to both types of music, would learn to prefer music of a more serious nature. The musicians had little choice: absent elite patronage, the survival of the orchestra depended on ticket sales.

Table V.3.1 shows the repertory of the New York Philharmonic over the first forty years of its existence, tabulated according to genre.[19] "Serious" genres are represented by symphonies, overtures, and concertos, plus chamber music, works for chorus and orchestra, and "other orchestral," which consists mostly of symphonic poems. Lighter genres include opera arias and scenes, songs for voice and piano, and music for solo instruments, which ranges from Chopin ballades to Liszt opera transcriptions to sets of virtuoso variations. The total number of pieces programmed in each five-year period varies somewhat from one column to the next.[20] The table shows that the proportion of "serious" music, initially high in keeping with the ideals of the founders, declined in the 1850s and '1860s, because vocal selections and instrumental solos were added to the programs, then increased in the 1870s back to about three-quarters of the repertory. The proportion of symphonies increased gradually from 1842 to 1872, then held steady at about a quar-

17 · New York Philharmonic Society, *Sixth Annual Report*, 10.

18 · Ibid.

19 · Data for table V.3.1 come from the New York Philharmonic's performance history archive, online at http://nyphil.org/about/archives.cfm. The procedures for counting works and assigning them to genres involved some arbitrary decisions. For example, sets of Chopin preludes or Schubert songs were counted as a single piece; duets of two instruments were counted as "solos," whereas quartets were counted as "chamber." These decisions make little difference in the proportions of various genres.

20 · The total number of works varied according to how many concerts the orchestra gave and whether shorter or longer pieces were programmed. Consequently the proportion of genres in the repertory is a better measure than absolute numbers of works.

TABLE V.3.1. New York Philharmonic repertory by genre, 1842–82

	1842–47	1847–52	1852–57	1857–62	1862–67	1867–72	1872–77	1877–82
"Serious" music								
Symphony	20	22	22	26	30	32	37	37
Overture	40	36	28	23	31	40	31	23
Concerto	16	17	18	24	22	27	21	16
Other orchestral	–	–	–	7	11	10	10	24
Chamber	6	2	–	–	–	1	–	2
Chorus + orchestra	2	1	3	2	4	5	1	–
Less "serious" music								
Opera aria, duet, scena	29	12	23	31	18	24	23	21
Other vocal (song, etc.)	3	4	13	12	11	2	10	5
Sacred vocal	2	1	5	1	3	2	–	1
Instrumental solo	6	11	23	20	21	6	17	2
Solo inst. + orch.	1	1	–	1	–	1	–	–
Dance	1	–	–	–	–	–	–	–
TOTAL	126	107	135	147	151	150	150	131
"SERIOUS"/TOTAL	.67	.73	.53	.56	.65	.77	.67	.78

ter of the repertory. The proportion of overtures declined, as overtures were replaced by tone poems—equally "serious" works. Concertos held more or less steady, while chamber music and works with chorus declined. Among the "lighter" genres, opera scenes and arias declined (though not steadily) from almost a quarter to less than a fifth of the repertory, and songs, after increasing in the 1850s, declined thereafter. Instrumental solos increased considerably in the 1850s, then declined at the end of the period. Save for one waltz in 1847 (an arrangement for men's chorus), dance music did not appear in the Philharmonic's repertory.

Table V.3.1 suggests the evolving dynamics of the Philharmonic's attempt to balance the musicians' commitment to musical idealism with their desire to increase their audience through accessible programming. It also may reflect the orchestra's finances—that is, whether money was available to pay for famous singers and touring instrumental virtuosos. Finally, it probably reflects the tastes of the orchestra's first two permanent conductors, Carl Bergmann in 1866 and Theodore Thomas from 1877. The evolution of programming over the forty-year period seems to show an enduring commitment to musical idealism, evident in the earliest programs of the 1840s, wavering during the 1850s, then establishing itself ever more strongly from the 1860s on.

Beginning in the 1860s, a few programs were given that realized the ambition of the founders as expressed in the sixth annual report that "the cause of Instrumental Music should stand or fall on its own merits." Here is one of the earliest of these programs, conducted by Carl Bergmann in 1872.

Program 2. New York Philharmonic Concert, January 6, 1872

PART I

Weber, Overture: *Euryanthe*

[Carl] Reinecke, Concerto for Piano in F-sharp Minor, op. 72

Haydn, Symphony no. 13 in G Major [Hob I:88]

PART II

[Joachim] Raff, Symphony: *Im Walde*

This program was groundbreaking not just because it excluded vocal music and instrumental solos unaccompanied by the orchestra, but also in that it was one of the earliest programs to begin with an overture rather than a symphony.[21] These practices became more frequent in the ensuing years, anticipating the programming practices of twentieth-century orchestras.

The Philharmonic's repertory can also be analyzed according to the representation of various composers over the years, as shown in table V.3.2.[22] The composers who formed the pantheon of the sixth annual report in 1848—Beethoven, Haydn, Mozart, Spohr, Weber, Mendelssohn—remained central through the 1850s. After that Weber declined slightly and Spohr precipitously, their places being taken by Schumann and Schubert, then by Wagner, Liszt, and Brahms. The Philharmonic had opened its inaugural concert with Beethoven's Fifth Symphony, and Beethoven continued to dominate Philharmonic programming to a remarkable extent. Through 1867 Beethoven's music made up from 10 to 15 percent of works programmed; thereafter the percentage rose to around 20 percent or more. From 1862 to 1882, at least one piece by Beethoven appeared on two-thirds of Philharmonic programs. Works by "other" modern German composers, such as Gade, Bargiel, and Lindpaintner, continued to be represented at about the same rate throughout the forty-year period. On the other hand, Italian, French, and English music all declined, reflecting the shift away from operatic selections and virtuoso display pieces seen in table V.3.1. American composers—mostly members of the orchestra and many of them German immigrants—gained a place in the repertory during the 1850s and 1860s, only to lose it again after 1867, when

21 · The first New York Philharmonic program that offered neither singers nor an instrumental solo was given on November 21, 1846. The first program to begin with an overture was May 20, 1846. Such programs remained uncommon until the 1870s.

22 · Table V.3.2, like table V.3.1, is based on the New York Philharmonic performance history archive online. The totals of the columns in table V.3.2 tend to be lower than the totals in table V.3.1 because a few of the composers could not be assigned to the nationality categories in the table and were omitted.

TABLE V.3.2. New York Philharmonic repertory by composer and nationality, 1842–82

	1842–47	1847–52	1852–57	1857–62	1862–67	1867–72	1872–77	1877–82
German "classic"								
Beethoven	16	8	13	18	21	31	26	27
Mozart	9	7	7	11	14	13	7	7
Haydn	3	–	1	2	3	3	8	2
German modern								
Weber	14	10	10	4	9	9	4	4
Mendelssohn	9	20	15	13	15	13	8	4
Spohr	6	7	7	4	1	2	4	–
Schumann	–	1	4	12	9	12	10	9
Schubert	–	2	4	6	4	4	3	6
Wagner	–	–	2	5	5	6	6	17
Liszt	–	–	–	8	9	10	10	6
Brahms	–	–	1	–	–	–	1	5
Other	23	23	24	22	21	23	25	13
Revival								
Bach	–	–	–	–	1	2	5	5
Handel	–	–	1	–	2	1	1	1
Other	–	–	1	2	2	3	3	1
Italian								
Rossini	8	2	1	–	2	2	3	–
Donizetti	8	1	2	3	3	2	–	–
Other	5	4	7	7	–	–	2	1
French								
Berlioz	2	–	2	1	6	3	5	7
Other	10	7	10	7	10	3	4	3
English	2	7	6	2	–	1	1	–
American	1	2	11	5	7	2	3	–
Polish/Russian	–	–	–	–	–	–	–	–
Chopin	1	–	4	3	7	1	8	3
Other	–	–	–	1	1	4	5	10
TOTAL	117	101	133	136	152	150	152	131
BEETHOVEN/TOTAL	.14	.08	.10	.13	.14	.21	.17	.21
GERMAN/TOTAL	.68	.77	.66	.77	.75	.86	.78	.81

Bergmann and then Thomas took over as conductors and reduced the number of instrumental solos on the programs.

The percentage of German music on Philharmonic programs, already above 65 percent at the orchestra's inception, continued to rise, surpassing 75 percent in the 1850s and 80 percent from 1867 on. Pieces revived from the "early music" repertory were mostly German as well, especially Bach and Handel and also Gluck. The "Germanization" of the Philharmonic's repertory in the 1860s was noticed by the public and commented on in the press.[23] But the Philharmonic had made a commitment to "the advancement of Instrumental Music" and to "enjoyment of the highest intellectual character," and to a considerable extent serious music meant German music.

Organization

The Philharmonic Society of New-York was established in 1842 by the musicians themselves, who, without any outside support or patronage, organized the orchestra as a cooperative. The musicians sacrificed time and money as needed to rehearse or perform with the orchestra, even if it meant giving up an evening's work at higher pay in the theater. "We are an Art-Democracy," the musicians proclaimed in their fifteenth annual report; the orchestra's survival depended on every member doing his civic duty.[24]

The absence of aristocratic or government patronage was a defining aspect of orchestral history in the United States vis-à-vis Europe. What New York had in its place was a long history of entrepreneurship, introduced by the first colonists, the Dutch, who made New Amsterdam the center of a free trade zone.[25] The spirit of risk-taking, together with rights of citizens to engage in commerce and to take part in public affairs, inscribed in the governance of New Amsterdam and reinscribed by the British under pressure from the citizens of newly renamed New York, was the spirit that energized the founders of New York's orchestra. Members boasted of the orchestra's economic independence, "unsustained ... by State patronage, or by the purses of an opulent few," and they proposed it as a model for American musical life: "self-existing, self-sustained, self controlling ... a salient instance of success among similar musical institutions."[26]

In its first decade, the Philharmonic gave "rough," even "amateurish" performances, according to Frédéric Louis Ritter, whose ideas about good orchestral playing had been formed in France and Germany, but the performances also had "a good deal of enthusiasm and life."[27] The musicians,

---

23 · See Krehbiel, *Philharmonic Society of New York*, 69; also Shanet, *Philharmonic*, 109.

24 · New York Philharmonic Society, *Fifteenth Annual Report of the New-York Philharmonic Society* (1857), 3. This report was written for the Philharmonic by Richard Storrs Willis, editor of the *Musical Times*. New York Philharmonic Society, Minutes of Meeting, August 22, 1857, New York Philharmonic Archives. See also Krehbiel, *Philharmonic Society of New York*, 64.

25 · See Russell Shorto, *The Island at the Center of the World: The Epic Story of Dutch Manhattan and the Forgotten Colony That Shaped America* (2004), 106.

26 · New York Philharmonic Society, *Fifteenth Annual Report*, 3.

27 · Frédéric Louis Ritter, *Music in America* (1883), 276.

however, seem to have been ready to do what was needed to raise the standard, even if that meant replacing some of the founding members with more gifted or conscientious players. "Ours being, comparatively, a young Society," they declared in the fourteenth annual report, it is "constantly gathering new strength, by adding now, only members of undoubted talent; many older members who formed the nucleus of our Society, having, in consideration of not constantly practicing their respective instruments, with commendable self-denial relinquished their places in the orchestra, and by their outside influence and maturer [counsel] at our meetings, show that conscious pride of having been instrumental in forming (may we be allowed to say it?) the noblest institution of the kind in America."[28]

Conductors of the Philharmonic were members of the society, and they served at the pleasure of the other players, who elected them yearly. During the first few seasons, conductors rotated from concert to concert; from 1849 to 1866 conducting duties were divided between two men, Theodore Eisfeld and Carl Bergmann. During this entire period conductors received exactly the same pay as the players, that is, an equal share of monies left over after expenses. When Carl Bergmann was elected sole conductor in 1866, the members granted him a salary of $500, far more than the players' yearly share.[29] Bergmann remained as conductor for ten years, followed by Leopold Damrosch for one.[30] In 1877 the orchestra elected Theodore Thomas, who conducted the orchestra (with one short gap) until he moved to Chicago in 1891.[31]

The shift to a single conductor had a significant effect on the Philharmonic's repertory, particularly in the balance of "serious" and lighter genres. Bergmann had only partial authority over programming: sometimes he was a member of the ad hoc committees that chose repertory and engaged soloists; other times he was not.[32] Yet a shift after 1866 away from songs and instrumental solos and toward symphonies and other orchestral music is read-

28 · New York Philharmonic Society, *Fourteenth Annual Report of the New-York Philharmonic Society* (1856), 1.

29 · According to the society's annual reports, Bergmann's salary was raised in 1868 to $600 and in 1869 to $1,000. For the 1874–75 season, he received only $750. Thanks to Gabe Smith for providing this and other information from the Philharmonic Archives.

30 · On Damrosch's brief tenure at the Philharmonic, see chapter III.3 in this volume.

31 · Thomas left the orchestra for one season to direct the Cincinnati College of Music and then returned to the Philharmonic. On the complex relations between Thomas, the Theodore Thomas Orchestra, and the New York Philharmonic, see Ezra Schabas, *Theodore Thomas: America's Conductor and Builder of Orchestras, 1835–1905* (1989), 78–84, 121–46. Also see Shanet, *Philharmonic*, 155–74.

32 · See, for example, New York Philharmonic Society, Minutes of Meeting, February 10, 1866, New York Philharmonic Archives.

ily apparent in table V.3.1, as is a shift toward even more German music in table V.3.2. During Bergmann's tenure, the orchestra featured not only more symphonies by Beethoven but also major works by Berlioz, Liszt, and Wagner, leading composers of the "modern" school. Thomas went even further in this direction. As he said later in his autobiography, Beethoven and Wagner became the "pillars" of his programming. "I placed them where they belonged," he said, "and then filled out the rest of the program."[33] During his first few seasons (1877–78, 1879–82), Thomas followed this plan, conducting six symphonies, two concertos, and five overtures of Beethoven and performing entire acts of *Rheingold* and *Götterdämmerung* (twice), as well as instrumental and vocal excerpts from *Meistersinger, Tannhäuser, Siegfried, Flying Dutchman,* and *Lohengrin.* Almost half of Thomas's concerts over the period were devoted exclusively to orchestral music. Here is the final program of Thomas's first season:

Program 3. New York Philharmonic Concert, April 6, 1878

Beethoven, Music to Goethe's *Egmont,* op. 84 (the songs by Madame
　Eugenie Pappenheim)
[Anton] Rubinstein, Symphony no. 2, *Ocean,* op. 42
Wagner, "Siegfried's Death" and finale from *Die Götterdämmerung*
　(Brunnhilde, Mme. Eugenie Pappenheim)

To be sure, this program included—indeed it featured—vocal music. And only one of the composers, Beethoven, was on the short list from the sixth annual report. But the selections that Mme. Pappenheim sang were eminently "serious" and manifestly "enjoyment of the highest intellectual character." Thirty-five years after the Philharmonic's inaugural concert, Theodore Thomas's programs came very close to realizing the idealistic goals of the founders.

The Audience for Idealism

In his seminal book on Boston's musical culture in the nineteenth century, Michael Broyles discusses the tensions that arose when an art with its roots in a hierarchical society was presented as an ideal for citizens of a democracy. Broyles notes that "the aristocratic basis of European music had not escaped American observers in the early nineteenth century, for music nurtured in the courts and cathedrals of Europe seemed out of place in the democratic

---

33 · Theodore Thomas, *Theodore Thomas: A Musical Autobiography* (1905), 2:15–16.

society America was producing."[34] In Boston at the mid-nineteenth century, such music had still not set down firm roots, despite the efforts of John Sullivan Dwight, editor of *Dwight's Journal of Music* and president of the Harvard Musical Association, and Samuel Eliot, president of the Boston Academy of Music and mayor of Boston. "By 1840," writes Broyles, "the view that there was a fundamental incompatibility between classical European music and American society had become widespread."[35]

New York, however, was a more cosmopolitan city than Boston and had by far the largest and most diverse population in the country. More than half of New Yorkers at midcentury were European born: one-quarter Irish, about 15 percent born in Germany, plus clusters of immigrants from France, Italy, and other countries.[36] Most of the rest were native born, including elites of Dutch and English origin, second- and third-generation immigrants, and a rather small African-American community. There was a sizeable middle class, native- and foreign-born, engaged in commerce, industry, and the professions, from which the Philharmonic drew its most numerous support.

New York's German community constituted an important portion of the Philharmonic's audience. According to Richard Grant White, writing in the *New York Times* in 1880, "The majority of the audiences are neither New-York nor American by birth and breeding, but chiefly German.... When I first attended the rehearsal and the concerts of the Philharmonic Society no speech was heard among the audience but English—with, of course, such rare exceptions as might occur in London or Liverpool or any large town. Now at these concerts, and particularly at Mr. Thomas's, there is a spraching of German all around me, in my in-going, in my down-sitting, and in my out-coming."[37] German ethnicity predisposed audience members toward music by German composers, but it did not guarantee that they wanted to hear symphonies, overtures, and tone poems or that they adhered to the tenets of musical idealism. And much of the non-German audience was unfamiliar with both repertory and the ideology of "serious" music. Therefore the Philharmonic, declared the annual report of 1856–57, "is or should be, an *educating* institution." The report went on to boast that "it is not too much to say, that during the period of its existence, it *has* succeeded in educating and securing a large public for itself, from among the most varied classes of

---

34 · Michael Broyles, *"Music of the Highest Class": Elitism and Populism in Antebellum Boston* (1992), 215.

35 · Ibid.

36 · Robert Ernst, *Immigrant Life in New York City, 1825–1863* (1949), 193. These figures are based on the census of 1855.

37 · Richard Grant White, "New York Taste: History of the Philharmonic Society," *New York Times*, December 26, 1880, 7.

the community.... We cannot think that in our choice of compositions for performance, our lofty and true aim will ever be lowered to an *ad captandum* and less worthy style."[38]

This optimistic assessment was written during precisely the period when, according to table V.3.1, the Philharmonic was presenting the lowest proportion of "serious" music. Between 1852 and 1857 the Philharmonic programmed more opera excerpts than symphonies and a large number of instrumental tours de force like the *Caprice Burlesque*, "Polchinelle," for piano by August Gockel (April 23, 1853) and a *Duo Concertante* by Baumann for two French horns and orchestra on the air "Araby's Daughter" (April 22, 1854). Perhaps the report's grand pronouncements about lofty aims were designed to assuage a bad conscience. By the late 1860s, as the Philharmonic's programming began to mirror its ideals more closely again, the annual reports leave off preaching idealism and restrict themselves to the details of soloists, repertory, and finance.

Not everyone agreed that the public, even a musically educated public, deserved a diet of exclusively "serious" and mostly instrumental music. A columnist in the *New York Herald*, a newspaper with a populist point of view, complained in 1866 that the Philharmonic offered no concerts of "popular music at popular prices."[39] The taste, he says, "in the community for good music is universal and is improving every day." But an "honest citizen" who wants to take his wife and children to a Philharmonic concert will have to pay $7.50—no half price for the children. And what, the writer asks, will they hear for their money?

Why, a "sonata" or a "symphony," or a "theme" at which a hundred musicians work like madmen for an hour, and produce, to these worthy folk, nothing but discord. As well they might purchase a Greek grammar for family fireside reading, as go to a "Philharmonic" for the music they seek.... These "high art" affairs in fact suit about a dozen musical amateurs who enter on free tickets, but the public don't care for them....

The trouble is that our rising musicians have taken to what they call "high art." The sublime and the incomprehensible music of the intellect is to them the only music worth hearing or playing.... What the public want is popular music, given by the best artists in a concert room large enough to seat comfortably the three or four thousand people who would go every night to hear it—if offered at prices as it ought to be—which would enable a man to

38 · New York Philharmonic Society, *Fifteenth Annual Report*, 4. *Ad captandum vulgus* means "pander to the crowd."

39 · *New York Herald*, October 6, 1866, 12.

take his wife and children for a couple of dollars, all told.... This is the great popular want—which *must* be filled at an early day, and which will realize a speedy fortune for the originator of such a series of concerts.[40]

This "great popular want" was already being filled—but not by the New York Philharmonic. Louis Antoine Jullien had filled it in 1853–54, not just in New York but on tour throughout the United States.[41] Bernard Ullman, the impresario, filled it in 1858 with promenade concerts by the Musard orchestra.[42] Theodore Thomas filled it with his summer concerts at Terrace Garden beginning in 1866 and then at Central Park Garden. Carl Bergmann, Nahan Franko, and a host of other conductors filled it with Sunday concerts in venues like the Terrace Garden, the Atlantic Garden, and Ebling's Casino.[43]

The New York Philharmonic, on the other hand, after trying during the 1850s and 1860s to balance artistic integrity with popular tastes, was moving by 1866 in the opposite direction, embracing "high art" and the repertory of serious, instrumental music. Musical idealism, whatever the *Herald* might say about it, was a viable marketing strategy in New York. Enjoying the commitment of its musicians, a base in the large German community, the patronage of professional and business elites, and the support of the press and the educational establishment, the Philharmonic was able to adhere to its ideals, perhaps even raise them. Audiences continued to grow, even after Leopold Damrosch organized a competing orchestra in 1878, which turned itself the next year into the New York Symphony Orchestra.[44] New York was large enough, economically strong enough, and its audiences familiar enough with symphonic repertory to support not one but two orchestras that played serious music.

40 · Ibid.
41 · On Jullien's American tour, see chapter IV.1 in this volume.
42 · On Ullman and the Musard orchestra, see chapter III.1 in this volume.
43 · On Sunday concerts and orchestras at the beer gardens, see chapter II.2 in this volume.
44 · On Damrosch's orchestra, see chapter III.3 in this volume.

Afterword: Coming of Age

RONALD G. WALTERS

The United States and its orchestras came of age at the same time.

Between 1840 and 1900—roughly the period covered by the chapters in this book—America reached its present continental limits and acquired Alaska, Hawai'i, and the Philippines. Its economy had become the most dynamic in the world, and it was emerging as a major military power. During those sixty years, the population of the United States grew from seventeen million to a little over seventy-six million, much of this fueled by a large influx of immigrants in the last decades of the century. Their countries of origin differed from those of their primarily northwestern European predecessors. Among the largest groups of newcomers in 1900 were southern Italians, Poles, and "Hebrews" (a newly invented category). All of this happened in spite of a devastating civil war. America in 1840 would be an alien place to us. In 1900 it would be recognizably familiar.

The same holds true for American orchestras. Finding anything resembling a modern orchestra would have been difficult in 1840. The institution of the "symphony" orchestra simply did not exist, in the sense of a standing ensemble that gives public concerts of symphonic music. Sixty years later, both older orchestras like the New York Philharmonic and the new ones that emerged in the 1890s would be familiar in repertory, in level of professionalism, and even in organizational structure, as the present "corporate" model began to take shape.

Parallels between the trajectory of American history in the last half of the nineteenth century and the history of America's orchestras are revealing and misleading. The story of both the nation and its orchestras is one of growth, as well as one of increasing specialization and prominence in the world. The rise of the corporate model for symphony orchestras, moreover, suggests a parallel with the rise of giant corporations like Standard Oil that by 1900 dominated the American economy. Yet the history of nineteenth-century orchestras seems in other ways significantly detached from several major currents that marked the period, one of bitter and violent racism and open conflict between capital and labor, scant mention of which appears in this volume. At a time when striking workers in steel, coal, and railroads fought pitched battles with company hirelings, symphony musicians formed unions with relative ease.

It is nonetheless tempting to read both the transit of American history in the nineteenth century and the history of symphonies as parallel triumphal narratives of progress, which is how contemporaries and early historians read them. For decades, however, scholars have been dismantling such a cheery view of nineteenth-century U.S. history. In their works, growth came with high costs—violence, corruption, imperialism, poverty, and racism among them. Some comparable dismantling also takes place in this volume: Deane Root's introduction locates the present authors in a revisionist relationship with their predecessors and with the story of American symphonic progress and musical triumph. Yet two questions immediately emerge: (1) is there a new narrative implied in this collection? and (2) if so, how does this narrative link up with other interpretations of nineteenth-century American history? I will briefly outline a "yes" answer to the first question. Following that, I will take up one particular theme in these chapters, the growing diversity of American public culture, as a case study for addressing the second question and as an opportunity to meditate on what perspective the story told here might give on the present state of American symphony orchestras.

First the new narrative.

These chapters subtly trace the growth of American orchestras out of a large, varied, and often vibrant antebellum musical culture to assume their twentieth-century form. Yet the story is not one of "progress" toward symphony orchestras. It is filled with alternatives and paths not taken. Failures are as interesting as successes; ephemeral orchestras as important as enduring ones. As in earlier narratives, remarkable individuals still matter, but so do figures that previous accounts omitted or kept in the shadows, notably amateurs, women, and the orchestra musicians themselves. Geographically, the story travels from the cities of Europe to transplanted immigrant musical cultures in the United States, and on to more peculiarly American settings, where local differences prove crucial. Spatially, the story moves across a similarly broad range of venues, from private balls, to public halls, to theater orchestra pits, to beer gardens, and at the century's end to new, specially designed symphony halls like those in Boston (1900) and Chicago (1904). Although it concludes with the rise of modern orchestras, this narrative is far from linear. It is full of fits and starts, contingencies, and possibilities.

The story told here is not entirely celebratory. There is an occasional sense of loss and curiosity about what might have been if, for example, amateurs had not been so effectively pushed to the margins of symphonic music, or if a more collective, less corporate, model for orchestras had persisted. There are also traces of nostalgia for the world of music that prevailed before the Civil War, a yearning for a time of a "rich shared public culture that once characterized the United States."[1] The words are those of Lawrence Levine, whose highly influential 1988 book, *Highbrow/Lowbrow: The Emergence of Cultural Hierarchy in America*, haunts these pages. In Levine's analysis, that "rich shared public culture" began to fragment around the time of the Civil War. Some elements came to be regarded as "lowbrow" popular culture, while others, including symphonic music, were withdrawn from the broader, cross-class audience that had once enjoyed them and "sacralized" as "highbrow" art. As "sacralization" progressed, Beethoven and beer no longer shared the same venues.

The new narrative suggested by these chapters is far more shaded than either the older histories of cultural triumph or Levine's tale of separation and loss. Although the chapters provide plenty of examples of the separation of "highbrow" and "lowbrow" cultures in the nineteenth century, they also show the process to have been more gradual and partial than Levine claims. Far from being triumphalist, moreover, the story told here is one of losses and missed opportunities along the way to the creation of modern American orchestras. In that respect, it may also resemble more mixed and darker tales historians in other fields are telling about nineteenth-century America, as they weigh the gains, costs, and intended and unintended consequences of, for example, Reconstruction, westward expansion, and the Progressive era.[2] White hats and black hats remain in such accounts (as here), but gray hats are more common.

That brings me to the second question: how does this fresh understanding of the origins of American symphony orchestras connect to other major themes in nineteenth-century U.S. history? A number of the authors suggest possibilities, notably links to the histories of gender, social and educational reform, class and taste, and labor and economic history. These chapters also speak to a current interest in "transnational history," represented here by the migration of music, ideas about music, musicians, and listeners back and forth across the Atlantic.

1 · Lawrence W. Levine, *Highbrow/Lowbrow: The Emergence of Cultural Hierarchy in America* (1988), 9.
2 · For three examples among many possible ones, see Eric Foner, *A Short History of Reconstruction, 1863–1877* (1990); Patricia Nelson Limerick, *The Legacy of Conquest: The Unbroken Past of the American West* (1987); and Michael E. McGerr, *A Fierce Discontent: The Rise and Fall of the Progressive Movement in America, 1870–1920* (2003).

I am going to examine a narrower connection between the history of nineteenth-century orchestras and the rapidly expanding universe of commercial popular culture. I address this theme, first, because it is less grand and more manageable than other candidates and, second, because it helps tie this collection to problems and possibilities confronting present-day symphony orchestras.

As highbrow and lowbrow cultures drew apart, orchestras found places for themselves on both sides of the divide. Orchestras were essential to many "popular" entertainments—spoken theater, vaudeville, circuses, dances, and more. At the same time "symphony" orchestras began to emerge that played a "purer" repertory of European "classics." What did Americans lose as the "shared public culture" faded? And what did they gain (this is a question scholars rarely ask) from the "sacralization" of high culture? The chapters in this volume help frame both these questions.

Calculating such gains and losses requires a brief excursion backward in time to a point before the "rich shared public culture" emerged—1800 will do—followed by a glance forward at 1900. This exercise merges the story of orchestras into a more general account, one of the intersections of commercial entertainment, class, and culture in nineteenth-century America.

In 1800 theaters were few and of limited capacity, as were performance venues of any sort. Admission was expensive, and the evening's entertainment was likely to be an import from London. By the 1840s American entertainment had begun to change in every respect. Larger theaters, cheaper tickets, and the construction of beer halls and other popular performance sites presented urban audiences with far more entertainment choices. Steamboats and railroads took music, theater, and opera well beyond the cities of the Atlantic coast. Improved print technologies brought newspapers, magazines, books, and sheet music to an expanding middle class, and even within the reach of the less well-to-do.

The universe of entertainment continued to expand. Mass markets inspired mass marketing, and by the end of the nineteenth century there were far more affordable leisure-time choices—amusement parks, dance halls, vaudeville, and early movies, for example. The balance of trade in popular culture, moreover, had begun to shift as the United States, formerly an importer, started exporting such native forms as minstrel shows, P. T. Barnum's various promotions, and Buffalo Bill's Wild West Show.[3] New technologies like the phonograph and player piano were signs that musical elements of public culture were moving more deeply into private spaces, a process that

3 · See Ronald G. Walters, "Buffalo Bill, Harry Houdini, and Real Magic," in *The Meanings of Magic: From the Bible to Buffalo Bill*, ed. Amy Wygant (2006).

continued with radio in the 1920s and by the twenty-first century had reduced private space to a pair of earbuds.

To a large extent, orchestras rode the same forces that propelled the nineteenth-century expansion of leisure-time activities, but in some instances less successfully or more ambiguously than their competitors. Like all other forms of entertainment, orchestras benefited from the larger markets—especially urban ones—that population growth produced. More people translated into larger potential audiences, more venues for orchestras, and more jobs for musicians. In the same fashion, the enormous improvements in transportation that enabled the Wild West Show to tour nationally and internationally also benefited touring orchestras. Here, however, a bit of divergence appears. A singular, spectacular show such as Buffalo Bill's faced no local competition. Traveling orchestras, such as the Thomas Orchestra, created local audiences and stimulated local competitors.

Orchestras were likewise unable to take full advantage of many of the technological and economic innovations that benefited popular culture. In entertainment, as in other American industries, labor was increasingly replaced by capital in the second half of the nineteenth century. Typesetters were replaced by linotype machines; portrait painters by photographers; magazine engravers by photogravure; and, in the 1890s, live actors by motion pictures. This last development posed both opportunities and threats for orchestras. Initially, it generated new jobs for orchestras, playing along with the silent cinema. In the 1920s, however, another innovation, movie sound tracks, lowered costs for theater owners, who replaced the continuing expense of hired musicians with the fixed cost of a sound system.[4] By 1935 thousands of theater orchestras had disappeared. The advent of phonograph recordings in the 1890s had similarly ambiguous results for the orchestra. Orchestras reproduced particularly badly with the early "acoustical" recording processes, so most recordings were made with bands and smaller combos. Not until well into the twentieth century did recordings give even a fair reproduction of a symphony on a home phonograph.

In these and other instances the demographic, marketing, technological, and entrepreneurial changes that enabled American commercial popular culture to flourish over the course of the nineteenth century had mixed implications for orchestras in general and symphony orchestras in particular. Orchestras benefited from urbanization, education, improved transportation, and the growth of a cultivated middle class. But orchestras in the nineteenth century benefited less from technological innovation than did

4 · James P. Kraft, "The 'Pit' Musicians: Mechanization in the Movie Theaters, 1926–1934," *Labor History* 35 (1994).

456 RONALD G. WALTERS

other forms of entertainment, and they began to drift toward the margins of popular culture.

That brings us back to tallying gains and losses.

From a present-day perspective some of each are obvious. Over the course of the nineteenth century common folk lost (perhaps willingly) such hallmarks of the newly "highbrow" culture as Shakespeare and Beethoven, which in the first half of the century had been part of a culture that many Americans shared. What did common folk gain in the bargain? The pleasures of the popular were multiple. For small amounts of money, immigrants and working-class Americans could see people like themselves on stage as performers and as characters. Young men and women could enjoy each other's company in new public spaces, including dance halls and amusement parks such as those at Coney Island, where (contrary to what we might expect) a fine symphony orchestra performed successfully in the 1890s.[5] Popular culture was a source of comfort, companionship, laughter, meaning, and opportunity.

What did orchestras gain and lose? Symphony orchestras lost a large portion of the earlier audience for their music, but they gained stability, a focused repertory, and international respectability. As new spaces for entertainment proliferated, symphonic music gradually withdrew into a special place, the symphony hall.

There are at least two ways to think about these developments. The first is positive and focuses on progress: symphonic music finally found its true audience, one capable of appreciating its artistry. It catered, often brilliantly, to a niche market. The other assessment carries with it a whiff of pessimism. It argues that symphonic music was doomed to lose once it competed for a broader audience's support. The contest was unequal from the start and became progressively more unequal over the course of the nineteenth century.

Looked at purely from a marketing perspective, the advantage was decisively with the new commercial popular culture. Of all the marketing ploys used by entertainment entrepreneurs, only one gave an undisputable competitive advantage to symphony orchestras—providing "culture." Although vaudeville sometimes made the same claim with an occasional Shakespearian performer, opera star, or other "high class" act, the rest of the bill belied this pretense. In the cases of two other promotion techniques, there was no contest. The first was *spectacle*, the second *novelty*. Popular culture in the second half of the nineteenth century thrived on both. While a symphony orchestra might advertise its size and "completeness," New York City's Hippodrome Theater in 1905 could (and did) encompass a whole circus on its stage.

<hr />

5 · See Joseph Horowitz, *Wagner Nights: An American History* (1994), chap. 11.

A bit later, the great magician Harry Houdini made an elephant disappear in front of his audience's eyes. When it came to spectacle, a larger string section didn't have a chance. The same was true with novelty. It was the essence of the new commercial popular culture. Whereas symphony orchestras increasingly focused on a canon of masterworks, popular music lived or died by change. Without a parade of ephemeral hits, each supplanting the last, the sheet music publishers of New York's "Tin Pan Alley" would have gone bankrupt. Novelty ruled.

Faced with this kind of competition for the public's attention and money, perhaps the only hope for symphonic music in America was in fact to cast its lot with "sacralization" (although, as this collection points out, there were alternative ways of getting there). "Sacralization," after all, had some advantages for orchestras. It brought better performances, better acoustics in better halls, more attentive and appreciative audiences, and more stable financial support. Its positive aspects were promoted not only by the cultured elite, but also by journalists, by educators, and by the orchestral musicians themselves.

Whether one takes the brighter or darker view of this narrative, the larger point is that the cultural moment in which the story took place was a new and dynamic one. If there was a widely shared public culture in the antebellum decades, it gave way over the next half century to increasing diversification, professionalization, and specialization—larger themes in nineteenth-century American society as well as in leisure-time activities. In the United States, the symphony orchestra assumed its modern form within those greater historical currents.

Where does that leave us?

This book not only provides a fresh history of the origins of American orchestras, but also provokes thoughts about the present condition of these orchestras. On the one hand, they are now among the best in the world—and it is a much larger world, encompassing countries bordering the Pacific as well as the Atlantic. On the other hand, pessimists view aging audiences and perilous finances as present challenges for symphony orchestras and ill omens for the future.

Perhaps two strategies pursued in the nineteenth century are still with us, in different clothing. The first is to embrace eclecticism and novelty in hope of reaching a larger audience for symphonic music and—in a twenty-first-century twist—in the name of musical creativity and innovation. This takes the form of exploring previously neglected musical sources, from American popular song to music from around the world. Some classically trained artists have done this in ways that attract audiences (Yo-Yo Ma comes to mind). How successfully this might be done and for what purpose remain open questions. To resituate symphonic music within a broader culture? To re-imagine a shared public culture? To reimagine music itself? Or simply to create a new kind of niche audience?

A second possibility would be to continue along the line set by 1900 — to strive to be the best in the world within a glacially changing symphonic canon. But how to do this in the face of enormous economic pressures (some of them nineteenth-century legacies like the expensive focus on star conductors and performers)? One answer is to seek new markets, and perhaps that is happening: any comparable collection of essays on the early twenty-first century would include Pacific as well as Atlantic crossings. Another answer might be a high-tech equivalent of touring orchestras—an effort to collapse time and space to reach a widely dispersed but devoted audience through live broadcasts of orchestral performances, thus enabling fans anywhere in the world to see the Philadelphia Symphony Orchestra in real time (as world-wide fans already see the Metropolitan Opera). By 2010, this phenomenon was successful enough to provoke concern about its effects on performances and audiences. It even acquired a label, "the HD-ification of the arts," a term evoking "sacralization" in an electronic format.[6]

Whether either approach (or some other) works is a matter for future historians.

In the end, this collection makes clear that contemporary American symphony orchestras are not simply the bearers of an uncontested tradition, but rather the products of the messy reality of history. We can take this insight as a cause for optimism or pessimism, or even as a call to action. If humans and history could create modern American symphony orchestras out of an earlier, very different musical world, there is no reason to think these orchestras cannot or will not be remade.

6 · See, for example, Daniel J. Wakin, "Orchestras on Big Screens: Chase Scene Needed?" *New York Times*, November 9, 2010, sec. A.

BIBLIOGRAPHY

Books, Articles, Dissertations, and Theses

Adler, Ayden Wren. "Classical Music for People Who Hate Classical Music: Arthur Fiedler and the Boston Pops, 1930–1950." Ph.D. diss., Eastman School of Music, 2007.

Ahlquist, Karen. *Democracy at the Opera: Music, Theatre, and Culture in New York City, 1815–60*. Urbana: University of Illinois Press, 1997.

———. "Musical Assimilation and 'the German Element' at the Cincinnati Sängerfest, 1879." *Musical Quarterly* 94 (2011): 381–416.

———. "Playing for the Big Time: Musicians, Concerts, and Reputation-Building in Cincinnati, 1872–82." *Journal of the Gilded Age and Progressive Era* 9 (April 2010): 145–65.

Albrecht, Henry. *Skizzen aus dem Leben der Musik-Gesellschaft Germania (Germania Musical Society)*. Philadelphia: King and Baird, 1869.

American Federation of Musicians. *Proceedings of the [First Annual] Convention, Indianapolis, Indiana*. Cincinnati, 1896.

———. *Proceedings of the Third Convention, Louisville, Kentucky*. Cincinnati, 1898.

Amerika, wie es ist. Ein Buch für Kunde der neuen Welt. Hamburg, Germany: Verlags-Comtoir, 1854.

Ammer, Christine. *Unsung: A History of Women in American Music*. 2nd ed. Portland, OR: Amadeus Press, 2001. First published 1980 by Greenwood Press.

Andreas, Alfred Theodore. *History of Chicago*. 3 vols. Chicago: A. T. Andreas, 1884.

Appleton's Dictionary of New York and Vicinity. Edited by Townsend Percy. New York: D. Appleton, 1880.

Apthorp, William Foster. "John Sullivan Dwight" [Obituary]. *Boston Transcript*, September 5, 1893. Reprinted in *Musicians and Music-lovers, and Other Essays*. New York: C. Scribner's Sons, 1894, 277–86. Reprint, Freeport, NY: Books for Libraries Press, 1972.

———. "Musical Reminiscences of Boston Thirty Years Ago." In *By the Way: Being a Collection of Short Essays on Music and Art in General, Taken from the Program-books of the Boston Symphony Orchestra*. Boston: Copeland and Day, 1898.

Bank, Rosemarie K. *Theatre Culture in America, 1825–1860*. Cambridge: Cambridge University Press, 1997.

Barnard, Charles. *Camilla: A Tale of a Violin*. Boston: Loring, 1874.

Baxter, Anne W. "Showplace of Central Parkway: The College of Music Administration Building." *Queen City Heritage* 57 (1999): 26–40.

Beck, Roger, and Richard Hansen. "Joseph Gungl and His Celebrated American Tour: November 1848 to May 1849." *Studia Musicologica Academiae Scientiarum Hungaricae* 36 (1995): 53–72.

Becker, Gottfried Wilhelm. *Ein Blick auf das Jahr 1832 in Beziehung auf Leipzig*. Leipzig: A. Fest, 1833.

Bender, Thomas. "Introduction: Historians, the Nation, and the Plenitude of Narratives." In *Rethinking American History in a Global Age*, edited by Thomas Bender, 1–22. Berkeley: University of California Press, 2002.

Bennett, Francis Cheney. *History of Music and Art in Illinois*. Philadelphia: Historical Publishing Co., 1904.

Bernheim, Alfred L. *The Business of the Theatre*. New York: Actors' Equity Association, 1932.

Bial, Bert. *Focus on the Philharmonic: In Celebration of the 150th Anniversary of the New York Philharmonic*. New York: Philharmonic Symphony Society of New York, 1992.

Blair, Karen J. *The Clubwoman as Feminist: True Womanhood Redefined, 1868–1914*. New York: Holmes and Meier, 1980.

———. *The Torchbearers: Women and Their Amateur Arts Associations in America, 1890–1930*. Bloomington: Indiana University Press, 1994.

Block, Adrienne Fried. "Matinee Mania, or the Regendering of Nineteenth-Century Audiences in New York City." *19th Century Music* 31, no. 3 (2008): 193–216.

———. "New York's Orchestras and the 'American' Composer: A Nineteenth-Century View." In *European Music and Musicians in New York City, 1840–1900*, edited by John Graziano, 114–34. Rochester, NY: University of Rochester Press, 2006.

———. "Two Virtuoso Performers in Boston: Jenny Lind and Camilla Urso." In *New Perspectives on Music: Essays in Honor of Eileen Southern*, edited by Josephine Wright and Samuel Floyd Jr., 355–71. Warren, MI: Harmonie Park Press, 1992.

Block, Adrienne Fried, and Carol Neuls-Bates. *Women in American Music*. Westport, CT: Greenwood Press, 1979.

Blum, Solomon. "Trade Union Rules in the Building Trades." In *Studies in American Trade Unionism*, edited by Jacob H. Hollander and George E. Barnett, 293–319. New York: Henry Holt, 1905.

Boder, Wolfram. *Die Kasseler Opern Louis Spohrs: Musikdramaturgie im sozialen Kontext*. Kassel, Germany: Bärenreiter, 2007.

Bomberger, E. Douglas. *"A Tidal Wave of Encouragement": American Composers' Concerts in the Gilded Age*. Westport, CT: Praeger, 2002.

Bonds, Mark Evan. "Idealism and the Aesthetics of Instrumental Music at the Turn of the Nineteenth Century." *Journal of the American Musicological Society* 50 (1997): 387–420.

Bornstein, David. *How to Change the World: Social Entrepreneurs and the Power of New Ideas*. 2nd ed. New York: Oxford University Press, 2007.

Boston Academy of Music. *Annual Report of the Boston Academy of Music, Read at the Anniversary Meeting, in the Odeon*. Boston, 1842.

———. *11th Annual Report of the Boston Academy of Music*. Boston: T. R. Marvin, 1843.

Bourdieu, Pierre. "The Production of Belief: Contribution to an Economy of Symbolic Goods." In *The Field of Cultural Production: Essays on Art and Literature*, edited by Randal Johnson, 74–111. New York: Columbia University Press, 1993.

Brainard's Biographies of American Musicians. Edited by E. Douglas Bomberger. Westport, CT: Greenwood Press, 1999.

Brown, Clive. *Louis Spohr: A Critical Biography*. Cambridge: Cambridge University Press, 1984.

Browne, Junius Henri. *The Great Metropolis: A Mirror of New York*. Hartford, CT: American Publishing, 1869.

Broyles, Michael. *"Music of the Highest Class": Elitism and Populism in Antebellum Boston*. New Haven, CT: Yale University Press, 1992.

Bunting, J. "The Old Germania Orchestra." *Scribner's Monthly* 11, no. 1 (1875): 98–107.

Butsch, Richard. "Bowery B'hoys and Matinee Ladies: The Re-Gendering of Nineteenth-Century American Theater Audiences." *American Quarterly* 46, no. 3 (1994): 374–405.

Cahall, Michael C. "Battle on Mount Olympus: The Nichols-Thomas Controversy at the College of Music of Cincinnati." *Queen City History* 53 (Fall 1995): 24–32.

———. "Jewels in the Queen's Crown: The Fine and Performing Arts in Cincinnati, Ohio, 1865–1919." Ph.D. diss., University of Illinois, 1991.

Camus, Raoul. "Bands." In *The New Grove Dictionary of American Music*, edited by H. Wiley Hitchcock and Stanley Sadie, 1:127. London: Macmillan, 1986.

Carse, Adam. *The Life of Jullien: Adventurer, Showman-Conductor and Establisher of the Promenade Concerts in England*. Cambridge: Heffer, 1951.

———. *The Orchestra from Beethoven to Berlioz*. New York: Broude Brothers, 1949.

Catalogue of Music: Band, U.S. Marine Corps. Washington, DC: Government Printing Office, 1885.

Celletti, Rodolfo. *A History of Bel Canto*. Translated by Frederick Fuller. Oxford: Clarendon Press, 1991. Originally published as *Storia di belcanto* (Fiesole, Italy: Discanto, 1983).

Charlton, David. "Hoffmann as a Writer on Music." In *E. T. A. Hoffmann's Musical Writings*, edited by David Charlton, translated by Martyn Clark, 1–20. Cambridge: Cambridge University Press, 1989.

Charter, Constitution and By-Laws of the Philadelphia Musical Association. Philadelphia, 1865.

Chase, Gilbert. *America's Music: From the Pilgrims to the Present*. Rev. 3rd ed. Urbana: University of Illinois Press, 1987. First published 1955 by McGraw-Hill.

Chitty, Alexis. "Zerr, Anna." In *Grove's Dictionary of Music and Musicians*, 3rd ed., edited by H. C. Colles. New York: Macmillan, 1935.

Christensen, Thomas. "Four-Hand Piano Transcription and Geographies of Nineteenth-Century Musical Reception." *Journal of the American Musicological Society* 52, no. 2 (1999): 255–98.

Cincinnati Symphony Orchestra: Centennial Portraits. Cincinnati: CSO, 1994.

Cipolla, Frank J. "Dodworth." In *New Grove Dictionary of American Music*, edited by H. Wiley Hitchcock and Stanley Sadie, 1:639–40. London: Macmillan Press, 1984.

Clague, Mark. "Chicago Counterpoint: The Auditorium Theater Building and the Civic Imagination." Ph.D. diss., University of Chicago, 2002.

———. *Making Music, Building Culture, Thinking City: Chicago's Auditorium Theater and the Social Engineering of American Culture*. Urbana: University of Illinois Press, forthcoming.

Clapp, William. *Record of the Boston Stage*. Boston: James Munroe, 1853.

Cockrell, Dale. "Can American Music Studies Develop a Method?" *American Music* 22, no. 2 (2004): 272–83.

Commons, John R. "Types of American Labor Unions: The Musicians of St. Louis and New York." *Quarterly Journal of Economics* 10, no. 3 (1906): 419–42.

Constitution and By-Laws of the Cincinnati Musicians' Protective Association No 1. Cincinnati: Schellenbaum, 1898.

Constitution and By-Laws of the Musicians' Protective Association of the United States. Philadelphia: M'Calla and Stavely, 1872.

Constitution der Musical Mutual Protective Union: Gegründet den 23. April 1863, organisirt und angenommen den 26. Juni 1863, revidirt und verbessert den 29. Sept. 1863. New York: New-Yorker Staats-Zeitung, 1863.

Cooke, George Willis. *John Sullivan Dwight, Brook-Farmer, Editor, and Critic of Music; A Biography.* Boston: Small, Maynard, 1898.

"Correspondence Connected with the Withdrawal of Mr. Theodore Thomas from the College of Music of Cincinnati." Cincinnati: Press of Robert Clarke and Co., 1880.

Crawford, Richard. *The American Musical Landscape: The Business of Musicianship from Billings to Gershwin.* Berkeley: University of California Press, 1993.

———. *America's Musical Life: A History.* New York: W. W. Norton, 2001.

———. *Studying American Music: With a Bibliography of the Published Writings of Richard Crawford.* I.S.A.M. Special Publication no. 3. Brooklyn: Institute for Studies in American Music, 1985.

Curtis, George H. "George Frederic Bristow." *Music* 3 (1893): 559.

Curtis, George William. *Early Letters of George Wm. Curtis to John S. Dwight; Brook Farm and Concord.* Edited by George Willis Cooke. New York: Harper and Brothers, 1898.

Czitrom, Daniel. "The Politics of Performance: From Theater Licensing to Movie Censorship in Turn-of-the-Century New York." *American Quarterly* 44, no. 4 (1992): 525–53.

Dahlhaus, Carl. *The Idea of Absolute Music.* Translated by R. Lustig. Chicago: University of Chicago Press, 1989. Originally published as *Die Idee der absoluten Musik* (Kassel, Germany: Bärenreiter, 1978).

Damrosch, Leopold. *Symphony in A Major.* Edited by Kati Agócs. Middleton, WI: A-R Editions, 2005.

Damrosch, Walter. *My Musical Life.* New York: Charles Scribner's Sons, 1923. Reprint, Westport, CT: Greenwood Press, 1972.

Daniel, Oliver. *Stokowski: A Counterpoint of View.* New York: Dodd Mead, 1982.

Davison, Henry. *From Mendelssohn to Wagner: Being the Memoirs of J. W. Davison, Forty Years Music Critic of the* Times. London: Wm. Reeves, 1912.

Deaville, James. "Damrosch, Leopold." In *Die Musik in Geschichte und Gegenwart,* 2nd rev. ed., *Personenteil,* 5:347–49. (Original article by Willi Kahl.)

———. "The Origins of Music Journalism in Chicago: Criticism as a Reflection of Music Life." In *American Musical Life in Context and Practice to 1865,* edited by James Heintze, 301–66. New York: Garland, 1993.

———. "'Westwärts zieht die Kunstgeschichte': Liszt's Symphonic Poems in the New World." In *Identität—Kultur—Raum: Kuturelle Praktiken und die Ausbildung von Imagined Communities in Nordamerika und Zentraleuropa,* edited by Susan Ingram, Markus Reisenleitner, and Cornelia Szabó-Knotik, 223–45. Vienna: Turia und Kant, 2001.

Dees, J. Gregory. *Enterprising Nonprofits: A Toolkit for Social Entrepreneurs.* New York: John Wiley and Sons, 2001.

De Koven, Anna Farwell. *A Musician and His Wife.* New York: Harper and Brothers, 1926.

Dictionary of American Biography. Edited by Allen Johnson and Dumas Malone. New York: Charles Scribner's Sons, 1928–40.

DiMaggio, Paul. "Cultural Entrepreneurship in 19th Century Boston: The Creation of an Organizational Base for High Culture in America." *Media, Culture, and Society* 4, no. 1 (1982): 33–50.

Directory of the Cincinnati Musicians' Protective Association No. 1 A. F. of M. No. 1. Cincinnati, 1899.

DuBois, Ellen Carol. *Feminism and Suffrage: The Emergence of an Independent Women's Movement in America, 1848–1869.* Ithaca, NY: Cornell University Press, 1978.

Dwight, John Sullivan. "History of Music in Boston." In *A Memorial History of Boston*, edited by Justin Winsor, 4:415–64. Boston: James R. Osgood, 1881.

———. "The Intellectual Influence of Music." *Atlantic Monthly* 26, no. 157 (December 1870): 614–26.

———. "Music." In *Aesthetic Papers*, edited by Elizabeth P. Peabody, 25–36. Boston: The Editor; New York: G. P. Putnam, 1849. Reprinted in *The Transcendentalists: An Anthology*, edited by Perry Miller. Cambridge, MA: Harvard University Press, 1950, 410–14.

———. "Music as a Means of Culture." *Atlantic Monthly* 26, no. 155 (September 1870): 321–32.

———. "The Proper Character of Poetry and Music for Public Worship." *Christian Examiner* 21, no. 2 (November 1836): 254–63.

Edwards, George Thornton. *Music and Musicians of Maine.* Portland, ME: Southworth Press, 1928. Reprint, New York: AMS Press, 1970.

Elson, Louis C. *The History of American Music.* New York: Macmillan, 1904. Rev. ed., 1915; rev. 3rd ed., edited by Arthur Elson, 1925. Reprint, New York: B. Franklin, 1971.

Elwart, Antoine. "Quelques mots sur la position des musiciens d'orchestre de nos trois scenes lyriques." *Revue et Gazette Musicale*, February 14, 1839, 53–54.

Epstein, Dena J. "Frederick Stock and American Music." *American Music* 10, no. 1 (1992): 20–52.

Ernst, Robert. *Immigrant Life in New York City, 1825–1863.* New York: King's Crown Press, 1949.

Erskine, John. *The Philharmonic-Symphony Society of New York: Its First Hundred Years.* New York: Macmillan, 1943.

European Music and Musicians in New York City, 1840–1900. Edited by John Graziano. Rochester, NY: University of Rochester Press, 2006.

Farwell, Arthur, and W[illiam] Dermot Darby. *Music in America.* Vol. 4 of *The Art of Music*, edited by Daniel Gregory Mason. New York: National Society of Music, 1915.

Faul, Michel. *Louis Jullien: Musique, spectacle et folie au XIXᵉ siècle.* Biarritz: Atlantica, 2006.

Fauquet, Joel-Marie. "Les debuts du syndicalisme musical en France." In *La musique du théorique au politique*, edited by H. Dufourt and J-M. Fauquet, 219–59. Paris: Klincksiek, 1991.

Feldman, Ann E. "Women Composers at the 1893 World's Columbian Exposition." *Notes* 47, no. 1 (1990): 7–20.

Feldman, Mary Ann. "George P. Upton: Journalist, Music Critic and Mentor to Early Chicago." Ph.D. diss., University of Minnesota, 1983.

Foner, Eric. *A Short History of Reconstruction, 1863–1877.* New York: Harper and Row, 1990.

Foster, Myles Birket. *History of the Philharmonic Society of London: 1813–1912.* London: John Lane, 1912.

Freeland, David. *Automats, Taxi Dances, and Vaudeville: Excavating Manhattan's Lost Places of Leisure.* New York: New York University Press, 2009.

Frey, Eugene Victor. "Jullien in America." Master's thesis, University of Cincinnati, 1943.

Frick, John W. *Theatre, Culture, and Temperance Reform in Nineteenth-Century America.* Cambridge: Cambridge University Press, 2003.

Friedman, Ruth Klauber. *History of the Musicians Club of Women, Formerly Amateur Musical Club, Chicago, Illinois*. Chicago: Musicians Club of Women, 1975.

Galinsky, Adam, and Erin V. Lehman. "Emergence, Divergence, Convergence: Three Models of Symphony Orchestras at the Crossroads." *European Journal of Cultural Policy* 2 (1995): 117–39.

Geertz, Clifford. "Thick Description: Toward an Interpretative Theory of Culture." In *The Interpretation of Cultures*, 3–32. New York: Basic Books, 1973.

Gere, Anne Ruggles. *Intimate Practices: Literacy and Cultural Work in U.S. Women's Clubs, 1880–1920*. Urbana: University of Illinois Press, 1997.

Gienow-Hecht, Jessica. *Sound Diplomacy: Music and Emotions in Transatlantic Relations, 1850–1920*. Chicago: University of Chicago Press, 2009.

Gilbert, Sandra M., and Susan Gubar. *The Madwoman in the Attic: The Woman Writer and the Nineteenth-Century Literary Imagination*. New Haven, CT: Yale University Press, 1979.

Goehr, Lydia. *The Imaginary Museum of Musical Works: An Essay in the Philosophy of Music*. Oxford: Oxford University Press, 2007.

Gramit, David. *Cultivating Music: The Aspirations, Interests, and Limits of German Musical Culture, 1770–1848*. Berkeley: University of California Press, 2002.

Grant, Margaret, and Harman S. Hettinger. *America's Symphony Orchestras, and How They Are Supported*. New York: W. W. Norton, 1940.

Grant, Mark N. *Maestros of the Pen: A History of Classical Music Criticism in America*. Boston: Northeastern University Press, 1998.

Grau, Robert. *Forty Years of Observation of Music and the Drama*. New York: Broadway Publishing, 1909.

Graziano, John. "Jullien and His *Music for the Millions*." In *A Celebration of American Music: Words and Music in Honor of H. Wiley Hitchcock*, edited by Richard Crawford, R. Allen Lott, and Carol J. Oja, 192–216. Ann Arbor: University of Michigan Press, 1990.

Green, Anna Weldon. "Musicians' Union of San Francisco." Master's thesis, University of California, 1929.

Greene, Stephen R. "Visions of a 'Musical America' in the Radio Age." Ph.D. diss., University of Pittsburgh, 2008.

Groh, Jan Bell. *Evening the Score: Women in Music and the Legacy of Frédérique Petrides*. Fayetteville: University of Arkansas Press, 1991.

Guyer, Isaac D. *History of Chicago, Its Commercial and Manufacturing Interests and Industries: Together with Sketches of Manufacturers and Men Who Have Most Contributed to Its Prosperity and Advancement, with Glances at Some of the Best Hotels; Also the Principal Railroads Which Center in Chicago*. Chicago: Church, Goodman and Cushing, 1862.

Habermas, Jürgen. *The Structural Transformation of the Public Sphere: An Inquiry into a Category of Bourgeois Society*. Translated by Thomas Burger with the assistance of Frederick Lawrence. Cambridge, MA: MIT Press, 1989.

Haley, William. "Amateurism." *American Scholar* 45, no. 2 (1976): 253–59.

Hamm, Charles. *Music in the New World*. New York: W. W. Norton, 1983.

A Handbook of American Music and Musicians. Edited by F. O. Jones. Canaseraga, NY: F. O. Jones, 1886. Reprint, New York: Da Capo Press, 1971.

Handford, Margaret. *Sounds Unlikely: 600 Years of Music in Birmingham, 1392–1992*. Birmingham, UK: Birmingham Midland Institute, 1992.

Harlow, Alvin F. *Old Bowery Days: The Chronicles of a Famous Street*. New York: D. Appleton, 1931.

Hart, Philip. *Orpheus in the New World: The Symphony Orchestra as an American Cultural Institution—Its Past, Present, and Future*. New York: W. W. Norton, 1973.

Haydu, Jeffrey. "Business Citizenship at Work: Cultural Transposition and Class Formation in Cincinnati, 1870–1910." *American Journal of Sociology* 107, no. 6 (2002): 1424–67.

Henderson, Ruth. "A Confluence of Impresarios: Max Maretzek, the Strakosches, and the Graus." In *European Music and Musicians in New York City, 1840–1900*, edited by John Graziano, 235–52. Rochester, NY: University of Rochester Press, 2006.

Henderson, W[illiam] J[ames]. *What Is Good Music? Suggestions to Persons Desiring to Cultivate a Taste in Musical Art*. New York: C. Scribner's Sons, 1898.

Hepner, Arthur W. *Pro bono artium musicarum: The Harvard Musical Association, 1837–1987*. Boston: Harvard Musical Association, 1987.

Herz, Henri. *Mes voyages en Amérique*. Paris: Faure, 1866. Translated by Henry Bertram Hill as *My Travels in America*. Madison: State Historical Society of Wisconsin, 1963.

Higginson, Henry Lee. *Life and Letters of Henry Lee Higginson*. Edited by Bliss Perry. Boston: Atlantic Monthly Press, 1921.

Higginson, Thomas Wentworth. "Ought Women to Learn the Alphabet?" In *Women and the Alphabet: A Series of Essays*, 1–36. Boston: Houghton, Mifflin, 1900. Reprint, New York: Arno Press, 1972. First published in the *Atlantic Monthly*, February 1859.

Hitchcock, H. Wiley. *Music in the United States: A Historical Introduction*. 3rd ed. Englewood Cliffs, NJ: Prentice-Hall, 1988. 4th ed., Upper Saddle River, NJ: Prentice-Hall, 2000.

Hoffmann, Ernst Theodor Amadeus. *E. T. A. Hoffmann's Musical Writings*. Edited by David Charlton. Translated by Martyn Clark. Cambridge: Cambridge University Press, 1989. See esp. chap. 4, "Beethoven's Instrumental Music."

Holliday, Joseph E. "Cincinnati Opera Festivals during the Gilded Age." *Bulletin of the Cincinnati Historical Society* 24, no. 2 (April 1966): 130–49.

———. "The Cincinnati Philharmonic and Hopkins Hall Orchestras, 1856–1868." *Bulletin of the Cincinnati Historical Society* 26, no. 2 (April 1968): 158–73.

———. "Notes on Samuel N. Pike and His Opera House." *Bulletin of the Cincinnati Historical Society* 25 (July 1967): 164–83.

Horowitz, Joseph. *Classical Music in America: A History of Its Rise and Fall*. New York: W. W. Norton, 2005.

———. "Reclaiming the Past: Musical Boston Remembered." *American Music* 19, no. 1 (2001): 18–38.

———. *Wagner Nights: An American History*. Berkeley: University of California Press, 1994.

Howard, John Tasker. *Our American Music: A Comprehensive History from 1600 to the Present*. 4th ed. New York: Thomas Y. Crowell, 1965. Originally published as *Our American Music: Three Hundred Years of It*. New York: Thomas Y. Crowell, 1931.

Howe, M. A. De Wolfe. *The Boston Symphony Orchestra: An Historical Sketch*. Boston: Houghton Mifflin, 1914. Revised and extended in collaboration with John N. Burk as *The Boston Symphony Orchestra, 1881–1931*. Boston: Houghton Mifflin, 1931.

Huneker, James Gibbons. *The Philharmonic Society of New York and Its Seventy-Fifth Anniversary: A Retrospect*. New York: Philharmonic Society of New York, 1917.

Jackson, Richard. *United States Music: Sources of Biography and Collective Biography*. I.S.A.M. Monographs no.1. Brooklyn: Institute for Studies of American Music, 1973.

Jennings, John Joseph. *Theatrical and Circus Life, or, Secrets of the Stage, Green-Room and*

Sawdust Arena: Embracing a History of the Theatre from Shakespeare's Time to the Present Day. St. Louis: Sun Publishing, 1882.

Johnson, H. Earle. "Longfellow and Music." *American Music Research Center Journal* 7 (1997): 7–98.

Kagan, Susan. "Camilla Urso: A Nineteenth-Century Violinist's View." *Signs* 2, no. 3 (1977): 727–34.

Kelley, Mary. *Learning to Stand and Speak: Women, Education, and Public Life in America's Republic*. Chapel Hill: University of North Carolina Press, 2006.

Kerber, Linda. *No Constitutional Right to Be Ladies: Women and the Obligations of Citizenship*. New York: Hill and Wang, 1998.

Kirk, Elise K. *Music at the White House: A History of the American Spirit*. Urbana: University of Illinois Press, 1986.

Koegel, John. *Music in German Immigrant Theater: New York City, 1840–1940*. Rochester, NY: University of Rochester Press, 2009.

Koury, Daniel J. *Orchestral Performances in the Nineteenth Century: Size, Proportions, and Seating*. Ann Arbor, MI: UMI Research Press, 1986.

Kraft, James P. "Artists as Workers: Musicians and Trade Unionism in America, 1880–1917." *Musical Quarterly* 79, no. 3 (1995): 512–43.

———. "The 'Pit' Musicians: Mechanization in the Movie Theaters, 1926–1934." *Labor History* 35, no. 1 (1994): 66–89.

———. *Stage to Studio: Musicians and the Sound Revolution, 1890–1950*. Baltimore: Johns Hopkins University Press, 1996.

Krasner, Orly Leah. "A Capital Idea: Reginald de Koven and the Washington Symphony Orchestra." In *Music, American Made: Essays in Honor of John Graziano,* edited by John Koegel, 123–59. Sterling Heights, MI.: Harmonie Park Press, 2011.

Krehbiel, Henry Edward. *Notes on the Cultivation of Choral Music and the Oratorio Society of New York*. New York: E. Schuberth, 1884. Reprint, New York: AMS Press, 1970.

———. *The Philharmonic Society of New York: A Memorial*. New York: Novello, Ewer, 1892. Reprinted in *Early Histories of the New York Philharmonic*, edited by Howard Shanet. New York: Da Capo Press, 1979.

Krohn, Ernst C. *Missouri Music*. New York: Da Capo Press, 1971. Originally published as *A Century of Missouri Music*. St. Louis: N.p., 1924.

Krummel, Donald W. *Bibliographical Handbook of American Music*. Urbana: University of Illinois Press, 1987.

Krummel, D[onald] W., Jean Geil, Doris Dyen, and Deane Root. *Resources of American Music History: A Directory of Source Materials from Colonial Times to World War II*. Urbana: University of Illinois Press, 1981.

Kupperman, Karen Ordahl. "International at the Creation: Early Modern American History." In *Rethinking American History in a Global Age*, edited by Thomas Bender, 103–22. Berkeley: University of California Press, 2002.

Lahee, Henry Charles. *The Orchestra: A Brief Outline of Its Development in Europe and America, with a Description of the Instruments and Their Functions*. Boston: Boston Musical and Educational Bureau, 1925.

Laurie, Joe, Jr. *Vaudeville: From the Honky-Tonks to the Palace*. New York: Henry Holt, 1953.

Lawrence, Vera Brodsky. *Strong on Music: The New York Music Scene in the Days of George Templeton Strong*. Vol. 1, *Resonances, 1836–1849*. Chicago: University of Chicago Press, 1995. Originally published New York: Oxford University Press, 1988.

————. *Strong on Music: The New York Music Scene in the Days of George Templeton Strong.* Vol. 2, *Reverberations: 1850–1856.* Chicago: University of Chicago Press, 1995.

————. *Strong on Music: The New York Music Scene in the Days of George Templeton Strong.* Vol. 3, *Repercussions: 1857–1862.* Chicago: University of Chicago Press, 1999.

Lawyers' Reports Annotated. Rochester, NY: Lawyers' Co-operative Publishing, 1888–1918.

Leavitt, M[ichael] B[ennett]. *Fifty Years in Theatrical Management.* New York: Broadway Publishing, 1912.

Lefeuvre, Gabriel. "L'Association des musiciens instrumentistes fondée en 1876." *Courrier de l'orchestre,* August 1902, 4–6.

Leiter, Robert David. *The Musicians and Petrillo.* New York: Bookman Associates, 1953.

Lerner, Laurence Marton. "The Rise of the Impresario: Bernard Ullman and the Transformation of Musical Culture in Nineteenth Century America." Ph.D. diss., University of Wisconsin, 1970.

Levine, Lawrence W. *Highbrow/Lowbrow: The Emergence of Cultural Hierarchy in America.* Cambridge, MA: Harvard University Press, 1988.

Lewis, Robert. "'Rational Recreation': Reforming Leisure in Antebellum America." In *Religious and Secular Reform in America: Ideas, Beliefs, and Social Change,* edited by David K. Adams and Cornelius A. Van Minnen, 121–32. New York: New York University Press, 1999.

Life of Harriet Beecher Stowe Compiled from Her Letters and Journals by Her Son, Charles E. Stowe. Boston: Houghton, Mifflin, 1889.

Limerick, Patricia Nelson. *The Legacy of Conquest: The Unbroken Past of the American West.* New York: W. W. Norton, 1987.

Locke, Ralph P. "Music Lovers, Patrons, and the 'Sacralization' of Culture in America." *19th-Century Music* 17, no. 2 (1993): 149–73.

Locke, Ralph P., and Cyrilla Barr. *Cultivating Music in America: Women Patrons and Activists since 1850.* Berkeley: University of California Press, 1997.

Loft, Abram. "Musicians' Guild and Union: A Consideration of the Evolution of Protective Organization among Musicians." Ph.D. diss., Columbia University, 1950.

————. "Richard Wagner, Theodore Thomas, and the American Centennial." *Musical Quarterly* 37, no. 2 (1951): 184–202.

Long, Clarence Dickinson. *Wages and Earnings in the United States, 1860–1890.* New York: Arno Press, 1975. First published 1960 by Princeton University Press.

Lott, R. Allen. "Bernard Ullman: Nineteenth-Century American Impresario." In *A Celebration of American Music: Words and Music in Honor of H. Wiley Hitchcock,* edited by Richard Crawford, R. Allen Lott, and Carol J. Oja, 174–91. Ann Arbor: University of Michigan Press, 1991.

————. *From Paris to Peoria: How European Piano Virtuosos Brought Classical Music to the American Heartland.* Oxford: Oxford University Press, 2003.

MacLeod, Beth Abelson. *Women Performing Music: The Emergence of American Women as Instrumentalists and Conductors.* Jefferson, NC: McFarland, 2001.

Mahling, Christoph-Hellmut. "Berlin: 'Music in the Air.'" In *The Early Romantic Era,* edited by Alexander L. Ringer, 109–39. Englewood Cliffs, NJ: Prentice-Hall, 1991.

————. "The Origin and Social Status of the Court Orchestral Musician in the 18th and Early 19th Century in Germany." In *The Social Status of the Professional Musician from the Middle Ages to the 19th Century,* edited by W. Salmen, translated by H. Kaufman and B. Reisner, 219–64. New York: Pendragon Press, 1983.

Maretzek, Max. *Revelations of an Opera Manager in 19th-Century America.* New introduction by Charles Haywood. New York: Dover Publications, 1968. Includes *Crotchets and Quavers* (New York: S. French, 1855) and *Sharps and Flats* (New York: American Musician Publishing Co., 1890).

Marks, Edward B. *They All Sang: From Tony Pastor to Rudy Vallée, as Told to A. J. Liebling.* New York: Viking Press, 1934.

Marquardt, Carl Eugene. "The German Drama on the New York Stage." Ph.D. diss., University of Pennsylvania, 1915.

Martin, George. *The Damrosch Dynasty: America's First Family of Music.* Boston: Houghton Mifflin, 1983.

Mathews, W[illiam] S[mythe] B[abcock]. *A Hundred Years of Music in America: ... A Full and Reliable Summary of American Musical Effort as Displayed in the Personal History of Artists, Composers and Educators, Musical Inventors and Journalists, with Upwards of Two Hundred Full Page Portraits of the Most Distinguished Workers, Together with Historical and Biographical Sketches of Important Personalities.* Chicago: G. L. Howe, 1889. Rev. ed., Philadelphia: Theodore Presser, 1900. Reprint, New York: AMS Press, 1970.

Mazzola, Sandy R. "Bands and Orchestras at the World's Columbian Exposition." *American Music* 4, no. 4 (1986): 407–24.

———. "When Music Is Labor: Chicago Bands and Orchestras and the Origins of the Chicago Federation of Musicians, 1880–1902." Ph.D. diss., Northern Illinois University, 1984.

McCabe, James D. *Lights and Shadows of New York.* Philadelphia: National Publishing, 1872.

McCrossen, Alexis. *Holy Day, Holiday: The American Sunday.* Ithaca, NY: Cornell University Press, 2000.

McGerr, Michael E. *A Fierce Discontent: The Rise and Fall of the Progressive Movement in America, 1870–1920.* New York: Free Press, 2003.

McNamara, Brooks. *The New York Concert Saloon: The Devil's Own Nights.* Cambridge: Cambridge University Press, 2002.

McVeigh, Simon. "Concert Promoters and Entrepreneurs in Late-Nineteenth-Century London." In *The Musician as Entrepreneur, 1700–1914: Managers, Charlatans, and Idealists,* edited by William Weber, 162–83. Bloomington: Indiana University Press, 2004.

Miller, Leta. "Racial Segregation and the San Francisco Musicians' Union, 1923–60." *Journal of the Society for American Music* 1 (2007): 161–206.

Miller, Zane L. *Boss Cox's Cincinnati: Urban Politics in the Progressive Era.* New York: Oxford University Press, 1968.

Moore, Martin. *Boston Revival, 1842: A Brief History of the Evangelical Churches of Boston, Together with a More Particular Account of the Revival of 1842.* Boston: J. Putnam, 1842. Reprint, Wheaton, IL: R. O. Roberts, 1980.

Mueller, John H. *The American Symphony Orchestra: A Social History of Musical Taste.* Bloomington: University of Indiana Press, 1951.

Mueller, Kate Hevner. *Twenty-Seven Major American Symphony Orchestras: A History and Analysis of Their Repertoires, Seasons 1842–43 through 1969–70.* Bloomington: Indiana University Studies, 1973.

Murdoch, William J. "Graupner Became a Papa, Too!" *Music Educators Journal* 35 (1948): 64–65.

Musical Mutual Protective Union. *Constitution and By-Laws.* New York, 1869.

———. *Constitution and By-Laws.* New York: Concord, 1886.

———. *Constitution and By-Laws.* New York: Machauer and Schmetterling, 1905.

Musical Yearbook of the United States, 1892–1893. Chicago: Summy, 1893.

Mussulman, Joseph A. *Music in the Cultured Generation: A Social History of Music in America, 1870–1900.* Evanston, IL: Northwestern University Press, 1971.

Myers, Margaret. *Blowing Her Own Trumpet: European Ladies' Orchestras and Other Women Musicians, 1870–1950, in Sweden.* Göteborg: University of Göteborg, 1993.

National League of Musicians. *Proceedings of the Convention of the National League of Musicians Held March 12–15, 1890, Inclusive in the City of Cincinnati Ohio.* N.p., 1890.

———. *Souvenir of the Seventh Annual Convention, Hotel Marlborough, New York, N.Y., Convening Tuesday March 15, 1892.* N.p., 1892.

Naylor, Blanche. *The Anthology of the Fadettes.* Boston: N.p., ca.1937.

Newhouse, Martin Jacob. "Artists, Artisans, or Workers? Orchestral Musicians in the German Empire." Ph.D. diss., Columbia University, 1979.

Newman, Nancy. "Gleiche Rechte, gleiche Pflichten, und gleiche Genüsse: Henry Albrecht's Utopian Vision of the Germania Musical Society." *Yearbook of German–American Studies* 34 (1999): 83–111.

———. "Good Music for a Free People: The Germania Musical Society and Transatlantic Musical Culture of the Mid-Nineteenth Century." Ph.D. diss., Brown University, 2002.

———. *Good Music for a Free People: The Germania Musical Society in Nineteenth-Century America.* Eastman Studies in Music. Rochester, NY: University of Rochester Press, 2010.

New York Philharmonic Society. *Fifteenth Annual Report of the New-York Philharmonic Society.* New York: Wm. C. Martin, 1857.

———. *Fourteenth Annual Report of the New-York Philharmonic Society.* New York: Wm. C. Martin, 1856.

———. *Sixth Annual Report of the New-York Philharmonic Society, Sept. 9, 1848.* New York: Wm. C. Martin, 1848.

———. *Tenth Annual Report of the New-York Philharmonic Society, Sept. 11, 1852.* New York: Wm. C. Martin, 1852.

New York Sabbath Committee. *First Five Years of the Sabbath Reform, 1857–62.* New York: Edward O. Jenkins, 1862.

Nicholls, Alex. *Social Entrepreneurship: New Models of Sustainable Social Change.* New York: Oxford University Press, 2008.

Notebook: Chicago Symphony Orchestra, 2007–2008 Season. Edited by Denise Wagner. Chicago: Chicago Symphony Orchestra, 2007.

Nutter, Charles R. ["History of the Harvard Orchestra."] *HMA Library Bulletin* 16 (April 1948); 17 (January 1949); 18 (January 1950); 19 (January 1951). Available online at http://www.hmaboston.org/bulletins.html.

Odell, George C. D. *Annals of the New York Stage.* 15 vols. New York: Columbia University Press, 1927–49.

Offenbach, Jacques. *Offenbach en Amérique: Notes d'un musicien en voyage.* Paris: Calmann-Lévy, 1877. Translated by Lander MacClintock as *Orpheus in America: Offenbach's Diary of His Journey to the New World.* Bloomington: Indiana University Press, 1957.

Olmstead, Andrea. *Juilliard: A History.* Urbana: University of Illinois Press, 1999.

The Opera Orchestra in 18th- and 19th-Century Europe I: The Orchestra in Society. Edited by N. M. Jensen and F. Piperno. Berlin: Berliner Wissenschafts-Verlag, 2008.

Osgood, Marion G. "America's First 'Ladies Orchestra.'" *Etude* 58, no. 10 (October 1940).

Otis, Philo Adams. *The Chicago Symphony Orchestra: Its Organization, Growth, and Development, 1891–1924.* Chicago: Clayton F. Summy, 1924.

Parker, J. C. D. *Seven Part Songs*. Boston: Oliver Ditson, 1875.

The Penal Code of the State of New York in Force December 1, 1882. Albany, NY: Banks, 1902.

Petrides, Frédérique. "Los Angeles Group: A Tested Veteran." *Women in Music* 1, no. 6 (February 1936).

Pieper, Antje. *Music and the Making of Middle-Class Culture: A Comparative History of Nineteenth-Century Leipzig and Birmingham*. Basingstoke, UK: Palgrave/Macmillan, 2008.

Pisani, Michael V. "Composing in the Theater: The Work of a Late Nineteenth-Century New York Music Director." Paper read at A Century of Composing in America, 1820–1920, Conference, CUNY Graduate Center, November 2004.

———— *Imagining Native America in Music*. New Haven, CT: Yale University Press, 2005.

Preston, Katherine K., ed. *George F. Bristow's Symphony No. 2 ("Jullien"): A Critical Edition*. Music of the United States of America 23. Madison, WI: A-R Editions, 2011.

————. *Music for Hire: A Study of Professional Musicians in Washington (1877–1900)*. Stuyvesant, NY: Pendragon Press, 1992.

————. *Opera on the Road: Traveling Opera Troupes in the United States, 1825–60*. Urbana: University of Illinois Press, 1993.

————. "Travelling Troupes–5: The USA." In *The New Grove Dictionary of Opera*, edited by Stanley Sadie. New York: New Grove Dictionaries of Music, 1992.

Ralph, Julian. "The Bowery." *Century Illustrated Monthly Magazine* 43 (n.s. 21), no. 2 (1891): 227–37.

Reblitz, Arthur A. *The Golden Age of Automatic Musical Instruments*. Edited by Q. David Bowers. Woodsville, NH: Mechanical Music Press, 2001.

Reichert, Matthew. "Carl Bergmann in New York: Conducting Activity, 1852–1876." D.M.A. diss., Graduate Center of the City University of New York, 2010.

Rice, Edwin T. "Personal Recollections of Leopold Damrosch." *Musical Quarterly* 28, no. 3 (1942): 269–75.

————. "Thomas and Central Park Garden." *Musical Quarterly* 26, no. 2 (1940): 143–52.

Ringel, Matthew L. "Opera in 'The Donizettian Dark Ages': Management, Competition and Artistic Policy in London, 1861–70." Ph.D. diss., King's College, University of London, 1996.

Ritter, Frédéric Louis. *Music in America*. New York: C. Scribner's Sons, 1883. 2nd edition with new introduction by Johannes Riedel, 1890. Reprint, New York: Johnson Reprint, 1970.

Robins, Brian. *Catch and Glee Culture in Eighteenth-Century England*. Woodbridge, Suffolk, UK: Boydell Press, 2006.

Rodger, Gillian. *Champagne Charlie and Pretty Jemima: Variety Theater in the Nineteenth Century*. Urbana: University of Illinois Press, 2010.

————. "Legislating Amusements: Class Politics and Theater Law in New York City." *American Music* 20, no. 4 (2002): 381–98.

Rogers, Carl Stanton. "The Songs of Alfred H. Pease (1838–1882)." Ph.D. diss., University of Illinois, 1980.

Rogers, Delmer Dalzell. "Nineteenth-Century Music in New York City as Reflected in the Career of George Frederick Bristow." Ph.D. diss., University of Michigan, 1967.

Root, Deane L. *American Popular Stage Music 1860–1880*. Ann Arbor, MI: UMI Research Press, 1981.

Ross, Steven J. *Workers On the Edge: Work, Leisure, and Politics in Industrializing Cincinnati, 1788–1890*. New York: Columbia University Press, 1985.

Rosselli, John. "Italy: The Decline of a Tradition." In *The Late Romantic Era from the Mid-Nineteenth Century to World War One*, edited by Jim Samson, 126–50. London: Macmillan, 1991.

Russell, Charles Edward. *The American Orchestra and Theodore Thomas*. Garden City, NY: Doubleday, Page, 1927. Reprint, Westport, CT: Greenwood Press, 1971.

Russell, Frank. *Queen of Song: The Life of Henrietta Sontag*. New York: Exposition Press, 1964.

Ryan, Thomas. *Recollections of an Old Musician*. New York: Dutton, 1899. Reprint, New York: Da Capo Press, 1979.

Saloman, Ora Frishberg. *Beethoven's Symphonies and J. S. Dwight: The Birth of American Music Criticism*. Boston: Northeastern University Press, 1995.

———. "John Sullivan Dwight." In *The American Renaissance in New England: Third Series*, edited by Wesley T. Mott, 96–103. *Dictionary of Literary Biography*, vol. 235. Detroit: Gale Group, 2001.

———. *Listening Well: On Beethoven, Berlioz, and Other Music Criticism in Paris, Boston, and New York, 1764–1890*. New York: Peter Lang, 2009.

———. "Presenting Berlioz's Music in New York, 1846–1890: Carl Bergmann, Theodore Thomas, Leopold Damrosch." In *European Music and Musicians in New York City, 1840-1900*, ed. John Graziano, 29–49. Rochester, NY: University of Rochester Press, 2006.

Sax, Alphonse, Jr. *Gymnastique des Poumons: La musique instrumentale au point de vue de l'hygiène des orchestres féminins*. Paris: L'auteur, 1865.

Schabas, Ezra. *Theodore Thomas: America's Conductor and Builder of Orchestras, 1835–1905*. Urbana: University of Illinois Press, 1989.

Schleis, Thomas H. "Balatka." In *The New Grove Dictionary of American Music*, edited by H. Wiley Hitchcock and Stanley Sadie, 1:117. London: Macmillan, 1986.

Schlicher, J. J. "Hans Balatka and the Milwaukee Musical Society." *Wisconsin Magazine of History* 27, no. 1 (September 1943): 40–55.

Schmaltz, Robert. "Organizing Orpheus: Protecting the American Orchestral Musician, 1890–1910." *Sonneck Society Bulletin* 25, no. 1 (1999): 1–5.

Schnapper, Laure. "Bernard Ullman-Henri Herz: An Example of Financial and Artistic Partnership, 1846–1849." In *The Musician as Entrepreneur, 1700–1914: Managers, Charlatans, and Idealists*, edited by William Weber, 130–44. Bloomington: Indiana University Press, 2004.

Scott, Derek. *Sounds of the Metropolis: The 19th-Century Popular Music Revolution in London, New York, Paris, and Vienna*. Oxford: Oxford University Press, 2008.

Sealander, Judith. *Private Wealth and Public Life: Foundation Philanthropy and the Reshaping of American Social Policy from the Progressive Era to the New Deal*. Baltimore: Johns Hopkins University Press, 1997.

Seeger, Charles. "Music and Class Structure in the United States." *American Quarterly* 9 (1957): 281–94. Reprinted in *Studies in Musicology, 1935–1975*, 222–36. Berkeley: University of California Press, 1977.

Segell, Michael. *The Devil's Horn: The Story of the Saxophone, from Noisy Novelty to King of Cool*. New York: Farrar, Straus and Giroux, 2005.

Shanet, Howard J. *Philharmonic: A History of New York's Orchestra*. Garden City, NY: Doubleday, 1975.

Sheahan, James W., and George P. Upton. *The Great Conflagration*. Chicago: Union Publishing, 1872.

Shear, Charlotte. *The First Hundred Years of the Friday Morning Music Club of Washington, D.C.* Washington, DC: privately printed, 1987.

Shirley, Wayne D. "Leopold Damrosch as Composer." In *European Music and Musicians in New York City, 1840–1900*, edited by John Graziano, 92–113. Rochester, NY: University of Rochester Press, 2006.

A Short History of the National Symphony Orchestra. Washington, DC: National Symphony Orchestra Association, 1949.

Shorto, Russell. *The Island at the Center of the World: The Epic Story of Dutch Manhattan and the Forgotten Colony That Shaped America.* New York: Vintage Books, 2004.

Silverman, Kaja. *The Acoustic Mirror: The Female Voice in Psychoanalysis and Cinema.* Bloomington: Indiana University Press, 1988.

Smith, Catherine Parsons. *Making Music in Los Angeles: Transforming the Popular.* Berkeley: University of California Press, 2007.

Smith, Jewel. *Music, Women, and Pianos in Antebellum Bethlehem, Pennsylvania: The Moravian Young Ladies' Seminary.* Bethlehem, PA: Lehigh University Press, 2008.

Solie, Ruth A. "'Girling' at the Parlor Piano." In *Music in Other Words: Victorian Conversations*, 85–117. Berkeley: University of California Press, 2004.

Sonneck, Oscar. *Early Concert-Life in America (1731–1800).* Leipzig: Breitkopf and Härtel, 1907. Reprint, New York: Da Capo Press, 1978.

Spitzer, John. "The Entrepreneur-Conductors and Their Orchestras." *Nineteenth-Century Music Review* 5, no. 1 (2008): 3–24.

Spitzer, John, and Neal Zaslaw. *The Birth of the Orchestra: History of an Institution, 1650–1815.* New York: Oxford University Press, 2004.

———. "Orchestra." In *The New Grove Dictionary of Music and Musicians*, 2nd ed., edited by Stanley Sadie, 18:530–48. London: Macmillan, 2001.

Stevenson, Robert, and Betty Bandel. "Hill, Ureli Corelli." In *The New Grove Dictionary of American Music*, edited by H. Wiley Hitchcock and Stanley Sadie, 2:386–87. London: Macmillan, 1986.

Swift, Lindsay. *Brook Farm: Its Members, Scholars, and Visitors.* New York: Macmillan, 1900.

Tawa, Nicholas E. *The Coming of Age of American Art Music: New England's Classical Romanticists.* Westport, CT: Greenwood Press, 1991.

———. *From Psalm to Symphony: A History of Music in New England.* Boston: Northeastern University Press, 2001.

Thomas, Louis R. "A History of the Cincinnati Symphony Orchestra to 1931." Ph.D. diss., University of Cincinnati, 1972.

Thomas, Rose Fay. *Memoirs of Theodore Thomas.* New York: Moffat, Yard, 1911.

Thomas, Theodore. *Theodore Thomas: A Musical Autobiography.* Edited by George P. Upton, with a new introduction by Leon Stein. Chicago: A. C. McClurg, 1905. Reprint, New York: Da Capo Press, 1964.

Tick, Judith. *American Women Composers before 1870.* Ann Arbor, MI: UMI Research Press, 1983. Reprint, Rochester NY: University of Rochester Press, 2010.

———. "Passed Away Is the Piano Girl: Changes in American Musical Life, 1870–1900." In *Women Making Music*, edited by Jane Bowers and Judith Tick, 325–48. Urbana: University of Illinois Press, 1986.

———. "Women as Professional Musicians in the United States, 1870–1900." *Anuario Interamericano de Investigación Musical* 9 (1973): 95–133.

Toll, Robert. *Blacking Up*. New York: Oxford University Press, 1974.

Tomlinson, Gary. "The Web of Culture: A Context for Musicology." *19th-Century Music* 7, no. 3 (1984): 35–62.

Upton, George P. *Musical Memories: My Recollections of Celebrities of the Half Century, 1850–1900*. Chicago: A. C. McClurg, 1908.

Upton, William Treat. *William Henry Fry: American Journalist and Composer-Critic*. New York: Thomas Y. Crowell, 1954.

Vitz, Robert C. *The Queen and the Arts: Cultural Life in Nineteenth-Century Cincinnati*. Kent, OH: Kent State University Press, 1989.

Von Glahn, Denise. *The Sounds of Place: Music and the American Cultural Landscape*. Boston: Northeastern University Press, 2003.

Wagner, Richard. *Das Kunstwerk der Zukunft*. Leipzig: Otto Wigand, 1850. Translated by William Ashton Ellis as *The Art-Work of the Future*. Lincoln: University of Nebraska Press, 1993.

Walters, Ronald G. "Buffalo Bill, Harry Houdini, and Real Magic." In *The Meanings of Magic: From the Bible to Buffalo Bill*, edited by Amy Wygant, 199–220. New York: Berghahn Books, 2006.

Warfield, Patrick. "John Esputa, John Philip Sousa, and the Boundaries of a Musical Career." *Nineteenth-Century Music Review* 6, no. 1 (July 2009): 27–46.

Waters, Edward. "John Sullivan Dwight: First American Critic of Music." *Musical Quarterly* 21 (1935): 69–88.

Weber, J. J. *Ganz Leipzig für acht Groschen: Neuer und vollständiger Wegweiser durch Leipzig für Fremde und Einheimische*. Leipzig: Weber, 1838.

Weber, William. *The Great Transformation of Musical Taste: Concert Programming from Haydn to Brahms*. Cambridge: Cambridge University Press, 2008.

———, ed. *The Musician as Entrepreneur, 1700–1914: Managers, Charlatans, and Idealists*. Bloomington: Indiana University Press, 2004.

———. *The Rise of Musical Classics in Eighteenth Century England*. Oxford: Clarendon Press, 1992.

———. "Wagner, Wagnerism, and Musical Idealism." In *Wagnerism in European Culture and Politics*, edited by David C. Large and William Weber, in collaboration with Anne Dzamba Sessa, 28–71. Ithaca, NY: Cornell University Press, 1984.

Whitesitt, Linda. "Women as 'Keepers of Culture': Music Clubs, Community Concert Series, and Symphony Orchestras." In *Cultivating Music in America: Women Patrons and Activists since 1860*, edited by Ralph P. Locke and Cyrilla Barr, 65–89. Berkeley: University of California Press, 1997.

Winsor, Justin, ed. *Memorial History of Boston*. 4 vols. Boston: Ticknor and Co. [Osgood and Co.], 1881.

Wister, Frances Anne. *Twenty-Five Years of the Philadelphia Orchestra, 1900–1925*. [Philadelphia]: Women's Committees for the Philadelphia Orchestra, 1925.

Wolf, Richard James. "A Short History of the Pittsburgh Orchestra, 1896 to 1910." Master's thesis, Carnegie Institute of Technology, 1954.

Worgan, T[homas] D[anvers]. *The Musical Reformer*. London: S. Maunder, 1829.

World's Columbian Exposition Bureau of Music. *Announcement regarding American Music at the Exposition*, October 20, 1893. Pamphlet in Theodore Thomas Felsengarten Collection, Rosenthal Archives, Chicago Symphony Orchestra.

Wright, John S. *Chicago: Past, Present, Future*. Chicago: Horton and Leonard, 1870.

Zboray, Ronald, and Mary Saracino Zboray. "Whig Women, Politics, and Culture in the Campaign of 1840: Three Perspectives from Massachusetts." *Journal of the Early Republic* 17, no. 2 (1997): 277–315.

Newspapers and Magazines

Indicated publication dates do not include predecessor and successor publications. Online availability: AHN = America's Historical Newspapers (http://www.newsbank.com/readex/?content=96); APS = American Periodical Series Online (http://www.proquest.com/en-US/catalogs/databases/detail/aps.shtml); CA = Chronicling America (http://chroniclingamerica.loc.gov/); PHN = Proquest Historical Newspapers (http://www.proquest.com/en-US/catalogs/databases/detail/pq-hist-news.shtml).

Albion (New York, 1822–76) [APS]
American Art Journal (New York, 1876–1905)
American Musician (New York, 1888–1915); also *American Music Journal*
Appleton's Journal of Literature, Science and Art (New York, 1869–76) [APS]
Arcadian (New York, 1870s)
Baltimore American and Commercial Advertiser (1802–83)
Birmingham Musical Examiner (Birmingham, England, 1845–46)
Boston Daily Advertiser (1813–1900) [AHN]
Boston Daily Atlas (1841–57) [AHN]
Boston Daily Globe (1872–)
Boston Evening Transcript (1842–56); also *Boston Transcript* [AHN]
Boston Musical Gazette (1838–39) [APS]
Boston Musical Times (1860–71)
Boston Post (1840–57) [AHN]
Boston Saturday Evening Gazette (1851–1906) [AHN]
Boston Sunday Times (1866–69)
Brainard's Musical World (Chicago, 1869–95)
Century Magazine (New York, 1881–1930); also *Century Illustrated Monthly Magazine* [APS]
Chicago Daily News (1875–1978)
Chicago Daily Tribune (1847–); also *Chicago Press and Tribune, Chicago Tribune* [AHN, PHN]
Chicago Inter Ocean (1879–1902); also *Daily Inter Ocean* [AHN]
Chicago Musical Review
Christian Inquirer (New York, 1846–64) [APS]
Christian Science Monitor (Boston, 1908–97) [PHN]
Christian Union (New York, 1870–93) [APS]
Church's Musical Visitor (Cincinnati, 1871–83); also *Musical Visitor* [APS]
Cincinnati Commercial (1882–83)
Cincinnati Commercial Gazette (1883–96)
Cincinnati Enquirer (1849–)
Cincinnati Gazette (1855–83); also *Cincinnati Daily Gazette*
Cincinnati Times-Star (1880–1958)
Cleveland Plain Dealer (1845–)
Cleveland Press (Cleveland, 1889–1960)
Courier [published by the College of Music of Cincinnati] (1882–1916)
Courrier d'orchestre (Paris, 1902–22)

Cummings' Evening Bulletin (Philadelphia, 1851–70); also *Daily Evening Bulletin*

Detroit Free Press (1851–)

Deutsche Musiker-Zeitung (Berlin, 1870–1933)

Dwight's Journal of Music (Boston, 1852–81); reprinted New York, Johnson Reprint, 1968

Frank Leslie's Illustrated Newspaper (New York, 1855–91)

Harbinger (Brook Farm, then New York, 1845–49) [APS]

Harper's Bazaar (New York, 1867–1912) [APS]

Harper's Weekly (New York, 1857–1976)

Illustrated London News (1842–2003)

L'art musical (Paris, 1860–94)

London Musical World (1836–90)

Los Angeles Times (1881–) [PHN]

Louisville Daily Journal (1833–68)

Message Bird (New York, 1849–51)

Metronome (Boston, 1871–74)

Music (Chicago, 1891–1902)

Musical Cabinet (Boston, 1841–42) [APS]

Musical Courier (New York, 1883–1961)

Musical Independent (Chicago, 1868–73)

Musical People (New York, 1881–83)

Musical Visitor (Cincinnati, 1883–97); also *Church's Musical Visitor* [APS]

Musical World and Times (New York 1852–60); also *New York Musical World*

Music Trade Review (New York, 1875–78)

National Intelligencer (Washington, DC, 1810–69) [AHN]

Neue New-Yorker Musik-Zeitung (1866–76+)

New-Hampshire Patriot (Concord, 1819–62)

New Orleans Daily Picayune (1837–) [AHN]

New Peterson Magazine (Philadelphia, then New York, 1842–98) [APS]

New York Clipper (1853–1923)

New York Courier and Enquirer (1829–61)

New York Daily Times (1851–57); same as *New York Times*

New York Dramatic Mirror (1889–1917)

New Yorker Musikzeitung (1865–78)

New-Yorker Staats-Zeitung (1834–1934)

New York Evangelist (1830–1902) [APS]

New York Evening Star (1833–40)

New York Herald (1840–1920) [AHN]

New York Independent (1848–1921) [APS]

New York Observer (1829–1912); also *New York Observer and Chronicle* [APS]

New York Post (1801–1920); also *Evening Post* [AHN]

New York Sun (1833–1916) [CA]

New York Times (1851–); also *New-York Times* [PHN]

New York Tribune (1842–1924); also *New-York Daily Tribune* [AHN, ChronAm]

Orpheus: A Repository of Music, Art and Literature (New York, 1865–80)

Philadelphia Inquirer (1860–) [AHN]

Richmond Enquirer (1804–63) [AHN]

Savannah Daily Morning News (1850–64)

Scientific American (New York, 1845–) [APS]

Scribner's Monthly (New York, 1870–81) [APS]
Souvenir (Milwaukee, 1890s)
Spirit of the Times (New York, 1837–61); also *Porter's Spirit of the Times* [APS]
Times (London, 1788–)
Utica Morning Herald & Daily Gazette (Utica, NY, 1857–1900)
Washington Post (1877–) [PHN]
Washington Star (Washington, DC, 1854–1972); also *Washington Evening Star*
Wheeling Daily Intelligencer (1852–1903)
York Sunday News [*York Daily Record*] (York PA, 1973–)

Archival Sources

American Antiquarian Society, Worcester, MA
    Broadsides (in general collection)
    Jennison Family Papers
    Newspaper Clippings File
    "Record Book 1849, of Women Invited to the Inauguration Ball 'In Honor of the Great and Good Zachary Taylor'" (Worcester, MA, Records, 1686–1941)
    Birmingham Central Library, Birmingham, UK
    Local History Collection, Musical Archive
Boston Public Library, Music Collection
    Boston Academy of Music, Programs of Concerts, 1833–1847
    Boston Philharmonic Society, Programs of Concerts, 1843–1863
    Programs of Concerts in Boston, 1817–1863, Scrapbooks, 3 vols. (microfilm), **M19.3
Chicago Historical Society
    Woman's Symphony Orchestra of Chicago Collection
Chicago Symphony, Rosenthal Archives
    CSO Programs
    Theodore and Rose Fay Thomas Felsengarten Collection
    Theodore Thomas Music Library
Cincinnati Historical Society Library
    Centennial Exposition of the Ohio Valley, Papers
    College of Music of Cincinnati Records, 1879-1899
    Ladies' Musical Club/Orchestra Association Scrapbook
    Wulsin Family Papers
Harvard Musical Association, Boston
    Boston Philharmonic Orchestra, Programs, 1843–1863, P.B65P
    Boston Philharmonic Orchestra, Programs, 1879–1883, P.B65P
    "Criticisms of HMA Symphony Concerts—1865 to 1881" [Scrapbook of clippings]. Archives 003
    "HMA Orchestra—1865 to 1882—Repertoire and Personnel," Archives, 101, frames 49–62
    "HMA Orchestra: Letters to Mr. Dwight," Archives, 088
    "HMA Symphony Concerts" [programs], Archives, 006
    Germania Musical Society, Programs 1851–1853, P.G31
    Orchestral Union, Programs, 1857–1868, P.Or17
    "Records of the Recording Secretary—Pierian Sodality and HMA," Archives, 018
    "Reports of Board of Directors, 1875–1879," Archives, 031.

"Reports on the Harvard Orchestra Concerts, 1865 to 1882," Archives, 033.
Harvard University, Houghton Library
    Harvard Theatre Collection, Program Collection
    Henry Wadsworth Longfellow Papers
    Music from the Collection of John Knowles Paine
Historical Society of Pennsylvania
    Philadelphia Musical Association, Records
Historical Society of Washington, DC
    General Photograph Collection
Huntington Library, San Marino, CA
Johns Hopkins University, Baltimore, MD
    Lester S. Levy Collection of Sheet Music
    Peabody Archives
Library of Congress, Music Division
    Damrosch-Blaine Collection, Papers of Leopold Damrosch
    Damrosch-Tee Van Collection, Papers of Leopold Damrosch
Martin Luther King, Jr., Memorial Library, Washington, DC, Washingtoniana Division
    Scrapbooks Compiled by Mattie Saxton
Museum of the City of New York
    Theater Collection
National Archives and Records Administration, Washington, DC, Record Group 127,
    Records of the U.S. Marine Corps (includes Marine Band)
National Portrait Gallery (London), Photograph Division
Newberry Library, Chicago, Theodore Thomas collection
New York City Municipal Archives
    "Mayors Papers"
    "Police Department, Licensing of Theatres"
New York Philharmonic Archives
    Bound Books of Printed Programs
    Hill, U.C. Diary, 1835–1837 (Manuscript), Box 500-01-01
    Minutes of Directors' Meetings of the New York Philharmonic Society
    "The Personnel of the New York Philharmonic and Those Orchestras Merging with
        That Organization, 1842–2001" (Norman Schweikert, comp.)
New York Public Library
    Americana Collection, George Bristow Collection
    Manuscripts and Archives Division, David Blakely Papers (Sousa Scrapbook)
    Music Division, Walter Damrosch Collection
    Oratorio Society of New York, Archives
    Reviews Symphony Society of New-York, 1877–1878
Providence Athenaeum
    Scrapbook, "Concert Programs, 1847–1854"
United States Marine Band Library
    Fowles Scrapbook, Programs
    Sousa Pressbooks
University of Iowa Libraries, Special Collections
University of Texas at Austin, Harry Ransom Humanities Research Center

CONTRIBUTORS

Karen Ahlquist teaches in the Department of Music at the George Washington University in Washington, D.C. She is the author of *Democracy at the Opera: Music, Theater, and Culture in New York City* (1997) and editor of *Chorus and Community* (2006).

Adrienne Fried Block (d. 2009) was a leading contributor to the history of nineteenth-century American music and of women in American music. She was the author of *Amy Beach, Passionate Victorian* (1998) and of *Women in American Music: A Bibliography of Music and Literature* (with Carol Neuls-Bates, 1979) and was codirector of the "Music in Gotham" project at the Graduate Center of the City University of New York.

Mark Clague is associate professor of musicology at the University of Michigan. His articles have appeared in *American Music* and the *Black Music Research Journal* as well as in the *International Dictionary of Black Composers* and *The Encyclopedia of Chicago*. He served for six years as Executive Editor for Music of the United States of America (MUSA).

Mary Wallace Davidson has directed the music libraries at Radcliffe, Wellesley College, the Eastman School of Music, and Indiana University. She chairs the Library Committee at the Harvard Musical Association.

James Deaville is professor in the School for Studies in Art and Culture: Music, Carleton University, Ottawa. He has published in the *Journal of the American Musicological Society*, *Journal of the Society for American Music*, and *Intersections*. Author of numerous entries in the Amerigrove, he edited the book *Music in Television: Channels of Listening* (2011).

Bethany Goldberg is a Ph.D. candidate in musicology at Indiana University. She has written for *American Music Review* and *The New Grove Dictionary of American Music* and currently teaches at Youngstown State University.

John Graziano, professor emeritus of music, The City College and Graduate Center, City University of New York, is the director of *Music in Gotham*, a National Endowment for the Humanities funded "We the People" project. He has published books and articles on various aspects of popular and art music in the nineteenth and early twentieth centuries and has served as president of the Society for American Music.

Barbara Haws has been the archivist and historian of the New York Philharmonic since 1984. She is Executive Producer of the Philharmonic's historic recordings label and the editor, with Burton Bernstein, of *Leonard Bernstein: American Original* (2008).

John Koegel, professor of musicology at California State University, Fullerton, investigates

U.S. and Mexican musical life. His articles and reviews appear in journals such as *American Music, Journal of the American Musicological Society, Heterofonía*, and *Latin American Music Review*. His *Music in German Immigrant Theater: New York City, 1840–1940* (2009) won the 2011 Irving Lowens Book Award of the Society for American Music.

Brenda Nelson-Strauss served as director of the Rosenthal Archives of the Chicago Symphony Orchestra from 1989 to 2002, where she worked to reassemble and catalog the Theodore Thomas Orchestra music library. She is currently the head of collections of the Archives of African American Music at Indiana University.

Nancy Newman is assistant professor of music and an affiliate of women's studies at the University at Albany–SUNY. Her writings include *Good Music for a Free People: The Germania Musical Society in Nineteenth-Century America* (2010) and an article on the 1950s film musical *The 5000 Fingers of Dr. T* (2008).

Katherine K. Preston is the David N. and Margaret C. Bottoms Professor of Music at the College of William and Mary. She has published extensively on various aspects of American musical culture of the nineteenth century. Among her books are *Opera on the Road: Travelling Opera Troupes in the United States, 1825–1860* (1994/2001) and *George F. Bristow's Symphony no. 2 in D Minor, op. 24 ("Jullien")* (2011). She is coeditor of *Emily's Songbook: Popular Music in 1850s Albany* (2011).

Deane Root is professor of music and director of the Center for American Music at the University of Pittsburgh and Editor in Chief of *Grove Music*. He is the author of *American Popular Stage Music 1860–1880* (1981), coauthor of *Resources of American Music History* (1981), and editor of the sixteen-volume-series *Nineteenth-Century American Musical Theater* (1994).

Ora Frishberg Saloman (d. 2011) was professor of music at Baruch College and Graduate Center of the City University of New York. She was the author of *Listening Well: On Beethoven, Berlioz, and Other Music Criticism in Paris, Boston, and New York, 1764–1890* (2009) and of *Beethoven's Symphonies and J. S. Dwight: The Birth of American Music Criticism* (1995).

Anna-Lise P. Santella is publishing editor of Grove Music / Oxford Music Online. She has written about American women's orchestras for *The New Grove Dictionary of American Music* and *Women Building Chicago, 1790–1990: A Biographical Dictionary* (2001).

John Spitzer teaches music history at the San Francisco Conservatory of Music. He is the author (with Neal Zaslaw) of *The Birth of the Orchestra: History of an Institution* (2004).

Ronald G. Walters is professor of history at Johns Hopkins University and the author or editor of five books and numerous articles on American history. His research is divided between an older interest in American reform movements and a more recent one in the evolution of commercial popular culture in the United States.

Patrick Warfield teaches in the Division of Musicology and Ethnomusicology at the University of Maryland. He has written extensively about John Philip Sousa and music in the Washington D.C. area and is the editor of *John Philip Sousa: Six Marches* in the series *Music of the United States of America*.

William Weber, professor of history emeritus at California State University, Long Beach, has published several books on music and society, including *Music and the Middle Class* (1975, 2003), *The Rise of Musical Classics in 18th-Century England* (1992), and *The Great Transformation of Musical Taste: Concert Programming from Haydn to Brahms* (2008).

Jonas Westover received his doctorate from the Graduate Center of the City University of New York. He has written extensively for *The New Grove Dictionary of American Music* and teaches in the Minneapolis area.

INDEX

The letter *f* denotes figures, *n* footnotes, and *t* tables.

and women, 289–309

See also Ahner, Henry; Albrecht, Henry;
Bergmann, Carl; Lenschow, Carl;
Schultze, William; Zerrahn, Carl

Germania Orchestra. *See* Germania Musical Society

German immigrants. *See* immigrants: German

Gilmore, Patrick, 28n7, 89, 93

Glackens, William, 143f

Gottschalk, Louis Moreau, 136n13, 226,
399, 420

Grau, Jacob, 38

Great Western Band (Chicago), 41n64, 42,
46, 47, 187

Gungl, Josef, 122, 292, 321, 334, 385–86,
400

Habermas, Jürgen, 308–9

Hagen, Theodore, 371, 438

Hamilton, Harley, 66–68

Hamm, Charles, 9–10

Handel and Haydn Society. *See* Boston

Hart, Philip, 11

Harvard Musical Association, 21, 378, 382

founded, 247–49

ideology and mission, 223–24

Harvard Musical Association Orchestra

decline, 260–63

finances, 221, 253, 261–62

founded, 251–53, 388

membership, 266–68

officers, 256

programs, 221, 252, 254, 255, 258–59, 263

See also Dwight, John Sullivan

Harvard Orchestra. *See* Harvard Musical
Association Orchestra

Hassard, John Rose Green, 271, 278, 281–82

Hauser, Miska, 292

Haymarket Square riot, 42n68

Helmsmuller, Frederick B., 306

Henderson, William James, 5

Herbert, Victor, 93, 422

Herz, Henri, 226

Higginson, Henry Lee, 8, 49, 164, 170, 205,
264–65

Higginson, Thomas Wentworth, 304

Hill, Ureli Corelli, 7n16, 348–64, 437–38

critical judgments, 314, 359–61

diary, 349

family and early career, 349

itinerary of trip to Europe, 348–49

and Jullien orchestra, 327, 337

and New York Philharmonic, 348,
362–63

study with Spohr, 349–50

Hitchcock, H. Wiley, 9

Horowitz, Joseph, 12

Horton, Mary Ann, 298

Howard, John Tasker, 7

Hoym, Otto, 139–40

immigrants

English, 86, 313, 362, 374

French, 96, 362

German: assimilation with American
culture, 41, 147, 152, 154, 282–83, 313–
15; in audiences, 157, 313, 315, 439;
in Boston, 256; choral societies, 40,
270; in Cincinnati, 157; conflict with
American culture, 137–38; and musicians' unions, 84, 117; in New York
City, 130, 132–34, 154–55, 398, 439; and
New York Philharmonic, 3, 363, 398,
437–38, 448; in orchestras, 3, 86, 98–
99, 103, 275, 313–14; and sacred concerts, 137–38, 147; socialist culture
among, 41. *See also* Aschenbroedel
Verein; beer gardens; festivals

Italian, 315, 370

instrumentalists. *See* musicians (orchestral)

Jaëll, Alfred, 220–21, 291f, 292, 302

Jennison, Ann Elizabeth, 296, 305–6

Jullien, Louis Antoine

and American composers, 7, 329–31,
340–41, 343–45, 398

American tour, 104, 220, 319–42

appearance and charisma, 221, 234, 320,
322, 323f

in Boston, 386–87

as composer, 331–33

conducting style, 322, 332

European career, 320–21, 340

legacy in United States, 339

marketing, 220, 222

as model, 230, 239, 400

New York concerts, 328, 450

programming, 328–33, 335

reception in United States, 337–39